The Notebooks of
HENRY JAMES

as the second of the two women whom he has had compunction about. ✗ ✗ ✗ ✗ ✗ ✗ ✗ ✗ Cornettons, this morning (April 20th,) the whole frank, bright, manly, human little comedy — in its initial steps at least — seems to come to me. Begin it — try it — a little; put your hand into the paste! ✗ Casa Biondetti, April 21st, 1894.

I know put my hand to it — I did yesterday, in a morning's limited scribble; but the subject, which is good, doesn't somehow speak to me for this particular purpose. It isn't the quite objective thing I want. The thing I want will come — will come "in its glory": the quiet, generous, patient mornings will bring it. They are everything; or only want to be, beg to be, so far as they are encouraged and permitted. Oh, soul of my soul — oh, sacred benef-icence of _doing_! Oh blest, oh blest Past! Consider many things — open the hospitable mind! Look at this, judge of that — turn over the other! ✗

A PAGE FROM HENRY JAMES' NOTEBOOKS

NOTE ON THE COVER TO THIS EDITION

Sir Max Beerbohm owned a copy of the first edition of The Notebooks of Henry James, *which is now in the Houghton Library of Harvard College. Besides a number of notes and comments, it contains two pencil sketches of Henry James. One, facing the leaf of Acknowledgments, shows a bearded Henry James, with the following comment:*

⟨ H. J. as he was in 1895. I would have supposed that a man so intensely secretive as he would never have have [sic] shaved, as he did, to the wonderment of all his friends and acquaintances, suddenly, in 1899 or so.

⟨ He had looked rather like a Russian Grand Duke. Afterwards he looked rather like a lay Cardinal.

On the verso of the title page, Max sketched Henry James as a "lay Cardinal."

Copies of these two sketches, reduced somewhat in size, are used on the front and back covers of this edition of The Notebooks.

The Oxford University Press is most grateful to Mrs. Eva Reichmann and to the Harvard College Library for permission to reproduce these two drawings and the accompanying description.

The Notebooks of
HENRY JAMES

EDITED BY F.O. MATTHIESSEN

AND KENNETH B. MURDOCK

A Galaxy Book

NEW YORK · OXFORD UNIVERSITY PRESS · 1961

CONTENTS

ACKNOWLEDGMENTS

TOWARDS the end of his life Henry James destroyed many letters and papers, but several working notebooks survived. Along with much other James family material, these have recently been deposited in the Houghton Library at Harvard University by the present Henry James, the nephew of the novelist, by whose permission they are now published. The editors also acknowledge with gratitude Mr. James' permission, and that of Charles Scribner's Sons, to use excerpts from the New York edition of Henry James' works and from *The Letters of Henry James*, edited by Percy Lubbock; the permission of the D. Appleton-Century Company to use a passage from Edith Wharton's *A Backward Glance*; and the permission of A. P. Watt and Sons, Ltd., of London, of the executors of Lord Tweedsmuir's estate, and of Houghton Mifflin Company, to quote from John Buchan's *Pilgrim's Way* (*Memory Hold-the-Door*). For the opportunity to print in its entirety James' 'Scenario' for *The Ambassadors* (previously printed in part in *The Hound and Horn*, Spring, 1934), the editors thank its present owner, Mr. A. Hyatt Mayor.

Among our many other debts are those to Mr. LeRoy Phillips for his invaluable bibliography of Henry James; to the President and Fellows of Harvard College for a generous grant from the William F. Milton Fund; to Mr. Allen Clark for his work as our research assistant; to Mr. Sterling Lanier for his help in research and in proofreading; to Mr. Leon Edel for his unsurpassed knowledge of James' biography, which he has bestowed with great generosity upon our entire manuscript; to Professor André Morize for helping us decipher James' French; to Mr. Donald Brien for permission to print some of James' correspondence with Horace Scudder; and to Eleanor E. Murdock for endless co-operation.

INTRODUCTION

THE notebooks of Henry James, which constitute the bulk of this volume, are a record of his work in progress for a period of more than thirty years. As early as 1873 he wrote to his brother William thanking him for his 'criticism on *Middlemarch*,' and adding: 'I have duly transcribed it into that notebook which it will be a relief to your mind to know that I have at last set up.' But 'the note-taking habit' did not come easily, since in 1881 he confessed that he had 'lost too much by losing, or rather by not having acquired,' it. By then, however, he had begun to set down each new theme that occurred to him for his fiction, and subsequent to his first entry about *Confidence*, in the autumn of 1878, all his finished novels and all but a handful of his stories are discussed or at least mentioned in his memoranda.[1]

Ideas for stories appear sometimes merely as bare statements, but more often with comments on the possibilities James saw in them. Often, too, there are further entries working out the technical problems presented, and showing how the finished story or novel took shape. In the cases of *The Princess Casamassima* and *The Tragic Muse*, the notes are obviously continuations from other outlines, and to judge from James' preparation of extensive 'scenarios' for *The Ambassadors* and *The Wings of the Dove*, it seems likely that he made separate notations for several of his other longer works.

Three of his surviving notebooks differ in character from the rest. Two deal with his non-fictional work. In one (1904-5), he recorded, for the most part at Coronado Beach, California, some of the memories of Cambridge he was to use in *The American Scene* and *Notes of a Son and Brother*; in the other (1907-9), he sketched some London scenes for a book about that city which he did not get around to writing. And in a third manuscript volume, started in 1881, at a marble-topped table in the Hotel Brunswick in Boston, he concerned

1. *In the Cage* (1898) is the longest story left unmentioned. The others omitted are *Nona Vincent, Collaboration*, and *The Visits*—published during 1892 when James was occupied primarily with writing for the stage—*The Third Person* (1900), *The Great Good Place* (1900), and three of his latest stories (1908-9), *Julia Bride, Crapy Cornelia*, and *The Velvet Glove*, which were written when he was no longer keeping his notebooks regularly.

himself less with his work than with his life, and made a rapid 'summing up' of the preceding six years, the years of his first uninterrupted experiment of living and working in Europe. Some of its superficial entries—the enumeration of the houses at which he had visited and even of a particular drink of milk one evening in the Alps—may remind us oddly of the triviality and emptiness for which James criticized similar material in Hawthorne's notebooks. But here James also gave voice to a conviction of great significance for his career, the conviction that, for a man of his temperament and capacities, the decision to live abroad had been the right one. He likewise expressed his belief that the American writer of fiction must deal, by implication at least, with Europe, whereas the European novelist who neglected America was not 'incomplete'—although 'fifty years hence . . . he will doubtless be accounted so.'

In this 'summing up' James spoke more intimately of some of his aspirations than he permitted himself to do in his published autobiographies. He evoked the freshness and vivacity of his earliest impressions, and insisted that 'never was an ingenuous youth more passionately and yet more patiently eager for what life might bring.' This mixture of passion and patience made him remarkable as an observer. He exemplified Stendhal's description of a novel as 'a mirror dawdling down a road,' but there was no coldness or indifference in his detachment. One of the recurrent themes in his memoranda is the one that found its quintessential expression through Lambert Strether in *The Ambassadors*. In 1891, as James neared fifty, he reflected: 'I have only to let myself go! So I have said to myself all my life—so I said to myself in the far-off days of my fermenting and passionate youth. Yet I have never fully done it. The sense of it—of the need of it—rolls over me at times with commanding force: it seems the formula of my salvation, of what remains to me of a future. I am in full possession of accumulated resources—I have only to use them, to insist, to persist, to do something more—to do much more—than I *have* done. The way to do it—to affirm one's self *sur la fin*—is to strike as many notes, deep, full and rapid, as one can. All life is—at my age, with all one's artistic soul the record of it—in one's pocket, as it were. Go on, my boy, and strike hard; have a rich and long St. Martin's summer.' But James spoke, unlike Strether, primarily as an artist, and concluded: 'Try everything, do everything, render everything—be an artist, be distinguished to the last.'

There are not many such generalizations in his notebooks. He often advised himself 'to live *in* the world of creation—to get into it and stay in it—to frequent it and haunt it—to *think* intently and fruitfully—to woo combinations and inspirations into being by a depth and continuity of attention and meditation—this is the only thing.' He disciplined himself in that attention by making his notes as concrete as possible.

In the preface to *The Altar of the Dead*, after reflecting how little any account of origins could tell about such fantasies as *Owen Wingrave* or *The Friends of the Friends*, he made his most explicit summary of how his memoranda had served him: 'The habitual teller of tales finds these things in old note-books—which however but shifts the burden a step; since how, and under what inspiration, did they first wake up in these rude cradles? One's notes, as all writers remember, sometimes explicitly mention, sometimes indirectly reveal, and sometimes wholly dissimulate, such clues and such obligations. The search for these last indeed, through faded or pencilled pages, is perhaps one of the sweetest of our more pensive pleasures. Then we chance on some idea we *have* afterwards treated; then, greeting it with tenderness, we wonder at the first form of a motive that was to lead us so far and to show, no doubt, to eyes not our own, for so other; then we heave the deep sigh of relief over all that is never, thank goodness, to be done again. Would we have embarked on *that* stream had we known? —and what mightn't we have made of this one *hadn't* we known! How, in a proportion of cases, could we have dreamed "there might be something"?—and why, in another proportion, didn't we *try* what there might be, since there are sorts of trials (ah indeed more than one sort!) for which the day will soon have passed? Most of all, of a certainty, is brought back, before these promiscuities, the old burden of the much life and the little art, and of the portentous dose of the one it takes to make any show of the other. It isn't however that one "minds" not recovering lost hints. . . Doesn't the fabulist himself indeed recall even as one of his best joys the particular pang . . . of parting with some conceit of which he can give no account but that his sense—of beauty or truth or whatever—has been for ever so long saturated with it?'

The notebooks clarify the question of how James went about writing the famous prefaces for his collected edition. Those prefaces aimed to reproduce the circumstances of composition for his various novels and stories, to reveal what James called 'the contributive value of the *accessory* facts in a given artistic case.' Many commentators have been surprised at James' feat of memory in repossessing both the time and place where a long-past story was written, and even its moment of inception in some fragmentary suggestion. But it now becomes apparent that he composed the prefaces with his notes at his elbow, and that it was to them he alluded in his seemingly general references to 'the scantest of memoranda,' in regard to *Pandora*, or, in regard to *Broken Wings*, to how 'any old note-book would show *that* laid away as a tragic "value." ' His varied evocations of the places where he had worked—perhaps the most vivid being that of 'the waterside life' of Venice, above the fascinating distractions of which he tried to concentrate upon *The Portrait of a Lady*—were also refreshed by what he had written on the spot.

When James began the first of the notebooks with his sketch of *Confidence*, he had completed more than twelve years of apprenticeship to his craft. Of his first two dozen stories he had collected only six in *A Passionate Pilgrim* (1875), but he had begun to find his stride as a novelist with *Roderick Hudson* in 1876, and *The American* in the following year. He had also issued the first of his travel books, *Transatlantic Sketches* (1875), and the first of his collections of criticism, *French Poets and Novelists* (1878). *Daisy Miller* had come out in the *Cornhill Magazine* that summer; and *The Europeans* had just been serialized by the *Atlantic Monthly*. But James' best work was still to come, and his notebooks were to serve him well in his achievement of it. To read them is to see at once many different ways in which they helped him gain that saturation in his material which he always held to be the first requisite for viable art. His notes on *Confidence*, probably the weakest of all his novels, were closely followed by his discussion of the structure of *The Portrait of a Lady*, and that discussion is an illuminating instance of how he used his memoranda in thinking out his themes. He also used them to clarify his *données*, to establish his characters and their backgrounds and connections so solidly that, once he began to compose, he could be sure that he possessed, as he said in relation to *The Coxon Fund*, 'a rich subject summarized.'

James did not rate himself highly as a thinker, and he kept deploring his too frequent vagueness of mind. He believed that 'one does nothing of value in art or literature, unless one has some general ideas.' But he knew as well as Mallarmé that novels, like poems, are written not with ideas, but with words. He knew that the fruitful generalization can be reached only through an abundant sequence of details, that the theoretical must be drenched with the actual. He knew that for the artist 'the only balm and the only refuge, the real solution of the pressing question of life,' lay in the repeated 'intimate battle with the particular idea, with the subject, the possibility, the place.' Of such battles his notebooks are the record—of upwards of eighty victories in completed stories and novels, and of thirty or forty more skirmishes with themes that he abandoned for one reason or another.

His ideas often came to him in the fashion described in his preface to *The Spoils of Poynton*, through a chance anecdote communicated by the lady to whom he sat next at some dinner. That would hardly seem a promising source for anything but the most superficial society fiction, and yet as we know, and as the notebooks reaffirm, James always stressed the importance of subject. When he felt some misgivings even about *The Altar of the Dead*, he reminded himself that 'solidity of subject, importance, emotional capacity of subject, is the only thing on which, henceforth, it is of the slightest use for me to expend myself. Everything else breaks down, collapses, turns thin, turns poor, turns wretched—betrays one miserably. Only the fine, the large, the human, the natural, the fundamental, the passionate things.' How he found such things while dining out may be attributed in part to some of the ladies whose names occur most often in his notes: to Thackeray's daughter, Mrs. Richmond Ritchie, and especially to Fanny Kemble, who, thirty-five years James' senior, brought him into connection 'with a thousand vanished and present things,' and whose warm and eloquent talk, as he celebrated it in a memorial essay, 'swarmed with people and with criticism of people, with the ghosts of a dead society. She had, in two hemispheres, seen everyone and known everyone, had assisted at the social comedy of her age.'

But mainly, like all greatly perceptive artists, James took from these interlocutresses what he brought himself, as the opening of his preface to *The Spoils of Poynton* declares:

It was years ago, I remember, one Christmas Eve when I was dining with friends: a lady beside me made in the course of talk one of those allusions that I have always found myself recognizing on the spot as 'germs.' The germ, wherever gathered, has ever been for me the germ of a 'story,' and most of the stories straining to shape under my hand have sprung from a single small seed, a seed as minute and wind-blown as that casual hint for *The Spoils of Poynton* dropped unwittingly by my neighbour, a mere floating particle in the stream of talk. What above all comes back to me with this reminiscence is the sense of the inveterate minuteness, on such happy occasions, of the precious particle—reduced, that is, to its mere fruitful essence. Such is the interesting truth about the stray suggestion, the wandering word, the vague echo, at touch of which the novelist's imagination winces as at the prick of some sharp point: its virtue is all in its needle-like quality, the power to penetrate as finely as possible. This fineness it is that communicates the virus of suggestion, anything more than the minimum of which spoils the operation. If one is given a hint at all designedly one is sure to be given too much; one's subject is in the merest grain, the speck of truth, of beauty, of reality, scarce visible to the common eye—since, I firmly hold, a good eye for a subject is anything but usual. Strange and attaching, certainly, the consistency with which the first thing to be done for the communicated and seized idea is to reduce almost to nought the form, the air as of a mere disjoined and lacerated lump of life, in which we may have happened to meet it. Life being all inclusion and confusion, and art being all discrimination and selection, the latter, in search of the hard latent *value* with which alone it is concerned, sniffs round the mass as instinctively and unerringly as a dog suspicious of some buried bone. The difference here, however, is that, while the dog desires his bone but to destroy it, the artist finds in *his* tiny nugget, washed free of awkward accretions and hammered into a sacred hardness, the very stuff for a clear affirmation, the happiest chance for the indestructible.

In a few cases James proceeded in the way habitual to Hawthorne, that is to say he started with an abstraction and sought an embodiment for it. 'What is there,' he asked himself, 'in the idea of *Too late*—of some friendship or passion or bond—some affection long desired and waited for?' Meditation on this theme yielded both *The Friends of the Friends* and *The Beast in the Jungle*. Or, again, he began with 'the notion of a young man (young, presumably) who has something— some secret sorrow, trouble, fault—to *tell* and can't find the *recipient*.' Further reflection persuaded him that 'there is probably something worth thinking of in the idea,' but that 'the thing needs working out— maturing.' Not until fifteen years after his first entry on this theme did he devise the right chain of events for *A Round of Visits*.

In his more usual procedure some concrete incident appealed to him by the possibilities it offered for development. Sometimes he seems to have been attracted first by the formal neatness of a subject, by the chance it gave for an 'intensely structural, intensely hinged and jointed preliminary frame,' but as he worked he almost always clothed the bare bones of structure so that the final effect of the tale depended not on symmetrical construction but on the depiction of relations between characters or on the full presentation of an individual. In *The Wheel of Time*, for example, he masks the schematic balance of the plot by his concentration on the heroine; similarly, in *What Maisie Knew*, his first efforts were toward the building of a squared pattern, but in the finished novel the strictness of the plan is carefully kept from seeming obvious. 'Form,' in the sense of ordered construction, was essential, but as a means not as an end. The end was the revelation of character.

Accordingly, most of the incidents that suggested stories to him did so because they offered material for portraits. When Mrs. Anstruther-Thompson told him at Lady Lindsay's about a son who had sued a mother for his property, he went ahead to create the *Spoils*, but on lines quite different from those of the original anecdote. His notes for *The Liar* and *Owen Wingrave* afford insight both into the way in which he evolved his characters and into another way in which his notebooks served him. The first suggestions for these stories, as his entries indicate, came to him from his reading, from Daudet's *Numa Roumestan* for the one, and from Marbot's *Memoirs* for the other. But when he wrote his prefaces he did not recall these details; he recalled instead a remarkably extravagant *raconteur* he had met one evening, and a young man in the next chair in Kensington Gardens who suddenly became Owen Wingrave. In these instances the fact that he had already mulled over a theme enabled the fusion between idea and image to take place at a flash.

James insisted, in the face of his brother's objection to his basing Miss Birdseye in *The Bostonians* too closely upon old Miss Peabody, that he had done nothing of the sort, that all his characters, no matter what external stimulus had helped to call them forth, had been 'evolved entirely from my moral consciousness.' That evolution is one of the most interesting to follow through the notebooks. The plot of *Washington Square* was suggested by Mrs. Kemble's story about her brother's engagement to a 'dull, plain, common-place girl'; but as James transferred the setting from England to New York, his Catherine Sloper took on a dignity of her own. On many other occasions we can observe James changing English material so that it will involve one of the international contrasts that he knew to be his most distinctive vein. Even when his anecdotes seem most shallow, recounting some liaison or divorce of the London set, we can discern how they became transformed into life. He described their impalpable growth when recalling how much he had garnered from his first country week-ends:

These delicious old houses . . . on the soil over which so much has passed and out of which so much has come, rose before me like a series of visions. I thought of a thousand things; what becomes of the things one thinks of at these times? They are not lost, we must hope; they drop back into the mind again, and they enrich and embellish it. I thought of stories, of dramas, of all the life of the past—of things one can hardly speak of; speak of, I mean, at the time. It is art that speaks of those things; and the idea makes me adore her more and more.

In such asides to himself James reveals the kind of American innocence that he never lost. This may have prevented him from becoming anything like as searching a critic of social corruption as the French and Russian masters of the novel had already shown themselves. But the value of what he brought to his *données* may be best realized in his imaginative transformation of the theme for *The Wings of the Dove* during the eight years between its first mention and the completed novel. He thought at the outset of the situation between a man and two girls as possibly fitted for a play, where, however, a happy ending seemed demanded. Only as an afterthought to a long notation did he conceive of his stricken heroine 'perhaps as an American.' At what point this outline merged with his long-buried memories of his cousin Minny Temple is impossible to say; but in Milly Theale he gave his fullest expression to the emotional qualities he understood best, to the innocent eagerness for life, and, none the less, to his deeply interfused consciousness of suffering and of evil.

Most of his notebook entries only skirt such major issues, and they will prove of interest in proportion to the reader's concern with the technical problems that any writer of fiction must face. As a contributor to American and English magazines, James was continually made aware of the limitations they imposed upon him, particularly in the treatment of sex, and he noted the greater freedom he would have enjoyed with a French audience. But he also recognized the fundamental divergence between the naturalists of the new school, and what he called 'the characteristic manner of H.J.' He knew himself to be far more concerned with the inner life and with ethical issues than they were, and from these preoccupations grew his chief contribution to the technique of the novel. Since he did not care for his plots half so much as for their psychological accompaniments, he became ever more dissatisfied, as his notebooks bear witness, with narratives in the first person, and kept devising methods by which his stories might be reflected through a central consciousness.

As he also became ever more interested in the projection of complex states of thought and feeling, he got into other difficulties with the magazine editors, who found his stories too long and not 'exciting' enough. His notebooks show him realizing the ironic fact that at the very time he was growing into fuller mastery of his resources, he was beginning to be rejected by magazines that had previously accepted him. He foresaw lucidly the widening gap between the slick popular magazine and the serious reader, and fought vigorously against each new sign of vulgarization of taste. His chief weapons in this fight were such stories as *The Next Time, The Death of the Lion,* and *The Figure in the Carpet,* which were designed as fables for critics.

But he did not shrug off the question of excessive length, since he knew it to be the danger in his method. His last secretary, Theodora Bosanquet, reported that all the five stories that made up *The Finer Grain* were produced as a succession of abortive attempts to meet *Harper's* request for a piece of five thousand words. We can observe him, again and again, conceiving his theme as 'a thing of a tiny kind,' only to have it expand, once he began to treat it, far beyond his reckoning. Short stories became *nouvelles,* and *nouvelles* became novels. He almost never held himself down to the limit he first specified, and when he did, for example, in *The Two Faces*, the shortest story in his collected edition, he signalized the occasion in his preface as a special triumph.

But these struggles also taught him some of the primary lessons of his craft. They enabled him to formulate his definition of the essential difference between 'the anecdotal' and 'the developmental,' between the story that could be handled as 'a single incident,' and the theme that necessarily demanded accretions. His greater fascination with the latter brought him to the mastery of a form in which Turgenieff and Flaubert had furnished him with examples—the story between twenty and forty thousand words in length, which James called the 'beautiful and blest' *nouvelle*, and in which he opened up the way for subsequent writers in English. Even when *The Spoils of Poynton* and *What Maisie Knew* dilated beyond those dimensions and grew into novels, James still maintained 'vivid concision' as his constant ideal. He often invoked 'the spirit of Maupassant' to come to his aid, and though his desire to portray a more and more intricate consciousness inevitably led him into greater length, he kept from first to last, to his resolution to be 'intensely objective.'

James wrote in his notebooks most frequently in the mid-eighteen-nineties, which means that they throw most light on his fiction at the period when he was just finishing his experiment of writing plays, and was looking for fresh resources. In his 'summing up' of 1881 he spoke of working for the stage as 'the most cherished of all my projects,' and of 'the dramatic form' as 'the most beautiful thing possible.' But not until ten years later, after he had produced a fairly successful acting version of *The American*, did he settle to that project in earnest. He then composed four comedies which failed to reach the stage, and *Guy Domville*, which was a failure. He found himself hampered and harried by the demands of the current commercial theater, and even while making every effort to meet them, he often dipped his pen for solace 'into the *other* ink—the sacred fluid of fiction.' It was also during this period that he discussed his aims most often, and reminded himself of 'the old, old lesson—that of the art of *reflection*. When I practise it the whole field is lighted up—I feel again the multitudinous presence of all human situations and pictures, the surge and pressure of *life*. All passions, all combinations, are there.'

Shortly after the disastrous opening night of *Guy Domville* there followed the most interesting sequence in all the notebooks. Instead of being crushed by the disappointment and by the apparent wastage of nearly five years of his career, James simply noted: 'I take up my *own* old pen again—the pen of all my old unforgettable efforts and sacred struggles. To myself—today—I need say no more. Large and full and high the future still opens. It is now indeed that I may do the work of my life. And I will.'

Within a month he made one of his most eloquent rededications to his craft: 'I have my head, thank God, full of visions. One has never too many—one has never enough. Ah, just to let one's self go—at last: to surrender one's self to what through all the long years one has . . . hoped for and waited for—the mere potential, and relative, increase of *quantity* in the material act—act of application and production. One has prayed and hoped and waited, in a word, to be able to work *more*. And now, toward the end, it seems, within its limits, to have come. That is all I ask. Nothing else in the world. I bow down to Fate, equally in submission and in gratitude. This time it's gratitude; but the form of the gratitude, to be real and adequate, must be large and confident action—splendid and supreme creation.'

During the next year his imagination was thronged with far more potential subjects than at any other period. He resumed the themes for both *The Wings of the Dove* and *The Golden Bowl*, both of which he had noted previously, and added that for *The Ambassadors*. But he undertook none of these big novels at this time. He was absorbed first with salvaging what he could from his recent experience: 'IF there has lurked in the central core of it this exquisite truth—I almost hold my breath with suspense as I try to formulate it; so much, so *much*, hangs radiantly there as depending on it—this exquisite truth that what I call the divine principle in question is a key that, working in the same *general* way fits the complicated chambers of *both* the dramatic and the narrative lock: IF, I say, I have crept round through long apparent barrenness, through suffering and sadness intolerable, to that rare perception—why my infinite little loss is converted into an almost infinite little gain.'

He was presently advancing confidently in his demonstration of that truth. *The Spoils of Poynton* and *What Maisie Knew* are the works that receive the most extensive discussion in his notebooks, and they also form the pivotal point between his earlier and later methods. He spoke, while outlining the *Spoils*, of the valuable economy of 'fundamental statement.' His plays had taught him how to work out what he now called a 'close, clear, full scenario'; and for *Maisie* in particular he thought of his structure as a succession of acts. He had arrived, as he said, at 'the acquired mastery of scenic presentation,' and the rest of his work would illustrate his conviction that 'the *scenic* method is my absolute, my imperative, my *only* salvation.'

With *The Awkward Age*, on which his notes are much less full, he carried as far as he could the experiment of making a novel consist entirely of dramatic dialogue. But he continued to advise himself of the necessity of dramatizing everything he touched. He turned again at intervals to the question of 'the really short thing,' and invoked new miracles of 'foreshortening.' But near the turn of the century he felt a renewed desire for 'the *big* (scenic, constructive, "architectural" effects).' This was to yield, in three successive years, his three major novels, and when he started these, his notebook entries virtually stopped.

The three related documents printed take us a few steps farther into his processes of work. After he had completed *The American Scene* and the prefaces for his collected edition (1907-9), he wrote Howells of having 'broken ground on an American novel.' The first result of that effort would appear to be his 'Note for the "K.B." Case,' and we find him reaffirming there once again what he had gained from his crucial experience of working for the theater, and how it had crystallized once for all his ability to conceive everything 'in the dramatic way.' He started to work out his *donnée* with the amplitude he was also to enjoy in his printed notes for *The Ivory Tower* and *The Sense of the Past*, and even began the opening chapter. But his work was interrupted by several months of nervous ill-health, and then, after William's death, he recaptured his memories of the past in his autobiographies. When he came back, four years later, to his plan for an American novel, he used, in *The Ivory Tower*, some of the names he had devised for the characters in 'Mrs. Max' (as he thought of calling 'The "K.B." Case'), but his theme was altogether different.

The outbreak of the war seems to have made it impossible for him to concentrate any longer upon contemporary society, and he returned to the theme for *The Sense of the Past*, which he had sketched in his notebook years before. The additional notes printed here reveal the way he went about re-absorbing himself in a theme, and carry him to the point where he could say, 'Above all I see . . .' With that phrase, so heavily freighted for a writer whose long career had been devoted to the farthest intensity of aesthetic and moral perception, he could break off his notes and resume the development of his novel.

The longest single outline included here, his 'scenario' for *The Ambassadors*, belongs in a somewhat different category from the rest of his notes, since it was written not for himself alone, but for his publisher, as a basis for serialization. Though dating from many years earlier than his final memoranda, it forms a fitting climax to the present volume, since its fullness of detail brings us to the very threshold of his completed fiction.

Readers of that fiction will find many uses for these notebooks, and many other threads of interest beyond those suggested in this introduction. Our commentary scattered through the volume is designed to place James' notes in relation to the stories and novels he evolved from them, and to indicate, in the briefest possible manner, the principal developments or alterations between the notes and their final treatment. We have drawn upon his prefaces wherever they amplified points raised by the notebooks themselves. We have left without commentary those themes that James did not work up into a specific story, but other readers may discover in his voluminous work partial handlings of some material that we have passed over. The chief value in these notebooks should remain for other practitioners of fiction to quarry out, since they will find them a more informal companion volume to his prefaces, which, as he told Howells, constitute 'a sort of comprehensive manual or *vademecum* for aspirants in our arduous profession.'

F. O. M.
K. B. M.

A NOTE ON THE TEXT

HENRY JAMES' notebooks and the other manuscripts printed in this volume were for the most part written hastily, simply for his own eyes. In printing them it has seemed more important to make an intelligible and easily readable version than to reproduce precisely all their peculiarities of abbreviation, punctuation, capitalization, and spelling. Anyone curious about such minutiae can be easily satisfied, since the original manuscripts, together with microfilm or typed copies, are in the Harvard College Library.

Pointed brackets have been used to indicate whatever necessary changes from the original have been made by the editors, wherever this could be done without impairing readability and wherever the alterations seemed important enough to note. Thus, pointed brackets enclose words added by the editors to replace obvious omissions in the manuscript, letters added to correct manifest errors in spelling or to fill out names indicated only by initials, and editorial conjectures (indicated by question marks) for words illegible in James' script. Editorial emendations that could not be indicated in the text without impairing the appearance and legibility of the printed page have been separately listed in an appendix on p. 417. To illustrate, when James writes 'take' for 'takes,' 'take <s>' is printed; '<wasted?>' appears for a word indecipherable in the manuscript; and James', 'He must be a great admirer of the physique of English race,' becomes 'He must be a great admirer of the physique of <the> English race.' But when he wrote 'in spite of in spite of,' the text has simply 'in spite of,' and the omission of the accidental repetition in the original is noted in the appendix.

Some minor changes have been made from the manuscripts without any notation in appendix or text. These fall into the categories listed in the following paragraphs.

The dates and places at the head of many entries were written by James in various forms. To improve the appearance of the printed page they have all been italicized and uniformly punctuated. In order to separate entries, to divide sections of the notebooks, or to mark unfinished sentences, the manuscripts often have rows of 'X's' or rows of dashes. These are reproduced in type as x x x x x.

The spelling of the manuscripts has been followed, with the exceptions noted here. When one word is spelled differently by James in various places, the usual current form has been chosen and consistently used. Patent misspellings, when they do not involve an error of more than one letter (or, in foreign words, an omission of, or mistake in, accents) and when the misspelling is not itself a word, have been correctly printed. For example, James sometimes wrote 'charing' for 'charming'; 'charming' has been printed. When the apparently misspelled form is itself a word, however, the correct version has been printed with an indication of the editorial correction given either by the use of pointed brackets, as explained above, or by a notation in the appendix.

'And' is commonly expressed in the manuscripts by a sign, presumably meant to be an ampersand, and this sign, followed by 'c' is often used for 'etc.' 'Would' and 'should' are sometimes abbreviated as 'wld' and 'shld.' These abbreviations are ignored, and 'would,' 'should,' 'and,' and 'etc.' are printed. James' other abbreviations are unchanged, except for a few noted in the appendix.

Foreign words and phrases were sometimes underlined in the manuscripts and sometimes not. They are all printed here in italics, except that a few words, like 'denouement,' which are in common English use, are printed unitalicized in their Anglicized forms. All titles of books, stories, and articles are printed in italics, without quotation marks. James sometimes underlined them and sometimes used quotation marks.

In the manuscripts many words were underlined, some singly, some doubly, and a few even triply or quadruply, to indicate varying degrees of emphasis. In the printed text the single underlinings are represented by italics; the double, triple, and quadruple, by small capitals. This destroys a few of James' distinctions of emphasis, but these distinctions do not seem to have been very carefully made and to have attempted to preserve them in type would have produced an ugly and confusing effect.

James occasionally struck out words or phrases and substituted others for them. The printed text follows his corrected version, without indication of his deletions, except for a few cases in which his corrections seem revealing. Such cases are commented on in footnotes.

Throughout, James' punctuation is erratic and often hard to decipher. His hasty writing often blurred, for example, the distinction between a comma and a dash. In the interest of readability the punctuation of the printed text follows conventional standards, but the original has been changed only when a change was necessary to make a passage quickly intelligible.

James' capitalization has been followed, except in a few passages in which his practice is inconsistent. In these the editors have adhered to conventional usage, but whenever the original capitalization has seemed to add to the meaning, it has been kept.

The use of parentheses and of square brackets is haphazard in the manuscripts. Sometimes a phrase begins with a parenthesis and ends with a bracket, or vice versa. Sometimes the beginning of a parenthetical phrase is marked and the end is not. Sometimes one parenthesis is enclosed within another. The printed text punctuates with parenthesis marks, whether they or brackets appeared in the original, except that where James included one parenthesis within another, parentheses are used for the outer one and square brackets for the inner.

In the lists of names for possible characters in stories, occurring throughout the notebooks, the punctuation of the manuscripts is inconsistent. The printed text punctuates them uniformly, separating each name from the next with a dash. This accords with James' own most usual practice.

Footnotes have been very sparingly used, and necessary comments have been included, wherever possible, in the tailnotes affixed to the various sections of the text. The interest of the notebooks, the editors believe, is not primarily historical or biographical, so that no attempt has been made to print identifications of all the persons mentioned or annotations on all the historical and geographical data. Where James refers to individuals simply by their initials, most of the identities inevitably remain in the realm of conjecture. The editors have supplied the full names only in the few cases where they felt most certain, and where such elucidation seemed useful for the interpretation of what James wrote.

The notebook entries are printed in the order in which they were written. This has sometimes involved putting passages from one notebook among passages from another, but all such transpositions have been pointed out in notes, as have the few omissions from James' text. The three manuscripts that conclude the volume are grouped together regardless of chronology, because of their obvious relation to each other and in order to give the most important of them the climactic position.

CHRONOLOGICAL LIST

This list includes the more important volumes published in James' lifetime and in the years immediately following his death, together with a listing of the two chief collected editions, and a tabulation of the volumes in the 'New York Edition.'

1875
A Passionate Pilgrim and Other Tales
  (A Passionate Pilgrim, The Last of the Valerii, Eugene Pickering, The Madonna of the Future, The Romance of Certain Old Clothes, Madame de Mauves)
Transatlantic Sketches

1876
Roderick Hudson

1877
The American

1878
Watch and Ward
French Poets and Novelists
The Europeans

1879
Daisy Miller
An International Episode
Daisy Miller, A Study; An International Episode; Four Meetings
Hawthorne
The Madonna of the Future, and Other Tales

  (The Madonna of the Future, Longstaff's Marriage, Madame de Mauves, Eugene Pickering, The Diary of a Man of Fifty, Benvolio)

1880
The Diary of a Man of Fifty; A Bundle of Letters
Confidence

1881
Washington Square
Washington Square; The Pension Beaurepas; A Bundle of Letters
The Portrait of a Lady

1883
The Siege of London; The Pension Beaurepas; The Point of View
Portraits of Places
Daisy Miller, A Comedy in Three Acts

1884
Tales of Three Cities
  (The Impressions of a Cousin, Lady Barberina, A New England Winter)

Maud-Evelyn, Miss Gunton of Poughkeepsie)

1901
The Sacred Fount

1902
The Wings of the Dove

1903
William Wetmore Story and His Friends
The Better Sort
(Broken Wings, The Beldonald Holbein, The Two Faces, The Tone of Time, The Special Type, Mrs. Medwin, Flickerbridge, The Story in It, The Beast in the Jungle, The Birthplace, The Papers)
The Ambassadors

1904
The Golden Bowl

1905
The Question of Our Speech; The Lesson of Balzac
English Hours

1907
The American Scene

1908
Views and Reviews, edited by LeRoy Phillips

1909
Julia Bride
Italian Hours

1910
The Finer Grain
(The Velvet Glove, Mora Montravers, A Round of

Visits, Crapy Cornelia, The Bench of Desolation)

1911
The Outcry

1913
A Small Boy and Others

1914
Notes on Novelists
Notes of a Son and Brother

1917
The Ivory Tower
The Sense of the Past
The Middle Years

1918
Within the Rim, and Other Essays, 1914-15
Gabrielle De Bergerac

1919
A Landscape Painter
(A Landscape Painter, Poor Richard, A Day of Days, A Most Extraordinary Case)
Travelling Companions
(Travelling Companions, The Sweetheart of M. Briseux, Professor Fargo, At Isella, Guest's Confession, Adina, DeGrey: A Romance)

1920
Master Eustace
(Master Eustace, Longstaff's Marriage, Théodolinde, A Light Man, Benvolio)
The Letters of Henry James, edited by Percy Lubbock

1921
Notes and Reviews, edited by Pierre de C. la Rose

The Novels and Tales of Henry James. The New York Edition.
Twenty-six Volumes.

I. Roderick Hudson

II. The American

III.
IV. The Portrait of a Lady

V.
VI. The Princess Casamassima

VII.
VIII. The Tragic Muse

IX. The Awkward Age

X. The Spoils of Poynton; A London Life; The Chaperon

XI. What Maisie Knew; In the Cage; The Pupil

XII. The Aspern Papers; The Turn of the Screw; The Liar; The Two Faces

XIII. The Reverberator; Madame de Mauves; A Passionate Pilgrim; The Madonna of the Future; Louisa Pallant

XIV. Lady Barbarina; The Siege of London; An International Episode; The Pension Beaurepas; A Bundle of Letters; The Point of View

XV. The Lesson of the Master; The Death of the Lion; The Next Time; The Figure in the Carpet; The Coxon Fund

XVI. The Author of Beltraffio; The Middle Years; Greville Fane; Broken Wings; The Tree of Knowledge; The Abasement of the Northmores; The Great Good Place; Four Meetings; Paste; Europe; Miss Gunton of Poughkeepsie; Fordham Castle

XVII. The Altar of the Dead; The Beast in the Jungle; The Birthplace; The Private Life; Owen Wingrave; The Friends of the Friends; Sir Edmund Orme; The Real Right Thing; The Jolly Corner; Julia Bride

XVIII. Daisy Miller; Pandora; The Patagonia; The Marriages; The Real Thing; Brooksmith; The Beldonald Holbein; The Story in It; Flickerbridge; Mrs. Medwin

XIX.
XX. The Wings of the Dove

XXI.
XXII. The Ambassadors

XXIII.
XXIV. The Golden Bowl

XXV. The Ivory Tower

XXVI. The Sense of the Past

1921-1923
The Novels and Stories of Henry James. New and Complete Edition.
Thirty-five Volumes.

The Notebooks of
HENRY JAMES

NOTEBOOK I

7 November 1878—11 March 1888

3 Bolton St., W., November 7th, 1878.

— A young Englishman, travelling in Italy twenty years ago, meets, in some old town—Perugia, Siena, Ravenna—two ladies, a mother and daughter, with whom he has some momentary relation: the mother a quiet, delicate, interesting, touching, high bred woman— the portrait of a perfect lady, of the old English school, with a tone of sadness in the picture; the daughter a beautiful, picturesque high-tempered girl; generous, ardent, even tender, but with a good deal of coquetry and a certain amount of hardness. As the incident which constitutes this momentary contact of Harold Stanmer and Bianca Vane—their names are perhaps provisional—the former may be imagined, in the course of making a sketch of some picturesque old nook in the Italian city, to have found the young girl's figure in the line of his composition, and to have appealed to her as she stands there, to kindly remain a moment and suffer him to introduce it. She consents and he makes a hasty sketch of her—which he presents to her. They are thus in a manner introduced; but they separate without learning each other's names; she however, having made a certain appreciable impression—not exclusively agreeable—on the young man.

2. Stanmer shortly afterwards receives a letter from an intimate friend, Bernard Longueville, begging him to come and join him at Baden Baden (or some other German watering-place), which Harold presently does. The two men are old friends—closely united friends. The interest of the story must depend greatly upon this fact of their strong, deep friendship and upon the contrast of their two characters. They are, in effect, singularly different. Harold must be represented as the (roughly speaking) complex nature of the two—the subtle, the re-fined, the fanciful, the eminently modern; as he is also, by four or five years, the younger. Longueville is simpler, deeper, more masculine, more easily puzzled, less intellectual, less imaginative. He is greatly under the influence of his friend and has a great esteem for his judge-ment. He concludes his letter, asking Harold to join him, with telling him he has something momentous to consult him about. A certain

[3]

rigid, formal element must be made appreciable in Longueville—a certain English deference to all the conventions and decencies of life; but it must not be made in any way contemptible. or ridiculous, for one must feel that at bottom his nature is rich and tender, and that when he is once moved, he is moved forever. Stanmer, on joining him, finds that he is with the two ladies whom he himself has met in Italy—and that it is on a subject connected with them that he wishes to consult him. Longueville, in a word, is in love with Bianca Vane, but is rather struggling with his passion. He has a certain indefinable mistrust of the young girl, at the same time that he is deeply smitten. He has proposed to her and she has refused him; but he has reason to believe that if he proposes again she will accept him. Longueville wants to know what Stanmer thinks of her and Stanmer is a good deal embarrassed. This appeal on the part of Longueville can be made natural only by the great simplicity and conscientiousness of the young man, and by his habit of putting faith in his friend's impressions and opinions. There has been recognition, of course, between Stanmer and the two ladies, but it has not gone far; before Longueville there has been nothing more than an allusion to his having seen them at Siena. Harold does not mention the episode of the portrait; he waits, by a natural instinct, for Miss Vane to do so; and, finding that she has not done so, he says nothing. On the whole, seeing more of her, he inclines not to like her; there is something in her that displeases him. He reserves judgement, however, and of course is in no hurry to talk of her unfavourably to his friend. It befalls that the latter is suddenly summoned away for a short time; he is obliged to go to England. He asks Stanmer to remain near the ladies while he goes—to give them his care and protection; and he adds that it will be <a> capital occasion for Harold to form an opinion about Miss Vane. He will expect him to be ready with one on his own return—and with this he takes his departure. Harold accepts the charge—rather protesting, but interested in the proposal that is made him. Longueville remains absent three weeks, and in his absence Stanmer attempts to study Bianca Vane. The result of his observations is that he perceives her, as he believes, to be a coquette—that she attempts to engage in a flirtation with him. I think it may be made very interesting here to mark the degree in which Stanmer—curious, imaginative, speculative, audacious, and yet conscientious, and believing quite in his own fair play—permits himself to *experiment* upon Bianca—to endeavor to draw her out and make her, if possible, betray herself. He holds that she does so—she makes a painful impression upon him. Longueville comes back and asks him what he thinks—candidly, literally—of Blanche. Stanmer hesitates; but then tells the simple truth. He thinks she is charming, interesting—but dangerous. She is false—she has tried to entangle him. He tells him, as a friend, what has passed between them. Longueville is greatly affected by it—greatly shocked.

'But after all,' says Stanmer, 'there was no literal infidelity, since she had given you no pledge. She had listened to you, but she had refused you.'

Longueville looks at him a moment. 'She had accepted me. After I had spoken to you—the evening before I went away, I proposed to her again. She then accepted me.'

Stanmer, in a good deal of horror, 'Ah, why didn't you tell me?'

Longueville. 'I'm glad I didn't.'

Stanmer. 'Ah, but my dear fellow.'

Longueville, turning away, 'I'm sorry I didn't!'

And Stanmer learns, the next day, that there has been a rupture; but that it has come from Bianca—not from Longueville. The latter gives him no explanation of it and he is a good deal perturbed. The parties separate; Harold has, on the whole, a certain compassion for Miss Vane; and a certain sense that he has done her an injury.

3. They separate, I say, and Stanmer parts from Longueville, as well <as> from the two ladies, who return to England, to live for a long time in the country, in seclusion. Time elapses and the intimacy of the two men suffers a sensible falling-off. There is no rupture nor quarrel—no acknowledged alteration; but, in fact, something has come between them and they see much less of each other than formerly. At last, at the end of three or four years, Stanmer learns that Longueville is on the point of marrying. The marriage takes place—Stanmer is present. The figure of the bride to be studied—an opposition to Bianca. At the end of a couple of years, Harold hears, and has reason to believe, that Longueville's marriage is not a happy one—though he does not learn it from Longueville himself. Then occurs the great stroke of the story: Stanmer meets Bianca Vane again—in England—and falls violently in love with her. This may be made, I think, both very striking and very natural. She is older—she is still unmarried—she is altered—she is sad. He has the sense of having wronged her—she seems to him deeply touching. His friend's marriage leaves him at liberty to address her, and she listens to him—accepts him. At this moment, before he has had time to let Longueville know of the situation, they learn that the latter has departed from his wife, who has been cruelly unfaithful to him; and immediately afterwards Longueville turns up. He presents himself—he learns that they are on the point of marrying. Then a terrible sense of outrage, out of the past, comes over him—he breaks out in reproaches against Stanmer, whom he calls the falsest, the most treacherous, of friends. Stanmer vainly protests that he has acted with

integrity—that it was with no ulterior or disinterested view that he set his friend against Miss Vane at Baden. He had no love for her at that time—it has all come since—since Longueville's own marriage. But in Longueville the sense of injury—the force of resentment—overmasters every other feeling; he continues to protest—he *forbids* Stanmer the marriage. He discloses that he himself has been *always* in love with her—that he has never ceased to dream of her, to long for her; that only the stubbornness and folly of pride has led into his other, this miserable, union.

Stanmer. 'But married you are, unfortunately, nevertheless! What good would <it> be to you that I should renounce Miss Vane? *You* wouldn't be able to marry her.'

Longueville. 'I shouldn't? You will see!'

— Three days afterwards he comes and tells them that he is free— that his wife is dead. Here is a terribly dangerous and delicate point. It is left to be supposed—it is not made definitely clear—that he has himself been the means of his wife's death. (The circumstances of this affair to be determined—most carefully.) Bianca guesses the horrible truth and of course, in bewilderment and terror, repudiates Longueville. But she also, almost as inevitably, breaks with Stanmer and flings herself back into retirement—into a religious life. Stanmer is left with Longueville and with the latter's terrible secret. He watches over them both.—The violence of this denouement does not I think disqualify it. It can, I believe, be made strongly dramatic and natural. There are of course very many details to be studied, and I have said, here, nothing about the character of Blanche, which is of the first importance.

[*James' novel,* Confidence, *grew out of the foregoing sketch. He wrote Grace Norton in June 1879, saying that he was just finishing it, and it began to appear serially in Scribner's Monthly in August. James told Miss Norton that it was 'worth being read,' but he probably came to realize its weakness, and he did not include it in the New York edition.*[1]

Except for the conclusion, the plot of Confidence *follows that outlined here. The name Stanmer, 'perhaps provisional,' is dropped, to be used later in* The Diary of a Man of Fifty. *The hero, instead of his friend (now named Gordon Wright), becomes Bernard Longueville,*

1. Throughout the editorial comments in this volume, the phrases 'collected edition' or 'New York edition' refer to *The Novels and Tales of Henry James: The New York Edition*, published in 26 volumes from 1907 to 1917. Except as otherwise noted, all quotations from James' works, included in this edition, follow its text. Individual volumes are referred to by their titles and not by their numbers in the set.

[6]

and Blanche (or Bianca) Vane is translated into Angela Vivian. The name Blanche is used for the girl whom Gordon marries, and Vane is thriftily kept for use in A Bundle of Letters. All these characters are made American, not English, and Angela's mother, instead of belonging to 'the old English school,' is 'of old New England stock,' 'animated by the genius of Boston.'

In the novel, after Wright's marriage to Blanche Evers, he comes with her to Paris, obviously unhappily mated, and discovers that Bernard is engaged to Angela. From this point Confidence entirely departs from the notebook plan. The only violence is verbal, in Gordon's passionate tirade on what seem to him to be his wrongs. He hears for the first time that Angela and Bernard met in Siena, and is sure that this proves there has been a plot against him. But for Bernard things turn out unexpectedly well. Angela tells him that on the evening after he gave his unflattering verdict upon her to Gordon at Baden, Gordon proposed (for the second time) and was refused, so that there was no question of the verdict's having driven her suitor from her. Gordon's protestation that in spite of this he did believe his friend and that his woes have come from that belief, carries no conviction whatever in the context.

Gordon's anger and any repinings that Bernard may still have are now swiftly disposed of by the sudden transformation of Angela, hitherto a slightly enigmatic or even 'mysterious' girl, intelligent but with no definable force of character, and willing to 'present herself as a beautiful tormentress,' into an all-wise ministering angel. Her mother, until now shown chiefly as a matchmaker for Angela, becomes her partner in benevolence. The men virtually fade out of the book before a demonstration of the power of pure women. Angela packs Bernard off to London in order that she may devote herself to reforming Gordon, and her mother meanwhile takes Blanche in hand. Angela has divined somehow—the reader does not share her insight—that the Wrights deeply love each other and need only a little wholesome guidance from the Vivians. Bernard has daily letters from Angela, telling him that the therapy goes on swiftly and successfully, but not explaining how or why. At last he comes back to Paris and the Wrights travel away, happy or at least resigned, leaving him free to marry Angela as placidly as the hero of any sentimental tale in the magazines of James' day.

The next two entries, listing names recorded by James for possible use in his stories, are the first of many similar ones in the notebooks. Many of them may be easily traced in his finished work, as the reader will quickly see; and the incidence of their first occurrence, as well as their collocations, often provide clues to some of the workings of James' mind.

[7]

His special concern for names, vividly shown in the notebooks, is also testified to elsewhere. In Mora Montravers (1909), for example, one of Mr. and Mrs. Traffle's difficulties as they contemplate Mora's marriage to Walter Puddick is their dislike—and hers—for his name. And in Edith Wharton's A Backward Glance there is a particularly revealing passage. James, she writes, was 'pleased' by 'the magic of ancient names, quaint or impressive, crabbed or melodious. These he would murmur over and over to himself in a low chant, finally creating characters to fit them, and sometimes whole families, with their domestic complications and matrimonial alliances, such as the Dymmes of Dymchurch, one of whom married a Sparkle, and was the mother of little Scintilla Dymme-Sparkle, subject of much mirth and many anecdotes.' Finally, James himself writes of his method of storing up names for his 'puppets' in a letter printed on page 63 below.]

A *name*. Mrs. Portier.

Mrs. Bullivant—Mrs. Almond.

December 12th. It has often occurred to me that the following would be an interesting situation.—A man of a certain age (say 48) who has lived and thought, sees a certain situation of his own youth reproduced before his eyes and hesitates between his curiosity to see at what issue it arrives in this particular case and the prompting to interfere, in the light of his own experience, for the benefit of the actors. Mortimer, for instance, goes abroad and in some foreign town he finds the daughter of a lady—the Contessa G.—whom, when he was five and twenty, on a visit to the same place, he had known and fallen in love with. That episode of his youth comes back to him with peculiar vividness—the daughter is a strange, interesting reproduction of the mother. The mother had been a dangerous woman and had entangled him in a flirtation; an unscrupulous charmer—an imperious Circe—on the brink of whose abysmal coquetry he trembled for an hour; or rather for many days. After a great struggle he took himself off, escaped from his danger by flight and breathed more freely. Then he had greatly regretted his discretion—he wished that he might have known what it was to love such a woman. Afterwards, however, he hears things that make him think he has had a great escape. The Contessa G. has an intrigue with another man, with whom, in consequence, her husband fights a duel. The Conte G. is killed and the Countess marries her lover. She is now dead—all this, for Mortimer, is a memory. But her daughter, as I say, strongly resembles her and stirs up in Mortimer's mind the depths of the past. She is a beautiful dangerous coquette. Hovering

[8]

near her Mortimer finds a young Englishman who is evidently much in love with her, and who seems to Mortimer a sort of reproduction of himself at twenty-five—the image of his own early innocence—his own timid and awkward passion. The young man interests him and he watches the progress of his relations with the lady. They seem to him to correspond at all points with his own relations with the mother —so that at last he determines to warn him and open his eyes. x x x x x (The above sketch worked out and finished Jan. 17th.—*The Diary of a Man of Fifty.*)   x   x   x   x   x

[*This story appeared in both* Harper's Magazine *and* Macmillan's Magazine *in July 1879. Its climax turns on the point that the young Englishman, Edmund Stanmer, is not persuaded, but marries his Countess. Through witnessing his young friend's happiness the narrator, now a retired English general, is quickened into questioning his own withdrawal of twenty-five years before, and thereby gives expression to a familiar kind of Jamesian regret. But James apparently decided that this story was too thin to warrant its inclusion in the New York edition.*]

January 22d. Subject for a ghost-story.

Imagine a door—either walled-up, or that has been long locked—at which there is an occasional knocking—a knocking which—as the other side of the door is inaccessible—can only be ghostly. The occupant of the house or room, containing the door, has long been familiar with the sound; and, regarding it as ghostly, has ceased to heed it particularly—as the ghostly presence remains on the other side of the door, and never reveals itself in other ways. But this person may be imagined to have some great and constant trouble; and it may be observed by another person, relating the story, that the knocking increases with each fresh manifestation of the trouble. He breaks open the door and the trouble ceases—as if the spirit had desired to be admitted, that it might interpose, redeem and protect.

x   x   x   x   x

Another theme of the same kind.

A young girl, unknown to herself, is followed, constantly, by a figure which other persons see. She is perfectly unconscious of it—but there is a dread that she may cease to be so. The figure is that of a young man—and there is a theory that the day that she falls in love, she may suddenly perceive it. Her mother dies, and the narrator of the story then discovers, by finding an old miniature among her letters and papers, that the figure is that of a young man whom she has jilted in her youth, and who therefore committed suicide. The girl *does* fall in love, and sees the figure. She accepts her lover, and never sees it again! [1]

[*The first of these two notes, though not developed into a story, looks back to Hawthorne as well as forward to James' most characteristic handling of the ghost story. The theme of unconscious obsession by a ghostly presence and of release through love was developed, a dozen years later, in Sir Edmund Orme (1891). Including it with other ghost stories in* The Altar of the Dead *volume of his collected edition, James remarked that he could remember 'absolutely nothing' about its origin. He pointed out that his treatment of such a theme against a Brighton background owed its leading interest to 'the strange and sinister' being 'embroidered on the very type of the normal and easy.'*]

January 18th.
    A. 'Don't you hate the English?'
    B. 'Hate the English—how?'
    A. 'Don't you hate them as a nation?'
    B. 'Hating a nation is an expensive affair. I have taken too much stock in the human race to be able to do so. I can't afford it. It would ruin me.'
    A. 'Ah, if you regulate your emotions upon economical principles . . . !'

January 22d. I heard some time ago, that Anthony Trollope had a theory that a boy might be brought up to be a novelist as to any other trade. He brought up—or attempted to bring up—his own son on this principle, and the young man became a sheep-farmer, in Australia. The other day Miss Thackeray (Mrs. Ritchie) said to me that she and her husband meant to bring up their little daughter in that way. It hereupon occurred to me (as it has occurred before) that one might make a little story upon this. A literary lady (a poor novelist)—or a poor literary man either—(this to be determined)—gives out to the narrator that this is their intention with regard to their little son or daughter. After this the narrator meets the parent and child at intervals, about the world, for several years—the child's peculiar education being supposed to be coming on. At last, when the child is grown,

1. The last lines of this paragraph are very much crowded in the manuscript, in order to get them all on the page. Note that the next entry, on the next page of the manuscript, has an *earlier* date.

there is another glimpse; the intended novelist has embraced some extremely prosaic situation, which is a comment—a satire—upon the high parental views.

[*This theme, which was finally to be developed in* Greville Fane (1892), *is recurred to and elaborated in James' entry for 27 February 1889 (page 93 below).*]

January 27th. A story upon some such situation as this. Henry Irving, the actor, broke with the Batemans and got rid of Isabel B. in order to get up *Hamlet* on a great scale, and replace poor Isabel by Ellen Terry, a much more brilliant attraction. Ellen Terry appears with immense *éclat* and the thing is a great success. Isabel lapses into obscurity and is quite forgotten. One may imagine that Ellen Terry falls ill, and that Irving is suddenly in want of a substitute. Casting about for one he bethinks himself of Isabel B.—rejected and wounded, having witnessed the triumph of the other, and brooding over her wrong. Suppose then that, after a short struggle with her wounded pride, she responds to Irving's appeal—she sacrifices her resentment—makes herself little— and resumes the part in which Ellen T. has so completely effaced her. The sacrifice is an heroic one—that of a woman's most passionate personal vanity. Explanation and revelation—because she is secretly in love with the great actor. These *circumstances* might easily be changed; the idea, otherwise arranged, would remain the special sort of sacrifice made by a woman—and its motive.

[*James' continuing interest in situations dealing with the life of the theater found its fullest expression, a decade later, in* The Tragic Muse (1890) *and in the story* Nona Vincent (1892).]

January 27th. A story told in letters written alternately by a mother and her daughter and giving totally different accounts of the same situation. The mother and daughter are closely united—there has never been a shadow between them. Both are very gentle and refined—and each is very subtle and resolute. Both also are highly conscientious. The girl is devoutly in love with a young man who is also in love with her—though no declarations or confessions have passed between them. The young man at last makes known his feelings to the mother and asks leave to pay his suit. The mother, thinking him an undesirable match, refuses consent, assuring him and herself that the girl doesn't care for him. He declares that she does—that he feels it, knows it; but the mother insists that she knows her daughter best, that she has watched her, studied her; that the girl is perfectly fancy-free. And she

[11]

makes up <her> mind to this—desiring and determined to believe it. The young man writes to the girl—three times; and the mother intercepts the letters. The girl, suspecting nothing of this, cherishes her secret passion, and keeps up, out of pride and modesty, that appearance which confirms her mother's theory of her indifference. Mutual attitude of the mother and daughter, with this secret between them and yet with their apparent affection for each other unchanged. Attitude of the daughter in particular, desirous not to *pain* her mother.

x   x   x   x   x

[*In the autumn of 1879 James' friend, Theodore Child, then editing 'an Anglo-American periodical,' the Parisian, asked him for a story. 'In a single long session' in Paris he wrote* A Bundle of Letters, *which Child printed on 18 December, just less than a year after James suggested in his notebook that he might tell a story 'in letters.'*

A Bundle of Letters *does present in letter form a group of characters 'giving totally different accounts of the same situation,' but has no other connection with the memorandum in the notebook. If James referred to it at all here, he took from his entry only the idea that he might use letters to tell a story (as he did later in* The Point of View), *and contented himself with doing one of his 'mere ingenious and more or less effective pleasantries' on his favorite and successful 'international' theme, with no attempt to develop the tale outlined in his note. Nothing of the complicated relation between the mother and daughter is kept; the letters instead point up with shrewd humor the contrasts in behavior and attitude shown by tourists of various nationalities, three of them American, thrown together in a Parisian boarding-house.*]

February 21st. Mrs. Kemble [1] told me last evening the history of her brother H.'s engagement to Miss T. H.K. was a young ensign in a marching regiment, very handsome ('beautiful') said Mrs. K., but very luxurious and selfish, and without a penny to his name. Miss T. was a dull, plain, common-place girl, only daughter of the Master of King's Coll., Cambridge, who had a handsome private fortune (£4000 a year). She was very much in love with H.K., and was of that slow, sober, dutiful nature that an impression once made upon her, was made for

1. Frances Anne Kemble, the actress and writer, was 69 when James made this entry. He had written to his mother a month before: 'She is certainly one of the women I know whom I like best. . . It is . . . a kind of rest and refreshment to see a woman who (extremely annoying as she sometimes is) gives one a positive sense of having a deep, rich, human nature and having cast off all vulgarities.' In April 1893, shortly after her death, he published an essay on her in *Temple Bar,* already alluded to in the Introduction.

ever. Her father disapproved strongly (and justly) of the engagement and informed her that if she married young K. he would not leave her a penny of his money. It was only in her money that H. was interested; he wanted a rich wife who would enable him to live at his ease and pursue his pleasures. Miss T. was in much tribulation and she asked Mrs. K. what she would advise her to do—Henry K. having taken the ground that if she would hold on and marry him the old Doctor would after a while relent and they should get the money. (It was in this belief that he was holding on to her.) Mrs. K. advised the young girl by *no means* to marry her brother. 'If your father does relent and you are well off, he will make you a kindly enough husband, so long as all goes well. But if he should not, and you were to be poor, your lot would be miserable. *Then* my brother would be a very uncomfortable companion—*then* he would visit upon you his disappointment and discontent.' Miss T. reflected a while; and then, as she was much in love with <him>, she determined to disobey her father and take the consequences. Meanwhile H.K., however, had come to the conclusion that the father's forgiveness was not to be counted upon—that his attitude was very firm and that if they should marry, he would never see the money. *Then* all his effort was to disentangle himself. He went off, shook himself free of the engagement, let the girl go. She was deeply wounded—they separated. Some few years elapsed—her father died and she came into his fortune. She never received the addresses of another man—she always cared in secret for Henry K.—but she was determined to remain unmarried. K. lived about the world in different military stations, and at last, at the end of 10 years (or more), came back to England—still a handsome, selfish, impecunious soldier. One of his other sisters (Mrs. S.) then attempted to bring on the engagement again—knowing that Miss T. still cared for him. She tried to make Mrs. K. join her in this undertaking, but the latter refused, saying that it was an ignoble speculation and that her brother had forfeited every claim to being thought well of by Miss T. But K. again, on his own responsibility, paid his addresses to Miss T. She refused him—it was too late. And yet, said Mrs. K., she cared for him—and she would have married no other man. But H.K.'s selfishness had over-reached itself and this was the retribution of time.

[*The characters sketched here bear considerable resemblance to Catherine Sloper and Morris Townsend in* Washington Square, *which was serialized in the* Cornhill Magazine *from June through November 1880, with illustrations by George Du Maurier, and in* Harper's *from July through December. The outlined situation is also fairly similar to the* central one in the novel, but James took the theme and fitted it to an entirely different background and milieu out of his own experience.]

Names. Mrs. Parlour—Mrs. Sturdy—Silverlock—Dexter Frere—Dovedale.

In a story, some one says—'Oh yes, the United States—a country without a sovereign, without a court, without a nobility, without an army, without a church or a clergy, without a diplomatic service, without a picturesque peasantry, without palaces or castles, or country seats, or ruins, without a literature, without novels, without an Oxford or a Cambridge, without cathedrals or ivied churches, without latticed cottages or village ale-houses, without political society, without sport, without fox-hunting or country gentlemen, without an Epsom or an Ascot, an Eton or a Rugby . . . ! !'

[*James presently incorporated this passage, almost word for word, into his biography of Hawthorne (1879), where he made it constitute his well-known enumeration of 'the items of high civilization, as it exists in other countries, which are absent from the texture of American life.' His one significant alteration was to drop 'a picturesque peasantry' and to add 'no museums, no pictures.' Many critics have noted that such an enumeration throws more light on James than on Hawthorne, and that fact, as well as the rhetorical flourish that has given the passage its quotability, seems accounted for by its having originally been conceived in the terms of James' own fiction.*]

March 18th. The figure of an American woman (in London) young, pretty, charming, clever, ambitious and conscious of her merits, desiring immensely to get into society, but handicapped by a common, vulgar, *impossible* husband. Her struggles—her appeals to the American minister, etc. (Mrs. H.L.)

A subject—The Count G. in Florence (Mme T. told me the other night) married an American girl, Miss F., whom he neglected for other women, to whom he was constantly making love. She, very fond of him, tried to console herself by flirting with other men; but she couldn't do it—it was not in her—she broke down in the attempt. This might be related from the point of view of one of the men whom she selects for this purpose and who really cares for her. Her caprices, absences, preoccupations, etc.—her sadness, her mechanical, perfunctory way of doing it—then her suddenly breaking it off and letting him see that she has a horror of him—he meanwhile being very innocent and devoted.

Names. Dainty—Slight—Cloake—Beauchemin—Lord Demesne.

Description of a situation, or incident, in an alternation of letters, written from an aristocratic, and a democratic, point of view;—both enlightened and sincere.

[*James picked up this theme during his visit to America in 1881-2, and worked it out in* The Point of View (Century Magazine, *December 1882). Cast in a series of letters, sent from America to Europe by returning travelers and by visiting Europeans, this story gave James an opportunity to gather together the many divergent impressions that struck him upon his own return after six years.*]

Names. Osmond—Rosier—Mr. and Mrs. Match—Name for husband in *P. of L.*: Gilbert Osmond—Raymond Gyves—Mrs. Gift—Name in *Times:* Lucky Da Costa—Name in Knightsbridge: Tagus Shout—Other names: Couch—Bonnycastle—Theory—Cridge—Arrant—Mrs. Tippet—Noad.

P. of a L. After Isabel's marriage there are *five* more instalments, and the success of the whole story greatly depends upon this portion being well conducted or not. Let me then make the most of it—let me imagine the best. There has been a want of action in the earlier part, and it may be made up here. The elements that remain are in themselves, I think, very interesting, and they only need to be strongly and happily combined. The weakness of the whole story is that it is too exclusively psychological—that it depends to<o> little on incident; but the complete unfolding of the situation that is established by Isabel's marriage may nonetheless be quite sufficiently dramatic. The idea of the whole thing is that the poor girl, who has dreamed of freedom and nobleness, who has done, as she believes, a generous, natural, clear-sighted thing, finds herself in reality ground in the very mill of the conventional. After a year or two of marriage the antagonism between her nature and Osmond's comes out—the open opposition of a noble character and a narrow one. There is a great deal to do here in a small compass; every word, therefore, must tell—every touch must count. If the last five parts of the story appear crowded, this will be rather a good defect in consideration of the perhaps too great diffuseness of the earlier portion. Isabel awakes from her sweet delusion —oh, the art required for making this delusion natural!—and finds herself face to face with a husband who has ended by conceiving a hatred for her own larger qualities. These facts, however, are not in themselves sufficient; the situation must be marked by important events.

[15]

Such an event is the discovery of the relation that has existed between Osmond and Madame Merle, the discovery that she has married Madame Merle's lover. Madame Merle, in a word, is the mother of Pansy. Edward Rosier comes to Rome, falls in love with Pansy and wants to marry her; but Osmond opposes the marriage, on the ground of Rosier's insufficient means. Isabel favours Pansy—she sees that Rosier would make her an excellent husband, be tenderly devoted and kind to her—but Osmond absolutely forbids the idea. Lord Warburton comes to Rome, sees Isabel again and declares to her that he is resigned, that he has succeeded in accepting the fact of her marriage and that he is now disposed, himself, to marry. He makes the acquaintance of Pansy, is charmed with her, and at last tells Isabel that he should like to make her his wife. Isabel is almost shocked, for she distrusts this sentiment of Lord Warburton's; and the reader must feel that she mistrusts it justly. This same sentiment is a very ticklish business. It is honest up to a certain point; but at bottom, without knowing it, Lord W.'s real motive is the desire to be near Isabel whom he sees, now, to be a disappointed, and unhappy woman. This is what Isabel has perceived; she feels that it would <be> cruel to Pansy, dangerous to herself, to allow such a marriage—for which, however, there are such great material inducements that she cannot well oppose it. Her position is a most difficult one, for by begging Lord Warburton to desist she only betrays her apprehension of him—which is precisely what she wishes not to do. Besides, she is afraid of doing a wrong to Pansy. Madame Merle, meanwhile, has caught a glimpse of Warburton's state of mind and eagerly takes up the idea of his marrying the girl. Pansy is very much in love with Rosier—she has no wish to marry Lord W. Isabel is <so> convinced at last of this that she feels absolved from considering her prospects with Lord W. and treats the latter with such coldness that he feels the vanity of hope and withdraws from the field, having indeed not paid any direct attention to Pansy, whom he cannot in the least be accused of jilting. Madame Merle, very angry at his withdrawal, accuses Isabel of having dissuaded him, out of jealousy, because of his having been an old lover of hers and her wishing to keep him for herself; and she still opposes the marriage with Rosier, because she has been made to believe by Lord Warburton's attentions that Pansy may do something much more brilliant. Isabel resents Madame Merle's interference, demands of her what she has to do with Pansy. Whereupon Madame Merle, in whose breast the suppressed feeling of maternity has long been rankling, and who is passionately jealous of Isabel's influence over Pansy, breaks out with the cry that she alone has a right—that Pansy is her daughter. (To be settled later whether this revelation is to be made by Mme Merle herself, or by the Countess

[16]

Gemini. Better on many grounds that it should be the latter; and yet in that way I lose the 'great scene' between Madame Merle and Isabel.) In any event this whole matter of Mme Merle is (like Lord W.'s state of mind about Pansy) a very ticklish one—very delicate and difficult to handle. To make it natural that she should have brought about Isabel's marriage to her old lover—this is in itself a supreme difficulty. It is not, however, an impossibility, for I honestly believe it rests upon nature. Her old interest in Osmond remains in a modified form; she wishes to do something for him, and she does it through another rather than by herself. That, I think, is perfectly natural. As regards Pansy the strangeness of her conduct is greater; but we must remember that we see only its surface—we don't see her reasoning. Isabel has money, and Mme Merle has great confidence in her benevolence, in her generosity; she has no fear that she will be a harsh stepmother, and she believes she will push the fortunes of the child she herself is unable to avow and afraid openly to patronize. In all this Osmond sinks a little into the background—but one must get the sense of Isabel's exquisitely miserable revulsion. Three years have passed—time enough for it to have taken place. His worldliness, his deep snobbishness, his want of generosity, etc.; his hatred of her when he finds that she judges him, that she morally protests at so much that surrounds her. The uncleanness of the air; the Countess Gemini's lovers, etc. Caspar Goodwood of course must reappear, and Ralph, and Henrietta; Mrs. Touchett, too, for a moment. Ralph's helpless observation of Isabel's deep misery; her determination to show him nothing, and his inability to help her. This to be a strong feature in the situation. Pansy is sent back to the convent, to be kept from Rosier. Caspar Goodwood comes to Rome, because he has heard from Henrietta that Isabel is unhappy, and Isabel sends him away. She hears from Ralph at Gardencourt, that he is ill there (Ralph, himself), that indeed he is dying. (The letter to come from Mrs. Touchett who is with him; or even it would be well that it should be a telegram; it expresses Ralph's wish to see her.) Isabel tells Osmond she wishes to go; Osmond, jealously and nastily, forbids it; and Isabel, deeply distressed and embarrassed, hesitates. Then Madame Merle, who wishes her to make a *coup de tête*, to leave Osmond, so that she may be away from Pansy, reveals to her her belief that it was Ralph who induced her father to leave her the £70,000. Isabel, then, violently affected and overcome, starts directly for England. She reaches Ralph at Gardencourt, and finds Caspar Goodwood and Henrietta also there: i.e., in London. Ralph's death—Isabel's return to London, and interview with Caspar G.—His passionate outbreak; he beseeches her to return with him to America. She is greatly moved, she feels the full force of his devotion—to which she has never done

[17]

justice; but she refuses. She starts again for Italy—and her departure is the climax and termination of the story.

x   x   x   x   x

With strong handling it seems to me that it may all be very true, very powerful, very touching. The obvious criticism of course will be that it is not finished—that I have not seen the heroine to the end of her situation—that I have left her *en l'air*.—This is both true and false. The *whole* of anything is never told; you can only take what groups together. What I have done has that unity—it groups together. It is complete in itself—and the rest may be taken up or not, later.

— I am not sure that it would not be best that the exposure of Mme Merle should never be complete, and above all that she should not denounce herself. This would injure very much the impression I have wished to give of her profundity, her self-control, her regard for appearances. It may be enough that Isabel should believe the fact in question —in consequence of what the Countess Gemini has told her. Then, when Madame Merle tells her of what Ralph has done for her of old—tells it with the view I have mentioned of precipitating her defiance of Osmond—Isabel may charge her with the Countess G.'s secret. This Madame Merle will deny—but deny in such a way that Isabel knows she lies; and *then* Isabel may depart.—The last (October) instalment to take place wholly in England. At the very last Caspar Goodwood goes to Pratt's hotel, and is told that Mrs. Osmond has left it the night before. Later in the day he sees Henrietta who has the last word—utters the last line of the story: a characteristic characterization of Isabel.

[*This undated discussion of* The Portrait of a Lady *would indicate a lapse of well over a year in James' entries in this notebook. As he remarked in his summary of these years (p. 29 below), he began this most ambitious of his early novels in Florence in the spring of 1880, or rather, he returned then to 'an old beginning, made long before.' He did not finish it until the summer of 1881, considerably after it had started to appear serially in both Macmillan's Magazine (October 1880– November 1881) and the Atlantic Monthly (November 1880–December 1881). There actually turned out to be six installments after Isabel Archer's marriage, and the analysis above furnishes, therefore, a fascinating instance of how James continued to develop and clarify his novels even while they were in the process of publication.*

[18]

His remarks about leaving his heroine's situation in a sense 'unfinished' are revelatory of his conception of structure, and correspond to what he was to say in the preface to Roderick Hudson: 'Really, universally, relations stop nowhere, and the exquisite problem of the artist is eternally but to draw, by a geometry of his own, the circle within which they shall happily appear to do so.' In the preface to the Portrait he discussed the problem caused for the novelist by starting with a character instead of with a story. But by then he was no longer worried that this novel had been 'too exclusively psychological.' He asserted that his source of interest lay not in the events but in Isabel's sense of them. He took pride that he had produced in her a center of consciousness comparable in intensity to what he later created in Lambert Strether. He singled out as 'obviously the best thing in the book' a chapter which he hardly reckons with in his outline, the chapter of entirely inward drama in which Isabel, sitting alone by the dying fire, begins to realize the relationship between Osmond and Madame Merle.

When he undertook the revision of the Portrait for his collected edition, James was still thinking of the 'great scene' he had passed up by not making the revelation of Pansy's parentage come through Madame Merle; and he therefore devoted his most extensive rewriting to building up the scene between Isabel and the Countess Gemini. Another detail of considerable importance in interpreting the ending of the novel is provided by James' remark at the end of the entry above, that the final speech by Henrietta Stackpole ('Look here, Mr. Goodwood, just you wait') is to be 'characteristic' of her rather than of Isabel. James' note thus makes it clear that he intended from the time of his first draft to have this speech be indicative of Henrietta's unquenchable optimism rather than what it has sometimes been interpreted to be, a sure forecast of Isabel's future action.][1]

January 17th, 1881. I heard an allusion yesterday to a matter in the history of Mme de Sévigné, which suggested the germ of a story. Mrs. Ritchie (Thackeray), who has been writing a little book about her, was mentioning her unbecoming conduct in siding with her daughter against the poor little *demoiselle de Grignan*, who was being forced into a convent, because her father, during her minority, had spent all her property and didn't wish to have to give an account of it. (It was more probably her stepfather: I don't remember.) This suggested to me a situation; unfortunately the convent has to come into it, and the convent is rather threadbare. The guardian or trustee of a young girl—

1. A fuller analysis of the ending of *The Portrait of a Lady*, in the light of these notebook entries, is given in F. O. Matthiessen's *Henry James: The Major Phase*, pp. 173-86.

he might be a distant blood-relation—has charge of her property for some time and perverts it to his own use, so that it is impossible to render it up when she comes of age or to give a faithful account of his stewardship. He tries to make her go into a convent (whereby however he would not really <be> absolved from handing in his accounts)—so that he shall be rid of her and of the danger of her making a noise. To his surprise—though he has strong reason to believe that she suspects his infidelity (she must be yet in her minority), she consents with great meekness—with a peculiar kind of sadness and sweetness that touch him. They touch him so much—her want of resentment and readiness to forgive him are so affecting—that, combined with his sense of having wronged her, they produce a great commotion in his mind, the result of which is a sudden consciousness that he has fallen in love with her. He then tries to keep her from executing her step, from retiring from the world; beseeches and implores her not to do so. But she persists, with the same sad gentleness, and turns away from him forever. Then he discovers that she had been in love with him and that her love had made her eager to forgive the wrong he had done her, and to forego all reparation. But his dishonourable act had made her also blush for her passion and desire to bury it in the cloister.

[The 'germ of a story' suggested by Mrs. Ritchie's allusion stuck in James' mind. He developed it into 'a sufficiently picturesque little donnée,' described in his notebook for 30 May 1883, and used a few months later in The Impressions of a Cousin. See page 52 below.]

January 18th, 1881. Mrs. T., living in America (say at Newport), has a son, young, unmarried, clever and selfish, who persists in living in Europe, and whom she therefore sees only at long intervals. He prefers European life, and takes his filial duties very lightly. She goes out to see him from time to time, but dares not fix herself permanently near him, for fear of boring him. At last, however, he comes home, to pay a short visit, and all her desire is to induce him to remain with her for some months. She has reason to believe that he will grow very tired of her quiet house; and in order to enhance its attraction she invites a young girl—a distant relative, from another part of the country—to stay with her. She has not the least desire that her son shall fall in love, seriously, with the girl; and does not believe that he will—being of a cold and volatile disposition and having a connection with some woman abroad. She simply thinks that the girl will make the house pleasant, and her son will stay the longer. That *she* may be sacrificed—that is, that *she* may become too much interested in the son, is an idea which she does not allow to stand in her way. The son arrives, is very pleasant for a week—then very much bored and disposed to depart. He stays a while longer, however, at the mother's urgency, and then does become interested in the girl. The latter, who is very intelligent and observant, has become aware of the part that she has been intended to play, and, after a little, has enough of it and departs. The son meanwhile is seriously in love; he follows the girl, leaves his mother alone, and spends the rest of the time that he is in America in vainly besieging the affections of the young lady—so that the mother, as a just retribution, loses his society almost altogether. The girl refuses him, and he returns in disgust and dudgeon to Europe, where he marries the other person, before-mentioned, while the mother is left lamenting! —The subject is rather trivial, but I think that something might be made of it. If the denouement just suggested appears too harsh, it may be supposed that the girl at last accedes to the son's passion and that he marries her—the separation from his mother being none the less complete. The story may be told as a journal of the mother.

[A New England Winter *grew out of this sketch. It was finished by February 1884, and printed in the August and September issues of the* Century Magazine. *James wrote Howells: 'It is not very good—on the contrary; but it will perhaps seem to you to put into form a certain impression of Boston.' Howells was enthusiastic in his response to the vividness and accuracy of James' 'impression,' but James did not include the story in his collected edition.*

In the story Mrs. Daintry arranges to have Rachel Torrance come to Boston to make life more interesting for her son, Florimond, but Rachel stays with a cousin, Mrs. Mesh. The young man goes to the Meshes' constantly, but Rachel does not fall in love with him, nor he with her. Instead, as Mrs. Daintry comes at last to realize, his interest is in Mrs. Mesh. The affair is innocent, but Mrs. Daintry is shocked, and the story ends with her forcing Florimond back to Europe by insisting that she must go herself. The 'subject' remains 'rather trivial' and James treats it lightly, making the young man vain and lazy—'poor little Florimond'—and contrasting his impulsive and none too clear-sighted mother with a shrewd Bostonian sister-in-law, who has little patience with her or her son, but likes Rachel. The notebook sketch would have made a 'harsh' or at least a serious tale; A New England Winter *is social comedy.*

After his entry for 18 January 1881, James wrote nothing more in Notebook I *until 22 December 1882. In the meanwhile, however, he began another notebook, with a passage dated 25 November 1881.*

[21]

This, and the entries which follow it, through one for 11 November 1882, are printed in the pages which follow, 23 to 45, in order to keep the chronological order of the entries. The printed text reverts to Notebook I on page 45.

Notebook II has, on its second fly-leaf, memoranda of club dues for the Athenaeum and the Reform. These are omitted in the printed text.]

NOTEBOOK II

25 November 1881—11 November 1882

Brunswick Hotel, Boston, November 25th, 1881.

If I should write here all that I might write, I should speedily fill
this as yet unspotted blank-book, bought in London six months ago,
but hitherto unopened. It is so long since I have kept any notes, taken
any memoranda, written down my current reflections, taken a sheet of
paper, as it were, into my confidence. Meanwhile so much has come
and gone, so much that it is now too late to catch, to reproduce, to
preserve. I have lost too much by losing, or rather by not having acquired, the note-taking habit. It might be of great profit to me; and
now that I am older, that I have more time, that the labour of writing
is less onerous to me, and I can work more at my leisure, I ought to
endeavour to keep, to a certain extent, a record of passing impressions,
of all that comes, that goes, that I see, and feel, and observe. To catch
and keep something of life—that's what I mean. Here I am back in
America, for instance, after six years of absence, and likely while here
to see and learn a great deal that ought not to become mere waste
material. Here I am, *da vero*, and here I am likely to be for the next
five months. I am glad I have come—it was a wise thing to do. I
needed to see again *les miens*, to revive my relations with them, and
my sense of the consequences that these relations entail. Such relations,
such consequences, are a part of one's life, and the best life, the most
complete, is the one that takes full account of such things. One can
only do this by seeing one's people from time to time, by being with
them, by entering into their lives. Apart from this I hold it was not
necessary I should come to this country. I am 37 [1] years old, I have made
my choice, and God knows that I have now no time to waste. My
choice is the old world—my choice, my need, my life. There is no need
for me today to argue about this; it is an inestimable blessing to me,
and a rare good fortune, that the problem was settled long ago, and
that I have now nothing to do but to act on the settlement.—My impressions here are exactly what I expected they would be, and I scarcely

1. He was actually 38.

see the place, and feel the manners, the race, the tone of things, now that I am on the spot, more vividly than I did while I was still in Europe. My work lies there—and with this vast new world, *je n'ai que faire.* One can't do both—one must choose. No European writer is called upon to assume that terrible burden, and it seems hard that I should be. The burden is necessarily greater for an American—for he *must* deal, more or less, even if only by implication, with Europe; whereas no European is obliged to deal in the least with America. No one dreams of calling him less complete for not doing so. (I speak of course of people who do the sort of work that I do; not of economists, of social science people.) The painter of manners who neglects America is not thereby incomplete as yet; but a hundred years hence—fifty years hence perhaps—he will doubtless be accounted so. My impressions of America, however, I shall, after all, not write here. I don't need to write them (at least not *à propos* of Boston); I know too well what they are. In many ways they are extremely pleasant; but, Heaven forgive me! I feel as if my time were terribly wasted here! x x x x x

It is too late to recover all those lost impressions—those of the last six years—that I spoke of in beginning; besides, they are not lost altogether, they are buried deep in my mind, they have become part of my life, of my nature. At the same time, if I had nothing better to do, I might indulge in a retrospect that would be interesting and even fruitful— look back over all that has befallen me since last I left my native shores. I could remember vividly, and I have little doubt I could express happily enough, if I made the effort. I could remember without effort with what an irresistible longing I turned to Europe, with what ardent yet timid hopes, with what indefinite yet inspiring intentions, I took leave of *les miens.* I recall perfectly the maturing of my little plan to get abroad again and remain for years, during the summer of 1875; the summer the latter part of which I spent in Cambridge. It came to me there on my return from New York where I had been spending a bright, cold, unremunerative, uninteresting winter, finishing *Roderick Hudson* and writing for the *Nation.* (It was these two tasks that kept me alive.) I had returned from Europe the year before that, the beginning of September, '74, sailing for Boston with Wendell Holmes and his wife as my fellow passengers. I had come back then to 'try New York,' thinking it my duty to attempt to live at home before I should grow older, and not take for granted too much that Europe alone was possible; especially as Europe for me then meant simply Italy, where I had had some very discouraged hours, and which, lovely and desirable though it was, didn't seem as a permanent residence, to lead to anything. I wanted something more active, and I came back and sought it in New York. I came back with a certain amount of scepticism, but with very loyal intentions, and extremely eager to be 'interested.' As I say, I was interested but imperfectly, and I very soon decided what was the real issue of my experiment. It was by no means equally soon, however, that I perceived how I should be able to cross the Atlantic again. But the opportunity came to me at last—it loomed before me one summer's day, in Quincy St. The best thing I could imagine then was to go and take up my abode in Paris. I went (sailing about October 20th, 1875) and I settled myself in Paris with the idea that I should spend several years there. This was not really what I wanted; what I wanted was London—and Paris was only a stopgap. But London appeared to me then impossible. I believed that I might arrive there in the fulness of years, but there were all sorts of obstacles to my attempting to live there then. I wonder greatly now, in the light of my present knowledge of England, that these obstacles should have seemed so large, so overwhelming and depressing as they did at that time. When a year later I came really to look them in the face, they absolutely melted away. But that year in Paris was not a lost year—on the contrary. On my way thither I spent something like a fortnight in London; lodging at Story's Hotel, in Dover St. It was November—dark, foggy, muddy, rainy—and I knew scarcely a creature in the place. I don't remember calling on anyone but Lady Rose and H. J. W. Coulson, with whom I went out to lunch at Petersham, near Richmond. And yet the great city seemed to me enchanting, and I would have given my little finger to remain there rather than go to Paris. But I went to Paris, and lived for a year at 29 Rue de Luxembourg (now Rue Cambon). I shall not attempt to write the history of that year—further than to say that it was time by no means misspent. I learned to know Paris and French affairs much better than before— I got a certain familiarity with Paris (added to what I had acquired before) which I shall never lose. I wrote letters to the *New York Tribune*, of which, though they were poor stuff, I may say that they were too good for the purpose (of course they didn't succeed). I saw a good deal of Charles Peirce that winter—as to whom his being a man of genius reconciled me to much that was intolerable in him.[1] In the spring, at Madame Turgenieff's, I made the acquaintance of Paul

1. James' reaction to Peirce was summed up in a letter home at the time: 'He is a very good fellow—when he is not in ill-humour; then he is intolerable. But, as William says, he is a man of genius. . .' Peirce wrote to William: 'Your brother is looking pretty well, but looks a little serious. . . He is a splendid fellow. I admire him greatly and have only discovered two faults in him. One is that his digestion isn't quite that of an ostrich and the other is that he isn't as fond of turning over questions as I am, but likes to settle them and have done with them. A manly trait too, but not a philosophic one.'

Joukowsky. *Non ragioniam di lui—ma guarda e passa.* I don't speak of Ivan Turgenieff, most delightful and lovable of men, nor of Gustave Flaubert, whom I shall always be so glad to have known; a powerful, serious, melancholy, manly, deeply corrupted, yet not corrupting, nature. There was something I greatly liked in him, and he was very kind to me. He was a head and shoulders above the others, the men I saw at his house on Sunday afternoons—Zola, Goncourt, Daudet, etc. (I mean as a man—not as a talker, etc.) I remember in especial one afternoon (a weekday) that I went to see him and found him alone. I sat with him a long time; something led him to repeat to me a little poem of Th. Gautier's—*Les Vieux Portraits* (what led him to repeat it was that we had been talking of French poets, and he had been expressing his preference for Théophile Gautier over Alfred de Musset—*il était plus français,* etc.). I went that winter a great deal to the Comédie Française—though not so much as when I was in Paris in '72. Then I went every night—or almost. And I have been a great deal since. I may say that I know the Comédie Française. Of course I saw a great deal of the little American 'set'—the American village encamped *en plein Paris.* They were all very kind, very friendly, hospitable, etc; they knew up to a certain point their Paris. But ineffably tiresome and unprofitable. Their society had become a kind of obligation, and it had much to do with my suddenly deciding to abandon my plans of indefinite residence, take flight to London and settle there as best I could. I remember well what a crime Mrs. S. made of my doing so; and one or two other persons as to whom I was perfectly unconscious of having given them the right to judge my movements so intimately. Nothing is more characteristic of certain American women than the extraordinary promptitude with which they assume such a right. I remember how Paris had, in a hundred ways, come to weary and displease me; I couldn't get out of the detestable *American* Paris. Then I hated the Boulevards, the horrible monotony of the new quarters. I saw, moreover, that I should be an eternal outsider. I went to London in November, 1876. I should say that I had spent that summer chiefly in three places: at Étretat, at Varennes (with the Lee Childes), and at Biarritz—or rather at Bayonne, where I took refuge being unable to find quarters at Biarritz. Then late in September I spent a short time at St. Germain, at the Pavillon Louis XIV. I was finishing *The American.* The pleasantest episode (by far) of that summer was my visit to the Childes; to whom I had been introduced by dear Jane Norton; who had been very kind to me during the winter; and who have remained my very good friends. Varennes is a little moated *castel* of the most picturesque character, a few miles from Montargis, *au coeur de l'ancienne France.* I well recall the impression of my arrival

[26]

—driving over from Montargis with Edward Childe—in the warm August evening and reaching the place in the vague twilight, which made it look precisely like a *décor d'opéra*. I have been back there since —and it was still delightful; but at that time I had not had my now very considerable experience of country visits in England; I had not seen all those other wonderful things. Varennes therefore was an exquisite sensation—a memory I shall never lose. I settled myself again in Paris —or attempted to do so (I like to linger over these details, and to recall them one by one); I had no intention of giving it up. But there were difficulties in the Rue de Luxembourg—I couldn't get back my old apartment, which I had given up during the Summer. I don't remember what suddenly brought me to the point of saying—'Go to; I will try London.' I think a letter from William had a good deal to do with it, in which he said, 'Why don't you?—That must be the place.' A single word from outside often moves one (moves *me* at least) more than the same word infinitely multiplied as a simple voice from within. I *did* try it, and it has succeeded beyond my most ardent hopes. As I think I wrote just now, I have become passionately fond of it; it is an anchorage for life. Here I sit scribbling in my bedroom at a Boston hotel—on a marble-topped table!—and conscious of a ferocious homesickness—a homesickness which makes me think of the day when I shall next see the white cliffs of old England loom through their native fog, as one of the happiest of my life! The history of the five years I have spent in London—a pledge, I suppose, of many future years—is too long, and too full to write. I can only glance at it here. I took a lodging at 3 Bolton St., Piccadilly; and there I have remained till today—there I have left my few earthly possessions, to await my return. I have *lived* much there, felt much, thought much, learned much, produced much; the little shabby furnished apartment ought to be sacred to me. I came to London as a complete stranger, and today I know much too many people. *J'y suis absolument comme chez moi.* Such an experience is an education—it fortifies the character and embellishes the mind. It is difficult to speak adequately or justly of London. It is not a pleasant place; it is not agreeable, or cheerful, or easy, or exempt from reproach. It is only magnificent. You can draw up a tremendous list of reasons why it should be insupportable. The fogs, the smoke, the dirt, the darkness, the wet, the distances, the ugliness, the brutal size of the place, the horrible numerosity of society, the manner in which this senseless bigness is fatal to amenity, to convenience, to conversation, to good manners—all this and much more you may expatiate upon. You may call it dreary, heavy, stupid, dull, inhuman, vulgar at heart and tiresome in form. I have felt these things at times so strongly that I have said—'Ah London, you too then are impossible?'

But these are occasional moods; and for one who takes it as I take it, London is on the whole the most possible form of life. I take it as an artist and as a bachelor; as one who has the passion of observation and whose business is the study of human life. It is the biggest aggregation of human life—the most complete compendium of the world. The human race is better represented there than anywhere else, and if you learn to know your London you learn a great many things. I felt all this in that autumn of 1876, when I first took up my abode in Bolton St. I had very few friends, the season was of the darkest and wettest; but I was in a state of deep delight. I had complete liberty, and the prospect of profitable work; I used to take long walks in the rain. I took possession of London; I felt it to be the right place. I could get English books: I used to read in the evenings, before an English fire. I can hardly say how it was, but little by little I came to know people, to dine out, etc. I did, I was able to do, nothing at all to bring this state of things about; it came rather of itself. I had very few letters— I was afraid of letters. Three or four from Henry Adams, three or four from Mrs. Wister, of which I only, as I think, presented one (to George Howard). Poor Motley, who died a few months later, and on whom I had no claim of *any* kind, sent me an invitation to the Athenaeum, which was renewed for several months, and which proved an unspeakable blessing. When once one starts in the London world (and one cares enough about it, as I did, to make one's self agreeable, as I did) *cela va de soi*; it goes with constantly increasing velocity. I remained in London all the following summer—till Sept. 1st—and then went abroad and spent some six weeks in Paris, which was rather empty and very lovely, and went a good deal to the theatre. Then I went to Italy, spending almost all my time in Rome (I had a little apartment flooded with sun, in the Capo le Case). I came back to England before Xmas and spent the following nine months or so in Bolton St. The club question had become serious and difficult; a club was indispensable, but I had of course none of my own. I went through Gaskell's (and I think Locker's) kindness for some time to the Travellers'; then after that for a good while to the St. James's, where I could pay a monthly fee. At last, I forget exactly when, I was elected to the Reform; I think it was about April, 1878. (F. H. Hill had proposed, and C. H. Roberts had seconded, me: or vice versa.) This was an excellent piece of good fortune, and the Club has ever since been, to me, a convenience of the first order. I could not have remained in London without it, and I have become extremely fond of it; a deep local attachment. I can now only briefly enumerate the landmarks of the rest of my residence in London. In the autumn of 1878 I went to Scotland, chiefly to stay at Tillypronie. (I afterwards paid a short visit at Gillesbie, Mrs.

Rogerson's, in Dumfriesshire.) This was my first visit to Scotland, which made a great impression on me. The following year, 1879, I went abroad again—but only to Paris. I stayed in London during all August, writing my little book on Hawthorne, and on September 1st crossed over to Paris and remained there till within a few days of Xmas. I lodged again in the Rue de Luxembourg, in another house, in a delightful little *entresol entre cour et jardin,* which I had to give up after a few weeks however, as it had been let over my head. Afterwards I went to a hotel in the Rue St. Augustin (de Choiseul et d'Égypte) where I was staying during the great snow-storm of that year, which will long be famous. It was in that October that I went again to Varennes; I had other plans for seeing a little of France which I was unable to carry out. But I did a good deal of work: finished the ill-fated little *Hawthorne,*[1] finished *Confidence,* began *Washington Square,* wrote a *Bundle of Letters.* I went that Christmas, as I had been, I think, the Xmas before, to Ch. Milnes Gaskell's (Thorne's). In the spring I went to Italy—partly to escape the 'season,' which had become a terror to me. I couldn't keep out of it—(I had become a highly-developed diner-out, etc.) and its interruptions, its repetitions, its fatigues, were horribly wearisome, and made work extremely difficult. I went to Florence and spent a couple of months, during which I took a short run down to Rome and to Naples, where I had not been since my first visit to Italy, in 1869. I spent three days with Paul Joukowsky at Posilipo, and a couple of days alone at Sorrento. Florence was divine, as usual, and I was a great deal with the Bootts. At that exquisite Bellosguardo at the Hotel de l'Arno, in a room in that deep recess, in the front, I began the *Portrait of a Lady* [2]—that is, I took up, and worked over, an old beginning, made long before. I returned to London to meet William, who came out in the early part of June, and spent a month with me in Bolton St., before going to the continent. That summer and autumn I worked, *tant bien que mal,* at my novel which began to appear in *Macmillan* in October (1880). I got away from London more or less—to Brighton, detestable in August, to Folkestone, Dover, St. Leonard's, etc. I tried to work hard, and I paid very few visits. I

---

1. James' *Hawthorne,* printed in 1879, was 'ill-fated' in the attacks it provoked. He wrote Elizabeth Boott on 22 February 1880: 'The American press, with 2 or 3 exceptions, seems furious over my poor little Hawthorne. It is a melancholy revelation of angry vanity, vulgarity and ignorance. I thought they would protest a good deal at my calling New England life unfurnished, but I didn't expect they would lose their heads and their manners at such a rate.' A letter to Howells a month earlier refers to some critics of the book as 'bloodhounds' eager to besplatter 'the decent public' with its author's 'gore.'

2. When he wrote the preface to *The Portrait of a Lady* James' memory betrayed him into misdating this visit to the spring of 1879.

had a plan of coming to America for the winter and even took my passage; but I gave it up. William came back from abroad and was with me again for a few days, before sailing for home. I spent November and December quietly in London, getting on with the *Portrait*, which went steadily, but very slowly, every part being written twice. About Xmas I went down into Cornwall, to stay with the John Clarks, who were wintering there, and then to the Pakenhams', who were (and still are) in the Government House at Plymouth. (Xmas day, indeed, I spent at the Pakenhams'—a bright, military dinner at which I took in Elizabeth Thompson [Mrs. Butler], the military paintress: a gentle, pleasing woman, very deaf.) Cornwall was charming, and my dear Sir John drove me far away to Penzance, and then to the Land's End, where we spent the morning of New Year's day—a soft moist morning, with the great Atlantic heaving gently round the outermost point of old England. (I was wrong just above in saying that I went *first* to the Clarks'. I went on there from Devonport.) I came back to London for a few weeks, and then, again, I went abroad. I wished to get away from the London crowd, the London hubbub, all the entanglements and interruptions of London life; and to quietly bring my novel to a close. So I planned to betake myself to Venice. I started about February 10th and I came back in the middle of July following. I have always to pay toll in Paris—it's impossible to pass through. I was there for a fortnight, which I didn't much enjoy. Then I traveled down through France, to Avignon, Marseilles, Nice, Mentone and San Remo, in which latter place I spent three charming weeks, during most of which time I had the genial society of Mrs. Lombard and Fanny L. who came over from Nice for a fortnight. I worked there capitally, and it made me very happy. I used in the morning to take a walk among the olives, over the hills behind the queer little black, steep town. Those old paved roads that rise behind and above San Remo, and climb and wander through the dusky light of·the olives, have an extraordinary sweetness. Below and beyond, were the deep ravines, on whose sides old villages were perched, and the blue sea, glittering through the grey foliage. Fanny L. used to go with me—enjoying it so much that it was a pleasure to take her. I went back to the inn to breakfast (that is, lunch), and scribbled for 3 or 4 hours in the afternoon. Then, in the fading light, I took another stroll, before dinner. We went to bed early, but I used to read late. I went with the Lombards, one lovely day, on an enchanting drive—to the strange little old mountain town of Ceriana. I shall never forget that; it was one of the things one remembers; the grand clear hills, among which we wound higher and higher; the long valley, swimming seaward, far away beneath; the bright Mediterranean, growing paler and paler as we rose above it; the splendid stillness, the infinite light, the clumps of olives, the brown villages, pierced by the carriage road, where the vehicle bumped against opposite doorposts. I spent ten days at Milan after that, working at my tale and scarcely speaking to a soul; Milan was cold, dull, and less attractive than it had been to me before. Thence I went straight to Venice, where I remained till the last of June—between three and four months. It would take long to go into that now; and yet I can't simply pass it by. It was a charming time; one of those things that don't repeat themselves; I seemed to myself to grow young again. The lovely Venetian spring came and went, and brought with it an infinitude of impressions, of delightful hours. I became passionately fond of the place, of the life, of the people, of the habits. I asked myself at times whether it wouldn't be a happy thought to take a little *pied-à-terre* there, which one might keep forever. I looked at unfurnished apartments; I fancied myself coming back every year. I *shall* go back; but not every year. Herbert Pratt was there for a month, and I saw him tolerably often; he used to talk to me about Spain, about the East, about Tripoli, Persia, Damascus; till it seemed to me that life would be *manquée* altogether if one shouldn't have some of that knowledge. He was a most singular, most interesting type, and I shall certainly put him into a novel. I shall even make the portrait close and he won't mind. Seeing picturesque lands, simply for their own sake, and without making any use of it—that, with him, is a passion—a passion of which if one lives with him a little (a little, I say; not too much) one feels the contagion. He gave me the nostalgia of the sun, of the south, of colour, of freedom, of being one's own master, and doing absolutely what one pleases. He used to say, 'I know such a sunny corner, under the south wall of old Toledo. There's a wild fig tree growing there; I have lain on the grass, with my guitar. There was a musical muleteer, etc.' I remember one evening when he took me to a queer little wineshop, haunted only by gondoliers and *facchini*, in an out of the way corner of Venice. We had some excellent muscat wine; he had discovered the place and made himself quite at home there. Another evening I went with him to his rooms—far down on the Grand Canal, overlooking the Rialto. It was a hot night; the cry of the gondoliers came up from the Canal. He took out a couple of Persian books and read me extracts from Firdousi and Saadi. A good deal might be done with Herbert Pratt. He, however, was but a small part of my Venice. I lodged on the Riva, 4161, *quarto piano*. The view from my windows was *una bellezza*; the far-shining lagoon, the pink walls of San Giorgio, the downward curve of the Riva, the distant islands, the movement of the quay, the gondolas in profile. Here I wrote, diligently every day and finished, or virtually finished, my novel. As I say, it was a charming life; it seemed to me, at times, too improbable, too festive. I went out in the morning—first to Florian's, to break-fast; then to my bath, at the Stabilimento Chitarin; then I wandered about, looking at pictures, street life, etc., till noon, when I went for my real breakfast to the Café Quadri. After this I went home and worked till six o'clock—or sometimes only till five. In this latter case I had time for an hour or two *en gondole* before dinner. The evenings I strolled about, went to Florian's, listened to the music in the Piazza, and two or three nights a week went to Mrs. Bronson's. That was a resource but the milieu was too American. Late in the spring came Mrs. V.R., from Rome, who was an even greater resource. I went with her one day to Torcello and Burano; where we took our lunch and eat it on a lovely canal at the former place. Toward the last of April I went down to Rome and spent a fortnight—during part of which I was laid up with one of those terrible attacks in my head. But Rome was very lovely; I saw a great deal of Mrs. V.R.; had (with her) several beautiful drives. One in particular I remember; out beyond the Ponte Nomentano, a splendid Sunday. We left the carriage and wandered into the fields, where we sat down for some time. The exquisite still-ness, the divine horizon, brought back to me out of the buried past all that ineffable, incomparable impression of Rome (1869, 1873). I re-turned to Venice by Ancona and Rimini. From Ancona I drove to Loreto, and, on the same occasion, to Recanati, to see the house of Giacomo Leopardi, whose infinitely touching letters I had been reading while in Rome. The day was lovely and the excursion picturesque; but I was not allowed to enter Leopardi's house. I saw, however, the dreary little hill-town where he passed so much of his life, with its enchanting beauty of site, and its strange, bright loneliness. I saw the streets—I saw the views he looked upon. . . Very little can have changed. I spent only an evening at Rimini, where I made the ac-quaintance of a most obliging officer, who seemed delighted to con-verse with a *forestiero*, and who walked me (it was a Sunday evening) all over the place. I passed near *Urbino*: that is, I passed a station, where I might have descended to spend the night, to drive to Urbino the next day. But I didn't stop! If I had been told that a month before, I should have repelled the foul insinuation. But my reason was strong. I was so nervous about my interrupted work that every day I lost was a misery, and I hurried back to Venice and to my MS. But I made an-other short absence, in June—a 5 day's *giro* to Vicenza, Bassano, Padua. At Vicenza I spent 3 of these days—it was wonderfully sweet; old Italy, and the old feeling of it. Vivid in my memory is the afternoon I arrived, when I wandered into the Piazza and sat there in the warm shade, be-fore a *caffe* with the smooth slabs of the old pavement around me, the big palace and the tall *campanile* opposite, etc. It was so soft, so mellow, so quiet, so genial, so Italian; very little movement, only the waning of the bright day, the approach of the summer night. Before I left Venice the heat became intense, the days and nights alike impossible. I left it at last, and closed a singularly happy episode; but I took much away with me. x x x x x

I went straight to the Lake of Como and over the Splügen; spent only a lovely evening (with the next morning) at Cadenabbia. I mounted the Splügen under a splendid sky, and I shall never forget the sensation of rising, as night came (I walked incessantly, after we began to ascend) into that cool pure Alpine air, out of the stifling *calidarium* of Italy. I shall always remember a certain glass of fresh milk which I drank that evening, in the gloaming, far up (a woman at a wayside hostel had it fetched from the cow), as the most heavenly draft that ever passed my lips. I went straight to Lucerne, to see Mrs. Kemble, who had already gone to Engelberg. I spent a day on the lake, making the *giro*; it was a splendid day, and Switzerland looked more sympathetic than I had ventured to hope. I went up to Engelberg, and spent nearly a week with Mrs. Kemble and Miss Butler, in that grim, ragged, rather vacuous, but by no means absolutely unbeautiful valley. I spent an enchanting day with Miss Butler—climbing up to the Trübsee, toward the Joch Pass. The Trübsee is a little steel grey tarn, in a high cool valley, at the foot of the Titlis, whose great silver-gleaming snows overhang it and light it up. The whole place was a wilderness of the alpine rose—and the alpine stillness, the splendour of the weather, the beauty of the place, made the whole impression immense. We had a man with us who carried a lunch; and we partook of it at the little cold inn. The whole thing brought back my old Swiss days; I hadn't believed they could revive even to that point. x x x x x

New York, 115 East 25th St., December 20th, 1881.

I had to break off the other day in Boston—the interruptions in the *morning* here are intolerable. That period of the day has none of the social sanctity here that it <has> in England, and which keeps it singularly free from intrusion. People—by which I mean ladies— think nothing of asking you to come and see them before lunch. Of course one can decline, but when many propositions of that sort come, a certain number stick. Besides, I have had all sorts of things to do, chiefly not profitable to recall. I have been three weeks in New York, and all my time has slipped away in mere movement. I try as usual to console myself with the reflection that I am getting impressions. This is very true; I have got a great many. I did well to come over;

[33]

it was well worth doing. I indulged in some reflections a few pages back which were partly the result of a melancholy mood. I *can* do something here—it is not a mere complication. But it is not of that I must speak first in taking up my pen again—I shall return to those things later. I should like to finish briefly the little retrospect of the past year's doings, which I left ragged on the opposite page. x x x x x I came back from Switzerland to meet Alice,[1] who had been a month in England, and whom I presently saw at the Star and Garter, at Richmond. I spent two or three days with her, and saw her afterwards at Kew; then I went down to Sevenoaks and to Canterbury for the same purpose, spending a night at each place. I paid during July and August several visits. One to Burford Lodge (Sir Trevor Lawrence's); memorable on which occasion was a certain walk we took (on a Sunday afternoon), through the grounds of the Deepdene, an artificial but to me a most enchanting and most suggestive English place—full of foreign reminiscences; the sort of place that an Englishman of 80 years ago, who had made the grand tour and lingered in Italy would naturally construct. I went to Leatherhead, and I went twice to Mentmore. (On one of these occasions Mr. Gladstone was there.) I went to Fredk. Macmillan's at Walton-on-Thames, and had some charming moments on the river. Then I went down into Somerset and spent a week at Midelney Place, the Lady Trevilian's. It is the impression of this visit that I wish not wholly to fade away. Very exquisite it was (not the visit, but the impression of the country); it kept me a-dreaming all the while I was there. It seemed to me very old England; there was a peculiarly mellow and ancient feeling in it all. Somerset is not especially beautiful; I have seen much better English scenery. But I think I have never been more *penetrated*—I have never more loved the land. It was the old houses that fetched me—Montacute, the admirable; Barrington, that superb Ford Abbey, and several smaller ones. Trevilian showed me them all; he has a great care for such things. These delicious old houses, in the long August days, in the south of England air, on the soil over which so much has passed and out of which so much has come, rose before me like a series of visions. I thought of a thousand things; what becomes of the things one thinks of at these times? They are not lost, we must hope; they drop back into the mind again, and they enrich and embellish it. I thought of stories, of dramas, of all the life of the past—of things one can hardly speak of; speak of, I mean, at the time. It is art that speaks of those things; and the idea makes me adore her more and more. Such a house as Montacute, so perfect, with its grey personality, its old-world

1. Henry James' sister.

[34]

gardens, its accumulations of expression, of tone—such a house is really, *au fond*, an ineffaceable image; it can be trusted to rise before the eyes in the future. But what we think of with a kind of *serrement de coeur* is the gone-and-left-behind-us emotion with which at the moment we stood and looked at it. The picture may live again; but *that* is part of the past. x x x x x

Cambridge, December 26th.

I came here on the 23d, to spend Xmas, Wilky [1] having come from the West (the first time in several years), to meet me. Here I sit writing in the old back sitting room which William and I used to occupy and which I now occupy alone—or sometimes with poor Wilky, whom I have not seen in some eleven years, and who is wonderfully unchanged for a man with whom life has not gone easy. The long interval of years drops away, and the edges of the chasm 'piece together' again, after a fashion. The feeling of that younger time comes back to me in which I sat here scribbling, dreaming, planning, gazing out upon the world in which my fortune was to seek, and suffering tortures from my damnable state of health. It was a time of suffering so keen that that fact might <claim?> to give its dark colour to the whole period; but this is not what I think of today. When the burden of pain has been lifted, as many memories and emotions start into being as the little insects that scramble about when, in the country, one displaces a flat stone. Ill-health, physical suffering, in one's younger years, is a grievous trial; but I am not sure that we do not bear it most easily then. In spite of it we feel the joy of youth; and that is what I think of today among the things that remind me of the past. The freshness of impression and desire, the hope, the curiosity, the vivacity, the sense of the richness and mystery of the world that lies before us—there is an enchantment in all that which it takes a heavy dose of pain to quench and which in later hours, even if *success* have come to us, touches us less nearly. Some of my doses of pain were very heavy; very weary were some of my months and years. But all that is sacred; it is idle to write of it today. x x x x x

What comes back to me freely, delightfully, is the vision of those untried years. Never did a poor fellow have more; never was an ingenuous youth more passionately and yet more patiently eager for what life might bring. Now that life has brought something, brought a measurable part of what I dreamed of then, it is touching enough to look back. I knew at least what I wanted then—to see something of the

1. Henry James' younger brother, Garth Wilkinson.

[35]

world. I have seen a good deal of it, and I look at the past in the light of this knowledge. What strikes me is the definiteness, the unerringness of those longings. I wanted to do very much what I have done, and success, if I may say so, now stretches back a tender hand to its younger brother, desire. I remember the days, the hours, the books, the seasons, the winter skies and darkened rooms of summer. I remember the old walks, the old efforts, the old exaltations and depressions. I remember more than I can say here today. x x x x x

Again, in New York the other day, I had to break off: I was trying to finish the little history of the past year. There is not much more to be said about it. I came back from Midelney, to find Alice in London, and spent ten days with her there, very pleasantly, at the end of August. Delightful to me is London at that time, after the horrors of the season have spent themselves, and the long afternoons make a cool grey light in the empty West End. Delightful to me, too, it was to see how *she* enjoyed it—how interesting was the impression of the huge, mild city. London is mild then; that is the word. And then I went to Scotland— to Tillypronie, to Cortachy, to Dalmeny, to Laidlawstiel. I was to have wound up, on my way back, with Castle Howard; but I retracted, on account of Lord Airlie's death. I can't go into all this; there were some delightful moments, and Scotland made, as it had made before, a great impression. Perhaps what struck me as much as anything was my drive, in the gloaming, over from Kirriemuir to Cortachy; though, taking the road afterward by daylight, I saw it was commonplace. In the late Scotch twilight, and the keen air, it was romantic; at least it was romantic to ford the river at the entrance to Cortachy, to drive through the dim avenues and up to the great lighted pile of the castle, where Lady A., hearing my wheels on the gravel (I was late) put her handsome head from a window in the clock-tower, asked if it was I, and wished me a bonny good-evening. I was in a Waverly Novel.

Then my drive (with her) to Glamis; and my drive (with Miss Stanley) to Airlie Castle, enchanting spot! Dalmeny is delicious, a magnificent pile of wood beside the Forth, and the weather, while I was there, was the loveliest I have ever known in the British Isles. But the company was not interesting, and there was a good deal of dreariness in the ball we all went to at Hopetoun for the coming of age of the heir. A charming heir he was, however, and a very pretty picture of a young nobleman stepping into his place in society—handsome, well-mannered, gallant, graceful, with 40,000£ a year and the world at his feet. Laidlawstiel, on a bare hill among hills, just above the Tweed, is in the midst of Walter Scott's country. Reay walked with me over to Ashestiel one lovely afternoon; it is only an hour away. The house has been greatly changed since the 'Sheriff's' day; [1] but the place, the country, are the same, and I found the thing deeply interesting. It took one back. While I was at the Reays' I took up one of Scott's novels—*Redgauntlet*; it was years since I had read one. They have always a charm for me—but I was amazed at the badness of R.: *l'enfance de l'art.*

x   x   x   x   x

Now and here I have only one feeling—the desire to get at work again. It is nearly six months that I have been resting on my oars—letting the weeks go, with nothing to show for them but these famous 'impressions'! Prolonged idleness exasperates and depresses me, and though now that I am here, it is a pity not to move about and (if the chance presents itself) see the country, the prospect of producing nothing for the rest of the winter is absolutely intolerable to me. If it comes to my having to choose between remaining stationary somewhere and getting at work, or making a journey during which I shall be able to do no work, I shall certainly elect for the former. But probably I shall be able to compromise: to see something of the country and yet work a little. My mind is full of plans, of ambitions; they crowd upon me, for these are the productive years of life. I have taken aboard by this time a tremendous quantity of material; I really have never taken stock of my cargo. After long years of waiting, of obstruction, I find myself able to put into execution the most cherished of all my projects—that of beginning to work for the stage. It was one of my earliest—I had it from the first. None has given me brighter hopes—none has given me sweeter emotions. It is strange nevertheless that I should never have done anything—and to a certain extent it is ominous. I wonder at times that the dream should not have faded away. It comes back to me now, however, and I ache with longing to settle down at last to a sustained attempt in this direction. I think there is really reason enough for my not having done so before: the little work at any time that I could do, the uninterrupted need of making money on the spot, the inability to do two things at once, the absence of opportunities, of openings. I may add to this the feeling that I could afford to wait, that, looked at as I look at it, the drama is the ripest of all the arts, the one to which one must bring most of the acquired as well as most of the natural, and that while I was waiting I was studying the art, and clearing off my field. I think I may now claim to have studied the art as well as it can be studied in the contemplative way. The French stage I have mastered; I say that without hesitation. I have it

1. The 'Sheriff' was Walter Scott, appointed Sheriff of Selkirkshire in 1799. He rented the house of Ashestiel, on the south bank of the Tweed, near Selkirk, in 1804.

in my pocket, and it seems to me clear that this is the light by which one must work today. I have laid up treasures of wisdom about all that. What interesting hours it has given me—what endless consideration it has led to! Sometimes, as I say, it seems to me simply deplorable that I should not have got at work before. *But it was impossible at the time,* and I knew that my chance would come. Here it is; let me guard it sacredly now. Let nothing divert me from it; but now the loss of time, which has simply been a maturing process, will become an injurious one. *Je me résume,* as George Sand's heroes say. I remember certain occasions; several acute visitations of the purpose of which I write come back to me vividly. Some of them, the earliest, were brought on merely by visits to the theatre—by seeing great actors, etc.—at fortunate hours; or by reading a new piece of Alex. Dumas, of Sardou, of Augier. No, my dear friend, nothing of all that is lost. *Ces emotions-là ne se perdent pas; elles rentrent dans le fonds même de notre nature; elles font partie de notre volonté.* The *volonté* has not expired; it is only perfect today. Two or three of the later occasions of which I speak have been among the things that *count* in the formation of a purpose; they are worth making a note of here. What has always counted, of course, has been the Comédie Française; it is on that, as regards this long day-dream, that I have lived. But there was an evening there that I shall long remember; it was in September, 1877. I had come over from London; I was lodging in the Avenue d'Antin—the house with a *tir* behind it. I went to see *Jean Dacier,* with Coquelin as the hero; I shall certain<ly not> forget that impression. The piece is, on the whole, I suppose, bad; but it contains some very effective scenes, and the two principal parts gave Coquelin and Favart a magnificent chance. It is Coquelin's *great* chance, and he told me afterwards in London that it is the part he values most. He is everything in it by turns, and I don't think I ever followed an actor's creation more intently. It threw me into a great state of excitement; I thought seriously of writing to Coquelin, telling him I had been his school-mate, etc.[1] It held up a glowing light to me—seemed to point to my own path. If I could have sat down to

1. James had been for a time Coquelin's schoolmate at the Collège Communal in Boulogne, as he tells us in *A Small Boy and Others* (1913). When he wrote that book he looked back on Coquelin as 'the most interesting and many-sided comedian, or at least the most unsurpassed dramatic *diseur* of the time.' As early as 1877, in his essay on *The Théâtre Français* in the *Galaxy* for April, he devoted several appreciative paragraphs to Coquelin, but it was the performance of Lomon's *Jean Dacier* in September that brought his enthusiasm to its peak. The experience proved indeed unforgettable, and ten years later, in his essay on Coquelin in the *Century* for January 1887, James described just as he does here in the notebook his emotional excitement and his late evening walk after leaving the theater. The play, a four-act tragedy in verse, he called Coquelin's 'highest flight in the line of rhymed parts.'

work then I probably should not have stopped soon. But I didn't; I couldn't; I was writing things for which I needed to be paid from month to month. (I like to remind myself of these facts—to justify my innumerable postponements.) I remember how, on leaving the theatre—it was a lovely evening—I walked about a long time under the influence not so much of the piece as of Coquelin's acting of it, which had made the thing so human, so brilliant, so valuable. I was agitated with what it said to me that I might do—what I ought to attempt; I walked about the Place de la Concorde, along the Seine, up the Champs Elysées. That was nothing, however, to the state I was thrown into by meeting Coquelin at breakfast at Andrew Lang's, when the Comédie Française came to London. The occasion, for obvious reasons, was unpropitious, but I had some talk with him which rekindled and revived all my latent ambitions. At that time, too, my hands were tied; I could do nothing, and the feeling passed away in smoke. But it stirred me to the depths. Coquelin's personality, his talk, the way the *artist* overflowed in him—all this was tremendously suggestive. I could say little to him there—not a tittle of what I wished; I could only listen, and translate to him what *they* said—an awkward task! But I listened to some purpose, and I have never lost what I gained. It excited me powerfully; I shall not forget my walk, afterwards, down from South Kensington to Westminster. I met Jack Gardner, and he walked with me to leave a card at the Speaker's House. All day, and for days afterward, I remained under the impression. It faded away in time, and I had to give myself to other things. But this brings it back to me; and I may say that those two little moments were landmarks. There was a smaller incident, later, which it gives me pleasure to re-call, as it gave me extreme pleasure at the time. John Hare asked me (I met him at dinner at the Comyns Carrs')—urged me, I may say— to write a play, and offered me his services in the event of my doing so. I shall take him at his word. When I came back from Scotland in October last I was full of this work; my hands were free; my pocket lined; I would have given a £100 for the liberty to sit down and hammer away. I imagined such a capital winter of work. But I had to come hither instead. If that however involves a loss of part of my time, it needn't involve the loss of all!

February 9th, 1882, 102 Mt. Vernon St., Boston.

When I began to make these rather ineffectual records I had no idea that I should have in a few weeks to write such a tale of sadness as today. I came back from Washington on the 30th of last month (reached Cambridge the next day), to find that I should never again see my dear mother. On Sunday, Jan. 29th, as Aunt Kate sat with her in the closing dusk (she had been ill with an attack of bronchial asthma, but was apparently recovering happily), she passed away. It makes a great difference to me! I knew that I loved her—but I didn't know how tenderly till I saw her lying in her shroud in that cold North Room, with a dreary snowstorm outside, and looking as sweet and tranquil and noble as in life. These are hours of exquisite pain; thank Heaven this particular pang comes to us but once. On Sunday evening (at 10 o'clock in Washington) I was dressing to go to Mrs. Robinson's—who has written me a very kind letter—when a telegram came in from Alice (William's): 'Your mother exceedingly ill. Come at once.' It was a great alarm, but it didn't suggest the loss of all hope; and I made the journey to New York with whatever hope seemed to present itself. In New York at 5 o'clock I went to Cousin H.P.'s—and there the telegram was translated to me. Eliza Ripley was there—and Katie Rodgers—and as I went out I met Lily Walsh. The rest was dreary enough. I went back to the Hoffman House, where I had engaged a room on my way up town and remained there till 9.30, when I took the night-train to Boston. I shall never pass that place in future without thinking of the wretched hours I spent there. At home the worst was over; I found father and Alice and A.K.[1] extraordinarily calm—almost happy. Mother seemed still to be there—so beautiful, so full of all that we loved in her, she looked in death. We buried her on Wednesday, Feb. 1st; Wilkie arrived from Milwaukee a couple of hours before. Bob[2] had been there for a month—he was devoted to mother in her illness. It was a splendid winter's day—the snow lay deep and high. We placed her, for the present, in a temporary vault in the Cambridge cemetery—the part that lies near the river. When the spring comes on we shall go and choose a burial place. I have often walked there in the old years—in those long, lonely rambles that I used to take about Cambridge, and I had, I suppose, a vague idea that some of us would some day lie there, but I didn't see just that scene. It is impossible for me to say—to begin to say—all that has gone down into the grave with her. She was our life, she was the house, she was the keystone of the arch. She held us all together, and without her we are scattered reeds. She was patience, she was wisdom, she was exquisite maternity. Her sweetness, her mildness, her great natural beneficence were unspeakable, and it is infinitely touching to me to write about her here as one that *was*. When I think of all that she had been, for years—when I think of her hourly devotion to each and all of us—and that when I went to Washington the last of December I gave her

1. 'A.K.' was 'Aunt Kate'—James' mother's sister, Katharine Walsh.
2. Henry James' youngest brother, Robertson.

my last kiss, I heard her voice for the last time—there seems not to be enough tenderness in my being to register the extinction of such a life. But I can reflect, with perfect gladness, that her work was done— her long patience had done its utmost. She had had heavy cares and sorrows, which she had borne without a murmur, and the weariness of age had come upon her. I would rather have lost her forever than see her begin to suffer as she would probably have been condemned to suffer, and I can think with a kind of holy joy of her being lifted now above all our pains and anxieties. Her death has given me a passionate belief in certain transcendent things—the immanence of being as nobly created as hers—the immortality of such a virtue as that—the reunion of spirits in better conditions than these. She is no more of an angel today than she had always been; but I can't believe that by the accident of her death all her unspeakable tenderness is lost to the beings she so dearly loved. She is with us, she is of us—the eternal stillness is but a form of her love. One can hear her voice in it—one can feel, forever, the inextinguishable vibration of her devotion. I can't help feeling that in those last weeks I was not tender enough with her— that I was blind to her sweetness and beneficence. One can't help wishing one had only known what was coming, so that one might have enveloped her with the softest affection. When I came back from Europe I was struck with her being worn and shrunken, and now I know that she was very weary. She went about her usual activities, but the burden of life had grown heavy for her, and she needed rest. There is something inexpressibly touching to me in the way in which, during these last years, she went on from year to year without it. If she could only have lived she should have had it, and it would have been a delight to see her have it. But she has it now, in the most complete perfection! Summer after summer she never left Cambridge—it was impossible that father should leave his own house. The country, the sea, the change of air and scene, were an exquisite enjoyment to her; but she bore with the deepest gentleness and patience the constant loss of such opportunities. She passed her nights and her days in that dry, flat, hot, stale and odious Cambridge, and had never a thought while she did so but for father and Alice. It was a perfect mother's life—the life of a perfect wife. To bring her children into the world—to expend herself, for years, for their happiness and welfare—then, when they had reached a full maturity and were absorbed in the world and in their own interests—to lay herself down in her ebbing strength and yield up her pure soul to the celestial power that had given her this divine commission. Thank God one knows this loss but once; and thank God that certain supreme impressions remain! x x x x x

[41]

All my plans are altered—my return to England vanishes for the present. I must remain near father; his infirmities make it impossible I should leave him. This means an indefinite detention in this country—a prospect far enough removed from all my recent hopes of departure.

August 3d, 1882, 3 Bolton St. W. From time to time one feels the need of summing-up. I have done it little in the past, but it will be a good thing to do it more in the future. The prevision with which I closed my last entry in these pages was not verified. I sailed from America on the date I had in my mind when I went home—May 10th. Father was materially better and had the strongest wish that I should depart; he and Alice had moved into Boston and were settled very comfortably in a small, pretty house (101 Mt. Vernon St.). Besides, their cottage at Manchester was rapidly being finished; shortly before sailing I went down to see it. Very pretty—bating the American scragginess; with the sea close to the piazzas, and the smell of bay-berries in the air. Rest, coolness, peace, society enough, charming drives; they will have all that.—Very soon after I had got back here my American episode began to fade away, to seem like a dream; a very painful dream, much of it. While I was there, it was Europe, it was England, that was dreamlike—but now all this is real enough. The Season is over, thank God; I came in for as much of it as could crowd itself into June and July. I was out of the mood for it, pre-occupied, uninterested, bored, eager to begin work again; but I was obliged, being on the spot, to accommodate myself to the things of the day, and always with my old salve to a perturbed spirit, the idea that I was seeing the world. It seemed to me on the whole a poor world this time; I saw and did very little that was interesting. I am extremely glad to be in London again; I am deeply attached to London; I always shall be; but decidedly I like it best when it is 'empty,' as during the period now beginning. I know too many people—I have gone in too much for society x x x x x

Grand Hôtel, Paris, November 11th. Thanks to 'society,' which, in the shape of various surviving remnants of the season, and to a succession of transient Americans and to several country visits, continued to mark me for its own during the greater part of the month of August, I had not even time to finish that last sentence written more than three months ago. I can hardly take up at this date the history of these three months: a simple glance must suffice. I remained in England till the 12th of September. Bob, whom I had found reclining on my sofa in Bolton St. when I arrived from America toward the last of May—(I hadn't even time, above, to mention my little disembarkation in Ireland

and the few days I spent there)—Bob, who as I say was awaiting me at my lodgings in London—greatly to my surprise, and in a very battered and depressed condition, thanks to his unhappy voyage to the Azores—sailed for home again in the last days of August, after having spent some weeks in London, at Malvern and at Llandudno, in Wales. The last days, before sailing, he spent with me. About the 10th of September William arrived from America, on his way to the Continent to pass the winter. After being with him for a couple of days, I came over to Paris via Folkestone (I came down there and slept, before crossing), while he crossed to Flushing, from Queenborough. All summer I had been trying to work, but my interruptions had been so numerous that it was only during the last weeks that I succeeded, even moderately, in doing something. My record of work for the whole past year is terribly small, and I opened this book, just now, with the intention of taking several solemn vows in reference to the future. But I don't even know whether I shall accomplish that. However, I am not sure that such solemnities are necessary, for God knows I am eager enough to work, and that I am deeply convinced of the need of it, both for fortune and for happiness. x x x x x

I scarcely even remember the three or four visits to which, in the summer, I succeeded in restricting my 'social activity.' A pleasant night at Loseley—Rhoda Broughton was there. Another day I went down there to lunch, to take Howells (who spent all August in London) and Bob. Two days at Mentmore; a Saturday-to-Monday episode (very dull) at Miss de Rothschild's, at Wimbledon; a very pleasant day at the Arthur Russells', at Shiere. This last was charming; I think I went nowhere else—having wriggled out of Midelney, from my promised visit to Mrs. Pakenham, and from pledges more or less given to Tillypronie. Toward the last, in London, I had my time pretty well to myself, and I felt, as I have always felt before, the charm of those long, still days, in the empty time, when one can sit and scribble, without notes to answer or visits to pay. Shall I confess, however, that the evenings had become dull? x x x x x

I had meant to write some account of my last months in America, but I fear the chance for this has already passed away. I look back at them, however, with a great deal of tenderness. Boston is absolutely nothing to me—I don't even dislike it. I like it, on the contrary; I only dislike to live there. But all those weeks I spent there, after Mother's death, had an exquisite stillness and solemnity. My rooms in Mt. Vernon St. were bare and ugly; but they were comfortable—were, in a certain way, pleasant. I used to walk out, and across the Common, every morning, and take my breakfast at Parker's. Then I walked back to my lodgings and sat writing till four or five o'clock; after which I walked out to Cambridge over that dreary bridge whose length I had measured so often in the past, and, four or five days in the week, dined in Quincy St. with Father and Alice. In the evening, I walked back, in the clear, American starlight.—I got in this way plenty of exercise. It was a simple, serious, wholesome time. Mother's death appeared to have left behind it a soft beneficent hush in which we lived for weeks, for months, and which was full of rest and sweetness. I thought of her, constantly, as I walked to Boston at night along those dark vacant roads, where, in the winter air, one met nothing but the coloured lamps and the far-heard jingle of the Cambridge horse-cars. My work at this time interested me, too, and I look back upon the whole three months with a kind of religious veneration. My work interested me even more than the importance of it would explain—or than the success of it has justified. I tried to write a little play ($D<aisy> M<iller>$) and I wrote it; but my poor little play has not been an encouragement. I needn't enter into the tiresome history of my ridiculous negotiations with the people of the Madison Square Theatre, of which the Proprietors behaved like asses and sharpers combined; this episode, by itself, would make a brilliant chapter in a realistic novel. It interested me immensely to write the piece, and the work confirmed all my convictions as to the fascination of this sort of composition. But what it has brought <me> to know, both in New York and in London, about the manners and ideas of managers and actors and about the conditions of production on our unhappy English stage, is almost fatally disgusting and discouraging. I have learned, very vividly, that if one attempts to work for it one must be prepared for *disgust*, deep and unspeakable disgust. But though I am disgusted, I do not think I am discouraged. The reason of this latter is that I simply can't afford to be. I have determined to take a year—even two years, if need be—more, in experiments, in studies, in attempts. The dramatic form seems to me the most beautiful thing possible; the misery of the thing is that the baseness of the English-speaking stage affords no setting for it. How I am to reconcile this with the constant solicitation that presses upon me, both from within and from without, to get at work upon another novel, is more than I can say. It is surely the part of wisdom, however, not to begin another novel at once—not to commit myself to a work of *longue haleine*. I must do *short* things, in such measure as I need, which will leave me intervals for dramatic work. I say this rather glibly —and yet I sometimes feel a woeful hunger to sit down to another novel. If I can only *concentrate* myself: this is the great lesson of life. I have hours of unspeakable reaction against my smallness of production; my wretched habits of work—or of un-work; my levity, my vagueness of mind, my perpetual failure to focus my attention, to absorb myself, to look things in the face, to invent, to produce, in a word. I shall be 40 years old in April next: it's a horrible fact! I believe however that I have learned how to work and that it is in moments of forced idleness, almost alone, that these melancholy reflections seize me. When I am really at work, I'm happy, I feel strong, I see many opportunities ahead. It is the only thing that makes life endurable. I must make some great efforts during the next few years, however, if I wish not to have been on the whole a failure. I shall have been a failure unless I do something *great!* x x x x x

[*There are three later entries in Notebook II, but they are omitted since they are all mere memoranda. One gives the date of the death of James' great-grandfather Barber, the second mentions the date of his moving to Lamb House in October 1897, and the third, the date of his sailing for America in August 1904. The text printed here reverts to Notebook I.*]

'English things and ways don't impress me nearly as much as they did three years ago. England is all clogged and stuffed with the great load of superfluities, the great rubbish-heap and sweepings of centuries that she drags after her, smeared in the fog and smoke. All other nations seem so light and intelligent in the Balance.'

W.J.,[1] Letter to his wife, from London, December 22nd, 1882.

'As to myself, I have learned to be cosmopolitan, but I cannot shake off the feeling that the Latin races need no longer to be reckoned with, even if they should conquer the world, which they won't.'

E. Gryzanowski to W.J., Livorno, December 18th, 1882.

'I must on Saturday save my life by escaping to Paris. Never did place seem to agree with me less than London, strange to say. I like the people more and more. Of all the *Kunst-produkte* of this globe the exquisitely and far-fetchedly fashioned structure called the English Race and Temperament is the most precious. I should think a poor Frenchman would behold with a kind of frenzy the easy and genial way in which it solves, or achieves without needing to solve, all those things which are for his unfortunate people the impossible.'

W.J., London, January 22nd, 1883.

1. W.J. is, of course, William James.

À *propos* of Sarah B. in Sardou's *Fedora:*

'She is a wonderful creature, but how a being as intelligent as she can so elaborate what has so little moral stuff in it to work upon, I don't comprehend. The play is hard, and sinister, and horrible, without being in the least degree tragic or pathetic; one felt like an accomplice in some cold-blooded bit of cruelty when it was over. I feel like giving up the French and calling to my own species to stand from under and let their fate overtake them. Such a disproportionate development of the external perceptions and such a perversion of the natural feelings, must work its nemesis in some way.' [1]

W.J., Paris, February 19th, 1883.

Boston, April 8th, 1883. I transcribe here part of a letter I have just written to J. R. Osgood, my publisher, in regard to a new novel.

'The scene of the story is laid in Boston and its neighbourhood; it relates an episode connected with the so-called "woman's movement." The characters who figure in it are for the most part persons of the radical reforming type, who are especially interested in the emancipation of women, giving them the suffrage, releasing them from bondage, co-educating them with men, etc. They regard this as the great question of the day—the most urgent and sacred reform. The heroine is a very clever and "gifted" young woman, associated by birth and circumstances with a circle immersed in these views and in every sort of new agitation, daughter of old abolitionists, spiritualists, transcendentalists, etc. She herself takes an interest in the cause; but she is an object of still greater interest to her family and friends, who have discovered in her a remarkable natural talent for public speaking by which they believe her capable of moving large audiences and rendering great aid in the liberation of her sex. They cherish her, as a kind of apostle and redeemer. She is very pleasing to look upon, and her gift for speaking is a kind of inspiration. She has a dear and intimate friend, another young woman, who, issuing from a totally different social circle (a rich conservative exclusive family), has thrown herself into these questions with intense ardour and has conceived a passionate admiration for our young girl, over whom, by the force of a completely different character, she has acquired a great influence. She has money of her own, but no talent for appearing in public and she has a dream that her friend and she together (one by the use of her money and the other by her eloquence) may, working side by side, really revolutionize the condition of women. She regards this as a noble and aspiring task,

1. This comment by William James was incorporated in Henry James' essay on Loti in *Essays in London* (1893).

a mission to which everything else should be sacrificed, and she counts implicitly on her friend. The latter, however, makes the acquaintance of a young man who falls in love with her and in whom she also becomes much interested, but who, being of a hard-headed and conservative disposition, is resolutely opposed to female suffrage and all similar alterations. The more he sees of the heroine the more he loves her, and the more determined he is to get her out of the clutches of her reforming friends, whom he utterly abominates. He asks her to marry him, and does not conceal from her that if she does so, she must entirely give up her "mission." She feels that she loves him, but that the sacrifice of the said mission would be terrible, and that the disappointment inflicted on her family and friends, and especially on the rich young woman, would be worse. Her lover is a distant relative of the rich young woman, who in an evil hour, by accident, and before she was acquainted with his opinions (he has been spending ten years in the West) has introduced him. She appeals to her friend to stand firm—appeals in the name of their intimate friendship and of all the hopes that are centred on the young girl's head. The tale relates the struggle that takes place in the mind of the latter. The struggle ends, after various vicissitudes, with her letting everything go, breaking forever with her friend, in a terrible final interview, and giving herself up to her lover. There are to be several other characters whom I have not mentioned—types of radical agitators—and as many little pictures as I can introduce of the woman's rights agitation.'—So much to Osgood. I must return to this, with more details. The subject is strong and good, with a large rich interest. The relation of the two girls should be a study of one of those friendships between women which are so common in New England. The whole thing as local, as American, as possible, and as full of Boston: an attempt to show that I *can* write an American story. There must, indispensably, be a type of newspaper man—the man whose ideal is the energetic reporter. I should like to *bafouer* the vulgarity and hideousness of this—the impudent invasion of privacy—the extinction of all conception of privacy, etc. Daudet's *Évangéliste* has given me the idea of this thing. If I could only do something with that *pictorial* quality! At any rate, the subject is very national, very typical. I wished to write a very *American* tale, a tale very characteristic of our social conditions, and I asked myself what was the most salient and peculiar point in our social life. The answer was: the situation of women, the decline of the sentiment of sex, the agitation on their behalf. x x x x x

[The Bostonians *was not finished until a couple of years later, and was then serialized in the* Century Magazine (February 1885—February

[47]

1886). James could hardly have taken more than an initial impulse from L'Évangéliste, which had just appeared in 1883, and which he analyzed in his essay on Daudet in the same year. He gave this account of the plot: 'It treats of a young girl (a Danish Protestant) who is turned to stone by a Medusa of Calvinism, the sombre and fanatical wife of a great Protestant banker. Madame Autheman persuades Eline Ebsen to wash her hands of the poor old mother with whom up to this moment she has lived in the closest affection, and go forth into strange countries to stir up the wicked to conversion.' Notwithstanding his general admiration for Daudet's vitality—'a novelist to his finger-tips' —James held that in L'Évangéliste he had 'got up' his material 'solely from the outside,' and that Madame Autheman in particular was 'quite automatic,' and 'psychologically . . . a blank.' Such criticisms point up his own different aim in The Bostonians.

He departed from his outline in several particulars, as he made his central subject a psychological study of Olive Chancellor and Verena Tarrant. Verena is the granddaughter rather than the daughter of transcendentalists, since her father is represented as false and cunning, as 'a moralist without moral sense,' who is willing to live off his daughter's talent in the name of specious reform. The true faith of the old reformers is only a diminishing aftershine in an endearing but futile old lady like Miss Birdseye: 'She was heroic, she was sublime, the whole moral history of Boston was reflected in her displaced spectacles.' James sharpened his dramatic contrast between Boston in its era of decline and the world of Basil Ransom by making his young man not a sojourner in the West but a native of Mississippi, a 'reactionary' whose social doctrines, according to a New York editor in the novel, were 'about three hundred years behind the age.'

Selah Tarrant lives for the world of publicity, and is naturally drawn to Matthias Pardon, the young journalist, the 'ingenuous son' of the age, for whom 'all distinction between the person and the artist had ceased to exist; the writer was personal, the person food for newsboys, and everything and every one were every one's business.' Through such varied facets did James attempt to reflect as many glimpses of Boston as possible. He sketched in the downtown streets and the horsecars, the Music Hall and the view over the Charles. He included also a few scenes from Harvard life, and in the latter portions of the book extended his canvas for a brief view of New York as well as of Olive's summer cottage on Cape Cod—which had very few chairs but 'all George Eliot's writings and two photographs of the Sistine Madonna.'

But despite this effort to make an American story, The Bostonians was the first of James' novels to be almost unanimously a failure with the American press, which did not enjoy his satire. This reception discouraged him enough to prevent him from trying another novel laid in this country until the very end of his career, in the unfinished Ivory Tower. He discussed some of his difficulties in producing The Bostonians in letters to his brother William. He agreed that he had been too redundant 'in the way of descriptive psychology,' but he had been led into this by 'the sense of knowing terribly little about the kind of life I had attempted to describe. . . I should have been much more rapid and had a lighter hand, with a subject concerned with people and things of a nature more near to my experience.'

Scribner's was to discourage him from including this novel in his collected edition, a decision which he regretted, since he believed in retrospect that the book had 'never received any sort of justice.' He said again, in the last year of his life: 'I should have liked to review it for the Edition—it would have come out a much truer and more curious thing (it was meant to be curious from the first) . . . I should have liked to write that Preface.']

x x x x x In this same letter to Osgood I gave a sketch of the plan of a short story of the 'international' family (like *Daisy Miller*, the *Siege of London*, etc.). 'The name of the thing to be *Lady Barberina*.[1] I have already treated (more or less) the subject of the American girl who marries (or concerning whom it is a question whether she *will* marry) a British aristocrat. This story reverses the situation and presents a young *male* American who conceives the design of marrying a daughter of the aristocracy. He is a New Yorker, a good deal of an Anglomaniac and a "dude"; and as he has a good deal of money she accepts him and they are united. The 1st half of the tale goes on in England. In the 2d the parties are transported to New York, whither he has brought his bride, and it relates their adventures there, the impressions made and received by the lady, and the catastrophe.' So much to Osgood.—I think something very good might be made of this—I see it quite vividly.

A good (American) comparison: 'As . . . and as silent as a chiropodist.'

Lady Barberina: Notes.   (*May 17th, 1883*)

He must be a young physician, the youth who marries the earl's daughter, for that will be very national and typical. It is only here that

1. In the collected New York edition this title is *Lady Barbarina*. When the story was first printed, the spelling was 'Barberina.' That seems to be the spelling in the notebooks, and it is used consistently in this text.

the son of a rich man—of a man as rich as his father—would have entered that profession, and that the profession itself is capable of being considered 'rather aristocratic.' His father leaves him a great fortune—but he is still 'Doctor Jeune' (say). He doesn't practice but he cares for medicine, and is very generous and beneficent to the suffering poor. He has a brother who is vulgar, and a mother who is charming; and the relations of these two with Lady Barberina after she gets to N.Y. are of course a feature in the story. Lady B.'s expectation of going before Mrs. Jeune (her mother-in-law, etc.). Of course the difficulty will <be> to make the marriage natural: but this difficulty is inspiring. On her part (Lady B.'s) his large fortune will go far toward explaining it. She is not a beauty, though a very fine creature, and she has no fortune to help her to marry in England. She is twenty-six years old, her father is a poor peer, and she has four sisters and five brothers. Her mother thinks that for her to marry a rich man *là-bas* will be a *pied à l'étrier* for the rest of the brood—that the boys in particular, some of them yet young, will be accommodated with ranches and monied wives in the U.S.—Besides Barberina likes the young man, and he must be made attractive. The novelty, the change, takes her fancy, everything American is so the fashion. The 'Dr.' is a big dose to swallow; and I think I must concede that, in London, as he has quite ceased to practice, he doesn't put forward the title. It is only after she is married and reaches New York that she finds every one giving it to him—his own brother always calling <him by> it, etc. One of her sisters, by the way, must come with them to America, and must be recommended as liking it awfully. She must marry a poor young man: a handsome minister of N.Y. The thing is to make the marriage with Lady B. seem natural and possible to my hero, without making him appear snobbish. But it surely can be done. To begin with, there is nothing in life to prevent him from falling in love with her. She must strike him as a splendid young woman—responding completely to his ideal of physical completeness, happy development, perfect health, etc., for all of which he must have an immense appreciation. He must be a great admirer of the physique of <the> English race and think her a beautiful specimen of it. He is a little fellow himself—not a physique which he wishes to perpetuate *telle quelle*; but very cool, very deliberate, very obstinate, and very much attached to his own ideas: opposition always puts him on his mettle; and his marriage to Lady B. is opposed. It is a point that *his* friends and relations, some of them, think it as strange that he should wish to marry her, as hers do that she should unite herself to him. He declines to see *why* it should be difficult for him to marry any woman in the world whom he may fancy; and he

[50]

is really urged to prosecute his suit by the determination that she *shall* find it natural and comfortable. Damn it, if he fancies an earl's daughter he will have an earl's daughter. The attitude of his mother to be defined, and the details of the episode in New York worked out. Then the *entrée en matière* in London. He must have a pair of confidants there, who bring him accidentally into relation with Lady B., and who watch his proceedings with amusement and dread. In addition to this he must have a friend—a Boston M.D. (of the type of J.P.[1]).

[Lady Barberina appeared in the Century from May through July 1884, and James used it as the title-story of a volume of 'international' tales in the New York edition. In his preface he said that his interest had been in reversing the usual situation of the American heiress marrying the English nobleman, and remarked that 'the essential . . . was to get my young man right.' Jackson Lemon, the Dr. Jeune of the notebook, must be given a 'natural and possible' reason for marrying Lady Barberina, and must not appear a snob. His qualities, as outlined in the notebook, explain his marriage, and in the story James added an episode in order to reveal them in action. Lemon refuses to have a marriage 'settlement' drawn up, because it seems to him a concession to a foreign standard and a reflection on his honesty and on his perfect equality with Barberina's family. But when his friends, the Freres, urge him to use the dispute about the 'settlement' as an excuse for breaking off the match, he changes his mind abruptly, and thereby reveals his defiance of opposition. Thus by introducing a single detail James is able to present dramatically and economically the characteristics of his hero which are indispensable for the story. With similar economy he telescopes the 'vulgar' brother and the 'handsome minister' of the original into Herman Longstraw, a vulgar and handsome Californian adventurer, 'a mere mustache' and 'a slightly mitigated cowboy,' who elopes with Agatha, Barberina's sister. This supplies a 'catastrophe' for the 'episode in New York.' Agatha's outraged mother asks that Barberina be allowed to visit her in England. Lemon knows that if she goes she will never return to America, but he cannot decently refuse her mother's request. The story ends with Lady Barberina and her husband established in London, where the Longstraws live off his charity.]

'The self-made girl'—a very good subject for a short story. Very modern, very local; much might be done.

1. This may refer to William James' friend, Dr. James Putnam.

[James turned to this theme again the following winter (p. 56 below).]

May 30th, 1883. I have promised to furnish three short stories to Osgood (for the *Century*); and Gilder now writes me that they want the two shorter ones first, before *Lady Barberina*, which I had begun and half finished. I have written to him that I will keep back this, and send him the little ones as soon as possible. Accordingly, I must select my tales —my subjects. A short time since I thought of a sufficiently picturesque little *donnée* which I was to call *The Impressions of a Cousin*. It is a modification of the thing suggested to me some time ago by Miss Thackeray and chronicled here—the history of the little *demoiselle de Grignan* who was forced into a convent because her father or step-father didn't wish to give an account of his false stewardship of her property. I won't go into the details of it here: sufficient that the false trustee here is a gentleman with whom the young girl owning the property is (very secretly) in love; and that his wish is to get her to marry his stepbrother who has a fortune of his own; so that the couple will not insist upon an exposure which will ruin him—deterred therefrom by near relationship, family pride, etc. The girl refuses the cousin absolutely, yet insists on no exposure, and puts up in silence with the injury she has suffered. Her trustee thus, *à qui ceci donne à penser*, discovers that she has loved *him* for three years and that if he had not been such an ass *he* might have married her and enjoyed her property honestly. Now she knows what he has done, she won't prose-cute—but of course she can't marry him in his dishonour and she doesn't go into a convent (my tale is too modern); but she retires, as it were, from the world with her property, her wound and her secret. The 'Cousin' of the title is a young woman who relates the story (in the form of a journal), living with her kinswoman as a companion, observing these events and guessing the secret. It is only in her journal that the secret 'transpires.' She herself of course to be a 'type.' I thought of infusing a little American local colour into it by making the story take place in New York and representing the Cousin as a Bostonian, with the Boston moral tone, etc. But that would be pale—the heroine living in 37th St., etc. The New York streets are fatal to the imagina-tion. At all events, I have lost my fancy for the theme, which is rather thin and conventional, and wanting in actuality. Actuality must be my line at present. I may work it with infinite profit. The thing is to do so!

[*The Impressions of a Cousin was printed in the Century in the last two months of 1883, and with Lady Barberina and A New England Winter, in Tales of Three Cities (1884)—one story of Boston, one of New York, and one of New York and London.*

The seed of The Impressions of a Cousin was given to James on 16 January 1881 (page 19 above). Deciding after all to lay the story in New York, he gave it an 'international' flavor by making the 'cousin,' through whose journal the narrative is told, an American woman, an artist, just returned from Italy and very dubious about the artistic possibilities of the United States. She is an actor in the story as well as an observer because the stepbrother of Mr. Caliph, the errant trustee, whom he tries to make marry the heroine, falls in love with the narrator instead.

The conclusion of the story differs from that which James proposed. The stepbrother learns the facts of the case, and gives up his fortune to repair the losses caused the heroine by Caliph. She knows that she has been cheated by Caliph, but that he has somehow been able to make restitution, and there is a typically Jamesian hint that her love for him is lessened as soon as loving him involves no sacrifice and little need for forgiveness. But this note is blurred by the strong suggestion at the end that she will marry him after all. If she does, the narrator promises to marry the noble stepbrother, so that the tender-minded reader may assume that a conventional 'happy ending' lies just ahead.

Telling the story by means of the journal of the 'observer' makes it essentially a narrative in the first person, and James' objections to this method, expounded later in his preface to The Ambassadors, apply here. The 'observer' becomes more vivid than the other characters, and James' feeling that the theme was 'rather thin' and 'wanting in actuality' seems justified, partly because the other characters can be seen only through the eyes of a woman who is herself, although intelligent, unable, without falling out of character, to reveal herself and the others fully in the pages of a journal.

In two of the three stories in Tales of Three Cities, James seems to have altered his original ideas in the direction of softening the conclusions, and in all three he strikes the 'international' note. Both he and Osgood had, no doubt, an eye for the ingredients which might make a popular success. To judge by the record of their printings, however, no one of the stories seems to have been especially successful with the public.]

London, January 2d, 1884.

Names. Daintry—Vandeleur—Grunlus—Christian names: Florimond—Ambrose—Mathias—Surnames: Benyon—Pinder—Vallance—Nugent—Maze—Dinn—Fiddler—Higgs. Most of them are out of the Times of the above date. Very rich.—Chancellor—Ambient.

January 29th, 1884. I heard the other day at Mrs. Tennant's of a situation which struck me as dramatic and a pretty subject. The story was told of young Lord Stafford, son of the Duke of Sutherland. It appears he has been for years in love with Lady Grosvenor whom he knew before her marriage to Lord G. He had no expectation of being able to marry her, however, her husband being a young, robust man of his own age, etc. Yielding to family pressure on the subject of taking a wife, he offered his hand to a young, charming, innocent girl, the daughter of Lord Rosslyn. He was gratefully accepted, and the engagement was announced. Suddenly, a very short time after this, and without any one's expecting it, Lord Grosvenor dies and his wife becomes free. The question came up—'What was Lord S. to do?'—to stick to the girl—or to get rid of her in the best way he could and—after a decent interval—present himself to Lady G.? The question, as a matter of ethics, seems to me to have but one answer; if he had offered marriage to Miss Rosslyn (or whatever her name) by that offer he should abide. But the situation might make, as I say, a story, capable of several different turns, according to the character of the actors. The young man may give up Miss R. and betake himself to Lady G., who may then refuse him, on account of his having done an act she deems dishonourable. Or Miss R., guessing or learning the truth, may sacrifice herself, and liberate him of her own free will. Or she may still, knowing the truth, cling to him because she loves him, because she cannot give him up, and because she knows that Lady G. has refused to marry him. (I use these initials simply as convenient signs—knowing nothing of the people.) This attitude Miss R. may maintain until she meets Lady G., when a revulsion may take place, born simply of her fears. She may feel, as the impression of the older more brilliant woman is stamped upon her, that though the latter refuses to marry him at the cost of his tergiversation, she *must* be queen of his thoughts and will finally end by becoming his mistress. A conviction of this—a real presentiment of it—may take possession of her; so that she renounces her brilliant marriage, her noble suitor, rather than face this danger. There is another line which one may imagine another sort of girl taking: a girl, ambitious, tenacious, *volontière*,[1] unscrupulous, even slightly cynical. The state of things becomes apparent to her—she *has* to recognize that her suitor would give millions to break off his engagement. But she says, 'No, I won't give you up, I can't, it would kill me, for I have set my heart on everything that a marriage with you would bring me— But I don't ask for your affection—if I hold you to our betrothal, I leave you free in conduct. Let me be your wife, bear your name, your coronet, enjoy your

1. *Volontière* is probably a slip for *volontaire*.

wealth and splendour; but devote yourself to Lady G. as much as you like—make her your mistress, if you will. I will shut my eyes—I will make no scandal.'—If I were a Frenchman or a naturalist, this is probably the treatment I should adopt.—These things all deal with the matter from the point of view of the girl. As I began by saying, the quandary of the man is dramatically interesting; and one may imagine more than one issue, though only one is rigidly honourable. Lord S. may determine to stick to the girl. He may resist the temptation and he may have a frank understanding with Lady G. about it; in which she (in love with him) even adds to the height of his own lofty view of the matter, agrees that they must give each other up, that he *must* marry Miss R. and that he and she (Lady G.) must see each other in future as little as possible. The girl, in this, remains innocent and unconscious, but the light of the pathetic is projected upon her by the narrator of the story. It might be told by a friend and confidant of Lord S., who is in the secret throughout. *He* knows the force of Lord S.'s passion for Lady G., he knows that his engagement to Miss R. was merely perfunctory, because a man in his position *must* marry and have an heir and his father has badgered him till he has done so. *He* knows also a good deal about Lady G., and what she is capable of. Therefore when they plan together this noble renunciation, he doubts and fears and he thinks it is of bad omen for the poor little bride and is sure that it is only a question of time that Lord S. shall become the other woman's lover. 'Ah, they have agreed to give each other up!— Poor little woman!' That is the note on which this particular story would close. This arrangement would be congenial to the characteristic manner of H.J.—I shall probably try it. In this case the whole story might be told by Lord S.'s friend, who has observed it while it went on. He may relate it to an American visitor. The *point de départ* of this might be the sight of Lord S. and Lady G. together somewhere, in public; which is an intimation that what the friend has foreseen has happened.

[Here we have an instance of James' constant awareness of the multiple points of view from which any situation might be handled. In presenting this situation in The Path of Duty (the English Illustrated Magazine, December 1884), he rejected, as he foresaw that he would, the treatment of 'a Frenchman or a naturalist.' He concentrated 'on the quandary of the man,' Sir Ambrose Tester, rather than on that of Lady Vandeleur or of Joscelind Bernardstone. He made the narrator an American woman living in London, an old friend and confidante, much given to 'American analysis,' who sets down the story for her own eyes alone. Its effectiveness is considerably diminished by an offhand lightness in the narrator's tone, which robs the story of 'the characteristic manner of H.J.' in treating the pathetic, and leaves it a rather cool piece of society fiction, where none of the characters are either strongly sympathized with or strongly satirized. James included it in Stories Revived (1885), but did not collect it thereafter.]

I don't see why I shouldn't do the 'self-made girl,' whom I noted here last winter, in a way to make her a rival to D<aisy> M<iller>. I must put her into action, which I am afraid will be difficult in the small compass (16 magazine pages which I now contemplate). But I don't see why I shouldn't make the thing as concise as Four Meetings. The concision of Four Meetings, with the success of Daisy M.; that is what I must aim at! But I must first invent the action! It must take place in New York. Perhaps indeed Washington would do. This would give me a chance to do Washington, so far as I know it, and work in my few notes, and my very lovely memories, of last winter. I might even do Henry Adams and his wife. The hero might be a foreign secretary of Legation—German—inquiring and conscientious. New York and Washington, say. The point of the story would naturally be to show the contrast between the humble social background of the heroine, and the position which she has made—or is making for herself and, indirectly, for her family. He must meet her first in New York, then in Washington, where she has come to stay (with Mrs. Adams), and is seeing the president's cabinet, etc.; then again in New York; then finally in the country, in summer. Her people—her impossible father and mother—the way she carries them, etc. The picture admiring and appreciative. It must be a case of 'four meetings,' each with its little chapter, etc., each a picture. The thing must have the name of the girl (like D.M.) for its title—carefully selected. Each chapter (if there are 4) 20 pp. of MS.—I may make the thing a 'little gem'—if I try hard enough.

[Pandora turned out to be half as long again as Four Meetings (1877), and is a nouvelle of about twenty thousand words, a form for which James developed a strong liking. He made his impression of 'the self-made girl,' of the girl who has gotten into society solely by her own wits and bold charm, a deliberate companion-piece to Daisy Miller (1878). Indeed, he introduced his serious young German diplomat as reading that earlier story in its Tauchnitz edition in preparation for the oddities of American life. But when Pandora appeared in the New York Sun, 1 and 8 June 1884, it did not cause anything like the stir that Daisy Miller did.

James sketched the Adams family with his lightest hand. Pandora Day does not actually stay with them in Washington but rather with a lady from the South, a relict of a commodore, who looks 'like the vieux jeu idea of the queen in Hamlet.' But for the reception at the Bonnycastles', where the earnest Count Otto Vogelstein is bewildered by the rapid progress of the little girl from Utica, James drew upon his friends. Mrs. Bonnycastle's parties were 'the pleasantest in Washington,' the only criticism ever voiced of her house being that 'it left out, on the whole, more people than it took in.' Her husband, Alfred Bonny-castle 'was not in politics, though politics were much in him.' He is made to chafe a bit at some of the restrictions of their circle: 'it struck him that for Washington their society was really a little too good.' His is the idea for the reception: 'Hang it, there's only a month left; let us be vulgar and have some fun—let us invite the President.'

James also wove in some of his fresh memories of Mt. Vernon, of scenes along the river, and of the Capitol, uplifting its 'isolated dome' above Pennsylvania Avenue, 'at the end of a long vista of saloons and tobacco-shops.']

March 26th, 1884. Edmund Gosse mentioned to me the other day a fact which struck me as a possible *donnée*. He was speaking of J.A.S., the writer (from whom, in Paris, the other day I got a letter), of his extreme and somewhat hysterical aestheticism, etc.: the sad conditions of his life, exiled to Davos by the state of his lungs, the illness of his daughter, etc. Then he said that, to crown his unhappiness, poor S.'s wife was in no sort of sympathy with what he wrote; disapproving of its tone, thinking his books immoral, pagan, hyper-aesthetic, etc. 'I have never read any of John's works. I think them most *undesirable.*' It seemed to me *qu'il y avait là un drame—un drame intime;* the opposi-tion between the narrow, cold, Calvinistic wife, a rigid moralist; and the husband, impregnated—even to morbidness—with the spirit of Italy, the love of beauty, of art, the aesthetic view of life, and aggravated, made extravagant and perverse, by the sense of his wife's disapproval. *Le drame pourrait s'engager—si drame il y a*—over the education of their child—the way he is to be brought up and to be taught to look at life; the husband drawing him one way and the wife another. The father wishes to make him an artist—the mother wishes to draw him into the church, to dedicate him to morality and religion, in order to expiate, as it were, the countenance that the family have given to god-less ideas in the literary career of the father, who, however, is perfectly decent in life. The denouement to be the fate of the child, who either bolts, as he begins to grow up, and becomes a lout and ignoramus, equally removed from both tendencies—leading a stupid and vegetative life; or else, more pathetically, while he is still a boy, dies, a victim to

[57]

the *tiraillements*, the heavy pressure, of his parents; not knowing what all the pother is about and not finding existence sufficiently simple. If it were not too gruesome, the mother might be supposed to sacrifice him rather than let him fall under the influence of the father. He has an illness during which they both hang over him, tenderly, passionately, as he apparently sinks, and in the course of which it becomes clear to the mother that her husband, with his pagan beliefs, his absence of Christian hopes, has no expectation of meeting the child in a future life. This brings home to her the sense of his pernicious views, the sense of what the child will be exposed to if he lives. She makes up her mind secretly, that it is better he should die; she determines not to save him. During one critical night she sits watching him sink— holding his hand—but doing nothing—allowing him for very tenderness to fade away. This, of course, does not 'transpire,' as the American newspapers say; the reader knows it (the husband never does) through its being guessed by an admirer and devotee of the father (whose genius is immensely prized by a select few) and who must be the narrator of the tale, as I may in courtesy call it. The story should be told by a young American who comes out to England and calls upon the poet (he should be a poet or novelist or both) to pay his *hommage*. He is very kindly received—he remains near them for some weeks, and it is his impression, afterwards related (*à propos*, say, of the death of the poet), that constitutes the narrative, which ought to be— which would only bear to be—extremely short. He guesses, and the wife sees that he has guessed, that she has let the child go; in her exaltation and excitement she virtually confesses it to him. He keeps his knowledge to himself—never imparts it to the husband. She is more conciliatory to the latter, it may be conjectured, after the death of the boy. All this would require prodigious delicacy of touch; and even then *is* very probably too gruesome—the catastrophe too unnatural. Still, I think I shall try it; for the general idea is full of interest and very typical of certain modern situations. The story should be called *The Author of (So-and-So)*, the name of the poet's principal work, for the love of which the young American had come to see him.

x x x x x

[James must have composed the twenty thousand words of The Author of Beltraffio very shortly after setting down this outline, since the story appeared in the English Illustrated Magazine in June and July 1884. James' remark in his preface that the anecdote which touched off his imagination had referred to 'an eminent author, these several years dead,' has often been misconstrued to mean Stevenson, instead of John Addington Symonds.

The Mark Ambient of the story is a novelist devoted to 'the gospel of art,' for whom all of life is 'plastic material.' Though James gives a sympathetic portrayal of him, he also includes some perceptive satire of the excesses of the aesthetic movement through his picture of Ambient's sister who, in her faded velvet robe and with golden fillets in her hair, harbored the vague notion that she 'made up very well as a Rossetti.']

Same date. Mrs. Kemble repeated to me the other night a story told her by Edward Sartoris and told him by his daughter-in-law, Mrs. Algie,[1] in which it seemed to me that there was a 'situation.' The story has only the *tort* to be very incredible, and almost silly: it sounds 'made up.' Mrs. A. relates at any rate that she knew of a young girl, in one of the far western cities of America, who formed an attachment to a young U.S. officer quartered in the town and of whose attentions to her her family wholly disapproved. They declared that under no circumstances would they consent to her marrying him, and forbade her to think of doing so or to hope for a moment for this contingency. Her passion, however, was stronger, and she was secretly married to the officer. But she returned to her father's house, and it was determined to keep the marriage absolutely secret. Both parties appear to have repented, to a considerable degree, of what they had done. In the course of time, however, the girl discovers that living is becoming difficult; she has the prospect of being confined. She is in despair, doesn't know what to do, etc.; and takes a friend, a married woman, into her confidence. This lady, pitying her, offers to take her to Europe and see that in some out-of-the-way place, the child is brought secretly into the world. The girl's parents consent to her making the journey, she goes to Europe with her friend, and in some small Italian town the young lady is delivered. The child is made over, with a sum of money, to a woman of the place, and the others go their way. In due time the young lady returns to her native town and her family, and is reinstated as a daughter of the house. The officer has been ordered to a distant post, and relations between them have ceased. After a while another *prétendant* presents himself, who is agreeable to the family and who ends by becoming agreeable to the girl. (I should mention—for it is the most important point of the whole!—that before she married the officer she extracted from him a promise that he would never demand of her to recognize their union, would never claim her publicly

1. Mrs. Algernon Sartoris, daughter of Ulysses S. Grant.

as his wife, etc. He has given this promise in the most solemn form.)
She marries the new suitor, the officer makes no sign, and she lives for
several years with her new husband, in great happiness, and has several
children. At the end of this time the officer turns up. He tells her that
it is all very well for *her* to be a bigamist, but that he doesn't choose to,
and that she must allow him to institute a divorce suit against her, on
the ground of desertion, in order that *he* too may marry a second time,
being much in love with another woman and desiring to do so. That he
may institute this suit she must release him from his old promise not
to claim her as his wife, etc. It was not made clear to me, in Mrs. K.'s
story, what the heroine did; but I was arrested by the situation I have
just indicated: that of two persons secretly married, and one of whom
(the husband, naturally) is tied by a promise to be silent, yet wishes to
break the marriage in order to recover his freedom—to marry again, to
beget legitimate children. The interest of the other is that the marriage
never be known—her honour, her safety concerned, etc. The husband
pleads that after the vow she has broken, he may surely break his
promise, etc. Her entreaties, in opposition, her distress at the prospect
of exposure, etc. The only endurable denouement that I can see is in
the officer's agreeing to let her off, giving up his own marriage—making
this sacrifice to his word. It will add to the tragic impression of this,
etc., that he is unable to account to his new fiancée, or, at any rate, his
new *inamorata*, for his backing out. He can't tell her why he gives her
up—can't explain to her his extraordinary conduct. His only alternatives
are to commit bigamy and to wait for the death of his bigamous wife.
The situation as presented in the foregoing anecdote (which is impu-
dently crude and incoherent) might be variously modified. The dropping
of the child in Europe would be an impossible incident. It isn't necessary that she should have had a child—though, of course, if she has
none at first it is almost necessary that she should have none afterwards.

[Mrs. John L. Gardner read James' Georgina's Reasons in the second
volume of his Stories Revived (1885), and scribbled to a friend a card
about the heroine: 'She is odious, but she is interesting—And the
story is a masterpiece.' It is not a masterpiece, but out of the idea given
him by Mrs. Kemble, James did make an interesting study of a peculiarly
'odious' girl, whose 'odiousness' is the core of the work. The plot outlined here is followed in the main, but the emphasis is on Georgina's
complete arrogance and heartlessness. The hero is made an officer in
the navy instead of the army, and the story opens in New York. By
another change, useful to develop the plot, the girl whom the 'hero,'

Benyon, eventually wants to marry, is made a connection by marriage of his wife, Georgina. He sees her portrait, recognizes it, and is told by her relatives of her second marriage, which he, of course, knows to be bigamous.

The story pretty well escapes the silliness and crudity that James feared, because Georgina's pride and cruelty are made credible. For example, her first secret marriage is displayed as largely a product of her resentment of her family's opposition, and this, although it does not fully explain her insistence on secrecy, at least helps to show her defiant love for her own way or even whim. The leaving of the child in Europe proved not to be 'an impossible incident,' when prepared for by the complete revelation, earlier in the story, of Georgina's passionate selfishness.

Late in the story two new characters are introduced—Kate Theory, with whom Benyon is falling in love, and her invalid sister, Mildred. Hitherto the story has been told on the basis of what Benyon, as participant and observer, might have known or later learned, but the two Theorys talk together without any possibility of his being aware of it. It may be that James thought the tale not worth including in the collected edition because it fell short of his later strictness about 'point of view.' More interesting is the fact that Mildred Theory is 'as beautiful as a saint, and as delicate and refined as an angel,' a girl who 'knew everything' and benignly watched over her sister. The kinship of the names Minny Temple, Mildred Theory, and Milly Theale, is plain; so is the correspondence in the situations of Mildred and of Minny Temple, whose beauty in her fatal illness deeply impressed James and gave him the impulse to create Milly in The Wings of the Dove. The Minny Temple theme was obviously already in his mind when he wrote Georgina's Reasons.

The first printing of the story was in the New York Sun, on 20 and 27 July and 3 August 1884.]

Names. Papineau—Beaufoy—Birdseye—Morphy.

Names. Tester—Frankinshaw—Tarrant—(Italian): Olimpino—Pagano—Avellana—Ginistrella—(English): Lightbody—R(h)ymer—Busk—Wybrow—Bernardistone—Squirl—Secretan—Ransome.

June 19th, 1884. One might write a tale (very short) about a woman married to a man of the most amiable character who is a tremendous, though harmless, liar. She is very intelligent, a fine, quiet, high, pure nature, and she has to sit by and hear him romance—mainly out of vanity, the desire to be interesting, and a peculiar irresistible impulse.

[61]

He is good, kind, personally very attractive, very handsome, etc.: it is almost his only fault though of course he is increasingly very *light*. What she suffers—what she goes through—generally she tries to rectify, to remove any bad effect by toning down a little, etc. But there comes a day when he tells a very big lie which she has—for reasons to be related—to adopt, to reinforce. To save him from exposure, in a word, she has to lie herself. The struggle, etc.; she lies—but after that she hates him. (*Numa Roumestan*.)

[*Daudet's Numa Roumestan came out in 1881. James praised it highly in his essay on Daudet in the Century Magazine in August 1883. The character of Numa is very like that outlined, and it seems probable that James got from Daudet the hint for making a tale out of a glib liar and a sensitive and honest wife. But, in his preface to The Aspern Papers, he said that The Liar grew directly out of his meeting at a dinner-party 'one autumn evening' a man who was 'the most unbridled colloquial romancer the "joy of life" had ever found occasion to envy.' He added that he never forgot the meeting. Since the story did not appear in the Century until May and June 1888, four years after the entry above, it seems more likely that the original germ for the story came from Daudet, and that James put it down in his notebook prior to the dinner party. Then, later, he met the 'liar' in the flesh, and wrote the tale—perhaps referring to the notebook or perhaps not remembering it or its relation to Numa Roumestan at all.*

The Liar opens with a dinner party, which is unparalleled in Daudet. The strength of the tale comes from James' centering, as in the notebook, not on the 'liar' but on the problem of his wife, and from the introduction of an emotional relation between the wife and an artist, through whose observation the story is told. He has wooed her vainly years before. Because he is still deeply interested in her and feels that she has once slighted him, he tries to find out how far she will go to protect her husband, hoping that she will give some sign of a feeling that if she had married the artist, 'her life would have been finer.' In the sketch she protects her husband, but 'after that she hates him'; in the story she is still in love with the 'liar.' This change in the ending increases the effectiveness of the story by making it almost a case of the 'possession' of a pure spirit by an impure one, and by saving it from the relative banality of a presentation simply of a wife loyal to her husband under unpleasant circumstances.

James' use of the name 'Capadose' for the 'liar' evoked an inquiry from a member of the Capadose family. He replied in a letter, printed in Isaäc Da Costa's Noble Families among the Sephardic Jews.

My dear Sir,

You may be very sure that if I had ever had the pleasure of meeting a person of your striking name I wouldn't have used the name, especially for the purpose of the tale you allude to.

It was exactly because I had no personal or private association with it that I felt free to do so. But I am afraid that (in answer to your amiable inquiry) it is late in the day for me to tell you how I came by it.

The Liar was written (originally published in the Century Magazine) 10 years ago—and I simply don't remember.

Fiction-mongers collect proper names, surnames, &c.—make notes and lists of any odd or unusual, as handsome or ugly ones they see or hear—in newspapers (columns of births, deaths, marriages, &c.) or in directories and signs of shops or elsewhere; fishing out of these memoranda in time of need the one that strikes them as good for a particular case.

"Capadose" must be in one of my old note-books. I have a dim recollection of having found it originally in the first columns of The Times, where I find almost all the names I store up for my puppets. It was picturesque and rare and so I took possession of it. I wish—if you care at all—that I had applied it to a more exemplary individual! But my romancing Colonel was a charming man, in spite of his little weakness.

I congratulate you on your bearing a name that is at once particularly individualizing and not ungraceful (as so many rare names are).

I am, my dear Sir,
Yours very truly
HENRY JAMES.']

June 19th. Mrs. H. Ward mentioned the other day to me an idea of hers for a story which might be made interesting—as a study of the histrionic character. A young actress is an object of much attention and a great deal of criticism from a man who loves the stage (he oughtn't to be a *professional* critic) and finally, though she doesn't satisfy him at all, artistically, loves the girl herself. He thinks something may be made of her, though he doesn't quite see what: he works over her, gives her ideas, etc. Finally (she is slow in developing, though full of ambition), she takes one, and begins to mount, to become a celebrity. She goes beyond him, she leaves him looking after her and wondering. She begins where he ends—soars away and is lost to him. The interest, I say, would be as a study of a certain particular *nature d'actrice*: a very

[63]

curious sort of nature to reproduce. The girl I see to be very crude, etc. The thing a confirmation of Mrs. Kemble's theory that the dramatic gift is a thing by itself—implying of necessity no *general* superiority of mind. The strong nature, the personal quality, vanity, etc., of the girl: her artistic being, so vivid, yet so purely instinctive. Ignorant, illiterate. Rachel.

[*Miriam Rooth, in* The Tragic Muse (*see pp. 90-91, 92-3 below*) *is a development of this idea for the portrait of an actress.*]

Another little thing was told me the other day by Mrs. R. about Mrs. D<uncan> S<tewart>'s little maid (lady's maid), Past, who was with her for years before her death, and whom I often saw there. She had to find a new place of course, on Mrs. S.'s death, to relapse into ordinary service. Her sorrow, the way she felt the change, and the way she expressed it to Mrs. R. 'Ah yes, ma'am, you have lost your mother, and it's a great grief, but what is your loss to mine?' (She was devoted to Mrs. D.S.) 'You continue to see good society, to live with clever, cultivated people: but I fall again into my own class, I shall never see such company—hear such talk—again. She was so good to me that I lived *with* her, as it were; and nothing will ever make up to me again for the loss of her conversation. Common, vulgar people now: that's my lot for the future!' Represent this—the refined nature of the little plain, quiet woman—her appreciation—and the way her new conditions sicken her, with a denouement if possible. Represent first, of course, her life with the old lady—figure of old Mrs. D.S. (modified)—her interior—her talk. Mrs. R.'s relations with her servants. 'My child—my dear child.'

[*Mrs. Stewart's 'lady's maid' was transmuted into the ineffable butler, Brooksmith, in James' story of that name. The theme is exactly that of the notebook entry; the change from lady's maid to butler was made because, as James said in his preface to the Daisy Miller volume, his 'little derived drama, in the event, seemed to require, to be ample enough, a hero rather than a heroine. I desired for my poor lost spirit,' he continued, 'the measured maximum of the fatal experience . . . the obscure tragedy of the "intelligent" butler present at rare table-talk, rather than that of the more effaced tirewoman.' The story is one of James' shortest, and admirable for its technical economy and sharpness of emphasis. Brooksmith's whole 'tragedy' is revealed through the eyes of a guest at many London houses who meets him first in his ideal milieu and then encounters him in successively less attractive circles, until at last he is discovered to have disappeared completely.*

Pelham Edgar suggests that the story is important because Brooksmith was 'the only representative of the servant class whom James ever thought worthy to commemorate,' but its real interest lies in the fact that it is a skillful and concise dramatization of a dilemma that constantly fascinated James—the dilemma of the highly sensitive intelligence frustrated and starved by the lack of fit material and a proper environment for its development.

The story appeared first in Black and White for 2 May 1891, nearly seven years after the notebook entry was made.]

July 9th, 1884. It was told me the other day of Lady Ashburton that she asked a young girl to come and stay with her in Scotland, asseverating to her (the girl's) mother that she would be the best of duennas, etc., and look after her in perfection. On these terms the girl is allowed to go, alone. She arrives, and finds that Lady A., having quite forgotten that she had asked her, has left home, the day before, on a yachting expedition. She is away from railways, etc., there is nothing for her but to stay, especially as the hostess is expected back in a day or two. She stays, and the next day a young man arrives, also invited and forgotten. The *beau jeune homme* and the girl are face to face—it is a situation out of which something might be made. Various developments possible. The thing might be done in letters—from each person concerned: the hostess after she remembers, on the yacht, included. The young man's scruples—yet desire to stay, etc. The girl's fears—yet hopes that he will. It is all perhaps rather cheap—yet may contain something.

July 9th, 1884. This idea has been suggested to me by reading Sir Lepel Griffin's book about America. Type of the conservative, fastidious, exclusive Englishman (in public life, clever, etc.), who hates the U.S.A. and thinks them a contamination to England, a source of *funeste* warning, etc., and an odious country socially. He falls in love with an American Girl and she with him—this of course to be made natural if possible. He lets her know, frankly, that he loathes her country as much as he adores her personally, and he begs her to marry him. She is patriotic in a high degree—a genuine little American—and she has the sentiment of her native land. But she is in love with the Englishman, and though she resists on patriotic grounds she yields at last, accepts him and marries him. She must have a near relation—a brother, say—who is violently American, an *anglophobiste* (in public life in the U.S.A.); and of whom she is very fond. He deplores her marriage, entreats her to keep out of it, etc. He and the Englishman *loathe* each other. After the marriage the Englishman's hostility to

[65]

the U.S. increases, fostered by the invasion of Americans, etc. State of mind of the wife. Depression, melancholy, remorse and shame at having married an enemy of her country. Suicide? There is a certain interest in the situation—the difficulty of choice and resignation on her part—the resentment of a rupture with the brother, etc. Of course internationalism, etc., may be found overdone, threadbare. That is to a certain extent a reason against the subject; but a weak, not a strong one. It is always enough if the *author* sees substance in it.

[*Two Countries appeared in Harper's Magazine (June 1888), with illustrations by Charles S. Reinhart, an appreciation of whose interpretative skill in black and white James was to include in Picture and Text (1893). When James put this story into a book with The Aspern Papers and Louisa Pallant (1888), he changed the title to The Modern Warning. The new phrase was taken from the title which Sir Rufus Chasemore, the English husband in the story, gives to his travel impressions of the United States, a book designed to warn his countrymen against contaminating influences from across the sea. Such also had been the intention of Sir Lepel Henry Griffin's The Great Republic (1884).*

Through the strictures of Macarthy Grice, the American brother, James balanced his sharp criticisms of the two countries, drawing again on his recent travel. As tends to be the case with his occasional use of violence, the suicide ending is inadequately prepared for, and not very effective. He may have excluded the story from his collected edition for that reason, or because he believed that he had enough better examples of international contrasts and that The Modern Warning did not justify its length of twenty-five thousand words.]

Names. Greenstreet—Wingrave—Major—Touchstone—Luna—Midsummer—Utterson—Pardon—Monkhouse—Prance—Basil—Blythe—Lancelot—Farrinder—Bigwood—Float—Hendrik—Joscelind—Mummery—Middlemas—Burrage—Prendergast—Scambler—Wager—Baskerville—Langrish—Robina—Crookenden—Pynsent—Loam—Amandus—Vau—Foot—Oriel (Xtian name)—(Lord) Inglefield: or name of a place—Severals (of a place)—Jump—Maplethorpe (place)—Catching—Quarterman—Alabaster—Muniment—Stark—Whiteroy (place)—Middle—Maidment—Filbert—Fury—Trist (person or place—house).

August 6th, 1884. Infinitely oppressed and depressed by the sense of being behindhand with the novel—that is, with the *start* of it, that I have engaged, through Osgood, to write for the *Century.* I go today for

36 hours to Waddesden, and on the 9th for the same stay to the Rallis'. These are old engagements, which I keep very *à contre coeur*: I would so far rather stick to my table and scribble. But it is far better to put them through—it is the braver course; but what a divine relief when I am back from the Rallis', on the 11th, with all this infernal survival of the season at rest, only *one* engagement, a Sunday at <Buxril?>, the 16th, ahead of me, and a clear stretch of work to look forward to. Then I shall possess my soul, my faculties, my imagination again, then I shall feel that life is worth living, and shall (I trust) be tolerably calm and happy. *A mighty will*, there is nothing but that! The integrity of one's will, purpose, faith. To wait, when one *must* wait, and act when one can act!

x   x   x   x   x

I haven't even a name for my novel, and fear I shall have to call it simply—*Verena*: the heroine. I should like something more descriptive —but everything that is justly descriptive won't do—*The Newness*— *The Reformers*—*The Precursors*—*The Revealer*—etc.—all very bad, and with the additional fault that people will say they are taken from Daudet's *Évangéliste*. x x x x x The heroine to be called Verena— Verena Tarrant. Her mother had seen the name in a book and liked it. Her father's name is Amariah. Her friend is Olive Chancellor. The hero is Basil Ransom. The 'other fellow' (her other lover) is Mathias Pinder. The little old lady is Miss Birdseye.

[*James soon changed Amariah to Selah, and Pinder to Pardon. Two months after making this entry he wrote to his brother William that he was calling this book* The Bostonians: '*I shall be much abused for the title, but it exactly and literally fits the story, and is much the best, simplest and most dignified I could have chosen.' He was attacked by outraged local critics precisely on the grounds that all Bostonians were not as false or as hyper-analytic as he had represented some of them. He found such criticism 'idiotic and insulting.'*

Over Miss Birdseye he engaged in a heated discussion with William, who had protested against his basing her on old Miss Elizabeth Peabody, Hawthorne's sister-in-law. James denied the charge in a passage that throws great light on the way he evolved his characters: 'I absolutely had no shadow of such an intention. I have not seen Miss P. for twenty years, I never had but the most casual observation of her, I didn't know whether she was alive or dead, and she was not in the smallest degree my starting-point or example. Miss Birdseye was evolved entirely from my moral consciousness, like every other person I have

[67]

ever drawn, and originated in my desire to make a figure who should embody in a sympathetic, pathetic, picturesque, and at the same time grotesque way, the humanitary and ci-devant transcendental tendencies which I thought it highly probable I should be accused of treating in a contemptuous manner in so far as they were otherwise represented in the tale. I wished to make this figure a woman, because so it would be more touching, and an old, weary, battered, and simple-minded woman because that deepened the same effect. I elaborated her in my mind's eye—and after I had got going reminded myself that my creation would perhaps be identified with Miss Peabody—that I freely admit. . . The one definite thing about which I had a scruple was some touch about Miss Birdseye's spectacles—I remembered that Miss Peabody's were always in the wrong place; but I didn't see, really, why I should deprive myself of an effect (as regards this point) which is common to a thousand old people. So I thought no more about Miss P. at all, but simply strove to realize my vision.']

Names. Croucher—Smallpiece—Corner—Buttery—Bide—Cash—Medley (place, country-house)—Dredge—Warmington—Probert—Henning—Beadle—Gallex—Bowerbank—Ermelinda—Lonely—Button—Filer—Dolman (Miss Dolman)—Rushout—Chad—Trantum—German (Xtian name)—Audrey (family name)—Ivy (the plant)—Castanet—Bavard—Rust—Plaster—Buxbridge—Peachey—Pillar—Pontifex—Trigg—Suchbury—Pinching—Pulse—Gleed—Constant—Six—Frowd—Terbot—Wherry.

Names (continued). Gamage—Fluid—Welchford—Fancourt—Trinder—Trender.

August 10th, 1885. It is absolutely necessary that at this point I should make the future evolution of the *Princess Casamassima* more clear to myself. I have never yet become engaged in a novel in which, after I had begun to write and send off my MS., the details had remained so vague. This is partly—or indeed wholly—owing to the fact that I have been so terribly preoccupied—up to so lately—with the unhappy *Bostonians,* born under an evil star. The subject of the *Princess* is magnificent, and if I can only give up my mind to it properly—generously and trustfully—the form will shape itself as successfully as the idea deserves. I have plunged in rather blindly, and got a good many characters on my hands; but these will fall into their places if I keep cool and think it out. Oh art, art, what difficulties are like thine; but, at the same time, what consolation and encouragements, also, are like thine? Without thee, for me, the world would be, indeed, a howling desert. The

Princess will give me hard, continuous work for many months to come; but she will also give me joys too sacred to prate about.—In the 3d installment of the serial Hyacinth makes the acquaintance of x x x x x

August 22d. Phrases, of the people.

. . . 'that takes the gilt off, you know.'
. . . a young man, of his *patron*, in a shop . . . 'he cuts it very fine.' . . . ' 'Ere today, somewhere else tomorrow: that's '*is* motto.'

x   x   x   x   x

[*The Princess Casamassima appeared serially in the Atlantic Monthly (September 1885–October 1886). James hoped that it would prove 'more popular' than The Bostonians, but at the beginning of 1888, he wrote to Howells, who had hailed the Princess as his greatest novel so far: 'I have entered upon evil days. . . I am still staggering a good deal under the mysterious and (to me) inexplicable injury wrought—apparently—upon my situation by my two last novels, the Bostonians and the Princess, from which I expected so much and derived so little. They have reduced the desire, and the demand, for my productions to zero. . .'*

These two books constituted James' attempt to handle the Dickensian type of social novel. Into the Princess he poured the distillation of his long observation of London's streets, in an effort to suggest the dark heaving of revolt, 'irreconcileably, subversively, beneath the vast smug surface.' His preface is one of his most eloquent defenses of the novel of intelligence, of the use of such 'intense perceivers' as his tragic young hero, Hyacinth Robinson.

In the third installment of the serial, Hyacinth has just made the acquaintance of the revolutionary Paul Muniment. James' broken sentence suggests that he may possibly have resorted here to another notebook. The 'Phrases, of the people' are such as he tried to record in presenting both the printer's shop where Hyacinth worked and the political meetings.]

August 22d. One does nothing of value in art or literature unless one has some general ideas, and if one has a few such, constituting a motive and a support, those flippancies and vulgarities (abusive reviews in newspapers) are the last thing one troubles about.

Names. Gamble—Balm—Stannary (of a place, seat)—Quibbler—Lonsgrove—Chick—Sholto—Ruffler—Booker—Longhurst (place)—Ambler—

Campion—Gus (or Guss)—Leolin (boy)—<Leolin>e (girl)—Starling—
Lumb—Merryweather—Yeo—Rix—Francina (girl).

x   x   x   x   x

[*The lapse of over a year before the next entry is presumably owing
to the work involved in finishing* The Princess Casamassima.]

Florence, January 12th, 1887.

A. mentions in a letter that Sir J.R. is to marry the Dowager Lady T.
—that 'he blushes whenever her name is mentioned, and that Mrs. S.C.
says it is simply forty years of her mother's life wiped out.' There is a
little drama here—at least a possible one—between a father and daughter on such an occasion; especially—I mean—when the 1st married life
has been a happy one—the 2 have cherished the memory of the wife
and mother together. The daughter's sense of the want of dignity of
her father's act—as an old, or elderly, man—of the difference between
her mother and the new love, etc. It sickens her—she goes to the fiancée,
etc. She must have—to make her opposition natural—the worship of
her mother's memory—and a kind of horror. I am not sure that there
is much of a subject—but a short tale might be made of it. The father
may be affected by his daughter's opposition so much as to repent
of his engagement. He is *ébranlé*, he is ashamed of it, he wishes to retreat. But he tells her it is there and that he can't get out of it. 'Very
well,' says she—*'je m'en charge.'* SHE goes to the fiancée again and
there she tells her something about the father—a pure fabrication—
she swears her to secrecy—which she flatters herself will prevent the
woman from wishing to go on with the marriage. (*What* she tells her
is a delicate point—to be settled; and of course it must be under the
empire of a passionate *idée fixe*.) This communication has its effect—
the intended wife shortly afterwards lets the father know that she repents of the engagement and that she releases him. He is pleased at
first—pleased that he has pleased his daughter—and she (the daughter) is delighted at what she has done. Before long, however, she
begins to see a change in her father—he is sad, brooding, sombre—he
looks at her in a different way. In fact, he is beginning to wonder *how*
she affected the lady—what she did, what arts she used—and to suspect that she *did* say something that was injurious to him. She perceives
this change in him—that he is resentful and unhappy—and suddenly,
weary of the whole thing, she gives up her opposition. She determines
to go to the lady and tell her that everything she said before was false.
She does so, and the latter replies—'I am very sorry—but I have just become engaged to Mr. So-and-So!' It may be represented—to make the

[70]

daughter's action a little less odious—that the intended wife has not really believed what she said—has seen through it as a manœuvre—but *has* thought that the father has lent himself to it and despises him accordingly. It wouldn't be a very 'sympathetic' tale.

x   x   x   x   x

[The Marriages, though not printed until August 1891 in the Atlantic Monthly, may have been written nearer to the date of the entry above, since in his letter to Howells about the reduction in the demand for his stories, James said: 'Though I have for a good while past been writing a number of good short things, I remain irremediably unpublished. Editors keep them back, for months and years, as if they were ashamed of them.'
In The Marriages James intensified the drama by eliminating the suggested element of the father's connivance, and by making the action depend wholly upon Adela Chart's almost hysterical objections to his remarrying. She goes in secret to Mrs. Churchley, and pretends that her mother's life had been devastated by her father's brutalities. When it is revealed at the close that Mrs. Churchley had not believed her, the reason for breaking off the match is also revealed. Mrs. Churchley had in turn denounced Adela to Colonel Chart, and had said that she would not live in the same house with such a girl. His refusal to sacrifice his daughter had brought on the rupture and Mrs. Churchley's subsequent acceptance of Lord Dovedale.
In discussing this story in the Daisy Miller volume, James noted its center of consciousness in 'the fond imagination, the possibly poisoned and inflamed judgement' of the suffering daughter. This is the kind of story in which a later writer would not have skirted the 'unsympathetic' element, and would have probed more deeply into the sexual pathology latent in the theme.]

Same date. Hamilton (V.L.'s brother) told me a curious thing of Capt. Silsbee—the Boston art-critic and Shelley-worshipper; that is of a curious adventure of his. Miss Claremont,[1] Byron's *ci-devant* mistress (the mother of Allegra) was living, until lately, here in Florence, at a great age, 80 or thereabouts, and with her lived her niece, a younger Miss Claremont—of about 50. Silsbee knew that they had interesting papers—letters of Shelley's and Byron's—he had known it for a long time and cherished the idea of getting hold of them. To this end he laid the plan of going to lodge with the Misses Claremont—hoping

1. Clairmont is the usual form of the name, and the one used by James in his preface to The Aspern Papers.

that the old lady in view of her great age and failing condition would die while he was there, so that he might then put his hand upon the documents, which she hugged close in life. He carried out this scheme —and things *se passèrent* as he had expected. The old woman *did* die —and then he approached the younger one—the old maid of 50—on the subject of his desires. Her answer was—'I will give you all the letters if you marry me!' H. says that Silsbee *court encore.* Certainly there is a little subject there: the picture of the two faded, queer, poor and discredited old English women—living on into a strange generation, in their musty corner of a foreign town—with these illustrious letters their most precious possession. Then the plot of the Shelley fanatic—his watchings and waitings—the way he *couvers* [1] the treasure. The denouement needn't be the one related of poor Silsbee; and at any rate the general situation is in itself a subject and a picture. It strikes me much. The interest would be in some price that the man has to pay—that the old woman—or the survivor—sets upon the papers. His hesitations—his struggle—for he really would give almost anything. — The Countess Gamba came in while I was there: her husband is a nephew of the Guiccioli—and it was *à propos* of their having a lot of Byron's letters of which they are rather illiberal and dangerous guardians, that H. told me the above. They won't show them or publish any of them—and the Countess was very angry once on H.'s representing to her that it was her duty—especially to the English public!— to let them at least be seen. *Elle se fiche bien* of the English public. She says the letters—addressed in Italian to the Guiccioli—are discreditable to Byron; and H. elicited from her that she had *burned* one of them!

x   x   x   x   x

[*The situation in James' The Aspern Papers is the one outlined in the first part of the note above, but Shelley has been disguised as an American poet, and Florence has become Venice.*

James added to the notebook sketch by suggesting strongly that the old lady, Juliana, schemed to make the seeker for Jeffrey Aspern's papers marry the 'younger one,' Tina, as the price of seeing them. After Juliana dies, Tina virtually offers him the relics if he will marry her. He runs away, then wavers—only to discover that Tina will not have him now that she realizes that he cannot love her. The story ends with her destruction of the papers and his discomfited departure. Juliana is made a kind of symbol of what James, as his preface shows, wanted to see in the 'Byronic' age, and her constant masking of her eyes heightens

---

1. Here James uses the infinitive of a French verb—*couver*—and adds an English termination. Cf. *regimbers* on page 137.

the mystery which hangs about her in a time very different from that in which she was a poet's mistress. Tina, whose transparent honesty borders on downright stupidity, supplies a sharp contrast, and in developing this James goes beyond the notebook to set up tension between the romantic charm of a 'Byronic' world, and the simpler aspect of later American characters.

James' interest in names, already alluded to (pp. 7-8 above), is here profitably used to enhance his characterization and setting. Tina talks of the days when she and Juliana first came to Italy, and says that they led a 'brilliant life.' 'It was Miss Tina who judged it brilliant. . . I asked her what people they had known and she said Oh very nice ones—the Cavaliere Bombicci and the Contessa Altemura, with whom they had had a great friendship! Also English people—the Churtons and the Goldies and Mrs. Stock-Stock, whom they had loved dearly.' The very sound of the names adds to the irony implicit in Tina's magnifying into brilliance a society sadly inglorious in comparison with Juliana's romantic past.

Evan Charteris, in his John Sargent, tells the same story that James heard about Captain Silsbee, and also quotes Vernon Lee on that 'typical American skipper' with a passion for Shelley. This suggests that 'Hamilton (V.L.'s brother)' was Eugene Lee-Hamilton, half-brother of Vernon Lee.

James wrote The Aspern Papers soon after he heard the story, for it was published in the Atlantic Monthly in March–May 1888.]

Same date. The idea of a worldly mother and a worldly daughter, the latter of whom has been trained up so perfectly by the former that she excels and surpasses her, and the mother, who has some principle of goodness still left in her composition, is appalled at her own work. She sees the daughter, so hard, so cruelly ambitious, so bent on making a great marriage and a great success at any price, that she is almost afraid of her. She repents of what she has done—she is ashamed. The daughter fixes a rich, soft, amiable young man as an object of conquest —and the mother finds herself pitying the lad. She is tempted to go to him and warn him. They may all be Americans—in Europe: since Howells writes to me that I do the 'international' far better than anything else. The story may be told by an elderly American—the uncle, or cousin, of the very rich lad whom the girl considers a *parti* worth her efforts. He has known the 2 ladies of old—he has seen the mother's great worldliness, and he observes the change. The mother shall have been an old flame of his and shall have thrown him over. After that their relations shall have become frank—intensely candid. She knows he knows her views and efforts—and they have openly talked of them.

[73]

He doesn't like the daughter—he is responsible for his rich young nephew—he warns the mother off—says the boy is not to be their game. The mother takes the warning—or perhaps it's not definitely given, for that after all might be too brutal. However, that's a point to be settled. She may see for herself that her old sweetheart fears their bagging the boy (for the girl is superficially charming), and determines to retrieve herself in the uncle's eyes by preventing the capture. She has always been ashamed of the way she has treated her old admirer. She sees that her daughter is determined to collar the young man. So she goes to the latter clandestinely, denounces the girl (after a fashion), and recommends him to go away. He consents—he is affected by what she says—and escapes. The mother is in a kind of exaltation —she feels as if she had purified herself. She goes to the uncle and says—'Ah, well, you must respect me now.' He admires her, and he must describe this in a good tone. But he feels even a little sorry for the girl, and after a little he even expresses this. Then the mother may reply, as a last word—'Oh, after all, I don't know that it matters! She will still get a prince!' * The narrator says—'She *is* now the Countess So-and-So.'

[Louisa Pallant *appeared in* Harper's Magazine *in February 1888, with illustrations by Reinhart, but James' brief mention of the story in the preface to* The Reverberator *volume notes that it was written in Florence in the February of the year before.*

All the characters are American, and the story opens in Homburg.

* [James' note] This business might begin and indeed take place wholly at some watering place—say Homburg—or perhaps better in Switzerland. No room for description. Perhaps Florence might do. At any rate the narrator meets the ladies after a long interval. The nephew arrives—joins him—later. The narrator must begin this story—'Never say you know the last word about any human heart! I once was treated to a revelation which startled and touched me in the nature of a person whom I knew well, whom I had been well acquainted with for years, whose character I had had good reason, Heaven knows, to appreciate, and in regard to whom I flattered myself I had nothing more to learn. It was on the terrace of the Kursaal at Homburg, nearly ten years ago, one lovely summer night. I was there alone, but I was waiting for my nephew, etc., etc. The band played—the people passed and repassed in front of me; I smoked my cigar and watched them. Suddenly I recognized Mrs. Grift and her daughter. I hadn't seen Linda since she was fifteen, but I had then seen how she was going. She had become exceedingly pretty —and wonderfully like what her mother was twenty years before.' They walk (the mother and daughter up and down together) and he watches them, unseen, for some time before he speaks to them. No one else does so; it is almost as if they were not respectable. (I don't know that that is very important.) I must give his little retrospect while he regards them. Then he gets up and goes to them—and the rest comes on. I don't see why this shouldn't be a little masterpiece of *concision*, all narrative—not too much attempt to *fouiller*, with every word telling. If M. Schuyler doesn't find *Cousin Maria* possible for his 'holiday number' of *Harper*, this might very well serve.

[74]

The marked difference from the outline is that the narrator, the boy's uncle, is entirely unsuspicious of Linda Pallant's nature. The story is given greater singleness of effect by the strength of Louisa Pallant's denunciation to her old suitor of the hardness of her daughter.

A glimpse of how James amplified as he wrote is provided by a comparison of the Harper's version with the first draft. He kept close to his initial sentences, and then began to accumulate a greater range of concrete detail: 'Never say you know the last word about any human heart! I was once treated to a revelation which startled and touched me, in the nature of a person with whom I had been acquainted (well, as I supposed) for years, whose character I had had good reasons, Heaven knows, to appreciate, and in regard to whom I flattered myself that I had nothing more to learn.

'It was on the terrace of the Kursaal at Homburg, nearly ten years ago, one lovely night toward the end of July. I had come to the place that day from Frankfort, with vague intentions, and was mainly occupied in waiting for my young nephew, the only son of my sister, who had been intrusted to my care by a very fond mother for the summer (I was expected to show him Europe—only the very best of it), and was on his way from Paris to join me. The excellent band discoursed music not too abstruse, and the air was filled, besides, with the murmur of different languages, the smoke of many cigars, the creak, on the gravel of the gardens, of strolling shoes, and the thick tinkle of beer glasses. There were a hundred people walking about, there were some in clusters at little tables, and many on benches and rows of chairs, watching the others with a kind of solemn dumbness. I was among these last—I sat by myself, smoking my cigar, and thinking of nothing very particular, while families and couples passed and repassed me.

'I scarcely know how long I had sat there when I became aware of a recognition which made my meditations definite. It was on my own part, and the object of it was a lady who moved to and fro, unconscious of my observation, with a young girl at her side. I had not seen her for ten years, and what first struck me was the fact, not that she was Mrs. Henry Pallant, but that the girl who was with her was remarkably pretty. . .']

I don't see why the three above things (the 2d and 3d are much the best—and I think the 2d really almost a gem) shouldn't be, if treated at all, treated effectively with great brevity.

[James handled The Marriages and Louisa Pallant in about twelve thousand words each, but The Aspern Papers grew into a nouvelle of three times that length.]

Florence, January 21st, 1887. A possible subject for something 'international' might be the situation of an English or American girl (presumably the latter) who has grown up in a polyglot and 'cosmopolite' society, like that of Florence—and is sick of it all—sick of the coming and going, the absence of roots and responsibilities in the people, the bad French, which is the medium of social intercourse—the absence of all that savours of her own race and tongue. For the latter she has a sort of consuming desire. She might be made a little literary—privately and unsatisfiedly—to carry this out. All around her Russians, Italians, vague French—English and Americans who are also vague. She is thought to have had great 'advantages'—linguistic and other—but she longs for some little corner of England or of the U.S. She must have a sister or two married in foreign lands. Some young Englishman or American meets her. A sketch—a portrait—of this kind, very briefly treated, might be interesting, and give an impression of such a place, 'socially,' as this.

Venice, June 20th, 1887 (Palazzo Barbaro).

Paul Bourget mentioned to me the other day, as the subject of a *nouvelle*, a situation (making it over to me to use if, and as, I liked) which, through alterations, has converted itself in my mind into an idea which I think excellent. The form in which he gave it to me was suggested by the suicide, in Rome, of his beautiful young friend, Mlle S. She jumped out of the window of an hotel at Milan, in her night-dress, at 6 o'clk., in the a.m. while in the delirium of a fever. Bourget had a theory about her—which was that she had believed that her mother had lovers, that this weighed upon her horribly and that she wanted to escape from the house, to get away and cease to be the witness of the maternal *dérèglements*. The only way for her to do this was to marry. A young man came often to the house, seemed to take pleasure in her society, etc. She thought he might rescue her— if an opportunity were given him—by asking for her hand. So one day —and the impulse was strange and desperate—she said to him: 'You come here so much—you seem to like me, etc. Why do you do it? Is it that you want to marry me? Speak if you do.' No sooner had she uttered these words than she perceived her mistake. The young man was evidently taken completely by surprise; he blushed, stared, stammered, said that certainly the honour of her hand was a thing to which one might well aspire—if one dared, etc. In short he was civil, vague—tried to behave gallantly, for a man caught. She looked at him a moment and burst into tears. 'Oh heavens, what have I done? From the moment you don't throw yourself at my feet with joy, I see

[76]

what my mistake has been. Go away, go away, this instant, and let me *never* see you again!' The young man retired, respectfully, and left the place altogether. The girl relapsed into the situation that surrounded her, saw no issue, and after a short time, disgusted, sick at soul, despairing, destroyed herself. I should add that a day or two after telling me this story, Bourget let me know that his interpretation of the *motive* of the suicide had probably been utterly fanciful. Nothing, in the real history, was clear but the fact that she had killed herself, and the mother's immorality and the appeal to the young man, relegated themselves to the vague. The girl simply had typhoid fever —had been cheerful and natural before it, etc. Bourget's version was very characteristic of himself—the facility of the hypothesis that the mother was an adulteress, etc. This however doesn't alter the suggestiveness of the drama as he imagined it. It would have been very possible in this form, whether actual or not. But to make something of it I must modify it essentially—as I can't, and besides, don't particularly want to, depict in an American magazine, a woman carrying on adulteries under her daughter's eyes. That case, I imagine, is in America so rare as to be almost abnormal. Something of this sort is the shape into which it has converted itself to my fancy. I see it as an episode in that 'international' series which, really, without forcing the matter or riding the horse to death, strikes me as an inexhaustible mine. Something of about the form of *Daisy Miller* or the *Siege of London*. An American girl, very pretty, but of a very light substance, easily depraved, marries a young Englishman and lives in the smart, dissipated set, the P. of W.'s, etc., in London. She is frivolous *outre mesure*, and a terrible young person 'for men.' Her husband is an idiot, though not a bad fellow, leading exclusively the life of amusement, sport, etc. It will be a very good chance to try and reproduce some of my London impressions of that order. Lady Davenant (say, for convenience), has a younger sister who has come out from America to stay with her, to make a long visit, and it must be of the essence of this girl's position that she has no other home or refuge—no other place to go. It must also be the essence of her nature that she is as different as possible from her sister—grave, sensitive, serious, honest, unadapted to the world in which Lady D. lives, troubled and tormented by it, and above all distressed and alarmed at the way she sees Lady D. going. She is poor, the parents are dead, she has no other brother nor sister—the father has 'failed,' characteristically, in New York, not long after the elder sister's marriage. This fact, by itself, is already a source of discomfort and humiliation to the younger. It makes her unhappy, uncertain of her footing. Lady D. has had a considerable *dot* paid down on her marriage; so that the failure, subsequent, has not compromised *her* fortune, though she and her husband are both so extravagant that they transcend their means, etc. This is necessary (the fact that the elder sister has had her portion and that Laura [say] has nothing), to make it possible to represent the latter as living with her, being supported by her. Laura has before her the spectacle of Lady D.'s frantic frivolity, and it pains and bewilders her—she doesn't know what to make of it. It is new to her—she not having come out to London for some years after the marriage; kept at home by the family troubles, looking after the father, broken by his reverses, the mother, after his death, ruined, etc. She is twenty-five or six by the time she comes; Lady D. is about thirty. Meanwhile the latter has had time to fall into the pace—to become thoroughly *lancée*. Her sister finds her immensely changed and <wasted?> when she comes; but it takes her some time to take it in—to understand what surrounds her. She is too innocent at first—too pure, too accustomed to optimistic interpretations. Add to this that her sister imposes upon <her> as her elder, by her beauty, her brilliancy, etc. This point must be insisted upon—that Laura has adored Lady D., admired her precisely for being so different from herself. This is necessary, to make the revulsion, the deep pain greater, when she finds what a good-for-nought she has become. She doesn't presume to judge her at first—it is only little by little. There must be an old lady—like Mrs. Duncan S<tewart>—only of rank—a genial, clever, worldly, old-fashioned, half comforting, half shocking old lady, whom she goes to see and talk with, and who half enlightens her, half reassures her. This old woman must have taken a great fancy to her—she tries to marry her. But this doesn't succeed—Laura having no money and not being a success in London. Accentuate the fact that she is of the kind, the American kind, that isn't. Lady D. has already had a lover before her sister comes; she is very considerably compromised, but that episode is over. The wretched woman, completely *brouillée* with her husband, who has none of the tact to manage her, and whose own tastes and pursuits only drive her deeper into the mire, *toute dorée qu'elle soit*, is hovering, drifting, all ready for another plunge. This situation gradually becomes clear to Laura—trace the incidents by which she takes it in. It goes hard with her to judge her sister, to warn her, to check her, but at last she does. She remonstrates, pleads, does her best to save her—and Lady D. pretends to listen, to resist, to cling to her, as a salvation. But this all *plaisir* and comedy—she is incorrigibly light. If I can only make a little masterpiece of Lady D.—as the portrait of a little heartless, shallow, *pretending* cat, who is yet capable of running off with a handsome guardsman if she takes a fancy to him. There must be 2 children in whom Laura takes an interest and whom she tries to view in a pathetic light. But she can't do this—they are such sturdy, happy healthy British infants, with the promise of no nerves—no capacity for self-bother: to grow up into the same world, in the same way, not *creuser*-ing anything and thinking everything natural. How the American Lady D.—the little New York scrap—has produced these perfect English youngsters—best both boys. Laura's relations with her brother-in-law, whom she likes, pities, despairs of, and also more or less despises —for his complicity, his acceptance, his inability to keep his wife straight, because it's all a part of the same business, the same life, and he hasn't the courage to give up any of it. He likes *her* greatly—tells her he wishes it had been she that he married. So I get my change—the young girl sore and sick over a sister's, instead of a mother's, irregularities. I think the American magazines can be made to swallow the sister, at least. The remainder very much as in what B. told me—save that I don't want the suicide. It's too rare, and I used it the other day in the *Two Countries*. (*To be continued.*)

My young girl in her desire to get away, to make a new life for herself, makes the same strange speech to a young man who comes to the house and as to whom it is open to her to believe that he comes to her—the same singular appeal that the heroine of B.'s anecdote is supposed to have made: a scene which it will take great art and tact to render credible and to keep from being displeasing. This can be done, however, and there is nothing inconceivable in the girl's conduct, once her feelings as to the whole situation are definitely marked. She is essentially a *sensitive*—a nature needing help and support and unable to stand alone. She must be interesting, touching as a tormented, anxious heroine—not as a free, high-stepping one. I must make my young man, an Englishman, a clerk in the foreign office, of the kind I have seen—*compassé*, ambitious, with a great sense of the *parti* and responsibility of his work, etc.; one of those competent, colourless, gentlemanly mediocrities of whom one sees so many in London and who have a career. Laura sees that her sister is going to 'bolt' with her new lover—that a catastrophe is impending—certain that she can't avert it, and that shame and disgrace hang over the house. She feels above all that they hang over *her*. She ceases almost to feel anything for her brother-in-law—he ends by striking her as a poor creature, cynical and abject, deserving of his doom. A desire has taken possession of her to provide for herself *before* the scandal becomes public—for she feels that there will be a horrible divorce case, with odious details —at least 2 corespondents, etc. After everything has come out she will be dishonoured, as the sister, the only sister, of a woman so dreadfully exposed. No one will marry her then—she will have to hide, to bury herself. She has a sort of terror of that fate, and this has been at the bottom of her appeal. She thinks the young man doesn't know—if he will only take her in time. Of course it will all come out *after* he has married her—but then she will be safe; and meantime she will have made her husband love her and esteem her so that he will regret nothing. This is not heroic, but, given the girl, it is natural and touching. She isn't obliged to care too much that her husband will have been taken in if her sister's shame comes out afterwards—for he won't (she knows how little) have been deceived in *her*. He will have acquired a treasure—she will be incomparably good to him—to make up. The scene follows that takes place in the original and she drives the young man from her sight. Meanwhile if I reject the denouement of the suicide I must have another—the following seems to me the best. Laura's remarkable old friend (Mrs. D.S.) takes, as I think I have noted, an interest in marrying her, all the more after having a glimpse of her state of mind in regard to the situation at home. She doesn't know personally the young man of whom I have spoken, at the time the scene between Laura and him takes place, but she knows him afterwards. Perhaps it ought to be that she, knowing how he comes to the house, though she has not seen him, advises the girl to challenge him— tells her that that's all he is waiting for. I think indeed, that that will be much the best—for it will help the denouement. After the scene with the girl has taken place the old lady learns, elicits from Laura, how painfully it has ended and feels that as she has precipitated it, she owes her young friend some reparation—some compensation. She determines to bring the young man back—she guesses that Laura's conduct has made a greater impression upon him than anything relating to her hitherto, and that he may very well be saying to himself—'after all, why not—why not?' She figures to herself that he has begun to be sad and angry at having been *chassé*. She sends to him to come and see her, and she has a very frank and original talk with him, such as she is capable of. She tells him she knows what has happened—praises Laura immensely to him—pleads for her, as it were, with him. Besides, she makes him in a measure responsible—makes him feel that in such a case a man of delicacy *ought* to marry the girl. Of course she can't do this save that of himself he is fermenting, internally: he wants very much to see Laura again. He determines to do so, and succeeds. Meantime her sister's proceedings have reached a climax: she knows that the worst is at hand—has taken place. Her sister has 'bolted' (under the plea of being in Paris): certain information of this has reached her. No one knows it as yet but herself and her brother-in-law—but it will all inevitably come out in a day or two, so that London society will ring with the scandal. She knows that her brother-in-law wants a divorce—to marry another woman; and that he can get it because he hasn't done, flagrantly, provably, what his wife has done. *Type this, particulier,* of the man of his kind who, in his situation, doesn't. Shall she now accept her suitor, who protests that the other day she completely mistook and misconceived him and that his dearest wish, at present, is that she shall be his wife? She feels that now to be impossible—she only wants to get away from it all, and she refuses him and goes off—vanishes—returns, as best she can, to America. That must be my denouement—it will be vulgarly judged—but it is the only possible one.

[James wrote A London Life in Venice, while staying with the Daniel Curtises, and evoked in his preface, as he had a fondness for doing, a luminous glimpse of his surroundings in the Palazzo Barbaro, the same palace that he was to draw upon so magnificently in The Wings of the Dove. A London Life was serialized in Scribner's from June through September 1888, and became the title-story of a volume in the following year. It ran to over forty thousand words, nearly double the length of Daisy Miller and considerably longer, too, than The Siege of London.

In his collected edition he did not group this nouvelle with his 'international' stories, but with The Spoils of Poynton (1897) and The Chaperon (1891). He noted that these three belonged to the same 'kind' by virtue of their heroines, Laura Wing, Fleda Vetch, and Rose Tramore, each one a register of 'acuteness and intensity, reflexion and passion.' He also remarked that there had been little necessarily 'international' in the situation of A London Life. Although he had made not only his heroine but also his young man, Mr. Wendover, an American, James came to see that he need not have been at such costs 'to bring him all the way from New York,' when he might easily have found his type in London. James also pointed out that he had struck a false note in trying to represent Laura's sister as an American, since the sort of sophisticated depravity she exhibited was essentially native to her London world, to the Prince of Wales' 'set' which he had thought of in his outline.

He made several minor departures from that outline. Lady Davenant became the name of the elderly confidante, and Laura's sister was married to Lionel Berrington. Laura's overstrained declaration to Wendover is worded much less bluntly, and it was not suggested beforehand by Lady Davenant. The scene with which James was least satisfied when he wrote his preface was that in which Lady Davenant calls Wendover back for an explanatory interview, since there James had broken the rules that he had set himself for such a story: to heighten its intensity by making every detail be reflected through the conscious-ness of his sensitive heroine.

The most important change is at the end. Laura rushes away in desperation to America, but Wendover follows her with the hope of ultimate success, an ending very remote from the implications of Paul Bourget's original anecdote.]

London, Thursday, November 17th, 1887.

Last winter, in Florence, I was struck with the queer incident of Miss McC.'s writing to the New York *World* that inconceivable letter about the Venetian society whose hospitality she had just been enjoy-ing—and the strange *typicality* of the whole thing. She acted in per-fect good faith and was amazed, and felt injured and persecuted, when an outcry and an indignation were the result. That she *should* have acted in good faith seemed to me to throw much light upon that mania for publicity which is one of the most striking signs of our times. She was perfectly irreflective and irresponsible, and it seemed to her pleasant and natural and 'chatty' to describe, in a horribly vulgar newspaper, the people she had been living with and their personal domestic ar-rangements and secrets. It was a striking incident and it seemed to me exactly the theme for a short story. One sketches one's age but imper-fectly if one doesn't touch on that particular matter: the invasion, the impudence and shamelessness, of the newspaper and the interviewer, the devouring *publicity* of life, the extinction of all sense between pub-lic and private. It is the highest expression of the note of 'familiarity,' the sinking of *manners*, in so many ways, which the democratization of the world brings with it. I was prompted to make use of the incident in question which struck me <as> a very illustrative piece of contem-porary life—the opposition of the scribbling, publishing, indiscreet, newspaperized American girl and the rigid, old-fashioned, conservative, still shockable and much shocked little society she recklessly plays the tricks upon. The drama is in the consequences for *her*, and it is of course interesting in proportion as the consequences are great. They are greatest if the thing brings about a crisis and a cataclysm in her 'pros-pects.' These prospects bear pre-eminently, of course, on the question of her marriage. Imagine the girl engaged to a young Italian or French-man of seductive 'position,' and pretty and *dotée* in order to have be-come so—and then imagine her writing to a blatant American news-paper 'all about' the family and domestic circle of her fiancé, and you have your story. I shouldn't have thought of the incident if in its main outline it hadn't occurred: one can't say a pretty and 'nice' American girl wouldn't do such a thing, simply because there was Miss McC.

[82]

who did it. One can't say she *isn't* 'nice'—when she belongs to *tout ce qu'il y a de mieux là-bas*—the daughter of an illustrious citizen. She was not indeed engaged to a Venetian, and her case thereby lends itself the less; but she might easily have been—she would have liked to be—and that addition is necessary. I have made up my mind, however, that it wouldn't do to take her case in its actuality—partly because I might seem to be 'copying' and partly because it can be much improved. So I leave it simply as a starting-point—an idea, and imagine different facts. These are quite my own. An American girl, abroad with her father and sister, becomes engaged to a young European who has been brought up and lived wholly *dans les vieilles idées*. (I give the subject in as few words as possible.) A young American admirer of hers, who has tried without success to woo and win her, is a journalist, of the most enterprising, and consequently the most vulgar, character. He has been with her, crossed the Atlantic with her, etc., before her engagement, and comes upon her again, in Paris, after this takes place. He thinks that if he can't get what he originally wanted out of her he may at least get something else; perceiving therefore all her new affiliations he endeavours to interview her—to make her tell him all about the family and the affairs of her intended—so that he may make of it a bright 'society' letter. *His* type and character therefore become almost the more salient one<s>. He of course hasn't a grain of delicacy in his composition (I must do him very well); he has no tradition of reserve or discretion—he simply obeys his gross newspaper instinct and thinks it a piece of uncommon good luck that he has had such a chance: that he is 'in' with a girl who can tell him so much. She likes him—her refusal to marry him has brought with it no rupture of relations—and thinks him wonderfully 'bright,' wonderfully amusing. She is simple, sweet, uncultivated, gentle, innocent, yet with the stamp <of> her antecedents (I must make them of the right—i.e., of the explanatory sort) upon her mind, her ideas. He means no harm in pumping her, and she means none in telling everything she knows about her prospective circle, who have made much of her, treated her charmingly, etc. (they have accepted the marriage), and with whom she has been staying, living. The result is a most fearful letter from the young man to his big catchpenny newspaper—preferably a Western sheet—'giving away' the girl herself and everyone she has mentioned —a letter as monstrous as Julian H.'s beastly and blackguardly betrayal last winter of J.R.L.[1] I must arrange that the young fiancé have gone

1. In October 1886, Julian Hawthorne printed in a New York newspaper his version of a conversation with Lowell about English affairs. Lowell wrote to a friend: 'He *knew* that I didn't know he was interviewing me. To any sane man the shimble-shamble stuff he has made me utter is the proof of it. I say "made me

[83]

over to America at the moment to look after affairs, property, etc.—which will acount the better for the journalist's having access to the girl. The young man, while he is in the 'States,' comes upon the horrible newspaper—opens it—finds himself, his family, his friends, his sisters, and their husbands, the most personal facts, mysteries, etc., including a family secret, proceeding from a past generation, which no one talks of—blazoned forth in the vulgarest terms. He is appalled, and rushes back to Europe for an explanation. Meanwhile his people have already seen the letter and share all his horror and wonder. The girl is confronted with the consequences of her act—and is amazed at the light in which they are presented to her. She has meant no harm, and scarcely understands the fuss. The attitude of her new family make<s> her indiscretion a little more clear to her—but *she* is resentful, too, of their scandalized tone, the row they make; her pride rises (all the more that the monstrosity of what she has done *does* begin to dawn upon her), and she draws back, after a scene with the fiancé, and throws up the engagement. The rumpus, the scandal, the crisis, in short are immense. Nothing of that sort has ever been known *dans ce monde là*: the newspaper is a thing of loathing to them. The end is a little difficult to determine. I think the truest and best and most illustrative would be this: that the young interviewer who has *his* virtuous indignation too, learning the scandal he has brought about, the rupture of the marriage, etc., threatens the bloated foreigners with a new horror—that is, to publish the scandal itself, with tremendous headings—the way they have treated the girl, etc. Appalled by this possibility they 'come round'—forgive, conciliate, swallow their grievance, etc., so that the marriage takes place. The newspaper dictates and triumphs—which is a reflection of actual fact. Such is the rough contour of my idea. The application has presented a real difficulty, which, however, I think I have solved: that difficulty was where to find people today in Europe who would really be so shocked as that comes to—shocked enough for my dramatic opposition. I don't in the least see them in England, where publicity is far too much, by this time, in the manners of society for my representation to have any verisimilitude here. The World and Truth, etc.,[1] stare one in the face—people write to the newspapers about everything—it is in short also a newspaperized

utter" deliberately, because, though he has remembered some of the subjects (none of my choosing) which we talked about, he has wholly misrepresented the tone and sometimes falsified the substance of what I said. . . . The worst of' his 'infidelity (I mean to keep my temper) is that it is like a dead rat in the wall—an awful stink and no cure.'

1. Alice James' journal has several references to *Truth*, one of which is to a slur on Henry James as a critic. Mrs. J. Comyns Carr in her *Reminiscences* calls the *World*, another English publication, 'that malicious society journal.'

world, and, allowing for a rather better form, there is about as little delicacy as *là bas*. The poor Venetians, living outside of modern enterprise, were shocked by Miss McC.; but they are too near, and I can't use them. Besides, their feelings are not interesting enough—the race is poor and represents today too little. A Roman or a Florentine lot wouldn't do either, for very much the same reasons (in a minor degree). So I came down to the French—imagined an old *claquemuré* Legitimist circle, as detached as possible from *tout ce que se fait, s'écrit et se pense aujourd'hui*. There would be great difficulties, however, there, not the least of which the difficulty of really making the picture. Besides I have taken a vow never again to do the French in any such collective way (as in the *American*); *à peu près* effects of that sort are too cheap, too valueless. So I found my solution where, with the help of Heaven, I hope to find many others in work to come; viz., in the idea of the Europeanized American. And it is that that represents not simply an easier way, but a greater reality. The thing is under my nose; imagine the ingredients of E. Lee Childe and D. S. Curtis rolled into one—and add a few of my own—and *je tiens mon affaire*. They would really be the people most detached and most scandalized; and in the light of their idea the whole little story straightens out. It fits together —it hangs together. I knew I should find something—and now I SEE it. *Cela se passe en France*—it begins in Paris and goes on mainly in Paris. Old Mr. Probert (call him) is of the oldest American *monde* there: his father will have come out in 1830. He is completely merged —thanks to wealth, sympathies—*dans le monde du Faubourg*. His 2 sisters have married old French names, his daughter and his other son *en ont fait autant*. His elder son is the fiancé of my young lady— he has *never* been willing to do like the others; he has always had the dream of marrying an American—like his mother. His family smile on it—if he will only pick out a nice one. It was not to be expected that he should come across my heroine—but he does, by accident, and falls in love with her. There are also very good elements of money. His people are glad of these latter and accept the girl, making rather a big mouth—especially to swallow her father and sister. These 2 figures I see, and shall see still better.

[James' memory was inexact when he said, in the preface to The Reverberator, that its incident had lain stored up with him for 'several years' until 'its illustrative worth' came fully into view. In point of fact he must have begun writing this short novel (of about fifty-five thousand words) soon after making this entry, since it ran in Macmillan's Magazine from February through July 1888.

His emphasis and tone changed. He did not center the story upon the shameless publicity of the modern world. Although he drew a sharp sketch of George Flack, the reporter for The Reverberator, and referred in the preface to the vogue of 'the recording slobbering sheet,' he noted also that Francie Dosson was the point around which he had constructed the novel. He spoke further of her kinship with Daisy Miller, Pandora Day, and Bessie Alden (of An International Episode).

He had struck, as he hoped he would, a new and rich vein in 'the Europeanized American,' in the Probert family, Catholics from Carolina who had settled in Paris at the time of Louis Philippe and had gradually become part of its aristocracy. He added too another version of innocents abroad through his portrayal of Francie's family. Mr. Dosson, the patient and ruminant American father, who liked 'to see the great markets, the sewers, and the Bank of France,' and who 'looked for the most part as if he were thinking over, without exactly understanding it, something rather droll that had just occurred,' is a creation of James' warmest humor. He is the kind of American in Paris who has had many successors: 'He liked to invite people and to pay for them, and disliked to be invited and paid for. He was never inwardly content on any occasion unless a great deal of money was spent, and he could be sure enough of the large amount only when he himself spent it.'

Because the theme had so many facets of lively interest, the sinister ending of the outline was abandoned. Mr. Flack and his newspaper are dropped after his first unhappy article, and no attempt is made to threaten the Proberts into allowing the marriage. Young Gaston defies their wishes by sticking to his friends of the Hôtel de l'Univers et de Cheltenham, and by persisting in his union with Francie, for love and not at all for her money. The novel is, therefore, a less serious piece of social criticism than James at first envisaged. He signalized it in the preface as a jeu d'esprit, and as such it especially delighted William James, who pronounced it 'masterly and exquisite,' and added: 'It shows the technical ease you have attained, that you can handle so delicate and difficult a fancy so lightly.']

January 5th, 1888.

The Patagonia. The name of the ship (a slow voyage, though in summer, from Boston—an old Boston Cunarder—to Liverpool); on which I shall place the little tragic story suggested to me by Mrs. Kemble's anecdote of Barry St. Leger and the lady (married and with a husband awaiting her in England) with whom he sailed from India. She was young and pretty and had been placed under the captain's care. At a certain stage of the voyage the captain was notified that the passengers were scandalized by the way she was flirting and carrying on with B.St.L. This came to her knowledge—and one night she jumped overboard. Admirable little dismal subject.

[*This idea is returned to and more fully developed just below.*]

Another came to me last night as I was talking with Theodore Child about the effect of marriage on the artist, the man of letters, etc. He mentioned the cases he had seen in Paris in which this effect had been fatal to the quality of the work, etc.—through overproduction, need to meet expenses, make a figure, etc. And I mentioned certain cases here. Child spoke of Daudet—his 30 *Ans de Paris*, as an example in point. 'He would never have written that if he hadn't married.' So it occurred to me that a very interesting situation would be that of an elder artist or writer, who has been ruined (in his own sight) by his marriage and its forcing him to produce promiscuously and cheaply— his position in regard to a younger *confrère* whom he sees on the brink of the same disaster and whom he endeavours to save, to rescue, by some act of bold interference—breaking off the marriage, annihilating the wife, making trouble between the parties.

[*In* The Lesson of the Master, *printed in the* Universal Review *in July and August 1888, James worked out the idea suggested by Child's remarks. Henry St. George, the older artist, whose work has suffered by his marriage, is strongly attracted by an admirer, Miss Fancourt. She recognizes the deterioration in his writing, and confides her fears to Paul Overt, a younger author, who is also charmed by her. St. George's 'bold interference' takes the form of a warning against marriage as damaging to the artist. Overt is impressed enough to devote himself single-mindedly to his work for many months—only to find at last that St. George, whose first wife has died, has married Miss Fancourt. This adds an ironic twist to the story and makes a neatly finished plot, but possibly blurs the main point by raising an ambiguity, and distracting the reader into conjectures about how far St. George's advice to Overt was sincere and how far it was dictated by his selfish wish to drive away a rival in love.*]

Sunday, March 11th, 1888. Here I sit: impatient to work: only wanting to concentrate myself, to keep at it: full of ideas, full of ambition, full of capacity—as I believe. Sometimes the discouragements, however, seem greater than anything else—the delays, the interruptions, the *éparpillement*, etc. But courage, courage, and forward, forward. If one must generalize, that is the only generalization. There is an immensity

to be done, and, without vain presumption—I shall at the worst do a part of it. But all one's manhood must be at one's side. x x x x x
Let me note a little more in detail one of the subjects just foregoing —the thing I have called *The Patagonia.* In the incident as mentioned to me by Mrs. Kemble the heroine was a married woman in charge of the captain of the ship—who presumably knew her husband and could tell him of her misbehaviour. I shall change that and make her simply 'engaged': not only because of the prejudices of the Anglo-Saxon reader, but because I really think that more touching—think it more touching, that is, that she should jump overboard to escape having to marry (as well as to be denounced to) the man she is going out to Europe to join. And yet, and yet x x x x x
At any rate let us suppose that she is a young woman no longer in her very 1st youth, who has been the victim of a 'long engagement.' Her intended is in Europe and they have never yet had means to marry. He is studying architecture, and his studies never come to an end. She doesn't care for him at the last as she did at first—she is weary, disillusioned, tepid, but she is poor and she feels she *must* marry. Her lover sends for <her> at last, tells her the union must take place, but he can't come home—can't interrupt his studies. She must come out to him; he will meet her at Liverpool.—They haven't met for four years. She goes, in a perfunctory way, but her heart is not in it. I must tell the story as an eye-witness; I am on the ship and partly an actor in the drama. I must have seen her once—just before starting, on shore. It is a slow Boston Cunarder—a summer passage. The ship is changed *la veille,* to an old substitute, as occurred when I went over, in 1874, in the *Atlas.* The girl must have been committed to the charge of a lady—an old lady, an old friend of mine, whom I call on, in Boston, just before sailing. I go to see her to ask if I can be of any use to her— to tell her we are to be fellow-passengers. It is a summer evening, in the empty town—in Mt. Vernon St. She has come up from the country (Beverly, etc.) to sail—to go to her daughter, in Germany—or some other natural pretext. She is alone at 1st—she tells me that there is a question of her son going with her, so that she won't have to count on me. If he doesn't go, however, she will look to me with pleasure. But he can't decide—he is wavering—he has just gone round to the club—it seems as if he couldn't make up his mind—wouldn't really know till the morrow. Suggestion of his rather dissipated type. He comes in presently and is still uncertain: he is waiting for a telegram— he doesn't know—he will go round to the club again and see if the telegram has come. No trouble about a cabin—1st of August—old ship— sure to be several free even at the last moment. He is very good-looking, etc. We sit in the dusky room—with fans and ices—the house is dis-

[88]

mantled—the windows look on the Back Bay with its lights. Oh, spirit of Maupassant, come to my aid! This may be a triumph of robust and vivid concision: and certainly ought to be. The girl comes in with her mother. Her mother isn't going; she has to send the daughter off alone. She doesn't know my old lady—save through some common friend—and it is a little 'pushing' (the good mother must be slightly vulgar, and also forlorn, poor and nervous) on her part to come and call and make her appeal. She wants my friend to look after the girl— so that she shan't feel she is quite alone. That is her excuse, her maternal tremors. The girl about 28—very handsome and rather proud and stiff. She lets her mother act—*la laisse faire*, with a little silent embarrassment. Attitude of my old lady—very good-natured condescension, mingled with a little sense of intrusion, etc. She consents to have an eye on the young lady—is very poor at sea—but will do her best. The visitors stay a little and have ices. Before they go the son comes back, is introduced to the visitors, talks with the daughter, wanders into the other room with her, etc.—to go on the balcony—there being none to the windows that look on the water. This lasts about half an hour, or less. Then the ladies go, with vows of meeting on the ship, etc. After they have gone the son announces to his mother that he *has* decided to sail. I take my departure and he comes down to the door with me. I have 3 words with him—Miss X. is mentioned. I wonder, as I walk home, if that glimpse of her is what has determined him. I must tell him she is going out to her fiancé—he has not known that —it having been mentioned, in her mother's chatter, only in his absence. His answer to that. This might make i. Then the middle, ii; and the denouement, iii. I fear that with all the compression in the world I can't do it in so very short a compass as Comyns Carr has demanded. Well, that is my start—and the rest ought to go. I can trust myself. It suddenly occurs to me, however, that to make the girl's dread of exposure a sufficient (partial) motive, I must be represented as knowing her intended—as having known him of old. My impression of him —in ten words. She must know that I know him and be afraid I shall tell him. Something must pass between us, in regard to this, just before she disappears. This knowledge of mine—this apprehension of hers, must play the part played by the scandalized public opinion of the ship (on the long Indian voyage) in Mrs. K.'s anecdote. That lady was known to be married—to be going back to her husband. If my heroine is only engaged I can't make out the visible scandal as so great. But the young man's mother must also be represented as shocked —she talks with me, very distressfully about the matter. She is greatly displeased with her son, etc. It is rather awkward he is her son— that makes her reprobation of the girl less direct and therefore less operative. But I must do my best with this—I must of course have some words with the young man—a little as the friend and representative of the injured fiancé. He must tell the girl that I have spoken, indignantly, for *him*—and that will increase her presumption that I *may* betray her when we land. Of course I must be a good deal older than my old lady's son—that is needed to justify my criticism and interference, if interference it may be called. What I mainly do is to remind him that—at the rate he is going on—the girl is engaged, and that if he makes trouble between her and her lover he must at least be prepared to marry her. This he is evidently not in the least disposed to. He behaves badly—the fault is primarily his—and the horror of the denouement such as to overcloud him forever more.

[The Patagonia was published in August and September 1888, in the English Illustrated Magazine. It had four parts instead of three, and James' effort for 'robust and vivid concision' failed to hold it down below twenty-three thousand words. It follows the sketch closely, and the only important addition is the character of Mrs. Peck. She is a Boston neighbor of the heroine, and on the voyage her gossip builds up the flirtation into a scandal.]

Continuation of sketch of xiii of *Tragic Muse*.

<. . .> between them, is peculiar—interesting—dramatic. Julia is delighted with him—this is the way she likes him—she is in love with him—she is ready for anything. She will marry him on the spot if he asks her. He is very conscious of this and he thinks he ought to ask her. She has done everything for him—for his election—she has been charming, effective, wonderful. She hasn't given money, of course —only Mr. C. has given that. But she *will* give money—she will give him her fortune. She tries to seduce him—she is full of bribery. I *must* make 2 scenes of it—one is not enough. Yet perhaps it is—with the 4th section of the instalment (the one scene should be the third) for his visit to Mr. C., to thank him. Mrs. Dallow virtually says to Nick: 'You have great talent—you *may* have a great future. But you have no money, and you can do nothing without that. I have a great fortune and it shall be yours. We will strike an alliance—I will marry you if I can count upon you. I want to be the wife of a great statesman—I am full of ambition—and my ambition is *that*. I will work with you and for you. Moreover I love you—I adore you. Only you must promise me—you are slippery and I must have some pledges. What did you mean that night in Paris? I love you—but I mistrust you. Therefore reassure me. The best way will be to love me—to possess me. See how

[90]

charming, how enchanting, soothing, sympathetic I can be—whom they call hard.' She appears soft, seductive—but in it all there lurks her *condition*—her terms. He is much *échauffé*—but he feels this—feels the *condition*. Yes, yes—*one* scene—the rest at St. Albans.

[*This continuation of an entry started, apparently, in a notebook that has not been preserved, was added here in red ink.*

It refers to the fifth installment (May 1889) of The Tragic Muse, *as printed in the Atlantic Monthly. This installment ends with the first part of Chapter* XIII, *which shows Julia Dallow's happiness about Nick Dormer's election, and in which not she but his mother urges upon him the advantages of his marrying her. The scene is ended in the sixth installment, for June. In* XIV *Nick becomes conscious of Julia's power over him, and in* XV *he proposes and is accepted. The June installment ends with* XVI, *the first of two chapters on the visit to Mr. Carteret. As often happened, James' idea, as he developed it, demanded more space than he had planned to allow.*

In the novel Julia nowhere openly makes any suggestion that could be called 'bribery.' It is Lady Agnes, his mother, who 'tries to seduce him' into marrying Julia. The change is an obvious improvement, since it makes it possible for Julia to keep the restraint which characterizes her throughout, and gives to Lady Agnes a part quite in keeping with her eagerness to feather her own family's nest.

At the bottom of the last page, James wrote, in red ink, a further note on Verena. (See also p. 67 above.)]

Verena. My divisions of instalments: pp. of MS.
2d no. (VI) begins page 86.
End of IX chapter (and second Part ?).
p. (MS.) 155. In type p. 97.

NOTEBOOK III

2 February 1889—3 November 1894

34 De Vere Gardens, February 2d, 1889.

I have been woefully interrupted in the composition of my long novel for the *Atlantic*; and must absolutely get on with it without further delay. I have had to write four articles (it was really stupid, and it was needless, to consent) since I last worked at it, in the autumn, with any continuity or glow. I had at 1st a great deal of that glow; and I must make it come back to me. I can do so soon and effectually with a little *attention suivie*. The first thing is to keep cool and not to worry and get nervous; above all to *think*—as little as I really manage that in general!—and *live back* into the conditions one has tried to imagine. It all comes, thank God, so soon as I give it a barely decent chance. It is there—it lives—it waits; the picture blooms again so soon as I really fix my eyes on it. It is this time really a good subject, I think: save that it's too pale a one. I have undertaken to tell and to describe too much—given my *data*, such as they are—one of the reasons being that I was afraid of my story being too thin. For fear of making it too small I have made it too big. This, however, is a good fault, and I see my way out of it. Variety and concision must be my formula for the rest of the story—rapidity and action. I have of course, as usual, spread myself too much in the 1st chapter—been too complacently descriptive and illustrative. But I can retrieve that if I only *will*—if I will only bring myself to be brief and quick in the handling of the different episodes. Unless I achieve this I can't possibly get them all in. Let me write it as if, at any stage, it were to be a short story. That is the only way to get on and to put it all there. I have very interesting things to relate, but I must only *touch* them individually. À *la Maupassant* must be my constant motto. I must depend on the collective effect. For instance I must make a little masterpiece in 30 pp. of MS. of Nick's visit to Mr. Carteret. How much I must put into this! The same of the next chapter, Sherringham's visit to the Comédie Française with Miriam—my impression of Bartet, in her *loge*, the other day in Paris. x x x x x

[*Although* The Tragic Muse *had begun to appear in the* Atlantic Monthly *in January 1889, James was still having trouble with the length of his story. The visit to Mr. Carteret takes two chapters, and two other chapters intervene before the visit to the theater. The excellence of the description of that visit testifies to the vividness of James' impression of the French actress, Bartet, and to the skill with which he could turn a personal impression into a central scene in a novel. Mlle Voisin is, no doubt, drawn from Bartet; what is more important is that she is used to light up the character of Miriam Rooth, whose absorbed delight in the actress's every word and movement dramatizes her own passionate determination to succeed upon the stage.*]

February 27th, 1889. I have promised Archibald Grove to write him a short tale in three parts for his new projected magazine; and I must get at work at it. The conditions are unsatisfactory—I am doing other work, which I have to interrupt, and I don't like the *form* of this task —the break into three parts each of which is very short—4500 words. Any subject will suffer from it: but I will do what I can: make as good a thing of it as possible and let the form of publication (till it's in a book) concern me as little as possible. x x x x x

[*Grove was editor of the* New Review. *James'* The Solution (*see p. 95 below*), *running to eighteen thousand words, was published in it in December, January, and February 1889-90.*]

There comes back to me with a certain vividness of solicitation, an idea that I noted a long time ago, suggested by something that Jennie Thackeray once said or repeated to me. That is, her story of Trollope's having had the plan of bringing up his son to write novels, as a lucrative trade. She added (as Mrs. R. Ritchie) that she and her husband had the same idea with regard to her little girl. They would train her up to it as to a regular profession. This suggested to me the figure of a weary battered labourer in the field of fiction attempting to carry out this project with a child and meeting, by the irony of fate, the strangest discomfiture. All sorts of possibilities vaguely occur to one as latent in it. The child is given a chance to 'see life,' etc., that it may have material, and sees life to such a tune that he (or she) is swamped and destroyed. That is one element. Then the mother (this especially if it be a 'lady-novelist') tries to enable the son to go out into the world for *her own* purposes—to see society, hear things, etc. The poor mother describes fashionable life and the upper classes—and wants data and material. She is frowsy and dingy herself—she can't go—and she is too busy. The stupidity of the children, who bring home nothing—have no observation, etc. But there must be an *action*, of some little sort—and this occurs to me. There is a daughter and she has appeared pretty and clever—she is the one (there is a son beside), whom there has been this attempt to *form*, to train. In the early years there must be the dim vision of a handsome, idle father, living upon his wife. The expense of the girl's education, etc.—and also the boy's, who is good-looking and unaddicted to any literary pursuit. The particular drama to be that the girl proves quite useless as a novelist, but grows up, marries a snob on the edge of good society, is worldly and hard and would be smart, and is ashamed of her mother. Thinks her novels are vulgar rubbish—keeps her at a distance—almost ignores her—makes her very unhappy. The poor lady is obliged to go on writing, meanwhile, to meet the demands of her son—whom she has thrown into the world to pick up information for her, and who has simply become idle, selfish, extravagant and vicious. She has all sorts of <lurking?> romanticisms and *naïvetés*—make a very vivid amusing pathetic picture of her mixture of queer qualities, etc.—her immorality, her natural penchant to license *à la Ouida*, of which her priggish daughter is ashamed. Her love of splendour, of the aristocracy, of high society—the wealth and beauty which she attributes to her people, etc. —contrasted with the small shabby facts of her own life. She dies at the end, worn out, disappointed, poor. The thing had much best be told by a witness of her life—a friend—a critic, a journalist, etc.: in the 1st person: rapid notes. I speak of the telegram from the editor of one of the big papers when she dies, asking for ½ a column about her. I saw and wrote the ½ column and made it kinder. Then for myself I wrote these other notes—kinder still.—The thing to be called by the *nom de plume* of the poor lady—some rather smart *man's* name.

This little sketch of which I think very well on the whole (Feb. 28th) would gain in effect by the supposititious narrator being himself a novelist but of the younger generation and of the modern psychological type. There would be touches there which might throw the poor woman's funny old art into contrast with his point of view—touches of bewilderment at his work on *her* side and of indulgence and humour on his.

[James picked up here a theme he had noted a decade before (p. 10 above), and produced Greville Fane, *whose seven thousand words constitute one of his shorter stories, what he called 'a minor miracle of foreshortening.' It appeared in the* Illustrated London News, *17 and 24 September 1892.*

He made an appealing presentation of the deluded lady novelist's devotion to her worthless children. Her frigid snobbish daughter grew to despise her as soon as she herself had become Lady Luard; and her son sponged on her shamelessly while pretending to be devoted to such exacting standards that he never produced a word. Through the device of having the story told by a serious younger writer who enjoyed the company of Greville Fane—her real name was Mrs. Stormer—because 'she rested him so from literature,' James also included some gentle satire of the best-selling novelist who 'could invent stories by the yard, but couldn't write a page of English. She went down to her grave without suspecting that though she had contributed volumes to the diversion of her contemporaries she hadn't contributed a sentence to the language.']

February 28th. Mightn't I do something fairly good with that idea I made a note of long ago—the idea of the young man on whom some companions impose the idea that he has so committed himself with regard to a girl that he must propose to her—he is bound in honour— and who does propose, credulously, *naïvement*, to do the right thing, and is eagerly accepted, having money and being something of a *parti*. This was suggested to me by an anecdote told me by Mrs. Kemble of something that had taken place years ago—in the diplomatic body in Rome—I think—under her observation. The young man married the girl—not caring for her at all—under this delusion which 2 or 3 of his colleagues (he was a young secretary, I believe) had amused themselves with fastening upon him—he being a naïf, tempting subject. I think the girl was English, one of two or three sisters with a loud, hard, worldly, pushing mother. 'Only not Olympia'—I made a note of that when the little tale was told me: the young fellow's cry when the others told him that there was one of the sisters who had a right to expect of him that he should make up to her. He thought Olympia too like her mother—but it was of course she whom the others pushed him into the arms of. His after life with Olympia, etc. Isn't this situation very considerably dramatic? There is something in it which might be made interesting—surely. The story should be told by one of the actors, one of the *jeunes étourdis* (an Englishman) who carried out the joke. He relates it late in life—as a very old retired diplomatist, full of memories. The old delicious, quiet, sunny, idle Rome of forty or fifty years ago! He has had great remorse since—he had it at the time—he tried to back out when he found how far the game had gone. I noted all this before—but it didn't seem quite enough. There should be a complete drama in it, a sequel and a conclusion. I began to write the story—but I gave it up—I have the commenced fragment somewhere. Perhaps it would serve my turn for the article for A. Grove, better than the idea recorded in this place yesterday. It would have movement but be short and divisible into three parts. The young fellow practiced upon is the American Secretary of Legation. His simplicity, good faith, etc., made natural—he is easily persuaded that he must act in accordance with European customs, and by that canon he has distinctly committed himself and even compromised the girl. The narrator's scare when he finds the consequences are serious. There must be three men in it —himself and two others. But what is the drama—the denouement— *voyons?* It all depends on that. I try to prevent it—I go to the mother —it is too late. She tells me that she will break off the arrangement— the engagement that has been entered into if *I* will 'take over' her daughter instead. But I *can't* bring my mind to that. I struggle—I hesitate—but I can't. x x x x x

I think *je tiens mon dénouement*—and the rest of the action. There must be another woman in the case; a woman whom I am rather in love with—a woman clever, accomplished, independent, etc. She can only be a widow—and that is rather conventional.

[*From this James worked out* The Solution, *and used it to carry out his promise to the editor of the* New Review (*p. 93 above*).

The story follows the notebook sketch closely, and the denouement is made by the introduction of another woman, with whom the narrator, who is also one of the perpetrators of the bad 'joke,' is in love. She hears of the trick played on the young American diplomat, admires his scrupulousness on what seems to him a point of honor, and saves him from his projected marriage by persuading him to turn over his fortune to his fiancée. She then marries him herself. By dropping his original idea of dealing with the later life of a man tricked into marriage, James abandoned a possibility for 'serious' treatment of the situation, and produced what is little more than a too lengthy anecdote of the 'biter bit' variety, unworthy, he decided later, to be included in his collected edition.

The name of the 'Olympia' of the sketch is Veronica Goldie—and Goldie is a name used also in The Aspern Papers *in a disparaging connection (*p. 73 above*).*

James' play, Disengaged, *published in* Theatricals, Two Comedies (1894), *is based on* The Solution.]

March 18th. Note here next (no time today) the 2 things old Lady Stanley told me the other day that the former Lady Holland had said to her—and the admirable subject suggested to me yesterday, Sunday, at Mrs. Jeune's by Mrs. Lynn Linton's (and Mrs. J.'s) talk about F.H.:

the man marrying for money to serve him for a great political career
and public ends.

March 25th, 1889 (Monday).

Last evening before dinner I took a walk with G. du Maurier, in the
mild March twilight (there was a blessed sense of spring in the air),
through the empty streets near Porchester Terrace, and he told me
over an idea of his which he thought very good—and I do too—for a
short story—he had already mentioned <it> to me—a year or two
ago, in a walk at Hampstead, but it had passed from my mind. Last
night it struck me as curious, picturesque and distinctly usable: though
the want of musical knowledge would hinder *me* somewhat in handling
it. I can't set it forth in detail here, now; I haven't the time—but I
must do it later. It is the history of the servant girl with a wonderful
rich full voice but no musical genius who is mesmerized and made
to sing by a little foreign Jew who has mesmeric power, infinite feeling,
and no organ (save as an accompanist—on some instrument, violin)
of his own. He carries her away, about the world—singing, for shillings,
in the streets of foreign towns, etc.—she performs wonderfully while
he is there, acting upon her. The man who relates the story—a poorish
artist—has known her in London as the stupid, handsome daughter of
his landlady, or as that of one of his friends. He meets the pair, abroad,
follows them, wonders (having recognized her—and having seen *him*
once of old—at an artist's supper in Newman St. [given by his friend]
where the girl has waited and been noticed—just enough noticed, by
the little Jew, for the story). She doesn't know him—she is changed,
strange, besides her wonderful singing—which she didn't have before—
and he is quite mystified. He has heard, already, after the girl's original
unexplained disappearance—two or three years after—of a wonderful
voice—that of a mere *chanteuse de café*, etc.—of which a dilettante
friend of his has spoken to him with rapture and which (the owner
of which) he tries to follow up and put his hand upon in order to
capture her for a party of Lady X.'s, a woman he wishes to please.
Say she is to have royalty, etc.—and he is keen in pursuit. But he
misses—the pair is vanished. It is *after* this that the narrator meets
them abroad—and recognizes them, both as the subjects of his friend's
anecdote and as the London *fille bête* and the wonderfully *doué* disreputable little foreigner. *Il s'y perd*—because the girl is really all the
while only galvanized by her mate. He makes them come to his rooms
somewhere—at Nuremburg or at Siena—and they perform wonderfully
for him (all this requires tact—in regard to the music) till the man

[97]

drinks too much and is disabled by it. Then *she* can do nothing, becomes helpless—drinks, *chancelle,* behaves as if she were vaguely tipsy
herself. She relapses, in short, into impotence. They disappear again—I
meet them once more—and now the man is dead or dying. He dies—
the girl becomes *Gros-Jean comme devant*—unable to raise a note.
She had only been a subject, and the whole thing was mesmerically
communicated to her. She had had the glorious voice, but no talent—
he had had the sacred fire, the rare musical organization, and had
played into her and through her. The *end,* as regards her, miserably
pathetic.

[*In an article on Du Maurier, in* Harper's Monthly *for September 1897,
James wrote: 'No companion of his walks and talks can have failed to
be struck with the number of stories that he had, as it were, put by;
none either can have failed to urge him to take them down from the
shelf. . . They dazzled me with the note of invention. He had worked
them out in such detail that they were ready in many a case to be served
as they stood.' Some remarks by Du Maurier about a conversation
with James were included by Joseph B. and Jeannette L. Gilder in
their* Trilbyana (*New York, 1895). Du Maurier said: 'It was one day
while we were walking together on Hampstead Heath. We were talking
about storywriting, and I said to him:—"If I were a writer, it seems to
me that I should have no difficulty about plots. I have in my head now
plots for fifty stories. I'm always working them out for my own amusement." "Well," he said, "it seems to me that you are a very fortunate
person; I wish you'd tell me one of those plots." Then I told him the
story of "Trilby." Yes, he praised it very generously. "Well," I said,
"you may have the idea and work it out to your own satisfaction." But
he refused to accept it. "You must write it yourself," he said: "I'm
sure you can do it, if you'll only try." ' With this stimulus Du Maurier
first tried his hand at a novel, beginning not with* Trilby *but with*
Peter Ibbetson. Trilby *did not appear, as a serial in* Harper's Monthly,
*until January 1894—about seven years after the conversation on Hamp-
stead Heath.*

*Du Maurier's development of the narrative differs in many ways from
that which James suggests, but it is impossible to say whether James'
version represents what Du Maurier planned in 1889, or whether it is
his own working out of the idea. We do know, however, from the notes
in* Trilbyana, *that Du Maurier, when he wrote the novel, had radically
altered his original scheme. He told his interviewer that his earliest
conception of the story was quite different from the one he finally
arrived at.*]

I interrupt some other work this moist still Sunday morning to make a few notes on the subject of the play I have engaged to write for Edward Compton. I needn't go over the little history of this engagement and the reasons—they are familiar enough—which led me to respond to the proposal coming to me from him while I was in Paris last December. I had practically given up my old, valued, long cherished dream of doing something for the stage, for fame's sake, and art's, and fortune's: overcome by the vulgarity, the brutality, the baseness of the condition of the English-speaking theatre today. But after an interval, a long one, the vision has revived, on a new and a very much humbler basis, and especially under the lash of necessity. Of art or fame *il est maintenant fort peu question*: I simply *must* try, and try seriously, to produce half a dozen—a dozen, five dozen—plays for the sake of my pocket, my material future. Of how little money the novel makes for me I needn't discourse here. The theatre has sought me out—in the person of the good, the yet unseen, Compton. I have listened and considered and reflected, and the matter is transposed to a minor key. To accept the circumstances, in their extreme humility, and do the best I can *in* them: this is the moral of my present situation. They are the reverse of ideal—but there is this great fact that for myself at least I may make them better. To take what there *is*, and use it, without waiting forever in vain for the preconceived—to dig deep into the actual and get something out of *that*—this doubtless is the right way to live. If I succeed a little I can easily—I think—succeed more; I can make my own conditions more as I go on. The field is common, but it is wide and free—in a manner—and <amusing?>. And if there is money in it that will greatly help: for all the profit that may come to me in this way will mean real freedom for one's general artistic life: it all hangs together (time, leisure, independence for 'real literature,' and, in addition, a great deal of experience of *tout un côté de la vie*). Therefore my plan is to try with a settled resolution—that is, with a full determination to return repeatedly to the charge, overriding, annihilating, despising the boundless discouragements, disgusts, *écœurements*. One should *use* such things—grind them to powder.

x   x   x   x   x

His proposal is that I shall make a play of the *American*, and there is no doubt a play in it. I must extract the simplest, strongest, baldest, most rudimentary, at once most humorous and most touching one, in a form whose main *souci* shall be pure situation and pure point combined with pure brevity. Oh, how it must not be too good and how very bad it must be! À *moi*, Scribe; *à moi*, Sardou, *à moi*, Dennery! —Reduced to its simplest expression, and that reduction must be my play, *The American* is the history of a plain man who is at the same time a fine fellow, who becomes engaged to the daughter of a patrician house, being accepted by her people on acct. of his wealth, and is then thrown over (by *them*) for a better match: after which he turns upon them to recover his betrothed (they have bullied her out of it), through the possession of a family secret which is disgraceful to them, dangerous to them, and which he holds over them as an instrument of compulsion and vengeance. They are frightened—they feel the screw: they dread exposure; but in the novel the daughter is already lost to the hero—she is swept away by the tragedy, takes refuge in a convent, breaks off her other threatened match, renounces the world, disappears. The hero, injured, outraged, resentful, feels the strong temptation to *punish* the Bellegardes, and for a day almost yields to it. Then he does the characteristically magnanimous thing—the characteristically good-natured thing—throws away his opportunity—lets them 'off'—lets them go. In the play he must do this—*but* get his wife.

[*With the composition of* The American, *which he thought for a while of calling* The Californian, *James hoped to begin the realization of his dream of writing successfully for the theater. He worked out a four-act structure, but by providing a happy ending he produced a piece less substantial and less moving than his novel. His letters at the time are filled with excitement and expectation over this new venture, as is the journal of Alice James, who in an English sanitarium at this juncture was her brother's close confidante.*

The American, *with Edward Compton in the role of Christopher Newman, and his wife, Virginia Bateman, in that of Claire de Cintré, went through a promising tour in the provinces. It came to London in the autumn of 1891 for only a moderate success—a two months' run— with Elizabeth Robins as Claire. Leon Edel has discussed this production and all other aspects of James' theatrical career in* Henry James: Les Années Dramatiques (1931).

By the time of the production James had also completed four other plays, Tenants, Disengaged, The Album, *and* The Reprobate, *though none of these reached the stage. But he was still full of hopes, and wrote to William James: 'I feel at last as if I had found my real form, which I am capable of carrying far.' But as Granville-Barker has remarked, it was too bad that James knew as his model the French theater at one of its worst periods.*]

Sunday, May 19th, 1889.

Very interesting meeting with Taine yesterday—at a lunch given by Jusserand at the Bristol Restaurant: company, M. and Mme Taine, their daughter, Dr. Jessopp, pleasant, clerical friend of Jusserand—George du Maurier—myself. The personal impression of Taine remarkably pleasant; much more *bonhomie*, mildness and geniality, than his hard, splendid, intellectual, logical style and manner had led me to expect. Charming talker—renewal of the sense of the high superiority of French talk. He has an obliquity of vision, yet is handsome in spite of it, with a fine head, a brown complexion, straight, strong, regular features—a fine, grave, masculine type. He talked about many things, and all well: about England with knowledge, friendliness, etc.—great knowledge; but what I wish especially to note here is his tribute to Turgenieff—to his depth, his variety, his form, the small, full perfect things he has left, which will live through their finished objectivity, etc. He rates T. very high—higher in form even than I have done. But his talk about him has done me a world of good—reviving, refreshing, confirming, consecrating, as it were, the wish and dream that have lately grown stronger than ever in me—the desire that the literary heritage, such as it is, poor thing, that I may leave, shall consist of a large number of perfect *short* things, *nouvelles* and tales, illustrative of ever so many things in life—in the life I see and know and feel—and of all the deep and the delicate—and of London, and of art, and of everything: and that they shall be fine, rare, strong, wise —eventually perhaps even recognized.

Taine used the expression, very happily, that Turgenieff so perfectly cut the umbilical cord that bound the story to himself.

January 23d. Dining last night at the Ch. Lawrences', Condie Stephen, who sat next to me, mentioned an anecdote—a case—of some man he had heard of, who fearing to suffer intensely in his last illness extracted a solemn promise from his wife that she would give him something that, at the last, would put an end to him. He fell ill, in due course, and then his wife's heart utterly failed her and she only did things—covert spoonsful of brandy, etc.—that would keep him alive longer—even from one day to the other. This struck me—a little tale might be made on it: especially with complications. Her promise, for instance, may be known to some other person, and her underhand restoratives (for she is ashamed of breaking it) be suspected to be doses of an opposite intention. In other words she looks as if she were poisoning her husband, while she is really keeping him alive. Denouement!

[101]

February 6th, 1890. (Sent the Act 2 of *The Californian* yesterday to E. Compton.) Perhaps the best formula for the fabrication <of> a dramatic piece *telle qu'il nous faut en faire,* in the actual conditions, if we are to do anything at all, is: Action which is never dialogue and dialogue which is always action.

Vallombrosa, July 27th, 1890. Subject for a short tale: a young man or woman who, in a far Western city—Colorado or California—surrounds himself with a European 'atmosphere' by means of French and English books—Maupassant, *Revue des 2 Mondes*—Anatole France, Paul Bourget, Jules Lemaître, etc.; and, making it really very complete, and a little world, intense world of association and perception in the alien air, lives in it altogether. Visit to him of narrator, who has been in Europe and knows the people (say narrator is a very modern impressionist painter); and contrast of all these hallucinations with the hard western ugliness, newspaperism, vulgarity, and democracy. There must be an American literary woman, from New England, 'pure and refined,' thin and intense. The sketch, picture, vision—*à la Maupassant.* The point that, after all, even when an opportunity offers to go over and see the realities—go to Paris and there know something of the life described—the individual *stays*—won't leave: held by the spell of knowing it all *that* way—as the best. It isn't much of a 'point'—but I can sharpen it; the situation, and what one can bring in, are the point.

Paris, Hotel Westminster, February 22d, 1891.

In pursuance of my plan of writing some very short tales—things of from 7000 to 10,000 words, the easiest length to 'place,' I began yesterday the little story that was suggested to me some time ago by an incident related to me by George du Maurier—the lady and gentleman who called upon him with a word from Frith, an oldish, faded, ruined pair—he an officer in the army—who unable to turn a penny in any other way, were trying to find employment as models. I was struck with the pathos, the oddity and typicalness of the situation—the little tragedy of good-looking gentlefolk, who had been all their life stupid and well-dressed, living, on a fixed income, at country-houses, watering places and clubs, like so many others of their class in England, and were now utterly unable to *do* anything, had no cleverness, no art nor craft to make use of as a *gagne-pain*—could only *show* themselves, clumsily, for the fine, clean, well-groomed animals that they were, only hope to make a little money by—in this manner—just simply *being.* I thought I saw a subject for very brief treatment in this *donnée*—and I think I do still; but to do anything worth while with it I must (as always, great Heavens!) be very clear as to what is in it and what I wish to get out of it. I tried a beginning yesterday, but I instantly became conscious that I must straighten out the little idea. It must be an idea—it can't be a 'story' in the vulgar sense of the word. It must be a picture; it must illustrate something. God knows that's enough—if the thing *does* illustrate. To make little anecdotes of this kind real *morceaux de vie* is a plan quite inspiring enough. *Voyons un peu,* therefore, what one can put into this one—I mean how much of life. One must put a little action—not a stupid, mechanical, arbitrary action, but something that is of the real essence of the subject. I thought of representing the husband as jealous of the wife—that is, jealous of the artist employing her, from the moment that, in point of fact, she begins to sit. But this is vulgar and obvious—worth nothing. What I wish to represent is the baffled, ineffectual, incompetent character of their attempt, and how it illustrates once again the everlasting English amateurishness—the way superficial, untrained, unprofessional effort goes to the wall when confronted with trained, competitive, intelligent, *qualified* art—in whatever line it may be a question of. It is out of *that* element that my little action and movement must come; and now I begin to see just how—as one always *does*—Glory be to the Highest—when one begins to look at a thing hard and straight and seriously—to fix it—as I am so sadly lax and desultory about doing. What subjects I should find—for *everything*—if I could only achieve this more as a habit! Let my contrast and complication here come from the opposition—to my melancholy Major and his wife—of a couple of little vulgar professional people *who know*, with the consequent bewilderment, vagueness, depression of the former—their failure to understand how such people can be better than *they*—their failure, disappointment, disappearance—going forth into the vague again. *Il y a bien quelque chose à tirer de ça.* They have no pictorial sense. They are only clean and stiff and stupid. The others are dirty, even—the melancholy Major and his wife remark on it, wondering. The artist is beginning a big illustrated book, a new edition of a famous novel—say *Tom Jones*: and he is willing to try to work them in—for he takes an interest in their predicament, and feels—sceptically, but, with his flexible artistic sympathy—the appeal of their type. He is willing to give them a trial. Make it out that *he* himself is on trial—he is young and 'rising,' but he has still his golden spurs to win. He can't afford, *en somme*, to make many mistakes. He has regular work in drawing every week for a serial novel in an illustrated paper; but the great project—that of a big house—of issuing an illustrated Fielding promises him a big lift. He has been intrusted with (say) *Joseph Andrews*, experimentally; he will have to do this brilliantly in order to have the engagement for the rest confirmed. He has already 2 models in his service—the 'complication' must come from *them*. One is a common, clever, London girl, of the smallest origin and without conventional beauty, but of aptitude, of perceptions—knowing thoroughly *how*. She says 'lydy' and 'plice,' but she has the pictorial sense; and can look like anything he wants her to look like. She poses, in short, in perfection. So does her colleague, a professional Italian, a little fellow—ill dressed, smelling of garlic, but admirably serviceable, quite universal. They must be contrasted, confronted, *juxtaposed* with the others; whom they take for people who *pay*, themselves, till they learn the truth when they are overwhelmed with derisive amazement. The denouement simply that the melancholy Major and his wife won't do—they're not 'in it.' Their surprise—their helpless, proud assent—without other prospects: yet at the same time *their* degree of more silent amazement at the success of the two inferior people—who are so much less nice-looking than themselves. Frankly, however, is this contrast enough of a *story*, by itself? It seems to me Yes—for it's an IDEA—and how the deuce should I get *more* into 7000 words? It must be simply 50 pp. of my manuscript. The little tale of *The Servant (Brooksmith)* which I did the other day for *Black and White* and which I thought of at the same time as this, proved a very tight squeeze into the same tiny number of words, and I probably shall find that there is much more to be done with this than the compass will admit of. Make it tremendously succinct—with a very short pulse or rhythm—and the closest selection of detail—in other words *summarize* intensely and keep down the lateral development. It *should* be a little gem of bright, quick, vivid form. I shall get every grain of 'action' that the space admits of if I make something, for the artist, hang in the balance—depend on the way he does this particular work. It's when he finds that he shall lose his great opportunity if he keeps on with them, that he has to tell the gentlemanly couple, that, frankly, they won't serve his turn—and make them wander forth into the cold world again. I must keep them the age I've made them—50 and 40—because it's more touching; but I must bring up the age of the 2 real models to almost the same thing. That increases the incomprehensibility (to the amateurs) of their usefulness. Picture the immanence, in the latter, of the idle, provided-for, country-house habit—the blankness of their *manière d'être*. But in how tremendously few words I must do it. This is a lesson—a *magnificent* lesson—if I'm to do a good many. Something as admirably compact and *selected* as Maupassant.

[In the preface to Daisy Miller, James said that The Real Thing 'sprang at a bound' after 'a momentary fond consideration' of Du Maurier's anecdote. It appeared in Black and White, 16 April 1892, and though it ran about two thousand words longer than he had originally figured, it was still 'a little gem of bright, quick, vivid form.'

In making his subject bear out an idea instead of just telling a 'story,' James created a condensed parable of some of his leading conceptions about art. His belief in realism was not in literal recording: he did not want to be held down by the accidents of a situation, but to penetrate to its essence by stylization. He was devoted to the nuances of character, and always resisted being ridden by fixed types. Mrs. Monarch is decidedly the real social thing, but she is 'always the same lady,' and put beside Miss Churm's imaginative improvising she comes to look 'singularly like a bad illustration.' The contrast between the stolid handsome Major and Oronte's mimetic gift is an even more compelling example of what the doctrine of imitation must mean for any art.

The painter-narrator is not doing illustrations for Joseph Andrews, but for Rutland Ramsay, the first volume of 'the projected édition de luxe of one of the writers of our day—the rarest of the novelists—who, long neglected by the multitudinous vulgar and dearly prized by the attentive (need I mention Philip Vincent?) had had the happy fortune of seeing, late in life, the dawn and then the full light of a higher criticism; an estimate in which on the part of the public there was something really of expiation.' When James wrote that sentence, he may have been indulging in oblique, playful concern with the possibility of his own later edition.]

Names. Beet—Beddington—Leander (surname)—Stormer—Luard—Void (name of a place) or Voyd would do for this.—Morn, or Morne—Facer — Funnel — Haddock — Windermere — Corner — Barringer — Jay—State—Vesey—Dacca—Ulick (Xtian name)—Brimble (or for a house)—Fade—Eily, the Irish name—good for a girl.

Marine Hotel, Kingstown, Ireland, July 13th, 1891.

I must hammer away at the effort to do, successfully and triumphantly, a large number of very short things. I have done ½ a dozen, lately, but it takes time and practice to get into the trick of it. I have never attempted before to deal with such extreme brevity. However, the extreme brevity is a necessary condition only for some of them—the others may be of varying kinds and degrees of shortness. I needn't go into all my reasons and urgencies over again here; suffice it that they are cogent and complete. I must absolutely *not* tie my hands with promised novels if I wish to keep them free for a genuine and sustained attack on the theatre. That is one cogent reason out of many; but the artistic one would be enough even by itself. What I call *the* artistic one *par excellence* is simply the consideration that by doing short things I can do so many, touch so many subjects, break out in so many places, handle so many of the threads of life. x x x x x

However, I have threshed all this out; it exists, in my mind, in the shape of absolutely digested and assimilated motive—inspiration deep and clear. The upshot of all such reflections is that I have only to let myself *go!* So I have said to myself all my life—so I said to myself in the far-off days of my fermenting and passionate youth. Yet I have never fully done it. The sense of it—of the need of it—rolls over me at times with commanding force: it seems the formula of my salvation, of what remains to me of a future. I am in full possession of accumulated resources—I have only to use them, to insist, to persist, to do something more—to do much more—than I *have* done. The way to do it—to affirm one's self *sur la fin*—is to strike as many notes, deep, full and rapid, as one can. All life is—at my age, with all one's artistic soul the record of it—in one's pocket, as it were. Go on, my boy, and strike hard; have a rich and long St. Martin's Summer. Try everything, do everything, render everything—be an artist, be distinguished, to the last. One has one's doubts and discouragements—but they are only so many essential vibrations of one's ideal. The field is still all round me, to be won; it blooms with the flowers that are still to be plucked. But enough of the *general*, these things are the ambient air; they are the breath of one's artistic and even of one's personal life. Strike, strike, again and again and again, at the *special*; I have only to live and to work, to look and to feel, to *gather*, to note. My *cadres* all there; continue, ah, continue, to fill them.

x x x x x

I made, I think, some time ago, a little note on the idea (suggested by a word of Mrs. Earle's on the situation of Mrs. M. and one of her daughters), of the adaptability of that particular little subject to a short tale. The situation is that of a woman who has compromised herself gravely while her child was young—made a scandal and a rumpus, quitted her husband for another man by whom, in turn, she was quitted, and who, living cold-shouldered by the world, though without another lover, ever since, finds herself confronted with her children when they <grow?> up. There must be a daughter, and a couple of sons.

The father has had them and brought them up; living separated of course from his wife, whom he has not chosen, or not been able, to divorce. They have occasionally seen her, have been allowed to go to see her, and are vaguely conscious of the peculiarity of her situation. The daughter grows up pretty and charming and people compassionate her, think it a pity she should have over her the cloud of her besmirched mother, whom she resembles—regret its effect on her prospects, etc. The idea, in a word, of the tale, is that the girl proves such a little person that she not only accepts, courageously, gaily, and quietly, keeping her own counsel and opening herself to no one, the facts of her mother's fate, the 'disadvantage' of such an association, etc., but determines to reverse the condition and be herself the poor lady's providence. Her mother can do nothing for her in society, can't 'take her out,' etc.; so she makes it her plan to bestow these services instead of receiving them. She will take her mother out—she will be *her* chaperon and protectress, she will make a place for her. The mother, in a word, is reinstated socially by the daughter's doing for *her* what she is not able to do for the daughter. I think there *must* have been a divorce—it makes the girl's action more difficult and her *tare* more marked. Type of the girl—pretty, very pretty, with charm; clever, quietly resolute, reticent and imperturbable. She is so attractive that she makes people accept her mother in order to have *her*. She becomes attractive to do it—being really serious, indifferent to vulgar success. She is proud, and she is in love with a clever, rather narrow-minded man, who is much taken with her but who has his reserves, is full of implied reservations and conditions. *Je vois tout ça d'ici*—the items and elements multiply and live. It is necessary that the girl must have elected to go and live with her mother. The father has died, expressing the strongest wish <that> his children shall do nothing of the kind. There are two others, a younger daughter and a son who don't. There must be a grandmother and an aunt, both paternal of course. So many types and figures—the observed London world—'Society' *telle que je l'ai vue*. The whole very short—with every touch an image, a step. The contrast between the mother and daughter—the mother flimsy and trivial, in spite of all her pathos and her troubles—the girl wondering at such yearnings—getting invited to parties, etc.—even while she makes herself their instrument. The mother is reinstated, the girl does it all for her; then she marries her *soupirant*, who must be a young soldier, of the peculiarly English moral and religious kind. She is left with a grievance, after all (I mean the mother), as against her daughter; she makes it a reproach to her that the stepson doesn't like or welcome her—a woman in such a position as hers! Can't she make him receive her differently—make him seem to wish more to see her in his house?

Last words of the tale: 'The girl turned away, with a sigh; she spoke wearily: "No, mamma, I'm afraid I can't do that too."' Her only allusion, to her mother, to what she has done.

Marine Hotel, Kingstown, July 21st, '91.

I have done my best for the foregoingly noted little subject, but it insists—it has insisted—on getting itself treated at somewhat greater length than I intended—in 2 parts, for the *Atlantic*. I have finished one of these sufficiently well, I think, to make it immensely my interest to straighten out to the very best effect the possibilities of the other. If I can make Part II all it may be, the thing will be very good indeed. Make it purely dramatic, make it movement and action. I have set the stage sufficiently in the first act. Make it a vivid London picture—the picture of what Rose Tramore does and how she does it. The idea is pretty enough and odd enough to express completely. But the right formula for the 2d part is a series of *scènes de comédie*, with a strong ironical taste. Plunge into the midst—set it going. There must be, as a core to the little action, some London woman who wants Rose for her son—her vision of the inducements and advantages made clear— but wants her *without* her mother, tries to get her away from her mother, deal with her singly, etc. Rose's absolute refusal, from the first, to be dealt with singly, and comprehension that with this rigid rule she will eventually succeed in her purpose. The chapter must open with some episode of apparent failure. I see it, and I can go on. It must be intensely brief and concise; only 45 pp. of MS.

[James' The Chaperon *is saved from being mere anecdote—in his preface he contrasted two methods by saying that he rejoiced in 'the anecdote' but revelled in 'the picture'—by the presentation of the narrative entirely through the sense that Rose Tramore, the heroine, has of its events and persons. The notebook outline is closely followed, but the conclusion is changed and the suggested 'last words of the tale' do not appear. The mother is left with no grievance, but is pictured as quite happy now that she is once more in society. The story ends with a conversation between Rose and her husband, in which each gives the other credit for the successful launching of the tarnished Mrs. Tramore. The change is effective because it keeps the concentration on Rose and her life rather than on her mother's, and avoids a possible interruption of the singleness of point of view which, James thought, gave virtue to the tale.*

The story was first printed in the Atlantic Monthly *in November and December 1891, so that it must have been finished very shortly after* the second of the two entries just above was written. Once again James' effort for brevity was unavailing; the second part, as printed in the *Atlantic*, has more than ten thousand words.]

Names. Wharton—Rosedew—Vaudrey (or Vawdrey)—Grutt—Stack—Fillingham—Smale—Morillion.

Kingstown, July 27th, 1891.

The Private Life (title of the little tale founded on the idea of F.L. and R.B.) must begin: 'We talked of London, face to face with a great bristling primeval glacier. The hour and the scene were one of those impressions which make up, a little, in Switzerland, for the modern indignities of travel—the promiscuities and vulgarities of the station and the hotel—the struggle for a scrappy attention, the reduction to the numbered state. The high valley was pink with the mountain rose and the pure air as cold as one's submission to nature.[1] The desultory tinkle of the cattle bells seemed to communicate a sociability with innocent things.'

[*James kept to this opening almost word for word until he came to the description of nature, which he amplified as follows: 'The high valley was pink with the mountain rose, the cool air as fresh as if the world were young. There was a faint flush of afternoon on undiminished snows, and the fraternising tinkle of the unseen cattle came to us with a cropped and sun-warmed odour.'*]

Names. Pickerel — Chafer — Bullet — Whitethorne — Dash — Elsinore (place)—Douce—Doveridge (person or place)—Adney—Twentyman (butler)—Firminger—Wayward (place)—Wayworth—Greyswood (place)—Nona (girl's name)—Runting.

Names (continued).—Scruby—Mellifont (a place, or still better, title. Ld. Mellifont)—Undertone (for a countryhouse)—Gentry—Butterton—Vallance—Ashbury—Alsager—Bosco (person or place)—Isherwood—Loder — Garnet — Antram — Antrim — Cubit — Ambler — Urban (Xtian name)—Windle—Trivet—Middleship—Keep—Vigors—Film—Philmor—Champ—Cramp—Rosewood—Roslin—Littlewood—Esdaile—Galleon—Bray—Nurse—Nourse—Reul—Prestige—Poland—Cornice—Gosselin—Roseabel (Xtian name)—Shorting—Sire—Airey—Doubleday—Conduit—Tress—Gallop—Farrington—Bland—Arrand—Ferrand—Dominick—

---

1. In this sentence James first wrote 'alpine' and then crossed it out, before 'mountain,' and similarly wrote and deleted 'tinkle' before 'pure.'

Heatherfield—Teagle—Pam—Locket—Brickwood—Boston-Cribb—Trend —Aryles—Hoyle—Flake—Jury—Porches (place)—Morrish—Gole.

Marine Hotel, Kingstown, August 3d, 1891.

The Private Life—the idea of rolling into one story the little conceit of the private identity of a personage suggested by F.L., and that of a personage suggested by R.B., is of course a rank fantasy, but as such may it not be made amusing and pretty? It must be very brief—very light—very vivid. Lord Mellefont is the public *performer*—the man whose whole personality goes forth so in representation and aspect and sonority and phraseology and accomplishment and frontage that there is absolutely—but I *see* it: begin it—begin it! Don't talk *about* it only, and around it.

x   x   x   x   x

[*In the preface to* The Altar of the Dead *volume, James remarked that the 'mild documentation' for* The Private Life *'fairly thickened' for him, since here was an instance where his imagination had started to work from the impressions made upon him by two celebrities of the London world. The contrast he noted was between 'a highly distinguished man, constantly to be encountered, whose fortune and whose peculiarity it was to bear out personally as little as possible . . . the high denotements, the rich implications and rare associations, of the genius to which he owed his position and his renown'; and another, 'that most accomplished of artists and most dazzling of men of the world whose effect on the mind repeatedly invited to appraise him was to beget in it an image of representation and figuration so exclusive of any possible inner self that, so far from there being here a question of an alter ego, a double personality, there seemed scarce a question of a real and single one, scarce foothold or margin for any private and domestic ego at all.'*

Lord Mellifont (as the name is spelled in James' story) is a painter who seems to be 'all public,' with 'no corresponding private life,' whereas Clare Vawdrey, a novelist and playwright, 'was all private and had no corresponding public.' James stated in his preface that Robert Browning—whom he was also to characterize in The Middle Years *as having been in public 'as little as possible a Bard,' all 'heterogeneous and profane'—had furnished the starting point for Vawdrey; and it appears likely that F.L. may indicate Frederick, Lord Leighton, the fashionable Victorian painter.*

James' treatment of this theme in terms of 'alternate identities' links the method of his fantasy, as he recognized, with that of his ghost stories.]

October 22d, 1891, 34 De Vere Gdns. I finished yesterday my difficult paper on J<ames> R<ussell> L<owell> for the January *Atlantic* and I must immediately get into the work promised to Kinloch-Cooke. I am emerging a little from all the *déboires* and distresses consequent on the production of *The American* by Edward Compton, and I needn't note them here to remind myself what the episode has been, and still, in a measure, *is*; nor to feel how much it gives me something to live for in the future. I shall live, I trust, for several things; but a very prominent one, surely, shall be the firm—the exquisitely still and deep-rooted resolution—to compass, in the theatre, the solid, the honourable (so far as anything can be honourable there!), the absolute and interesting success. Meanwhile the soothing, the healing, the sacred and salutary refuge from all these vulgarities and pains is simply to lose myself in this quiet, this blessed and uninvaded workroom in the inestimable effort and refreshment of art, in resolute and beneficent production. I come back to it with a treasure of experience, of wisdom, of acquired material, of (it seems to me) seasoned fortitude and augmented capacity. Purchased by disgusts enough, it is at any rate a boon that now that I hold it, I feel I wouldn't, I oughtn't, to have missed. Ah, the terrible law of the artist—the law of fructification, of fertilization, the law by which everything is grist to his mill—the law, in short, of the acceptance of all experience, of all suffering, of *all* life, of *all* suggestion and sensation and illumination. To keep at it—to strive toward the perfect, the ripe, the only best; to go on, by one's own clear light, with patience, courage and continuity, to live with the high vision and effort, to justify one's self—and oh, so greatly!—all in time: this and this alone can be my only lesson from *anything.* Vague and weak are these words, but the experience and the purpose are of welded gold and adamant. The consolation, the dignity, the joy of life are that discouragements and lapses, depressions and darknesses come to one only as one stands *without*—I mean without the luminous paradise of art. As soon as I really re-enter it—cross the loved threshold—stand in the high chamber, and the gardens divine—the whole realm widens out again before me and around me—the air of life fills my lungs—the light of achievement flushes over all the place, and I believe, I see, I *do.*

x   x   x   x   x

What of this idea for a very little tale?—The situation of a married woman who during her husband's lifetime has loved another man and who, after his death, finds herself confronted with her lover—with the man whom, at least, she has suffered to make love to her, in a certain particular way. The particular way I imagine to be this: the husband

is older, stupider, uglier, but she has of course always had a bad conscience. I imagine a flirtation between her and the younger man, who is really in love with her, which she breaks off on becoming aware that her husband is ill and dying. He is kind, indulgent, unsuspicious to her and she is so touched by his tenderness and suffering that she is filled with remorse at her infidelity and breaks utterly with her lover. She devotes herself to her husband, nurses and cherishes him— but at the end of a short time he dies. She is haunted by the sense that she was unkind to him—that he suspected her—that she broke his heart—that she really killed him. In this state she passes 6 months, at the end of which she meets again the man who has loved her and who still loves her. His hope is now that she will marry him—that he has gained his cause by waiting, by respecting her, by leaving her alone. x x x x x
I interrupt myself, because suddenly, in my imagination the clearing process takes place—the little click that often occurs when I begin to straighten things out pen in hand, really tackle them, sit down and look them in the face. I catch hold of the slip of a tail of my action— I see my little drama. There are 4 persons—2 men and 2 women— not 1 woman and 2 men. The revelation about her husband's behaviour is made to the heroine by the 2d woman, not by the man who loves her. This is a calculated act on the 2d woman's part—she being in love with the 2d man. This sounds awfully crude, but it isn't, as I see it all. It is a subject, and I can make it do for the *English Illust.* I needn't take time, with expatiating on it here—but only *begin* it, in good faith—and it will go.

[*Despite the definiteness of this note, James wrote no such story for the* English Illustrated Magazine. *That periodical was for a time edited by Sir Clement Kinloch-Cooke whom he mentioned just above.*]

34 De Vere Gdns., October 23d.

To live *in* the world of creation—to get into it and stay in it—to frequent it and haunt it—to *think* intently and fruitfully—to woo combinations and inspirations into being by a depth and continuity of attention and meditation—this is the only thing—and I neglect it, far and away too much; from indolence, from vagueness, from inattention, and from a strange nervous fear of letting myself go. If I vanquish that nervousness, the world is mine. x x x x x
Surely it would be possible to make another and a less literal application of the idea of poor H.W.[1] and the queer tragedy of his relation

1. Possibly Henry Wycoff, whom James discusses in A *Small Boy and Others* (pp. 133 ff.).

with Cousin H. I might make a little tale of it in which the motive would really *be* an idea, and a pretty and touching one—the idea of the *hypnotization* of a weak character by a stronger, by a stronger will, so that the former accepts a certain absolute view of itself, takes itself from the point of view of another mind, etc., and then, by the death of the dominant person, finds itself confronted with the strange problem of liberty.

February 5th, 1892. I find myself wrenched away from the attempt to get on with the drama—wrenched only for the hour, fortunately—by the necessity of doing *au plus tôt* some short tales. Once I get into this current the spell works, the charm, the faith comes back to me; but the effort—at the start—is great. But there is all the big suggestive, swarming world around me, with all its life and motion—in which I only need to dip my ladle. But I must dip with a free and vigorous hand.

x   x   x   x   x

It is all one quest—in the way of subject—the play and the tale. It is not one *choice*—it is two deeply distinct ones; but it's the same general *enquête*, the same attitude and *regard*. The large, sincere, attentive, constant quest would be a net hauling in—with its close meshes—the two kinds.

x   x   x   x   x

I was greatly struck, the other day, with something M. d'Estournelles, whom I met at Lady Brooke's, said to <me> about P.B.'s life and situation—in regard to his marriage, his prospects: that his only safety —*their* only safety, as a *ménage heureux*, resided in their remaining *loin de France*—abroad—far from Paris. From the moment they should return there their union would *have* to go to pieces—their safety as a *ménage heureux*—their mutual affection and cohesion. It was sad, but it was *comme ça*. Paris wouldn't *tolerate* a united pair; would inevitably and ruthlessly disintegrate it. When Lady B. said, 'C'est bien triste!,' the speaker said, 'Mon Dieu, madame, c'est comme ça!' Something probably to be done with the tragedy, the inevitable *fate*, of this; the prevision of it, on the part of a young couple, the mingled horror and fascination of the prospect.

x   x   x   x   x

Henry Adams spoke to me the other day of the end <of> certain histories of which, years ago, in London he had seen the beginning— poor Lady M.H., who broke off her engagement with X.Y.Z. on the

[113]

eve of marriage and now trails about at the tail of her mother—or some other fine lady—a dreary old maid. Then the situation of two other girls of the same noble house, one of whom, Augusta, now gives music lessons for a living. The other, the elder sister, was the daughter of a French mistress—dancer or someone—and of Lord A.B. (before his marriage) and was adopted by him and by his wife—it was a clause of the contract—as his own daughter and grew up on this footing. There is the suggestion of a situation in this—that is, in the relation of the sisters. Express it rapidly and crudely thus. The relation is one—for the younger, the legitimate, of jealousy—she is in love with the same man as Cynthia. He comes to the house—has seemed to hesitate between them, but really is taken by Cynthia. Augusta suffers, resents—but doesn't know the secret of her sister's birth. *Sur ces entrefaites* her mother—her own mother (ill and dying, say), tells her, so as to put into her hand a weapon, as it were, against Cynthia—to enable her to disclose the real fact and thereby disenchant—put off—the valuable suitor. (The idea is that Augusta should tell his sister—trusting *her* to communicate it.) But Augusta is overtaken by better feelings. She does tell his sister, then repents, has herself in horror and afterwards goes back to her and beseeches her not *to* tell the brother. The lady has no intention of doing so, and as she holds her tongue Augusta, stoically, sees the marriage take place. (She may at least have the temptation to tell the sister herself, I mean Cynthia—to relieve and *soulager* herself—but even this she resists.) But meanwhile the lady whom she has taken into her confidence is so struck with her behaviour that she mentions it, as a *beau trait*, to a friend—a young man (must *she* be in love with him?—YES, and she's a married woman!) on whom it makes such an impression that he is haunted by Augusta, as it were, seeks her acquaintance, falls in love with her and marries her: so that Augusta *is* rewarded for her magnanimity and *does* get a husband. It sounds, all, rather bald and thin here, but as a little homogeneous drama might, I think, be concisely told.

x   x   x   x   x

[*James continued to think about this theme (p. 119 below) and again the following year (pp. 135-6). When he returned to it once more, in 1899 (p. 297), he still found his grasp on it 'superficial.'*]

An *idée de comédie* came to me vaguely the other day on the subject of the really terrible situation of the young man, in England, who is a great *parti*—the really formidable assault of the mothers, and the *filles à marier*. I don't see, quite, my comedy in it yet—but I do see a little tale of about this kind.—A young nobleman—or only (perhaps better) commoner of immense wealth, feels himself, on the eve of the London Season, in such real discomfort and peril that he makes a compact with a girl he has known for years, and likes, to see him through the wood by allowing it to be supposed and announced, that they are engaged. His mother must have put him up to it. He has come into the whole thing suddenly—unexpectedly. He has known the girl before—for years. He doesn't dream he's hurting her. She consents and the device succeeds. But in the middle of the season she gets a real chance to marry—by feeling that there is a man who would marry her if it were not for this supposititious engagement. So she asks the *parti* if she mayn't drop the comedy. She thinks he *may* refuse—ask her to make it a real engagement. But he doesn't refuse—he's inconvenienced, reluctant—but he lets her go. She marries her *real* suitor—though she is secretly in love with the *parti*—and he afterwards finds that they were at cross purposes: she was *really* in love with him—and he has become so with her—but didn't want to press her lest he should have seemed to attribute to her the cupidity they had both thought to *soustraire* him from. Too great delicacy on his part, etc.—Try and do three for M. Morris, with the other little thing—the one I thought of in Ireland—the thing of which I scratched a beginning—the young man who dines out.—

x x x x x

[James wrote this story, called at first Lord Beauprey and then Lord Beaupré, very soon after he made his sketch for it in the notebook. It came out from April through June 1892 in Macmillan's Magazine, of which Mowbray Morris was editor.

The tale seems to have been difficult to manage. The 'afterwards' drops out, and the parti, Lord Beaupré, never discovers that his pretended fiancée, Mary Gosselin, was really in love with him. The only person who is, or says she is, aware of all the facts, is her mother. She, not Beaupré's mother, arranges the whole scheme and entices Mary into it. She does so because she is a designing parent, of just the type Beaupré fears—and secretly hopes that the mock engagement may lead to a real one. She is implausibly omniscient about Mary's feelings and Beaupré's, and the climax is weakened because only her gloomy forebodings suggest that her daughter's marriage, to a young American, will turn out badly. Her son, Hugh, who opposes her plan, supplies a neat contrast for her, and serves as someone to whom she may talk about her real acts and motives. But James' fictional contrivings, even in the space of more than 20,000 words, are relatively powerless against

the improbability and the essentially anecdotal character of the story.
He did not include it in the New York edition.]

Could not something be done—in the 'international' line—with the
immense typical theme of the *manless* American woman, in Europe
—the way everything social is in their hands *là bas*, etc.? The suggestion embodied in Mrs. L. of N. Y. The total suppression of the husband. I seem to catch hold of the tail of an action—2 women—2 husbands. Their description of each other: *minus* the husband:—or *to*
each other (of their lives), with the utterly unmentioned husbands turning up afterwards—as revelations, etc. One of the women may describe to
the other—then the other meets the husband—likes him (she being
unmarried, etc.) and finds that he *is* the appendage of her new acquaintance. There is distinctly, I think, the making of something in
this.

[*James was to handle such a theme, though on somewhat different lines,
in* Fordham Castle (1904). *He began to develop it afresh several years
later (pp. 267-8 below).*]

February 28th, 1892. A very good little subject (for a short tale), would
be the idea—suggested to me in a roundabout way by the dreadful E.D.
'tragedy' in the south of France—of a frivolous young ass or snob of a
man, rather rich, and withal rather proper and prim, who marries a
very pretty girl and is pleased with the idea of getting her into society
—I mean into the world smart and fast, *ou l'on s'amuse*; the sort of
people whom it most flatters his vanity to be able to live with. There
is no harm in him save that he's an ass and a snob. His wife is really
much more of a person, clever, independent, whimsical and easily-
bored. She tires of him, and of his platitude, and of that of the world
they live in, and takes a lover. She has already had 2 children. She
commits herself, is compromised, discovered and divorced. The lover is
an *homme sérieux*, he marries her. Change of scene and situation. She
becomes a serious 'earnest' woman—deploring the levity of her 1st
husband, the way he brings up their children, whom he has been able
to keep. *He* marries again and has another child—as *she* has. 2d wife
a goose but 'good.' She *dies*. The 1st wife's deplorings of the sort of
people they are. Renewal of relations in which the divorcée has the
moral, earnest, superior attitude—trying to rescue the others from their
frivolity. *Rapprochement* of the children. She resents the example of
her 1st lot, for her second. Lastly her husband's last daughter (of his
second wife), wishes to marry her son (that of her 2d husband) and

[116]

she breaks it off and the tale—purely ironic and satiric—ends. Told by *me*—the friend and observer.

March 16th. Idea of a servant suspected of doing the mean things— the base things people in London take for granted servants do— reading of letters, diaries, peeping, spying, etc.; turning out utterly innocent and incapable of these things—and turning the tables of scorn on the master or mistress, at a moment when, much depending on it, they are (the servant is) supposed to have committed all the little basenesses.

[*James listed a similar theme among possible subjects for short stories at page 236 below.*]

March 26th. The idea of the *responsibility* of destruction—the destruction of papers, letters, records, etc., connected with the private and personal history of some great and honoured name and throwing some very different light on it from the light projected by the public career. Might not a little drama be built on this—on the struggle, the problem, the decision *what* to do, the interest of truth, etc.? The famous personage may have been a high figure in politics—successful to the world—but with a secret history revealed in compromising documents, revelations of insincerity, tortuosity, venality, etc. They must come into the hands of a poor young man—not a relation—a young man poor enough to be tempted by their pecuniary value and having nothing at stake, for his honour, in their being made public. He must—he at least *may*—be a poor young man of letters, discouraged, depressed by his conscious<ness> of failure and intrinsic inability to produce, 'create' —his want of talent and gift. The manner in which he comes into possession of them to be determined—a dramatic accident. He appreciates their value, as well as the damage they will do to a great reputation, and a publisher or editor offers him money for them. There are no *relations*—no one to suffer. He is tempted, strongly, being in want of the money and not in sympathy with the great man's character or opinions—and *almost* consents to let the publisher have them. But a strange indefeasible instinct—a curious inner repulsion holds him back, makes him, each time he is on the point of concluding the bargain, conscious of an insurmountable feeling. The editor—the publisher— puts before him the public duty, the rights of truth, etc., very eloquently and interestedly. Meanwhile he has encountered a girl—a woman—poor like himself, whom he falls in love with. I see it from here—I needn't go on with the details. She is poor like himself—an actress, a singer or an artist. She lives in his house, say; has the rooms below. Her type, her charm for him. She has a little girl, etc. She must, I think, be somewhat more famous and fortunate than he. That constitutes his difficulty in making up to her—little to offer as he has. But he sees her, knows her, talks with her and to a certain extent makes love to her. x x x x x I see the rest of this so clearly now that I will go straight on with it.

[As he went ahead with Sir Dominick Ferrand, James endowed his young widow, Mrs. Ryves, with psychic intuition which enables her to foresee trouble as a result of Peter Baron's accidental discovery of the late Sir Dominick's papers, even though she does not know anything about what he has found. After Peter has responded to her impulses and has destroyed the scandalous papers without ever having told her what they were, he learns from her that she is the famous man's illegitimate daughter. This fact does not prevent their marriage on the unexpectedly large proceeds from a song she has composed and for which Peter has written the words. James printed this story in the Cosmopolitan (July–August 1892) under the title of Jersey Villas, and in The Real Thing and Other Tales (1893). He did not include it in his collected edition.]

March 26th, 1892. The idea of the soldier—produced a little by the fascinated perusal of Marbot's magnificent memoirs. The image, the type, the vision, the character, as a transmitted, hereditary, mystical, almost supernatural force, challenge, incentive, almost haunting, apparitional presence, in the life and consciousness of a descendant—a descendant of totally different temperament and range of qualities, yet subjected to a superstitious awe in relation to carrying out the tradition of absolutely military valour—personal bravery and honour. Sense of the difficulty—the impossibility, etc.; sense of the ugliness, the blood, the carnage, the suffering. All these things make him dodge it—not from cowardice, but from suffering. Get something it is enjoined upon him to do—etc. I can't complete this indication now; but I will take it up again, as I see in it the glimmer of an idea for a small subject, though only dimly and confusedly—the subject, or rather the idea, of a brave soldierly act—an act of heroism—done in the very effort to evade all the ugly and brutal part of the religion, the sacrifice, and winning (in a tragic death?) the reward of gallantry—winning it from the apparitional ancestor. This is very crude and rough, but there is probably something in it which I shall extract.

x   x   x   x   x

[*James proceeded, a few weeks later, to develop the theme for* Owen Wingrave.]

I get, it seems to me, a really very good little theme, by infusing an important alteration into the idea suggested by Henry Adams (*vide ante*), the story of Augusta, Cynthia, the *bâtardise*, etc.—making my heroine a hero, my Augusta an Augustus, and making the question hinge upon money—an inheritance. The secret of the bastardy of one of the brothers told in dying by the mother to the other (the illegitimate son is not hers, but the husband's, now dead), and make the motive the desire to prevent a rich relation (her *own* relation), from leaving the bequest to the wrong one—from favouring him—or there are other things, other possibilities in it. The rich possible benefactor may be really the relation of the bastard—his father's brother—and the bastard may be *her* child. Thresh it out, make it at any rate a young man's struggle and the motive the money question.

Yellowley—Chemney—Monier, or Monyer—Branch—Farthing—Perch—Barber—Pudney—Leal—Carrier—Coil—Paramore (place)—Chichley—Pardie—Verus (baptismal name)—Vera—Gerald—Harley—Crisford—Tregant—Pottinger—Drabble—Landsdale—Ryves (place)—Faith—Sisk (place)—Gaye (name of house)—Taunt—Tant (Miss Tant, name of governess)—Carrow—Hardwig—Punchard—Chivers—Bawtry—Nassington (place)—German—Germon—Potcher—Dunderdale—Martle.

May 8th, 1892, 34 De Vere Gardens.

Can't I hammer out a little the idea—for a short tale—of the young soldier?—the young fellow who, though predestined, by every tradition of his race, to the profession of arms, has an insurmountable hatred of it—of the *bloody* side of it, the suffering, the ugliness, the cruelty; so that he determines to reject it for himself—to break with it and cast it off, and this in the face of every sort of coercion of opinion (on the part of others), of such pressure not to let the family honour, etc. (always gloriously connected with the army), break down, that there is a kind of degradation, an exposure to ridicule and ignominy in his apostasy. The idea should be that he fights, after all, exposes himself to possibilities of danger and death for his own view—acts the soldier, *is* the soldier, and of indefeasible soldierly race—proves to have been so—even in this very effort of abjuration. The thing is to invent the particular heroic situation in which he may have found himself—show just *how* he has been a hero even while throwing away his arms. It is a question of a little subject for the *Graphic*—so I mustn't make it 'psychological'—they understand that no more than a donkey understands a violin. The particular form of opposition, of coercion, that he has to face, and the way his 'heroism' is *constatée*. It must, for prettiness's sake, be *constatée* in the eyes of some woman, some girl, whom he loves but who has taken the line of despising him for his renunciation—some *fille de soldat*, who is very *montée* about the whole thing, very hard on him, etc. But what the subject wants is to be distanced, relegated into some picturesque little past when the army occupied more place in life—poetized by some slightly romantic setting. Even if one could introduce a supernatural element in it—make it, I mean, a little ghost-story; place it, the scene, in some old country-house, in England at the beginning of the present century—the time of the Napoleonic wars.—It seems to me one might make some *haunting* business that would give it a colour without being ridiculous, and get in that way the sort of pressure to which the young man is subjected. I see it—it comes to me a little. He must die, of course, be slain, as it were, on his own battle-field, the night spent in the haunted room in which the ghost of some grim grandfather—some bloody warrior of the race—or some father slain in the Peninsular or at Waterloo—is supposed to make himself visible.

x   x   x   x   x

[Owen Wingrave appeared in the Christmas number of the Graphic (1892). For this story, his single eloquent denunciation of the stupidity and barbarism of war, James did not fit his theme to a romantic setting in the past. He made it one of his characteristic ghost stories by bringing the Hawthornesque spirit of Colonel Wingrave, Owen's brutal ancestor of the time of George II, into the haunted room of the country house in which the young man's grandfather still lives. Taunted by Kate Julian as a coward for refusing to follow the military career of his family, Owen spends a night's vigil in that room, and is found dead there. James' concluding sentence reads: 'He was all the young soldier on the gained field.'

The passage in the preface to The Altar of the Dead dealing with Owen Wingrave shows how James' notebook themes were sometimes catalyzed by a figment of immediate observation, and then fused into their concrete form. After speaking of how one's old notebooks 'sometimes explicitly mention, sometimes indirectly reveal, and sometimes wholly dissimulate' the clues of origination, James went on: 'It comes back to me of "Owen Wingrave," for example, simply that one summer afternoon many years ago, on a penny chair and under a great tree in Kensington Gardens, I must at the end of a few . . . visionary mo-

[120]

ments have been able to equip him even with details not involved or not mentioned in the story. Would that adequate intensity all have sprung from the fact that while I sat there in the immense mild summer rustle and the ever so softened London hum a young man should have taken his place on another chair within my limit of contemplation, a tall quiet slim studious young man, of admirable type, and have settled to a book with immediate gravity? Did the young man then, on the spot, just become Owen Wingrave, establishing by the mere magic of type the situation, creating at a stroke all the implications and filling out all the picture? That he would have been capable of it is all I can say—unless it be, otherwise put, that I should have been capable of letting him; though there hovers the happy alternative that Owen Wingrave, nebulous and fluid, may only, at the touch, have found himself in this gentleman; found, that is, a figure and a habit, a form, a face, a fate, the interesting aspect presented and the dreadful doom recorded; together with the required and multiplied connexions, not least that presence of some self-conscious dangerous girl of lockets and amulets offered by the full-blown idea to my very first glance. These questions are as answerless as they are, luckily, the reverse of pressing—since my poor point is only that at the beginning of my session in the penny chair the seedless fable hadn't a claim to make or an excuse to give, and that, the very next thing, the pennyworth still partly unconsumed, it was fairly bristling with pretexts. "Dramatise it, dramatise it!" would seem to have rung with sudden intensity in my ears. But dramatise what? The young man in the chair? Him perhaps indeed—however disproportionately to his mere inoffensive stillness; though no imaginative response can be disproportionate, after all, I think, to any right, any really penetrating, appeal. Only, where and whence and why and how sneaked in, during so few seconds, so much penetration, so very much rightness? However, these mysteries are really irrecoverable; besides being doubtless of interest, in general, at the best, but to the infatuated author.']

D. V. G., *May 12th, 1892.* The idea of the old artist, or man of letters, who, at the end, feels a kind of anguish of desire for a respite, a prolongation—another period of life to do the *real* thing that he has in him—the things for which all the others have been but a slow preparation. He is the man who has developed late, obstructedly, with difficulty, has needed all life to learn, to see his way, to collect material, and now feels that if he can only have another life to make use of this clear start, he can show what he is really capable of. Some incident, then, to show that what he *has* done *is* that of which he is capable— that he has done all he can, that he has put into his things the love of perfection and that they will live by that. Or else an incident acting just the other way—showing him what he might do, just when he must give up forever. The 1st idea the best. A young doctor, a young pilgrim who admires him. A deep sleep in which he dreams he *has* had his respite. Then his waking to find that what he has dreamed of is only what he has *done*.

[*In* The Middle Years (*Scribner's Magazine, May 1893*) *James objectified a theme that was deeply involved with his own experience. He may have felt something of that sort when he later borrowed this story's title for the third, unfinished volume of his autobiography.*

Dencombe, the writer in the story, says 'I've outlived, I've lost by the way,' and thereby gives refracted expression to such anxieties as James had expressed to Howells (pp. 69, 71 above), and was to repeat to him after the failure of Guy Domville at the opening of 1895: 'I have felt, for a long time past, that I have fallen upon evil days—every sign or symbol of one's being in the least wanted, anywhere or by any one, having so utterly failed. A new generation, that I know not, and mainly prize not, has taken universal possession.' James had also experienced a deep personal loss through the death of his sister Alice two months before this entry.

Dencombe, convalescent after a serious illness, longs for another span of life in which to produce 'a certain splendid "last manner," the very citadel, as it would prove, of his reputation, the stronghold into which his real treasure would be gathered.' But such a final period is not to be granted him. James dropped the dream-motif, but Dencombe dies with the satisfaction at least of knowing his work deeply appreciated by young Doctor Hugh. Knowing also that his death is at hand, Dencombe rallies above all anxieties to voice one of James' strongest convictions: 'We work in the dark—we do what we can—we give what we have. Our doubt is our passion and our passion is our task. The rest is the madness of art.'

James confined his discussion of this story, in the preface to The Author of Beltraffio, *entirely to technical matters. He had been asked by Scribner's for a story of six thousand words, and was determined to squeeze his treatment within that limit. (He remarks a little proudly that the finished job consists of 'some 5550,' but the actual count is nearer eight thousand.) What interested him most was that he had imposed the form 'of the concise anecdote' upon a subject that might well have seemed to demand 'developmental' treatment. As a result he could remember 'finding the whole process and act (which, to the exclusion of everything else, dragged itself out for a month) one of the* most expensive of its sort in which I had ever engaged.' He could also speak of his anxious efforts as having been comparable to those 'of some warden of the insane engaged at a critical moment in making fast a victim's straitjacket.' Yet, in retrospect, he could take satisfaction that such strenuous efforts and such rigorous control tended to make 'the very short story' one of the solidest of forms.

The description of the dream, abandoned here, may possibly be the first faint stirring of one of the themes for The Great Good Place (1900). The possibility is heightened by the fact that the author in that story, who dreams of a utopian respite and retreat, is named Dane, and that name appears in the list just below (p. 126).]

34 De Vere Gdns., May 18th, 1892.

Little subject suggested by some talk last night with Lady Shrewsbury, at dinner at Lady Lindsay's: about the woman who has been very ugly in youth and been slighted and snubbed for her ugliness, and who, as very frequently—or at least sometimes—happens with plain girls, has become much better-looking, almost handsome in middle life, and later—and with this improvement in appearance, charming, at any rate, and attractive—so that the later years are, practically, her advantage, her compensation, her *revanche*. Idea of such a woman who meets, in such a situation, a man who, in her youth, has slighted and snubbed her—who has refused a marriage perhaps—a marriage projected by the two families, and, out of fastidiousness, and even fatuity and folly, has let her see that she was too ugly for him. Mustn't there be a second woman, the woman he *has* married and who has turned plain, as it were, later in life, on his hands? Mightn't something be done with this little fancy of the *beau rôle* that the other one has—taking her revenge in protecting, assisting, cheering up the man whose own attitude and situation are now so different? Say she has always loved him—and now he is poor. His wife dies—and he has a son of marriageable age, the son of this wife, the ex-beauty, but who, as it happens, is hideous. He gets a chance to marry this son well (some reason for this must be given) if he can only do something for him. Say he has a fine old name which the other people will take as a *part* of the compensation for his being so hideous. The charming woman, who has money, makes up the rest. Or the charming woman (much better this) *has* also, later, married and she has a son who is very handsome. The disappointed man has a daughter, who is nice but very ugly. The magnanimous *revanche* of the charming woman—the way she shows her 'protection'—is by persuading her son (or perhaps only *trying*) to marry the ugly girl. It is probably better to make this only a trial—a vain one. The son *regimbers* too much—says the girl is too ugly.

'She'll grow better-looking when she's older.'

'She? Jamais de la vie!'

'She'll do as I have done. I was hideous.'

'I don't believe it—it's false.—Show me your photograph, to prove it.'

'I was too ugly ever to be taken.'

He doesn't believe it. She has to say to her friend: 'Que voulez-vous? My son won't believe it!'—*She* must have had money, or the prospect of money, as a girl. That's why the marriage was planned by his mother—an old friend, say, of her mother. That's why she has been able to marry later. The thing must begin with *his* mother, years ago, breaking the idea to him—he hasn't yet seen the girl. Then her qualificative:

'But I must tell you she's very plain.—BUT she has, etc., etc.' He promises to try, sees her, tries still, makes her fall in love with him—then finds he *can't!*

[*This idea had obvious possibilities for a neatly symmetrical plot of the sort that James loved, and in* The Wheel of Time, *which he printed in the* Cosmopolitan *in December 1892, and January 1893, he developed those possibilities fully. Lady Greyswood has a son who needs a rich bride; Mrs. Knocker has a daughter, Fanny, who has money but no looks. The two mothers try to arrange a marriage, but the son, Maurice, is so put off by Fanny's lack of beauty that he runs away to the continent. Years later he returns, a widower, with a homely daughter, and finds that Fanny, now Mrs. Tregent and a widow, has become strikingly attractive and has a handsome son. Maurice now wants to marry her, but although she has forgiven him and still loves him, she refuses. She has chosen as her 'remedy' or her 'revenge' devotion to others, and she longs to bring his daughter and her son together. History repeats itself. The young man runs off to Spain, and Maurice's daughter dies.*

James prevents the story from seeming too mechanical, in spite of its rigid pattern, by concentrating on the character of Fanny. The real climax comes when Maurice discovers that he has been the one great passion of her life and that she fully realized the situation and his reasons when he abandoned her. He sees how she has consoled herself by trying to help others—her husband, her son, and now Maurice's daughter. The essential theme of the story is the complex emotional relation between Fanny and Maurice. As he so often did, James started here with a carefully squared plot and then used it simply as a foundation on which to rest an action depending on the shrewd portraiture of a character in its emotional interplay with others.]

May 22d, 1892. Read last night admirable article in the *Revue des 2 Mondes* of 1st April last on *La Vie Américaine* by André Chevrillon, which somehow gave to my imagination a kind of impulse making it want to do something more with the American character. Another man —not a Newman, but more completely civilized, large, rich, complete, but strongly characterised, but essentially a *product.* Get the action —the action in which to launch him—it should be a big one. I have no difficulty in *seeing* the figure—it *comes*, as I look at it.

[*This impulse could have led to the creation of both Lambert Strether and Adam Verver.*]

Hotel Richemont, Lausanne, August 4th, 1892.

Last evening, at Ouchy, Miss R. said, after the conversation had run a little upon the way Americans drag their children about Europe:
    'A girl should be shown Europe—or taken to travel—by her husband —she has no business to see the world before. *He* takes her—*he* initiates her.'
Struck with this as the old-fashioned French view and possible idea for a little tale. The girl whose husband is to show her everything— so that she waits at home—and who never gets a husband. *He* is to take her abroad—and he never comes, etc. The daughter of a conservative 'frenchified' mother, etc. A pretext for the mother's selfishness, neglect, etc.—*she* travelling about. The girl's life—waiting—growing older—death. The husband comes in the form of death, etc.

x   x   x   x   x

[*James included this theme in a list of possible stories at page 235 below.*]

Some painter (Pasolini) in Venice said, after painting the Empress Frederick: [1] 'It is only Empresses who know how to sit—to *pose*. They have the habit of it, and of being looked at, and it is three times as easy to paint them as to paint others.'—Idea of this—for another little 'model' story; pendant to the *Real Thing.* A woman comes to a painter as a paid model—she is poor, perfect for the purpose and

1. The editors have found no record of any painter named Pasolini. The Empress Frederick was Victoria, Empress of Germany, and daughter of Queen Victoria. James' reference may be to Count Giuseppe Pasolini, who as a statesman and diplomat had many connections with England in Victoria's time, and may mean only that the story of the painter came from the Count. Or perhaps, as Miss E. L. Lucas suggests, Count Pasolini was himself an amateur painter and did a portrait of the Empress.

very mysterious. He wonders how she comes to be so good. At last he discovers that she is a deposed princess!—reduced to mystery! as to earning her living.

x   x   x   x   x

Situation of that once-upon-a-time member of an old Venetian family (I forget which), who had become a monk, and who was taken almost forcibly out of his convent and brought back into the world in order to keep the family from becoming extinct. He was the last *rejeton*—it was absolutely *necessary* for him to marry. Adapt this somehow or other to today.

[*This would seem to be the first hint for Guy Domville, which deals with a young English Catholic at the end of the eighteenth century. In the first act of James' play, which was composed in the summer of 1893, the hero is on the point of taking holy orders when he finds himself the inheritor of a great fortune, and is persuaded to assume its responsibility. The second act shows his sad disillusion with worldly society, and in the third he reverts to his original decision.*]

Names. Beague—Vena (Xtian name)—Doreen (ditto)—Passmore—Trafford—Norval—Lancelot—Vyner—Bygrave—Husson—Domville—Wynter—Vanneck—Bygone—Bigwood (place)—Zambra—Negretti—Messer—Coucher—Croucher—Woodwell—Chamley—Dann—Dane—Anderton (place)—Hamilton-finch (or with other short second name)—Byng—Bing—Bing-Bing—Oldfield—Briant—Dencombe—Tyrrel—Desborough—Morland—Bradbury—Messenden—Ashington—Jewel—Billamore—Windle—Chiddle—Vernham—Illidge—Tertius (Xn. name)—Poynton—Monmouth.

34 De Vere Gardens, W., November 12th, 1892.

— Two days ago, at dinner at James Bryce's, Mrs. Ashton, Mrs. Bryce's sister, mentioned to me a situation that she had known of, of which it immediately struck me that something might be made in a tale. A child (boy or girl would do, but I see a girl, which would make it different from *The Pupil*) was *divided* by its parents in consequence of their being divorced. The court, for some reason, didn't, as it might have done, give the child exclusively to either parent, but decreed that it was to spend its time equally with each—that is alternately. Each parent married again, and the child went to them a month, or three months, about—finding with the one a new mother and with the other a new father. Might not something be done with the idea of an odd and particular relation springing up 1st between the child and each of these new parents, 2d between one of the new parents and the other —through the child—over and on account of and by means of the child? Suppose the real parents die, etc.—then the new parents marry each other in order to take care of it, etc. The basis of almost any story, any development would be, that the child should prefer the new husband and the new wife to the old; that is that these latter should (from the moment they have ceased to *quarrel* about it), become indifferent to it, whereas the others have become interested and attached, finally passionately so. Best of all perhaps would be to make the child a fresh bone of contention, a fresh source of dramatic situations, *du vivant* of the original parents. *Their* indifference throws the new parents, through a common sympathy, together. Thence a 'flirtation,' a love affair between them which produces suspicion, jealousy, a fresh separation, etc. —with the innocent child in the midst.

[*In his preface to* What Maisie Knew, *James traces the ripening of his idea for it from 'the little acorn' of an 'accidental mention' of a child in the joint custody of divorced parents. The notebook entry above places and dates the 'accidental mention' and shows how James at once began to think about developing a symmetrical set of complications to surround the 'innocent child.' Nine months later, on 26 August 1893 (p. 134 below), he came back to the theme and recorded the further shaping he had given it in the interim.*]

Names. Mackle—Spavin—Alabaster—Pollard—Patent—Waymouth—George—Allaway (or Alloway)—Barran—Count—Currier—Arden—Damant—Malling—Coldfield (place)—Malin—Cushion—Merino—Ramage—Helder—Harrish—Mariner (Marriner)—Chuck-(or Check-)borough (title)—Cressage (place)—Edenbrook—Gravener—Hine—Millard—Linthorne—Mountain—Checkley—Pilling—Humber—Comrad—Maddock—Benefit—Blankley (or—like 'Mountain'—*place*)—Hue—Ashdown—Bycroft—Gunning—Wintle—Port—Braid—McBride—Goldring—Beaver—Berridge—Christmas—Pook—Devenish—Clarence (surname).

34 De Vere Gardens, W., November 24th, '92.

— Surely if I attempt another comedy for Daly, and a 'big part' for A.R., as I see myself, rather vividly, foredoomed to do, the subject can only be (it is so designated, and imposed, by the finger of opportunity), the American woman in London society. I see my figure—my type—it stands before me, and the problem opening up is of course the question of a great comedy-action. If this action is a strong one, a right one, a real one, the elements of success ought to be there in force. But, ah, how *charming*, how interesting, how noble, as it were, the subject ought to be. It must be something as remote, as *different*, as possible, from that of my little tale of *The Siege of London*; with its little picture of an innocent adventuress and its vague *rappel* of the 'situation' in Dumas's *Demi-Monde*—the situation of a man of honour who has to testify about the antecedents of a woman he has known in the past. This must be a totally different kind of *donnée*—with no *rappel* of anything familiar or conventional or already done—fresh, charming, superior, with a distinct elevation, a great comedy-'lift' in it. My heroine mustn't be one of the crudities—she must only be (and that with great intensity), one of the newnesses, the freshnesses, the independences, the freedoms. What I must show is the great thing, above all, the blank page, the clear fine-grained surface of the famous 'adaptability.' If I can do the thing I *see*, it will be too good for Ada R.; but I must thank heaven it be not for some one worse. The *idea* of the comedy must reside in the fact of the *renversement*, the altera-tion of the relations of certain elements of intercourse; the reversal of what the parties traditionally represent. (I am stating it very sketchily and crudely.) What my American woman must represent, at any rate, is the idea of attachment to the past, of romance, of history, continuity and conservatism. She represents it from a fresh sense, from an indi-vidual conviction, but she represents it none the less—and the action must be something in which she represents it effectively—with a power to save and preserve. In other words, she, intensely American in temperament—with her freedoms, her immunity from traditions, super-stitions, fears and *riguardi*, but with an imagination kindling with her new contact with the presence of a *past*, a continuity, etc., represents the conservative element among a cluster of persons (an old house, family, race, society) already in course of becoming demoralized, vul-garized, and (from their own point of view), Americanized. She 'steps in,' in a word, with a certain beautiful beneficence and passion. *How* she steps in, how she arrests and redeems and retrieves and appeals and clears up and *saves*—it is in the determination of this that must reside the *action* of my play: a matter as to which the clear and sacred light can only come to me with prayer and fasting, as it were, and little by little. But charming and interesting, it seems to me, should be the problem of representing the combination of this function of hers, this work, this office, this part she plays, and the intensity, the vividness, the unmistakableness and individuality of her American character. There glimmers upon me already an admirable first act—the act of her introduction, her presentation, initiation, amid all the elements—the surging of them before her with their appeal, their

[128]

fascination for her, and the culmination, at the end of the act, of her sense that she can *do* something—that she *must* undertake and achieve it. Of course—oh, how utterly!—there must be a 'love-interest'— which is one and the same with the other parts of the situation. It dimly shines before me that my heroine ought to love a younger son— a younger brother, a poor cousin, contingent heir or next of kin to a territorial magnate. Perhaps he's an advanced radical, a tremendous theoretic democrat, etc. Rather, I should say, must she be brought into contact and conflict, *not* amorous, with the theoretic one. A chance for a striking satiric picture—the radical English aristocrat, the democrat in a high place, etc., etc.

x   x   x   x   x

[Apparently James did do a 'light comedy,' Disengaged, for Ada Rehan some time before November 1893. It reached the rehearsal stage but was then withdrawn. (Elizabeth Robins, Theatre and Friendship, New York, 1932, pp. 137-43.) It was not on the theme noted here, which he began to develop into Covering End a couple of years later (pp. 185-6 below), but based on his story The Solution (pp. 95-6 above).]

November 26th, 1892. Curiously persistent and comically numerous appear to be the suggestions and situations attached to this endless spectacle—the queer crudity of which is a theme for the philosopher— of the Anglo-American marriage. The singular—the intensely significant circumstance of its being all on one side—or rather in one form; always the union of the male Briton to the female American—*never* the other way round.[1] Plenty of opportunity for satiric fiction in the facts involved in all this—plenty of subjects and situations. It seems to me all made on purpose—*on n'a qu'à puiser*. One has only to dip it out. The contrast between the man the American girl marries and the man who marries the American girl. This opens up—or *se rattache* to—the whole subject, or question, about which Godkin, as I remember, one day last summer talked to me very emphatically and interestingly—the growing divorce between the American woman (with her comparative leisure, culture, grace, social instincts, artistic ambitions) and the male American immersed in the ferocity of business, with no time for any but the most sordid interests, purely commercial, professional, democratic and political. This divorce is rapidly becoming a gulf—an abyss of inequality, the like of which has never before been seen under the sun. One might represent it, picture it, in a series of

1. James had treated the Anglo-American marriage 'the other way round' in *Lady Barberina* (pp. 49-51 above).

[129]

illustrations, of episodes—one might project a lot of light upon it. It would abound in developments, in ramifications.

x   x   x   x   x

November 28th. Situation, not closely connected with the above, suggested by something lately told one about a simultaneous marriage, in Paris (or only 'engagement' as yet, I believe), of a father and a daughter—an only daughter. The daughter—American of course—is engaged to a young Englishman, and the father, a widower and still youngish, has sought in marriage at exactly the same time an American girl of very much the same age as his daughter. Say he has done it to console himself in his abandonment—to make up for the loss of the daughter, to whom he has been devoted. I see a little tale, *n'est-ce pas?* —in the idea that they all shall have married, as arranged, with this characteristic consequence—that the daughter fails to hold the affections of the young English husband, whose approximate mother-in-law the pretty young second wife of the father will now have become. The father *doesn't* lose the daughter nearly as much as he feared, or expected, for her marriage which has but half gratified her, leaves her *des loisirs,* and she devotes them to him and to making up, as much as possible, for having left him. They spend large parts of their time together, they cling together, and weep and wonder together, and are even *more* thrown together than before. The reason of all this, for the observer (and I suppose the observer, as usual, must tell the tale—or, rather, *No*—this time I see it *otherwise*—especially in the interest of brevity)—the reason, I say, is not far to seek, and resides in the circumstance that the father-in-law's second wife has become much more attractive to the young husband of the girl than the girl herself has remained. *Mettons* that this second wife is nearly as young as her daughter-in-law—and prettier and cleverer—she knows more what she is about. *Mettons* even that the younger husband has known her before, has liked her, etc.—been attracted by her, and would have married her if she had had any money. She was poor—the father was very rich, and *that* was her inducement to marry the father. The latter has settled a handsome *dot* on his daughter (leaving himself also plenty to live on), and the young husband is therefore thoroughly at his ease. Relations are inevitably formed between him and his father-in-law's wife—relations which, in the pleasure they find in each other's society, become very close and very intimate. They spend as much of their time together as the others do, and for the very reason that the others spend it. The whole situation works in a kind of inevitable rotary way —in what would be called a vicious circle. The *subject* is really the

[130]

pathetic simplicity and good faith of the father and daughter in their abandonment. They feel abandoned, yet they feel consoled, with *each other*, and they don't see in the business in the least what every one else sees in it. The rotary motion, the vicious circle, consists in the reasons which each of the parties give<s> the other. The father marries because he's bereft, but he ceases to be bereft from the moment his daughter returns to him in consequence of the *insuccès* of his marriage. The daughter weeps with him over the *insuccès* of *hers*—but her very alienation in this manner from her husband gives the second wife, the stepmother, her pretext, her opportunity for consoling the other. From the moment she is not so necessary as the father first thought she would be (when his daughter seemed wholly lost), this second wife has also *des loisirs*, which she devotes to her husband's son-in-law. Lastly, the son-in-law, with the sense of his wife's estrangement from him, finds himself at liberty, and finds it moreover only courteous to be agreeable to the other lady in the particular situation that her 'superfluity,' as it were, has made for her. A necessary basis for all this must have been an intense and exceptional degree of attachment between the father and daughter—he peculiarly paternal, she passionately filial. The young husband may be made a Frenchman—*il faut*, for a short tale, *que cela se passe à Paris.* He is poor, but has some high social position or name—and is, after all, morally only the pleasant *Français moyen*—clever, various, inconstant, amiable, cynical, unscrupulous—charming always, to 'the other woman.' The other woman and the father and daughter all intensely American.

[Nearly twelve years were to elapse between this entry and James' composition of The Golden Bowl. Instead of using this outline for 'a little tale,' he produced one of his longest novels, but he held to the main subject as he saw it here. The Italian Prince Amerigo is of firmer moral fiber than the suggested French husband, but the essential 'simplicity' and 'good faith' of Adam and Maggie Verver remained as sketched. James also presented the 'exceptional degree' of attachment between them without pondering it as an abnormality. This attachment produces in its innocence the chief deviations from the outline. Maggie thinks, after her own marriage, that her father is too much alone and should marry again; and it is she who persuades him to choose Charlotte Stant. She does not weep with her father over her unsuccessful marriage. She does not suspect for some time that it is unsuccessful; she simply continues to be with her father a great deal because of their mutual devotion. When the situation dawns upon her and she resolutely determines to win back her husband, it is part of James' exacting

[131]

method that no words about the situation ever pass between father and daughter.

James recurs to this theme in his entry for 14 February 1895 (p. 187 below), and thinks of it then in relation to a projected short 'international' novel. By the time he finally came to its embodiment, he was able to enrich it with his most mature technical resources. Instead of using the device of the observer, he made the Prince his chief reflector for the first half of the novel, the Princess for the second. He also introduced the golden bowl as a central symbol, and brought his most masterly handling to the endless implications latent in it.]

34 De Vere Gardens, December 18th, 1892.

Intensely picturesque impression of visit yesterday afternoon to the Tower of London—to the 'Queen's House'—by invitation from Miss M., whom I found alone. Very English—quite intensely English, impression—the whole thing: the old homely, historic nook in the corner of a military establishment—the charming girl, daughter of the old Governor of the Tower, etc.—the memories, the ghosts, Anne Boleyn, Guy Fawkes, the block, the rack and the friendly modern continuity. *Ah, que de choses à faire, que de choses à faire!*

x   x   x   x   x

December 27th. 'I am disappointed in Greece, as I was disappointed in England'—phrase quoted to me by G<race> N<orton>—from letter of her nephew (Dick) and commented on by her as example of the joyless vagueness, the want of temperament and (I suppose) 'passion' of the modern youth (American in particular), as she sees them. Interesting view to see taken of it, almost comedy or tragi-comedy view. Suggestion to me of the 'culture' that has no assimilation nor application—the deluge of cultivated mediocrity, etc. The possibility of a little tale on it—the reaction against the overdose of education, on the part of a youth *conscious* of his mediocrity—a reaction frantic, savage, primitive and forming a grotesque commentary on all that has been expected of him and pumped into him. The *form* of the reaction to be determined and to constitute, really, the subject. This subject possibly obtainable by introduction of 2d concomitant and contrasted figure—the yearning (for culture) barbarian. A woman?

Names. Bernal—Veitch (or Veetch)—Arrow—Painter—Melina (Xtian name)—Peverel—Chaillé (de Chaillé) for French person—Brasier—Chattock—Clime—Lys—Pellet—Paraday—Hurter—Collop—Hyme—Popkiss—Lupton—Millington—Mallington—Malville—Mulville—Wiffin—Christopher (surname)—Dark—Milsom—Medway—Peckover—Alum—Braby (or of place)—Longhay—Netterville—Lace—Round—Ferrard—Remnant (noted before)—Polycarp (Xtian name)—Masterman—Morrow (house—place)—Marrast—Usher—Carns—Hoy—Doy—Mant—Bedborough—Almeric (Xtian name)—Jesmond—Bague—Misterton (place)—Pruden—Boys—Kitcat—Oldrey—Dester—Wix—Prestidge.

x   x   x   x   x

Said in defence of some young man accused of being selfish—of self-love: 'He doesn't love *himself*—he loves his *youth!*' or 'It isn't *himself* he loves—it's his *youth*—and small blame to him!'
'The most beautiful word in the language?—Youth!'

Hotel Westminster, Paris, April 8th, 1893.

The strange *genius* of Pierre Loti—so exquisite even in a thing so *mince*, so comparatively shrunken and limited, as *Matelot*, which I am just reading—and expressed somehow in the beauty of a passage that strikes me (with that indefinable charm of his) so much that I transcribe it.

'Donc, ils en venaient à s'aimer d'une également pure tendresse, tous les deux. Elle, ignorante des choses d'amour et lisant chaque soir sa bible; elle, destinée à rester inutilement fraîche et jeune encore pendant quelques printemps pâles comme celui-ci, puis à vieillir et se faner dans l'enserrement monotone de ces mêmes rues et de ces mêmes murs. Lui, gâté déjà par les baisers et les étreintes, ayant le monde pour habitation changeante, appelé à partir, peut-être demain, pour ne revenir jamais et laisser son corps aux mers lointaines. . .'

[*In writing to Edmund Gosse a few weeks later James urged him to read aloud this passage, 'and perhaps you will find in it something of the same strange eloquence of suggestion and rhythm as I do: which is what literature gives when it is most exquisite and which constitutes its sovereign value and its resistance to devouring time.'*]

Hotel National, Lucerne, May 7th, '93.

I have been worrying at the dramatic, the unspeakably theatric form for a long time, but I am in possession now of some interposing days (the reasons for which I needn't go into here—they are abundantly chronicled elsewhere), during which I should like to dip my pen into the *other* ink—the sacred fluid of fiction. Among the delays, the disappointments, the *déboires* of the horrid theatric trade nothing is so soothing as to remember that literature sits patient at my door, and that I have only to lift the latch to let in the exquisite little form that is, after all, nearest to my heart and with which I am so far from having done. I let it in and the old brave hours come back; I live them over again—I add another little block to the small literary monument that it has been given to me to erect. The dimensions don't matter—one must cultivate one's garden. To do many—and do them perfect: that is the refuge, the asylum. I must *always* have one on the stocks. It will be there—it will be started—and little by little it will grow. I have among the rough notes of this old book ½ a dozen decent starting-points. I don't say to myself, here, a 10th of the things I might—but it isn't necessary. So deeply I know them and feel them.

August 26th, 1893 (34 De Vere Gdns.).

I am putting my hand to the idea of the little story on the subject of the *partagé* child—of the divorced parents—as to which I have already made a note here. The little *donnée* will yield most, I think—most *ironic* effect, and this is the sort of thing mainly to try for in it—if I make the old parents, the original parents, *live*, not die, and transmit the little girl to the persons they each have married *en secondes noces*. This at least is what I ask myself. May I not combine the ironic and the *other* interest (the 'touch of tenderness'—or sweetness—or sympathy or poetry—or whatever the needed thing is), by a conception of this sort; viz.: that Hurter and his former wife each marry again and cease to care for the child—as I have originally posited—as soon as they have her no longer to quarrel about? The new husband and the new wife then take the interest in her, and meet on this common ground. The Hurters quarrel with *them* over this, and they separate: I mean each of the Hurters separate afresh. Make *Hurter* die? His 1st wife survives and becomes extremely jealous of his 2d. I must remember that if Hurter dies, the situation breaks, for his wife then gets the whole care of Maisie; which won't do. No, they both live.

x   x   x   x   x

[In What Maisie Knew the Hurters become the Faranges, both marry again and 'both live.' James had not yet reached what was to be the core of the story, as he at last saw it, but he had taken a step along the road he traces in his preface. 'I recollect, however, promptly thinking that for a proper symmetry the second parent should marry too,' he writes, and continues: 'The second step-parent would have but to be correspondingly incommoded by obligations to the offspring of a hated predecessor for the misfortune of the little victim to become altogether exemplary. The business would accordingly be sad enough, yet I am not sure its possibility of interest would so much have appealed to me had I not soon felt that the ugly facts, so stated or conceived, by no means constituted the whole appeal.' 'The whole appeal' was not revealed in the notebooks until James*had pondered further. (See p. 236 below.)]

August 30th. The desire to escape from the cramp of the *too* intensely short possesses me; crowds back upon me and pulls me up—making me ask myself whether I am not creating myself needless difficulties. God knows how dear is brevity and how sacred today is concision. But it's a question of degree, and of the quantity of *importance* that one can give. That importance is everything now. To try and squeeze it into a fixed and beggarly number of words is a poor and a vain undertaking—a waste of time. There are excellent examples of the short novel—and one that has always struck me as a supremely happy instance is poor Maupassant's admirable *Pierre et Jean*. Octave Feuillet is also, with all his flimsiness, singularly wise as to length. I want to do something that I can do in three months—something of the dimensions of *Pierre et Jean*. I should be glad also to make my story resemble it in other ways. The great question of *subject* surges in grey dimness about me. It is everything—it is everything. I have 2 or 3 things in mind, but they happen to be purely ironic. They will serve for some other time: the particular thing I want to do now is not the ironic. I want to do something fine—a strong, large, important human episode, something that brings into play character and sincerity and passion; something that marches like a drama. A truce to all subjects that are not superior! I have two things in mind, and the best thing is for me to thresh them out a little here. It all comes back to the old, old lesson—that of the art of *reflection*. When I practice it the whole field is lighted up—I feel again the multitudinous presence of all human situations and pictures, the surge and pressure of *life*. All passions, all combinations, are there. And oh, the luxury, the value of having time to *read!* As to this, however, the long ache is too deep for speech—sad, hungry silence covers it. x x x x x

One of the things which hangs before me just now, but which needs, in its actual vagueness and mere formal presence, a great deal of vivification, is the subject as to which, in 2 different places, I have scratched a few lines here already—referring to it as suggested by an anecdote, a mention, of Henry Adams's. I have sketched something very dimly (*vide ante*), which is a large, vague expansion of that suggestion. Then there is the subject that I have been turning over as a theme for a play, and tackled very superficially the 1st act of, under the designation of *Monte Carlo*. It will be no waste of time to straighten these things out a little. The question, as regards the latter, comes up as to how willing one can be to give up to the temporary presence of the need to produce a story, a *donnée*, that has presented itself as valuable for a play—the form as to which good *données* are so rare. That, however, is an independent question. In the 1st case (H.A.'s suggestion), the struggle, the drama, enacts itself round a question of legitimacy. As I have stated it before (as H.A. described the original situation to me), there were two girls brought up as sisters, as equal daughters, of a *cadet* of a good English house. However, I needn't recapitulate this. One of them, the younger, is informed by her mother, on the latter's deathbed, that the other is illegitimate. She is the child of the late father by a former liaison (pre-matrimonial), taken over, adopted by the wife and brought up as her own child. However, I have stated this situation before, with the *variante* of making the sisters brothers, and the matter, the interest at issue, being not a marriage, but an inheritance, a question of money. Let me see a little what this may give. It gives primarily the advantage of a hero, a male central figure, which I prefer. This young man is the younger son. But what force of *deterrence* can the information given, the revelation made, for her reasons, by the dying mother be supposed as having if imparted to the person from whom the money is expected? Say it's expected in the form of a daughter with a fortune and offered to the family by a x x x x x

34 De Vere Gardens, W., December 24th, 1893.

Three little histories were lately mentioned to me which (2 of the 3 in particular) appear worth making a note of. One of these was related to me last night at dinner at Lady Lindsay's, by Mrs. Anstruther-Thompson. It is a small and ugly matter—but there is distinctly in it, I should judge, the subject of a little tale—a little social and psychological picture. It appears that the circumstance is about to come out in a process-at-law. Some young laird, in Scotland, inherited, by the death of his father, a large place filled with valuable things—pictures, old china, etc., etc. His mother was still living, and had always lived, in this rich old house, in which she took pride and delight. After the death of her husband she was at first left unmolested there by her son, though there was a small dower-house (an inferior and contracted habitation) attached to the property in another part of the country. But the son married—married promptly and young—and went down with his wife to take possession—possession *exclusive*, of course—according to English custom. On doing so he found that pictures and other

treasures were absent—and had been removed by his mother. He en-
quired, protested, made a row; in answer to which the mother sent
demanding still other things, which had formed valuable and interesting features of the house during the years she had spent there. The
son and his wife refuse, resist; the mother denounces, and (through
litigation or otherwise), there is a hideous public quarrel and scandal.
It has ended, my informant told me, in the mother—passionate, re-
bellious against her fate, resentful of the young wife and of the loss
of her dignity and her home—resorting to <the> tremendous argument (though of no real *value* to her) of declaring that the young man
is not the son of his putative father. She has been willing to dishonour
herself to put an affront upon *him*. It is all rather sordid and fearfully
ugly, but there is surely a story in it. It presents a very fine case of
the situation in which, in England, there has *always* seemed to me to
be a story—the situation of the mother *deposed*, by the ugly English
custom, turned out of the big house on the son's marriage and relegated.
One can imagine the rebellion, in this case (the case I should build
on the above hint), of a particular sort of proud woman—a woman
who had *loved* her home, her husband's home and hers (with a knowledge and adoration of artistic beauty, the tastes, the habits of a col-
lector). There would be circumstances, details, intensifications, deepen-
ing it and darkening it all. There would be the particular type and
taste of the wife the son would have chosen—a wife out of a Philistine,
a tasteless, a hideous house; the kind of house the very walls and furniture of which constitute a kind of *anguish* for such a woman as I suppose the mother to be. That kind of anguish occurred to me, precisely, as a subject, during the 2 days I spent at Fox Warren (I didn't
mean to write the name), a month or so ago. I thought of the strange,
the terrible experience of a nature with a love and passion for beauty,
united by adverse circumstances to such a family and domiciled in
such a house. I imagine the young wife coming, precisely, out of it.
I imagine the mother having fixed on a girl after her own heart for
the son to marry; a girl with the same exquisite tastes that *she* has and
having grown up surrounded with lovely things. The son doesn't in
the least take to this girl—he perversely and stupidly, from the mother's
point of view, takes to a girl infatuated with hideousness. It is in this
girl's people's house, before the marriage, that the story opens. The
mother meets there the other girl—the one that pleases her: the one
with whom she discovers a community of taste—of passion, of sensibility and suffering.

[*James went into more thorough discussion of* The Spoils of Poynton
than of any other work recorded in his notebooks. The entry above,

[137]

read with those for 13 and 15 May, 11 August, 8 September, and 15 October 1895; and for 13 and 19 February and 30 March 1896 (pp. 198 ff., 207 ff., 214 ff., 247 ff. below) will yield illuminating insight into his detailed processes.

He was to begin his preface to this short novel (for it again far exceeded the 'little tale' he at first envisaged) with the account of how his stories had generally sprung from such a small seed as that dropped unwittingly by his dinner companion. He emphasized how the first tiny prick of suggestion was all that the imagination needed, how anything more than that minimum would spoil 'the operation' by giving too much. He made his well-known discrimination between 'life being all inclusion and confusion, and art being all discrimination and selection,' and insisted that for his purposes the conclusion to his companion's anecdote was both clumsy and sordid, another 'full demonstration of the fatal futility of Fact.'

His adaptation of the theme is evidence of what he meant. The property remained the core, but James' handling of it is quite different, say, from what Balzac's might have been, since Mrs. Gereth is not motivated by greed but by aesthetic devotion for her 'old things.' She makes no brutal denunciation of her son Owen, and, in fact, the drama shifts away from their quarrel to find its real center in the 'intenser consciousness' of Fleda Vetch who, quite without property herself, is one of James' most extreme embodiments of imagination, taste, and renouncing sensibility.]

Names. Gisborne—Dessin—Barden—Carden—Deedy—Gent—Kingdon (before)—Peregrine King (name in *Times*)—Brendon—Franking—Crevace—Covington (house)—Ledward—Bedward—Dedward—Deadward—Olguin—Alguin—Gannon—Leresche—Pinhorn—Loynsworth (Loinsworth)—Gallier—Parminter (Parmenter)—Count—Rouch—Carvel—Hilder—Medwick—Rumble (place)—Rumbal (person)—Ariel—Cork—Gulliver—Nesfield—Nest (place, house)—Rainy—Saltrem (or Saltram)—Cline—Stransom—Coxon—Derry—Lupus—Stamper—Creston—Cheston—Berry—Anvoy.

December 26th, 1893 (34 De Vere Gardens).

I have been sitting here in the firelight—on this quiet afternoon of the empty London Xmastide, trying to catch hold of the tail of an idea, of a 'subject.' Vague, dim forms of imperfect conceptions seem to brush across one's face with a blur of suggestion, a flutter of impalpable wings. The prudent spirit makes a punctual note of whatever may be least indistinct—of anything that arrives at relative concreteness. Is there something for a tale, is there something for a play, in something that might be a little like the following? It is the *play* that I am looking for, but it is worth noting, all the same, for the *other* possibility.

Very briefly, I imagine a young man who has lost his wife and who has a little girl, the only issue of that prematurely frustrated union. He has very solemnly, and on his honour, promised his wife, on her deathbed, that, *du vivant* of their child, he will not marry again. He has given her this absolutely sacred assurance and she has died believing him. She has had a reason, a deep motive for her demand—the overwhelming dread of a stepmother. She has had one herself—a stepmother who rendered her miserable, darkened and blighted her youth. She wishes to preserve her own little girl from such a fate. For five years all goes well—the husband doesn't think of marrying again. He delights in the child, consoles himself with her, watches over her growth and looks forward to her future. Then, inevitably, fatally he meets a girl with whom he falls deeply in love—in love as he hadn't *begun* to be with his poor dead wife. She returns his affection, his passion; but he sees the phantom of his solemn vow, his sacred promise rise terribly before him. In the presence of it he falters, and while the girl obviously stands ready to surrender herself, he hangs back, he tries to resist the current that sweeps him along. Or, there is another figure intensely engaged in the action—and without whom it would present no drama. This is the figure of a young woman who loves him, who has loved him from the moment she has seen him, who has seen him, known him, *du vivant* of his wife. The circumstances of this personage are all questions to determine. What is of the essence is that she was a friend and perhaps even a relation of his wife, who admired and trusted her and who more or less bespoke her sympathy and protection for the little girl that was to be left motherless. *Mettons*, provisionally, supposititiously, that she was a relation, and at the time of the wife's death a married woman—a woman young, ardent, and already, at that time, secretly in love, with my hero. Stay—better still than making her married will it be, I think, to make her *engaged*—engaged to a fine young man whom the dying wife knows, approves of, takes comfort in thinking of as the girl's *futur*, her caretaker through life. In the first chapter of my story this young man is present—the 1st chapter of my story—by which I mean the 1st act of my play! Their engagement is a thing established—their marriage is not to be distant. Well, very briefly, the wife dies, exacting the promise that I have mentioned, and which is imparted to the girl at the time—probably by the wife herself. In the early part of the act the condition of the wife is uncertain—her end not positively near. When her fate *becomes* certain, the girl, by a strange abrupt *revirement*, in face of a renewed

[139]

importunity of her lover, an 'appeal to name the day,' suddenly *breaks* with him, to his amazement, says she can't, that their engagement is at an end. He goes off in dismay, and it is *after* he goes off that she learns what the vow is that the hero has taken. There are also present in this first act the doctor, and a second young girl—my heroine proper, who has great subsequent importance and who is only introduced in the 1st. This 1st is of the nature of a prologue. Very, very briefly, so as to give the vaguest skeleton and *enclose* the statement in a definite loop, I go on with the mere essence of the story. The curtain rises on Act II, 5 years later. My Hero has never married, of course—no more has my Bad Heroine. She is fearfully in love with my Hero. He meanwhile has fallen in love with my Good Heroine, who ignorantly and innocently returns his passion. My Bad Heroine is frightfully afraid the two will marry; so, knowing what the other girl is, she makes up her mind to tell her of the vow he has made his wife, believing that will make her despise him if he violates it. Then, somehow, *this* is what I saw ½ an hour ago, as I sat in the flickering firelight of the winter dusk. The women have a talk—I won't answer, nor *attempt* to, now, here, of course, for links and liaisons—the women have a talk in which the good girl learns with *dismay* that it is the life of the child that keeps her from her lover. The effect of this revelation upon her is not, to the bad girl's sense, what she expected from it. She rebels, she protests, she is far from willing to give him up. Then my young lady takes a decision—she determines to poison the child—on the calculation that suspicion will fall on her rival. She does so—and on the theory of *motive*—suspicion *does* fall on the wretched girl. There are two persons to figure as the *public*, the judging, wondering, horrified world, the doctor and a convenient older woman who has been in the first act. Suspicion descends—it is *constatée* that the child is poisoned: the question is who has done it? The Hero, *seeing* the horrible fact and believing, for the moment, the good Heroine *is* responsible, has a moment of horror and anguish, and then, to *shield* her, takes a sublime decision, tells a noble dramatic lie, assumes the guilt (since the 'motive' may be shown to have all its force for him, too) and says '*I* did it!' That I am supposing to be the end of Act II. But I am also supposing that something has happened in Act I, and something more in Act II, which have combined to lay a magical hand on the gate of the denouement. The dismissed lover of the Bad Heroine has come back at the end of Act II—come back unexpectedly and from afar—in time to catch this last declaration, to be on the spot and astounded by it. Can't I, mustn't I, in the first act, have introduced some incident between himself and his fiancée of that hour, which now comes up again as a solution of the horrible predicament? Can't he have given her something, which she has kept ever since then and used in connection with her attempt on the child's life? May not this object have been found in the child's room, near the child's person, so that he recognizes it when it is again produced? I seem to see something like *this*—that in the 1st act something on the subject of the small object in question may have passed between the doctor and himself—on the subject of its being a strange and little-known poison, of which my young man happens to have brought, from a far country, this rather valuable specimen. It is in a locket, say: some woman gave it to him. *He* gives it to the Bad Heroine, *before* she throws him over. She *uses* it in Act ii—he recognizes it in Act iii. He has in Act iii a scene with her about it. The doctor has also been in love with her—*is* in love with her up to the time of this strange exposure. The doctor's a bachelor. The 2d *amoureux* is the means of disproving the heroic lie of the Hero. In the 1st act either the 2d *amoureux or the doctor* must have emptied the locket and substituted something innocuous for the fatal fluid. The child recovers, demanding the Good Heroine, and the attempt of the Bad One is condoned and covered up by the doctor—who has aspired to her hand!—and the man who first loved her. The Hero at the *'request'* of his little daughter determines on a union with the Good Heroine; and the other woman is got off by the doctor and the 2d *amoureux*. As I so barbarously and roughly jot the story down, I seem to feel in it the stuff of a play, of the particular limited style and category that can only be dreamed of for E.C. But I <am> not so much struck with there being in it a Part for an actor manager. A moment's reflection, however, suggests to me that that is only because of my very imperfect and inarticulated way of stating the matter. *Je me fais fort* to state it again in such a manner as that the Part of the Hero will appear—will take and hold its place.

x   x   x   x   x

[*This sketch James made into a plan for a three-act play, which, according to a letter to Auguste Monod, he laid aside after only one manager had seen it. It was unused until in May 1896 he began to rework it into a novel,* The Other House. *This was sent to Clement Shorter, editor of the* Illustrated London News, *who had been persuaded by Mrs. W. K. Clifford, a novelist and a friend of James, to ask him for a serial. James had told Mrs. Clifford of his idea for 'a play "of incident"—or . . . a novel—of the same,' and he wrote Shorter in February 1896 that it would do for a 'love story' of the sort the* News *wanted. He assured the editor that he would 'endeavour to be thrilling,' and added: 'My material is such that I think I shall succeed.'*

He wrote the novel quickly, since he had not begun it at the time of this letter, and it was printed in the News from 4 July to 26 September 1896. Although Shorter said that it was not popular as a serial, it had two editions in book form, in London, in 1896 and 1897. Later James did it over again into a play, but neither the original play nor the revised version was ever acted.

The first section of the novel, easily recognizable as a possible first act for a play, states the situation substantially as the notebook outlines it. But the promise to the dying wife is announced to all the main characters as soon as it is made, and James adds a scene in which the 'Bad Heroine,' Rose Armiger, urges Tony Bream, the husband, to take the oath his wife demands, but suggests the stipulation that his vow not to remarry be binding only during the lifetime of the child. The effect of the novel depends on the character of Rose, upon the clear portrayal of her calculated determination to win Tony. Her advice to him about the promise prepares for the denouement—her murder of the child—by suggesting that from the first she is scheming to capture him. The announcement of the promise to Jean (the 'Good Heroine'), to Rose's erstwhile fiancé and the others, means that everyone involved has grounds for fear, as the story develops, lest the child be in danger from Rose. The reader's sense of her evil nature is further heightened by the fact that she is not shown as eager to take care of the child of her friend, the dead wife, but instead as a woman who does not like children and will have nothing to do with the unfortunate baby.

The changes in the plan for Part (or Act) I necessitated others in II. There can be no revelation of the promise to Jean, since she already knows of it. Consequently Rose's desperate determination cannot proceed from a meeting between her and Jean, but comes instead from her realization that Tony does not love her and from her passionate jealousy of the 'Good Heroine.' Jean refuses an eligible suitor and Rose's fear and hatred increase, and she does her best to make Tony believe that Jean is not to be trusted with the child. To disarm suspicion of herself, Rose not only tries to make Jean suspected but announces that she herself has accepted once more her former fiancé, Dennis Vidal, who has unexpectedly reappeared. Rose then murders the child, not by poison but by drowning. Tony, as in the sketch, insists that he is the murderer, to protect Jean and to salve his bad conscience about his relation to Rose.

In Part III Dennis, who has seen Rose with the child in her arms, just before the drowning, is able to exonerate both Tony and Jean. The family doctor decides to hush up the whole ugly affair, and to help in this, Dennis takes Rose away with him. He no longer loves her and he is in no danger of being implicated, but since he has appeared as her suitor and since she has announced that he has engaged himself to her, he feels in honor bound to save her, although he tells her frankly that he will never marry her.

In the original sketch, with the poison in the locket, the recovery of the child, and the breaking of the promise at its request, the story was one for melodramatic comedy. As it was written in The Other House, it is melodramatic still, but James' concentration on Rose, and his skill in showing both her coldly villainous character and her curious fascination for, and power over, the men who know her, quite separate it from comedy.

Any reader of the novel will discover other changes from the sketch, but they all relate to the creation of a dramatic action centered on Rose's scheming, her frustration, and the brutal passion that drives her to murder.

The Other House was not included by James in his collected edition, nor does it appear in the Macmillan edition of his novels and tales.]

34 De Vere Gardens, January 9th, 1894.

Last night, as I worried through some wakeful hours, I seemed to myself to catch hold of the tail of an idea that may serve as the subject of the little tale I have engaged to write for H. Harland and his *Yellow Book*.[1] It belongs—the *concetto* that occurred to me and of which this is a very rough note—to the general group of themes of which *The Private Life* is a specimen—though after all it is a thing of less accentuated fantasy. I was turning over the drama, the tragedy, the general situation of disappointed ambition—and more particularly that of the artist, the man of letters: I mean of the ambition, the pride, the passion, the idea of greatness, that has been smothered and defeated by circumstances, by the opposition of life, of fate, of character, of weakness, of folly, of misfortune; and the drama that resides in—that may be bound up with—such a situation. I thought of the tragic consciousness, the living death, the helpless pity, the deep humiliation, etc., etc., of it all. Then I thought of the forces, the reverses, the active agents to which such an ambition, such pride and passion, may succumb —before which it may have to lay down its arms: intrinsic weakness, accumulations of misfortune, failure, marriage, women, politics, death. The idea of *death* both checked and caught me; for if on the one side it means the termination of the consciousness, it means on the other the beginning of the drama in any case in which the consciousness

1. For the stories James actually did write for Henry Harland, see page 149 below.

survives. In what cases *may* the consciousness be said to survive—so that the man is the spectator of his own tragedy? In the cases of defeat, of failure, of subjection, of sacrifice to other bribes or other considerations. There came to me the fancy of a sacrifice to political life—in combination with a marriage. A young man who has dreamed that he has the genius of a poet—a young man full of dreams of artistic glory—full of brilliant gifts as well—makes, in a political milieu, a worldly, showy, advantageous marriage, a marriage that pushes him, commits him, vulgarizes him, destroys his faith in his faculty. He forsakes, for this end, a girl whom he has originally loved and who is poor and intelligent. She has been the confidante of his literary, his poetic dreams; she has listened to his verses, believed in his genius and his future. He breaks with her, in an hour of temptation, and casts his lot the other way. That is the *death* my *donnée* supposes and demands. It hasn't form and value however till one determines the manner, the form in which one imagines his 'consciousness,' his observant life, his spectatorship of his own history, standing over and becoming an element of the case. I suggest this in the shape of the survival of his relation to the woman he had originally loved. He comes back to her, at the very behest of this consciousness. The woman he marries has taken him away; but he has died, as it were, in her hands. His corpse is politically, showily, galvanized; he has successes, notorieties, children, but to himself, in the situation, he is extinct. He meets the first woman again—and the dead part of him lives again. She too has married, after a while—and her husband and her children are dead. She is surrounded with death—and yet she lives with life. The other woman—his wife— is surrounded with life, and yet she lives with death. The thing can only be, like the *Private Life,* impressionistic: with the narrator of the story as its spectator. Stated, pen in hand, the whole *concetto* strikes me as thinner and less picturesque than when it first occurred to me. I must think it over a little more and perhaps something more in the nature of an *image*—as in the *P.L.*—will come out to me. Say (it occurs to me), that my hero dies ½ way through the story—dies really —and that *this,* to the woman who still loves him, becomes the crowning sign of his 'life' for *her.* She is in mourning *pour tous les siens* and at this she goes into radiant colours.* She has him now—he is all hers. He has come to her from his blighting wife. His verses, his poems, the things he has done for *her,* must play a part in the business.

x   x   x   x   x

* [James' note] This incident, as the essence of the matter, very possible, I think, for a *very short* thing. *Vide* red morocco notebook.

[*James came back to this theme of 'death in life' and 'life in death' a year later (pp. 183-4 below).*]

34 D.V.G., *January 23d, 1894.*

Plus je vais, plus je trouve that the only balm and the only refuge, the real solution of the pressing question of life, are in this frequent, fruitful, intimate battle with the particular idea, with the subject, the possibility, the place. It's the anodyne, the escape, the boundlessly beneficent resort. No effort in this direction is vain, no confidence is idle, no surrender but is victorious.—I failed the other day, through interruption, to make a note, as I intended, of the anecdote told me some time since by Lady Gregory, who gave it me as a 'plot' and saw more in it than, I confess, I do myself. However, it is worth mentioning. (I mean that I see in it all there is—but what there is is in the rather barren [today], and dreary, frumpy direction of the pardon, the not-pardon, of the erring wife. When the stout middle-aged wife has an unmentionable 'past,' one feels how tiresome and charmless, how suggestive of mature petticoats and other frowsy properties, the whole general situation has become.) At any rate, Lady G.'s story was that of an Irish squire who discovered his wife in an intrigue. She left her home, I think, with another man—and left her two young daughters. The episode was brief and disastrous—the other man left her in turn, and the husband took her back. He covered up, hushed up her absence—perhaps moved into another part of the country, where the story was unknown; and she resumed her place at his *foyer* and in the care and supervision of her children. *But* the husband's action had been taken on an inexorable condition—that of her remaining only while the daughters were young and in want of a mother's apparent, as well as real, presence. 'I wish to avoid scandal—injury to their little lives; I don't wish them to ask questions about you that I can't answer or that I can answer only with lies. But you remain only till they are of such and such ages, to such and such a date. Then you go.' She accepts the bargain, and does everything she can, by her devotion to her children, to repair her fault. Does she hope to induce her husband to relax his rigour—or does she really accept the prospect that stares her in the face? The story doesn't say: what it does say is that the husband maintains his conditions, and the attitude of the wife, maintained also for years, avails in no degree to attenuate them. He has fixed a particular date, a particular year, and they have lived *de part et d'autre*, with her eyes upon this dreadful day. The two girls alone have been in ignorance of it, as well as of everything else. But at last the day comes—they have grown up; her work is done and she must go. I suppose there isn't much question of their 'going out'; or else that it is just this function of taking them into the world, at 17, at 18, that he judges her most unfit for. She leaves them, in short, on the stroke of the clock, and leaves them in a bewilderment and distress against which the father, surely, should have deemed it his duty to provide—which he must from afar off have seen as inevitable. The way he meets it, in Lady G.'s anecdote, at any rate, is by giving the daughters the real explanation—revealing to them the facts of the case. These facts *appal* them, have the most terrible effect upon them. They are sensitive, pure, proud, religious (Catholics); they feel stained, sickened, horrified with life, and they both go into a convent—take the veil. That was Lady G.'s anecdote. I confess that as I roughly write it out, this way, there seems to me to be more in it—in fact, its possibilities open out. It becomes, indeed, very much what one sees in it or puts in it; presenting itself even as the possible theme of a rather strong short novel—80,000 to a 100,000 words. Jotting roughly what it appears to *recéler*, or suggest. I see the spectacle of the effect on the different natures of the 2 girls. I see a kind of drama of the woman's hopes and fears. I see the question of the marriage of one of the girls or of both —and the attitude, *là-dedans*, the part played, by the young men whom it is a question of their marrying. I see one of the girls 'take after' her mother on the spot. The other, different, throws herself into religion. The 1st one, say, has *always known* the truth. The revelation has nothing new to teach her. Something doubtless resides in such a subject, and it grows, I am bound to say, as one thinks of it. The character, the strange, deep, prolonged and preserved rigour of the husband— and above all his responsibility: that of his action, his effect upon his daughters. His stupidity, his worthlessness, his pedantry of consistency, his want of conception, of imagination of how they will feel, will take the thing. The absence of imagination his main characteristic. Then the young man—the lover of one of them—and his part in the drama, his knowledge in advance, his dread of it. He is the lover of the girl who goes into religion. The other one—reckless, cynical, with the soul of a *cocotte* has another tie: a secret relation with some bad fellow to whom, say, she gives herself. And the mother—and her lover? What becomes of her? The lover, say, has waited for her?—or the husband relents after he has seen the ravage made by his inhuman action and is reunited to her on the ruins of their common domestic happiness. x x x x x

Quite the subject of a story as well as of a play—it occurs to me— may be the idea, of the dramatic form of which I the other day commenced a rough sketch under the *étiquette* of The Promise. Oh yes, there is a story in that—a story of from 80,000 to a 100,000 words, which would greatly resemble a play. In the story wouldn't one make the thing begin by a visit to the young wife from her stepmother, the stepmother whom she hated and from whom she had suffered? This lady would meet in the house—it would be the first incident or scene—the other woman, the bad girl, the heroine of the later events.

x   x   x   x   x

[Here James reverts to his plot for The Other House, seeing in it possibilities for a story as well as for the play it had originally suggested (pp. 138-43 above). In the novel he does not begin with the stepmother—she and her visit are only referred to—and, recognizing that his 'Bad Heroine' was to be the center of the action, he soon confronts the two heroines in a scene in which they are at once contrasted, one as an embodiment of innocence and the other as the exponent, at least potentially, of evil.]

Another incident—'subject'—related to me by Lady G. was that of the eminent London clergyman who on the Dover-to-Calais steamer, starting on his wedding tour, picked up on the deck a letter addressed to his wife, while she was below, and finding it to be from an old lover, and very ardent (an engagement—a rupture, a relation, in short), of which he never had been told, took the line of sending her, from Paris, straight back to her parents—without having touched her—on the ground that he had been deceived. He ended, subsequently, by taking her back into his house to live, but *never* lived with her as his wife. There is a drama in the various things, for her, to which that situation —that night in Paris—might have led. Her immediate surrender to some one else, etc., etc., etc. x x x x x

It reminds me of something I meant to make a note of at the time —what I heard of the W.B.'s when their strange rupture (in Paris, too) immediately after their almost equally strange marriage became known. He had agreed, according to the legend, to bring her back to London for the *season*, for a couple of months of dinners—of *showing*, of sitting at the head of his table and wearing the family diamonds. This, in point of fact, he did—and when the season was over he turned her out of the house. There is a story, a short story, in that.

x   x   x   x   x

34 *De Vere Gdns., February 3d, 1894.* Could not something be done with the idea of the great (the distinguished, the celebrated) artist—

man of letters he must, in the case, be—who is tremendously made up to, *fêted*, written to for his autograph, portrait, etc., and yet with whose work, in this age of advertisement and newspaperism, this age of interviewing, not one of the persons concerned has the smallest acquaintance? It would have the merit, at least, of corresponding to an immense reality—a reality that strikes me every day of my life. If I can devise a little action, a little story, that will fit and express the phenomenon I mean, I think the thing would be really worth while. The phenomenon is the one that is brought home to one every day of one's life by the ravenous autograph-hunters, lion-hunters, exploiters of publicity; in whose number one gets the impression that a person knowing and *loving* the thing itself, the work, is simply never to be found. (The little tale might be called *The Lion*.) It should—the whole situation—be resolved, somehow, into a little concrete drama. The drama must reside in a close, an intense connection between the author's personal situation and this question of whether any one (in the crowd of lionizers) does know, really, when it comes to the point, the first word of the work the hero's reputation for having produced which is the very basis of their agitation. Something must depend, for him, on their knowing it—depend, perhaps, for his honour, for his memory (something important, I mean, something intimate, something vital), and the revelation of their chattering ignorance only becomes complete. They must *kill him, hein?*—kill him with the very fury of their selfish exploitation, and then not really have an idea of what they killed him *for*. *Trouve donc, mon bon*, an ingenious and compact little action, which will bring all this out. I seem to see, dimly, the possibilities of the thing in the situation of a man to whom public recognition has come late in life. The whole intention of the tale should be admirably satiric, ironic. The bewildered old hero is murdered by the interviewers—but the *consciousness of the moral* should probably reside only in the person telling the story, a friend, a companion, an observer and spectator of the drama. Shouldn't it, the little drama, take, in part, the form of this narrator's defending, attempting to defend—and attempting vainly—his precious friend against this invasion of the interviews, the portraitists and such; to defend him in particular against the appropriation of some arch and ferocious lion-huntress? This part of the story presents itself to me as tolerably easy to conceive; the difficulty is in what one may be able to find to express the crisis, as it were; the *other* half of the action—to embody the *exposure*, as it were, of the mere selfish interests on which the lionization rests. The whole thing might rest on a complete mistake and blunder as to the nature, the *form*, of the man's work. I *see*, however, the essence of the thing; and the party at the country-house, and the ultra-modern hostess, and

the autograph hunters and interviewers—and the collapse, the extinction of the hero, and the possible (for the interviewers) simultaneously
rising star: the alternative of that A.B., the new woman who writes
under a man's name, or B.A., the new man who (in order to be in
the swim—profit by the predominance of the women) writes under a
woman's. Say, too, the battle (of the narrator, the friend, the lover,
the knower, the protector) with the destructive horde, with the lion-
hunting hostess in particular, be the result of the hero's having imparted to him, read to him, talked of to him, the project of a splendid
new unwritten thing which he wants time and strength still to do, and
which the young man, said friend, yearns to *save* him, to keep him
alive for. x x x x x

I seem to catch hold (Feb. 9th) for the foregoing subject of the two or
three indispensable joints or hinges. Suppose I call it *The Death of
the Lion,* and make my narrator, my critical *reflector* of the whole
thing, a young intending interviewer who has repented, come to consciousness, fallen away. 'I had simply what is called a change of heart—
and it began, I suppose, when they sent me back my manuscript'—
that's the way I see it begin.

[*James began his discussion of* The Death of the Lion, *in the preface
to* The Lesson of the Master, *with an account of his association with
the Yellow Book. The Death of the Lion had the leading place in
its opening number (April 1894); and James also contributed to its pages
The Coxon Fund (July 1894) and The Next Time (July 1895). He was
to feel uneasy about some of his associates in 'the small square lemon-
coloured quarterly,' but this shows in his preface only to the extent of
obliquely expressed relief that Aubrey Beardsley had never been stimulated to a perverse illustration of 'my comparatively so incurious text.'
    What he was most pleased to recall was his gratitude to Harland for
allowing him as much space as he wanted. That had seemed to James
to inaugurate 'the millennium' for the short story. 'One had so often
known this product to struggle, in one's hands, under the rude prescrip-
tion of brevity at any cost, with the opposition so offered to its really
becoming a story, that my friend's emphasized indifference to the
arbitrary limit of length struck me, I remember, as the fruit of the finest
artistic intelligence.' He remembered too how he and the young editor
'had been at one . . . on the truth that the forms of wrought things,
in this order, were, all exquisitely and effectively, the things.' With the
example of France to refer to, they had also shared as their 'ideal' among
forms that of 'the beautiful and blest nouvelle.' The Death of the Lion
and The Next Time, running to between fourteen and fifteen thousand*

words, may still be regarded as short stories of the Jamesian order; but The Coxon Fund, with its somewhat more than twenty thousand, has passed over into the class of the nouvelle.

He observed that these three pieces 'have this in common that they deal all with the literary life, gathering their motive, in each case, from some noted adventure, some felt embarrassment, some extreme predicament, of the artist enamoured of perfection, ridden by his idea or paying for his sincerity.' He added further that though most of his work had depended upon 'some pencilled note on somebody else's case,' here he had drawn preponderantly, as in his other stories dealing with writers, 'from the depths of the designer's own mind.'

But how little he was ever inclined to treat his own case subjectively or with self-pity may be remarked from the plot and tone of The Death of the Lion. The story finds its crisis in the fatal illness of Neil Paraday, who has been worn out by the fatuous lion-hunters that have pursued him after his sudden vogue. Although the intelligent young critic who tells the story gives expression to Flaubert's 'refrain about the hatred of literature,' the handling of the whole is lightly ironic, even comic. Mrs. Weeks Wimbush, 'wife of the boundless brewer,' is also 'proprietress of the universal menagerie' at Prestidge. There she has lured not only poor Paraday but also such flashes of the moment as Guy Walsingham, author of Obsessions, whose real name is Miss Collop, and Dora Forbes, author of The Other Way Round, who turns out to be a gentleman with showy knickerbockers and a big red moustache. As Paraday lies dying upstairs, the guests chatter about his latest masterpiece, though none of them has read beyond page twenty, and though Lady Augusta Minch has lost the manuscript in which he set down the 'scheme' for what was to have been his next great work.]

34 De Vere Gardens, Sunday, February 17th, 1894.

Last night, at Mrs. Crackanthorpe's, Stopford Brooke suggested to me 2 little ideas.

(1) The man (à propos of S.B.) who has become afraid of himself when alone—vaguely afraid of his own company, personality, disposition, character, presence, fate; so that he plunges into society, noise, sound, the sense of diversion, distraction, protection, connected with the presence of others, etc.

(2) The notion of the young man who marries an older woman and who has the effect on her of making her younger and still younger, while he himself becomes her age. When he reaches the age that *she* was (on their marriage), she has gone back to the age that *he* was.—Mightn't this be altered (perhaps) to the idea of cleverness and

stupidity? A clever woman marries a deadly dull man, and loses and loses her wit as he shows more and more. Or the idea of a *liaison*, suspected, but of which there is no proof but this transfusion of some idiosyncrasy of one party to the being of the other—this exchange or conversion? The fact, the secret, of the *liaison* might be revealed in that way. The two things—the two elements—beauty and 'mind,' might be correspondingly, concomitantly exhibited as in the history of two related couples—with the opposition, in each case, that would help the thing to be dramatic.

x   x   x   x   x

[*James came back to this idea for* The Sacred Fount (*p. 275 below*).]

There came to me a night or two ago the notion of a young man (young, presumably), who has something—some secret sorrow, trouble, fault—to *tell* and can't find the *recipient*. x x x x x

[*Some of the phases through which this Hawthornesque abstraction passed before reaching its final embodiment in* A Round of Visits (1910) *may be remarked under the entries for* 21 April 1894, 7 May 1898, *and* 16 February 1899 (*pp.* 158, 266, 281 *below*).]

March 16th, 1894. Note at 1st leisure the idea suggested to me by George Meredith's amusing picture—the other night (Boxhill, March 11th)—of the bewilderment of A.M. in the presence of the immense pretensions to 'conquest' (to 'having repeatedly overthrown Venus herself') of A.A. It suggested to me a subject—or at any rate a type, a study—the man who celebrates his own great feats and triumphs of love, his irresistibility. The confrontation of another man with it, a man who has really *had* immense successes—in his younger past—and has kept deeply silent about them: the mystification, sadness, comedy, etc., of this (and especially of the A.A. type), seems to contain the germ of something that might be threshed out.—

[*James continued to try the possibilities of this theme* (*pp.* 155-8 *below*).]

Casa Biondetti, Venice, April 17th, 1894.

Here I sit, at last, after many interruptions, distractions, and defeats, with some little prospect of getting a clear time to settle down to work again. The last six weeks, with my 2 or 3 of quite baffling indisposition before I left London, have been a period of terrific sacrifice to the ravenous Moloch of one's endless personal, social relations—one's eternal exposures, accidents, disasters. *Basta.*

x   x   x   x   x

All the little subjects I have lately noted here seem to me good and happy—that is, essentially susceptible of further threshing out and development. x x x x x

In reading Dykes Campbell's book on Coleridge—it is so good that one almost forgets how much better a little more of the power of evocation might have made it—I was infinitely struck with the suggestiveness of S.T.C.'s figure—wonderful, admirable figure—for pictorial treatment. What a subject some particular cluster of its relations would make for a little story, a small vivid picture. There was a point, as I read, at which I seemed to see a little story—to have a quick glimpse of the possible drama. Would not such a drama necessarily be the question of the acceptance by someone—someone with something important at stake—of the general *responsibility* of rising to the height of accepting him for what he is, recognizing his rare, anomalous, magnificent, interesting, curious, tremendously suggestive character, vices and all, with all its imperfections on its head, and *not* being guilty of the pedantry, the stupidity, the want of imagination, of fighting him, deploring him in the details—failing to recognize that one *must* pay for him and that on the whole he is magnificently worth it. The individual whom I have described as having something at stake *does* pay for him, as it were—whereas there is another who doesn't, who won't. The figure of the rare eccentric, the bone of contention himself, is so (potentially) fine, I think, that one must hold one's little story—*je tiens mon effet*—from the moment one puts one's hand on the action that throws him into relief. Does it not seem to one that that action is, to a certain extent and in its general outline, fundamentally designated, indicated—that one puts one's hand on it as soon as one disengages that degree and quantity of it that are *implied* in the very personality and presence, the *obviousness* of fate, of the hero? He has the great Coleridge-quality—he is a splendid, an incomparable *talker.* He has the other qualities—I needn't name them here, I see them admirably, all, with the high picturesqueness of their anomalous, their baffling, despairing, exasperating cluster round the fine central genius. *Or*, what is 'obvious' in the action required, the action capable of making the thing a little masterpiece in 20,000 words, is precisely the element of opposition in the two modes, the unimaginative and the imaginative, the literal and the constructive manner of dealing with him. If I can embody this opposition in a little drama containing adequately the magic of suspense, <make it> amount effectively to a story, I may do something capable of being admirable. It is just this story, this chaste but workable and evincible young freshness of the inevitable, that I must shut myself up with in the sacredest and divinest of all private commerces. Live with it a little, *mon bon*, and the happy child will be born. x x x x x

The contender, the believer, the acceptor of responsibility, must, tolerably clearly, be a woman. The forces she is opposed to are the man's own belongings. What belongings can these be—on the assumption imperative, I think, as a solution of certain difficulties, of his being *young*, a wonder of *promise*, with all his infirmities already budding and all his genius already sensible to those susceptible of feeling it? (When I say 'young,' can he be less than 40? I must remember that I must give some of the people time for exhausted patience—for the determination of their disbeliefs and chuckings-up.) He must have a wife—a wife who divorces him? Yes, and the girl, the heroine, must incur imputations, by association, by induction, in regard to her own virtue. One of the sacrifices she makes is a big sacrifice of money? Assuredly, and the drama, the story, is the anecdote of this sacrifice, of the determination of it, in the face of scandal, etc.—the money being a high responsible trust. The trust is a bequest—an 'endowment of research' on the part of a rich, well-meaning relative, a woman (Bostonian?), an aunt, a cousin, or even simply a friend who feels her responsibilities to culture. The story may thus be excellently named *The So-and-So Fund*, of which the girl has, in a manner, the administration. Let it be constituted *after* the girl has made the acquaintance of the hero, begun to be interested in him and to wonder privately, secretly, with a certain conscious diffidence, whether he isn't one of those great ones who should have something done for them. She keeps this dawning conception from her relative (in pure innocence), at the time that relative (in dying and perhaps unable to be explicit about all her testamentary intentions) delegates to her summarily, leaving it, as a high expression of · affectionate trust in her wisdom, partly to her discretion, the execution, the administration of a certain legacy in a particular spirit already discussed with her, explained to her. (*The Coxon Fund.*) Put Saltram (Coleridge—or something like) on his feet from the first: present him to the girl, make her get her impression. Also his wife and the question of their divorce. He is staying with someone (à la Coleridge) whom she goes to see; the wife (of the host, patron) has been a former friend of hers. She appeals to Mrs. Saltram *not* to divorce him—appeals before her aunt's death: I set down things as they occur to me. She is engaged to a young man approved by her aunt and who is co-administrator of the fund with her. She therefore makes a sacrifice of marriage. He marries sister of Mrs. Saltram. The action, therefore, is the contention between the girl and her young man about the application of the fund—and it must be *d'un serré*. x x x x x

It must indeed be *d'un serré!* but after a single morning (April 18th) spent in starting the above (*The Coxon Fund*) and starting it fairly well, I recognize that the theme is far too fine and brave to be spoiled by mutilation—compression into the compass of 20,000 words. Indeed that operation is utterly impracticable—I see the folly of undertaking it. 20,000? A good 100,000 are already required. Some day it shall have them. It is so much to the good. Let it stand there as the admirable subject of a fine short (1 vol.) novel, all ready to my hand; and let me for my present job address myself patiently to something much simpler.

[The Coxon Fund, which appeared in the second issue of the Yellow Book (July 1894), owed its title to Lady Coxon, the aunt of the American girl who becomes so interested in Frank Saltram's genius. To account for her eccentricity in establishing such a fund, James made her not only a Bostonian but a 'thin transcendental' one. Although she has been in England forty years, her 'happy frumpy' marriage with Sir Gregory Coxon 'never really materialised her.'

In the preface to The Lesson of the Master, James discussed some of the probems raised for the writer of fiction when he bases one of his creations upon an historical figure. His imagination had been richly fertilized by the account of Coleridge's personality; but Saltram 'pretends to be of his great suggester no more than a dim reflexion and above all a free rearrangement.' James' main point was that 'more interesting still than the man—for the dramatist at any rate—is the S. T. Coleridge type; so what I was to do was merely to recognize the type, to borrow it, to re-embody and freshly place it; an ideal under the law of which I could but cultivate a free hand.' His criterion, therefore, for success in such matters was not that the result should be like its model, but rather that the model should have been transformed into something fresh, in proportion to its saturation in the novelist's imagination.

The Coxon Fund was one story in which James did not exceed the limitations of space that he first conceived. How he managed to treat its complex theme in a little over twenty thousand words is clarified by his entries for 25 and 29 April 1894 (pp. 160-63 below). There he works out the details in more nearly their final form.]

Casa Biondetti, April 19th, 1894.

The idea I noted here the other day—the situation suggested to me by an allusion of George Meredith—to A.A., *Vainqueur de Vénus*, and A.M.'s confused, anxious consideration of him (he, of so different a type, who had *really* been loved), recurs to me as an excellent little theme. It belongs, however, I think, essentially to the ironic, to the order of fine comedy, satiric observation, and is not exactly what I want for a story of emotion, a history of some passion, some tender relation. What it is, and what it is capable of being, I must add, is only determinable after it shall have been mated with some action, some element requisite for making it a tale. As I have it now it is only an idea—and everything is wanting to make it a story. The situation, primarily, is wholly wanting, and the 'moral' wholly to be disengaged. There must of course be a woman in it, or the thing has no sense. It is the action of the little drama that must reveal itself—the relation to the real forces of love (i.e., to some woman or some women) as well as to each other that the 2 men find themselves in. What essentially *takes* me in the *concetto* is, I think, the chance to have a fling at the general attitude of swagger and egotism in this particular matter—to have a dab at the *French* attitude, as I may call it for convenience. What I want to oppose to it dramatically is something that I may call for convenience the English attitude. I must, *voyons*, have something at stake for my genuine man—something in operation, in question; some passion, some devotion, some success—something perhaps that comes back out of the past, the past of his own personal triumphs. He WONDERS so at the little man's own achievements, *vanteries*, successes, confidences, exhibitions—is stupefied, mystified, depressed by them (being simple, impressible, etc., in his credulity), so that they make him say that if this is the kind of person that women succumb to, his own history must be all a delusion and a myth. Various little possibilities seem to loom and hover before me—disengaging themselves faintly in the divine way, the dear old blessed healing, consoling way in which they *always* respond to real solicitation and the pure, generous loyalty of which (one's own grateful sense of it), brings tears to my eyes as I write. Isn't there a potentiality of 3 men instead of 2—to give me the YOUNG man whose aspirations are nipped in the bud—by which I mean discouraged by the spectacle of the anomaly of the prosperous *vantard*, rendered 'mythic' to him in the future, as those of the elder man, originally conceived, are rendered 'mythic' (*to him*) in the past. Confraternity of these two men, exchange of bewilderments, mutual communication of melancholies and questions. Doesn't the 'action' become, this way, in *spite* of themselves, in spite of their modesty, their discovery of the falsity of the pretensions of the other? I want to establish, to illustrate, somehow, that these pretensions (i.e., of the kind), are *not* the real thing—that the real thing is silence and sanctity. I want to 'do' the egotist, the self-celebrator. I want to make the women themselves bring about the denouement, testify to my moral: I want it to come *by* them. My elder man is there with something that comes back to him out of his past—my younger one is there with something that *may* come to him out of his future. I seem to see my elder man coming back at some bidding of his conscience, that of some memory of an old wrong done —coming back devoutly and tenderly to repair it. He thinks he has hurt a woman in his youth—he thinks he has hurt two women. He comes back (from India?) to see *which* woman he has hurt (i.e., jilted, disappointed) most, in order that he may, if possible, marry her, make it all up to her now. My notion is that his reflections (upon A.A.) make him think he has exaggerated his responsibility and his compunction. I seem to get hold of the slippery tail of a fine idea in seeing something in the nature of a demonstration of the beauty and virtue of silence, and in particular of this truth that it is in their very movement of flight for *defense*, as it were, that the women have thrown themselves into the PRETENSE of victimization by A.A.—because they know he will betray them. He is their shield against the men who are silent—that is his very function: and it is only because there is nothing to betray that they let him appear to betray it. May I not imagine *this* position—these 2 positions—for my older and my younger man respectively—that the woman whom the former wishes to make the reparation to lends herself to A.A. from pride (precisely because she still so loves her old 'wronger'), and the woman whom the young man wishes to make up to (she must be married), seeks the same refuge from dread—dread of succumbing to the young man, the instinct of letting him think she belongs to another man, so that he may not pursue her. The *vantard* is USED, in the manner the most disrespectful of himself—that is the real ironic fact about him—and that is the moral of my little comedy, which will be difficult, thank God!, to write. The *vantard*, the swaggerer, is *always* used—while it is the silent man who *uses*; that is the generalization, the salient truth. Is it all too alembicated, too subordinate and subtle? I ask myself this, and the right answer seems to be that it *needn't* be, and that if I really take hold of the thing *autant cela qu'autre chose*. If it remains muddled, and vague—abstract and suggested—it will be 'too subtle'; if it is a clear,

[156]

straight, lucid action, a thing after my own heart, I don't see why
the little drama of it shouldn't be fine and interesting. The *form* of
this drama is what I have to determine: if it is happily determined
the sense of it all will come out, vividly, of itself. Make your little story,
find your little story, tell your little story, and leave the rest to the
gods! Ah, how the gods are on one's side the moment one enters the
enchanted realm! Ah, consoling, clarifying air of *work*—inestimable
sacred hours! Every doubt of them is an outrage—every act of faith is a
triumph! x x x x x

My two sincere men must be united, somehow—united by a meeting,
by a friendship, by a confidence or a series of confidences; and there
must not be too great a difference in their age. Say one is fifty-three
and the other, the 'young' one, thirty-six. The elder man, I think, must
be a soldier; convenient, indispensable attribution! The younger has
political aspirations. They must meet first before they both meet the
swaggerer. But the swagger<er> must have had some contact with
one of them—the swaggerer too must have political aspirations. Say
he is indeed the only one that has them, and that my young man of 36
is something else, a barrister, even a city man. There is perhaps indeed
no particular need of his being something else—they may be different
types of the political *genus*. This, however, is manageable enough: what
requires consideration is the particular plausibility of circumstance in
which the men are brought together. Say the two other men are fellow
contributors to a newspaper which the General (or Colonel) has bought.
Or say the swaggerer—or one of the others, the man of 36—is a diplomatist. *C'est encore bien* arrangeable—for these are details; what is
of the essence is the whole question, difficult to present to English
readers, of the 'sexual' side of the business, the element of pursuit,
possession, conquest, etc., on the men's part and of danger, response,
desire, surrender, etc., on the part of the women. However, one makes
one's appeal in all this, as one has always made it, to frankness, truth
and taste; to the *interesting*, as usual, wherever it resides and abides.
I seem, at any rate, to see *both* the women as antecedently connected
with the General—the one whom the younger man is in love with as
the second of the two women whom he has had compunctions
about. x x x x x

Somehow, this morning (April 20th) the whole frank, bright, manly,
human little comedy—in its initial steps at least—seems to come to me.
Begin it—try it a little; put your hand into the paste!

x   x   x   x   x

[157]

Casa Biondetti, April 21st, 1894.

I *have* put my hand to it—I did yesterday, in a morning's limited scribble; but the subject, which is good, doesn't somehow speak to me for this particular purpose. It isn't the quite *objective* thing I want. The thing I want will come—will come 'in its glory': the quiet, generous, patient mornings will bring it. They are everything; or only want to be, beg to be, so far as they are encouraged and permitted. Oh, soul of my soul—oh, sacred beneficence of *doing! Ohne Hast, ohne Rast!* Consider many things and open the hospitable mind! Look at this, judge of that and turn over the other! It all helps and fructifies and enriches x x x x x

There is apparently something worth thinking of in the idea I barely noted, a few weeks ago, of the young man with something on his mind —the young man with a secret, a worry, a misery, a burden, an oppression, that he carries about with him and suffers from the incapacity to tell—from the want of a confidant, a listening ear and answering heart, an intelligent receptacle for. He *tries* to communicate it, in the belief that it will relieve him. He goes from house to house and from person to person, but finds everywhere an indifference, a preoccupation too visible, a preoccupation, on the part of every one, with other things, with their own affairs, troubles, joys, pleasures, interests—an atmosphere that checks, chills, paralyses the possibility of any appeal. Some have pleasures they're entirely concerned with, others have troubles of their own which he thinks they make a strange excessive fuss about— being so much slighter and smaller than his. So he wanders, so he goes—with his burden only growing heavier—looking vainly for the ideal sympathy, the waiting, expectant, responsive recipient. My little idea has been that he doesn't find it; but that he encounters instead a sudden appeal, an appeal more violent, as it were, more pitiful even than his own has had it in it to be. He meets in a word a *demand* where he had at last been looking for a supply—a demand which embodies the revelation of a trouble which he immediately feels to be greater than his own. In the presence of this communication which he has to receive instead of giving it he forgets his own, ceases to need to make a requisition for it. His own ache, in a word, passes from him in his pity and his sympathy; he is healed by doing himself what he wanted to have done *for* him. Such is the little idea—which is perhaps as pretty as another. The charm and interest of the thing must necessarily be in the picture—the little panorama of his vain contacts and silent appeals, the view of his troubled spirit and of the people, the places, he successively turns to only to find that everywhere his particular grief is a false note. No one says to him—it *occurs* to no one to say: 'You've got something very painful on your mind—do tell us if we can help you—and what it is!' Don't I see that there is one person whom he has been counting upon most, inevitably a woman, a woman whom he has been occupied with, confusedly, anxiously, tenderly, whom he hasn't been sure about and as to his feeling for whom he has been by no means sure? He thinks it clears up that feeling that now, instinctively, it is to *her* his imagination turns most. He takes this as a *sign*, this confidence that he has in her; declaring to himself that if she meets it it will settle the matter for him, prove to him that she *is* the fine creature he has not been certain she is. She is unfortunately absent—away from London, and he is intensely impatient for her return. It is in the meantime, as a substitute, as a resource that *may* meet his case, that he goes to the other places, the other people. I think I see the little story begin with his visit to her house, after his grief, his disaster: his 1st movement is toward her. I describe, don't I?, his discomfiture, his disappointment as he learns that she is away, has gone to Paris—gone for some time, the servant not knowing when she will be back. The young man has absolutely expected to find her—had reason to count upon it. Her absence is really connected with the great trouble of her own which he doesn't know or suspect. He turns away from her door, deeply dejected and disappointed. He must go about with his burden for a week or ten days—trying vainly to *place* it, to dispose of it. Then a sort of intuition, a hope against hope, after his other failures and discomfitures, prompts him to return, to see if by a miracle she may not have happened to come back. She has—she *has!* and they are so soon face to face. Of extreme moment, and quite the keystone of my little arch, the question of what each of these two 'troubles' consists of. They must both be grave, painful, ugly; belong more or less to the horrors, the shocks, the treacheries, the disillusionments, the real sufferings of life. I must put my hand very exactly upon them; for as I make this blessed little statement I seem to see that my situation does hold something, that the thing is distinctly, within its dimensions, a subject. I seem to see *this* element in it—that the thing on which the woman makes her appeal, her demand to him (turns the tables on him, as it were), proves a matter as to which his participation, his knowledge, his compassion can bring him no profit, no personal advantage. If he is relieved by pity for another it is by pity for the sake of pity—not for the sake of the reward his pity will bring him. To illustrate simply, off-hand, what I mean, let me suppose that she is a married woman, a woman living apart from her husband x x x x x

[*James treated, in* A Round of Visits, *the theme of unexpected re-lease from pain through pity for the greater suffering of someone else. But he did not develop the plot suggested here. He did not begin to find the situation that he finally used until five years later (pp. 281-2 below).*]

Casa Biondetti, Venice, April 25th, 1894.

I have committed myself to the *Yellow Book* for 20,000 words, and I swing back, on 2d thought, to the idea of *The Coxon Fund*—asking myself if I can't treat it in a way to make it go into that limited space. I want to do something very good for the Y.B., and this subject strikes me as superior. The formula for the presentation of it in 20,000 words is to make it an *Impression*—as one of Sargent's pictures is an impression. That is, I must do it from my own point of view—that of an imagined observer, participator, chronicler. I must picture it, summarize it, impressionize it, in a word—compress and confine it by making it the picture of what I see. That has the great advantage, which perhaps after all would have been an imperative necessity, of rendering the picture of Saltram an implied and suggested thing. I should probably have had, after all, to have come to this—should have found it impossible to content myself with any literal record—anything merely narrative, with the detail of narrative. But if the thing becomes *what I see*—what is it I see—in the way of action, sequence, story, climax? The subject remains the same, but the great hinge must be more salient perhaps, and the whole thing simplified. A strong subject, a rich subject *summarized*—that is my indispensable formula and memento. x x x x x

Casa Biondetti, April 29th. I have begun my little tale, and written neatly enough, upwards of 3000 words—3300 rather say—p. 28 of MS. —stating, putting sufficiently well *en scène* my Frank Saltram and my George Gravener—but having left less than 17,000 to do all the rest. This will be sufficient, however, if I get the proper *grasp* of my drama. *Voyons un peu, mon bon*, what that grasp must be. I don't fail one jot of the faith—nor flinch in it—that the subject is admirable; but that very sense it is that makes me particularly nervous. I want so to squeeze out of it the perfection of a condensed action. Essentially, the pivot and climax of that action is the girl's decision, in circumstances of the highest import for her, that Saltram's 'morality,' i.e., his conduct, don't in such an exceptional case, matter. It seems to me that what I must get is an *intensification* of the drama of her situation by making doubly-much depend and hinge upon her determination.

That she forfeits her lover goes without saying; but she must do more than this—she must forfeit money, somehow; forfeit the money of the 'fund.' The manner in which she does this—the special provisions of the founder—I shall arrive at with a little patience. What I must CONSISTENTLY establish is the summarized *exhibition* of Saltram's incorrigibility—make the climax of it, as it were, match with the climax of her exaltation about his deserving the endowment. The picture becomes the picture of the opposition of these two states. I see that my leaps and elisions, my flying bridges and great comprehensive loops (in a vivid, admirable sentence or two), must be absolutely bold and masterly. I see, I think, that the thing must consist, that my safety and facility must reside, in a division into numbered sections which insist on remaining short and succeed in being rich and each one a fine dramatic and pictorial step; so that, each making from 12 to 15 pp. of my MS., there shall be some 15 in all. I think I catch my next step and a happy idea in making *Saltram himself* put the girl in relation with the narrator—that makes a long *enjambée*. That is III—she doesn't then know George Gravener; but she is presented, I introduce her, and she makes her first impression, for me, and gets her 1st as regards Frank Saltram. Four or five years have elapse<d>, and *two*, say, must elapse before the next section—the IV. This is a rough computation of everything; but it helps me, divinely, to make it. What it presses to interweave *quickly* is the element of the eccentric will-making aunt; and what it presses above all to render lucid is the terms of her will and the precise nature and degree of Saltram's want of character—the IMAGE of his laxity, his abandonment *des siens*, his want of all the qualities of will, exemplified in some deep vice, some abyss. There must be *one whole brief section* devoted to an impressionism of the beauty of his personal genius and the kindling effect of his talk. Perhaps I can't make IV, at that stage, comprehensive enough without making it both III and IV. The most treatable-in-a-short-compass infirmity that I can give him is his abandonment *des siens*—his intolerance of the family tie. He must endure *no liens*—and he must have NATURAL CHILDREN. The section about his genius must deal with the NOBLENESS of his intellect—his lectures, his *conférences*. May the girl not turn up at a *lecture?*—slip in that way first? I must care about the girl—but I mustn't get her. The girl must have met Mrs. Saltram—must have known her. Mrs. Saltram must have done something for the girl's aunt. That's why she has come to the lecture—to the *conférence*. There must be one at which Saltram himself has failed—through being drunk—through being 'off.' *That* is the one at which the girl and the narrator meet—*that* is III. She must, in regard to her aunt's bequest, have an option—a discretion. She is not *travelling* with her aunt; she has come out to see her. There are certain good little reasons which I think *prevail* for making her American. Though in relation (of help given) with Mrs. Saltram, the aunt never *dreams* of *his* being the sort of person who may be, or become, the object of her bounty. She is vague, highly disapproving about him—as an element in Mrs. Saltram's life. She can *only* be an 'eccentric.' I don't see how I can manage the question of the girl's option unless I make the question of the bequest for the fund come after her engagement, and during it. I must meet her at the (failure) lecture—and she mustn't *there* see Saltram. She must only hear about him from me. I must have a little talk with her—to explain. Then she disappears—the time elapses. I must have put her *au courant*—about everything. The III may open with her appeal to me to know if Mr. Saltram will really come; or with the words: 'If that first night was one of the liveliest, or at any rate was the freshest, of my exaltations, there was another, four years later, that was one of my disgusts. He had been announced to lecture (in the little St. J.'s Wood Assembly Rooms) but he didn't turn up'—or words to that effect. I *tell* the strange young lady—the pretty American girl—more or less about him. That's a short III. She also tells me how she comes to be there—and this strikes the note of the eccentric aunt—all in the III. Oh, the minimum of dialogue! The girl disappears—till IV; or till later. *Je crois que je tiens* my element of the Coxon bequest: Ah, *miséricorde divine*, ah, exquisite art and privilege and joy! The girl has the assurance of money— or thinks she has—and it is on this basis, the basis of what her father will be able to do for her, that she becomes engaged to George Gravener. After her engagement her aunt, who is not very rich and has some other claims, tells her of the provision existing in a will already made, a provision for the endowment of a fund for the disinterested pursuit of truth—the formula to be made perfectly felicitous. It doesn't at first seem to cover Saltram's case at all: it only becomes susceptible of this afterward by the girl's interpretation. The aunt, *on the girl's engagement,* offers to alter her will and give her the money instead—but she *declines* (after a discussion with her lover)—can't bear to deprive struggling merit of the advantage of the endowment. Tension of Gravener's attitude—*he* doesn't like it, and would much rather she would take the money. But he swallows the sacrifice—is consoled by the hopes from the father. The aunt is so pleased with the girl's response that, as a great compliment and honour, she makes her an administrator of the fund—a trustee, an executrix. She then— the aunt—dies and the marriage is retarded a little. Then the girl's father either dies or fails—or both; she loses all her prospects—all save £500—or

[162]

less—a year. This retards the marriage and produces a certain luke-warmness on Gravener's part. *Then* the girl—or before this—makes the full acquaintance of Saltram's talk. She must do so just *as* her father fails. Gravener wants her at least to dispose of it so that Mrs. Saltram shall get the use of it. But her reflection—objection? 'It's for *him*— how else does it meet the idea of the bequest?' Gravener makes it a condition that she doesn't do that with it. *She may even keep the money*—somehow; ARRANGE THIS. Yes, her knowledge of Mrs. Saltram, her wrongs, her story, her representations, which I work in with *my* corresponding knowledge, must pervade the part stretching from the lecture-night to her real meeting with Saltram; and it must be through Mrs. Saltram that I partly know these dispositions—incidents, conditions. Query?—doesn't this almost dispense with *my* knowing Gravener? No!!

[Here we can see again how James' notebooks served him as a pre-liminary means of clarifying the basis for his narrative. In the finished story there is far less space given to Lady Coxon than the passage above might suggest, and the tension and break between Ruth Anvoy and George Gravener is briefly sketched rather than presented at length. James kept the detail of the narrator's having previously known Gravener—at Cambridge—in order to bring all his characters into relation around a central point.

He worked out a remarkably symmetrical structure of twelve short chapters of almost equal length. But the chief device by which he kept this story within its neat compass was by holding to his formula of 'a rich subject summarized.' In particular his presentation of Saltram is nearly all indirect. He is hardly ever on the scene. His brilliant talk and erratic actions are foreshortened through reports by the others. No wonder that James singled out The Coxon Fund as meeting his test for the nouvelle, of preserving 'economy' and yet sacrificing 'no real value.' 'A marked example of the possible scope, at once, and the possible neatness of the nouvelle, it takes its place for me in a series of which the main merit and sign is the effort to do the complicated thing with a strong brevity and lucidity—to arrive, on behalf of the multiplicity, at a certain science of control.'

As is the case with several of James' stories dealing with the prob-lems of the artist, the tone of The Coxon Fund is less serious than the situation might have produced. James hardly dealt here with the tragedy or suffering involved in the waste of genius. His handling was on the plane of social comedy, and his conclusion was again ironic. The fund did Saltram no good. 'Its magnificence, alas, as all the world

now knows, quite quenched him; it was the beginning of his decline. . . The very day he found himself able to publish he wholly
ceased to produce.']

Casa Biondetti, Venice, May 13th, 1894.

I am struck, in reading in the *Fortnightly Review* of May, 1894,
an article on 'English and French Manners,' with there being in these
lines, perhaps, something of a 'subject.' 'When it is thoroughly understood in England that the majority of French people (exception
being made for the Anglomaniacs of advanced society) consider that
"flirting" is a dishonourable amusement and that a woman who has
once listened to the overtures of a man considers it an act of justice to
console him, this side of the French character will be more compre-
hensible to the English mind.' Make the 2 women—with their *opposed
views of 'conduct.'*

[*James returned to this quotation a year and a half later, and began to
develop the theme of* The Given Case (p. 234 below).]

15 Beaumont St., Oxford, September 29th, 1894.

I seem to see a pretty idea for a short tale in a small fancy to which I
should give the name of *The Altar of the Dead*. The name, at least,
is happy; if the story may be half as much so! I imagine a man whose
noble and beautiful religion is the worship of the Dead. It is the only
religion he has; and it is a refuge and a consolation to him. He cherishes
for the silent, for the patient, the unreproaching dead, a tenderness in
which all his private need of something, not of this world, to cherish,
to be pious to, to make the object of a donation, finds a sacred, and
almost a secret, expression. He is struck with the way they are forgotten, are unhallowed—unhonoured, neglected, shoved out of sight;
allowed to become so much more dead, even, than the fate that has
overtaken them has made them. He is struck with the rudeness,
the coldness, that surrounds their memory—the want of place made for
them in the life of the survivors. The essence of his religion is really
to make and to keep such a place. This place I call—he calls—their
altar; an altar that, in the obscurity of his spiritual spaces, seems to
blaze with lights and flowers. *His* dead, at least, are there, and there
is a great perpetual taper for each of them. The situation, the action,
that makes the idea a subject, comes to me vaguely as something like
this. Let me first say that I had first fancied the 'altar' as a merely spiritual
one—an altar in his mind, in his soul, more splendid to the spiritual

eye than any shrine in any actual church. But I probably can't get an adequate action unless I enlarge this idea. Let me suppose for the moment, at any rate, that he has set up a spiritual altar—either in some Catholic church or in some apartment or chapel of his own house. The latter alternative is, I think, much the *least* practicable. The idea of the story, in its simplest expression, is that, loving and cherishing his altar, he feels that it doesn't become complete—that it won't be, can't be, till his *own* taper is lighted there. It's to that end, as a climax, that the little tale must work. I think I see it, and that it comes to me. He begins it with the death of his mother—or at any rate with the loss of some dear friend. The thing takes place in London, vaguely, fancifully, obscurely, without 'realism' or dots upon the *i*'s. He wanders in his bereavement into a Catholic church. He sits there—in the darkness of a winter afternoon—before a lighted altar; and the comfort and the peace are sweet to him. It could all be much better abroad; but that is a detail, and tact, and art, the divine, circumvent everything. Abroad or in London, at any rate, he sees an old woman paying for a taper—for one of *her* poor dead; and that gives him the fancy, the hint. He finds one of the side-altars of the church obscure and neglected —and he makes an arrangement by which, on payment of a sum of money, *he* may establish certain perpetual candles there.

x   x   x   x   x

34 De Vere Gardens, October 2d, 1894.

I came back to town yesterday—and I see my little subject comparatively clear—I think. My hero's altar has long been a 'spiritual' one— lighted in the gloom of his own soul. Then it *becomes* a material one, and the event is *determined* in a manner that the story relates. He wanders into <a> suburban (of course, Catholic) church on a winter afternoon. He is under the *coup*, the effect, of some *fresh* perception of the way the Dead are forgotten, dishonoured, in the manner I have hinted at.

x   x   x   x   x

October 24th, 1894. I broke off there—but I wrote the greater part of a very short tale on those lines: with the effect, unusual for me, of quite losing conceit of my subject, within sight of the close, and asking myself if it is worth going on with: or rather feeling that it isn't. I shall put it by—perhaps it will, the humour of it, come back to me. But the thing is a 'conceit,' after all, a little fancy which doesn't hold a great deal. Such things betray one—that I more and more (if possible)

[165]

feel. *Plus je vais,* the more intensely it comes home to me that solidity of subject, importance, emotional capacity of subject, is the only thing on which, henceforth, it is of the slightest use for me to expend myself. Everything else breaks down, collapses, turns thin, turns poor, turns wretched—betrays one miserably. Only the fine, the large, the human, the natural, the fundamental, the passionate things. It is true, of course, that in the case of a little thing like this *Altar of the Dead,* a short thing, as to which its modest dimensions speak for it, it need not be of much moment, one way or the other, if one *does* go on with it. What one *has* seen in it is probably there, and pressing a little will bring it out. One's claim for it is, on the very face of the matter, slight. Let me remember that I have always put things through. x x x x x

[*In James' preface to* The Altar of the Dead—*which had been first printed in his volume of tales,* Terminations (1895)—*he says that its theme was one which, in a sense, he had always had in mind, since 'what sort of free intelligence would it be that, addressed to the human scene, should propose to itself, all vulgarly, never to be waylaid or arrested, never effectively inspired, by some imaged appeal of the lost Dead?' It is puzzling, therefore, that in the notebook entry just above he thinks of it as so slight and so empty. Possibly the passage represents no more than a momentary discouragement with the working out of the idea rather than with the idea itself, a feeling that, however rich the potentialities in a treatment of the relation of the living to the dead, the story itself did not live up to them. Certainly his inclusion of it as a title-story to a volume in the New York edition, and his preface to it, suggest no dissatisfaction, and it has often been counted among the best of his tales.*

The essential situation is that outlined in the notebook, but the dramatic action is supplied by the addition of a woman character who also worships before Stransom's altar to his dead, and, as he realizes, regards it as a shrine to the memory of a man whom she has loved and whose betrayal of her she has forgiven. This man, it turns out, was also a dear friend of Stransom's but did him a great injury, and has therefore no candle on the altar. The revelation of the man's identity breaks Stransom's relation with his fellow-worshipper. She can come to the altar no more until it supports a candle for her lover, and Stransom cannot include him among the dead he honors. She, at last, changes her attitude and, for Stransom's sake, comes to the church again; he, aging and sick, finally manages to forgive, and intends that the one candle needed to complete the display on the altar shall be for the man who was unworthy of his friendship, instead of for himself. But before the situa-

tion is resolved, he dies in the arms of the woman who has shared his 'religion,' his consecration to the memory of the dead.

The additions to the original outline of the story not only give it 'plot' of a sort, but also make possible a fuller realization of Stransom's character, a realization essential if the tale is to carry its theme effectively. His struggle against his own vengeful spirit and his eventual triumph do much to turn him from a relatively abstract symbol into a man who, although an eccentric in his cultism, is at least sufficiently a creature of common emotions to be credible.]

Meanwhile Henry Harper, the other day at McIlvaine's gorgeous dinner at the Reform (given to *him*, H.H., Oct. 17th), brought me a kind of message from Alden of the *Magazine*; a message strongly backed up by himself, to the effect that they wanted to 'see me in the Magazine again.' Henry Harper, who is a very pleasant, clear-faced fellow, even suggested, as coming (partly) from Alden, the rough idea of a subject for me!—a subject on which an international tale, a tale of the *Daisy Miller* order, might be based. The odd part of it is that there is probably something in it, that it doesn't strike me as very bad, or as very empty! It is—vaguely speaking—the eternal question of American snobbishness abroad; the vividness of which appeared to have been brought home to *ces messieurs* by the situation and proceedings of W.A. I think they were rather out in their example—I should say he wasn't, for various reasons, a good signal instance. But the proposal seems to represent something to me, and I ask myself if it isn't—if it may not be—the moment for me to see something in such an overture? Henry Harper evidently wants another *Daisy Miller*; and *je ne demande pas mieux*; only there are various things to be said: such as that above all, first, I can't (if I *do* thresh the subject out into something good) undertake to handle the thing within the short compass of *Daisy M.* Anything I shall see in it must resolve itself into the form of something of about the length of Daudet's *Immortel*—or it's not worth doing. *L'Immortel* is, to speak vulgarly, upwards of eighty thousand words long. *The Reverberator* is less than 30,000.[1] x x x x x

Innumerable questions and alternatives (*questions d'art*, alternatives of work—of present immersion) have been surging round me all these last days; especially these 2 last—3 last—that I have been shut up with a sickly cold—the cold I brought home from the Millets on the 22d. (I write this Oct. 25th, 1894.) I have felt nervous and embroiled— but that's not worth mentioning here. x x x x x

1. James' memory betrayed him. The actual length of *The Reverberator* is about fifty-five thousand words.

November 3d, 1894. Isn't there a little drama in the idea of such a situation as A.L.'s—that of an extremely clever and accomplished man, a man much prized and followed up in society, a great favourite there as a talker and a 'brilliant' person, whose interior is 'impossible' through the dreariness of his wife and children, their inferiority to himself, their gross, dense, helpless stupidity and commonplaceness? If one were to give him *one* child—a daughter—who is like himself, bright, intelligent, sympathetic, there would perhaps be more in the little story. One can imagine his fellowship with this child, their sympathy, their foregatherings, confidences, mutual *entente* and the rest. Yet that makes, on the whole, another story, and complicates the simple effect that I see in the thing. This effect is that of the almost insoluble problem of his social life with such belongings: the absence of *acute* tragedy in it, yet the presence of all misery. His daughter utterly unmarriageable, his sons mere louts. One would have to constitute the picture in some little *action*, build the situation round some climax. The climax his having to give up everything—leave London, take them all off and bury them somewhere in the country—and himself with them. The story might be told, the episode witnessed, by a person, a friend, who has foreseen it from the first of his coming into the London horizon, has been asked advice and has hesitated, and been much troubled, seeing the germs of the situation. The poor man comes to take leave of him, to say 'good-bye—I chuck it up—it's impossible.' However, all that would be *à trouver.* What I seem to see is that there is a little subject in the picture, the predicament of such a man, with society catching at him hard, and such a family to carry.

[The notebook ends with a few jotted memoranda of addresses, and a record of James' weekly bill at a hotel in Lucerne in 1893.]

NOTEBOOK IV

3 November 1894—15 October 1895 [1]

34 De Vere Gardens, W., November 3d, 1894.

Isn't perhaps something to be made of the idea that came to me some time ago and that I have not hitherto made any note of—the little idea of the situation of some young creature (it seems to me preferably a woman, but of this I'm not sure), who, at 20, on the threshold of a life that has seemed boundless, is suddenly condemned to death (by consumption, heart-disease, or whatever) by the voice of the physician? She learns that she has but a short time to live, and she rebels, she is terrified, she cries out in her anguish, her tragic young despair. She is in love with life, her dreams of it have been immense, and she clings to it with passion, with supplication. 'I don't want to die—I won't, I won't, oh, let me live; oh, save me!' She is equally pathetic in her doom and in her horror of it. If she only could live just a little; just a little more—just a little longer. She is like a creature dragged shrieking to the guillotine—to the shambles. The idea of a young man who meets her, who, knowing her fate, is terribly touched by her, and who conceives the idea of saving her as far as he can—little as that may be. She has known nothing, has seen nothing, it was all beginning to come to her. Even a respite, with one hour of joy, of what other people, of what happy people, know: even this would come to her as a rescue, as a blessing. The young man, in his pity, wishes he could make her taste of happiness, give her something that it breaks her heart to go without having known. That 'something' can only be—of course—the chance to love and to be loved. He is not in love with her, he only deeply pities her: he has imagination enough to know what she feels. His impulse of kindness, of indulgence to her. She will live at the most but her little hour—so what does it matter? But the young man is entangled with another woman, committed, pledged, 'engaged' to one—and it is in that that a little story seems to reside. I see him as having somehow to risk something, to lose something, to sacrifice something in order to be kind to her, and

1. Three sheets, two of them written on on both sides, and one, written on on one side, have been torn out at the beginning of this notebook.

to do it without a reward, for the poor girl, even if he loved her, has no life to give him in return: no life and no personal, no physical surrender, for it seems to me that one must represent her as too ill for *that* particular case. It has bothered me in thinking of the little picture—this idea of the physical possession, the brief physical, passional rapture which at first appeared essential to it; bothered me on account of the ugliness, the incongruity, the nastiness, *en somme*, of the man's 'having' a sick girl: also on account of something rather pitifully obvious and vulgar in the presentation of such a remedy for her despair—and such a remedy only. 'Oh, she's dying without having had it? Give it to her and let her die'—that strikes me as sufficiently second-rate. Doesn't a greater prettiness, as well as a better chance for a story, abide in her being already too ill for that, and in his being able merely to show her some delicacy of kindness, let her think that they might have loved each other *ad infinitum* if it hadn't been too late. That, however, is a detail: what some dim vision of a little dramatic situation seems to attach to is the relation that this encounter places him in to the woman to whom he is *otherwise* attached and committed and whom he has never doubted (any more than this person herself has) that he loves. It appears inevitably, or necessarily, preliminary that his encounter with the tragic girl shall be *through* the other woman: I mean that *she* shall know all about her too (they may be relatives—brought together after an absence or for the first time) and shall be a close witness of the story. If I were writing for a French public the whole thing would be simple—the elder, the 'other,' woman would simply be the mistress of the young man, and it would be a question of his taking on the dying girl for a time—having a temporary liaison with her. But one can do so little with English adultery—it is so much less inevitable, and so much more ugly in all its hiding and lying side. It is so undermined by our immemorial tradition of original freedom of choice, and by our practically universal acceptance of divorce. At any rate in this case, the anecdote, which I don't, by the way, at all yet *see*, is probably more dramatic, in truth, on some basis of marriage being in question, marriage with the other woman, or even with both! The little action hovers before me as abiding, somehow, in the particular complication that his attitude (to the girl) engenders for the man, a complication culminating in some sacrifice for him, or some great loss, or disaster. The difficulty is that the beauty of the thing is precisely in his not being in love with the girl—in the disinterestedness of his conduct. She is in love with him—that is it: she has been already so before she is condemned. He *knows* it, he learns it at the same time that he learns—as *she* has learnt—that her illness will carry her off. Say that she swims into his ken as the cousin

—newly introduced—of the woman he is engaged to. Say he *is* definitely engaged to this elder girl and has been engaged some time, but that there is some serious obstacle to their marrying soon. It is what is called a long engagement. They are obliged to wait, to delay, to have patience. He has no income and she no fortune, or there is some insurmountable opposition on the part of her father. Her father, her family, have reasons for disliking the young man; the father is infirm, she has to be with him to the end, he will do nothing for them, etc., etc. Or say they have simply no means—which indeed has the drawback of not being very creditable to the hero. From the moment a young man engages himself he ought to have means: if he hasn't he oughtn't to engage himself. The little story *que j'entrevois* here suddenly seems to remind me of Ed. About's *Germaine*, read long years ago and but dimly remembered. But I don't care for that. If the young couple have at any rate, and for whatever reason, to *wait* (say for her, or for *his*, father's death) I get what is essential. *Ecco.* They are waiting. The young man in these circumstances encounters the dying girl as a friend or relation of his fiancée. *She* has money—*she* is rich. She is in love with him—she is tragic and touching. He takes his betrothed, his fiancée, fully into his confidence about her and says, 'Don't be jealous if I'm kind to her—you see *why* it is.' The fiancée is generous, she also is magnanimous—she is full of pity too. She gives him rope—she says, 'Oh yes, poor thing: be kind to her.' It goes further than she quite likes; but still she holds out—she is so sure of her lover. The poor child *is*—most visibly—dying: what, therefore, does it matter? She can last but a little; and she's so in love! But they are weary of their waiting, the two fiancés—and it is their own prospects that are of prime importance to them. It becomes very clear that the dying girl would marry the young man on the spot if she could.

November 7th, 1894. I dropped the foregoing the other day—I was pressed for time and it was taking me too far. There are difficulties in it —and what I meant was really only to throw out a feeler. I had asked myself if there was anything in the idea of the man's *agreeing with his fiancée that he shall marry the poor girl in order to come into her money and in the certitude that she will die and leave the money to him*—on which basis (his becoming a widower with property) they themselves will at last be able to marry. Then the sequel to that?—I can scarcely imagine any—I doubt if I can—that isn't ugly and vulgar: I mean vulgarly ugly. This would be the case with the girl's not, after all, dying—and that's not what I want, or mean. Moreover if she's as much in love with the young man as I conceive her, she would leave him the money without any question of marriage. I seem to get hold of the tail of a pretty idea in making that happiness, that life, that snatched experience the girl longs for, BE, *in fact*, some rapturous act of that sort—some act of generosity, of passionate beneficence, of pure sacrifice, to the man she loves. This would obviate all 'marriage' between *them*, and everything so vulgar as an 'engagement,' and, removing the poor creature's yearning from the class of egotistic pleasures, the dream of being possessed and possessing, etc., make it something fine and strange. I think I see something good in *that* solution—it seems dimly to come to me. I think I see the thing beginning with the 2 girls—*who must not love each other*. This idea would require that the dying girl, whom family or personal circumstances have brought into relation with the other, should not be fond of her, should have some reason to dislike her, to do *her* at least no benefit or service. One may see the story begin with them—the two together; brought a little nearer by the younger girl's illness and trouble—so that the *other* is the FIRST witness of her despair and has the FIRST knowledge of her doom. The poor girl breaks out to her, raves, can't help it. The elder girl is privately, secretly engaged to the young man, and the other hasn't seen him when the doom aforesaid is pronounced. She sees him and she loves him—he becomes witness of her state and, as I have noted, immensely pities her. It is with a vision of what she could do for *him* that she renewedly pleads for life. *Then* she learns, discovers—or rather she doesn't discover at first—that the 2 others—her relative and the young man—are engaged. I seem to see what passes between the young man and his fiancée on the subject. The fiancée has a plan—she suddenly has a vision of what may happen. She forbids her lover to tell the girl they are engaged. Her plan is that he shall give himself to her for the time, be 'nice' to her, respond, express, devote himself to her, let her love him and behave as if he loved her. She foresees that, under these circumstances, the girl will become capable of some act of immense generosity—of generosity by which her own life, her own prospect of marriage will profit—and without her really losing anything in the meanwhile. She therefore *checks* her lover's impulse, and he rather mystifiedly and bewilderedly assents. He 'reads her game' at last—she doesn't formally communicate it to him. She knows the girl dislikes her—say she has jilted the girl's brother, who has afterwards died. At any rate there is a *reason* for the dislike— and she, the elder woman, knows it. So much as this the latter tells her lover—for she has, after all, to *give* him a reason—explain to *him*, too, the dislike. In fact, in giving it, she virtually communicates her idea. 'Play a certain game—and you'll have money from her. But if she knows the money is to help you to marry me, you *won't* have it; never in the world!' My idea is that the poor (that is the rich) girl *shall*, at last, know this—learn this. *How* does she learn it? From the inexorable father? From the jilted brother (if he be *not* dead)? From the man (some other man, that is) whom the inexorable father *does* want her (i.e., want the elder girl) to marry; and who, disgusted with her, turns, in a spirit both vindictive and mercenary, to the rich little invalid? I seem to see, a little, THAT. I seem to see a penniless peer, whom my elder girl refuses. Her father will help her if she does that —if she makes the snobbish alliance. Her merit, her virtue is that she *won't* make it, and it is by this sacrifice that she holds her lover— *en le faisant valoir*—and makes him enter, as it were, into her scheme. Lord X. is a poor creature and has *nothing* but his title. The girl's sacrifice is a sacrifice of that—but of nothing else. If Lord X. goes, then, rebuffed, mercenarily and vindictively to the dying girl and tells her the other woman's 'game' (that is, her presumed, divined, engagement, from which she little by little, piece by piece, or in a vivid flash of divination, *constructs* the engagement), I seem to get almost a little 3-act play—with the main part for a young actress. I get, at any rate, a distinct and rather dramatic *action*, don't I?—*Voyons un peu.* The poor dying girl has an immense shock from her new knowledge— but her passion, after a little, is splendidly proof against it. She rallies to it—to her passion, her yearning just to taste, briefly, of life *that* way —and becomes capable of still clinging to her generosity. She clings, she clings. But the young man learns from her that she *knows*—knows of his existing tie. This enables him to measure her devotion, her beauty of soul—and it produces a tremendous effect upon him. He becomes ashamed of his tacit assent to his fiancée's idea—conceives a horror of it. In that horror he draws close to the dying girl. He tells his prospective bride that she knows—and yet how she seems determined to behave. 'So much the better!' says the prospective bride. My story pure and simple, very crudely and briefly, appears to be that the girl dies, leaving money—a good deal of money—to the man she has so hopelessly and generously loved, and whom it has become her idea of causing to contribute to her one supreme experience *by* thus helping, thus, at any cost, testifying to a pure devotion to. Then the young man is left with the money face to face with his fiancée. It is what now happens between them that constitutes the climax, the denouement of the story. She is eager, ready to marry now, but he has really fallen in love with the dead girl. Something in the other woman's whole attitude in the matter—in the 'game' he consented in a manner to become the instrument of: something in all this revolts him and puts him off. In the light of how exquisite the dead girl was he sees how little exquisite is the living. He's in distress <about> what to do —he hangs fire—he asks himself to what extent he can do himself vio-

[173]

lence. This change, this regret and revulsion, this deep commotion, his betrothed perceives, and she presently charges him with his infidelity, with failing her now, when they've reached, as it were, their goal. Does he want to keep the money for himself? There is a very painful, almost violent scene between them. (How it all—or am I detached?—seems to map itself out as a little 3-act play!) They *break*, in a word—he says, 'Be it so!'—as the woman gives him, in her resentment and jealousy (of the other's memory, now) an *opening* to break—by offering to let him off. But he offers her the money and she *takes* it. Then vindictively, in spite, *with* the money and with her father's restored countenance, she marries Lord X., while he lives poor and single and faithful—faithful to the image of the dead. Of course in the case of a play that one might entertain any hope of having acted, this denouement would have to be altered. The action would be the same up <to> the point of the girl's apparently impending death—and the donation of money would be before the EVENT. The rupture between the two fiancés would take place also before—he would buy her off with the money, the same way—and the hero would go back to the poor girl as her very own. Under this delight she would revive and cleave to him, and the curtain would fall on their embrace, as it were, and the *possibility* of their marriage and of her living. Lord X. and the betrothed's flunkeyizing father would be characters, and there would have to be a confidant of the hero's *evolution*, his emotions. I seem to see a vivid figure, and perhaps, for the hero, THAT figure—i.e., the 'confidant'—in the dying girl's *homme d'affaires*. I seem to see her perhaps as an American and this personage, the *homme d'affaires*, as a good American comedy-type. His wife would be the elderly woman. I seem to see Nice or Mentone—or Cairo—or Corfu—designated as the scene of the action, at least in the 1st act, and the gatherability of the people on some common ground, the salon of an hotel or the garden of the same. x x x x x

[In a manner comparable to his preliminary outline for The Golden Bowl, James thought his way here into the situation that he was to develop several years later in The Wings of the Dove (1902). But again the emotional possibilities were to be deepened and enriched by his final handling. He was writing the above at about the time Guy Domville went into rehearsal, which probably accounts for his thinking in terms of a possible play. But by now his bitter experience with the current standards of the stage made him take it for granted that he would have to sacrifice much of his essential theme for the sake of a happy ending.

In view of the fact that Milly Theale became his quintessential ex-

pression of the American girl, 'the heiress of all the ages,' it is interesting
to note that he began to think of her 'perhaps as an American' only in
the final sentences of this outline. He opened his preface with the
statement that The Wings of the Dove 'represents to my memory a
very old—if I shouldn't perhaps rather say a very young—motive; I can
scarce remember the time when the situation on which this long-drawn
fiction mainly rests was not vividly present to me.' In this case he was
to bring to his sketched outline not the kind of immediate observation
that suddenly made a young man on the next bench into Owen Wingrave, but rather the stored-up accumulation of one of the primary emotional experiences of his youth. In presenting Milly Theale he drew—
to a more penetrating extent than with any of his other characters—
upon someone he had known, upon his cousin Minny Temple. This
vivid brilliant girl who had died of tuberculosis at twenty-four was to
remain for him 'the supreme case of a taste for life as life.' He was to
end his Notes of a Son and Brother (1914) with a chapter dealing with
her, and to say that in her death William and he had felt together
the end of their own youth. The extent to which James' image of the
American girl, in Isabel Archer as well as in Milly Theale, depended
upon Minny Temple may be read in that commemoration, and also in
several of James' letters.[1]

His remembrance of Minny's thirst for life helped him solve one of
the problems of his story, the problem—which he came back to in the
preface—of presenting a sick heroine. James knew that it is 'by the act
of living' that characters appeal, and he created a heroine less tenuous
than the outline might suggest. She has made no such high-pitched
renunciation of love. James probed the deep connection between love
and the will to live, and when Milly learns of the relation between
Merton Densher and Kate Croy, she does not 'rally to it.' Instead, she
'turns her face to the wall.' Her generosity to Densher remains, but
she had wanted something more than to immolate herself in sacrificial
devotion. Just as James wrote about Minny on the final page of Notes
of a Son and Brother: 'Death, at the last, was dreadful to her; she
would have given anything to live.'

His matching of the forces arrayed against Milly also became more
affecting, especially in the kind of character he created in Kate Croy.
She possesses finally a terrifying force of will, but she is by no means
wholly brutal. There is no dislike posited between her and Milly, no
introduction of a jilted brother. James gave the bulk of his opening
book to accounting for her later actions as a result of her impoverished
background, in particular through her natural desire to escape her flashy

1. See also Matthiessen, Henry James: The Major Phase, pp. 43 ff.

sordid father. Lionel Croy is very different from the character in the outline; the role of social ambition is taken over by Kate's Aunt Maud. Kate becomes ruthless as she is swept along by the forces she has set in motion, but she is never a 'vindictive' villainess. The question whether she accepts Densher's offer of the money is, as so often in James, left to the reader to decide—on the basis of the impression produced by her whole character. But there is no possibility of her marrying Lord Mark 'in spite.' Densher is transformed by the action in the way suggested, but James did not give him a confidant, and as a result the handling of the denouement, with Milly dying offstage, is the most indirect that even James ever attempted.

When he recurred to the theme for his only other discussion of it in these notebooks, in the following February (p. 187 below), Guy Domville had failed, and James was no longer encumbered with thoughts of how to make his material suit the theater. When he finally brought it to expression, he had moved as far from the plays of Scribe as from any reminiscences of a plot of Edmond About's. His accumulated resources of pity and terror enabled him to produce his principal tragedy.]

November 8th, 1894. The other day, when at McIlvaine's dinner, as I have noted *ante* (in another old finished book), Henry Harper told me how he and Alden wanted me to do a little international story on American snobbishness abroad.[1] Three weeks later, meeting H.H. at lunch at the R<eform> C<lub> he returned to the question, urgently, again. I seemed to feel it in me to respond a little—to see it as an idea with which something might be done. But *voyons un peu* what it might possibly amount to. The thing is not worth doing at all unless something tolerably big and strong is got out of it. But the only way that's at all luminous to look at it is to see what there may be in it of most eloquent, most illustrative and most human—most characteristic and essential: what is its real, innermost, dramatic, tragic, comic, pathetic, ironic *note*. The primary interest is not in any mere grotesque picture of follies and misadventures, of successes and sufferings: it's in the experience of some creature that sees it and knows and judges and feels it all, that has a part to play in the episode, that is tried and tested and harrowed and exhibited by it and that forms the glass, as it were, through which we look at the diorama. On the very threshold one sees the difficulty that the subject is too big—too big for treatment on the *Daisy Miller* scale: which is what the *Harper* people have in their mind. And, alas, there is no inspiration or in-

1. See p. 167 above.

centive whatever in writing for *Harper* save the sole pecuniary one. They want, ever, the smaller, the slighter, the safer, the inferior thing; and the company one keeps in their magazine is of a most paralysing dreariness.

November 18th, 1894 (34 De Vere Gdns. W.).

Isn't there perhaps the subject of a little—a very little—tale (*de moeurs littéraires*) in the idea of a man of letters, a poet, a novelist, finding out, after years, or a considerable period, of very happy, unsuspecting, and more or less affectionate, intercourse with a 'lady-writer,' a newspaper woman, as it were, that he has been systematically *débiné*, 'slated' by her in certain critical journals to which she contributes? He has known her long and liked her, known of her hack-work, etc., and liked it less; and has also known that the *éreintements* in question have periodically appeared—but he has never connected them with her or her with them, and when he makes the discovery it is an agitating, a very painful, revelation to him. Or the reviewer may be a man and the author anonymously and viciously—or, at least, abusively —reviewed may be a woman. The point of the thing is whether there be not a little supposable theme or drama in the relation, the situation of the two people after the thing comes to light—the pretension on the part of the reviewer of having one attitude to the writer *as* a writer, and a totally distinct one as a member of society, a friend, a human being. They *may* be—the reviewer may be—unconsciously, disappointedly, *rég<u>lièrement*, in love with the victim. It is only a little situation; but perhaps there is something in it.

x   x   x   x   x

[*James came back to this theme a year later (p. 235 below), and thought of doing 'a very small something' and of calling it* The Publisher's Story. *He was to consider the possibility once more on 7 May 1898 (p. 266), and again in 1899 (p. 275).*]

It occurs to me that there may also be a situation, a small drama, in the conception of the way certain persons, closely connected, are affected by an event occurring, an act performed, which reflects strongly and grievously on the unspotted honour of their house, their family —an event embodied presumably in an individual, a dishonoured, dishonouring, misguided, sinning, erring individual—a strong difference as to the treatment of whom breaks out between them and constitutes the action. It must be, somehow, the contrasted opposition of the 2

[177]

forms of pride—the pride that can harden and stiffen its heart, its stare, its apparent, studied, unflinching unconsciousness of what has happened, and face out and live down the shame, disown, repudiate, inexorably *sacrifice* the guilty party—and the pride that suffers, and suffers *otherwise*, shrinks, hides, averts itself from the world and yet, while suffering, feels a solidarity with, can't too inhumanly dissociate itself from, the criminal. These things—I mean this situation—would depend wholly on what one should imagine in a way of a relation between the 2 representations, as it were—and on what one should imagine in the way both of a compromising act on the part of the 3d party and of a 'sacrifice' of him or her. The unchaste woman is too stale and threadbare, I think.

[*James continues his speculation on this subject on page* 197 *below*.]

Names. Hanmer—Meldrum—Synge—Grundle—Adwick—Blanchett—Sansom—Saunt—Highmore—Hannington (or place)—Medley (house)—Myrtle—Saxon—Yule—Chalkley—Grantham—Farange—Grose—Corfe—Lebus—Glasspoole (or place)—Bedfont, Redfont (places?)—Vereker—Gainer—Gayner — Shum — Oswald — Gonville — Mona (girl)—Mark—Floyer—Minton—Panton—Summervale—Chidley—Shirley—Dreever—Trendle—Stannace—Housefield—Longworth—Langsom—Nettlefold—Nettlefield—Beaumorris—Delacoombe—Treston—Mornington—Warmington—Harmer—Oldfield—Horsefield—Eastmead.

Saturday, January 12th, 1895. Note here the ghost-story told me at Addington (evening of Thursday 10th), by the Archbishop of Canterbury: the mere vague, undetailed, faint sketch of it—being all he had been told (very badly and imperfectly), by a lady who had no art of relation, and no clearness: the story of the young children (indefinite number and age) left to the care of servants in an old country-house, through the death, presumably, of parents. The servants, wicked and depraved, corrupt and deprave the children; the children are bad, full of evil, to a sinister degree. The servants *die* (the story vague about the way of it) and their apparitions, figures, return to haunt the house *and* children, to whom they seem to beckon, whom they invite and solicit, from across dangerous places, the deep ditch of a sunk fence, etc.—so that the children may destroy themselves, lose themselves, by responding, by getting into their power. So long as the children are kept from them, they are not lost; but they try and try and try, these evil presences, to get hold of them. It is a question of the children 'coming over to where they are.' It is all obscure and imperfect, the picture, the story, but there is a suggestion of strangely gruesome effect in it. The story to be told—tolerably obviously—by an outside spectator, observer.

[The Turn of the Screw (Collier's Weekly, 5 February–16 April 1898) *has in recent years been frequently interpreted in Freudian terms—as a fantasy conjured up by the children's governess (who is the narrator) as a result of her own neurotic repression. It is therefore worth noting that the anecdote from which James started posited both that the children had been corrupted and that they were still being influenced by the apparitions of the dead servants. James is again explicit on this point in his preface, where he discusses the kind of ghost story he was attempting in his imagined treatment of demonic possession. He added his incisive formulation of how to create a sense of evil: 'Only make the reader's general vision of evil intense enough . . . and his own experience, his own imagination, his own sympathy (with the children) and horror (of their false friends) will supply him quite sufficiently with all the particulars. Make him think the evil, make him think it for himself, and you are released from weak specifications.'*]

34 De Vere Gardens, W., January 23d, 1895.

I take up my *own* old pen again—the pen of all my old unforgettable efforts and sacred struggles. To myself—today—I need say no more. Large and full and high the future still opens. It is now indeed that I may do the work of my life. And I will. x x x x x I have only to *face* my problems. x x x x x But all that is of the ineffable—too deep and pure for any utterance. Shrouded in sacred silence let it rest. x x x x x

[*The significance of this entry is that James had just faced the un-favorable reception of* Guy Domville. *But instead of being crushed by the collapse of his hopes of working for the theater, or bewailing that he had spent so much time in vain, he felt a resurgence of new energy. He had written to Howells, just the day before making this note, the letter already quoted on page 69 above; but though he was aware of 'evil days,' he also said: 'I mean to do far better work than ever I have done before. I have, potentially, improved immensely and am bursting with ideas and subjects—though the act of composition is with me more and more slow, painful and difficult.' He noted, as a challenge to himself: 'Produce again—produce; produce better than ever, and all will yet be well.'*]

January 26th, 1895. The idea of the poor man, the artist, the man of letters, who all his life is trying—if only to get a living—to do something *vulgar,* to take the measure of the huge, flat foot of the public: isn't there a little story in it, possibly, if one can animate it with an action; a little story that might perhaps be a mate to *The Death of the Lion?* It is suggested to me really by all the little backward memories of one's own frustrated ambition—in particular by its having just come back to me how, already 20 years ago, when I was in Paris writing letters to the *N. Y. Tribune,* Whitelaw Reid wrote to me to ask me virtually *that*—to make 'em baser and paltrier, to make them as vulgar as he could, to make them, as he called it, more 'personal.' Twenty years ago, and so it has been ever, till the other night, Jan. 5th, the *première* of *Guy Domville.* Trace the history of a charming little talent, charming artistic nature, that has been exactly the martyr and victim of that ineffectual effort, that long, vain study to take the measure above-mentioned, to 'meet' the vulgar need, to violate his intrinsic conditions, to make, as it were, a sow's ear out of a silk purse. He tries and he tries and he does what he thinks his coarsest and crudest. It's all of no use—it's always 'too subtle,' always too fine—never, never, vulgar enough. I had to write to Whitelaw Reid that the sort of thing I had already tried hard to do for the *Tribune* was the very worst I *could* do. I lost my place—my letters weren't wanted. A little drama, climax, a denouement, a small tragedy of the *vie littéraire*—mightn't one oppose to him some contrasted figure of another type—the creature who, dimly conscious of deep-seated vulgarity, is always trying to be refined, which doesn't in the least prevent him—or her—from succeeding. Say it's a woman. *She* succeeds—and she *thinks* she's fine! Mightn't *she* be the narrator, with a fine grotesque *inconscience?* So that the whole thing becomes a masterpiece of close and finished irony? There *may* be a difficulty in that—I seem to see it: so that the necessity may be for the narrator to be *conscient,* or SEMI-CONSCIENT, perhaps, to get the full force of certain efforts. The narrator at any rate, a person in the little drama who is trying bewilderedly the opposite line—working helplessly for fineness.

x x x x x

[In writing to his brother William, just after the disastrous opening night of Guy Domville, James had said: 'You would understand better the elements of the case if you had seen the thing it followed (The Masqueraders) and the thing that is now succeeding at the Haymarket —the thing of Oscar Wilde's. On the basis of their being plays, or successes, my thing is necessarily neither. Doubtless, moreover, the want of a roaring actuality, simplified to a few big familiar effects, in my subject—an episode in the history of an old English Catholic family in the last century—militates against it, with all usual theatrical people, who don't want plays (from variety and nimbleness of fancy) of different kinds, like books and stories, but only of one kind, which their stiff, rudimentary, clumsily-working vision recognizes as the kind they've had before. And yet I had tried so to meet them! But you can't make a sow's ear out of a silk purse.'

He worked out, four months later, the scheme that he actually used for The Next Time (pp. 200 ff. below).]

February 5th, 1895. Last evening, as, by a tremendous clear cold, I rolled along in a rattling four-wheeler (to go to dinner with the Lovelaces, who, by agreement—the only other guest being Miss De Morgan, a person much initiated—showed me some of their extremely interesting Byron papers; especially some of those bearing on the absolutely indubitable history of his relation to Mrs. Leigh, the sole *real* love, as he emphatically declares, of his life)—as I rolled along there came to me, I know not why, the idea of the possible little drama residing in the existence of a peculiar intense and interesting affection between a brother and a sister. It was an odd coincidence that this should have suggested itself when I was in the very act of driving to a place where I was to see the Byron-Leigh letters—some of them. But this (as regards the particular documents) I knew nothing about in advance—didn't know I was to see *those*, at all. Also, the little relation that occurred to me presented itself to me with none of the nefarious—abnormal—character of the connection just mentioned.[1] There may be nothing in it—probably is; but what I vaguely thought of (scarcely distinctly enough indeed for the purposes of this note) was the incident of such a union (of blood and sympathy and tenderness) that, on the part of each, it can only operate for intelligence and perception of the other's conditions and feelings and impulses—not in the least for control or direction of them—as is the case with *most* affectionate wisdoms, guiding devotions, which enter into the nature of the loved object *for its good* and to protect it sometimes against itself, its native

1. John Buchan in *Memory Hold-the-Door* says 'an aunt of my wife's, who was the widow of Byron's grandson, asked Henry James and myself to examine her archives in order to reach some conclusion on the merits of the quarrel between Byron and his wife. She thought that those particular papers might be destroyed by some successor and she wanted a statement of their contents deposited in the British Museum. So, during a summer week-end, Henry James and I waded through masses of ancient indecency, and duly wrote an opinion. . . My colleague never turned a hair. His only words for some special vileness were "singular"—"most curious"—"nauseating, perhaps, but how quite inexpressibly significant." ' Presumably the occasion described in the text above was a forerunner of the 'summer week-end.'

dangers, etc. I fancy the pair understanding each other too well—
fatally well. Neither can protect the character of the other against itself
—for the other in each case is, also, equally the very self against whom
the protection is called for—can only abound in the same sense, see
with the same sensibilities and the same imagination, vibrate with the
same nerves, suffer with the same suffering: have, in a word, exactly,
identically the same experience of life. Two lives, two beings, and *one*
experience: that is, I think, what I mean; with the question of what
situations, what drama, what little story, might possibly come of it.
The manner in which the thing (the climax) hovered before me was
the incident of their dying together as the only thing they *can* do
that does not a little fall short of absolutely ideally perfect agreement.
I imagined such a feeling about life as that when one, under the
influence of it, 'chucks up' the game, the other, from a complete understanding of the sensibilities engaged, the effect produced, must do
exactly the same—in a kind of resigned, inevitable, disenchanted,
double suicide. It's a reflection, a reduplication of melancholy, of
irony. They may be twins, but I don't think it's necessary. They
needn't even be brother and sister: they may be 2 brothers or even
2 sisters. Brother and sister, however, probably most recommend
themselves—and not as twins. I remember now—it comes back to
me—what little image led to the fancy: the idea of some unspeakable
intensity of feeling, of tenderness, of sacred compunction, as it were,
in relation to the *past*, the parents, the beloved mother, the beloved
father—of those who have suffered before them and *for* them and
whose blood is in their veins—whose image haunts them with an almost
paralysing pathos, an ineffability of pain, a sense of the irreparable,
of a tragic reality, or at least a reality of sadness, greater than the
reality of the actual. What it is probable that the little *donnée* would
rightly present is the image of a deep, participating devotion of one to
the other (of a brother to a sister presumably), rather than that of
an absolutely equal, a mathematically divided affection. The brother
suffers, has the experience and the effect of the experience, is carried
along by fate, etc.; and the sister understands, perceives, shares, with
every pulse of her being. He has to tell her nothing—she *knows*: it's
identity of sensation, of vibration. It's, for *her*, the Pain of Sympathy:
that would be the subject, the formula. The denouement would be:
to what that conducts you—conducts the victim. It conducts to a
sharing of the fate of the other, whatever this fate may be. The story
is the fate.

February 5th, 1895. What is there in the idea of *Too late*—of some
friendship or passion or bond—some affection long desired and waited

for, that is formed too late?—I mean too late in life altogether. Isn't there something in the idea that 2 persons may meet (as if they had looked for each other for years) only in time to feel how much it might have meant for them if they had only met earlier? This is vague, nebulous—the mere hint of a hint. They but meet to part or to suffer—they meet when one is dying—'or something of that sort.' They may have been dimly conscious, in the past, of the possibility between them —been groping for each other in the darkness. It's love, it's friendship, it's mutual comprehension—it's whatever one will. They've heard of each other, perhaps—felt each other, been conscious, each, of some tug at the cord—some vibration of the other's heartstrings. It's a passion that *might* have been. I seem to be coïnciding simply with the idea of the married person encountering the *real* mate, etc.; but that is not what I mean. Married or not—the marriage is a detail. Or rather, I fancy, there would have been no marriage conceivable for either. Haven't they waited—waited too long—till something else has happened? The only *other* 'something else' than marriage must have been, doubtless, the wasting of life. And the wasting of life is the implication of death. There may be the germ of a situation in this; but it obviously requires digging out. x x x x x

There comes back to me, *à propos* of it, and as vaguely and crookedly hooking itself on to it, somehow, that *concetto* that I have jotted down in another notebook [1]—that of the little tragedy of the man who has renounced his ambition, the dream of his youth, his genius, talent, vocation—with all the honour and glory it might have brought him: sold it, bartered it, exchanged it for something very different and inferior, but mercenary and worldly. I've only to write these few words, however, to see that the 2 ideas have nothing to do with each other. They are different stories. What I fancied in this last mentioned was that this Dead Self of the poor man's lives for him still in some indirect way, in the sympathy, the fidelity (the relation of some kind) of another. I tried to give a hint in my former note, of what this vicarious self, as it were, might amount to. It will require returning to; and what I wanted not to let slip altogether was simply some reminder of the beauty, the little tragedy, attached perhaps to the situation of the man of genius who, in some accursed hour of his youth, has bartered away the fondest vision of that youth and lives ever afterwards in the shadow of the bitterness of the regret. My other little note contained the fancy of his *recovering* a little of the lost joy, of the Dead Self, in his intercourse with some person, some woman, who knows what that

1. Pages 143-4 above.

self was, in whom it still lives a little. This intercourse is his real life. But I think I said that there was a banality in that; that, practically, the little situation will have often enough been treated; and that therefore the thing could, probably, only take a form as the story, not of the man, but of the woman herself. It's *the woman's sense of what might <have been>* in him that arrives at the intensity. (The link of connection between the foregoing and this was simply my little feeling that they each dealt with might-have-beens.) *She is his Dead Self: he is alive in her and dead in himself*—that is something like the little formula I seemed to *entrevoir.* He himself, the man, must, *in* the tale, also materially die—die in the flesh as he had died long ago in the spirit, the *right* one. Then it is that his lost treasure revives most— no longer *contrarié* by his material existence, existence in his false self, his wrong one.—But I fear there isn't much in it: it would take a deuce of a deal of following up.

[*James was always concerned with 'the wasting of life,' with passions 'that might have been.' Such later stories as* The Friends of the Friends *and especially* The Beast in the Jungle *pick up this theme, though with different situations than that projected for the story of 'the Dead Self.'*]

February 6th, 1895. I went yesterday, by appointment, to see Ellen Terry; and I won't pretend here, now, to go into the question of the long, tragic chapter with which my consideration (so troubled, so blighted for the time at least) of the proposal contained in the note of hers which led to our interview, was—and still is—associated. I make this allusion, this morning, simply because it has reference to my talk with her, and to what may come of it, to ask myself *de cette triste plume tâtonnante,* whether, for such a little one-act or two-act play as Ellen Terry wants, there is possibly anything in the idea of a *Mme Sans-Gêne,* as it were, turned the other way, reversed, transposed: I mean not a woman of the people, who in consequence of a stroke of fortune has to play the *grande dame,* but a *grande dame* who in consequence of a stroke of fortune has to play a woman of the people. It is by no means impossible that this image may not be void: everything would depend on the story that embodies it, on what the stroke of fortune is, may be conceived as being. This to be admirably figured out.

x   x   x   x   x

Another little possibility dances before me—I only just catch the tip of its tail—in the fancy of something faintly suggested by Miss Terry's happening to have said, rather in the air, that she would have a fancy to do an American woman! A couple of years ago, in a note previous to this, in an hour of deep delusion (like perhaps even *this* hour), I jotted down something very vague (with an eye to some part for Ada Rehan),[1] on the subject of an American woman as the beneficent intervening agent in the drama of an English social, an English family, crisis—some supreme dramatic, probably tragic, but possibly some comic, juncture in the affairs of an old English race—her stepping in as the real conservative, more royalist than the king, etc.; stepping in with some charming, clever enthusiasm and infatuation of her own which repairs and redeems—which rescues and restores. The mere tail of the image which I catch hold of for the moment is the confused vision of the American woman (a rich widow) coming down, *en touriste*, to see an old house she has heard of, seen a photograph or picture of, dreamed about, and alighting *so* upon the dramatic crisis as to which she becomes a saviour and redeemer. This will probably permit (God forgive me if it doesn't!) of some following up; particularly because I seem to see in it the adumbration of a short tale *aussi bien* as of a play. However, what I see in it as yet is just merely that figure and its background, with everything else confused and crude; I mean the bright, kind, comic, clever, charming creature—in the agitated, convulsed, threatened, somehow troubled and exposed *show* house. I seem to see the 'show' element—the trooping visitors, the other tourists—salient and usable as an effect of comedy. Even as I write, just God, something seems to come to me!—seems to come as a sort of faint ramification of there swimming before me a certain phantasmagory of the charming woman *showing the house herself*, showing it better than any of *them* can. *Elle s'improvise*, somehow, *cicerone*. I have a confused dream of a rupture, a breakdown or crisis, on the part of the people of the house, with regard to this question of farming it out to an *entrepreneur* (as I believe Knole is farmed), to their want of returns, of proceeds, their immediate need of the money, their making some better arrangement, necessitated by extreme pressure. *She* takes it over—and the younger son with it. *Or*—an alternative swims before me: the presence of some vulgar English people, very new and very dreadful, who, coming down to look at it, think of buying it, want to buy it, propose for it. She saves it from *them*. I fancy I see a wild ostensible radical of an eldest son, of an owner, and a sympathetic and sensible younger brother, the 'hero,' whom she hits it off with. But all this is troubled and confused—very mixed and crudely extemporized: I must

1. Page 127 above.

[185]

come back to it. All I mean, for the moment, is that the little picture, the localised and animated *act*, shines out at me. x x x x x

[James worked the theme outlined here into a play which he named Summersoft, but consistently referred to as 'Mrs. Gracedew.' He gave it to Ellen Terry, who kept it, as James wrote to H. G. Wells on 9 December 1898, 'for three mortal years.' He added, 'I had simply to make up a deficit and take a small revanche. . . I couldn't wholly waste my labour. The B.P. [British Public] won't read a play with the mere names of the speakers—so I simply paraphrased these and added such indications as might be the equivalent of decent acting—a history and an evolution that seem to me moreover explicatively and sufficiently smeared all over the thing.' 'The thing' was the story Covering End, printed in James' The Two Magics in 1898.

The play has not been printed, but Covering End is obviously, as James says, a close paraphrase of it in story form. The heroine is Mrs. Gracedew, a rich American widow. She does come to an old house, Covering End, does show other tourists about, discovers that there is a family crisis, and eventually straightens it out. The device is simple. The house is heavily mortgaged and Captain Yule, a young radical politician, who has inherited it, has not money enough to redeem it. Mr. Prodmore, one of the vulgar and 'very dreadful' people suggested in the sketch, holds the mortgages. He will give the house to Yule if Yule will stand for Parliament as a Tory, and also marry his daughter, Cora Prodmore. Mrs. Gracedew argues Yule into a love for the house and the ancient tradition it represents, and in so doing makes him love her and falls in love with him. She discovers that Cora will not marry him, because she cares for someone else, and with this knowledge she proceeds to buy off Mr. Prodmore and wins for herself both the house and Captain Yule.

The story had a further history. In 1899, both George Alexander and Forbes-Robertson sent James 'pressing requests' for the play from which the tale was written. James refused but then relented, only to have it rejected. The New Century Theatre also considered 'Mrs. Gracedew,' and William Archer wrote a favorable report on it, but it was finally decided not to produce it. In 1907, however, Forbes-Robertson, who saw great dramatic possibilities in Covering End, persuaded James to make a new play of it. He rewrote it in three acts, working on it less than a month. After discussions with Forbes-Robertson, and after revisions, one of which was the introduction, as a character, of 'a young man,' Cora's suitor, who is only alluded to in the story, the play was produced in Edinburgh on 26 March 1908, with considerable success. On 18 February 1909, it began a series of five London matinée performances and was favorably received.]

34 *D. V. G., W., February 14th, 1895.*

I have my head, thank God, full of visions. One has never too many —one has never enough. Ah, just to let one's self go—at last: to surrender one's self to what through all the long years one has (quite heroically, I think) hoped for and waited for—the mere potential, and relative, increase of *quantity* in the material act—act of application and production. One has prayed and hoped and waited, in a word, to be able to work *more*. And now, toward the end, it seems, within its limits, to have come. That is all I ask. Nothing else in the world. I bow down to Fate, equally in submission and in gratitude. This time it's gratitude; but the form of the gratitude, to be real and adequate, must be large and confident action—splendid and supreme creation. *Basta.* x x x x x

I have been reading over the long note—the 1st in this book—I made some time since on the subject of the dying girl who wants to live— to live and love, etc.; and am greatly struck with all it contains. It is there, the story; strongly, richly there; a thing, surely, of great potential interest and beauty and of a strong, firm artistic *ossature*. It is *full*—the scheme; and one has only to stir it up *à pleines mains*. I allude to my final sketch of it—the idea of the rupture at last between the 2 fiancés: his giving her the money and her taking it and marrying Lord X. Meanwhile I am haunted by the idea of doing something for Henry Harper, as he put it before me in the autumn: something that I may do *now*, soon, in 3 months, and get the money for. In other words, as I sit here, it goes against my grain to relinquish without a struggle the idea of the short 'International' novel the Harpers want —little as H.H.'s suggestion of the particular thing at first appealed to me. Something probably lurks in it—something that I have only to woo forth. Let me live with it a while—let me woo it; even if I have to sit with it here in mere divine *tâtonnement* every patient morning for a week or two. If I don't find it I shall at least find something else, *much* else perhaps, even, by the way. Dimly the little drama looms and looms; and clearly it will come to me at last. Meanwhile in my path stands—appears at least to stand—brightly soliciting, the idea I jotted down a year ago, or more, and that has lain there untouched ever since: the idea of the father and daughter (in Paris, supposably), who marry—the father for consolation—at the same time, and yet are left more together than ever, through their respective *époux* taking such a fancy to each other. This has many of the very elements required: it is intensely international, it is brief, dramatic, ironic, etc.; and this mere touching of it already makes my fingers itch for it. I seem to see in it something compact, *charpenté*, living, touching, amusing. *Everything* about it qualifies it for *Harper* except the subject—or rather, I mean, except the adulterine element *in* the subject. But may it not be simply a question of *handling* that? For God's sake let me try: I want to plunge into it: I *languish* so to get at an immediate creation. This thing has for my bang-off purpose the immense merit of having no prescribed or imposed length. I seem to see it as a nominal 60,000 words: which *may* become 75,000. *Voyons, voyons:* may I not instantly sit down to a little close, clear, full scenario of it? As I ask myself the question, *with* the very asking of it, and the utterance of that word so charged with memories and pains, something seems to open out before me, and at the same time to press upon me with an extraordinary tenderness of embrace. Compensations and solutions seem to stand there with open arms for me—and something of the 'meaning' to come to me of past bitterness, of recent bitterness that otherwise has seemed a mere sickening, unflavoured draught. Has a *part* of all this wasted passion and squandered time (of the last 5 years) been simply the precious lesson, taught me in that roundabout and devious, that cruelly expensive, way, *of the singular value for a narrative plan too* of the (I don't know *what* adequately to call it) divine principle of the Scenario? If that *has* been one side of the moral of the whole unspeakable, the whole tragic experience, I almost bless the pangs and the pains and the miseries of it. IF there has lurked in the central core of it this exquisite truth—I almost hold my breath with suspense as I try to formulate it; so much, so *much*, hangs radiantly there as depending on it—this exquisite truth that what I call the divine principle in question is a key that, working in the same *general* way fits the complicated chambers of *both* the dramatic and the narrative lock: IF, I say, I have crept round through long apparent barrenness, through suffering and sadness intolerable, to that rare perception—why my infinite little loss is converted into an almost infinite little gain. The long figuring out, the patient, passionate little *cahier*, becomes the *mot de l'énigme*, the thing to live by. Let me commemorate here, in this manner, such a portentous little discovery, the discovery, probably, of a truth of real value even if I exaggerate, as I daresay I do, its *partée*, its magicality. <Now?> something of those qualities in it vivifies, backwardly—or appears to, a little—all the horrors that one has been through, all the thankless faith, the unblessed work. But how much of the precious there may be in it I can only tell by trying. x x x x x

[188]

[*The themes for* The Wings of the Dove *and* The Golden Bowl, *both recurring to James as he meditated here upon 'large and confident action, splendid and supreme creation,' remained together in his mind when, at the close of this year, he listed them first and second in a group of subjects for possible novels (p. 233 below).*]

34 De Vere Gardens, February 27th, 1895.

For a very short thing the idea of a Girl—the idea suggested to me, in a word, by learning *par où E.B. a consenti à passer* in the matter of her engagement to C.K. His family would give her, first, no sign whatever—his mother wouldn't write to her: they being Florentines *de vieille souche*, proud, 'stuck up,' etc. They demanded that she should write first—make the overture. She brought a fortune; she brings, in short, almost everything. But she consented—she wrote first. One can imagine a case in which the Girl—an American Girl—wouldn't: would have taken her stand on her *own* custom—her own people—that of the bride's being *welcomed*, always, by the mother, in the family into which she is to enter. One can imagine a situation arising out of this. The young man, distressed by her refusal, yet having his own family attitude, his mother's stiffness, etc., to count with, tries to make the latter make a concession—write 1st. She may not like the marriage or the girl, though having had reasons not definitely to oppose it; or she may be, merely, stiffly and *bêtement*, inexorably proud. She waits for the girl to write—says that if she does she will then herself do everything proper. But write first herself—never! This is exactly what the girl says: it's an *idée fixe* with her, she can't—she won't—she oughtn't. She takes exactly the same stand as the mother. What comes of the young man, of the engagement, of the marriage, between them? The girl asks him if he wants her to humiliate herself. He says no, and consents to *passer outre*. But she then says she won't come into the family without the letter from the mother. That is perhaps too hard an attitude to attribute to her. Imagine him devoted to his mother, *à l'italienne*—and yet consenting to the girl's not writing. There are the germs of trouble in that. Say the mother writes at last, but writes too late. The state of tension has warped the situation. The relation between the 2 lovers is injured, spoiled; and not less so—not less fatally damaged—the relation of the son to his mother.

x x x x x

[*In* Miss Gunton of Poughkeepsie, *printed first in the* Cornhill Magazine *for May 1900, this sketch is developed. An Englishwoman, Lady Champer, serves as an observer and commentator on the affair, and the Prince's worries lest his American fiancée draw too heavily on her fortune before she marries him add an amusingly vulgar touch to his character. At the end, after the rupture, the story is given a twist by Lady Champer's pointing out to the astonished Prince that what the American girl had really loved was his family tradition, and that it was her admiration of it that had made her so stubbornly insistent on her own 'tradition' and so determined to be 'welcomed' by his mother.]*

I was greatly struck, the other day, with something that Lady Playfair told me of the prolongation—and the effects of it—of her aunt, old Mrs. Palfrey, of Cambridge, Mass. She is, or was, 95, or some such extraordinary age; and the little idea that struck me as a small *motif* in it was that of the consequences of this fact on the existence of her 2 or 3 poor old maid daughters, who have themselves grown old (old enough to die), while sitting there waiting, waiting endlessly for her to depart. She has never departed, and yet has always been supposed to be going to, and they have had endlessly to be ready, to be near her, at hand—never to be away. So Sarah P., whom I vaguely remember, has come to be 70. They have never been anywhere, never done anything—their lives have passed in this long, blank patience. Some small thing might perhaps be done with the situation, with the picture. One of the daughters—the eldest—might die—of old age; and the thing, all the while, have to be kept from the old woman. She wonders what has become of her, tries to find out; and then, at last, one of the others tells her—tells her So-and-So has died. The old woman stares. 'What did she die of?' She died of old age. This makes the old woman realize—it finishes her. Or 2, the 2 elder, must die (of old age!) and *one* be left simply to watch—to conceal it. Only I think that 2 sisters is the right number originally—there had better not be more.

x   x   x   x   x

[James wrote 'Europe' four years later, and printed it in Scribner's (June 1899). As its title suggests, he had found a somewhat different center for his anecdote—in the daughters' longing for Europe. He recorded, in the preface to The Author of Beltraffio, his distinct memory of its genesis: 'I had preserved for long years an impression of an early time, a visit, in a sedate American city—for there were such cities then —to an ancient lady whose talk, whose allusions and relics and spoils and mementoes and credentials, so to call them, bore upon a triumphant sojourn in Europe, long years before, in the hey-day of the high scholarly reputation of her husband, a dim displaced superseded

celebrity at the time of my own observation.' In such terms did he recall Mrs. John Gorham Palfrey, the widow of the historian.

But his story took its spring of life from the old lady's malice. Mrs. Rimmle's three untraveled daughters were longing only to share in something of the rich world she had known, but 'on the occasion of each proposed start,' she 'announced her approaching end—only to postpone it again after the plan was dished and the flight relinquished. So the century ebbed, and so Europe altered—for the worse—and so perhaps even a little did the sisters who sat in bondage; only so didn't at all the immemorial, the inextinguishable, the eternal mother.'

Becky in particular knew already so much about Europe that it was hard to believe that her 'limit of adventure . . . consisted only of her having been twice to Philadelphia. The others hadn't been to Philadelphia, but there was a legend that Jane had been to Saratoga.' At this point James changed his plot further. He allowed Jane finally to escape and boldly join the Hathaways on a summer's trip. Once in Europe, she stoutly refuses to come back, and poor Becky secretly finances her. From then on her remorseless mother pronounces that Jane is 'dead.' And when Becky does actually die, 'the centenarian mummy in the high chair' can still summon enough strength to say to her visitor, in the closing words of the story: 'Have you heard where Becky's gone? . . . To Europe.'

By the time James included this theme in a list of possible stories, on 7 May 1898 (p. 266 below), he had seen his way to this ending. He pointed out in his preface that the 'merit' of this seven-thousand-word story consisted 'in the feat . . . of the transfusion' of his complex matter into its form: 'the receptacle (of form) being so exiguous, the brevity imposed so great. I undertook the brevity, so often undertaken on a like scale before, and . . . arrived at it by the innumerable repeated chemical reductions and condensations that tend to make of the very short story, as I risk again noting, one of the costliest, even if, like the hard shining sonnet, one of the most indestructible, forms of composition in general use.']

Reading, at the Athenaeum the other night, a little volume of *Notes sur Londres* by one 'Brada,' with a very, and on the whole justly, laudatory preface by that intelligent, but just at the end always slightly vulgar (*ça ne manque jamais*) Augustin Filon: skimming through this, I say, I was greatly struck with all that may be of dramatic, of fertile in subject, for the novel, for the picture of contemporary manners, in 2 features of current English life on which he much insists. One of them is perhaps fuller than the other; but what strikes me in both of them is that they would have as themes, as *données* dealt with, with the real right art, a very large measure of a sort of ringing and reverberating actuality. What I speak of, of course, is manners in this country. What 'Brada' speaks of in particular, as the 2 most striking social notes to him, are *Primo,* The masculinization of the women; and *Secondo,* The demoralization of the aristocracy—the cessation, on their part, to take themselves seriously; their traffic in vulgar things, vulgar gains, vulgar pleasures—their general vulgarization. x x x x x I must go on with that: I must copy the passage out of 'Brada.'

March 4th, 1895. The idea of the little London girl who grows up to 'sit with' the free-talking modern young mother—reaches 17, 18, etc.—comes out—and, not marrying, has to 'be there'—and, though the conversation is supposed to be expurgated for her, inevitably hears, overhears, guesses, follows, takes in, becomes acquainted with, horrors. A real little subject in this, I think—a real little situation for a short tale—if circumstance and setting is really given it. A young man who likes her—wants to take her out of it—feeling how she's exposed, etc. Attitude of the mother, the father, etc. The young man hesitates, because he thinks she already knows too much; but all the while he hesitates she knows, she learns, more and more. He finds out somehow how much she *does* know, and, terrified at it, drops her: all her ignorance, to his sense, is gone. His attitude to her mother—whom he has liked, visited, talked freely with, taken pleasure in. But when it comes to taking *her* daughter—! She has appealed to him to do it—begged him to take her away. 'Oh, if some one would only marry her. I know—I have a bad conscience about her.' She may be an ugly one —who has also a passion for the world—for life—likes to be there—to hear, to know. There may be the contrasted clever, *avisée* foreign or foreignized friend or sister, who has married her daughter, very virtuously and very badly, unhappily, just to get her out of the atmosphere of her own talk and entourage—and takes *my* little lady to task for her inferior system and inferior virtue. Something in this really, I think—especially if one makes it take in something of the question of the non-marrying of girls, the desperation of mothers, the whole alteration of manners—in the sense of the *osé*—and tone, while our theory of the participation, the *presence* of the young, remains unaffected by it. Then the type of the little girl who is conscious and aware. 'I am modern—I'm supposed to know—I'm not a *jeune fille,*' etc. x x x x x

[*The Awkward Age is not, of course, a short tale, which was all that James saw in his original idea. When it came to supplying 'circumstance and setting' he added so much, and became so fascinated with the tech-*

nical problems he posed for himself, that the result was a long novel. It was serialized in Harper's Weekly (1 October 1898–7 January 1899) but did not succeed as a book. In a letter to Henrietta Reubell on 12 November 1899, James ascribed its failure to the scenic form of the novel and to the lack of people clever enough to see what he meant. He defended Mrs. Brookenham as the best character he had done, and as late as 1912 he wrote to R. W. Chapman that he was prepared to stand a 'stiff cross-examination on that lady.' She becomes the focal point of the novel; it is the mother rather than the daughter who commands James' attention more and more as the story develops. This was natural, since Nanda's plight can be realized only if the character of her mother's little circle is made clear, and it could hardly become so without a strong portrayal of its presiding genius.

To judge by his preface, what fascinated James most in writing the novel were the technical excitements offered by composing it in a series of 'scenes' like concentric rings drawn around the theme outlined here. To supply the rings, more characters were needed than those suggested above and James created them in such figures as Tishy Grendon, Mitchy, and, most important of all, Mr. Longdon. He, a representative of the manners of an older generation, who once loved Nanda Brookenham's grandmother, is shocked at Nanda's being allowed to frequent her mother's drawing-room, and his attitude, of course, points up and dramatizes the central idea. Through Mr. Longdon, James also makes use of the theme he was speculating on just above—the theory that English society shows signs of decay. Vanderbank is the young man whose scruples about Nanda's sophistication keep him from marrying her, the Duchess is the 'foreign friend,' and there are a handful of others, each of whom aids in one way or another in dramatizing the lack of innocence in Mrs. Brookenham's favorite society.

In this book James, as he did so often, tightens the web by introducing among his characters relationships not foreseen in the original scheme. For example, the Duchess's daughter does make a failure of her marriage—and her husband is Mitchy, who has been a suitor for Nanda, and Mrs. Brookenham's preferred candidate. The Duchess herself has a lover who is a friend of the other characters. There is Nanda's brother, Harold; there is Lady Fanny, always on the eve of running away from her husband until Harold supplies attractions which keep her at home; there is the philandering Mr. Cashmore, who seems to be enamored of Tishy's sister. The effect of this interlocking of characters is to throw Nanda and her mother into sharp relief against a closely woven background of people more or less directly involved with each

[193]

other, and, singly or in pairs, both actors in, and observers of, the dramatic development of the story.]

Names. Genneret—Massigny—Mme d'Ouvré (or Ouvray)—Ince—Haffenden—Moro—Snape—Gossage—Goldberg—Vandenberg—Vanderberg—Beauville—Duchy—Pillow—Warry—Garry—Brigstock—Bransby—Gracedew — Tregarthen — Gable — d'Audigny — Callow — Seneschal—Bounce—Bounds (house, place)—Grander—Rix—Bembridge—Waterbath (? place)—Mme de Jaume or Geaume—(Mme J. or G.)—Mordan—Gwither (or Gwyther)—Able—Mme de la Faye—Robeck—Roebeck—Crimble—Birdwhistle—Ardrey—Acherley—Gysander—Gésandre—Heffernan—Considine—Limbert—Mellice—Thane—Turret—Atherfield—Otherfield—Gereth—Vanderbank—Desborough—Markwick—Dedborough—Mysander—Bonnace—Bender (American—might do for the Father [and daughter], in the novel of the *Mystification* [1]—even if written Benda)—Messent—Bloore—Cheshire—Shirving—Pelter—Maryborough—Marsac—Russ—Counsel—Smout—Daft (place—house)—Umber—Umberley—Umberleigh—Ombré—Mme d'Ombré—Rimmington—Roof—Carvick—Corvick—Burbeck—Longdon—Silk—Mme de Vionnet—Iffield—Buddle—Manders—Barningham—Pugsley—Parm—Fradalon—Brere—Vizard.

> 'Donald Macmurdough lies here low,
> Ill to his friends and waur to his foe,
> Leal to his maister in weal and woe.'

Some extremely well-said and suggestive things (oh, the common, general French *art de dire*, as exemplified even in a nobody like this!) in *Notes sur Londres* by one 'Brada,' alluded to above. The idea of his little book is the Revolution in English society by the *avènement* of the women, which he sees everywhere and in everything. I saw it long ago—and I saw in it a big subject for the Novelist. He has some very well uttered passages on this and other matters.

'Tel Gladstone, aujourd'hui Anglais jusqu'aux moelles, même dans une salutaire hypocrisie. Oui, assurément salutaire, et elle s'en va, elle disparait: encore quelques années et il n'en restera plus rien; et ce sera un grand dommage, car c'était une belle chose après tout, que de voir une puissante aristocratie, une société si riche et si forte, tant d'êtres divers tenus en respect par quelques fictions que suffisaient à défendre l'édifice social; c'était une salutaire illusion que de supposer toutes les femmes chastes, tous les hommes fidèles, et d'ignorer, de chasser résolu-

---

1. James may conceivably have referred thus to the theme of *The Golden Bowl*.

ment ceux qui portaient quelque atteinte visible à cette fiction. Ce respect des mots, cette pudeur de convention, provoquaient et développaient néanmoins de réelles vertus: cela s'en va; dans certaines milieux cela a déjà disparu!' x x x x x

And on the excellent subject of the *déchéance* of the aristocracy; its ceasing to have style, to take itself seriously: 'A vouloir être trop liberale et de bon accueil, à se moquer elle-même de ses vieux préjugés, l'aristocratie anglaise joue une grosse partie, et sans être un grand prophète on peut croire que dans sa forme actuelle ses jours sont comptés. Tout est permis à une caste fermée qui est persuadée de sa supériorité, mais du moment qu'elle abdique elle-même, prétend à la liberté d'allures du premier plébéien venu, on ne sait plus très bien ce qu'elle signifie, et il est à craindre qu'un beau jour on ne le lui demande un peu rudement. Aussi longtemps' (also) 'que les femmes entretiennent le feu du sanctuaire on peut avoir bon espoir, mais du moment qu'elles se rient et du sanctuaire et du feu sacré, il est probable qu'il ne tardera pas à s'éteindre, et le grand mouvement d'émancipation qui s'accomplit à cette heure en Angleterre vient de la femme. Il y a plusieurs courants, mais tous tendent au même but: s'affranchir de la tutelle de l'homme—vivre d'une vie personelle.'

'Le succès de l'Américain s'explique par un côté particulier du caractère anglais, cette volonté d'ignorer certaines choses; l'Américain est un personnage anonyme, pour ainsi dire; on peut commodément feindre ne rien savoir de son passé ni de la source de sa fortune, ce qui est moins facile vis-à-vis du nouveau riche qui est de provenance nationale. L'amour propre souffre moins d'avouer une épousée de New York ou de Washington que de la prendre à l'ombre d'une usine; il y a là une nuance qui a été très commode à l'orgueil héréditaire; puis l'Américaine est un être particulier dont à l'occasion, la vulgarité sera traitée de couleur locale; ce qui n'est pas le cas pour un compatriote. Il ne faut pas oublier non plus que cette uniformité de gens bien élevés n'existe pas en Angleterre—que les manières de voir, les façons, les habitudes de la grande classe moyenne ne sont pas du tout celles de la classe supérieure; on ne s'y trompe pas lorsqu'on connait l'un et l'autre, et par conséquent la fusion est bien plus difficile. x x x x x

Malgré tout l'Américain à Londres ne peut être qu'un accident, et le jour qu'on voudra le boycotter, rien de plus facile.

x   x   x   x   x

Les 1ers à être corrompus par le changement de la vieille société ont été les jeunes gens; autrefois les bonne<s> grâces des nobles maîtresses de maison leur étaient nécessaires pour faire leur chemin dans le monde, aujourd'hui ce sont eux qui sont nécessaires aux maîtresses de maison. La plupart du temps ils sont invités par des tiers; le sans-façon qu'ils ont apporté chez les parvenus indignes ou étrangers, ils le conservent comme manière definitive; la politesse la plus élémentaire est mise de côté, celle même de se faire présenter à son hôtesse. De l'excès de conventionalité on est tombé à l'excès du cynisme: des fils de famille n'ont pas rougi de servir (moyennant finance) de recruteurs à des tapissiers ou à des couturières; eux-mêmes sont devenus couturiers et recommandent l'article à leurs danseuses; il y a là le plus lamentable renoncement à la dignité personelle, la veritable nécessité n'ayant rien à invoquer là-dedans, et une société aristocratique qui ne saurait pas sauver ses membres d'une telle humiliation serait indigne d'exister.' x x x x x

I have copied the above for convenience of statement; and it appears to me that the general direction of *all* these observations swarms with subjects and suggestions. As I have noted before there is a big comprehensive subject in the *déchéance* of the aristocracy through its own want of imagination, of nobleness, of delicacy, of the exquisite; and there is a big comprehensive subject in the *avènement,* or rather in the masculinization of women—and their *ingérence,* their *concurrence,* the fact that, in many departments and directions, the cheap work they can easily do is more and more all the 'public wants.' The 'public wants' nothing, in short, today, that they *can't* do. I seem to see the great broad, rich theme of a large satirical novel in the picture, gathering a big armful of elements together, of the *train dont va* English society before one's eyes—the great modern collapse of all the forms and 'superstitions' and respects, good and bad, and restraints and mysteries—a vivid and mere showy general hit at the decadences and vulgarities and confusions and masculinizations and feminizations—the materializations and abdications and intrusions, and Americanizations, the lost sense, the brutalized manner—the publicity, the newspapers, the general revolution, the failure of fastidiousness. *Ah, que de choses, que de choses!*—I am struck with there being the suggestion of something in the *last* lines quoted above from this neat 'Brada'—I mean of something in the way of a little objective tale. She speaks ('Brada,' too, is a She) [1] of the prevention by the general aristocratic body of the *déchéance,* the commercialization, the shopkeeping, the mounting upon *les planches,* etc., of its unfortunate members. She implies that an aristocracy worthy to exist comes to the rescue of that sort of thing

1. Brada was the pen-name of Henriette Consuelo (Sansom), contessa di Puliga.

and sees that it shall not take place. Well, when it does, it can mainly assist and prevent and interfere by *alms,* by giving money, making the individual dependent, etc. This is what suggests a little situation, and the situation *se rattache* (in my mind—vaguely) to that vague one I hinted at, somewhere, very sketchily (in this *cahier de notes*),[1] that of the different view taken by 2 (or more) members of an 'old family,' of some dishonour or abomination that has overtaken someone *qui leur tient de près:* that is, the different view taken of the question of the treatment of it—the treatment before the world: the alternatives of disowning, repudiating, sinking the individual, or of covering him (or her) with the mantle of the general honour, being imperturbable and inscrutable, and presenting to the world a marble, unconscious face. It seemed to me that there might be a small drama in the embodiment in 2 opposed persons, on a given occasion, of these conflicting, irreconcilable points of view. One would arrange, one would invent and vivify the particular circumstances—construct the illustrative action. It occurs to me that, with a given little *donnée,* the 'illustrative action,' precisely, might include the picture of such a predicament as those foreshadowed in the aforementioned citation from 'Brada.' There, too, is a chance for the opposed, the alternative views. On the one side the demoralized aristocrat opens a shop, or wants to, engages, in short, or desires to, in some mercenary profession. On the other, he is saved from doing so by accepting 'relief' from the persons who would be ashamed of seeing him do it. Oppose these conflicting theories of relief and of 'vulgarity'—dramatise them by making something depend on them, depend on the question at issue, for certain persons who are actors in the little story. Make the conflict, in other words, a little drama—or make it so perhaps by thickening the situation, interweaving with it pictorially the other element, the situation of the individual who has been guilty (of something or other serious), and of the treatment of whom the family, the relations, the others, take a different view. This individual would be, as it were, the *pretext* of the little drama: the actors, the sufferers, the agents are the conflicting others. x x x x x

[*James may have taken from this memorandum a hint for his* Paste, *published in* Frank Leslie's Popular Monthly *in December 1899. The story, as James wrote in the preface to* The Author of Beltraffio *volume, originated from the idea of reversing the situation of de Maupassant's* La Parure, *in which a supposedly genuine necklace is found to be false, by centering the action on a string of pearls, thought to be worthless but proved to be real. Nothing in this or in the denouement of the*

1. Pages 177-8 above.

story suggests the notebook entry, but the idea of how members of a family might react differently to the discovery of a relative's fault is made use of. A woman, who has given up a stage career to marry a vicar, leaves hidden at her death a lot of tinsel jewelry that she has worn on the stage, among which is one pearl necklace that turns out to be genuine. Her step-son is shocked by the discovery, since he believes the jewels must have been the gift of a lover; his cousin is less interested in the moral aspect of the case than fascinated by the new romantic light in which the finding of the necklace places her aunt.]

May 13th, 1895. I have just promised Scudder 3 short stories for the *Atlantic.* I have a number of things noted here to choose from; but wish, in general, to remind myself that, more and more, every thing of this kind I do must be a complete and perfect little drama. The little idea must resolve itself into a little action, and the little action into the *essential* drama aforesaid. *Voilà.* It is the way—it is perhaps the only way—to make some masterpieces. It is at any rate what I want to do. x x x x x

There comes back to me the memory of a little idea I took up a year or two ago to the extent of writing a few pages—pages which I have just rummaged out of my desk: the idea suggested to me by one Mrs. Anstruther-Thompson, whom I sat next to at a Xmas dinner at Lady Lindsay's. She told me an anecdote that I noted at the time, in another book (than this) and have just hunted up.[1] Reading over my little statement I find the case vividly enough, though very briefly, presented, and I can probably go on with my beginning. What is wanting is a full roundness for the action—the completeness of the drama-quality. I see the action up to a certain point, but what can be the solution, the denouement? The action is the mother's refusal to give up the house, or the things. But that is, in itself, no conclusion, no climax. What is it that follows on that? (*May 15th, 1895.*) I seem to see the thing in three chapters, like 3 little acts, the 1st of which terminates with the son's marriage to one—the dreaded one—of the Brigstocks. In this 1st act Mrs. Gereth takes the girl—her own girl (Muriel Veetch)—to her own house and adopts her there, as it were, shows her its beauty. Her initiation—their relation. A scene with Albert there, before the marriage. Mrs. Gereth's threat of rupture if it takes place. She must have had a scene with Nora Brigstock at Waterbath— the scene that determines her. All this splendidly foreshortened, as it

1. Pages 136-7 above.

were; as the whole thing must be. Then, Act II, the little drama of Mrs. Gereth's attitude, her preparations to leave the house—her going over it in farewell; then her collapse, her inability to *s'en arracher* and surrender her treasures. Of course in Act I all due prominence given to the element of Albert's 'want of taste'—his terrible, fatal *penchant* to ugliness, the thing that has made his mother precisely *want* so to redeem him, to safeguard, by a union with such a girl as Muriel Veetch—and makes her feel that the union with a Brigstock precisely loses him forever. All this crystalline in Act I. It surely gives me plenty of material for that act. Each act is 50 pages of my MS. Well then, in II, I give her collapse, her refusal to surrender. But I must carry the action on a step, a stride *beyond* that, to get the climax of my Chapter II. What can this climax be? May it be some act or step on the part of the son—some resolution, some violence of his? And then the denouement, the solution, the climax that Chapter III leads up to, may that be something done by Muriel Veetch? I have a dim sense that the denouement must be *through* her. One thing strikes me as certain, that she must really be in love with Albert. The battle between Albert and his mother must be arrayed—and she in some way intervenes. His 'taking up the glove' ends Act II. Muriel takes the field in Act III— she interposes, she achieves. I seem vaguely to disembroil something like THIS: That Mrs. Gereth's *démarche* in II, the circumstance of her deciding to fight, is that she determines to have all the most precious things removed to the dower-house. She not only determines it—she *does* it. The element of her resentment at the way 'the mother' is treated in England is an active force in this. Perhaps she has a sister married in France—a silhouette, a thumbnail sketch chalked in—who sharpens the contrast and eggs her on. She *despoils* Umberleigh, or whatever the name is—she *skims* it, she strips it. She has everything that is really precious and exquisite carted away to her own house. *She does it in Muriel's absence*—while Muriel is away on a family errand (her dying father or something of that sort). She does it too without telling Albert of what she intends. He comes and finds it done—comes back from his wedding-tour—or from some later absence. This discovery, on his part, is the 'climax' of Chapter II. The mother and son are face to face in a 'row.' He threatens to prosecute—his wife eggs him on. Muriel's intervention takes the form of trying to avert all this hideousness, getting Mrs. Gereth to make the terrible concession and restore what she has taken away. She secretly loves the young man—that is why. She prevails, Mrs. Gereth has the things restored. The horrible, the atrocious conflagration—which may at any rate, I think, serve as my working hypothesis for a denouement. x x x x x

[*In discussing* The Spoils of Poynton *and* What Maisie Knew *in particular, James shows how his experience of writing for the theater has led him to think more and more interchangeably of narrative and dramatic structure. As he worked out the* Spoils, *he departed from the clear-cut divisions that would have been necessary on the stage. Owen's marriage to Mona Brigstock does not take place until near the end of the novel, whereas Fleda's concern with the affairs of both Mrs. Gereth and Owen starts developing almost from the outset.*

James dropped, as a needless complication, his intention of introducing a sister of Mrs. Gereth's, but mentioned in two or three sentences her friend Madame de Jaume, in order to point out the different disposition of property in France.

Since his normal manuscript pages ran at this time to between 110 and 140 words each (see pp. 104, 160 above, p. 229 below) James seems first to have conceived the whole as approximately fifteen to twenty thousand words, instead of the ten thousand which, as he remarks (at p. 211 below), Horace Scudder had asked for. James recalled in his preface the painful consequences of his delusion that he could ever handle this theme in the dimensions of three short installments, and concluded that 'the sole impression' the work made upon the editor was, 'I woefully gathered . . . that of length, and it has till lately . . . been present to me but as the poor little "long" thing.' But though Scudder had objected, without much perception of the quality involved, he had still run The Old Things *serially in the* Atlantic *from April through October 1896. Its final length was close to seventy thousand words. Considering the later connotations of the phrase, it is more than fortunate that James abandoned, as another possible title,* The House Beautiful.]

34 De Vere Gdns., W., June 4th, 1895.

The question of doing something in a very short compass—10,000 (or 8000) words with the little idea that I noted some time back[1]—the notion of the little drama that may reside in the poor man of letters who squanders his life in trying for a vulgar success which his talent is too fine to achieve. He wants to marry—he wants to do at least once something that will sell; BUT—do what he will—he *can't* make a sow's ear out of a silk purse. It's in this sad little baffled, almost tragically baffled, attempt that the small action must reside. He succumbs, somehow, he has to fail, to give up, to collapse materially, because the worst he can do, as it were, is too good to succeed—too good for the market. It is the old story of my letters to the *N.Y.T.* where I had to write

1. Page 180 above.

to Whitelaw R. that they 'were the worst I could do for the money.' It is against a little series of cases of this kind, of dismissals, of misfortunes, of failures to catch the tone in spite of wanting and *needing* to, that the talent incapable of adequate vulgarity *se rompt*—'every time.' The little story would be the story of what depends on it—of what he is prevented from doing (marrying, living, keeping his head above water), by his not hitting it off. I don't know what I can hope to do in my short 8000 words except show 3 or 4 cases. One of them—the one to begin with—might be just a little case similar to, identical with, my adventure with the *Tribune*. I lost that work, that place—so *he* loses it and is left stranded. Only for me everything didn't depend upon it; while for my imagined little hero everything *does*. Has he married on the prospect?—one must figure it out. In 8000 words—which is what I must try for—I probably can't show more than 3 cases. I seem to see them as three striking, crucial ones, observed at intervals by the narrator. In my former note of this I seemed to catch hold of the tail of a dim idea that my narrator might be made the ironic portrait of a deluded vulgarian (of letters too), some striving *confrère* who *has* all the success my hero hasn't, who *can* do exactly the thing he can't, and who, vaguely, mistily conscious that he hasn't the suffrages of the *raffinés*, the people who count, is trying to do something distinguished, for once, something that they will notice, something that WON'T sell. This person, man or woman, has become, *through* selling, rich enough to *se passer cette fantaisie*—which comes to him, or to her, through the stirring of the spirit communicated by contacts with our friend. Is this person the narrator—and do I simplify and compress by making him so? The difficulty is that the narrator must be fully and richly, must be ironically, *conscient*: that is, *mustn't* he? Can I take such a person and make him—or her—narrate my little drama *naïvement*? I don't think so—especially with so *short* a chance: I risk wasting my material and missing my effect. I must, I think, have my real ironic painter; but if I take that line I must presumably include the vulgarian somehow in my little tale. *I* become the narrator, either impersonally or in my unnamed, unspecified personality. Say I chose the latter line, as in the *Death of the Lion*, the *Coxon Fund*, etc. *Voyons un peu* what, saliently, in that case, my little vision of the subject gives me. Say, as the 1st example, the episode of the newspaper correspondence, the letters from London to some provincial sheet. He has married on this?—or has he only planned to marry? Oh yes, the latter—that gives me more drama. He is just going to be able to, when the dismissal from the paper comes. He has to put it off—to wait. Then he writes his novel, and it is, for the *raffinés*, so fine, that it's accepted. It is published and has no sale at all; so he again can't marry. His fiancée must have a grim, vulgar, worldly, interfering mother *qui s'y oppose*—makes an income a condition. May not she have pretensions to 'smartness'—to family?—and be broken-down and mercenary and selfish as well, very reluctant to part with the convenience of her daughter; hating her marriage and attaching conditions. She has some money to leave—she holds the girl to a certain extent by it. The girl's a lady and is extremely pretty. Her mother thinks her a beauty and that she might have contracted a much more elegant connection. Or may not the mother be a snobbish, pretentious, tyrannical FATHER, so as not to have 3 women? That's a detail—*nous verrons bien*. I seem, at any rate, to see my vulgarian, the successful novelist, as the sister (or the brother?) of the girl my hero's engaged to. *Mettons, sister,* for the sake of the little ray, the little play of added irony that comes from the question, here, of sex. It is she, started, *lancée,* as a novelist, who brings the young man her sister's engaged to, to my notice as a struggling young writer. I get him the engagement on the provincial paper. The successful sister isn't then —isn't *yet*—the great success she afterwards becomes. She is fearfully ugly. *She* marries perhaps a publisher, or (if that is too like Miss Braddon), a man of business who makes her bargains for her. When she develops the fancy to do something 'literary'—i.e., that won't sell —it sells more than ANYTHING she has done! I seem to catch hold of the tail of a glimpse of my own personality. I am a critic who doesn't sell, i.e., whose writing is too good—attracts no attention whatever. *My* distinguished writing fairly damages *his* distinguished—by the good it tries to do for <him>. To keep me *quiet* about him becomes one of his needs—one of the features of his struggle, that struggle to manage to do once or twice, remuneratively, the thing that will be popular, the exhibition of which (pathetic little vain effort) is the essence of my subject. I try not to write about him—in order to help him. This atti-tude of mine is a part of the story. I am supposing, then, that his novel (he must have written 2 or 3 before) fails, commercially, thanks to the attitude of the mother or the father about his marriage. But the marriage must take place, for the sake of what takes place after it. It is AFTER it that he tries to do the work that will meet Whitelaw Reid, etc. Then the pressure, the necessity to do that becomes great. He writes a 2d disinterested novel—and I get a magazine to 'serialize' it. It is on *that* money that he hopefully marries. But (the money having been paid down in a lump!) the serial is a deadly failure; and he is, with his wife and children on his hands, face to face with his future. *Or,* into what 2 or 3 salient, crucial cases can I summarize, to illustrate his vain effort, that future? What are the things that, thanks to his quality, he has successively to give up? There must be one or two of these, and then an illustrative denouement. May it be a question of some place—an editorship that he loses because he will only put in things of quality—and can't get them: won't put in certain vulgarities? He chucks up the thing on the question of a certain vulgar contribution which the publisher wants to force in, and which he can't bring himself to publish. He will himself work to sell, because he knows what he will do, or rather what he *won't* do; but he won't publish the rot of others when it belongs precisely to this class of what he won't do. He sacrifices the editorship—has the courage to do it—because this time, precisely, he holds—*il tient*—the idea that will make the selling novel. He puts the novel through, and it proves (I think it at least) finer than ever. I want to say so—but he begs me to keep my hands off it. He says, 'Can you abuse it? *That* may help it.' I say I will see, I will try. But I find I can't—so I say nothing. I seem to myself to want my denouement to be that in a final case I *do* speak—I uncontrollably break out (without his knowing I'm going to: I keep it secret, risk it); with the consequence that I just, after all, dish him. There is something that must depend, for him, on his book's selling—something that he will get or that he can do: I mean in this final case, which constitutes the denouement. *Voyons.* He is ill and must go abroad—go to Egypt. Then it is that wanting to help him and carried away by the beauty of the thing, I risk it. I secretly—that is without asking his leave, blow my trumpet for him. Yes—I dish him. The book *doesn't* do, this time, any more than the other times (he keeps changing publishers), and on my head is the responsibility. I am the *blighting* critic. He can't go abroad—he has to give it up—he dies for want of it, and his wife, in her frenzy, comes down on me. But she repents, retracts, says now that he is dead I *can* praise him. The good natured, vulgar sister-in-law's effort (she must have a hard stingy husband, who prevents her from charities and *largesses*)—this effort, *not* to sell, for once, and which also fails, must be in some manner synchronous with my hero's. She wants me to praise her, so that THAT may help her not to sell. But I *can't*—so sell she does. I think I may call the thing *The Next Time*. And begin it—'Yes, my notes as I look them over bring it back to me.' Or begin it with the visit of the selling sister-in-law (after his death, on the errand just stated) and hark back from that? This last, I think. Oh, it will take 10,000 words.

[*James must have written* The Next Time *quite rapidly, since it appeared in the* Yellow Book *for July 1895. His account of its origin, in his preface to* The Lesson of the Master, *is a very oblique refraction of what he says here.*

This entry furnishes an opportunity of watching James arrive at one of the most distinguishing features of his method, the character of his projected narrator. He dropped his first notion of having the story told by the successful lady novelist, since he soon realized that he wanted— as he generally did—to have his narrator 'conscient.' He ended with making the attitude of the critic-narrator such an integral part of the story that it even contributes a double refinement to James' game: added to Ralph Limbert's inability to make money by his magnificent novels is the fact that the devotion of his friend the critic is also 'the love that kills.'

The story opens with the conversation between the critic and Mrs. Highmore, 'one of the most voluminous writers of the time,' who yearns to be like her late brother-in-law, 'but of course only once, an exquisite failure.' (Miss Braddon, whom James had thought of in passing, was the author of Lady Audley's Secret and eighty other novels, and wife of the publisher, John Maxwell.) The critic recalls some of the episodes of poor Limbert's career, beginning with the time when he, the narrator, had used his little influence to get the young novelist the position of correspondent for the Blackport Beacon. Limbert had to have more means, since his prospective mother-in-law, Mrs. Stannace, quite disgusted with the career of her husband ('he had published pale Remains or flat Conversations of his father'), had an eye only for the main chance. In the view of the critic, Limbert did almost too well with his column—'The tone was of course to be caught, but need it have been caught so in the act?'—but to the astonishment of both young men, the editor found it nowhere near 'chatty' enough, and Limbert lost the job. He then managed to have The Major Key serialized, but in volume form it didn't even get the publisher's money back. It met the critic's (and James') test for a novelist's greatness— 'when of a beautiful subject his expression was complete.' 'It converted readers into friends and friends into lovers; it placed the author, as the phrase is—placed him all too definitely; but it shrank to obscurity in the account of sales eventually rendered.'

Then, by a stroke of fortune, Limbert happened to attract Mr. Bousefield, the proprietor of a 'high-class monthly,' who thought that he wanted 'literature,' since 'literature' was 'the way the cat was going to jump.' He thought also that Limbert's name would be an ornament on his cover, and made him his editor. But the break came when Limbert refused to publish 'a series of screaming sketches' by Minnie Meadows, while at the same time Mr. Bousefield took violent exception to the critic's column: 'Your "Remarks" are called "Occasional," but nothing could be more deadly regular; you're there month after month and you're never anywhere else. And you supply no public want.'

Thereafter, even the critic realized that 'the next time' would never be different, and watched how even The Hidden Heart, planned as an adventure story to bring in the receipts that Limbert by then desperately required for his health, 'proved, so to speak, but another female child.' The worst he could ever contrive was 'a shameless merciless masterpiece.']

June 26th, 1895, 34 De Vere Gdns., W.

A little idea occurred to me the other day for a little tale that Maupassant would have called *Les Lunettes*, though I'm afraid that *The Spectacles* won't do. A very pretty, a very beautiful little woman, devoted to her beauty, which she cherishes, prizing, and rejoicing in it more than in anything on earth—is threatened, becomes indeed absolutely afflicted, with a malady of the eyes which she goes to see oculists about. She has had it for a long time, and has been told that she must wear spectacles of a certain kind, a big strong unbecoming kind, with a *bar* across them, etc.—if she wishes to preserve her sight. (The little notion of this was given me by my seeing a very pretty woman in spectacles the other day on the top of an omnibus.) She has been unable to face this disfigurement—she has evaded and defrauded the obligation (wearing them only in secret and sometimes changing them for glasses, etc.) and she has got worse. She *adores* her beauty, and it has other adorers. The story must be told by a 3d person, as it were, a spectator, an observer. He knows her case—sees her 1st at the oculist's, where he has gone for himself. At any rate he is witness of her relations with an adoring young man, whom she cold-shoulders, makes light of, treats, *du haut de son orgeuil et de sa beauté,* as not worth her trouble. He must be ugly—rather ridiculously ugly—and not brilliant in other ways. Then she *has* to take to the spectacles and disfigure herself. She must have been a married woman—separated from her husband. Or she may marry—THIS IS BETTER—a rich man from whom she keeps the secret of her infirmity. May it not be *in order* to catch him, nail him, that she so keeps it? She is in dread of losing him if she lets him know how she may be afflicted and disqualified in the future. He marries her (or *doesn't* he?—does he chuck her at the last, on a suspicion?) and what I, as narrator, see is a poor blind helpless woman (but beautiful in her blindness still), with the old rejected and despised lover now tenderly devoted to her, giving up his life to her—in short, as it must be, married to her. I think one *must* make her MISS the preferred lover—miss him at the very last, through his getting an accidental glimpse of her doom, and so be left alone and without fortune, with that doom staring her in the face.

[205]

[*The climax of Glasses is laid in the theater where the 'observer,' the artist who tells the story, visits Flora Saunt in her box, and discovers, when he kisses her hand, that she is blind.* She has married the 'ugly' young man, has discarded the disfiguring spectacles, and lives contentedly, secure in her husband's devoted admiration of her beauty.

In order that the 'observer' may know enough about Flora to understand her situation, he is supplied with a friend, Mrs. Meldrum, who tells him of Flora's background, her vulgar associations, her vanity about her looks, and her stubborn determination not to wear glasses and to risk everything to make a good marriage. Mrs. Meldrum is tied into the story not only by her friendship with the 'observer' but also by her obvious liking for the 'ugly' suitor and by the fact that it is she who steps in and supports Flora when her fortune is used up and the young nobleman whom she had hoped to marry discovers the state of her eyes and jilts her. Moreover, Mrs. Meldrum herself wears glasses of just the sort that Flora is supposed to wear, and so serves as a constant reminder of the doom that threatens the girl.

James likened his story to a string of beads, leading back to the first impression, which is not, however, that of a meeting at the oculist's, but of Flora's full beauty as she is surrounded by admirers at Folkestone. The truth about her eyes, told to the 'observer' by Mrs. Meldrum, is then dramatically presented in a scene in a toyshop where Flora, thinking she is not watched, slips on her spectacles for a moment and is seen by her 'preferred' lover.

James did not begin Glasses until after 8 September 1895, as his note on page 212 below shows, and the story was published in the Atlantic for February 1896. This latter note makes it clear that his interest in the idea for the story arose from his feeling that it had 'singleness' and could be briefly treated. But the ten-thousand-word limit was doubled for reasons that a letter to Scudder explains: 'As I wrote you the other day, I find, in my old age, that I have too much manner and style, too great and invincible an instinct of completeness and of seeing things in all their relations, so that development, however squeezed down, becomes inevitable—too much of all this to be able to turn round in the small corners I used to. I select very small ideas to help this—but even the very small ideas creep up into the teens. This little subject—of an intense simplicity—was tiny at the start, but in spite of ferocious compression—it has taken me a month—it has become what you see. Of course, if it's absolutely too long for you—in spite of its high merit—you will return it.'

James did not include this story in the New York edition, but did revise it for the Uniform Edition of his tales, printed in London, 1915-1919.]

34 De Vere Gardens, W., July 15th, 1895.

Yesterday at the Borthwicks', at Hampstead, something that Lady Tweedmouth said about the insane frenzy of futile occupation imposed by the London season, added itself to the hideous realization in my own mind—recently so deepened—to suggest that a 'subject' may very well reside in some picture of this overwhelming, self-defeating chaos or cataclysm toward which the whole thing is drifting. The picture residing, exemplified, in the experience of some tremendously exposed and intensely conscious individual—the deluge of people, the insane movement for movement, the ruin of thought, of life, the negation of work, of literature, the swelling, roaring crowds, the 'where are you going?,' the age of Mrs. Jack, the figure of Mrs. Jack, the American, the nightmare—the individual consciousness—the mad, ghastly climax or denouement. It's a splendid subject—if worked round a personal action—situation. x x x x x

The Americans looming up—dim, vast, portentous—in their millions—like gathering waves—the barbarians of the Roman Empire.

x   x   x   x   x

Osborne Hotel, Torquay, August 11th, 1895.

Voyons un peu où j'en suis in the little story of the situation between the mother and the son, in the little tale I have called the *House Beautiful* and of which I have hammered out some 70 pp. of MS. It is a question of a concision—for the rest of my 150 pp. in all, my rigid limit, for the *Atlantic*—truly masterly. Mona Brigstock and her mother are down at Poynton, brought by Owen Gereth, who considers that Mona shows to great advantage there and is having a great success. This infatuated density, this singleness and stupidity of perception, so often characteristic of the young Englishman in regard to the inferior woman, is the note of his attitude throughout. It makes Fleda wonder, marvel—and marvel without jealousy—see clearly how much more *doué* he is for marital than for filial affection. He cares, comparatively, nothing for his mother—would sacrifice her any day to his virtuous, Philistine, instinctive attachment to Mona. It is only *for* Mrs. Gereth that Fleda is, as it were, jealous; she says, in the face of Mona: 'Good heavens, if she were *my* mother, how common and stupid she would make, in comparison and contrast, such a girl as that, appear!' What I should like to do, God willing, is to thresh out my little remainder, from this point, tabulate and clarify it, state or summarize it in such a way that I can go, very straight and sharp, to my climax, my denouement. What I feel more and more that I must arrive at, with these things, is the adequate and regular practice of some such economy of clear summarization as will *give* me from point to point, each of my steps, stages, tints, shades, every main joint and hinge, in its place, of my subject—give me, in a word, my clear order and expressed sequence. I can then *take* from the table, successively, each fitted or fitting piece of my little mosaic. When I ask myself what there may have been to show for my long tribulation, my wasted years and patiences and pangs, of theatrical experiment, the answer, as I have already noted here, comes up as just possibly *this*: what I have gathered from it will perhaps have been exactly some such mastery of fundamental statement—of the art and secret of it, of expression, of the sacred mystery of structure. Oh yes—the weary, woeful time has done something for me, has had in the depths of all its wasted piety and passion, an intense little lesson and direction. What that resultant is I must now actively show. x x x x x

What then is it that the rest of my little 2d act, as I call it, of *The House Beautiful* must do? Its climax is in the removal—*must absolutely and utterly be: voilà*—from the house, by Mrs. Gereth, of her own treasures. What are the steps that lead to that? Well, these.

1st. Owen must have a morsel with Fleda in which he shows how happy he is with the result of their visit, and which she doesn't retail to his mother.

2d. Mrs. G., the morning they go (the Brigstocks), does take the alarm, though Owen doesn't give her the news himself. He hasn't got it yet—Mona doesn't speak till they get back to town. But Mrs. Brigstock has spoken more or less, and Owen has shown, does show, to Mrs. Gereth, how pleased he is. There must be a scene of some sort between the young man and his mother—and between Mrs. G. and Mona. Yet surely all this must be very, *very*, VERY brief and rapid— for it is after all preliminary, and the centre of gravity of the piece, which is that Owen marries Mona, is in danger of being thrust much too far forward, out of its place. As it is I've almost no room at all for my people to talk. What I think I want to make take place between Mrs. Gereth and Owen and Mona is the striking utterance on her part of some note of warning—some expression to them of her own ground, of what she expects, how she feels. It must take place before Fleda. Make it, *n'est-ce pas?*, that the pieces follow each other in this order.

(a) Owen shows himself to his mother *and* Fleda in the morning; and Fleda, after a vision of what is going on between them, goes out, leaves them together. She goes out into the grounds and finds Mona

[208]

there; ten words about what passes between the 2 women. They come in again, and then it is that Fleda has the sense of what Mrs. G. has said to Owen—has probably, dreadfully said—about *her*.

(b) The scene, for Mrs. G., before Owen and Fleda, with Mona—the scene that as Fleda feels, practically settles and clinches Mona. (It is Owen's own indications that have, after the night when they went downstairs, alarmed Mrs. G.) They depart, the ladies and Owen, leaving Mrs. G. under the impression that she has frightened them away. *But Fleda knows better*—though she pretends to agree. It is then —after they are gone—that Mrs. Gereth lets her know or suspect, to her horror, what she has already seemed to divine, to apprehend—that she *did* speak (while F. was in the garden with M.) about her, F., being *her* ideal for a daughter-in-law. This it is that makes F. doubly sure that the engagement to Mona will now be precipitated. Owen comes down alone in a few days, in fact, to announce it. What action does his mother then take? There must be the scene, *before* Fleda, about her surrender of the house—the scene of her, Mrs. G.'s, waiting for him to say, passionately, grievingly giving him a chance to say, that she may stay, that feeling as she does, he won't turn her out—or even that he'll give him up some of the things. But he doesn't say it. x x x x x

Rather, indeed, why may he *not* say this last? Doesn't his mother have, there, her long-smothered outbreak—flash about upon him about Mona's barbarism and the horrors of Waterbath? It's a dreadful, fatal scene: Fleda sees it or knows it. *Then* it is she has the scene with Owen that is to come after her knowing what his mother has said to him about her. It leads to the fact that Owen *does* offer to let his mother keep some of the things. Fleda puts in her own plea for this and makes her own reflection. Owen tells his mother, before he leaves, what he'll do. Before the marriage, however, he retracts—he lets her know that his wife has refused to part with anything. It was as he showed her Poynton, that day, that she wants to have it. It was the sight of it that day, that settled her. Therefore he must keep faith with her—and after all isn't he within his absolute rights? The marriage takes place—all in Act III. Fleda isn't present at it—the young couple go to Italy. But after she is settled in her own house Fleda goes down to see Mrs. Gereth. The 1st thing she perceives in her house—her little dower-cottage—are the things Mrs. G. has removed from Poynton. Voilà. That was to have been the climax of my 2d act, as it were; but I don't see how it *can* be, with any feasible adjustment to my space, if I try to make my 2d act one with my second chapter or section—my little 'II.' My only issue, here, is in multiplying, throughout the whole, my divisions. x x x x x

[As James practices the economy of 'fundamental statement,' we can observe, nevertheless, his material expanding under his hand. The seven to eight thousand words he had written before Mrs. Brigstock and Mona come down from Waterbath to Poynton took him only part way into the third chapter; and there were finally to be twenty-two. He did manage to compress and foreshorten the details he outlined. He left out the proposed scene between Mrs. Gereth and Mona, and introduced here no open debate about the property between Mrs. Gereth and Owen. As a result, he dispatched the Brigstocks' visit by the end of the third chapter. But as he looked ahead, he could already foresee his outline taking on accretions.

The remainder of Notebook IV is given to an entry dated 15 October 1895, which is printed in its chronological order, on page 214.]

NOTEBOOK V

8 September 1895—26 October 1896

Osborne Hotel, Torquay, September 8th, 1895.

I am face to face with several little alternatives of work, and am in fact in something of a predicament with things promised and retarded. I must thresh out my solutions, must settle down to my jobs. It's idiotic, by the way, to waste time in writing such a remark as that! As if I didn't feel in all such matters infinitely more than I can ever utter! x x x x x

My immediate necessity is to tackle again the question of one of the little stories that I have promised to do for Scudder: the question round which, in general, as I have found before this, such tragic little accidents are apt to cluster. By tragic little accidents, I mean the tragic accident of the waste of labour to which I have often found myself condemned in trying to do the short (the really, I mean, the very short) thing. I am just crawling out of one of them, in this particular connection: the attempt, in *The House Beautiful*, to meet Scudder on the basis of 10,000 words—an attempt that has ended, irremissibly, incurably, in almost 30,000—leaving on my hands a production that *he* doesn't want and that I must try to make terms for in some other way, terms bad, terms sadd<en>ing, at the best. Ah, but let me not go, here, into the question of the reason for which this larger manner now imposes itself upon me—as it has every right and power to do: reasons with which my spirit is sufficiently saturated! Suffice it that I'm simply face to face with the little question: 'Can I do the thing in 10,000 words or can I not?' The answer to it is surely that I'm not prepared to say I can't. The difficulty has been, I think, when I've failed, that I haven't tried *right*. I've lost sight too much of the necessary smallness, necessary singleness of the subject. I've been too proud to take the very simple thing. I've almost always taken the thing requiring developments. Now, when I embark on developments I'm lost, for they are my temptation and my joy. I'm too afraid to be *banal*. I needn't be afraid, for my danger is small. I must try now, to do the thing of 10,000 words (which there is *every* economic reason for my recovering and holding fast the trick of). I must try it, I say, on the basis of rigid limitation of subject. That is, I must take, and take only, the single incident. I know what I mean by the single incident. *The Real Thing, The Middle Years, Brooksmith,* even, *The Private Life, Owen Wingrave,* are what I call single incidents. Many others are essentially ideas requiring development. *Cherchons, piochons, patientons—tenons-nous-en* to the opposite kind. Try to make use, for the brief treatment, of nothing, absolutely *nothing,* that isn't ONE, as it were—that doesn't begin and end in its little self. x x x x x

I noted the other day the little *concetto* that I might call *The Spectacles. Voyons,* let me consider a little how to turn it. It has the needed singleness, hasn't it? Surely, if anything *can* have. x x x x x

[Glasses defied James' efforts to achieve the brevity he wanted, as noted at page 206 above.]

Torquay, September 22d, 1895.

Note here more fully, later, 2 little *sujets de nouvelle* suggested to me, one by Mme Bourget, the other by both P.B. and his wife.— The 1st came up through our talking of Hugues L<e Roux> and his elaborate imitation—personal, manual, literary and other—of Bourget. The idea of such an imitation—of the person making it—operating as a source of disenchantment (through accentuation of the points least liked) to a person deeply interested in the model—in the individual imitated. More concretely a woman, say, is in love with the great artist (poet, soldier, orator, actor—whatever), A. She doesn't know him well, but has been taken, smitten, though protesting—and has had, somehow, to lose him, to give him up. She meets B., the imitator, and, being struck with the great analogy, hails him at 1st as a source of interest, a consoler, a substitute. Then the way he brings out all the sides of the other man that she has liked least rises before her and creates a disillusionment—a dislike. It must be on *them* the imitation most bears. The imitator must *make* it so bear—in his fatuity and also (oh yes!) his *sincerity,* with the very design of pleasing, capturing her. He wants to get her for himself—his attempt upon her is a conscious one. But his admiration of his model is real—profound. He thinks he sees resemblances—is sure he does, and very artfully cultivates them. The Denouement, it strikes me, offhand, must be determined by the chance—by *a* chance the woman has to recover the great man—meet him again, have him again—know him better. *He* wants to give it to her—he has liked her. Unexpectedly, etc.—somehow —he has come back. But now she doesn't want him—she refuses, flees, waves him off, hides herself: the imitator has been fatal. *This*, at least, strikes me, offhand, as a case in which the narrator may be personal—first-personal. I seem to see that 'I' may figure. I seem to see that the thing may begin with my meeting the imitator 1st and being the source of his contact with the woman. I go on to see her somewhere, after this meeting—I find my friend under the impression of her separation from, her loss of, the original. I mention to her the other man who is such an extraordinary reproduction of him, and that *he* is coming, also, in a day or two. Isn't that a good beginning? I assist, there, at the little drama. I must, of course, have had my own independent knowledge or observation of the original. And I have a glimpse of the *finis*—the FINAL finish. The original *does* 'come on'—to the place, wherever it is—and only disappointedly to find the woman missing, absent, or whatever it may be—having, as it were, chucked him up. I meet him, I am with him, I explain.—'Well, you see So-and-So—the Imitation—was here.' 'Oh, I see! She has taken *him!*' 'On the contrary—she has him in horror.' The Great Man is puzzled. 'And yet he is awfully like me.' 'He is too much so!' But the great man never understands.

x   x   x   x   x

Note here, at leisure, the other small subject—the situation of Cazalis and Jean Lahor: [1] the *médecin de ville d'eau* with his great *talent de poète*, changing his name to a 'pen-name'—at his worldly wife's behest, to write poetry—frivolous and compromising for a doctor who has to make his way and feed his children, etc.—and then when the poetry brings him honour, some money, etc., having to change back again, so that—in fine the thing is to be figured out. There is a subject. The loss and confusion of identity, etc.

[James included both of these last two subjects in a list for possible stories on page 265 below.]

Make, later on, a statement of idea for treatment of Gualdo's charming little subject of *The Child*.

[James elucidates this subject a little in connection with his discussion of the themes both for Maud-Evelyn and The Tone of Time (p. 265 below). He mentioned it further on pages 280, 302 and 306. Gualdo was, presumably, Luigi Gualdo, an Italian novelist and story-writer, born in 1847.]

1. The real name of Jean Lahor, the Parnassian poet, author of *L'Illusion Suprême*, was Cazalis.

Osborne Hotel, Torquay, October 15th, '95.[1]

My little story has grown upon my hands—I am speaking of *The House Beautiful*—and will make a thing of 30,000 words. But though I have been scared at the dimensions it was taking—scared in view of the meagerness of the little subject—yet I think I see the way to make it fill out its skin and be very fairly solid and fine. x x x x x

Fleda Vetch is down at Ricks—has come down to find Mrs. Gereth installed and in possession of most of the treasures of Poynton. I did what I could yesterday to handle her arrival, but I must thresh out finely every inch of the action from that point to the end. The sense of what her friend has done quite appals the girl, and what has now passed between her and Owen prepares her for a great stir of feeling in his favour—a resentment on his behalf and pitying sense of his spoliations. I am here dealing with very delicate elements, and I must make the operation, the presentation, of each thoroughly sharp and clear. If this climax of my little tale is confused and *embrouillé* it will be nothing; if it's as crystalline as possible it will be worth doing. I have, a little, to guard myself against the drawback of having,[2] in the course of the story determined on something that I had not intended —or had not expected—at the start. I had intended to make Fleda 'fall in love' with Owen, or, to express it *moins banalement*, to represent her as loving him. But I had not intended to represent a feeling of this kind on Owen's part. Now, however, I have done so; in my last little go at the thing (which I have been able to do only so interruptedly), it inevitably took that turn and I must accept the idea and work it out. What I felt to be necessary, as the turn in question came, was that what should happen between Fleda and Owen Gereth should be something of a certain intensity. My idea was that it should be, whatever it is, determining for *her*; and it didn't seem to me that I could make it sufficiently intense and sufficiently determining without making it come, as 'it were, *from* Owen. *Je m'entends.*—Fleda suddenly perceives that on the verge of his marriage to Mona—he is, well, what I have in fact, represented. My present question—not to waste words about it—is as to what takes place between them when he comes down to Ricks. For I seem to see it so—that he does come down to Ricks. Mrs. Gereth must have achieved her devastation by a *coup de main*— proceeded with extraordinary celerity: this is made clear as between her

1. The following entry is the last in Notebook IV, inserted here in its proper chronological place.
2. The text now reverts to Notebook V, with James' note: '(continued from last page of Red Book: Osborne Hotel, Torquay, October 15, '95).'

[214]

and Fleda: the way she proceeded—got off in a night, as it were—is made perfectly distinct. Definite questions and answers about this. Fleda's night, after this, in the 'lovely' room Mrs. Gereth had arranged for her—her suffering under it, hatred of it, hatred of profiting by such things at Owen's cost, as it were. What has happened makes her think only of Owen. His marriage hasn't as yet taken place, but it's near at hand—it's there. She expects nothing more from him —has a dread of its happening. She wants only, as she believes, or tries to believe, never to see him again. She surrenders him to Mona. She has a dread of his not doing his duty—backing out in any way. That would fill her with horror and dismay. But she has no real doubt that he'll go through with his marriage. In going down to Ricks she has only seemed to herself to be going further away from him. She has had no prevision—she *could* have none—that he would turn up there. All she has wanted is to hear of his marriage. Touch the note that it has seemed to her even unduly delayed—delayed in a way to act on her nerves. She has got no invitation, but she hasn't expected that. The light on Mrs. Gereth's action, however, that she encounters at Ricks, changes the whole situation; causes her to hold her breath— making her not know exactly WHAT may happen. Now, *voyons un peu, mon bon:* the whole idea of my thing is that Fleda becomes rather fine, DOES something, distinguishes herself (to the reader), and that this is really almost all that has made the little anecdote worth telling at all. It gives me a lift—an air—and I must make it give me as much of these things as it ever possibly can. But I am confronted with a little difficulty which requires my looking it as coolly and calmly as I can in the face and figuring it out. What I have seen Fleda do is operate successfully (to state it as broadly as possible), to the end that the things be mainly sent back to Poynton. Now there are 2 necessary facts in regard to this. One is that a certain event, or certain events, certain forces, *lead up* to it, with their irresistible pressure on the girl. The other resides in the particular way in which she responds to that pressure. She gets the things back. *How* does she get them back? My idea had been that she successfully persuades Mrs. Gereth to send them. That seemed possible and adequate so long as my thought was simply that she had a sentiment for Owen: it seemed in the key of that little suppressed emotion. But now that the emotion is developed more and Owen himself is made, as it were, active, I feel as if I wanted something more—I don't know what to call it except *dramatic*. Let me make out first, however, exactly what precedes, and then I shall see my way a little more into what follows. Owen is brought down to Ricks by his discovery of the spoliation of Poynton. He has gone over, after his mother's departure, and taken in the scene. He has notified

Mona, and Mona has then come over with him and seen for herself, and the upshot has been that—having had the matter out between them—he has come down to his mother to demand a surrender. I must *motiver* his coming—his coming in person. Mona has wanted him to communicate only through their solicitor. He won't do that—he will be more tender: but Fleda sees that he takes his own way first because Mona has been strenuous about hers. I must represent Owen as not coming down with a preoccupation about Fleda: he doesn't know she's there—he thinks she in fact isn't. He has come because he simply *has* to. The reason WHY he simply has to, comes out in what takes place between him and Fleda. His mother refuses to see him—he is over at the inn. She makes Fleda see him for her. This takes place the day after Fleda's arrival. The girl thinks of refusing—then she consents. She has tried to refuse—for the trouble and torment the thing inflicts upon her—and because she has made it her rule, now, not to meet him, not to 'encourage' him, not to let herself go to this 'lawless love.' It seems to me I have really here the elements of something rather fine. The fineness is the fineness of Fleda. Let me carry that as far as possible—be consistent and bold and high about it: allow it all its little touch of poetry. She is forced again, as it were, by Mrs. Gereth, to renew a relation that she has sought safety and honour, tried to be 'good,' in *not* keeping up. She is almost, as it were, thrown into Owen's arms. It is the same with the young man. He *too* has tried to be good. *He* has renounced the relation. He has determined to stick to Mona. He is thrust by his mother into danger again. Mrs. Gereth is operating with so much more inflammable material than she knows. The young people meet at first as if that scene in Kensington Gdns. hadn't occurred; and Fleda says to herself that he repents of it, is ashamed of it. But they get into deeper waters. He informs her of the *sommation* he bears to his mother. Then briefly, quickly, *de fil en aiguille*, they come to the question of his alternative—his alternative or contemplated course if Mrs. Gereth refuses. Owen lets her know—practically what it is. It is Mona who now determines it. Mona has insisted on his *insisting*—and if he doesn't insist she will break off their marriage. She has made it a *condition* of their marriage. This is the climax of the 'scene' between the 2. It helps to constitute whatever beauty I may put into the thing. It is Fleda's opportunity—Fleda's temptation. If Mrs. Gereth doesn't surrender Mona will break, and if Mona breaks —*her* opening seems to lie there before her. Well—it's a part of what the girl does that she *resists*. She *sees* this, yet she does her best, heroically, to shut her eyes to it. She sees that Owen is ashamed of his disloyalty to Mona, and she has such a feeling about him that she doesn't want, she can't bear, to see him disloyal. That's about the gist of it.

If I want *beauty* for her—beauty of action and poetry of effect, I can only, I think, find it just there; find it in making her heroic. To *be* heroic, to achieve beauty and poetry, she must conceal from him what she feels. I have it then that he shows, but that she doesn't. What's the matter with Owen is that he has never known a girl like her, and that it's a girl like her he wants. She reads it all for him and in him, and we see it as she sees it, without his telling, his coming out with it. It's all on *his* part inarticulate and clumsy; but we *see*—though she doesn't let him give Mona away. What does she do then?—how does she work, how does she achieve her heroism? She does it in the first and highest way by urging him on to his marriage—putting it before him that it must take place without a week's more delay. She settles this, as it were—she fixes it: she says *she'll* take care of the rest. It's the question of *how* she takes care of it that is the tight knot of my *donnée*. She sends Owen off, sends him back to Mona, answers to him for it that what they demand shall be done. At least, rather (for she can't of course really 'answer'), she gives him her word that she will do her utmost to bring the restitution about; and it's on this he leaves her, promising her, as it were, to get married immediately. That confronts me with the question of the action Fleda exercises on Mrs. Gereth and of how she exercises it. My old idea was that she worked, as it were, on her feelings. Well, eureka! I think I have found it—I think I see the little interesting turn and the little practicable form. How a little click of perception, of this sort, brings back to me all the strange sacred time of my thinkings-out, this way, pen in hand, of the stuff of my little theatrical trials. The old patiences and intensities—the working of the old passion. The old problems and dimnesses —the old solutions and little findings of light. Is the beauty of all that effort—of all those unutterable hours—lost forever? Lost, lost, lost? It will take a greater patience than all the others to see!—My new little notion was to represent Fleda as committing—for drama's sake—some broad effective stroke of her own. But that now looks to me like a mistake: I've got hold, very possibly, of the tail of the right thing. Isn't the right thing to make Fleda simply work upon Mrs. Gereth, but work in an interesting way? She proceeds to the execution of Owen's commission *auprès de sa mère*, but she is conscious that she can proceed to it only by an appeal. *She* has no idea of there being anything else she can do. She appeals therefore, frankly, strongly— has the most strenuous and *equal* sort of scene with her friend that she has ever had. She places her behaviour in the light of honour, duty, etc.—of the failure of Owen's contract with Mona, which was to give her the house as Mona came down that day and saw it. She produces an impression—she shakes and influences Mrs. Gereth; but it isn't from the point of view of these special arguments that she uses. It's by the very fact of her urgency, the very accent of her earnestness, of her hidden passion. Mrs. Gereth guesses that hidden passion, and by this she's affected—she throws herself into the possibility. She pricks up her ears—she stares—she exclaims: she suddenly breaks out and charges the girl with the sentiment which is her motive, the sentiment that she has divined in her. Fleda, taken aback at first, upset, bewildered, sees in a moment the chance (towards her ideal end) that it will give her to admit to Mrs. Gereth the truth. She admits then—but admits nothing else; nothing of what has supremely passed between Owen and herself. There must be an absolute definiteness about what *has* passed: the promise, as it were, in exchange for *her* promise to act, that Owen has made her to go and get married. There must have been an opening here for the question of date, of postponement. Owen tells Fleda, in their interview, that Mona has postponed, so as to give him time to act and his mother time to restitute. (The *original* date of the marriage was otherwise close at hand.) Fleda makes Owen PROMISE to make Mona fix a day—make it by telling her that she (Fleda) undertakes for what Mrs. Gereth will do, and that she (Fleda) desires him to inform her to that effect. This constitutes a definite transaction between him and Fleda. It is on this transaction that the girl, to Mrs. Gereth, observes a studied silence. (Fleda, by the way, has coerced Owen into this agreement, or transaction, as I call it, by being in possession—entering into possession—of his secret, as it were, without having surrendered to him her own. This secret of his change about Mona is *used* by her in her 'heroism.') She not only keeps Mrs. Gereth off the scent of finding out, of perceiving or inferring, Owen's condition, but she tells a virtuous, 'heroic' *lie* on the subject. 'Does he know?' 'Thank God, no!' Fleda can say that with truth; but when— at some turn of her investigation—Mrs. Gereth has a gleam of wonder sufficient to make her say: 'Can it be possible he doesn't feel as he did about Mona—that he likes *you*?,' Fleda emphatically denies this. But Mrs. Gereth insists. 'He has not said a word to you that could give colour to such a possibility?' 'He has not said a word to me.' *Reste* the question of the postponement. She learns, Mrs. G., that the wedding *is* postponed. It is really postponed to give her time to send back the furniture; but Fleda doesn't tell her this. She doesn't tell her of Mona's condition, as communicated by Owen; for in her appeal to her she has not put it on that ground—she has put <it> on the ground of Owen's honour, etc. But she *works*, as it were, the fact of the postpone-ment—allows Mrs. Gereth to see a reason, an encouragement and hope in it. 'If he *should* break with her—*should* ask you to marry him, would you take him?'

'I'd take him,' says Fleda, profoundly. After this they *still* don't hear of the marriage. This determines Mrs. Gereth and she takes action in consequence. She sends back all but a few things—sends them all back and goes *abroad.* x x x x x

From the point I have reached (Oct. 16th) it must all be an absolute and unmitigated *action.* I have in VII Fleda's impression of the situation at Ricks. This must go to p. 210 of MS.—to Owen's arrival and include what passes between the 2 women on the subject of it.

VIII—p. 211-240. The 'Scene' at Ricks between Fleda and Owen, including the latter's departure.

IX—p. 241-271: the whole business of the Restitution, between Mrs. Gereth and Fleda, including the former's decision.

X.

                x   x   x   x   x

[In reckoning with the consequences of the added complication introduced by his making Owen come to love Fleda, James reveals what in his eyes made his story 'worth telling.' Everything would depend upon her 'fineness,' upon the 'beauty of action and poetry of effect' which would constitute her 'heroism.' His drama did not consist in the outer conflict. It had become the inner drama of Fleda's appreciation. He formulated it further in his preface: 'The progress and march of my tale became and remained that of her understanding. Absolutely, with this, I committed myself to making the affirmation and the penetration of it my action and my "story"; once more, too, with the re-entertained perception that a subject so lighted, a subject residing in somebody's excited and concentrated feeling about something—both the something and the somebody being of course as important as possible—has more beauty to give out than under any other style of pressure.'

It was characteristic of James that he found such a sensitive being as Fleda an important register. It was equally characteristic that, as he proceeded, he did not make the action depend upon 'some broad effective stroke' by his heroine. She delivers no strong declaration. She *is* surprised by Mrs. Gereth into tacit admission of her love for Owen. When James came to writing that scene, he also altered his intention of having Fleda say 'I'd take him.' She keeps her own troubled counsel.

In the effort to hold himself now to thirty thousand words, James finished his seventh chapter, wherein Fleda comes down to the dower-house at Ricks, within the projected compass. But the chapter between Fleda and Owen ran to five thousand words; and the subsequent discussion between Fleda and Mrs. Gereth took three chapters rather than one. And when, at their close, instead of deciding to send 'the

[219]

things' back to Poynton, Mrs. Gereth determines to keep them longer
to see whether that won't cause Mona to break with Owen, James has
obviously let himself in for further extensions.]

Torquay, October 18th, 1895.

The little subject there may, somehow, be in the study of a romantic
mind.—That term is a very vague and rough hint at what I mean. But
it may serve as a reminder.

The idea of the picture, fully satiric, in illustration of the 'Moloch-
worship' of the social hierarchy in this country—the grades and shelves
and stages of relative gentility—the image of some succession or ladder
of examples, in which each stage, each 'party,' has something or someone below them, down to extreme depths, on which, on whom, the
snubbed and despised from above, may wreak resentment by doing,
below, as they are done by. They have to take it from Peter, but they
give it to Paul. Follow the little, long, close series—the tall column
of Peters and Pauls. x x x x x

Torquay, October 24th, 1895.

I seem to see a little subject in this idea: that of the author of certain
books who is known to hold—and to declare as much, *au besoin,* to
the few with whom he communicates—that his writings contain a very
beautiful and valuable, very interesting and remunerative *secret,* or
latent intention, for those who read them with a right intelligence—
who see *into* them, as it were—bring to the perusal of them a certain
perceptive sense. There's a general idea *qui s'en dégage:* he doesn't tell
what it is—it's for the reader to find out. 'It's there—it's *there,*' he says;
'I can't—or I won't—tell you what it is; but my books constitute the
expression of it.' I should premise that I think I see these books necessarily to be NOVELS; it is in fact essentially as a novelist that the personage *se présente à ma pensée.* He has such qualities of art and style and
skill as may be fine and honourable ones presumably—but he himself
holds that they don't *know* his work who don't know, who haven't felt,
or guessed, or perceived, this interior thought—this special *beauty* (that
is mainly the just word) that pervades and controls and animates them.
No reviewer, no 'critic,' has dreamed of it: lovely chance for fine irony
on the subject of that fraternity. *Mettons* that he mentions, after all,
the fact of the thing to only one person—to *me,* say, who narrate, in
my proper identity, the little episode. Say *I'm* a 'critic,' another little
writer, a newspaper man. I am in relation with him, somehow—relation, admiring, inquisitive, sympathetic, mystified, sceptical—whatever

it may be. *I* haven't, in the books, seen anything, but just certain pleasant and charming things—or whatever these things, merits, features, may superficially and obviously be. No, *I* haven't discovered anything. But he tells *me*: say (yes), I'm the only person he tells. (I can't go into the stages and details here—this is the barest of summaries.) That is, he tells me the fact: the *existence* of the latent beauty: oh, what it *is*, what it consists of, he doesn't tell me or tell anybody, at all. This he confides to no one, and is serenely, happily content not to confide to any one. There it is, there it is: there let it stay! His great amusement in life is really to see if any one will ever see it—if the great race of critics, above all, will ever be sufficiently perceptive for it some day to flash upon them. '*Does* it flash—is that the way it comes —in a sudden revelation?,' I ask him. My worriment, my wonderment— my little torment about what the devil it can be. My questions, my readings-over—and his answers, his indifference, his serenity, his amusement at all our densities and imbecilities: but without a shadow of *real* information. His answers only play with my curiosity—and he doesn't care. It isn't the 'esoteric meaning,' as the newspapers say: 'it's the *only* meaning, it's the very soul and core of the work.' I wonder if he's only joking—or if he's mad. I somehow don't believe he's joking (circumstances contradict it), and if he's mad, how can he have made his work so *perfect*? How can it be, in form and substance, so sane and sound? Decidedly, it must be distinguished, the work, must have the qualities of charm that are patent. That is needed to preclude the idea of madness. *Voyons*, then: after he makes his communication to me (tells me the thing is there), I, immediately, in turn, make it to another friend of mine, a young man of letters, say. He is interested in our author—he is much interested in the fact, in the revelation, imperfect as it is. Just after this the author tells me that I had better not mention or repeat what he has told me—it was for *me*: it wasn't for the vulgar world. I tell him that I *have* already repeated it to my young friend, etc.; but that I will tell him not to tell others. The Author says, 'Oh, it doesn't matter!'—he doesn't seem really to care, after all. I do tell my young friend what he has said to me—his caution about diffusing his statement; and my young friend says: 'I'm very sorry —I've already told So-and-So!' So-and-So is a young lady in whom he is much interested. 'Well, tell her to keep it to herself,' I say. He does so—he tells me afterward that she will. But he tells me also that she is much interested—she is an 'admirer,' and she wants to find out—if she can—what the reference bears upon. The young man, the 2d young man (my friend), does too—and it is *his* torment, *his* worry, *his* study of the pretty books, that I perhaps mainly represent. *I* have given them up—the game isn't worth the candle. It's all a bad joke and a mystifica-

[221]

tion: *that's* the ground I take. But I know that he talks the matter over with his young lady, goes into it with her, wonders, worries, seeks, renounces, with her. Say *I* take the ground of our hero's madness, or mere persistent pleasantry amounting almost to madness—and that it's he who take<s> the side of the outright beauty and sanity of the work. He too is a critic—only he's the shamed one, the one sensitive to the reproach. I'm not, I don't care, I cling to my vulgar explanation: I've not been a particular admirer of the novels. My friend has always seen more in them than I do. He has his theories—he has his explanations, his clues and glimpses—he puts forward one, then another, then a third—which he successively renounces—they won't hold. The young lady has hers—which he tells me about and which break down, too. They quarrel about them—they are quite possessed with their search. Does the young man, my friend, know the author, meet him, talk with him? A point to be settled, but I think not: he *wants* to, but he wants to wait till he can really say, 'Eureka!,' and then go and submit his solution to him and get a reply: say 'Isn't *that* it?'—and have perhaps at last the great assent. Well, before this, the Author dies—and that test, that light, that disclosure, become forever inaccessible. No one knows, now—he carries the secret away with him. But (to make a long story—it's really—it must be really—of the briefest—short) my young man continues to be haunted by it. At last he lets me know—from a distance—that he has discovered it. He has, he *has*, this time—it's a revelation—it's wonderful. Or I must learn, perhaps from the young woman, that this has occurred. Yes, that's the way I'll have it! He's at a distance and *she* has heard from him. She doesn't at all know what it is—but he's to tell her. I am then devoured with curiosity and suspense. 'When is he to tell you?' 'Well, after we're married,' she replies with some embarrassment. 'You're to be married?' I have thought they had quarrelled—but it appears they have made it up. She tells me *when*—he is coming on to London (he's abroad, or in the East, or in Scotland) and it will then take place. I write to him, however, before that—I ask him to appease my curiosity. He replies that he is coming on to his wedding and will do so then. I write that I shall not be in London, alas, for it, and that he had better make me the revelation by letter. He rejoins that he can do it much better *viva voce*, and would rather so do it; and I have to rest content with that. He has specified some near time at which we *shall* be likely to meet. But we don't meet—we never meet. I leave town before he comes—and he is married in my absence. Three months later, before I get back, he is killed—by an accident. He carries away his discovery with him—save in so far as he *has*, after marriage, told it to his wife. I must KNOW that he *has* so told it. But somehow I feel it to be a thing

I can't ask her and she can't tell me. There is evidently, about it, a strange mystifying uncomfortable delicacy. She never offers to satisfy me—though I meet her and she has a chance and knows how curious I am. So I have to go unsatisfied. I do so for a long time. The strange thing is that now, somehow, I feel the mystery to be a reality. I feel that the deceased wasn't mad. I almost want to marry the widow—to learn from her *de quoi*, in the name of wonder, *il s'agit*. I feel as if she might tell me if we should be married—but that she'll never tell me otherwise. But I don't marry her—I *can't*, simply for that! At last she marries some one else. I feel sure she tells *him*. I want to ask him—I hover about him—I come very near it. But I don't—I don't think it, when I come to the point, quite delicate or fair. I don't—I forbear. In the course of time—in childbirth—*she* dies. Then, after an interval, I get my chance. She is the 3d person who has carried the mystery to the grave; but she, at last will have left, in the person of her husband, a depositary. I am able to approach him, and I do so. I put the question to him, ask him if his wife didn't tell him. He stares—he's blank—he doesn't know what I'm talking about. 'So-and-So? The secret of his books—?' He looks at me as if *I* am mad. She has never told him anything: she has carried the mystery uncommunicated to the grave. x x x x x

Two little things, in relation to this, occur to me. One is the importance of my being *sure* the disclosure has been made to the wife by her 1st husband. The other is the importance of *his* having been sure he had got hold of the right thing. The only way for this would be to have made him submit his idea to the Author himself. To this end the Author's death would have *not* to precede his discovery. Say I make him get *at* the Author, with his 'discovery,' and the latter's death occurs, away from London, therefore, between that event and my ascertainment of the intended marriage. The form in which I hear of it from the girl is that her fiancé HAS submitted it to the Author. *Then* the Author dies—abroad, ill, in a climate. It's *there* my young man has gone to him—is with him. All this mere suggestion—to be figured out. The thing to be REALLY brief. x x x x x

[By devising this highly complicated plot for The Figure in the Carpet (Cosmopolis, January–February 1896), James produced for his reader an effect not unlike that of opening a series of ingeniously mystifying Russian boxes in search of an ultimate kernel. If all of life seems somehow sacrificed to the baffled critic's curiosity, he and his friend George Corvick and Gwendolen Erme are indefatigable players of James' favorite game: 'For the few persons, at any rate, abnormal or not, with whom my anecdote is concerned, literature was a game of skill, and skill meant courage, and courage meant honour, and honour meant passion, meant life.'

He admitted in his preface to having been asked, 'Where on earth, where round about us at this hour, I had "found" my Neil Paradays, my Ralph Limberts, my Hugh Verekers and other such supersubtle fry.' His answer was: 'If the life about us for the last thirty years refuses warrant for these examples, then so much the worse for that life.' He had designed The Figure in the Carpet in particular as 'a significant fable,' as an 'ironic or fantastic' protest against the general 'numbness' of Anglo-American sensibility. Through Hugh Vereker's plea for perception of the animating design of his work, James again took his stand against 'our so marked collective mistrust of anything like close or analytic appreciation.' His own prefaces were to be his ripest demonstration of the value of such analysis.]

Torquay, October 28th, 1895.

I remember how Mrs. Procter once said to me that, having had a long life of many troubles, sufferings, encumbrances and devastations, it was, in the evening of that life, a singular pleasure, a deeply-*felt* luxury, to her, to be able to *sit and read a book*: the mere sense of the security of it, the sense that, with all she had outlived, *nothing could now happen*, was so great within her. She had, as it were, never had that pleasure in that way or degree; and she enjoyed it afresh from day to day. I exaggerate perhaps a little her statement of her individual ecstasy —but she made the remark and it struck me very much at the time. It comes back to me now as the suggestion of the tiny little germ of a tiny little tale. The thing would be, of course, only a little picture— a little scrap of a vignette. One would tell it one's self, one would have seen it, and would retail it as an impression. There would be an old, or an elderly, person whom one would have known, would have met—in some contact giving an opportunity for observation. This old person—in the quiet waters of some final haven of rest—would manifest such joy—such touching bliss—in the very commonest immunities and securities of life—in a quiet walk, a quiet read, the civil visit of a friend or the luxury of some quite ordinary *relation*, that one would be moved to wonder what could have been the troubles of a past that give such a price to the most usual privileges of the present. What could the old party (man or woman) have been through, have suffered? This remains a little suggestive mystery. The old party (the time of life a thing to determine properly) is reserved, obscure, uncommunicative about certain things—but ever so weary and ever so rested. One wonders, but one doesn't really want to know—what one is really interested in is guarding and protecting these simple joys. One watches and sympathises, one is amused and touched, one likes to think the old party is safe for the rest of time. Then comes the little denouement. Isn't the little denouement, must it *not* only be, that some horrid danger becomes real again, some old menace or interruption comes back out of the past? The little safeties and pleasures are at an end. What I seem to see is that somebody, a fatal somebody, turns up. *Voyons:*—I seem to see something like an old fellow whose *wife* turns up. The *mot* of his present ease is that it's his wife who has been the source of the complications, the burdens that preceded. But she comes back as a repentant, reconciled, compunctious, reunited wife. She abounds in this sense—but all the more, on that account, *sein' Ruh ist hin.* She invades him still more with her compunction than with her—whatever it was of old. She has come (genuinely, but selfishly, for peace and quiet—*she* wants to read a book, etc.) but hers, somehow, puts an end to his. I note this, I see it all, I feel for him. It's the old life—in essence—back again. At last, abruptly, he disappears—he vanishes away, leaving the wife in possession. Then I see *her*—having exterminated him—given up to the same happy stillness as *he* was. She is in his chair, by his lamp, at his table: she expresses just the same quiet little joy that he did. 'It's such a luxury to just sit and read a book.' It's the same book—one I have seen *him* read. My old party, let me note, must (it seems to me) be, necessarily and essentially, of the specifically refined and distinguished order—a man of the world, absolutely, in type, a man of quality, as it were, in order to make this contentment with small joys, this happiness in the mere negative, sufficiently striking. It wouldn't *be* adequately striking in a person of very simple or common kind. The same, I suppose, is, or ought to be, true of the type of the wife. Mayn't one imagine them both *raffinés*—who have undergone a considerable loss of fortune?

[*James listed this subject again, under the general title* Les Vieux (*p. 234 below*).]

Names. Wilverley—Perriam—Boel—Beaudessin—Poyle—Jerram—Stanforth—Overmore—Undermore—Overend.

Torquay, October 31st, 1895.

I was struck last evening with something that Jonathan Sturges, who has been staying here 10 days, mentioned to me: it was only 10 words, but I seemed, as usual, to catch a glimpse of a *sujet de nouvelle* in it.

We were talking of W.D.H. and of his having seen him during a short and interrupted stay H. had made 18 months ago in Paris—called away—back to America, when he had just come—at the end of 10 days by the news of the death—or illness—of his father. He had scarcely been in Paris, ever, in former days, and he had come there to see his domiciled and initiated son, who was at the Beaux Arts. Virtually in the evening, as it were, of life, it was all new to him: all, all, all. Sturges said he seemed sad—rather brooding; and I asked him what gave him (Sturges) that impression. 'Oh—somewhere—I forget, when I was with him—he laid his hand on my shoulder and said à propos of some remark of mine: "Oh, you are young, you are young —be glad of it: be glad of it and *live*. Live all you can: it's a mistake not to. It doesn't so much matter what you do—but live. This place makes it all come over me. I see it now. I haven't done so—and now I'm old. It's too late. It has gone past me—I've lost it. You have time. You are young. Live!" ' I amplify and improve a little—but that was the tone. It touches me—I can see him—I can hear him. Immediately, of course—as everything, thank God, does—it suggests a little situation. I seem to see something, of a tiny kind, springing out of it, that would take its place in the little group I should like to do of *Les Vieux*—The Old. (What should I call it in English—*Old Fellows?* No, that's trivial and common.) At any rate, it gives me the little idea of the figure of an elderly man who hasn't 'lived,' hasn't at all, in the sense of sensations, passions, impulses, pleasures—and to whom, in the presence of some great human spectacle, some great organization for the Immediate, the Agreeable, for curiosity, and experiment and perception, for Enjoyment, in a word, becomes, *sur la fin*, or toward it, sorrowfully aware. He has never really enjoyed—he has lived only for Duty and conscience—his conception of them; for pure appearances and daily tasks—lived for effort, for surrender, abstention, sacrifice. I seem to see his history, his temperament, his circumstances, his figure, his life. I don't see him as having battled with his passions—I don't see him as harassed by his temperament or as having, in the past, suspected, very much, what he was losing, what he was not doing. The alternative wasn't present to him. He may be an American—he might be an Englishman. I don't altogether like the *banal* side of the revelation of Paris—it's so obvious, so usual to make Paris the vision that opens his eyes, makes him feel his mistake. It might be London—it might be Italy—it might be the general impression of a summer in Europe—abroad. Also, it *may* be Paris. He has been a great worker, a local worker. But of what kind? I can't make him a novelist—too like W.D.H., and too generally *invraisemblable*. But I want him 'intellectual,' I want him *fine*, clever, literary almost: it deepens the irony,

[226]

the tragedy. A clergyman is too obvious and *usé* and otherwise impossible. A journalist, a lawyer—these men WOULD in a manner have 'lived,' through their contact with life, with the complications and turpitudes and general vitality of mankind. A doctor—an artist too. A mere man of business—he's possible; but not of the intellectual grain that I mean. The Editor of a Magazine—that would come nearest: not at all of a newspaper. A Professor in a college would imply some knowledge of the lives of the young—though there might be a tragic effect in his seeing at the last that he hasn't even suspected what those lives might contain. (They had passed by him—he had passed them by.) He has married very young, and austerely. Happily enough, but charmlessly, and oh, so conscientiously: a wife replete with the New England conscience. But all this must be—oh, so light, so delicately summarized, so merely touched. What I seem to see is the possibility of some little illustrative action. The idea of the tale being the revolution that takes place in the poor man, the impression made on him by the particular experience, the incident in which this revolution and this impression embody themselves, is the point *à trouver*. They are determined by certain circumstances, and they produce a situation, his issue from which is the little drama. I am supposing him, I think, to have 'illustrated,' as I say, in the past, by his issue from some *other* situation, the opposite conditions, those that have determined him in the sense of the sort of life and feeling I have sketched and the memory, the consciousness of which roll over him now with force. He has sacrificed some one, some friend, some son, some younger brother, to his failure to feel, to understand, all that his new experience causes to come home to him in a wave of reaction, of compunction. He has not allowed for these things, the new things, new sources of emotion, new influences and appeals—didn't realize them at all. It was in communication with *them* that the spirit, the sense, the nature, the temperament of this victim (as now seems to him) of his old ignorance, struggled and suffered. He was wild—he was free—he was passionate; but there would have been a way of taking him. Our friend never saw it—never, never: he perceives that—ever so sadly, so bitterly, now. The young man is dead: it's all over. Was he a son, was he a ward, a younger brother—or an elder one? Points to settle: though I'm not quite sure I like the *son*. Well, my vague little fancy is that he 'comes out,' as it were (to London, to Paris—I'm afraid it *must* be Paris; if he's an American), to take some step, decide some question with regard to some one, in the sense of his old feelings and habits, and that the new influences, to state it roughly, make him act just in the opposite spirit—make him accept on the spot, with a *volte-face*, a wholly different inspiration. It is a case of some other person or persons, it is some other young life in regard to which it's a question of his interfering, rescuing, bringing home. Say he 'goes out' (partly) to look after, to bring home, some young man whom his family are anxious about, who won't *come* home, etc.— and under the operation of the change *se range due côté du jeune homme,* says to him: 'No; STAY:—*don't* come home.' Say our friend is a widower, and that the *jeune homme* is the son of a widow to whom he is engaged to be married. *She* is of the strenuous pattern— she is the reflection of his old self. She has money—she admires and approves him: 5 years have elapsed since his 1st wife's death, 10 since his own son's. He is 55. He married at 20! Displeasing the strenuous widow is a sacrifice—an injury to him. To marry her means rest and security *pour ses vieux jours.* The 'revolution' endangers immensely his situation with her. But of course my denouement is that it takes place—that he makes the sacrifice, does the thing I have, vaguely, represented him, *supra,* as doing, and loses the woman he was to marry and all the advantages attaching to her. It is too late, too late *now,* for HIM to live—but what stirs in him with a dumb passion of desire, of I don't know what, is the sense that he may have a little super-sensual hour in the vicarious freedom of another. His little drama is the administration of the touch that contributes to—that prolongs— that freedom.

[*James wrote to Howells, after finishing* The Ambassadors *in the summer of 1901, to tell him about their young friend Jonathan Sturges' repetition of 'five words you had said to him one day on his meeting you during a call at Whistler's. I thought the words charming—you have probably quite forgotten them; and the whole incident suggestive —so far as it was an incident; and, more than this, they presently caused me to see in them the faint vague germ, the mere point of the start, of a subject. I noted them, to that end, as I note everything; and years afterwards (that is three or four) the subject sprang at me, one day, out of my notebook. I don't know if it be good; at any rate it has been treated, now, for whatever it is; and my point is that it had long before —it had in the very act of striking me as a germ—got away from you or from anything like you! had become impersonal and independent. Nevertheless your initials figure in my little note; and if you hadn't said the five words to Jonathan he wouldn't have had them (most sympathetically and interestingly) to relate, and I shouldn't have had them to work in my imagination. The moral is that you are responsible for the whole business. . . May you carry the burden bravely!'*

Here, in contrast with both The Wings of the Dove and The Golden Bowl, James started, not with the outlines of a situation, but with the emotional center of his novel. Strether's declaration for life was the fullest expression of one of James' most recurrent themes. As he proceeded to fit his hero to a chain of events that could lead to this declaration, James gave up the notion of Strether's having failed in the past to understand some passionate son or younger brother. The only mention of Strether's family is that he has lost through death years ago both his wife and then his only son.

In keeping Paris as the scene for Strether's liberation, James presented the seductive charm of the city to which—in Tom Appleton's mot—'all good Americans go when they die.' But James avoided any shade of banality by making that liberation also an intense ethical drama. His imagination, when once aroused, also went on to find the human material it needed. To fill out Strether's desire 'of I don't know what,' it found the exquisite Madame de Vionnet.

The detailed preliminary draft or 'scenario' of The Ambassadors, which James submitted to Harper as a basis for serialization, is printed below on pages 372 ff. When he came to write his preface to this novel, James spoke of it confidently as 'the best, "all round," of all my productions.' He rejoiced particularly that his hero had afforded him the 'opportunity to "do" a man of imagination,' and that he had produced thereby his most effective center of consciousness.]

34 De Vere Gardens, November 4th, 1895.

I am thinking of trying the little *sujet de nouvelle* I noted the other day at Torquay—the one on the Author's Secret—for the 1st no. of the new review, *Cosmopolis*, to which the editor has asked me to contribute; but I must make it fit neatly into 11,000 words or, in other words, into a hundred (*close*) pages of my MS. *Voyons, voyons.* x x x x x I must make 10 little chapters of 10 pages of my MS. each. So! x x x x x

1. The visit from my friend who, owing to his *empêchement* (specify) asks me to do—to oblige him—a review of the Author's new novel, which he has made himself responsible for. He has to go off—to meet the girl who subsequently figures—meet her and her mother—returning from abroad: strike—yes—the note of the appearance of the girl here. He hasn't time—I must do it; and besides, it's a chance for me. I recognize the chance—I introduce the incident, in the very 1st words of my narration—as my FIRST real or good chance: the beginning of my little success or little career. I accept; we speak a moment or two of the Author—during which our note of divergence appears—and I mention, as a coincidence, that I have accepted an invitation to go

from the following Saturday to Monday down to a place in the country where it has been mentioned to me that I may meet him. 'Oh, then, you'll write handsomely—if you are going to look him in the face.—You must tell me all about him.' 'Yes, I'll tell you: I *will* look him in the face!' He goes off—I write my notice—I go down to the place. But I needn't detail here, so much, the points—only broadly indicate them.

II. I report to Corvick—I communicate: I set, in a word, the ball in motion. I see Vereker again and he warns me. I repeat this to Corvick and he tells me he has told the girl. x x x x x

I have brought the little subject treated of in the foregoing to p. 68 of my MS. (Nov. 22d), and must be sharply definite as to the skeleton of the rest. I have at the most 40 pages more. But they are, thank God, enough. *These*, at the point I've reached, are the facts still to be handled:—

Corvick has gone to the East on a commission from a newspaper.

Mrs. Erme is still alive and he is not yet engaged to Gwendolen.

She tells me that he writes to her from (Bombay?) that he has 'found it.'

What is it?

She doesn't know—he hasn't told her. (He says he'll tell her 'when we're married.') (She marries to find out [?]) He's to stop and see Vereker at Mentone and submit his idea to him. THEN he'll tell—if it's *right*—if it proves so. I hasten to Gwendolen to learn. Yes—it's right. Vereker says so. He's *with* Vereker. 'Then what is it?' 'He says he'll tell me when we're married.' 'You're engaged?' 'We've become so—but we can't marry in my mother's lifetime.' I don't ask after her mother's health, but I wonder—just wonder—! Corvick has told me before leaving England that they're *not* engaged. I write to him—he replies, telling me to wait. I am called away before his return: so I haven't the chance to see him face to face. I go to America—Vereker dies. Corvick dies 4 months after his marriage. The foregoing in 2 sections—leaving the last one for all that follows. Each to be of 12 pp. MS.

[The Figure in the Carpet *finally required eleven short chapters, and about fourteen thousand words.*]

Names.   Rotherfield—Fresson—Count—Delafield—Ash—Burr—Barb—Faber—Beale—Venning—Dandridge—Overmore—Balbeck—Bulbeck—Armiger—Gibelin—Beddom—Gerse—Nish—Bath—Brookenham—Fernanda ('Nanda')—Maliphant—Sneath.

December 21st, 1895, 34 De Vere Gardens.

The idea, for a scrap of a tale, on a scrap of a fantasy, of 2 persons who have constantly heard of each other, constantly been near each other, constantly *missed* each other. They have never met—though repeatedly told that they ought to know each other, etc.: the sort of thing that so often happens. They must be, I suppose, a man and a woman. At last it has been arranged—they really *are* to meet: arranged by some 3d person, the friend of each, who takes an interest in their meeting—sympathetically—officiously, blunderingly, whatever it may be: as also so often happens. But before the event one of them dies—the thing has become impossible forever. The other then comes, after death, to the survivor—so that they *do* meet, in spite of fate—they meet, and if necessary, they love.—They see, they know, all that would have been possible if they *had* met. It's a rather thin little fantasy—but there is something in it perhaps, for 5000 or 6000 words. There would be various ways of doing it, and it comes to me that the thing might be related by the 3d person, according to my wont when I want something—as I always do want it—intensely objective. It's the woman who's the ghost—it's the woman who comes to the man. I've spoken to them of each other—it's through me, mainly, that they know of each other. I mustn't be too much of an *entremetteur* or an *entre-metteuse:* I may even have been a little reluctant or suspicious, a little jealous, even, if the mediator is a woman. If a woman tells the story she may have this jealousy of her dead friend after the latter's death. She suspects, she divines, she feels that the man, with whom she is herself more or less in love, *continues* to see the dead woman. She has thought, she has believed, he cares for *her;* but now he is sensibly detached. Or if I don't have the '3d person' narrator, what effect would one get from the impersonal form—what peculiar and characteristic, what compensating, effect *might* one get from it? I should have in this case—shouldn't I?—to represent the *post-mortem* interview? Yes—but not necessarily. I might 'impersonally' include the 3d person and his (or her) feelings—tell the thing even *so* from his, or her, point of view. Probably it would have to be longer so—and really 5000 words is all it deserves.

x   x   x   x   x

[*The development of this theme into* The Friends of the Friends *is made more fully later at pages 241-4 below.*]

Thus I come back, inveterately—or at any rate necessarily—to the little question of the really short thing: come back by an economic necessity.

I can *place* 5000 words—that is the coercive fact, and I require, obviously, to be able to do this. It will help me so much to live that—really—I must make a more scientific trial of the form—I mean, of the idea of this extreme brevity. I needn't take time to make that formal declaration here: God knows I know what I mean, what I think, what I see, what I feel. My troubled mind overflows with the whole deep sense of it all—overflows with reflection and perception. The little things to do will all come to me—things of observation and reflection and fancy: life is full of them—they meet me at every turn. One thing is certain—they will come more and more the more I want them. Let them all proceed from my saturation—let them all be handed me straight by life. They'll come—they'll come: they *do* come: they have come: illustrations, examples, figures, types, expressions—I hold out my arms to them, I gather them in. À *l'oeuvre, mon bon, à l'oeuvre—roide!* x x x x x

Note, at my 1st leisure, briefly and concisely *all* the subjects for 'short' novels (80,000 to 100,000 words) I have *en tête*, and especially the 2 things that lately came to you: *The Advertiser* (magnificent, I think —[H<all> C<aine> etc.]) and the thing suggested by what was told me the other day of the circumstances of the W. K. Vanderbilt divorce: his engaging the *demi-mondaine*, in Paris, to *s'afficher* with him in order to force his virago of a wife to divorce him. I seem to see all sorts of things in that—a comedy, a little drama, of a fine colour, either theatrised or narrated: a subject, in short, if one turns it in a certain way. The way is, of course, that the husband doesn't care a straw for the *cocotte* and makes a bargain with her that is wholly independent of real intimacy. He makes her understand the facts of his situation—which is that he is in love with another woman. *Toward* that woman his wife's character and proceedings drive him; but he loves her too much to compromise her. He can't let himself be divorced on *her* account—he can on that of the *femme galante*, who has nothing—no name—to lose: a conspicuity the more, indeed, only to gain. The *femme galante* may take, of course, a tremendous, disinterested fancy to him: at any rate the thing has the germ of the *point de départ* of something—I think.

x   x   x   x   x

[As James handled this material in The Special Type *(1903), what he called 'the characteristic manner of H.J.' operated to its extreme. Even in these initial sentences he had departed from what would have been a naturalistic novelist's concern with the animal passions involved.*

By the time he had written his short story—not the novel he was think-ing of here—he had transformed the original data almost out of recog-nition. James' central character is neither Frank Brivet, nor Mrs. Caven-ham, the woman he is in love with and wants to marry. It has become Mrs. Dundene, who is nothing of a cocotte. Though she serves some-times as a model for the painter who tells the story, she is a lady of delicacy and tenderness who falls hopelessly in love with Brivet the first time she sees him in the painter's studio. Thereafter she consents to go through the role that will gain him his divorce, but her sacrifice, as she knows from the start, is all for nothing. In her final line she says to the painter that during their supposed affair she never even once saw Brivet alone.

James would appear to have been considerably interested in the possibilities of this theme, since he included it in three of his lists—immediately after (p. 234), and again in 1898 (p. 265) and 1899 (p. 292). He also discussed it a little more at page 288. But after printing the story in The Better Sort (1903), he seems to have realized that his handling was too special to produce a result of much human substance, and he did not collect it again.]

I was greatly struck, the other day, with Sargent's account of McKim, the American architect, given me in the train while we went together to Fairford (Wednesday, Dec. 18). I mean of his princely gallantry (de procédés) to women—to ladies—with whom his relations are irre-proachable, etc.: the scale of it, the practical chivalry of it, etc., etc. It might be something to do—as very characteristically American. Do the old grand seigneur in a 'new bottle'—Frank H.'s cabling his eloping wife £100,000, a case in point: the sort of thing which a 1000 French pens would have commemorated of the Duc de Richelieu. x x x x x

Here, by the way, are the approximate or provisional labels of the sujets de roman that I just alluded to one's having en tête.
    1° La Mourante: the girl who is dying, the young man and the girl he is engaged to.
    2° The Marriages (what a pity I've used that name!): the Father and Daughter, with the husband of the one and the wife of the other entangled in a mutual passion, an intrigue.
    3° The Promise: the donnée that I sketched (I have it all), as a 3-act play for poor E.C.
    4° The Awkward Age: to be completely ciphered out. It exists as yet only in a brief, former note and in my head—but I can produce it the moment I sit down to it—certainly with the help of my former note.
    5° The Advertiser (Hall Caine): The idea, as I hinted it, the other

night when I was dining with the former, to Colvin and Barrie (it came to me on the spot roughly and vividly), strikes me as really magnificent.

6° Call it, for the moment, *The Vanderbilt Story: vide supra.*

[*The titles of the first three became* The Wings of the Dove, The Golden Bowl, *and* The Other House. *James did not elucidate further in these notebooks the theme of* The Advertiser, *though he listed it as a possible 'anecdote' four years later (p. 292 below), and mentioned it again in passing (p. 309). The Vanderbilt Story, as noted just above, became* The Special Type.]

Let me just jot down, in this remnant of a beguiled morning, 3 or 4 things that I have noted before and may identify with a small label—3 or 4 little ideas that I can put a *present* hand on in 5000 words apiece: 50 pages of my MS. The very essence of such a job is—let me with due vividness remember it—that they consist each, substantially, of a *single incident*, an incident definite, limited, sharp. I must *cultivate* the vision, the observation and notation of that—just as I must sternly master the *faire*, the little hard, fine, repeated process. x x x x x

<1.> I have, to begin with, *Les Vieux*—the thing noted, at Torquay, on the memory of something said to me by Mrs. Procter.

<2.> I have the suggestion found in the Frenchman's article in the *Fortnightly Review* about the opposition of view of the *Française* and the *Anglaise* as to the responsibility incurred by a flirtation: one thinking of the compensation *owed* (where the man is really touched), the other taking the exact line of backing out. 'It's serious'—they both see —but the opposed conclusion from that premise. This seems to me *exactly* treatable in my small compass. In a correspondence—in a series of colloquies that reflect the facts—or in some other way? Shall I put the 2 men together?—or shall I put the 2 women? The law of EVERY job of this kind can only be intensely, *powerfully*, to simplify. I shall come to the treatment—the subject, at any rate, *y est*. I can't get brevity here—or anywhere—obviously, save by some tremendous foreshortening; but that effort, so remunerative, is a part of the general high challenge of the whole business. Don't I see my *biais* here, don't I see my solution, in my usual third person: the observer, the *knower*, the confidant of either the 2 women or the 2 men? The 2 women seem, decidedly, the really designated characters. That gives me the *notes*, the confidences, the reflections, the sharp, bright anecdote of some acute and clever person, some elderly woman, presumably, who was in relation with them—*devant laquelle la chose se passa.* Voilà.

3. The mother who takes the line that her daughter's husband must show her everything—the husband who never comes. (The little idea suggested by a remark of Miss Reubell.)

4. The child whose parents divorce and who makes such an extraordinary link between a succession of people. (Suggested by something mentioned to me several years ago, at dinner at the J. Bryces', by Mrs. Ashton, Mrs. Bryce's sister-in-law.)

5. The lying fine lady who *assumes* that her maid has spied on her, has read her letters—knows certain things about her doings 'because maids always do.' The figure of the maid: innocent, incapable of such tortuosity, and losing her place—*mise à la porte*—because, in a crisis of some misconduct of the mistress, she can't—*à l'improviste*—help her—save her—by acting for her as if—without explanation—she has the knowledge—the nefarious clue—which she could only have got by nefarious watching and peeping.

6. The reviewing woman who *éreinters* her friend—the man of letters who comes to see her—in the paper for which she does novels, *because she is RAGEUSEMENT* in love with him. The publisher finds it out—it might be called *The Publisher's Story*. There must be, of course, some climax: the idea must be: '*What is the way to make her stop?*' 'Try a sweet review of her, and let her know it's yours.' 'But I hate her work.' 'Well, nevertheless, pump out something.' The novelist tries this—it has no effect.—I check myself: there may be something in the *concetto* (a very small something indeed—even for 5000 words), but it doesn't lie in that direction. *Laissons cela* till something more seems to come out of it. x x x x x

[*In this group the first item refers back to an anecdote recorded on 28 October 1895 (p. 225 above). The second, referring to an article quoted by James on 13 May 1894 (p. 164 above), formed the basis for The Given Case (Collier's Weekly, 31 December 1898 and 7 January 1899), a somewhat mechanical contrast—in nine thousand words— between two English women, one engaged and the other unhappily married, who reached the opposite conclusions from the given premise. James did not take advantage here of the suggested device of highlighting his story through the clever reflections of an observer, but told it as direct narrative.*

The third theme—'the husband comes in the form of death'—had been suggested to him three years before, as recorded at page 125. In developing the fourth into What Maisie Knew, James gave up all thought that it belonged to the category of 'the single incident,' manageable within five thousand words.

A *theme similar to the fifth had been briefly noted on* 16 March 1892 (p. 117 *above*). *The sixth was outlined on* 18 November 1894 (p. 177 *above*).]

December 22d. Promising H. Harland a 10,000 (a *real* 10,000) for the April *Yellow Book*, I have put my pen to the little subject of the child, the little girl, whose parents are divorced, and then each marry again, then die, leaving her divided between the 2d husband of the one and the 2d wife of the other. But the thing, before I go further, requires some more ciphering out, more extraction of the subject, of the drama—if such there really *be* in it. *Voyons un peu*—what little drama *does* reside in it?—I catch it, I catch it: I seize the tail of the little latent action *qu'il recèle.* I made a mistake, above, in thinking—in speaking—of the divorced parents as 'dying': they live—the very essence of the subject is in that. Make my point of view, my *line*, the consciousness, the dim, sweet, scared, wondering, clinging perception of the child, and one gets something like *this.* The parents become indifferent to her as soon as they cease to have her to quarrel about; then each marry again. The father *first*—it's *his* new spouse who first takes an interest in the child. But let me state it, rather <in> 8 or 10 little chapters. x x x x x

I. 12½ pages about the parents.

II. 10 pages: the child's perceptions of the situation at first—its wonderings, bewilderments, then gradual clever little perception of what it must do. Boyd first takes her—his pretended arrangement of his life for it, his playing at being occupied with her and devoted to her. His talk to her about her mother—her dread and awe of going to her. Then her going—the mother's wild caresses, and her getting from the child all the father has said of her. The results of this—her behaviour on going back to her father, etc. The results don't show the *1st* time: she repeats to her father what her mother has said, as she has repeated to her mother what her father has said. Then, on her 2d visit to her mother, she takes the line of *not* telling—she gets a glimpse, in her little prematurely troubled and sharpened mind, of what she can do in the way of *peace.* This disappoints and angers her mother on the second visit—so that, with her vicious activity dropping, her mother neglects her, neglects her badly, and she is eager to return to her father. On her return she finds a governess. Or does her MOTHER get her the governess? I seem to see reasons for that. The mother hires the governess for the last three months of the visit—but under penalty of her displeasure if she goes to the other place with the child. She's to wait and take her six months later—that has been the arrangement under which she is hired. But she takes such a fancy to Maisie that she breaks the vow and goes, knowing what displeasure she incurs, and offers herself to Boyd. He is horrified, learning that she comes from his wife—from Maisie under that roof. But he relents on finding what promise she has broken, and binds her by another not to go back there. *She* gives it—her line is now, secretly, to keep the child at the father's. She falls in love with Boyd. The scene between Boyd and the governess takes place before Maisie. This is all in ii.

iii. Relation between Maisie and the governess. Then Maisie goes back once again to her mother, and stays there without the governess —with another, who also gets embroiled about her. Her mother *drops* her, after this third period, and she stays on—on and on. A young man comes to her father's, in the latter's absence, to see about her. He proves to be her mother's new husband. He has been put up to it— egged on by the embroiled governess—who adores the child and wants to get her back or get back *to* her. Essence of the little drama this— the strange, fatal, complicating action of the child's lovability. It occurs to me, however, that instead of making the young man come himself, outright (a little unnatural and *invraisemblable*), I had better make the 'embroiled governess'—the second, elder, plain one—come herself, hungrily, desperately, to see if the child *isn't* coming back to her mother. She has come to see Boyd Farange, but he is away. She sees *his* governess, the pretty one, my second 'heroine'; and the scene between the 2 women takes place before Maisie. The plain governess, the honest frump, *tells* of Mrs. Farange's marriage—this is the 1st they know of it. She has married Captain So-and-So—she tells who: she is abroad—it has taken place at Florence. She has written to the frump, character-istically—enclosing the portrait of her *sposo*—younger than herself, very handsome. (The 'Pretty' governess must not be very handsome—too much beauty—only a marked type.) *The* sposi *are coming home*— hence the poor woman's officious, pathetic errand. Her passion for the child—it breaks out. She catches her up, hugs her. She must be a widow—mrs. Something: she has lost her only little girl. Movement between the women precipitating the younger one's announcement of the kind of place she holds—the authority with which she speaks: she is engaged to be married to Boyd Farange.

iv. I must handle freely and handsomely the years—treat my *intervals* with art and courage; master the little secrets in regard to the expression of duration—be superior I mean, on the question of time. Maisie *does* go back to her mother—she sees her new stepfather—she stays a year. Her new stepfather—the Captain—attaches himself to her tenderly. Simple, good, mild chap, bullied, hustled by his wife, and not destined, as he is already sure, or at any rate definitely apprehensive, to have a child of his own: the thing he has almost predominantly married for—

and not *been* married, grabbed and appropriated, by Mrs. Farange. (I must get a name, a Xtian name, for Mrs. F. early—so as not to speak of her by a *changed* surname.) It occurs to me that it will be well to make Ida have a confinement—a *very*, VERY prompt one—which is what, in its results, dashes the Captain's hopes of paternity. She is awfully ill—the child dies—her convalescence is long—her attitude about another episode of the same kind unmistakable. It is during this—for him —worried and lonely time that the Captain fraternizes and foregathers with Maisie, who is as 'lonely' as himself—*délaissée* in a way that touches him. The year that she is now by way of staying with her mother is to make up for the time that Ida DIDN'T insist, antecedently to that event. It is the Captain, really, who, from his fancy for the child, carries out the rule of the time to be made up, stickles for it, puts it through. Trace as vividly as may be, *mark strongly*, the *drop*, the cynical surrender, on each side, of the *real parents'* responsibility— of their sense of it and pretension *to* it, and tolerance of the trouble of it. Mark the point of the *full change*—the change that leaves only the step-parents to keep the matter up. It is, e.g., the Captain who now keeps Maisie—the Captain only. All this in section IV. Section IV must terminate with the second wife's visit to the Captain, to *get back* the child. This is their MEETING—their 1st being brought face to face over Maisie. It takes place before Maisie—EVERYTHING TAKES PLACE BEFORE MAISIE. That is a part of the essence of the thing—that, with the tenderness she inspires, the rest of the essence, the second of the golden threads of my *form*. Maisie is really more—much more—than a year with the Captain and her mother. It is as married to Boyd Farange— married now *depuis bientôt 2 ans*—that the pretty governess presents herself. She has realised, too, that she will have no children. She may have been confined (yes, that is right) and lost her little girl. Yes, yes, she *tells* that to the Captain. This 1st meeting marks practically the middle of my tale. I am not SURE, now, that it will be well for her— at the end of III—to have ANNOUNCED to the frumpy governess her engagement to Boyd. And yet why not? When I can prepare so little, and must take such jumps, so much preparation as that may be valuable to me. *Nous verrons bien*. This relation established between the 2 step-parents evidently, at any rate, flows over into section V.

SECTION V consists, therefore, of the sharp, vivid establishment of the contact in question and of:—

(b) The second wife's second visit to the Captain to *continue* the effort to get Maisie. Ida is away—Boyd is away: this marks what has become of *their* duty. The Captain is at the seaside somewhere—in lodgings—with the child: say at Brighton. The second wife, this second time, comes down to Brighton. The frumpy governess is back again with the little girl—now 10 years old. She has come to her (in spite of everything?)—she clings to her: she is her only REAL guardian. Sound that note in her feeling—in her sense, her deep foreboding. She sees what is to happen between the younger pair—SHOW that she sees it.

(c) Maisie's return to her father and her stepmother.

(d) The Captain's going to see her there. *Boyd consents* to this—is jolly over it, seeing how unhappy he too is with Ida. This *rapprochement* between the 2 men takes place in the child's presence. The frumpy governess is meanwhile forbidden the house by the second wife—who is jealous and suspicious of her, has *her* vague foretaste and foreknowledge of what may happen, and an intuition of the old woman's perception of it which makes her keep her at a distance. The old woman gets in once—to express this to Maisie. That is, she formulates to the child exactly what *I* have just formulated. Everything is formulated and formulatable to the child. May not v terminate with this formula?—leaving vi to consist virtually of the *growth* of the extraordinary relation between the step-parents as witnessed by Maisie? Yes, that is it. The formula from the frump at the end of v *facilitates* my making the child witness the phenomenon in question—prepares the mirror, the plate, on which it is represented as reflected. Therefore we have:—

vi. (*sixth*) The freedom, the facility, of the step-parents together over the child. *Cela se passe chez* Boyd—since the Captain can come there. *Description of it in form of picture of the child's dim sense.* It terminates in irruption of Ida—an outbreak of jealousy. The Captain is out somewhere with Maisie in Kensington Gardens—out with her, *as brought from Boyd's house*—where they suddenly encounter Ida, who is there with a strange gentleman—strange to Maisie, but known, very well, to the Captain. Scene of jealousy from Ida to anticipate, to FORESTALL her 2d husband's (the Captain's) suspicion of her relations with the strange gentleman. The strange gentleman takes Maisie off—at Ida's request—to walk a little. That moment is, in 3 lines, described (*the gentleman* PERFECTLY SILENT—Maisie also), and the situation the child finds on their rejoining the others. vi ends with Maisie going back to her mother,[1] who has to have her to back up the grievance she has hurled at the Captain, but who really doesn't care for it a bit, *ou* that her being there only keeps the Captain more on the premises—or *may* do so: a state of affairs that doesn't suit her book, as she has her lover to receive and be with. However, the chapter terminates with the little girl's redomicilement under her mother's roof.

1. The rest of this sentence is encircled with a red line in the manuscript.

[239]

vii embodies:—(a) What I have surrounded with a red line just above. (b) The Captain's veto on the tattling frump. (c) The incident of Maisie being out with her stepmother—out from her mother's house —and meeting (as a counterpart of the incident of vi) her father with a strange lady, a lady strange to Maisie but known, well known, to her stepfather. The same things happen as before. There is the same scene between the 2 *sposi*. Maisie is taken off to walk a little by the strange lady—only the strange lady is extraordinarily loquacious, almost violently chatters. The *bout de scène* that, before the child, Boyd makes his wife, is a scene of *insincere jealousy*—like the scene Ida has made the Captain. But before introducing the incident I must have made it clear that the Captain has forbidden the frumpy governess his house— kept her off. Maisie knows the reason from him—knows that, to be well with Ida and get *at* the child (since Mrs. Farange no. 2 has turned her out—has banged *her* door in her face), she (the frump) has communicated to Ida her idea about the 2 step-parents. This to make Ida bring the child home, where she (the frump) may see her. She has reckoned without the Captain's divination (or knowledge *through* Ida) and resentment, which does not keep her out. He says *he* will teach Maisie.

In viii, Ida 'bolts' with the strange little gentleman. The Captain formulates this to Maisie. He takes her to her stepmother and there she learns—through the latter's formulation—that Boyd Farange has bolted with the strange little lady.

In ix, Maisie sees her step-parents very definitively come together— unite in devotion to her. *They* will take care of her, take care of her together—they will both be to her everything she has lost. She is wonderstruck and charmed with this—she sees them *really exalted and magnificent over it*; and she accepts the prospect, tells them it's them she prefers, etc., and prepares to give herself altogether to them. Then, with—

x, The old frumpy governess arrives, intervenes, has her great scene with them, *leur dit leur fait*, grandly, vividly (put everything into her mouth), and carries off the child, to rescue her, to save her. *She* will bring her up.

[*In this passage James reverts to the plan for* What Maisie Knew. *In entries for 12 November 1892 and 26 August 1893, he had already recorded the idea (pp. 126-7 and 134 above), and he listed it as a possible subject on page 235.*

Now, as he began to write, he discovered at last the real 'essence' of his subject. He was fascinated by the vision of the child's charm and innocence, which influenced the relations, often evil, of the other characters, and by the technical problem of presenting the whole through Maisie's consciousness, even when she was unable to understand the meaning of what she saw and heard. To meet the problem and to express what he had come to see as the true theme, he needed far more than 10,000 words and his '8 or 10 little chapters' grew to thirty-one in the finished novel.

Most of the basic features of the story are outlined here, but there were to be important changes, as can be seen in later entries beginning on page 256.]

34 D. V. G., W., January 10th, 1896.

I am doing for Oswald Crawfurd—in 7000 words—the little subject of the 2 people who never met in life. I see it in 5 little chapters, all very, very tiny and intensely brief—with every word and every touch telling. I have only put pen to paper; but before I go further I must be crystal-clear. Voyons un peu what must be immitigably brought out. The salient thing, up to the death of the woman, must be the condition, the state of things, or relation between the pair, brought about by its being—there being—so often a question, a lively question of their meeting, and nothing ever coming of it. They perpetually *miss* each other—they are the buckets in the well. There seems a fate in it. It becomes, *de part et d'autre*, a joke (of each party) with the persons who wish to bring them together: that is (in the small space) with *me*, mainly—the interested narrator. They say, each, the same things, do the same things, feel the same things. It's a JOKE—it *becomes* one— *de part et d'autre*. They each end by declaring that it makes them too nervous, *à la fin*—and that really it won't *do*, for either, at last, to see the other: so possible a disappointment, an anticlimax, may ensue. Each knows that the other knows—each knows just how the other is affected: a certain self-consciousness and awkwardness, a certain preoccupied shyness has sprung up. So it goes. This colours the whole situation so that, necessarily (as it happens), the thing is left very much to accident. It is the *idea* that it shall be so left. It's too *serious* to arrange it in any other way. *Chance* must bring the meeting about. So it's by way of being left to chance. It's a joke, above all for *me*: that is, it's an element of the little action to perceive in the joke a little serious side that makes me say 'Tiens!' Ah, divine principle of the 'scenario!'—it seems to make that wretched little past of patience and pain glow with the meaning I've waited for! I seem to catch hold of the tail of the very central notion of my little 'cochonnerie,' as Jusserand used to say. The LAST empêchement to the little meeting, the supreme one, the one that caps the climax and makes the thing

'past a joke,' '*trop fort*,' and all the rest of it, is the result *of my own
act*. I prevent it, because I become conscious of a dawning jealousy.
I become conscious of a dawning jealousy because something has taken
place between the young man (the man of my story; perhaps he's
not in his 1st youth) and myself. I was on the point of writing just
above that 'something takes place just before the last failure of the
2 parties to meet—something that has a bearing on this failure.' Well,
what takes place is *tout simplement* THAT: I mean that he and the
narrator become 'engaged.' It's *on* her engagement that her friend,
her woman-friend, wants, more than ever, to see the man who has
now become the fiancé. It is this (comparative eagerness) and a vague
apprehension that determines her jealousy. It makes her *prevent* the
meeting when it really might have (this time) occurred. The other
failures have been by accident: this one, which might have come
off (the narrator sees that there would have been no accident), has
failed from active interference. What do I do? I write to my fiancé
not to come—that *she* can't. (She mustn't live in London—but [say]
at Richmond.) So he doesn't come. *She* does—and she sits with me,
vainly waiting for him. I don't tell *her* what I have done; but, that
evening, I tell *him*. I'm ashamed of it—I'm ashamed, and I make that
reparation. She, in the afternoon, has gone away in good faith, but
almost painfully, quite visibly disappointed. She is not well—she is
'odd,' etc. I am struck with it. The form my reparation takes is to
take him the next day straight out to see her. Is she then, as we find,
dead—or only very ill—i.e., dying? The extreme brevity of my poor
little form doubtless makes it indispensable that she shall be already
dead. I can't devote space to what passes while she is dying, while her
illness goes on. I must jump that—I must arrive (with all the little
merveilleux of the story still to come) at what happens *after* this event.
—Or rather, on second thoughts, have I got this—this last bit—all
wrong? Don't I, *mustn't* I, see it, on reflection, in another way? V*oyons,
voyons*. Say the narrator with her impulse of reparation (having TOLD
her fiancé)—*confessed* to him—in the p.m., as I stated it just now: say
she goes ALONE out to Richmond. She does this in the a.m. of the
next day. She finds her friend has died that night. She goes home,
with the wonder of it; and there befalls the still greater wonder of
her interview with him in the afternoon. He tells her his marvellous
experience of that evening—how, on going home, he has found her
there. BUT that only comes out—is shaken out—in the *secousse*—of *my*
announcement that she's dead—that she died at 10 o'clock that evening. Ten o'clk.—the stupefaction, the dismay, the question of the
hour, etc. I see this—I see this: I needn't detail it here. I see what has
(to his sense) happened—how she hasn't spoken, etc.—has visibly only

come to see him, to let him see her: as if to say, 'Shouldn't we, now, have liked each other?' He puts it that way to the narrator. The narrator says, utterly wonderstruck: 'Why, she was dead *then*—she was dead already.' The marvel of this, the comparison of notes. The possible doubt and question of whether it was after or before death. The ambiguity—the possibility. The view we take—the view *I* take. The effect of this view upon *me*. From here to the end, the attitude, on the subject, is mine: the return of my jealousy, the imputation of the difference that seeing her has made in *him*; the final rupture that comes entirely from ME and from my imputations and suspicions. I am jealous of the dead; I feel, or I imagine I feel, his detachment, his alienation, his coldness—and the last words of my statement are: 'He sees her—he sees her: I know he sees her!' x x x x x

The ground on which the idea is originally started and the claim made that they shall know each other is that of this extraordinary peculiarity that each have had in their pretended (*constatée*), recognized, etc., experience of having had, each of them, the premonition, on the announcement of the death of a parent—he of his mother, she of her father after death—had it at a distance, at the moment, or just before, or just after. This known, recognized, etc.—whether generally, publicly or not; at any rate by the narrator. I've had it from each—I've repeated it to each. Others—yes—have done the same. Yes, there must be— have been—as much publicity as that: to make the needed consensus —the thing that follows them up and amuses and haunts them—the 'point' of the 1st ½ of the *morceau*. If instead of beginning the thing as I began it yesterday I give my first 10 (CLOSE ten) pages to a summary statement of this just-mentioned hearsay-business between them, and how it went on for long, each knowing and knowing the other knows, etc.—then I have my *last* 10 (all of premised closeness) for the state of mind, the imputations, suspicions, interpretations, etc., of the narrator—as a climax. That leaves me thirty for the rest: say, roughly 10 of these for the engagement and what surrounds it relative to *her*. But I've only to reflect to see that under this latter head must come in —then and there—the question of the last occasion for meeting. Perhaps I must make 10 little chapters. Try it so: each of 25 close pages. Let us see what this gives. But isn't, on the other hand, the best way to do so to see first what *five* give? FIRST. The statement of the peculiarity of the pair, and the way in which, for 3 or 4 years, it was followed by their dodging, missing, failing. SECOND. The narrator's engagement. Her jealousy. The day the 2d woman comes, when she (the narrator) has put off the man. THIRD. Her compunction, her confession to the man. Her going to Richmond. Her return with the news—with a certain relief. Her seeing her fiancé. FOURTH. His story to her. The recrudescence of her jealousy. FIFTH. Their going on with their engagement—her wonder and *malaise* about him. Then its coming over her —the *explanation's* coming over her (of what she sees). Her imputation. The rupture. Now let me try the little subdivisions into smaller fractions—a series of tenths.

1-10. 1st. The 2 persons and their story.

10-16. 2d. The long, odd frustration of their encounter.

16-20. 3d. The engagement. The others to meet because of it. The nearing of the day—my jealousy. I'm engaged—if now at the last *moment* something should intervene! I will—putting him off.

20-25. 4th. Her visit—her waiting—my dissimulation—her departure.

25-30. 5th. My compunction, my confession—scene with him—pendant to preceding.

30-35. 6th. My going to Richmond. What I learn there; and my return with the news—with a certain relief.

35-40. 7th. My scene with him—his revelation. My stupefaction.

8th. The ambiguity—the inquiry (mine). The return of my jealousy.

9th. Our approaching marriage—my theory—my suspicions—my imputations.

10th. The rupture. He goes on, unmarried, for years. Then I make up to him (?)—seek a reconciliation. *Il s'y soustrait par la mort* (?).

[The Way It Came *appeared in the* Chap Book *for 1 May 1896, and in the same month in* Chapman's Magazine of Fiction, *of which Oswald Crawfurd was editor. It was included in the collected edition with the title,* The Friends of the Friends. *In his preface James uses this story, along with* The Altar of the Dead, Owen Wingrave, *and others, as a basis for discussion of the 'ghost story' and of the importance of presenting the wonderful and strange 'by showing almost exclusively the way they are felt, by recognizing as their main interest some impression strongly made by them and intensely received.' Here the 'impression' is the jealousy roused in a woman who believes that her lover is visited by the ghost of a dead girl, because there is a bond between them, an 'irresistible call' from her to him. At the end of the story he dies. 'It was sudden, it was never properly accounted for, it was surrounded by circumstances in which—for oh I took them to pieces! —I distinctly read an intention, the mark of his own hidden hand.' The 'call' had been too strong.*

The substance of the story is as outlined here, except that the narrator makes no effort at reconciliation after her break with her lover. The idea of having her go alone to Richmond is kept; her jealousy, which leads to her preventing the planned meeting, is shown to have been increased by the news of the death of her estranged husband, which frees her to marry again. Her doubt as to whether the other woman first appeared to the young man before or after she died is enhanced because she is known to have seen his address on the back of a photograph. The story is introduced by a brief section explaining that it is taken from a diary. This helps verisimilitude, by accounting for the narrator's frankness in revealing her own motives and emotions.

The story finally ran to about ten thousand words, and has seven sections. Of these the first three correspond to those listed above, the fourth combines the fourth and fifth, the fifth includes the sixth and seventh, the sixth corresponds to the eighth in the outline, and the seventh covers the ninth and tenth. James was trying for condensation, but some parts of the story could not, he felt, be compressed. A comparison of what he condensed with what he did not affords an index of what seemed to him the relative importance of the elements in the tale. The exposition of the situation, the lover's revelation of the visit, and the presentation of the 'ambiguity' as to whether the visitor was alive or dead, are given all the space originally allotted to them. It proved possible to shorten the treatment of the initial jealousy, the prevention of the meeting, the frustrated visit, the confession, and the trip to Richmond, and the last two sections on the continuing jealousy and the breaking of the engagement were compressed into one. The exposition had to be full if the story was to have any point, and James' keeping of the original scale for the scene between the living lovers on the day after the death shows his wish to concentrate not on the 'apparition' itself but on its effect upon those whose lives it was immediately to concern.

The theme of a man's love for the memory of a dead woman is, of course, used for the climax of The Wings of the Dove.]

34 D. V. G., W., February 13th, '96.

R. U. Johnson's letter to me the other day, returning my little paper on Dumas as shocking to their prudery, strikes me as yielding the germ of a lovely little ironic, satiric tale—of the series of *small* things on the life and experiences of men of letters, the group of the little 'literary' tales. Isn't there an exquisite little subject in his sentence about their calculation that my article on A.D. would have been unobjectionable through being merely personal? It's the beauty of that, when one thinks of it, that is suggestive and *qui paraît se prêter* to the ironic representation of some illustrative little action—little action illustrative of the whole loathsomely prurient and humbugging business. The wondrous matter is their conception, their representation of their public

—its ineffable sneakingness and baseness. Oh, the whole thing *does* open up as a *donnée!* Their hope that one would have given a 'personal' account of a distinguished man, a mere brief, reserved, simply intelligible statement of the subject matter <of> whose work is too scandalous to print. They want to *seem* to deal with him because he is famous—and he is famous because he wrote certain things which they won't for the world have intelligibly mentioned. So they desire the supreme though clap-trap tribute of an *intimate* picture, without even the courage of saying on what ground they desire any mention of him at all. One must figure out a little story in which that *bêtise* is presented. There must be the opposition—embodied in 2 young men, the serious, intelligent youth who, *à propos* of a defunct great, fine, author, makes an admirable little study or statement; and the other fellow who, canny, knowing, vulgar, having the instinct of journalistic vulgarity, doesn't say a valuable thing, but goes in for superficial gossip and twaddle. The success of the latter, the failure of the former. The whole thing must of course reside in some little objective, concrete, DRAMA—which I must cipher out. This is a mere bald hint. I seem to see something like the DAUGHTER of the great defunct (who has only come up, say, into *vulgar* recognition, after, or at the moment of, his death). Don't I see a furious magazine-hunt, newspaper-hunt for a PORTRAIT, and the 2 men, the 2 attitudes, presented to, confronted with HER—the clear, loyal, ardent daughter—over the question of the obtention of the photog. for engraving—publishing. The story, this time, not told in the 1st person—but presented from outside.—There has never been but that sole photog. x x x x x

[*The rejection, by the editor of the* Century Magazine *of James' essay on the younger Dumas (which was printed in the* New York Herald *and the* Boston Herald *on 23 February 1896, and promptly accepted by the* New Review, *for March 1896), points up ironically his often repeated objection to the stupid prudery of American and English magazines. The irony is that this essay discusses in particular the confusions created, 'in the presence of a work of art,' by 'confounding the object . . . with the subject.' James' chief contention about Dumas is that the Frenchman's concern with 'bad cases' should not distract us from perceiving that he was above all else 'a professional moralist.' To illustrate the difference between Dumas' 'determined observation' and its absence in certain of 'our innocent writers . . . innocent even of reflection,' James wrote: 'One of his great contentions is, for instance, that seduced girls should under all circumstances be married'—by somebody or other, failing the seducer. 'This is a contention that, as we feel,* barely concerns us, shut up as we are in the antecedent conviction that they should under no circumstances be seduced.' That is doubtless the kind of passage that shocked Robert Underwood Johnson.

The 'illustrative little action' suggested by this experience was worked out in John Delavoy (Cosmopolis, January–February 1898). James altered his outline to the extent that instead of presenting two young men, he confronted his narrator-critic with the weighty opposition of Mr. Beston, the editor of the Cynosure, who controlled 'a body of subscribers as vast as a conscript army.' He also changed the late author's daughter to an admiring younger sister, whose pencil portrait is the only likeness of this 'most unadvertised, unreported, uninterviewed, unphotographed, uncriticised of all originals.' The critic, deeply impressed by Delavoy's undistracted devotion to his craft as well as by the greatness of his novels, determines to make a decisive estimate of them. Miss Delavoy recognizes his essay as the only one commensurate with its subject, but Mr. Beston finds it 'indecent.' Pressed to elucidate what he means, he pontificates: 'You're not writing in The Cynosure about the relations of the sexes. With those relations, with the question of sex in any degree, I should suppose you would already have seen that we have nothing whatever to do. If you want to know what our public won't stand, there you have it.'

It does the critic no good to protest that the editor's phrases are 'too empty and too silly, and of a nature therefore to be more deplored than any, I'm positive, that I use in my analysis. . . I simply try to express my author, and if your public won't stand his being expressed, mention to me kindly the source of its interest in him.'

Mr. Beston flatly rejects his essay and gets from elsewhere the 'anecdotes, glimpses, gossip, chat' that he wants. Even when Miss Delavoy asks him whether he doesn't care about his responsibility for furthering a great author's reputation, Mr. Beston rejoins: 'It's not my business to care. That's not the way to run a magazine.'

James included this story in The Soft Side (1900), but did not add it to his collected edition.]

February 13th, '96. I am pressingly face to face with the FINISH, for the Atlantic, of The Old Things, as the House Beautiful seems now destined, better, to be called. I must cipher out here, to the last fraction, my last chapters and pages. As usual I am crowded—my first two-thirds are too developed: my third third bursts my space or is well nigh squeezed and mutilated to death in it. But that is my problem. Let me state first, broadly, what I have now to show. The crude essence of what I have to show is this: that Mrs. Gereth sends back the things, that the marriage of Owen and Mona then takes place and

[247]

that after the treasures are triumphantly relodged at Poynton the house takes fire and burns down before Fleda's eyes. Those are the bare facts. *Voyons un peu les détails.* Mrs. Gereth surrenders the things partly because she believes—has reason to—that Fleda will eventually come into them. But that calculation won't—doesn't—appear a sufficient motive: she must have another to strengthen it. She surrenders them therefore, furthermore, because she appears to see that the knowledge of their being back again at Poynton, as an incentive, a heritage, a reward, a future (settled there again immutably, this time), will operate to make Fleda do what she has so passionately appealed to her to do—get Mona away from Owen. She, Mrs. G., is seeing if Mona WON'T break. She does at first what the end of x shows her as doing—she keeps on the things as she threatens. xi must begin, I think, this way. It is that same evening.

FLEDA: 'Well, then what answer am I to write Mr. Owen?'

MRS. G.: 'Write him to come up to town to meet you there.'

FLEDA: 'For what purpose?'

MRS. GERETH: 'For any purpose you like!'

She sets the girl on him—cynically, almost, or indecently (making her feel AGAIN how little account—in the way of fine respect—she makes of her. Touch *that*, Mrs. G.'s unconscious brutality and immorality, briefly and finely). She presses Fleda—yes—upon him: would ALMOST like her, in London, to give herself up to him. She has a vision of a day with him there as 'fetching' him—IN SPITE of Fleda's fine fit about the young man's not caring for her. *She'll* see, Mrs. G. will, if he won't care. The very *essence* of this turn of the story is that the escape of the girl's 'secret,' the revelation to Mrs. G. that she loves Owen, completely alters (in a manner still for the better—as regards at least the mother's attitude) the relations of the two women. It develops them further—develops Mrs. Gereth's feeling *for* Fleda—though not Fleda's (with all her dimnesses and delicacies) for her pushing, urging, overwhelming, hinting, suggesting friend. It is on this basis of her 'love' that Mrs. G. now extravagantly handles her. She is free with her on it, bold, frank, urgent, humorous, cynical with her on it, beyond what Fleda's fineness enjoys. She alludes perpetually, wonderingly, *admiringly* to it—all the while—attributing to her a FIERCER kind of sentiment (judging by herself) than Fleda's sacrificial exaltation really *is*—making her wince and draw back in this flood of familiarity. At the same time I catch for her, here, in this connection—ADMIRABLY, I think—a prime element of my denouement. Fleda is left 'sick' at the end of x by her companion's threatened postponement of the surrender —but that only spurs her to renewed, to confirmed, action and endeavour. It is an *idée fixe* with her that she shall serve Owen—bring about the disgorgement. She becomes hereby capable of lending herself *in appearance* to Mrs. G.'s inflamed view of her possible effect on Owen and routing of Mona. The thing she still cherishes is Owen's secret (his shy, barely revealed feeling for her); everything else has been blown upon and she is willing to accept that condition of things and *use* it as far as she can. What I see is, here, that she MUST have one more personal meeting with Owen. It is the last time she sees him. She must go up to town—with a 'subtle' appearance of profiting by Mrs. Gereth's directions and injunctions and suggestions—she must go up to town and have, somehow and somewhere, an hour with him. Say at her father's in West Kensington. I just suggest to myself that. If I can from this point on only clarify this to the SCENIC intensity, brevity, beauty—make it march as straight as a pure little dramatic action—I shall, I think, really score. What Fleda writes to Owen after that opening bit of dialogue with Mrs. G. is that, 1st, he is to hold on, that it's difficult, but that she is helping him; and that 2d, she will come and meet him in town. It comes to me that her meeting with him in town must be *une scène de passion*—yes, I must give my readers that. Don't I get a glimpse, this way, of the real and innermost mechanism of my end? Fleda breaks down—lets Owen see she loves him. It is all *covert*—and delicate and exquisite: she adjures him to do his literal duty to Mona. They arrive at some definite and sincere agreement about this. That is the ground, the *fond*, the deep ground TONE of their scene. It must be for MONA to break—only for Mona. He mustn't—by all that's honourable—do it if she *doesn't*. He agrees to this—he sees it, feels it, understands it, gives her his word on it.

'But she WILL break if mamma doesn't send back the things. Therefore she mustn't NOW,' says Owen. Fleda's *aveu* has changed all.

'You mustn't say that—you mustn't. You so must do your part—impeccably. I've worked your mother up to it.'

'Very good—leave it so. But she won't—she WON'T!' says Owen jubilantly.

What I have my glimpse of as my *right* issue is that even while they are talking, as it were, Mrs. Gereth DOES. She does it because, 1st: she has a visit from Mrs. Brigstock in which she reads a virtual revelation that the marriage is off; and 2d: she does it to fetch Fleda. To make these things possible I must represent the meeting between Owen and Fleda as an incident of an ABSENCE that Fleda makes from Ricks. She goes up to town for a week—goes to her father, goes to escape Mrs. G.'s hounding on, AND to prove to Mrs. G. that she *will* go at Owen in the sense *she* (Mrs. G.) pleads for. So I have roughly something like this.

[249]

xi. The new situation at Ricks between the 2 women, on the basis of Fleda's *aveu*. Fleda's attitude on this new footing, and the letter she 1st writes to Owen. It tells him to hold on: she is serving him—it is difficult—he must be patient. She *1st declines* Mrs. G.'s suggestion about meeting him—then at last (after a *fortnight* [?]) she turns, changes, can't stand it at Ricks, pleads that she must go up to town. She goes with Mrs. G.'s high approbation. What Mrs. G. sees in it.

xii. Her meeting with Owen in town.

xiii. Her meeting, their meeting, with Mrs. B.

xiv. Her return to Ricks to find everything gone. The last have just left. Mrs. Gereth has ACTED. She shows WHY. Fleda is partly prepared. There has appeared that a.m. in the *Morning Post* an announcement that the marriage, etc., will not take place. Then she describes Mrs. B.'s visit—a stupid frightened visit—*to complain of Fleda*. For it comes to me that they must have had in London—Owen and Fleda—an encounter with Mrs. B. SHE COMES TO SEE FLEDA—for news of Mrs. G.'s intentions and she finds Owen there. As an old acquaintance—her hostess, in Chap. I, at Waterbath, she knows her whereabouts or address. Yes—SHE COMES TO COMPLAIN. That encourages and determines Mrs. G.—she will, I have said, make it sure, 'fetch' Fleda and act on her. There she is—in the nudity of Ricks; but the news in the *Morning Post* rejoices her; and though Fleda, NOW THAT THE THINGS ARE GONE BACK, practically has her doubts and fears (*which she doesn't communicate*) the two women have together, an hour, a week of happiness and hope, *vis-à-vis* of the future. FLEDA MUST NOW HAVE LET OUT OWEN'S SECRET.

xv. The news that the marriage has taken place. This must (with other indispensable things) be a chapter by itself. They wait—the 2 women, first—for Owen to come down—almost immediately to propose for Fleda. The situation altered again—by a further shift—(I mean by Fleda's *aveu*, now, of Owen's 'caring for her') in a degree equivalent to that in which it has been altered *in x* by her *aveu* of her caring for him. They wait, they wait. Fleda tells Mrs. G. of Owen's offer to her of something from Poynton—anything: any small thing she can pick out. She rejoices: she says there is something at Ricks—the Maltese Cross. She will have THAT. (*It occurs to me that she had better not go back to Ricks—but that Mrs. G. comes up to town. The house is despoiled—the packers have been at it. Fleda has been on the* POINT *of going when she arrives. She learns from her that everything has gone —including the Maltese Cross. She arrives the evening of the day the M.P. gives the news of the rupture. She stays at an hotel. Owen is at Poynton.*) It is thus in London that the news comes to them together of the marriage HAVING taken place. It comes at the end of about

[250]

10 days. Mrs. G. then (her *state*, just Heaven, her condition) determines to go abroad. But she hears the young couple are going. LAST CHAPTER. —Fleda goes down to rescue the Maltese Cross and finds the house in flames—or already burnt down to the ground.

[*What James referred to as the 'first two-thirds' of The Spoils of Poynton was really the first half. The five remaining chapters turned out to be eleven. He wrote to Scudder a couple of weeks later: 'You catch me, as you have done before, in the act of finding my problem irreducible to all the brevity that my optimism has originally deluded itself into a belief in. My subject always refuses, I find, to be scraped down beyond a certain point—stiffens and hardens itself like iron. In this particular thing the very simplicity of my action forces me, I feel, to get everything out of it that it can give—as the real way, and the best way, to be interesting: if I am interesting—which I hope.'*

A typical feature of his method may be noted again in the number of details which, listed in positive form, were finally treated negatively. For instance, Fleda's letter to Owen does not say that she will meet him in London. She runs into him there by chance. Her tacit admission of her feelings to Mrs. Gereth hardly constitutes an aveu. The two women do not have 'a week of happiness' together at Ricks, nor does Fleda let out to Mrs. Gereth Owen's 'secret' until she no longer has any real hope of marrying him. Even the device of the Morning Post is transformed into a negative. Mrs. Gereth watches that paper from day to day to see whether the Brigstocks have set the date for the marriage, but she is lulled into false security by never finding any announcement there.]

February 19th, 1896.

I shall push (*D. V.*) bravely through *The Old Things*; but I must, a little, look into the matter of Fleda's second meeting with Owen in London, and Mrs. Brigstock's finding them together. *Il me faut en tirer* everything—especially in the way of beauty—it can possibly give. It *can* give, surely, some little *scène de passion*; but I want also, from this point on, the whole thing closely and admirably *mouvementé*. It must be unmitigatedly objective narration—unarrested drama. It must be in a word a close little march of cause and effect. Fleda is a week in London without anything happ\<en\>ing. Then Owen comes to West Kensington. He comes because his mother has let him know she is there. Fleda immediately challenges him—and he gives her that reason. His mother has written to him that Fleda has come up and has something to ask him on her behalf. He tells Fleda this. He has

[251]

come to see *what* she has to ask him. She, painfully disconcerted, thinks Mrs. G. has been capable of meaning that she (Fleda) shall communicate to Owen *her* (Mrs. G.'s) idea. She is revolted—but Owen gives her a clue—in *his* having, as he shows, taken for granted what his mother *does* mean by Fleda's errand. Fleda actively CHALLENGES him on this—finds out instantly, before she lets him go further, as it were, what he has thus assumed—assures herself in other words that what she has *first* feared is NOT the case—that Mrs. Gereth has not put him up to the idea that she is in love with him. She actually cross-questions him about this; and his answers show—clearly enough —that Mrs. G. has *not* gone so far—that she has been still AFRAID to. Fleda *breathes*, at this—feels more free to receive him. Then *his* communicated vision of what his mother HAS *entendu* by her message gives her the cue for a basis to let him stay a little without her giving herself away by *emotion* of any sort. WHAT Owen has assumed is that his mother has commissioned her to ask him, for her, whether if she engages to send back the things he will break with Mona—on the basis that Mona's delay, Mona's WAITING, seems obviously to have suggested the reality of. Besides, nothing is more natural than that he should *rush* to Fleda for more news than her note and her silence have given, of *où ils en sont, tous,* in the interminable transactions—of *où il en est, lui,* as to what he may really hope. She has been 'working for him,' she has said: 'Well then, has nothing at all been done?' His mother's note has sent him to Fleda to hear what *has* been done. It is of the essence—or at least of the necessity—of this scene, that Fleda shall with real directness question him. She didn't talk of Mona before— she talks of her NOW. She questions him straight—as he questions her. He asks her what has happened, on her side, since their hour together at Ricks—she asks him what has happened on *his*. What does Owen tell her?—Her questions must DRAW OUT what he tells her. He must be categoric. So, on *her* side, to meet and satisfy *him*, HER information must be. What *has* he, then, to tell her? What has she to tell *him?* He has to tell her that they are still waiting—that Mona is—and he must speak of that young woman more plainly, as it were, than Fleda has let him do at Ricks. He must speak very plainly indeed. He must tell the extreme and, to him, humiliating tension of the things not coming. AT THE SAME TIME HE MUST let her know that if they DON'T come he is free, he is hers. He must tell her that he hasn't seen Mona for a fortnight—but that he has had to describe to her—*had* described to her fully his scene with Fleda at Ricks, every detail of that visit. Mona knows therefore that he is dealing with Fleda—that Fleda has absolute *charge* of their affairs. This knowledge is part of the tension —of his present trouble and embarrassment and worry. He *must* tell her all—he *tells* her all, every scrap. I mustn't interrupt it too much with elucidations or it will be interminable. IT MUST BE AS STRAIGHT AS A PLAY—that is the only way to do. Ah, *mon bon*, make *this, here*, justify, crown, in its little degree, the long years and pains, the acquired mastery of scenic presentation. What I am looking for is my joint, my hinge, for making the scene between them pass, at a given point, into passion, into pain, into their facing together the truth. Some point that it logically reaches must DETERMINE the passage. I want to give Fleda her little hour. She can only *get* it if Owen fully comes out. Owen can only fully come out if he sees what is really in her. He must offer to give up Mona for her—and she must utterly refuse that. What her response IS is that she will take him if Mona really breaks. Yes, here I get my evolution don't I?—an understanding between them dependent on the things not coming. The difference is now, with the other scene (at Ricks), that they are *really*—morally—face to face and that they *speak* of it all. But *voyons, voyons*, I must be utterly crystalline and complete, and my *charpente* must be of steel. What must be thrown up to the surface is the coming back, through Owen, of Mrs. Gereth's OFFER of Fleda at Poynton. Owen has understood it since—*lived* on it—and it all is *in* him now. Thus it is a prime necessity that Mrs. G.'s attitude shall be absolutely—NOW—recognized between them. Owen must KNOW, from Fleda—must get it out of her, that his mother WILL absolutely surrender if he'll marry Fleda. Now it comes to me, in connection and accordance with this, that I must separate this London episode into 2 chapters, 2 occasions: making the 1st culminate in the arrival of Mrs. Brigstock at West Kensington. She then and there takes Owen away with her. She has come to get information and satisfaction from Fleda. She knows what Mona knows—that Fleda has charge of Owen's case *auprès de sa mère*. Owen, moreover, must have told Fleda that he has told Mona (by letter) of his having learned from Mrs. G. that she, Fleda, is in town. This is how Mrs. Brigstock knows it. She has more faith in the girl than her daughter has; and she comes to say: 'Do you realise this hideous deadlock?' Then she finds her daughter's worst suspicions and her jealousies confirmed, by what she seems to have surprised between the young couple upon whom she comes in. Owen must have told Fleda definitely that Mona is jealous. That is the prompt hinge or joint of his fuller frankness. But what I want to mark just here is the evolution of the second chapter of the pair. *This* is the chapter of passion—determined by Mrs. B.'s intervention. She has made him a scene of jealousy. By the chapter of 'passion' I mean the scene of Fleda's *aveux*. I don't see what it can do but take place the next day. Owen comes back to tell her what has happened between Mrs. Brigstock and himself. HE DOESN'T KNOW *she has made* up her mind to go straight down to Ricks. What over-whelms me, however, is the reflection that I have almost no space. FORTY PAGES of small (my smallest) penmanship (like this) [1] must do it all. There can be almost no dialogue at all. This is an iron law. It is absolute. I can squeeze *what* I can into 40 pp.; but I can't have a line more. Therefore in XIII, at least, it must be pure, dense, summarized narration. How can I bring in Mrs. Brigstock, in the tiny space, if it isn't? But above all what I must fix is what is the basis of emotion on which the 2d meeting between Owen and Fleda takes place? They feel that the situation has altered by Mrs. B.'s intervention. MONA WILL BREAK. Fleda surrenders herself—she tells him that she will marry him if Mona does break. On this they get their little duet. It is their hour of illusion—it is their fool's paradise. But it is indispensable to make clear that Fleda won't listen to anything but freedom by Mona's rup-ture; and therefore to have made clear antecedently exactly what Mona's actual attitude IS—at the point the affair has reached. Mona—*voyons* —must have given an *ultimatum*—a date: if the things are not sent back by such and such a day she *will* break. This day is near at hand. Mrs. Brigstock has been ANGRY—therefore she will be angering Mona by the description of how she found the pair together in West Ken-sington. Fleda's *aveux* are all qualified—saddened and refined, and made *beautiful*, by the sense of the IMPOSSIBLE—the sense of the infinite improbability of Mona's not really hanging on—and by the perfectly firm and definite ground she takes on the absolute demand of Owen's honour that he shall go on with Mona if she DOESN'T break.

[*The kind of character James was creating in Fleda is underscored by another small but significant change. She does not 'actively challenge' Owen about his mother's letter; he shows it to her as soon as they meet. James pointed out in his preface that he did not want Fleda to have any quantity of aggressive will. Mona was to be stupid and 'all will'; Mrs. Gereth was to be 'clever,' but aggressive and blinded. Fleda alone was to be 'intelligent,' but 'only intelligent, not distinctively able.' Those who object that Fleda's passivity in yielding Owen is abnormal and neurotic should at least ponder James' full awareness of what he was trying for. He wanted to present Fleda as the quintessence of 'the free spirit,' possessing taste, of which Mona should have no glimmering, and possessing tenderness and moral imagination beyond Mrs. Gereth's scope. But he knew who would win the battles of the world: Mona 'loses no minute in that perception of incongruities in which half Fleda's passion is wasted and misled. . . Every one, every thing, in the story is accordingly sterile but the so thriftily constructed Mona, able at any*

1. James here writes as small as possible.

moment to bear the whole of her dead weight at once on any given inch of a resisting surface.' He knew likewise that 'the free spirit, always much tormented, and by no means always triumphant, is heroic, ironic, pathetic or whatever, and, as exemplified in the record of Fleda Vetch, for instance, "successful," only through having remained free.' Just as William James was sympathetic with the underdog in our aggressive world of 'the bitch goddess, Success,' so Henry James had a partiality for the drama of renunciation.

Once again the six thousand words that, by writing as small as possible, he indicated as his limit proved wholly inadequate, since he needed over thirty thousand from this point on before he was done. But such continual expansion should mislead no one into thinking that the Spoils is diffuse. James had learned his own kind of concentration from his experience of writing plays. The two projected scenes between Fleda and Owen are intensely dramatic, but it inevitably takes time—and space—in James' method for the unspoken to pass over into the spoken, and for his characters to come 'morally face to face.' The economy of which he was a master may be instanced by the entrance of Mrs. Brigstock, when a single small biscuit lying on the carpet betrays to her the great agitation through which Fleda has passed.]

March 30th, 1896.

I am face to face now with my last part of *The Old Things*, and I must (D.V.) put it through with the aid of every drop that can be squeezed from it. It will take 10 days of real application—and then I shall have to get straight at the 65,000 for Clement Shorter. x x x x x

What I have, here, is that, in xviii, Fleda perceives what it is that Mrs. Gereth has done and why she has done it: the full proportions of the bribe, the bid, the pressure of her friend's confidence. I must do it all in 3 chapters of 35 pages each. In xviii the impression on Fleda, the overwhelmedness, the sense that everything is lost, and her confession of everything to Mrs. Gereth—their complete intimacy and exchange of all emotion and explanation over the matter. I see the whole instalment as *between* them—but this chapter as especially between them. They have it out together as it were—they are more face to face than they have ever been. What they are together, face to face with, is the question of what Owen will have done—Fleda lets Mrs. Gereth see that *she* believes it's too late, believes that Mona holds him. Mrs. Gereth denounces him with passion—denounces him for a milksop and a muff, declares that he's less than a man and that she's horribly ashamed of him. Fleda defends him, and the chapter

(18) which ought, after all, to be of 3000 words at most, terminates on their suspense. What I am asking myself is whether I bring back Owen at all. I am not well this a.m. and still shaky from a sick cold, a small assault of influenza; though convalescent, I'm not quite in my *assiette* and must puzzle my little problem out here with a mild patience and a considerable imperfection. But patience and courage—through endless small botherations and interruptions—will see me through—and I have only to *me cramponner*—and add word to word. *Se cramponner* and add word to word, is the endless and eternal receipt. *Owen is married*—that's what has happened; that is what I have to deal with in 19 and 20. HOW do I deal with it? How is the revelation made to the 2 women? It seems to me indispensable that OWEN should NOT come back. That's impossible—absolutely, and gives me ½ a dozen impossibilities and *gaucheries* of every kind. The whole thing *must* be between the two women, and the little problem of art is, finely, inspiringly, keeping it between them, to make it palpitate, make it close and dramatic and full to the very end. Little by little, as I press, as I ponder, it seems to come to me, the manner of my denouement—it seems to fall into its proportions and to *compose*. I see 4 little chapters, rather, of 25 pages each. I think, at any rate, I see Fleda return to Maggie's at the end of XVIII. There, after 2 or 3 days, Mrs. Gereth comes to her. Yes, Mrs. Gereth must *see* her there. This gives me the manner of my revelation to Fleda—it is Mrs. Gereth who makes it. Mrs. Gereth has had it herself from Owen: HE HAS COME TO HER IN TOWN TO THANK HER FOR WHAT SHE HAS DONE: he has been at Poynton and seen the things restored. Yes, that is it. That has clinched Mona, and they have been married at the registrar's on the spot. This scene of reproduction of these occurrences takes place between Mrs. G. and Fleda at Maggie's.

[*James finished up the Spoils virtually as indicated, except that he required five chapters and nearly fifteen thousand words. In sending off the final installment to Scudder, he added: 'I find that with hopes repeatedly deluded and every effort to forecast one's dimensions, one has to do these things as one can (at least I have) and as one "can" depends on the whole artistic life of one's donnée.' The projected '65,000 for Clement Shorter' became the seventy-seven thousand words of The Other House.*]

The Vicarage, Rye, September 22d, 1896.

I've brought my little history of 'Maisie' to the point at which I ought to be able to go on very straight with it; the point at which the child comes back to her father and the domesticated Miss Overmore *after* her 1st period with Mrs. Wix at her mother's. The relations between Miss Overmore and Beale exist—she is his mistress. This is my v, I find, and it must include the *prolongation* of Maisie's stay and the visit of Mrs. Wix as noted *supra.* x x x x x

[By this time James had apparently written, substantially as they stand in the finished novel, its first four sections. v reveals the relation between Beale Farange and Miss Overmore, but vi and vii were needed to cover the prolongation of Maisie's stay and the visit of Mrs. Wix. This visit, outlined on page 237 above, is the occasion of Mrs. Wix's telling 'the pretty governess' that Mrs. Farange is engaged (not married as in the original scheme) to Sir Claude (the Captain of the original). Miss Overmore retorts by announcing her marriage to Beale Farange. The changes make the scene a more complete defeat for Mrs. Wix, since now that Miss Overmore is the child's stepmother, she has an authority far greater than that of a mere governess.]

34 De Vere Gardens, October 26th.

I have brought this little matter of Maisie to a point at which a really detailed scenario of the rest is indispensable for a straight and sure advance to the end. Let me not, just Heaven—not, God knows, that I *incline* to!—slacken in my deep observance of this strong and beneficent method—this intensely structural, intensely hinged and jointed preliminary frame. In proportion as this frame is vague do I directly pay for the vagueness; in proportion as it is full and finished do I gain, do I rejoice in the strength. Sir Claude—in my viii—has come for the child to Mrs. Beale and taken her to her mother's. What then is the function and office of my ix? To develop the relation between Maisie and Sir Claude and, through her, between him and Mrs. Beale. It must picture a little Ida's *intérieur*—poor Sir Claude's relation to *her*—her own relation to Maisie, etc. She's very much in love with Sir Claude. She mustn't be too monstrous about Maisie—she must welcome her at 1st. Mrs. Wix is there—Mrs. Wix must explain things to the child. She adores—they вотн adore—Sir Claude. He must be very nice, very charming to Maisie, but he must get a little tired of her. As the whole thing is an action, so the little chapter is its little *piece* of the action; and to what point must the latter be brought by it? *Voyons, voyons.* Don't I best see the whole thing reflected in the talk, the confidences, the intercourse of Mrs. Wix? Something very pretty may be made of this—her going a little further and further, in the way of communication, of 'crudity,' with the child than her own old dingy decencies, her old-fashioned conscience quite warrants—her helpless pathetic sighs at what she *has*, perforce, to tell her, at what Maisie *already* has seen and learnt—so that *she* doesn't make her any more initiated—any 'worse': etc., etc., and thus serves as a sort of a dim, crooked little reflector of the conditions that I desire to present on the part of the others. The rest of my story—*voyons*—consists of the sharp notation, at a series of moments, of these conditions. Each little chapter *is*, thereby, a moment, a stage. What is this ix, then, the moment, the stage, *of*? Well, of a more *presented*, a more visible *cynisme* on the part of everybody. But what *step* does the action take in it? *That of Sir C.'s detachment from Ida—Mrs. Beale's from Beale*—OVER the little opportunity and pretext of Maisie. Furthermore the distinct indifferent parental surrender of Maisie. Beale has 'surrendered' her practically in viii—her mother, getting her back through Sir Claude, and putting up with her, to please him, at 1st (exhibit this through Mrs. Wix, to the child), her mother breaks down and resents her presence—or rather resents Beale's shirking—at the last. Yes, I *see* thus, I think, my little *act* of my little drama here. Ah, this *divine* conception of one's little masses and periods in the scenic light—as rounded ACTS; this patient, pious, nobly 'vindictive' * application of the scenic philosophy and method—I feel as if it still (above *all*, YET) had a great deal to give me, and might carry me as far as I dream! God knows how far—into the flushed, dying day—*that* is! *De part et d'autre* Maisie has become a bore to her parents—with Mrs. Wix to help to prove it. They must still hate each other, and Ida must be furiously jealous—of Mrs. Beale. Beale is more indifferent, but he won't (if he can help it) have back Maisie. What my ix brings me to is the coming together of Sir Claude and Mrs. B. on this basis of 'What the devil are they to do with the child?' Sir Claude says that Ida at last demands that Beale shall do, again, his turn; Mrs. Beale says that her husband is tremendously recalcitrant. Then they are *together*—with the child on their hands. *They* have a moment together, to this effect—a moment which seems to me to be the right climax of my ix. I must *enjamber* my period— my time for the child with her mother—from the 1st: hold out my cup—of this year—and then pour my little chapter—express my little act—into it. It must 'transpire' that Claude's visit to Mrs. Beale, his snatch at Maisie, has been 'unbeknown' to Ida. This has been his little way of doing it—quite sincere and generous and really tender to the child—in his pretty, pleasant, weak, bullied, finally disgusted nature —disgusted, of course, with Ida. Ida refuses to see Maisie at first—and Mrs. W. puts her *au courant*. Then Ida's relenting and what Maisie

* [James' note] 'vindicating.'

does see—the painted Idol, the sharp, showy, fiercely questioning mamma. She 'gets it out' of Maisie—the scene at Mrs. Beale's. It's the way it has been done—his going there to that woman—that she resents. But to the child she is at first pretentiously endearing. She must, however, take Sir Claude AWAY a great deal at 1st—through her absorption in him—her passion for him. He resents her neglect of her child and makes up for it to the little girl: comes up to the nursery or school-room, rather, to see her, charms Mrs. Wix more and more (she's in love with him), braves ridicule by going out with them when he can, taking them to the theatre, etc. Then comes the transition, the change. Ida becomes unfaithful. Beale becomes unfaithful. Sir Claude and Mrs. Beale come together on it and on 'What's to be done with Maisie?' I seem to see that I must keep Mrs. Beale AWAY for a year. I show it through Mrs. W.'s presentation of it to the child. Mrs. Wix shows Maisie that it's impossible she should come. Maisie knows fully how jealous her mother is of her (Mrs. B.). So there's an interval after the beginning, that I have shown in VIII, of the relations between Mrs. Beale and Sir Claude. The climax of the act, then, the *resumption* of them, the confrontation of the pair (at Brighton?), the 'Will *you* take her?' the 'Can't *you* keep her?' etc. They must have been, before this, in correspondence—toward the end of the year—ABOUT her. Mrs. Wix *clutches* her. But Sir Claude, in spite of Mrs. Wix, and not wishing in the least to pain her, but *having* to act, to do something, and wishing to see again—for Maisie's sake—Mrs. Beale, in whose tender-ness for her he *believes*—Claude *does act*, takes her off alone, takes her down to Brighton.

x.

What then does my x give me? It gives me primarily 2 things: one of them that Maisie *goes* back to her father's; the other that I get, till the end, rid of Mrs. Wix. I *must* get rid of Mrs. W., to give effect to her return *at* the end, when everything else has failed. And I must replace Maisie at her father's as the only possible basis for the carrying on of the intrigue between her step-parents. Claude can go there—Mrs. Beale could never go to Ida's. Claude is now Mrs. Beale's lover, and it is in this x that I must make the scene in Kensington Gardens occur—the outbreak of 'jealousy' on Ida's part when she—being there with a lover of her own—meets her husband and her daughter. I have sketched this scene *supra*—and here refer myself to it. It must *begin* my x—for the little picture of Sir Claude's *fréquentation* of Beale's house must come *after* it—resting *upon* it. Beale is constantly away—after *his* woman; and this x must contain a passage between him and Maisie. But what's to be its climax?—that of the chapter—this passage of the child with her father? Or must *that* come AFTER the pendant-scene to the foregoing—the scene of Maisie's being out with Mrs. Beale and meeting Beale with a strange lady as, out with Sir Claude, she has *met* Ida with a strange gentleman?

[*This entry is continued in the next notebook, and is commented upon on page 263 below.*]

NOTEBOOK VI

26 October 1896—10 February 1909

(James' note: *continuation of note on* Maisie *of Oct. 26th, 1896, from last page of black covered book with gilt line.*) I think it *must* come after XI (brief), must consist of this second episode and the passage between the child and her father. The latter, it seems to me, can really be *fine* in its picture of the brutality of Beale's cynicism and baseness. It prepares for the 'bolt' and it is the climax of the little chapter. I must now *leave* Maisie under his roof—I can't take her back again to her mother's. But do we *see* Ida again?—after the scene of the meeting? I *think* so—I think I can get an effect from it. Yes, Maisie has her passage with her father—she has her passage with her mother. Then if the former, following the *second* meeting, forms the climax of XI, the latter must be the *beginning* of XII. I imagine Ida coming—oh yes, oh yes, frankly, brazenly, to see the child *at* Beale's to tell her that—well, she's weary of the struggle—she surrenders her to her father. She is strange—she cries, she lies, she hugs her as she used to do of old—and she disappears. This is my 1st half of XII. The next thing Maisie 'knows' is that her mother has 'bolted.' Sir Claude arrives at her father's, where she is, with this news for Mrs. Beale. He is a 'free man,' but they greet the news as a supreme trick she has played Beale—about the child; unfitting herself—by her act—for further bother about it. Sir Claude, on this, asks Maisie if she will come now and live—stay with him: he will do her mother's turn for her. She must have had, over her mother's flight, a burst of grief and shame—her *one* EXPRESSION of perceptive violence: she cries, she breaks down. Her *one* break down. This *moves* Sir Claude; makes him want more to have her. He *urges* her—but on this Mrs. Beale protests. No— *she'll* keep her: he'll come and see her there. It reaches almost a dispute between them. I must have it that Mrs. Beale *really* clings to her —partly from her old affection, the charm of the child (formulate *to* the child—*for* the reader, *through* Mrs. Wix or Sir Claude, this charm so complicating and entangling for others); and partly because her presence is a way of *attracting* Sir Claude and making a tie *with* him. But he is the person, who, after Mrs. Wix, loves her most and he does get her

[261]

away from Mrs. Beale—for a week; succeeds in taking her to the empty house, where, abandoned of Ida, they moon about, vaguely and tenderly, together. That is, I *think* he takes her to the empty house: this is to settle, to *creuser*. V*oyons, voyons—arrangeons un peu cela*. What I seem to want is that a little interval should occur before the revelation that Beale, too, has bolted with a 'paramour.' If I can only keep this —that is, *make* it, really dramatic, it may perhaps be something of a little triumph. Mrs. Beale must come down, somewhere, *to* Sir Claude and Maisie with her great news for the former and her 'Now we're free!' My climax is that what this freedom conveys for them is the freedom to live together—to do now what they like—with the rather perplexed and slightly ashamed consciousness that now, charged with the child, if they keep her they keep her mixed up with their *malpropreté*, their illegitimate tie. The embarrassment, the awkwardness, the irony, the *cynisme*, the melancholy comedy, or whatever one may call it, of this. *Then* poor Mrs. Wix's descent—her indignant rise in her might, her putting before them the horror (for *her*, at least), of what they're doing; the way, in a word, in which *elle leur dit leur fait*, winding up with her *taking* Maisie to her own poor, bare shabbiness of home and life—her rescuing her, declaring that *she* will do for her. That is my clear climax and denouement; BUT what I've been asking myself is whether I may not with effect, whether I, indeed, *must* not, represent a little prior descent of Mrs. Wix's *after* Ida's flight and *before* Beale's—in the interval that I'm obliged to make. (Put it in the episode of the empty house?) It is not only that this interval— the wait for the effect of Mrs. Beale's advent with *her* news, the tidings of what has happened to *her* home—it is not only that this little interval requires to be filled; but, further, that there are 2 other reasons. One of these is that, given the attitude already imputed to Mrs. W. toward Sir Claude, it seems to me she mustn't reprobate him, break with him *tout d'un coup*. The other is that I do well to give her a chance to *appeal* to him—do it well from the point of view of dramatic prettiness and pathos. Isn't there a grotesque *pathos*, in especial, in her turning up on learning (I must settle *how* she learns—with her relation to Ida *that* is manageable very naturally) of her ladyship's flight and hurrying down to him to put his present chance for beauty and virtue (of behaviour) before him. She sees how the event must throw him into Mrs. Beale's arms, and *elle se démène* as *against* that. She pictures to him his chance—his chance to come off now with Maisie and *her*. They will be together—they will make a *trio*. The small touching oddity (with her secret passion for him) of her offering *herself* as a rescue from the temptation, the impropriety of Mrs. Beale. ADMIRABLE, this. He resists—he doesn't see it yet; and she *has* to go off, with her return, her next entrance, prepared for, as it were, and led up to. I seem to see this out of town—at Brighton, at a watering-place *quelconque*. I see Mrs. W. 'come down';—I see Mrs. Beale 'come down';—I see Mrs. W. 'come down' again. She leaves, in snatching up Maisie. Mrs. Beale and Sir Claude to go *abroad*. Yes, she goes back with the child to London. They stay there—behind—together: to embark together for the continent. Don't I get an effect from *Folkestone*? It's to Folkestone Sir Claude has taken Maisie, and, after Mrs. Beale, on Beale's 'bolt,' has rushed down, it is *there*, a *very* good place, I think, that they find themselves with the problem of having her between them in their adulterous relation. I thought of making Mrs. Wix arrive the same day as Mrs. Beale—in the afternoon—but I think I strengthen my effect by making her not come till 3 or 4 days after. A part of the ugly little comedy is their—the 'guilty couple's'—at once exalted and rueful *consideration* of what they are face to face with—and I must give that a little time—a few days—to go on. They go about with her—looking over to France and 'abroad'—meanwhile; and it is this *accomplished* situation that Mrs. Wix breaks into. Susan Ash is also with the child—Susan Ash has accompanied her and Sir Claude down to Folkestone when he goes and possesses himself of *Maisie* after Ida's flight. And Susan Ash *too* is a hussy, whom Mrs. Wix also *dit son fait* to—or about.

December 21st, 34 De Vere Gdns., W.

I realise—none too soon—that the *scenic* method is my absolute, my imperative, my *only* salvation. The *march of an action* is the thing for me to, more and more, *attach* myself to: it is the only thing that really, for *me*, at least, will *produire* L'ŒUVRE, and L'ŒUVRE is, before God, what I'm going in for. Well, the scenic scheme is the only one that *I* can trust, with my tendencies, to stick to the march of an action. How reading Ibsen's splendid *John Gabriel* a day or two ago (in proof) brought that, FINALLY AND FOREVER, home to me! I must now, I fully recognize, have a splendid recourse to it to see me out of the wood, at all, of this interminable little *Maisie*; 10,000 *more words* of which I have still to do. They can be magnificent in movement if I resolutely and triumphantly take this course with them, and *only if I do so.*

[This long entry, continuing that begun on page 257, seems to have been written after James had finished eight sections of What Maisie Knew.

In IX, in the novel, Ida does not welcome Maisie but refuses to see her for several days. The idea that Mrs. Wix's talk to Maisie is to reflect 'the whole thing' is used. But one section could not contain all that James planned for IX, so the expansion continued, and the stage scheduled for the beginning of X does not come until XIII, when Sir Claude takes Maisie to Mrs. Beale, leaving Mrs. Wix behind. The meeting in Kensington Gardens (sketched for X) occupies XV and XVI in the novel. Maisie does not see her father until XVIII when, accompanied by Mrs. Beale, she meets him with his 'countess' and is whisked off by him. Her talk with him at his mistress's rooms comes in XIX, and its climax is Maisie's realization that she is abandoned by him and that he is about to 'bolt.' This corresponds to the proposed XI, and the meeting with Ida, suggested for XII, occurs in the novel in XX, at Folkestone, where Sir Claude has taken Maisie. The remaining eleven chapters of the novel bring Mrs. Wix to France to join Sir Claude and Maisie before Mrs. Beale comes, and center on Mrs. Wix's further revelations to the child and their discussion of Maisie's 'moral sense,' ending, of course, with the struggle between Mrs. Beale and Mrs. Wix and the latter's final carrying off of her protégée. They depart considerably from the outline proposed here. Mrs. Wix 'comes down' but once—comes to France—and stays to the end, first with Maisie and Sir Claude, then with Maisie alone, then with Maisie and Mrs. Beale, and finally with both lovers and the child. This was the working out of James' determination to make the 'scenic' method see him 'out of the wood' of the 'interminable' novel, and was effective because it rendered it possible to present virtually the whole story through Mrs. Wix's successive encounters with the other characters. It also made it easier for him to live up to his decision to reveal everything through Maisie. To have had Mrs. Wix come '3 or 4 days after' Mrs. Beale joined Claude, in order to give the 'guilty couple' time for 'exalted and rueful consideration,' would have made difficulties, since there would have been only Maisie's unaided impressions to rely upon. But with Mrs. Wix at hand, what Maisie saw and felt could be enriched by what she could glean from her governess. Mrs. Wix was indispensable, because she extended the range of Maisie's consciousness and because only through her relation to Maisie could the little girl's 'moral sense' be dramatically conveyed.

James' fascination with the theme and method of Maisie is testified to by the care with which he recorded in his notebooks the progress of the book. A close study of the differences between the novel and some of the plans he considered while writing it illuminates not only his zeal to keep Maisie's consciousness the center, and his increasing insistence on the 'scenic,' but also other characteristic elements of his technique. To mention but one, in Maisie as in his other work he sought for symmetry and balance in the structure of the story, felt the need for an 'intensely structural, intensely hinged and jointed preliminary frame,' but at the same time saw the need of keeping the design from becoming too obvious. He liked, for example, the idea of the two parallel meetings—one when Maisie and Sir Claude come upon Ida and her lover and the other when Maisie and Mrs. Beale meet Farange and the 'brown lady.' Originally both meetings were to have been closely alike in situation and development, but eventually the second was altered—differently prepared for and differently worked out. The fundamental parallelism remains and is effective, but the danger of its appearing too rigidly contrived is neatly avoided.

What Maisie Knew ran serially in the Chap Book from 15 January to 1 August 1897.]

May 7th, 1898.

1. The thing suggested by what Aug. Birrell mentioned to me the other night, at Rosebery's, of Frank Lockwood—that is, of his writing, so soon after his death and amid all his things, F.L.'s *Life*—past tense—and 'feeling as if he might come in.'

2. *Les Vieux.*

3. 'Vanderbilt' story—the Cocotte (for the Divorce) 'covering' the real woman he wants to marry.

4. The Lady R.C. (Bourget) vindictive, bad, dressing of young wife incident.

5. The 'Cazalis' wife ('pen-name' and doctor's name) situation.

6. The Miss Balch and Lady G. incident. Imagine the protectress (Respectability) dealing death upon the person coming to denounce. She (Respectability) *must get her money,* etc.

7. The resemblance-of-Hugues-L.-to-Bourget-story—the woman affected.

8. Gualdo's story of the child *retournée*—the acquisition, construction (by portrait, etc. ???) of an ANCESTOR, instead of *l'Enfant.* The setting up of some one who must *have lived: un vrai mort.* Imagine old couple, liking young man: 'You must have married our daughter.'

'Your daughter?'

'The one we lost. You were her fiancé or her *mari.*' Imagine situation for young man (as regards some living girl) who has more or less accepted it. He succumbs to suggestion. He has sworn fidelity to a memory. He ends by believing it. He lives with the parents. They leave him their money. I see him later. *He is a widower.* He dies, to rejoin his wife. He leaves their fortune to the girl he doesn't marry. 35 pages. (Subject—subject.)

9. (In same key.) The woman who wants to have *been* married—to *have become* a widow. *She* may come, *à la Gualdo,* to the painter to have

[265]

the portrait painted—the portrait of her husband. The painter does it. Very pretty too I think. Young man—friend of painter's: 'Lord, I wish *I* looked like it—or it looked like *me!*' (Extraordinary old girl is rich.)

10. *Les Vieux* again or *The Waiters:*—Lady P.'s story of the Miss Palfreys. The last one—she remains. Or perhaps there is only *one* who waits. The mother survives her. (25 pages.) The daughter dies. The way they put it to the mother, or *she* puts it. 'Oh, I knew, I *knew* she would: she has gone to Europe!'

11. The young man who can't get rid of his secret—his oppressive knowledge—with solution of his *taking* one—HAVING to, from some one else—to keep it company.

12. Etta R.'s case of maturing, withering daughter. 'Her *husband* will *show* her the world, travel with her—a girl—in our *monde*—waits for *that.*'

13. 'The Publisher's Story.' Mrs. X.—a literary woman—ÉREINTERS *pendant de longues années* a writer—preferably novelist or poet. I (the Publisher) ask: 'Why can't you let him alone? You *know* him—like him.' 'Yes, but I don't like his work.' Then—about his never seeing what she says: *elle est rageuse.* I put my finger on the place: 'You love him.' She has to admit it. 'Well, try another tack.' She writes a eulogy, which he *sees*; and learns the authorship of, and in consequence of which he does notice her work. x x x x x I see the *other* woman or girl, who, then, on the accident of his seeing at last the back numbers and learning who *has* slated him (it needn't have been for so long; a year or two) says '*I* wrote them'; to save her friend. But *my* thought, on this, of how *she*, the 2d girl, must love. Try 1st (May 7th, 1898) the Frk. Lockwood, the Playfair, Palfrey, the Young Man who has Married the dead Daughter, and the wonderful feat of the poor fine lady (Miss B.) who, taking the money to put the *tarée* one through, *kills* the upsetter who comes to make her job worthless. Only the killing is difficult.

[During the sixteen months since the last entry James had produced In the Cage, The Turn of the Screw, and Covering End. He seems to have wanted to take stock now of the themes that he had on hand for potential short stories. He had already included 2, 12, and 13 in his similar list at the close of 1895 (pp. 233-7 above).

(1) furnished the starting point for The Real Right Thing (Collier's Weekly, 16 December, 1899) in which George Withermore, the admiring young critic, felt so strongly the actual presence of the late Ashton Doyne, mutely protesting against any biography, that he gave up working on one.

(2) presumably refers to the anecdote told James by Mrs. Procter (p. 224 above), though he also used Les Vieux as a general title for a possible group of stories that might include The Ambassadors (p. 226 above) as well as 10, 'Europe.'

(3) was to become The Special Type (as we have noted at p. 232 above). James mentioned it again the following year (p. 288 below).

He was to outline 4, The Two Faces, at pages 284-5 below; and 6, Mrs. Medwin, at pages 278-9. He had already outlined 5 and 7 at pages 212-13 above.

(8) became the theme for Maud-Evelyn (the Atlantic Monthly, April 1900), where James' love for the dead and for passions that might have been, carried him to a strange extreme.

He continued to develop 9, The Tone of Time, and 11, A Round of Visits (pp. 283-4, 280-81 below).]

Names. Dedrick—Emerick—Bauker—Flickerbridge—Marsock—Sandbeach—Chirk—Rivory—Reever—Dirling—Catchmere—Catchmore—Cashmore—Pewbury (place)—Gallery—Mitchett—Mitcher—Stilmore (place)—Tribe—Pinthorpe (place)—Cutsome.

34 De Vere Gdns., W., May 8th, 1898.

L'honnête femme n'a pas de roman—beautiful little 'literary (?)' subject to work out in short tale. The trial, the exhibition, the proof:—either it's not a '*roman*,' or it's not *honnête*. When it becomes the thing it's guilty; when it doesn't become guilty it doesn't become the thing.

[*James begins to develop the theme for* The Story in It *on page 275 below.*]

May 11th. Notion given me by G<aillard> T. L<apsley> yesterday on leaving with him a 'drawing-room tea' at the American Embassy. The 2 American girls there (Miss C.'s) whose history led him to touch the American phenomenon of the social suppression of the parents. They had suppressed theirs, etc., etc.—and *de fil en aiguille* the little idea comes to me: a case in which 2 children, daughter and *son*, I think—but the son essentially as his ambitious and 'successful' sister's mandatory and underling, so *conceal* their homely mother—with the aid of her own subjection and effacement—that, having almost, practically, given out that she is *dead*—brought to this by the scare of learning that she's supposed to be concealed because she *is* compromising—they, in a given case or crisis, are so ashamed and embarrassed at having to show she *isn't*, and that they *have* sacrificed her, that they

[267]

get her—for the occasion—till it's tided over and they are safe, etc.—
get her to FEIGN death, to lend herself—which it is part of the pathos
and drollery of the thing that she submissively and bewilderedly—*de-
votedly*, above all—does. The son is WITH her—works it FOR the sister
as (also) submissively as he must—and as tenderly as he *can*.

[*This 'notion,' altered and added to, resulted in Fordham Castle
(see pp. 274, 293-4 below).*]

Names. Leon—Brivet (place)—Trete (place)—Ure (place or person)—
Hessom—Manger—Hush (person or place)—Mush—Issater—Ister (Ice-
ster)—Elbert—Challen—Challice (or *is*)—Challas—Syme—Dyme—
Nimm—Etchester—Genrick (Genneric)—Dluce—Bagger—Clarring—
Compigny—Cavenham—Grendon—Treck—Randidge—Randage—Ban-
didge—Neversome—Witherfield—Withermore—Chering (place)—Smar-
den—Addard—Petherton—Kirl—Rosling—Ulph (place)—Treffry—Curd
('Lucy Curd')—Lutley (or place)—Staverton—Brissenden—Traffle—Ver-
ver (or, for place, Ververs)—Heighington—Hington—Hingley—Braddle
—Gostrey—Beveridge—Waldash (Waldish)—Dadd—Charl—Chelver—
Iddings—Branson—Brinton—Laud—Blessingbourne—Mapleton—With-
ermore—Shirrs—Damerel—Dreuil (Mme le Dreuil)—Bonair—Keel (Keal)
—Tocs.

Lamb House, January 22d, 1899.

George Alexander writes me to ask for *Covering End*,[1] for 'him and
Miss Davis' to do, and I've just written to him the obstacles and
objections. But I've also said I *would* do him a *fresh* one-act thing;
and it's strange how this little renewal of contact with the vulgar
theatre stirs again, in a manner, and moves me. Or rather, it isn't at
all the contact with the theatre—still as ever, strangely odious: it's
the contact with the DRAMA, with the divine little difficult, artistic,
ingenious, architectural FORM that makes old pulses throb and old
tears rise again. The blended anguish and amusement again touch me
with their breath. This is a grey, gusty, lonely Sunday at Rye—the tail of
a great, of an almost, in fact, *perpetual* winter gale. The wind booms
in the old chimneys, wails and shrieks about the old walls. I sit,
however, in the little warm white study—and many things come back
to me. I've been in London for 3 weeks—came back here on the 20th;
and feel the old reviving ache of desire to get back to work. Yes, I
yearn for that—the divine unrest again touches me. This note of
Alexander's is probably the germ of something. I mean of a little

1. See page 186 above.

wooing of something ingenious. Ah, the one-act! Ah, the 'short story!' It's very much the same trick! Apropos of the latter, Edmund G. gave me the other night, in town, something that was kindly intended for a possible tip—something retailed lately to himself as such. Some lady had seen an incident and told him. She was in a railway-carriage x x x x x (But note later on Gosse's incident of the *éplorée* mourning widow, observed by narrating fellow-traveller in corner of carriage, who gets into train with relations of dead husband so sympathetically seeing her off, and then at next station with a changed aspect meets handsome gentleman, who gets in and with whom she moves into other carriage—with a sequel, etc.)

Lamb House, January 27th, 1899.

How, through all hesitations and conflicts and worries, *the* thing, the desire to get back only to the *big* (scenic, constructive 'architectural' effects) seizes me and carries me off my feet: making me feel that it's a far deeper economy of time to sink, at *any* moment, into the evocation and ciphering out of *that*, than into any other *small* beguilement at all. Ah, once more, to let myself go! The very thought of it soothes and sustains, lays a divine hand on my nerves, and lights, so beneficently, my uncertainties and obscurities. *Begin* it—and it will grow. Put in now some strong short novel, and come back from the continent, with it all figured out. I must have a long *tête à tête* with myself, a long ciphering bout, on it, before I really start. *Basta.* I've other work to do this a.m. and I only just now overflowed into this from a little gust of restless impatience. I'm somehow haunted with the *American* family represented to me by Mrs. Cameron (*à propos* of the 'Lloyd Bryces') last summer. Yet that is a large, comprehensive picture, and I long to represent an *action*: I mean a rapid, concrete action is what I desire, yearn, just now, to put in: to build, construct, teach myself a mastery of. But *basta* again. À *bientôt*.

Lamb House, February 10th, '99.

Dear old George Meredith the other day (on Sunday the 5th at Boxhill) threw out an allusion (in something he was telling me) that suggested a small subject—5000 words. Some woman was marrying a man who knew very little about her. He was in love—intensely: but something came up about her 'past.' 'What *is* it? Is there anything . . . ? Anything I ought to know?' 'Give me 6 months,' she answers. 'If you want to know it *then*—I promise you I will tell you.' That was all his allusion—but it made me, on the spot, tie a knot in my handkerchief. There *is* a little subject—but what is it? I seem to see different possibilities. I see the thing, at any rate, as distinctively *ironic*. What appears to come out most is *this*:—

The woman is a woman who *may* have had a past; of an age, of a type. The question, the suspicion, the possibility, the idea, in short, comes up for the man who is making up to her, who has proposed and whom she has accepted. Thence the question, the answer, I have quoted. She is not in love with him—she is in love with another man; a man he knows. Well, he finds he can't accept her condition. 'Tell me *first*. It won't make any difference. I won't mind. Only I want to know. You ought to tell me. If you believe it's something that *will* make no real difference, why *can't* you tell?'

'Ah, but I can't. I won't. Yes, I'll marry you. I believe I shall suit you. But you must trust me so far. I swear that if six months hence you still *want* to know—!'

'Ah, but then I shall be married to you.'

'Yes, but what will you have lost by that—?'

'You mean if I *don't* want to know?'

'Yes—and if you do. If you care for me *now*—'

'I shall care for you then?—What if it's anything very bad?—*Is* it something very bad?'

'I don't know what you'd think it. If you must know it, you'll estimate it when you do know it. I don't know how it would strike you.' x x x x x

However, I find I can't figure this out today, through extreme seediness from convalescent influenza. I just catch the tail there—the 2d man, to whom the 1st tells his predicament. He backs *out*—the first—he can't accept the condition. The '2d man' is a man she does love—and the 1st (not knowing this) has told him (being a friend) of his predicament and then of his collapse. The 2d is so interested and touched that he approaches her—*he* in turn makes up to her—he mentions to her what the 1st has told him. He 'falls in love' with the woman, and intimates that *he* would accept her condition. *This* is what she has dreamed of, and she says 'Well, then—!' and she renews, *with* him, the condition; promises that if, after 6 months, he does want to know *what* there has been in her past, she will then make a clear statement. On this he marries her. They are happy—she charms and satisfies him; he is highly pleased with his own magnanimity and delicacy, and when at the end of 6 months she says to him: 'Now *do* you' want to know?' he waves away the thought. He *doesn't*. He wouldn't know for the world. He forbids her to tell him—and she of course (confessing it is quite what she hoped), happily concurs and

[270]

mildly triumphs. She says still: 'Whenever you like, you know!'—but he *doesn't* like: he won't hear of it. What he *does* like is the beauty of his own trust and confidence, his relinquishment—and on that they go on and on. The 1st man, meanwhile, has vanished into space—has gone off, after the marriage of his friend, the easier suitor, or has heard of it, rather, at a distance. But in time, restless, dissatisfied with himself, he comes *back*. He has been as little pleased with his own insistence as the happy husband has been much so with *his* own generosity: he continues to care for the woman, to be haunted and restless. He has never married another. He thinks of her perpetually—he wonders and wonders. (Oh, divine old joy of the 'Scenario,' throbbing up and up, with its little sacred irrepressible emotion, WHENEVER I give it again the ghost of a chance!) He tries to find out about her—he does get on her trace—comes across traces of her 'past,' looks into it, rakes it up. But nothing he gets a scent of is at all a *guilty* business or a compromising relation: only, really, traces of her courage and *bonne grâce;* difficulties, struggles, patience, solitude—all things to her honour. (Say she's a little music-mistress—a 'lady' adrift or say, even, she 'paints.') He is all the *more* perplexed and dissatisfied—feeling what he perhaps has lost. Yet, too, if she herself has admitted something, what does it mean? In fine he reappears. He comes back to her. The husband is still his friend—so he has a certain freedom. When they meet alone, he and the wife (he has met, again—renewed with—the husband first), he brings it up to her, tries to have it out.

'Have you ever told *him?*'

'Never.'

'And he doesn't want to know.'

'Absolutely not.—*You* wouldn't,' she adds—'if you had only believed it.'

'Well,' the old lover replies, sighing, pained, wretched: 'Will you at least tell me *now?*'

'Ah, no, *par exemple!*' That's too much for him to ask.

'You're afraid I'll go and tell your husband?'

'No—not *that*. He wouldn't let you.'

'Well, what then prevents you?'

He lets her know—*has* let her know—that he is in love with her still; but, at any rate, they separate without her having in any way satisfied him. He comes back; he sees her again; and then at last he brings out his thought. 'I've rifled and ransacked your life—so far as I could get near it and *at* it. But I've found, I *can* find, *nothing.* What was it—when was it? I believe there *was* nothing? Is it so? For God's sake, *tell* me.'

She considers. 'Will you give me a promise?'

'*Any* promise!'

'Will you swear on your sacred honour?'

'I'll swear.' He does so—swears, I mean, to repeat what she says to *no one*.

'Well, then—there *was* nothing.'

'Nothing?'

'Nothing.'

He's overwhelmed with the strangeness—the bitterness. 'What then were you to have told *me*?'

'Nothing. For you wouldn't have wanted it.'

'How could you be *sure*—?'

'Well, I would simply then have told you there *was*, there *is*, nothing.'

'Then why did <you> speak as if there was?'

'I didn't. It was *you* who did—from the first.'

'Ah, but you left the matter in an obscurity. You were willing to let me think an evil.'

'Certainly—that was your punishment.'

'At your expense? That of your reputation?'

'My reputation for what? For being too proud, simply, to go into explanations—!' x x x x x

— But my developments are carrying me too far at a moment when I'm still sick and seedy. *Basta*. My denouement is the *éclaircissement* between these 2: the explanation, the presentment she gives of the case. He says: 'And you don't want your husband to *know* that there's nothing—?'

'I want the subject left as he prefers to leave it—untouched, again, forever.'

'And let him believe every evil—?'

' "Every?" Why, my dear man, he scarcely believes ANY!'

'I like your scarcely! You mean he doesn't think it was so *very* bad—?'

'Well, he sees I'm, at all events—whatever may have happened—a good creature; and I have the benefit of that. I've been very nice to him.'

Un temps. 'You *really* wouldn't like me to tell him—as from my own belief—that there was nothing . . . ?'

Her positive irony of amusement. 'Don't you think it a delicate matter to offer such a reassurance?'

'I mean only as an amends for my former talk with him. I can tell him that with time I've felt that a burden to my conscience.'

[272]

'Well, however it may occur to you to put it, I don't recommend you to speak of it to him.'

Un temps. 'Oh, of course I can't—after my vow, my oath, to you.' *Encore un temps.* 'But I see now—of course—why you exacted that vow.' He shows her he sees why; puts his finger on that fact of the husband's 'hugging' his sense of the beauty of his own behaviour and forgiveness which is the psychological *nœud* or *concetto* of the matter.

She *accepts* this interpretation—and I, so far, *give* it, with my lucidity and authority. Then he tells her, the ex-lover, that he *now*, *par exemple*, does rage with jealousy, his passion re-excited by the thought of all this peculiar bliss that the husband enjoys. It does make him want to blight it—to spoil the other man's (self-)complacency. He is tempted to break his vow.

'Ah, you can't.'

'No—I can't.'

'That you see is your punishment.'—This speech of hers is the logical last note of the thing—the climax and denouement: but I seem to want to tuck in before it 2 or 3 things. I mean that any other (2 or 3) things I *do* want to tuck in must be *put* before it—so as to leave it in final possession. Above all I 'feel that I feel' that I don't absolutely get what I want in making *her* give up her 'past' *as* simply nothing. *Don't make her formulate that too much.* Let her rather, simply, *take it from* her ex-lover, since this is the way his researches have made it strike him. 'Oh, well—if you think so . . . !'—*that* is her attitude. She assents at most. 'Oh, well, if you can't *find* it—!' *That's* the way she puts it, as if with light, vague relief. That he hasn't been able to 'find' it is what he speaks of telling the husband.

[The Great Condition *ends with Mrs. Chilver's 'It's only your punishment,' which concludes the climactic scene between her and her ex-suitor, Braddle. In the finished story the substance of the sketch is kept and even some scraps of the suggested dialogue, but the emphasis is slightly shifted so that Mrs. Chilver becomes the one important character. Braddle is simply a stupid man obsessed by suspicion and curiosity, and Chilver is a relatively colorless figure, at first the observer of Braddle's state of mind and later little more than a complaisant foil for his highly intelligent wife. Her attitude is dignified throughout; she understands both men and is wiser than either; and her 'condition' is a test that reveals the weakness of one and the strength of the other and, as she sees, enhances her husband's happiness and his confidence in himself.*

The story first appeared in the Anglo-Saxon Review *in June 1899. James did not include it in the collected edition.]*

February 15th (Lamb House), 1899.

Would the little idea of the 'suppressed (American) mother' be feasible in 5000 words? It would be worth trying—for I seem to see I shall never do it in any other way. Try it so for what it is worth. DO THESE IN 5000 AT WHATEVER COST. IT IS ONLY THE MUTILATED, *the indicated thing that is feasible.* It occurs to me that it would be possible, and make for brevity, to do the thing *from* the vision, as it were, and the standpoint *of* the mother; i.e., make the mother show and present it. I see no effective brevity *but* in that. (I count 30 pages of author's 'pad' MS.) (This makes 5 divisions of 6 pages or 6 little sections of 5.) Oh, if I could only arrive at a definite firm fixed form of that exact dimension. How it *would* help to make the pot boil! Well, *cela ne tient qu'à moi—qu'à ma volonté. Tâchons, tâchons.* It's a question of throwing up, under the pressure of necessity, the right thing.—In this little subject I see the Daughters 1st; see them as I saw them, the pair, the Misses So-and-So, that day at the American Embassy, last spring—fresh from the Drawingroom. I recall my walk away, afterwards, in company with G. T. Lapsley—my stroll, in the budding May—or June—sunshine along the Mall of St. James's Pk. There he told me— charmingly—sounded the note of the sort of thing in which I instantly saw <a> little *donnée.* 'And in all kept their mother so out of the way, somehow—!' It was the way they had done it.—Well, narrating, I have (in 1) met the 2 girls. I give my little talk about them—the little talk I have with my (American also) hostess. *They have a chaperon —a dame de compagnie.* 'As usual, after everyone had gone—it was what I always outstaid them all for—my hostess, on her sofa by the fire, answered my questions and met my wonderments.' I begin about in *that* sort of little way. 'The 2 sisters?—oh, the Miss P.'s—they come to be presented.' Lapsley—sketch of them, and note of the ambiguity —obscurity—of the mother question more or less sounded.

II. I meet the mother—in Dresden or Switzerland—at *pension.* She tells me about her daughters. I 'fit' them together.

III. I re-meet the daughters—in London, Paris, Rome, or somewhere, in situation in which I *see* them pass as *without* the appendage. 'Mother?—oh, they *have* none.' I am going to interfere when the *chaperon—D. de C.*—checks me. 'Don't—I'll tell you *why.*' She tells me. (The thing might be told *by* the *dame de compagnie.*) x x x x x Pursue this some other time—keeping hold of the idea that the mother consents, for the given occasion, not to exist.

x   x   x   x   x

[Fordham Castle did not prove 'feasible in 5000 words' but expanded to nearly 10,000. Nor was James' scheme here sufficient for what he wanted. It was only later (p. 293 below) that he hit upon the added material he needed to make the story.]

Don't lose sight of the little *concetto* of the note in former vol. that begins with fancy of the young man who marries an old woman and becomes old while she becomes young. Keep my play on idea: the *liaison* that betrays itself by the *transfer* of qualities—qualities to be determined—from one to the other of the parties to it. They *exchange*. I see 2 couples. One is married—this is the *old-young* pair. I watch *their* process, and it gives me my light for the spectacle of the other (covert, obscure, unavowed) pair who are *not* married.

x   x   x   x   x

[*The concetto referred to here was suggested to James by Stopford Brooke and recorded by him in his notebook entry for 17 February 1894 (p. 150 above).*

The Sacred Fount (1901) presents the husband who ages as his wife grows younger, and a woman whose intelligence seems to wane while that of a man increases. To the uncannily acute and obsessedly curious observer who tells the story, this suggests that there must be a liaison, and the novel is the record of his attempt to discover the truth. Some critics have maintained the novel to be a serious study of the sexual 'fount' of personality; to others it has seemed an over-elaborate working out of a device, in which any possible symbolism is pretty well swamped by the detail with which the observer's relentless inquiry is displayed.]

Keep in view 'The Publisher's Story.' Also *L'honnête femme—n'a pas de roman* story. Worry something out of that. There is something *in* it. And, for the Publisher's story, revert to what I seem to have (in this vol.) got hold of the tail of—the idea of the 2d woman (girl), who falsely takes upon *herself* the authorship of the 'slatings' and who is *the* one that the narrator attributes the secret passion to. x x x x x

In the 'Honnête Femme' may there not be something like *this?*—very, very short: 3000 or 4000 words. A man of letters, an artist, *represents*, *expresses*, to a young, 'innocent,' yearning woman (a widow, say), that contention, in respect of the *honnête femme*. She must have wrestled with him about it—*à propos* of 'the French novel,' books, pictures, etc. —'art' I mean, generally—with her 'Anglo-Saxon' clinging to the impossible thesis. He is very clear. If she's *honnête* it's not a *roman*—if it's a *roman* she's not *honnête*. *He's* married—he's the artist—the man of frank, firm attitude. All the while she's in love with him—*secretly*, obscurely, with nothing coming out. But she has a relation, a witness, a friend who is also in love with him and is present at, assists at, this innocent contentious relation. *She* has let herself go—the man is her lover. It is successfully hidden. I show, however, that the passion, the relation, ardently, tormentedly, clandestinely, exists. Finally—after scenes and passages—to *confute* her friend (who *agrees*, to her, with the artist), she says: 'And all the while he talks thus he doesn't *know!*' 'Know what?' 'Why, that I *adore* him.' The friend, whose relations with the artist must have been *given*, unmistakeably, to the reader, wonders, winces, but controls herself. 'Then don't you want him to?' '*Never!*' 'Why, then—?' 'Because where then would be my (decency) *honnêteté?*' The other woman's deep, sore, tragic answer: 'But without it, triple idiot, where then is your romance?' '*Here.*' She strikes her heart. 'Oh!' says the other. I seem to wish to require, to have a passage, for finality and lucidity, between the artist *and* his mistress—in which the latter 'gives' him the foregoing. 'She calls *that*,' she says, 'a romance. But how, where? A romance is a *relation*: Well—like yours and *mine*. Where is—for *her*—the relation? There *is* none.' The artist turns it over, ponders, feels it. 'A relation—yes. But mayn't it be, after all, also a (sort of) *consciousness?*' 'How? What is there in that? What does it do for her?' *He* must say *he* has one too. 'Well then—constituted as she is—what does *yours* do for her?' He has to take this. 'I see. It only does—what it *can* do—for ME!' *That* I see as the climax. But I see also there must have been—*n'est-ce pas?*—2 or 3 other things. That is, it must be struck out that, as *she* (the 'lost' woman) puts it—'It all depends on what you *call* a relation.' Further, oughtn't the thing to *begin* with the fact of the relation (which she *does* call one) existing between the artist and the thorough-going woman. But it will be pretty, though, in making that plain, not to crudify the statement of it. Give her acceptance, vision of it, simply, *as* a relation. x x x x x I see it as *London* thing—the above.

x   x   x   x   x

[James stated, in the preface to Daisy Miller, that 'for the pure pearl' of his idea for The Story in It, he had had to take 'a dive into the deep sea of a certain general truth. . . The general truth had been positively phrased for me by a distinguished friend, a novelist not to our manner either born or bred, on the occasion of his having made such answer as he could to an interlocutor (he, oh distinctly, indigenous and glib!) bent on learning from him why the adventures he imputed to his heroines were so perversely and persistently but of a type impossible to ladies respecting themselves.' James' friend, who may very well have been Bourget, had replied with the question: 'A picture of life founded on the mere reserves and omissions and suppressions of life, what sort of a performance—for beauty, for interest, for tone— could that hope to be?' James had pursued the issue afterwards, and had reiterated once more his lasting belief that 'a human, a personal "adventure" is no a priori, no positive and absolute and inelastic thing, but just a matter of relation and appreciation.'

In dramatizing this truth, James did not make his man another artist, but a retired colonel, whose 'reputation for gallantry mainly depended now on his fighting Liberalism in the House of Commons.' The scene is the country house of Mrs. Dyott, with whom he is carrying on a secret affair. Mrs. Dyott's guest, Mrs. Blessingbourne, is a great reader of D'Annunzio and modern French novels, in contrast to her hostess, who does not care for books but for life.

When Colonel Voyt calls, he and Mrs. Blessingbourne discuss fiction. They agree on the emptiness and puerility of most current British and American novelists, but when the Colonel praises the continental writers for their greater 'sense of life,' she demurs. She doesn't agree that 'they feel more things than we'; she has found herself disappointed rather that the French 'give us only again and again, for ever and ever, the same couple.' They never present 'a decent woman.' He declares that they are necessarily restricted to 'the fact of a relation. . . The subject the novelist treats is the rise, the formation, the development, the climax and for the most part the decline of one. And what is the honest lady doing on that side of the town? . . . If a relation stops, where's the story? If it doesn't stop, where's the innocence? It seems to me you must choose.'

Maud Blessingbourne does not press her point further, but she is not convinced. After the Colonel has left, she does not declare her love for him to Mrs. Dyott, as James first intended her to do. Instead, as was far more typical of his method, Mrs. Dyott silently guesses the object of Maud's devotion. When she later tells her discovery to the Colonel, he ends the story with the reflection that Maud's 'consciousness, if they let it alone—as they of course after this mercifully must— was, in the last analysis, a kind of shy romance. Not a romance like their own, a thing to make the fortune of any author up to the mark—one who should have the invention or who could have the courage; but a small scared starved subjective satisfaction that would do

[277]

her no harm and nobody else any good. Who but a duffer—he stuck to his contention—would see the shadow of a "story" in it?'

James' lifelong conviction was that he could find stories in just such hidden states of consciousness. In commenting on this particular illustration of his belief, he added: 'Even after I had exerted a ferocious and far from fruitless ingenuity to keep it from becoming a nouvelle—for it is in fact one of the briefest of my compositions [1]—it still haunted, a graceless beggar, for a couple of years, the cold avenues of publicity; till finally an old acquaintance, about to "start a magazine," begged it in turn of me and published it (1903) at no cost to himself but the cost of his confidence, in that first number which was in the event, if I mistake not, to prove only one of a pair. I like perhaps "morbidly" to think that the Story in it may have been more than the magazine could carry.' LeRoy Phillips was unable to discover the magazine to which James alludes, or any publication of this story prior to its inclusion in The Better Sort (1903).]

Look also, a little, *mon bon*, into what may come out, further, of the little something-or-other deposited long since in your memory—your fancy—by the queer confidence made you by the late Miss B. (B . . . h) on the subject of what she had undertaken to do for the *tarée* Lady G. —her baffled, defeated undertaking. I say 'look into it a little' because I find I dashed off last summer, at the beginning of this vol., a reference to some gleam it appeared then to have thrown up. Miss B., say (her equivalent) *took* the money—that is, has had *half*—and is to receive the rest when the job is done. Frustration threatens her in the person of some interfering, protesting, fatal marplot of a *revealer*, a maker definite of the facts, of the *tarée* woman's actual history. This is dreadful to Miss B., who is in want of her money. She must oppose it, must prevent it. If she *is* frustrated she won't get her precious money. What does she do? I appear to have been visited by the flight of fancy that she 'kills' her upsetter. There is something fine in that—but 'kills' is soon said. 'The Killing,' I find I remarked, 'is the difficulty.' It is indeed! But I must let it simmer—I must worry it *out!* The whole essence of the thing is of course not in the very *usé* element of the *tarée* woman's desire to creep in—but in the situation of the Miss B. woman, with her *gagne-pain* of these offices, the way she *works* her *relations*, etc., etc. The essence is that she does something bold, big and prompt. x x x x x

It comes to me that she does something better than any 'killing'—comes through the portal of one's seeing how 'boldness' and promptness shows

1. It runs to a little over six thousand words.

itself as a sort of anticipating, forestalling and turning of the tables. Again, however, the thing becomes a little drama, and from the moment it becomes that, strains for more space. Well, one must only *sacrifice* more: that's all. This would be really a little cynical comedy. Miss B. has a suppressed, disowned appendage of a horrid, disreputable kind— I don't see what he can be but a fearfully *taré* and impossible brother, who turns up sometimes to ask for money, to exasperate and mortify her, to try and beg or bully her into getting him back into society. He has been the subject of a 'scandal' years before, and has more or less vanished—but leaving a name that is known. He can't be a brother —he must be a cousin; of another name. *Mettons* that he isn't a 'sponge'—that he has means, that he's even rich. Only he's out of society. I wish I could make him a murderer! x x x x x

February 16th. I've been ill again (with beastly little trail of influenza)— which was what broke the above off. But let me try to go on with this, and 2 or 3 more things in more or less stammering accents and very briefly. x x x x x

I see the 'appendage' of 'Miss B . . . h' must be—say—a stepbrother —with a different name; and that he must, decidedly, *not* be rich, as that has obvious interference. He is discredited, disgraced, has had to leave England; but he comes back after an interval and wants money from his sister-in-law. I put this crudely and temporarily. He and Lady G. have both been with her the day of the visit of the *protesting* friend. Well—well—I needn't (feeling rather seedy and sickish) worry this out now further than just to state simply that one's little climax and subject consists in the 'light' that comes to Miss B. on seeing her visitor (on some trace or gleam!) suddenly flash into a curiosity, a desire to see, to know, THIS *taré* one. He comes *up* between them. 'And he too—drat them all—wants to get back into society! But I can do nothing for *him*. I wash my hands!' x x x x x Effect of this on visitor. 'You think him hopeless?' 'Utterly'—but she has MENTIONED that it's some of her MONEY he wants, has *told* of this in fact to explain her need for the sum (£300) which the defeat of the effort for Lady G. will deprive her of. This is the beginning. The visitor warms to *him*—the PICTURE of the 'warming' given; and the climax becomes the bargain struck: the intermeddling woman allowing Miss B. to operate in peace on *condition* of her presenting *her* to—allowing her to take in hand the *case* of—the peccant and compromised stepbrother. But *how* must he have been compromised? There's the difficulty. I must leave it vaguish—or put *cards*. Cards will probably do. His poverty a proof of the baselessness of the allegations against him. x x x x x

[*The idea James got from Miss Balch's 'queer confidence' was used in Mrs. Medwin. The grim possibilities he saw in it at first were abandoned; 'the Killing' was, indeed, 'difficult.' James turned instead to the plan of having his Miss Balch—Mamie Cutter, in the story— do something which if not 'big' was at least 'bold,' 'prompt,' and also clever. Her poor and disgraced half-brother appears and meets Lady Wantridge just when that formidable critic of Mrs. Medwin has refused to help Mamie get her into society. Mamie detects the 'trace or gleam' of Lady Wantridge's liking for him and uses him as a bribe. The scheme is simplified by dropping the notion of making him socially ambitious. All he wants is part of his sister's earnings, so that he is content to obey her and refuse Lady Wantridge's invitation to Catchmore, until she has agreed to meet Mrs. Medwin as Mamie wants. He is simply an acquiescent assistant to his sister and not a 'case' to be taken in hand, so that it was easy to avoid any difficulty about the nature of his disgrace or his real guilt or innocence. There is a suggestion of 'cards,' but Mamie insists that she knows no details about his past.*

The 'international' note was introduced by making Mamie and her brother Americans, and Mrs. Medwin and the others British. Possibly James was amused by thus reversing the usual situation of the American who buys her way into English society under British sponsorship.

The changes from his original ideas for the story seem to proceed from James' realization that the theme was fit only for comedy and from his eagerness for brevity. In his list of themes on page 292 he says the idea must be treated 'concentratedissimo' in four sections of seven pages each, and the finished story, in The Better Sort (1903), has four sections, twenty-seven pages, and less than ten thousand words. He succeeded here in writing the 'little, scenic, self-expository thing' in small compass, although he could not keep down to the three or five thousand words he thought might suffice (p. 295 below).

The story was first printed in Punch in August and September 1901. James included it in the collected edition but did not comment on it in his preface.]

I pick up for a minute the idea of the portrait à la Gualdo—it haunts me: oh, what things, what *swarms* haunt me! (As for instance this little gleam of the notion of a man who, *bourru*, unamiable, ungracious, though absolutely 'straight' in some relation, becomes visibly, increasingly mild, gentle, gracious, GOOD—to the point of attracting the attention of some observer and spectator, who, struck, mystified, finding it strange, too marked, even suspicious, watches him till he finds it is the concomitant just of some adopted vice or pursued irregularity, 'impropriety,' wrong. It's his wishing to *se faire pardonner*. But *what*, *donc?* The narrator watches, studies, discovers. The thing has to fix on the vice.) (Don't lose, after this, the tail of the little *concetto* of the poor young man with the burden of his personal sorrow or secret on his mind that he longs to work off on some one, roams restlessly, nervously, in depression, about London, trying for a *recipient,* and finding in the great heartless preoccupied city and society, every one taken up with quite other matters than the occasion for listening to *him.* I had thought, for the point of this, of his being suddenly approached by some one who demands *his* attention for some dreadful complication or trouble—a trouble so much greater than his own, a distress so extreme, that he sees the moral: the balm for his woe residing not in the sympathy of some *one* else, but in the coercion of giving it—the sympathy—to some one else. I see this, however, somehow, as obvious and banal, *n'est-ce pas?*— 'goody' and calculable beforehand. There glimmers out some better alternative, in the form of his making some one *tide over* some awful crisis by listening to him. He learns afterwards what it has been—I mean the crisis, the *other* preoccupation, danger, anguish. [The thing needs working out—*maturing.*])

[By the time James had matured this theme, a decade later, in A Round of Visits (1910), he had freed it from a too expected moral. He also changed the locale from London to New York, and drew on some of the impressions of the harsh and violent life of the city that he had formed during his return to America in 1904-5.

He increased Mark Monteith's sense of his own burden by plunging him into the peculiar loneliness of the modern metropolis, to which he has just come back after a long absence abroad. He has discovered, upon his arrival, that he has been swindled by Phil Bloodgood, his supposed best friend, to whom he had entrusted the management of his property. But he finds no solace among the women of his acquaintance who—in the hotel world which James created through images of a luxuriant oppressive tropical jungle—are entirely preoccupied with their own concerns, about which they chatter as heedlessly and as heartlessly as so many gaudily plumaged birds. Only when he goes, as a last resort, to call on Newton Winch, whom he had remembered from Law School days as ordinary and common, does Mark encounter something that lifts him out of his own anxieties. For Newton is strangely transformed, and here James found his way in part by utilizing something like the theme recorded just above, that of the man who has been changed for the better through some 'irregularity.' Newton is filled with perceptive sympathy, but as Mark pours out the misery of his betrayal, he begins to be conscious that Newton's new quality has been begotten by suffering. He also begins to think—in a

further characteristic twist of the theme—of the suffering Phil Bloodgood must now be going through. Only at the end does he discover
that Newton, like Phil, has been deeply involved in larceny. But by
then the police are at the door, and Newton, with an image before
him of the kind of anguish his act has caused, ends his career by
suicide.

A Round of Visits, completed by James for the English Review
(April–May 1910) was the last short story that he published.]

(Don't let me let go either the idea of the 2 artists of some sort—male
and female—I seem to see them—as a writer and a painter—who keep
a stiff upper lip of secrecy and pride to each other as to how they're
'doing,' getting on, working off their wares, etc., till something sweeps
them off their feet and breaks them down in confessions, AVEUX, tragic
surrenders to the truth, which have at least the effect of bringing them,
for some consolatory purpose, together. Mustn't they have been somehow originally acquainted and separated? The fact, the situation that
BREAKS DOWN THEIR MUTUAL PRIDE [that's the *nuance*] to be of course
worked out. x x x x x)

[In Broken Wings (the Century Magazine, December 1900) James
dramatized the situation of such a middle-aged pair, each of whom had
once had a following in the country-house world, only to see it fall
away. Though they had tried to keep up a good front, each had come
to the conclusion that 'everything costs that one does for the rich,'
since they even take one's imagination and give nothing in return.
But Stuart Straith, the painter, and the novelist, Mrs. Harvey, finally
face their diminished future together, with the resolution to do their
work for its own sake.

In the preface to The Author of Beltraffio, James said that he failed
'to disinter again the buried germ' of this story, but went on to ask:
'When had I been, as a fellow scribbler, closed to the general admonition of such adventures as poor Mrs. Harvey's, the elegant representative of literature at Mundham?—to such predicaments as Stuart Straith's,
gallant victim of the same hospitality and with the same confirmed
ache beneath his white waistcoat?' He also reflected on a further aspect
of the situation: 'The appeal of mature purveyors obliged, in the very
interest of their presumed, their marketable, freshness, to dissimulate
the grim realities of shrunken "custom," the felt chill of a lower professional temperature—any old note-book would show that laid away
as a tragic "value" not much less tenderly than some small plucked
flower of association left between the leaves for pressing.']

At last I come back to the woman who wants a portrait of some non-existent (*never*-existent) person. I've noted the notion before as that of a woman who wants to 'have been' a *widow*—she wants to have in her house the portrait of her husband. What is there *in* it? I seem to catch the glimmer of something. Is she an old enriched *femme galante*? I *think* not—I think, though I'm not sure. She must be an odd creature. A mere intense old maid? No—there are reasons, I see immediately, against that. Well, what she is, what she has been, transpires, is implied. She is an *ancienne*, an ex-*femme galante*, but it comes out as it can. She calls on a painter of distinction.

'I want you to paint my husband.'

'*Fort bien.* When will he sit?'

'He can't sit. He's dead.'

'Ah, from some other memorial—from photographs?'

'No—I've *no* photographs: I've *no* other memorial.'

'Then how, Madam—?'

Un temps. 'Can't you do it from a—from a— No—I can't give you that. Can't you do it from imagination?'

In short she has a talk with him, the consequence of which is that he goes to see a friend, a lady artist. In a scene with *her* he tells her of his interview with the visitor—he comes with the visitor's (*final*) *assentiment*, to hand on the commission. He gives the whole thing— of which, directly, I have only given the opening notes. She wants— the odd lady—to have been married: she wants to be a widow. She wants a tall fine portrait of her late husband. She has no view—he must only be a *très-bel homme*. He must not moreover be a portrait from life of any one in particular: he must be a fancy creation. The artist must invent him—a perfection. *Elle y mettra bien le prix.* Well, this fantastic commission the painter can't take—but he thinks his old friend and comrade *may*, and wanting to give her the benefit of it if it is possible, he comes to her with the story. She is a rare copyist— but she has painted some charming things and that all look old. Who is she—? *What* is she? He says, more or less. (But this to be determined.) The lady-artist paints the picture—doing a thing, as she believes and tries, from imagination. But *what* she does, she does really from memory—the memory of the one man she *herself* has loved. He was the handsomest, the most irresistible: he jilted, forsook her, etc., in youth: she too has never married. She has reason to—more or less— *execrate* him: *aussi* she has thought of him with, always, as much of the passion of bitterness as of the passion of the other thing. She paints it almost in hate. *Bref*—when that woman sees it she recognizes it as a man she too has known and the only one she would have married, or can think of now (so base her view of those men she *has* known) as

[283]

the one she would have a portrait of. Situation—the lady-artist has really evoked and represented a (dead) reality—the man they both had loved. The *Ancienne* is eager for the picture—but then it is the lady-artist turns. Ah, *now* she can't have it. The other woman doubles the price—offers money, money. Ah, *now* she can't have it—*no*. She refuses the money—keeps the picture for herself. It has taken her resentment, her bitterness to produce, to paint it—it has been painted in hate. And now she sees, moreover, for whom it was he abandoned her. A reality is *added* to his reality for her—the reality of the other woman's connection with him. *But*, all the same, for herself, she now suddenly prizes this image of his cruelty and falsity that she hasn't produced *for* herself—but for another—yet that she can't part with. She refuses everything, keeps the picture, begins to *love* it. One day her comrade, the R.A. is there—it is over her chimney-piece. A visitor, a sitter, comes and asks, 'Who is it?' 'He's my late husband.' (Though this perhaps a little extravagant and *de trop*.)

[*The Tone of Time, published in* Scribner's Magazine *for November 1900, drops the possibly too 'extravagant' final episode suggested here, but keeps the rest. The story is told by the artist who gets for his friend the commission to paint the 'très-bel homme.' The two women never meet; the situation is revealed entirely through the narrator's observation of them. Their understanding of the curious relationship that exists between them comes from what they read into what he tells them. The result is a story concentrated into a few scenes between the narrator and the 'lady-artist' and between him and the Ancienne. The subject, as it was phrased in James' list on page 265, was material for hardly more than an anecdote, but his additions made it capable of relatively serious treatment. The finished work is a picture of how two women, responding to 'the tone of time,' were emotionally affected by their sudden rediscovery of the past.*

James did not include the story in his collected edition.]

The notion of the Lady R.C.'s little vengeance on the bride might be done this way. The lover who has *lachéd* her, taken to wife the charming simple young girl, comes to me—before going up to town—and says, 'What shall I do? How shall I proceed with her? I'm thinking of playing a very frank, bold game—of throwing myself on her magnanimity. She's generous, she's not *mean*'—and 'Addie'—or whatever—is charming. She can't help liking her. Therefore isn't the really superior policy to ASK her to be kind to her, to appeal to her for guidance, for patronage for his little wife? Hum!—*I* don't know! *I'm* not sure. I'm not so positive of Lady X.'s magnanimity. This takes place—this inter-view—abroad. I meet them on their wedding-tour. The talk is of what to do when they get to London. Well, I leave my friend to determine for himself. *Je me récuse*—I'm vague and elude the question. Then I see them later, in town. I HAVE the situation in my head—only this has come to me in regard to it: that I make, as a narrator, the point, that *fagotée* by her terrible friend's hands the little bride *is* hideously attired, while Lady X. is consummately so: a revelation of taste and distinction. But the faces! (*The Faces* might <be> the name of the little story.) The bride dimly, vaguely conscious of the trick played on her, pathet-ically lovely under her hideous toggery—angelic in her bewildered fair-ness: the other woman infernal in expression over all the perfection of her appearance. The husband speaks to me—we *mark* it so: we formu-late and phrase it. Or rather isn't it some *new* lover she (Lady X.) is trying for, that *catches* it, phrases it, puts it to me? Yes—and it's thus *herself* she dishes.

[*James listed The Two Faces at page 265 above, and again at page 292 below. This was the shortest story of his maturity, and almost kept to the limit of five thousand words. He managed to hold it down by elimi-nating the proposed preliminary discussion. Nor is there any interview abroad. The whole consists of the impression gained by Mr. Shirley Sutton, Mrs. Grantham's new lover, first in London and then in the country. He is present when Lord Gwyther comes to Mrs. Grantham with his extraordinary appeal to her that, as 'someone thoroughly kind and clever,' she should take his young wife Valda by the hand and lead her through her introduction to society. Sutton watches Mrs. Grantham very closely both then and later, at Burbeck, where the cruelly managed introduction takes place. The contrast between the two faces tells him all that he needs to know about Mrs. Grantham's hardness.*

This story appeared as The Faces in Harper's Bazar (15 December 1900), with illustrations by Albert Herter, and under its final title in the Cornhill Magazine (June 1901). James spoke of it, in the preface to The Aspern Papers, in connection with 'the writer's rueful hopeful assent to the conditions known to him as "too little room to turn round" . . . The value of The Two Faces—by reason of which I have not hesitated to gather it in—is thus peculiarly an economic one. It may conceal rather than exhale its intense little principle of calculation; but the neat evolution, as I call it, the example of the turn of the whole coach and pair in the contracted court, without the "spill" of a single] passenger or the derangement of a single parcel, is only in three or four cases (where the coach is fuller still) more appreciable.' Those other cases would presumably have included The Middle Years (p. 121 above), The Tree of Knowledge (p. 289 below), and The Abasement of the Northmores (pp. 296-7 below).]

February 19th.

Struck an hour ago by pretty little germ of small thing given out in 4 or 5 lines of charming volume of Miss Jewett—*Tales of N.E.* A girl on a visit to new-found old-fashioned (spinster-gentlewoman) relation, 'idealized her old cousin, I've no doubt; and her repression and rare words of approval, had a great fascination for a girl who had just been used to people who chattered and were upon most intimate terms with you directly, and could forget you with equal ease.' That is all—but they brushed me, as I read, with the sense of a little—a very tiny—subject. Something like *this*. I think I see it—*must* see it—as a young *man*—a young man who goes to see, for the first time, a new-found old-fashioned (spinster-gentlewoman) cousin. He hasn't known about her. She hasn't known about *him*. He has been ill—is convalescent—doesn't get well very fast—has had infernal influenza. He's a young barrister—young journalist. He's poor—but he's engaged. Well, his old cousin's type and manner and old-fashionedness are a revelation. Her absence of chatter—of excess—of familiarity are a cool bath to him—living as he does in a world of chatter, of familiarity, of exploiting of everything, of *raving* above all. Yes, he lives in that world, and the girl he's engaged to lives in it. *She* chatters, she raves. She writes—she's clever—(she masculine?) she's conscious and appreciative of everything. Well, the form that the effect, the impression his relative makes on the young man, *takes* on the form of wishing to keep her—for his private delectation—just *as* she is; keep her from getting approached, known and spoiled. He has a horrible fear that she'll herself *like* the chatter-element, the chatter people, if once she knows them. And oh, she *rests* him so! She'll think them so clever—and they'll appeal and rave and treat her as enchanting and picturesque and make her conscious. She doesn't *know* what and how she is—and the people actually about her don't know either. So he feels about her as we feel about a little untouched *place* that we want to keep to ourselves—not put in the newspapers and draw a railway and trippers and vulgarities to. So when she asks about his fiancée even, he has a terror. She's the great raver. *She'll* chatter about her and *to* her. She'll write her up. Yet the cousin wants to see her—wants her to come. She has to—he has to consent. Well, she comes, and his worst fears are verified. She does all he fears, and with the effect. The old woman becomes a show old woman. She likes it. He is overwhelmed with melancholy and regret—which the fiancée sees as jealousy and resents. *Bref*, the old cousin becomes completely *public*, exploited and demoralized, and after a rupture with his young woman, he retreats, *flees*, leaving *her* in chattering and raving possession.

[In Flickerbridge (Scribner's, February 1902), James made his young man, Frank Granger, an American painter who is learning his craft in Paris. There he has also come to know Addie Wenham, a fellow American of much more energy than he. 'She had thirty stories out and nine descriptive articles. His three or four portraits of fat American ladies— they were all fat, all ladies and all American—were a poor show compared with these triumphs.'

When over in London on a commission, he falls sick, and Addie arranges for him to recuperate at Flickerbridge, the country home of a distant English cousin whom she has just discovered and whom she has not yet had time to visit. By making the cousin hers instead of Granger's, James increased the inevitability that Addie must sooner or later join him there.

Granger takes in immediately a full visual image of the 'clear still backwater' of Flickerbridge, 'so little to be preconceived in the sharp north light of the newest impressionism.' As he becomes intimate with his hostess, he foresees how 'quaint' Addie will find her. In the climactic declaration of the story, Granger breaks out: 'She'll rave about you. She'll write about you. You're Niagara before the first white traveller —and you know, or rather you can't know, what Niagara became after that gentleman. Addie will have discovered Niagara. She'll understand you in perfection; she'll feel you down to the ground; not a delicate shade of you will she lose or let any one else lose. You'll be too weird for words, but the words will nevertheless come. You'll be too exactly the real thing and to be left too utterly just as you are, and all Addie's friends and all Addie's editors and contributors and readers will cross the Atlantic and flock to Flickerbridge just in order so—unanimously, universally, vociferously—to leave you. You'll be in the magazines with illustrations; you'll be in the papers with headings; you'll be everywhere with everything. You don't understand—you think you do, but you don't. Heaven forbid you should understand! That's just your beauty—your "sleeping" beauty.'

Granger has determined to have no part in the awakening of the old lady of Flickerbridge to any such 'consciousness.' His appreciation of her has made him realize how little he really has in common with

Addie. There is no final scene between them. He leaves Flickerbridge before she arrives to exploit it, and he knows that their engagement is off.

In his preface—to the Daisy Miller volume—James made no allusion to A Lost Lover, the story by Sarah Orne Jewett which had suggested his 'tone' here, the tone of their shared reverence for the local color of the old. He said rather that the 'highly-finished little anecdote' of Flickerbridge had thoroughly covered its tracks in his memory, that he could hardly recall the successive stages of his long-accumulating awareness of 'the whole thick-looming cloud of . . . the dark and dismal consequences, involved more and more to-day in our celebration, our commemoration, our unguardedly-uttered appreciation, of any charming impression.' He thereby indicated what he meant by saying that he was concerned here—as in The Story in It—with illustrating 'a certain general truth.' Taking up the pitch of Granger's declaration, James carried it even higher in a rhetorical cadenza on the age of journalism that he so much disliked: 'Living as we do under permanent visitation of the deadly epidemic of publicity, any rash word, any light thought that chances to escape us, may instantly, by that accident, find itself propagated and perverted, multiplied and diffused, after a fashion poisonous, practically, and speedily fatal, to its subject—that is to our idea, our sentiment, our figured interest, our too foolishly blabbed secret. Fine old leisure, in George Eliot's phrase, was long ago extinct, but rarity, precious rarity, its twin-sister, lingered on a while only to begin, in like manner, to perish by inches—to learn, in other words, that to be so much as breathed about is to be handed over to the big drum and the brazen blare, with all the effects of the vulgarised, trampled, desecrated state after the cyclone of sound and fury has spent itself. To have observed that, in turn, is to learn to dread reverberation, mere mechanical ventilation, more than the Black Death; which lesson the hero of my little apologue is represented as, all by himself and with anguish at his heart, spelling out the rudiments of.'

James recognized how high his rhetoric had flown by concluding: 'Of course it was a far cry, over intervals of thought, artistically speaking, from the dire truth I here glance at to my small projected example, looking so all unconscious of any such portentous burden of sense.']

Take some occasion to cipher out a little further the 'Vanderbilt'— arrangement with *cocotte* to *cover* real preferred woman and enable hated wife to bring divorce suit—subject. There is probably something in it—but to be a great deal pulled out. The *cocotte s'y prête*—from real affection for him: knowing the terms, etc.

Palazzo Barbaro, May 1st, 1899.

Note the 'Gordon Greenough' story told me by Mrs. C.—the young modern artist-son opening the eyes of his mother (his sculptor-father's *one* believer) to the misery and grotesqueness of the Father's work: he, coming back from Paris (to Florence, Rome, the wretched little *vieux jeu*—of the American and English set, etc.) to 'set her against' the father and unseal her eyes. She *has* so admired him. I must see the son, *also*, I think, as stricken in production—as too intelligent and critical to wish to do anything but what he *can't*—and the mother, between the pair: the son *in fact* NOT consoling her pride for the ridiculousness of the father. The latter serenely and most amiably *content de lui*. G.G. *died*.

[*In the preface to* The Author of Beltraffio *James described further 'the tiny air-blown particle' that had yielded* The Tree of Knowledge: 'In presence of a small interesting example of a young artist long dead, and whom I had yet briefly seen and was to remember with kindness, a friend had made, thanks to a still greater personal knowledge of him and of his quasi-conspicuous father, likewise an artist, one of those brief remarks that the dramatist feels as fertilising.'*

In writing this story James made no effort to reproduce the career of Horatio Greenough, whose vigorous functional theory of art—long forgotten by James' day—had far outrun his mediocre performance. Nor did James dwell upon the tragic implications of his theme. It is a shock to young Lance Mallow to perceive, on his return from Paris to his father's studio at Carrara Lodge, Hampstead, how utterly deluded he had been in his former innocent belief in his father's greatness. But the climax of James' story lies in Lance's discovery that Peter Brench, his father's closest friend, and even his mother have known, separately and secretly for years, that 'the Master' with 'the becoming beretto, the "plastic" presence, the fine fingers, the beautiful accent in Italian,' possessed 'everything of the sculptor but the spirit of Phidias.' Each has believed that he has loyally kept that knowledge from the others.

Although The Tree of Knowledge *was among James' very shortest pieces, he could not place it in a magazine. Its first appearance was in* The Soft Side (1900). *In his discussion of this story, he linked it with* The Abasement of the Northmores (pp. 296-7 below) *as a further instance of the war between the 'anecdotal' and the 'developmental':* 'Nothing . . . could well have been condemned to struggle more for . . . harmony than The Abasement of the Northmores and The Tree of Knowledge: the idea in these examples (1900) being develop-*

mental with a vengeance and the need of an apparent ease and a general congruity having to enforce none the less—as on behalf of some victim of the income-tax who would minimise his "return"—an almost heroic dissimulation of capital. These things, especially the former, are novels intensely compressed, and with that character in them yet keeping at bay, under stress of their failing else to be good short stories, any air of mutilation. They had had to be good short stories in order to earn, however precariously, their possible wage and "appear"—so certain was it that there would be no appearance, and consequently no wage, for them as frank and brave nouvelles. They could but conceal the fact that they were "nouvelles"; they could but masquerade as little anecdotes. I include them here by reason of that successful, that achieved and consummate—as it strikes me—duplicity: which, however, I may add, was in the event to avail them little—since they were to find nowhere, the unfortunates, hospitality and the reward of their effort.' The Tree of Knowledge was 'the production' that had cost him, 'for keeping it "down," even a greater number of full revolutions of the merciless screw than The Middle Years.']

Rome, Hotel de L'Europe, May 16th.

Note the idea of the knock at door (*petite fantaisie*) that comes to young man (3 loud taps, etc.) *everywhere*—in all rooms and places he successively occupies—going from one to the other. *I* tell it—am with him: (*he* has told *me*); share a little (though joking him always) his wonder, worry, suspense. I've my idea of what it means. His fate, etc. 'Sometime there *will* be something there—some one.' I am *with* him once when it happens, I am with him the 1st time—I mean the 1st time *I* know about it. (He doesn't notice—I do; then he explains: 'Oh, I thought it was only—' He opens; there *is* some one—natural and ordinary. It is my *entrée en matière*.) The denouement is all. What *does* come—at last? What *is* there? This to be ciphered out.

Mrs. Elliot (Maude Howe) on Sunday last (while I was at her charming place near St. Peter's—flowered terrace on high roof of Palazzo Rusticucci, with *such* a view) told me of what struck me as such a pretty little subject—her mother's (Julia W. H.'s) *succès de beauté*, in Rome, while staying with her, the previous winter: her coming out (*après*) at the end of her long, arduous life and having a wonderful unexpected final moment—at 78!—of being thought *the* most picturesque, striking, lovely old (wrinkled and *marked*) 'Holbein,' etc., that ever was. 'All the artists raving about her.' AWFULLY good little subject

—if rightly worked. *Revanche*—at 75!—of little old ugly, or plain (un-appreciated) woman, after dull, small life, in 'aesthetic' perceptive 'European' 'air.' Element in it of situation of some other American woman (who *has* had lots of 'Europe' always)—thought so pretty (and so envied by my heroine) when younger—and now so 'gone.' Work it out.

[*James saw in the story of Julia Ward Howe's belated 'succès de beauté,' 'a stray spark of the old "international" flame,' and used it in* The Beldonald Holbein, *printed in Harper's Magazine for October 1901. He dropped the neat contrast between the woman once lovely and now 'gone' and the homely one now discovered to be beautiful, and concentrated instead on the single impression of an old lady imported to Europe by a handsome and vain relative, Lady Beldonald, who wanted a plain companion to enhance her own charms. But the old lady was greeted in European artistic circles as a marvel of beauty, a perfect 'Holbein.' The 'action' comes from Lady Beldonald's realization of the situation and her sending the 'Holbein' back to obscurity in the United States. What might have been merely an ingeniously contrived anecdote becomes instead a brief but effective dramatization of an international contrast in aesthetic standards.*

The story was included with the other 'international' ones in the Daisy Miller *volume of the collected edition.*]

For W. W. Story. Beginning. 'The writer of these pages—(the scribe of this pleasant history?) is well aware of coming late in the day. . . BUT the very gain by what we see, *now*, in the contrasted conditions, of happiness of old Rome of the old days.' x x x x x

[*James kept nothing of this phraseology in his* William Wetmore Story and His Friends, *published in 1903, but in the last paragraph of its first chapter he struck a closely similar note. He writes of the 'charm' in the words 'vanished society.' Behind them 'is necessarily the stuff of pictures,' 'the sweetness of old music faintly heard, something of the mellowness of candlelight in old saloons.' We think of people in such a society 'as having had . . . a better "time" than we.'*][1]

Names. Steen—Steene—Liege—Bleat—Bleet (place)—Crawforth—Masset—Mulroney—Perrow (or place)—Drydown (place)—Harbinge—Belpatrick—Beldonald—Belgeorge—Grigger—Dashley—Belgrave ('Lord B.')—Counterpunt—Prime—Mossom—Birdle—Brash—Fresh—Flore (place)—Waymark—Dundeen—Prevel—Mundham—Thanks (place or person)—Outreau (d'Outreau—Mme d'O.).

Names. Pilbeam—Kenardington—Penardington—Ardington—Lindock —Sturch—Morrison-Morgan—Mallow—Newsome—Ludovick—Bream— Brench—Densher—Ilcombe—Donnard—Camberbridge—Marl (or place) —Norrington—Froy (or place)—Trumper—Husk—Vintry—Dunrose— Milrose—Croy—Match—Midmore.

For 'Anecdotes.'

1. 'The Sketcher'—some little drama, situation, complication, fantasy. to be worked into small Rye-figure of woman working away (on my doorstep and elsewhere).
2. The Coward—*le Brave.* The man who by a fluke has done a great bravery in the past; knows he can't do it again and lives in *terror* of the occasion that shall put him to the test. DIES of that terror.
3. 'The Advertiser'—the CLIMAX: (NOT, for 5000 words, told by '*me*').
4. The Faces.
5. THE NAME: Cazalis—Jean Lahor: wife's action and effect as told me by Bourget.
6. The idea of the man who looks *like* the other (Hugues L.–P.B.) to the degree of effect on woman. *Vide ante.*
7. The 2 couples (*vide ante*: Stopf. B).
8. The *Roman de l'Honnête Femme.*
9. The supposedly (assumedly) letter-reading servant.
10. The Biographer (after death: A.B. and F.L.).
11. The V..drb..t (Cocotte-Divorce) thing.
12. The (Cocotte) Portrait (of supposed Husband) thing. *Vide ante.*
13. The Mother and Husband (American) Meeting thing.
14. Yes—literally: The Miss B. and Lady G. idea—concentrated-*issimo*: 4 sections of 28 pages—7 (with 'talk') each.

[*James had previously listed or discussed all of these subjects, except the first two. He had included 3 and 11 in his group of possible novels at the close of 1895, and 9 among possible short stories at the same time (pp. 233-5 above). 4, 5, 6, 10, 11, 12, and 14 had appeared in his list for 7 May 1898 (p. 265 above).*

7 refers to the idea Stopford Brooke had suggested to him five years before (p. 150 above), the idea that James developed into The Sacred Fount. He had discussed 8, The Story in It at pages 267, 275-6, 288 above; and 13 would seem to indicate the lines on which he finally worked out Fordham Castle (*compare pp.* 267-8, 274 *above with pp.* 293-4 *below*).]

The idea of the rich woman *nuancée*, condemned, who *has every-thing*—so everything to lose and give up—wanting to arrange with little poor woman to *die for* her: the latter having *nothing* to lose—to give up. (Lady R.—the condemned.)

October 5th, 1899. Don't forget the little *Gordon-Greenough-and-his-mother-and-his-father* (*as to the latter's sculpture, etc.*) *idea.* Practicable on the rigid Maupassant (at extremest brevity) system.

I seem to see something in the idea of 2 contrasted scenes between (1) a 'corrupt' London pair—friends or lovers—who are treating of something on the basis, the supposition, assumption, that 'one's maid (and one's man) of course read all one's letters'; and (2) a pair of servants (maid and man) who show themselves somehow *not* so de-praved, nearly, as their employers assume. The man believes his man so good—the woman believes hers so bad. One would like to make some little gleam of an action hinge on it—and something is doubtless to be ciphered out. (Oh, the kind little, sweet little spell, the charm, that still lurks in that phrase and process—small, sacred relic of those strange *scenario* days! To use it at all is really to yearn, quite to let one's self go to it. Well, one does—one *is* letting one's self: oh, it will come again! Lamb House, Oct. 9th, 1899.) One feels in it some small situation—reflected in the up-stairs and the downstairs view. Of course there must be an IRONY—*tout est là.* One must fumble it out.

So one must fumble out the conjunction of the 2 Ameri<can> ap-pendages—the shunted mother (of 'presented,' etc., daughters) and the relegated husband (of presented, etc., wife) who meet somewhere (in the absence of their launched correlatives) and exhibit the situation to each other (unconsciously) in a series of confidences, communications, comparings of notes, etc., of the rarest and most characteristic *naïveté.* They go from one thing to another—they have the IV little passages (for 5000 words). As always, one must disengage an action—something they are respectively *in*, from day to day, in respect to the 2 prominent daughters and the voyaging wife. I work into this in thought, that idea (*vide supra*) of the mother consenting temporarily to be *dead* (as it were) to help the daughter *through* something—some social squeeze, 'country-house,' etc. One seems to see the husband as becoming the subject of some similar convenience for his wife—which mustn't be quite the same, but *matching*, and in the same 'note.' 'Separated?' 'Ill?'

—at a 'cure,' which he doesn't require? I feel the pair to be somewhere at an hotel in Switzerland, or Germany—in a kind of waiting *perdu* way. It may turn out that the wife of the poor man is in—as chaperon —with the daughters of the poor woman. I think I see Death and 'Separation.' They meet—they talk—the little affair *is* their talk. They learn from EACH OTHER *what each learns that they, respectively, are made, by the correlatives—thus together—to (temporarily) pass for.* That's about the little formula for the very short thing.

[*James here adds to the idea of the 'shunted mother,' which had attracted him earlier (pp. 267-8, 274), a 'relegated husband.' He has been exiled under a false name by his ambitious wife, who regards him as a social clog. The accidental conjunction of the banished pair, both Americans in Europe, gave James the material for Fordham Castle. The daughters are reduced to one. News of her progress in social climbing supplies part of the required 'action,' but most of it is in the record of how the lonely husband gradually falls in love, after a fashion, with the self-sacrificing mother. 'Death' and 'Separation' come at the end when the daughter is successfully betrothed and allows her mother to join her, leaving the still banished husband to a full sense of his virtual lifelessness. The center of the 'little affair' is the picture of the kind of death in life imposed upon the abandoned couple, the impression of the extent to which they cease to live when they are forced to give up all the external signs of identity in a world of make-believe.*

The story was included in The Author of Beltraffio volume of the collected edition, but James reserved his discussion of it for the preface to the Daisy Miller volume. There he says that in Fordham Castle he could only 'fumble again in the old limp pocket of the minor exhibition,' 'finger once more . . . a chord perhaps now at last too warped and rusty for complicated music at short order.' The 'chord' was his old favorite 'international' theme. His search was for some means of giving it freshness by variety of treatment; his hope was that by 'ingenuity' he might give a 'scrap of an up-town subject . . . a certain larger connexion.' By making the banished mother and husband 'bear the brunt' he hoped the tale might 'fairly hint . . . at positive deprecation . . . of too unbroken an eternity of mere international young ladies.' But he felt that in Fordham Castle the artistic 'miracle' did not happen. The 'stray emitted gleam,' 'the particular supreme "something" those who live by their wits . . . most yearningly look for' never 'turned up,' and the story remained a 'scrap' without the 'larger connexion' he had hoped for.]

I see such chances in these little scenic, self-expository things—dramatic, ironic passages and samples. I seem to see just now, say 4 small subjects as so treatable—on the (that is) 'dialogue' (more or less) plan. The 2 foregoing: the (what I call) 'Miss B . . . h and Lady G . . . ly' situation; and the little thing noted a long time ago as on a word dropped by Miss R.—the way for a woman (girl) to see the world, to travel, being for her husband to show her. The foreignized American mother who takes that line—and the *un*foreignized ditto—or, rather, American girl herself—who represents the idea of the young woman putting in all she can *before*—either to show it herself to her husband, or because she will, *after*, with the shelved and effaced state of so many, precisely, *by* marriage, have no chance. I might give the 3 images: the girl *à la* Miss Reubell (I mean evoked by her word); and the 1st and second, *both*, of these last-mentioned cases. They would make a little presented 'scenic' trio. *Et puis, vous savez, il n'y a pas de raison pour que je n'arrive pas à me dépêtrer*—in even 3000!

Ne lâchez donc pas, vous savez, mon bon, that idea of the little thing on the *roman de l'honnête femme.* It may be made charming—and 5000 words are ample!

Note here the little 'ironic' subject of 'H.A.' and the life of country-houses as against—fill it out—the memorandum. (Suggested by H.A.'s verses among the celebrities in M. de N.'s wonderful album.) [1]

Names. Berther—Champer—Server—Yateley—Lender—Casterton—Taker—Pouncer—Dandridge—Wantridge—Wantrage—Gunton—Medwin—Everina (fem. Xtian)—Obert—Burbage—Bellhouse—Macvane—Murkle (or place)—Mockbeggar (place)—Cintrey—Kenderdine—Surredge—Charlick—Carrick—Dearth—Mellet—Pellet—Brine—Bromage—Castle Dean (place).

November 11th, 1899 (L<amb> H<ouse>).

Subject of, for, a one-act thing with *male* part equivalent to what Mrs. Gracedew, in *Covering End,* is for female, suggested by the idea of *transposing* the small *donnée* (transposing *and* developing, *mon bon!*) noted *supra* as the 'episode of Miss B. and Lady G.' Idea of making Miss B. a *man*—an amiable London celibate, favorite of ladies, humorous, kindly, ironic, amusing, expert—fond of them (the ladies), applied to by them in troubles and difficulties and always helping one or another out of some hobble. I seek in the situation, the elements, of

1. Mme A. F. de Navarro (Mary Anderson) had an album that James described, in a letter to her in 1899, as 'priceless.'

the little 'Miss B . . . h' incident for an analogue, a similarity, drawn from circumstances of such a London bachelor; and giving, as in *C.E.*, the whole act, after effective preparation, to the alert presence and happy performance of that personage. After all, I brought the subject of *C.E.* from much further away still, and dug it out of much more unprepared earth. There *is* a man-situation in the 'B. and Lady G.' affair—I mean there is *the* one, the right one. Dig—dig! *creusons, fouillons!* The idea of the *exchange* effected by the protagonist in the interest at once of his encumbrance and of his petitioner—the bargain made as the result of a happy inspiration to practice on the ravening *Londonism* of the *grande dame* representing the stronghold the petitioner—applicant for help—(the compromised Lady G.) wishes to scale: this is more of a nucleus, *much,* than I had to start with for Ellen Terry. It seems to me that given the general idea—in its most general form—the successful 'placing' socially of some one he doesn't really care about by working the acquaintance, availability, of some one else (much worse, etc., etc.) as a bribe—sounding, searching, ciphering, from there down—on that *ground*—MUST, with patience, lead to anything. Difficulties, of course, but that's what it all means; and *turn and turn and turn about* is the gospel of it. It glimmers before me as the picture of a situation in which 3 or 4 more or less panting and pushing little *femmes du monde* all want something of him: all except one who wants nothing at all. Or perhaps the *clou* lies elsewhere: the thing, only, now is to let the matter Simmer. *Muse* it out till light breaks.

November 12th. Tiny fantasy of the projected 2 *vols. of posthumous letters* of 2 men who have had their course and career more or less side by side, but been rivals and unequal successes (one a failure)—watched, recorded by the wife (widow—or attached woman) of one of them (the failure), who has also known intimately of old (been loved and misused by) the success. Both die—and the bitter and sore (about her husband's —the failure's—overshadowing) has ever felt how really more brilliant (for the expert, the knowing) he was than the other. Then she hears the *Letters* of the other are to be published—and this excites, moves her: if it comes to *that*, why not publish the letters of *her* husband (the success's wife—an idiot, *quoi!*—publishes *his*) which *must* have been so far superior and which will so ineffably score. She appeals —right and left—to his friends: and lo! no one has kept any. There *are* none to publish. Beneath this last humiliation—no one *keeping* them—she feels quite crushed; and has only to wait, pale and still more embittered, the issue of the rival's. The<y> appear—and lo, they are an anti-climax, for mediocrity and platitude, a grotesqueness (for his reputation—turning it inside out), that makes it almost seem as if it were *as* grotesques and exposures that they were, by his correspondents, cynically and cunningly preserved. They fall with a flatness—they blast his hollow fame! She feels with a great swing round of her spirit—*avenged!* Then (I am thinking) she publishes the letters of her OWN (her husband's *to* her) that she has kept. *Those* SHE *has kept! (rather!!)* but delicacy, etc., the *qu'en dira-t-on?* has prevailed. Now it goes. She doesn't care. She wants to score. She publishes—and does.—*Or is there anything* ELSE *in it?—in connection with the letters she eventually publishes* ????—???—???

[*In The Abasement of the Northmores James followed this outline quite closely until he came to the conclusion. The widely-trumpeted letters of Lord Northmore turn out to be 'an abyss of inanity': 'pompous and ponderous and at the same time loose and obscure, he managed by a trick of his own to be both slipshod and stiff.' Then Mrs. Warren Hope has two possibilities of carrying her avengement further. She has kept her love letters from John Northmore, written years ago when he had hoped to marry her; and these issued now, in their full fatuity, might complete his deflation. She has also her own cherished collection of Warren's letters to her. But when she sees how deeply Lady Northmore has been affected by misfortune, she feels only pity for her, and destroys her damaging letters. Of the beautiful collection by her husband, she has a single copy struck off, with provision made for an edition only after her death.*

James included this story in The Soft Side (1900). His discussion of it in his preface, in connection with The Tree of Knowledge, has already been given at pages 289-90 above.]

December 14th, '99.— In my superficial (as yet) vision of what I call 'the H. Adams story,' the dying mother tells the younger son (her son) that the elder is not legitimate; and with the motive that he shall tell a certain person, a relation and presumable benefactor, who wants to benefit *her* child. The elder son is *not* her child, but a child of her husband (of before marriage) adopted and brought up, by agreement, *as* her own: the son of the father's early mistress in short. Well, my idea is a situation of magnanimity and heroism (*comme qui dirait*) for the young man—a young *man*, oh, at last preferably, instead of girl (2 girls) as in H.A.'s dim little germ of an anecdote. What does the relation propose to do?—seem likely to do? It must be a *definite* thing: say settle money on condition of a marriage x x x x x

Well, I seem to catch hold of the tail of something in supposing his encounter, somehow, with the girl destined to this purpose, through which it 'transpires' that she, too, is illegitimate. That is, a vision dimly rises of the check of his *use* of the knowledge imparted in respect to his brother by the x x x x x

[Here James picked up again, momentarily, the theme Adams had first suggested to him nearly eight years before (p. 113 above).]

January 28th, 1900. Note at leisure the subject of the parson-and-bought-sermon situation suggested to me by something mentioned by A. C. B<enson>. My notion of the unfrocked, disgraced cleric, living in hole, etc., and writing, for an agent, sermons that the latter sells, type-written, and for which there is a demand.

Names. Chattle—Voyt—Podd—Tant—Murrum—Glibbery—Wiggington —Gemham—Blay—Osprey—Holder—Dester—Condrip—Cassingham— Dyde—Questrel—Glint—Stroker—Brothers ('Brothers and Brothers')— Goldridge—Slate (or place)—Culmer—Frale (place)—Drack—Drook— Gellatly—Gellattly—Welwood—Lauderdale—Bridgewater—Bree—Blint.

L.H., April 17th, 1900.

Note the little idea of the 'Jongleur' as I caught it in talking with J<onathan> S<turges> this afternoon—as we lingered, talking, in the dining room after tea: that of the deluge, the vulgarity, the banality of *print* being at last such that the 'real' artistic thing isn't committed to it: is composed, *parachevé*, then talked, said, *dit*: hence idea of artist having his little person to whom he commits his repertory and who says it, on occasion, before a real audience. What's the situation—little drama—that can, that might, result from that—this committal of the thing to the perishable individual?

Names. Waterworth—Waterway—Pendrel—Pendrin—Cherrick—Varney —Castledene—Castledean—Coyne—Minuet—Fallows—Belshaw—Quarrington—Dammers—Beldom—Deldham—Tangley.

Lamb House, August 9th, 1900.

I've a great desire to see if I can worry out, as I've worried out before, some possible *alternative* to the 50,000 words story as to which I've been corresponding with Howells, and as to which I've again attacked —been attacking—*The Sense of the Past.* I fumble, I yearn, *je tâtonne,* a good deal for an alternative to *that* idea, which proves in execution so damnably difficult and so complex. I don't mind, God knows, the mere difficulty, however damnable; but it's fatal to find one's self in for a subject that one can't possibly treat, or hope, or begin, to treat, in the space, and that can only betray one, as regards that, after one is expensively launched. The ideal is something as simple as *The Turn of the Screw*, only different and less grossly and merely apparitional. I was rather taken with Howells's suggestion of an 'international ghost'—I kindle, I vibrate, respond to suggestion, imaginatively, so almost unfortunately, so generously and precipitately, easily. The formula, for so short a thing, rather caught me up—the more that, as the thing *has* to be but the 50,000, the important, the serious, the sincere things I have in my head are all too ample for it. And then there was the remarkable coincidence of my having begun *The Sense of the Past*, of its being really 'international,' which seemed in a small way the finger of providence. But I'm afraid the finger of providence is pointing me astray. There are things, admirably beautiful and possible things, in the *S. of the P.*, but I can't gouge them out in the space, and I fear I must simply confess to my funk at the danger, the risk, the possibility of the waste of *present*, precious hours. Let me lay the many pages I've worried out of it piously away—where some better occasion *may* find them again. I must proceed now with a more rigorous economy, and I turn about, I finger other things over, asking, praying, feel something that will do instead. I take up, in other words, this little blessed, this sacred small, 'ciphering' pen that has stood me in such stead often already, and I call down on it the benediction of the old days, I invoke the aid of the old patience and passion and piety. They are always there—by which I mean *here*—if I give myself the chance to appeal to them. There are *tails* of things that one must, with one's quick expert hand, catch firm hold of the tip of. They seem to whisk about me—to ask only for a little taking of the time, a little of the old patient mystic pressure and 'push.' Adumbrations of 'little' subjects flash before me, in short, and the thing is to make them condense. I *had* a vague sense, last autumn when I was so deludedly figuring out *The S. of the P.* for 'Doubleday,' that, as a no. 2 thing (in 'Terror') for the same volume, there dwelt a possibility in something expressive of the peculiarly acute Modern, the current polyglot, the American-experience-abroad line. I saw something; it glimmered on me; but I didn't in my then uncertainty, follow it up. *Is* there anything to follow up? *Vedremo bene.* I want something *simpler* than *The S. of the P.*, but I don't want anything, if may be, of less dignity, as it were. *The S. of the P.* rests on an idea—and it's only the idea that can give me the situation. *The Advertiser* is an idea—a beautiful one, if one could happily fantasticate it. Perhaps one *can*—I must see, I must, precisely, sound that little depth. Remember this is the kind of sacred process in which ½ *a dozen days*, a WEEK, of depth, of stillness, are but all too well spent. THAT kind of control of one's nerves, command of one's coolness, is the real economy. The *fantasticated* is, for this job, my probable formula, and I know what I mean by it as differentiated from the type, the squeezed sponge, of *The T. of the S.* 'Terror' *peut bien en être,* and all the effective *malaise,* above all, the case demands. Ah, things swim before me, *caro mio,* and I only need to sit tight, to keep my place and fix my eyes, to see them float past me in the current into which I can cast my little net and make my little haul. Hasn't one got hold of, doesn't one make out, rather, something in the general glimmer of the notion of what the quasi-grotesque Europeo-American situation, in the way of the gruesome, may, *pushed to the full and right expression of its grotesqueness,* has to give? That general formula haunts me, and as a *morality* as well as a terror, an idea as well as a ghost. Here truly *is* the tip of a tail to catch, a trail, a scent, a latent light to follow up. Let me, in the old way that I can't *think* of without tears, scribble things as they come to me, while little by little the wandering needle and the wild stitch makes the figure. I see the *picture* somehow—saw it, that night, in the train back from Brighton— the picture of the 3 or 4 'scared' and slightly modern American figures moving against the background of three or four European *milieux,* different European conditions, out of which their obsession, their visitation is projected. I seemed to see them *going*—hurried by their fate—from one of these places to the other, in search of, in flight from, something or other, and encountering also everywhere the something or other which the successive *milieux* threw up for them, each with the tone and stamp of its own character x x x x x—an awfully loose expression of something too faintly glimmering. It's only by way of saying that I seemed on the scent of an English, a French, an Italian terror—with an American to wind up? That was as far as I got with my formula—and it's not very far and I am now wondering whether one or other of the little American situations 'abroad' that have been running in my head as things of irony, of satire, *voire* of considerable comedy, may not lend themselves, if one really looks, to some sort of little fantastication that will be effective. x x x x x

What was at the basis, as I thought, of almost the prime beauty of the idea of the *S. of the P.* but the fancy of the *revealed* effect of 'terror,' the fact that the young man had himself become a source of it—or, to speak more lucidly—the fact of the consciousness of it as given, not *received,* on the part of the central, sentient, person of the story? That seemed to me charmingly happy, a real solution and working *biais*—and it seems so still: so that I am not sure that, 'dear God!' as the Brownings would say, I don't still see <it> again as sufficiently vivid to make me feel that by still clinging to the whole *essence* of the

[300]

conception, I may not ride a wave that will yet float me through. *Voyons un peu* what SIMPLIFICATION of the presentation as originally dreamed of may not be hammered out. It comes over me, for the hundredth time, as really so beautiful—the germ-idea—that I oughtn't even temporarily to shelve it without trying a little more for *all* that simplification can do to it. One of my old flushes and flutters seems to come to me as I begin perhaps to *entrevoir* that one's ingenuity and *expertise* may, God help them, possibly STILL save it. It glimmers before me that it's somehow attackable at a different angle and from a different side altogether—that is *almost*. A difficulty indeed immediately rises—when did I abjure the fond faith that a difficulty stated can, for me, only be a difficulty half solved? When I think of the expedient of making the narrator's point of view that of the persons outside—that of one of them—I immediately see how I *don't* get that way, the presentation by the person who is the source of the 'terror' of his sense of being so. On the other hand I don't, if I tell the thing from his point of view *in* the '1st person' get, easily, that I can see, the intense simplification. At the same time, I seem clearly to see, I don't get the hope, and the chance, of real simplification save *by* the first-person. What I feel I roughly make out is that if, under this rubric, I can arrange anything simple enough to be told in the first person, I shall manage: but if that, if, it won't go so, there's no use in it. My 'prologue,' it more than ever comes to me, is my overwhelming space-devourer; my exposition encroaches awfully on the time, on the field, of the poor little drama itself. I believe I could *do* my drama itself, if I could only launch my narrator, speaking for himself, straight into it.

[On 29 June 1900 James wrote to Howells, agreeing to do for him a novel of fifty thousand words. 'I brood with mingled elation and depression,' he wrote, 'on your ingenious, your really inspired, suggestion that I shall give you a ghost, and that my ghost shall be "international." I say inspired because, singularly enough, I set to work some months ago at an international ghost, and on just this scale . . . entertaining for a little the highest hopes of him. . . He was to have been called . . . The Sense of the Past.' The story had been planned in answer to a request, later withdrawn, from a publisher who wanted a pair of tales of 'terror' to make 'another duplex book like the Two Magics.'

Howells wrote again, and James replied on the same day that he made the entries above, saying that he had gone to work again on The Sense of the Past. But, as usual, space was a problem; he needed seventy or eighty thousand words. James did not mail his answer until 14 August and by then had heard from Howells that he no longer wanted a ghost story. This was welcome news since the 'damnable difficulty' of The Sense of the Past had forced James to put it aside. 'My tale of terror did . . . give way beneath me. It has . . . broken down for the present. I am laying it away on the shelf for the sake of something that is in it.' On the shelf it stayed until 1914, when he undertook to finish it. His 'preliminary' sketch, written then, is printed on pages 361-9 below.

The 'no. 2 thing,' the second of the two stories suggested by 'Doubleday' for a volume, was never done.]

Names. Strett (Allan Strett)—Strether—Sound—Wildish—Wickhamborough—Yarm—Crispin—Longhurst.

Names. Ferring—Leapmere—Longersh—Beddingham—Baberham—Billingbury—Warlingham—Poynings—Pallingham—Storrington—Ovingham—Warlingham—Worthingham—Maudling—Lillington—Wittering—Ashling—Bruss—Bress—Hillingly [1]—Lissack—Mant—Cordner—Bayber—Berridge—Wrent—MARCHER—Mild—Montravers—Gasper—Brocco—Rashley—Darracott—Barrick.

Lamb House, September 11th, 1900.

Two or three small things have lately struck me as possibilities for the short tale—one or two in particular mentioned by Alice [2] (not for that purpose!). Let me say first, by the way, that I learned last month from P.B. what makes the little 'Gualdo' notion of 'The Child' really, it seems to me, quite disponible to me on my own lines. They know nothing of his ever having written or published such a tale—they only meant in mentioning the thing to me at Torquay, that he had mentioned it to them. That he ever treated it, or what he made if he did, they wholly ignore—and it is moreover a question for me of a mere point de départ: that a young childless couple comes to a painter and ask him to paint them a little girl (or a child quelconque) whom they can have as their own—since they so want one and can't come by it otherwise. My subject is what I get out of that. Several pretty little things, it seems to me. Me voilà donc libre. Bon! x x x x x

Alice, in a little walk with her to-day—the eve of her leaving for the U.S., with W. at Nauheim—mentioned to me something that had passed between her and Mme F. at Geneva, on the subject of the pos-

1. In the margin James has written 'Essex local,' indicating the names from 'Ferring' through 'Hillingly.'
2. Mrs. William James.

sible marriage of her daughter to a young man, the son <of> old friends, who combined, as regards fortune, position, etc., *toutes les convenances* save ONE. This one was that he was stone-deaf, and hereditarily; not born so, I believe (so that he was not dumb), but having become so early, and now, at 28, or whatever, quite completely so. *Everything good*, else, was there; only that one stumbling-block. It was grave—very grave; but they were thinking; and what should they do? Alice *se récria:* but how *can* you think? how *can* you be willing, with such a terrible *tare?* It was Mme F.'s answer that gave me my hint. 'Well, there is one side even to THAT, that isn't absolutely without its compensation or virtue. It will in some respects protect her—it will be in a manner a guarantee that *elle peut être tranquille* (as to his relations with other women) as so many of us, *hélas, Madame,* even here, are not—and in *his* family (where there have been specimens!) that is not to be overlooked.' The idea, in other words, would be—*comme cela*—that he would be more faithful, *moins coureur,* less attractive to other women, and find *liaisons,* etc., less workable. It somehow suggested to me a girl married *so,* on that reasoning, and on those lines, and what might come of it: the one particular thing that would form the little situation. What would this particular thing be? Two things come to one: the irony of the 'sell' (both things are inevitably ironic) for the family, for the wife: it proving that, deaf as he is, he is *coureur* (or rather not that, for that would be compatible) but, rather, *galant* and unfaithful *comme pas un;* so that the wife has all the bore and fatigue of his deafness and none of the safety— and may perhaps be imagined as not *knowing* her lot, pitying him and unconsciously permitting. Or else, better, but *more* 'cynical,' she, *se privant,* takes advantage of his infirmity to take her own course, he unknowing—so that what the infirmity does protect and assure is just *her* flirtations and her license. He is the sacrificed, thus, the 'pathetic' figure; the fiction being kept up that her happiness is complete in their union and what the deafness does for her ideal of it. Her *mother's* attitude on this. There's *something* in it—very, very ironic. x x x x x

Alice related a day or two ago another little anecdote, of New England, of 'Weymouth' origin, in which there might be some small *very* good thing. Some woman of that countryside—some woman and her husband—were waked at night by a sound below-stairs which they knew, or believed, must be burglars, and it was a question of the husband's naturally going down to see. But the husband declined —wouldn't stir, said he wasn't armed, hung back, etc., and his wife declared that in that case *she* must. But her disgust and scorn. 'You mean to say you'll *let* me?' 'Well, I can't prevent you. But *I* won't—!' She goes down, leaving him, and in the lower regions finds a man—a young man of the place—whom she *knows*. He's not a professional housebreaker, naturally, only a fellow in bad ways, in trouble, wanting to get hold of some particular thing, to sell, realise it, that they have. Taken in the act, and by *her*, his assurance fails him, while hers rises, and her view of the situation. He too is a poorish creature—he makes no stand. She threatens to denounce him (he keeps her from *calling*) and he pleads with her not to ruin him. The little scene takes place between, and she consents at last, this first time, to let him off. But if ever again—why, she'll *this*: which counts all the *more* against him —so, look out! He does look out, she lets him off and out, he escapes, and she returns to her husband. He has heard the voices below, making out, however, nothing, and he knows something has taken place. She admits part of it—says there *was* somebody, and she has let him off. Who was it then?—he is all eagerness to know. Ah, but this she won't tell him, and she meets curiosity with derision and scorn. She will *never* tell him; he won't be able to find out; and he will never know— so that he will be properly punished for his cowardice. Well, his baffled curiosity *is* his punishment, and the subject, the little subject, would be something or other that this produces and leads to. Tormenting effect of this withholding of his wife's—and creation for him, by it, of a sense of a relation with (on her part) the man she found. There is something in it, but for very brief treatment, for the simple reason that the poltroon of a husband can't be made to have a consciousness in wh<ich> the reader will linger long. x x x x x

[*James returned to this theme, at much greater length, more than a decade later (pp. 336-40 below).*]

Note on some other occasion the little theme suggested by Lady W.'s account of attitude and behaviour of their landlord, in the greater house, consequent on their beautiful installation in the smaller and happy creation in it—beyond what he could have dreamed—of an interesting and exquisite milieu. Something in the general situation— the resentment by the bewildered and mystified proprietor—of a work of charm beyond anything he had conceived or can, even yet, understand. It's a case—a study <of> a peculiar kind of jealousy, the resentment of supersession. The ugly hopeless, helpless great house—the beautiful, clever, unimitable small one. The *mystification*—the original mistake.

Don't give up—DON'T give up the American girls and their suppressed mother; the meeting of the latter and the man whose wife is to the fore.[1]

Names. Pembrey—Landsbury (place)—Belph—Loveless—Duas—Styart—Tryart—Brabally—Lane-Lander—Nevitt—STANT—Wain—Etcher—Wisper (person)—Wispers (place)—Mora (girl)—Fencer—Dyas—DREED—Churcher—Bartram—Pletch (or place)—Lowsley—Chapple—Perdy—Lewthwaite—Malham—Stanyer—Bilham—Barrace—Anning—Cavitt—Scruce (place)—Went—Crenden—Ferrand—Banyard—Boyer—Borron—Budgett—Rance—Daltrey—Casher—Gadham—Garvey—Pester—Astell—Formle—Assingham—Padwick—Lutch—Marfle—Bross—Crapp—Didcock—Wichells—*Putchin*—Brind—Coxeter—Cockster—Angus—Surrey—Dickwinter—Dresh—Ramridge—Pardew—FAWNS (country-house)—Jakes—Talmash—Bract—Chorner—Chawner—Colledge—Maule—Mawl—Hazel—Chance—Bundy—Flurrey (or place)—Belton—Messiter—Motion—Pannel (place)—Flodgeley—Mitton.

Names. Drewitt—Courser—Tester—Player—Archdean—Manningham—Matcham—Matchlock—Marcher—Everel—Aldershaw (or place)—Leakey—Pemble—Churley (or place)—Wetherend—or Weatherend (place or person)—Larkey—Shrive—Betterman—Say—Shreeve—Gray.

Lamb House, May 23d, 1901.

I seem to see little subject in the small idea—tiny enough, no doubt—of some person who discovers after the death of some other person nearly, intimately, related (one seems to see it inevitably as husband and wife), some unsuspected, some concealed, *side* or gift, which the survivor's own personality has had the effect of keeping down, keeping in abeyance, in *their* intercourse, but which has come out in intercourse with others. The form in which this occurs to me is the notion—put it frankly, for convenience, of husband and wife—that the wife may have been a charming *talker*—and the husband never had an inkling of it *because* he has been himself so overwhelming and inconsiderate a chatterbox. Think, in this connection, of F.T.P.: say HE had discovered that his wife *could* talk—discovered after her death, some relation in which this had come out. But the denouement?—for is *that* enough? Does he marry again—as an atonement—some talkative woman, to give her a chance? But what can come of that? Work it out. It's a little germ—to be possibly nursed. *N.B.* How, after a long intermission, the charm of this little subject-noting for the 'S<hort>-S<tory>' glimmers out to me again—lighting up for me something of the old

1. See page 293 above.

divine light, re-kindling the little old sacred possibilities, renewing the little link with the old sacred days. Oh, sacred days that are still somehow *there*—that it would be the golden gift and miracle, to-day, still to find *not* wasted!

x   x   x   x   x

Lamb House, June 12th, 1901.

The other day at Welcombe (May 30th or 31st) the Trevelyans, or rather Lady T., spoke of the odd case of the couple who had formerly (before the present incumbents) been for a couple of years—or a few—the people in charge of the Shak<e>speare house—the Birthplace—which struck me as possibly a little *donnée*. They were rather strenuous and superior people from Newcastle, who had embraced the situation with joy, thinking to find it just the thing for them and full of interest, dignity, an appeal to all their culture and refinement, etc. But what happened was that at the end of 6 months they grew sick and desperate from finding it—finding their office—the sort of thing that I suppose it is: full of humbug, full of lies and superstition *imposed* upon them by the great body of visitors, who want the positive impressive story about every object, every feature of the house, every dubious thing—the simplified, unscrupulous, gulpable *tale*. They found themselves *too* 'refined,' too critical for this—the public wouldn't have criticism (of legend, tradition, probability, improbability) at any price—and they ended by contracting a fierce intellectual and moral disgust for the way they had to *meet* the public. That is all the anecdote *gives*—except that after a while they could stand it no longer, and threw up the position. There may be something in it—something more, I mean, than the mere facts. I seem to see them—for there is no catastrophe in a simple resignation of the post, turned somehow, by the experience, into strange sceptics, iconoclasts, positive negationists. They are forced over to the opposite extreme and become rank enemies not only of the legend, but of the historic *donnée* itself. Say they end by denying Shakespeare—say they do it on the spot itself—one day—in the presence of a big, gaping, admiring batch. *Then* they must go.—THAT seems to be arrangeable, workable—for 6000 words. In fact, nothing *more* would be—nothing less simple. It's that or nothing. And told *impersonally*, as an anecdote of *them* only—not, that is, by my usual narrator-observer—an inevitably much more copious way.

P.S. I don't quite see why this and the foregoing and the Gualdo ('Child') thing shouldn't make a trio.

[Commenting upon The Birthplace, in the preface to The Altar of the Dead, James saw it as a recurrence of one of his favorite themes, since it 'deals with another poor gentleman—of interest as being yet again too fine for his rough fate.' It had also struck him 'that here, if ever, was the perfect theme of a nouvelle.' As a short nouvelle he had worked it out—'with a confidence unchilled by the certainty that it would nowhere, at the best (a prevision not falsified) find "acceptance."' He had included it in The Better Sort (1903). Written at about the same time as The Wings of the Dove (which also failed of serialization), The Birthplace is more in the tone of a jeu d'esprit like The Reverberator.

James' ending, as so often, gives a new turn to the recorded anecdote. Morris Gedge and his wife are at first delighted to move on from being in 'charge of the library at Blackport-on-Dwindle—'all granite, fog and female fiction'—to 'the early home of the supreme poet,' whose name is never directly stated in the story. But soon Mr. Gedge finds that he can't bear to tell all the lies that are expected of him. When he begins to demur against some of the legends that his clientele want to believe, Mr. Grant-Jackson descends upon him with the Committee's complaint that he is 'giving away the Show.' He determines to mend his ways in order to keep his job, and soon finds that if he will only let himself go, he has a considerable talent for holding his audience spellbound. Poor Mrs. Gedge then warns him that he 'could dish them by too much romance as well as by too little,' but having desperately taken this new line, Mr. Gedge can't hold his imagination in check. Mr. Grant-Jackson again ominously calls, and the Gedges foresee that now it is all up. But they discover that you can't overdo it for such a public, and that the Committee has just voted to double Mr. Gedge's stipend.]

Lamb House, June 15th, 1901.

Reading in a small vol. of tales of Howells's a thing called a *Circle in the Water* I seem to see in a roundabout way a little idea suggested to me. His story deals, not very happily, I think, with the situation of a man released from 10 years in prison for swindling and the question of whether his daughter shall be told about him. She is with relations who have taken her, blinded her, and who wish her never to: but other friends—former friends of the father—are for putting them (*he* wants it so) face to face. There is a difference—an opposition, etc. However, I mention this (of which very little directly comes) only for the notion of small small possibility it made *arrive* at thinking of—*de fil en aiguille.* I seem to see some girl, some woman, in relation to whom, by no fault of her own, some very painful fact exists, and 2 men who 'care for' her and one of whom thinks she should know it, and the other that she shouldn't. Is it something about her mother?—is it the question of her *seeing* her mother? (like the seeing the father in H.'s tale), the latter being discredited and dishonoured, but re-emergent for the occasion. I seem to see something come of it—but not very much. They are each trying to marry her, and each takes a line on the question *in* that interest. The crisis passes—she *doesn't* see her mother (or isn't reached by the knowledge, whatever it is) and she marries the man who has been for this result, whatever the case may have been. Say it is a mother who has been horrid. The father has deeply suffered from her and is dead—partly *by* her. This is what the girl believes. *She* has adored her father. The mother has turned up, wishing, pressing to see her. Shall she, the girl, be told? A. opines Yes—B. insists No. The mother waits. B.'s side carries the day—the mother goes off, dies, disappears. The girl, who has learned, followed this, marries B. Time passes and she isn't very happy with B. The dismissed A. reappears. What she knows about *him* is mainly that he was for her seeing her mother. Her husband, who had been so against it, had not seen her himself. A. had seen her, did see her—continued to see her afterwards. This draws her to A.—draws her *from* B. It becomes A.'s merit now. He had thought ill of her for not wanting, not *re-calling,* the poor woman. They meet on it, grow frequent and intimate on it, on much talk of it. The thing is from a point of view—some old woman (a non-narrator) as in *Miss Gunton of Poughkeepsie.* She is the observer, recipient, confidant. The husband comes to her—has his last word for her—or she hers for *him.* 'Oh, you see, *you* wouldn't let her see her mother.' 'But that was just what she liked me, *married* me, for.' (Say *they* were engaged—and A. what? a cousin, a discarded one?) Then the old lady's reply—which I must get right.—Perhaps the thing isn't very much. But don't lose sight, by the way, of the subject that I know— I've marked it somewhere, as the E. Deacon subject.[1]

L.H., June 19th. Note the idea, here, suggested to me by Louisa Loring's mention of the girl, 'Chicago girl,' engaged to 'Boston man,' who, making a serious illness (fever) showed herself on recovery to have *forgotten* completely both the man she had been engaged to and the fact of her engagement. He, in face of difficulty of re-establishing his identity for her, *gave her up,* etc.—could only accept the strange accident. But scrabble down here the one or two notions in connec-

1. This would seem to refer to 'the E.D. tragedy,' mentioned at page 116 above.

[308]

tion—as sequences—that confusedly occur to you—on 1st leisure. (No time tonight.)

1st. It's being suggested to her fiancé that it possibly will come back to her (*he* will) if she sees him apparently interested in another woman. 'Ah, but how *can* I be?'—Then the 'apparently,' etc., etc.

2d. The girl *feigns* it as a KIND way of getting rid of him—or there is a question of whether she *isn't* feigning. 'I' tell the story; my suspicion, wonderment, doubt, etc.—thus my *clue* or whatever—the *dénouant* all to be worked out.

L.H., July 28th, 1901.

Scrabble here (happy word!) at 1st leisure some note of the 2 small notions:—

1st. The suggestion (utterly vague) conveyed by passage in Funck-Brentano's *Affaire du Collier* (about the servants of the *ancien régime*) which quote (p. 115).[1]

2d. The suggestion, equally vague, conveyed by passage in recent letter to me from E.F., which I've destroyed—passage characteristically advising me—and in the strongest good faith—to go to the U.S. and give readings from my work—for the money and the boom. I seem to see *that* possible result and then, as a sequel, a quenching of every other result: the whole interest swallowed up in and annihilated by, the satisfied, sated, gorged curiosity and publicity, and the thing working so into something of my old little notion of *The Advertiser*. Puzzle out—something perhaps in it.

Lamb House, August 22d, 1901.

Note the notion suggested to me by George Ashburner's allusion to something said to Sir J.S. by the man with whom his niece had 'bolted' and was living: 'If I marry her I lose all control of her. ('I will if you insist, etc.—*but*—etc.') They *did* insist, and what he foretold happened—he lost all control. But imagine the case in which (*given the nature of the girl*) one of the parties interested or connected *doesn't* insist, while the other does, for the appearance, and the situation springing from that—the opposition, the little drama for short thing.

[*Mora Montravers, printed in the* English Review *for August–September* 1909, *and in the volume of stories,* The Finer Grain, *in* 1910,

---

1. The passage deals with the self-sacrificing devotion of some of the servants of aristocratic masters before the French Revolution.

uses the substance of this. The 'opposition, the little drama' develops between a husband and wife who disagree about how to 'save' an errant niece. As in the note, Mora's marriage means that her husband loses all control over her, but the effect of the story rests in the humorously ironic interplay between her uncle and aunt. The interest is heightened by the introduction of a favorite Jamesian theme, that of the man suddenly wakened to a realization of the too narrowly respectable bonds that hamper him and to a regretful sense of the 'fun' and the 'life' he has missed.]

L.H., *August 27th*, 1901.

An idea, perhaps a 'first rate' one, seems to me to reside in passing allusion made this p.m., by William, to general attitude observed by Mrs. W. (of Boston) to her late husband—he is just dead. He was insignificant, common, inferior, and she was—well, all that one knows. She could scarcely bear it of him; bear above all the way he gave away, as it were, their earlier time, when he *was* good enough for her, *was* a possible match. She had always stuck to him and done the letter of her duty by him, while disliking him and ashamed of him, and, above all, while *showing* that she was. My 'story' seemed struck out in one of the small quick flashes in which such things come, when William, speaking of these things, said, 'Ah, the mistake, in such a case, of the American sort of *honnête femme* tradition! Better for her, surely, to have left him, to have gone her way—that is, as it were, *not* have been faithful, have been perpetually exemplary and, as it were, exasperated.' Those were not perhaps his exact words, but such was the query he threw off. On the spot it suggested to me a little novel of American types and manners, following pretty well the facts, or appearances, of the W. case. I seem to see that case, and to see opposed to it, and dramatically, the case of the woman who *does* take the line of W.'s query, does not stick and 'virtuize' and suffer, but who appears somehow to seek, to have found, *her* solution somewhere other than in the *honnête femme* line, the good conscience *quand même—quand même* she (like Mrs. W.) despises and shows she despises. She does in short the opposite of what Mrs. W. did (though *outwardly* 'sticking'— that is outwardly not 'bolting,' etc.) and she thereby suffers, despises and generally 'minds' less. There seems to me much in this—in the dramatic complexity formed by the 2 cases, etc.—to be gouged out, and it especially strikes me as working rather particularly into my old idea of something to illustrate and *mettre en scène* the big typical American case of the growing separation of the 2 sexes *là bas* by the growing superiority of the woman, getting all the culture, etc., to the man immersed in business and money. I've wanted a *hinge* for that, a pivot and platform; but wouldn't they here, precisely, appear to be '*archi*'-found? Lots of things, it strikes me, would come in under it; and I must hammer at it—that is, turn it round a bit—with more time and a better occasion x x x x x

Meanwhile there is something else—a very tiny *fantaisie* probably—in small notion that comes to me of a man haunted by the fear, more and more, throughout life, that *something will happen to him:* he doesn't quite know what. His life *seems* safe and ordered, his liabilities and exposures (as a *result* of the fear) a good deal curtailed and cut down, so that the years go by and the stroke doesn't fall. Yet 'It *will* come, it will still come,' he finds himself believing—and indeed saying to some one, some second-consciousness in the anecdote. 'It will come before death; I shan't die without it.' Finally I think it must be *he* who sees—not the 2d consciousness. Mustn't indeed the '2d consciousness' be some woman, and it be she who *helps* him to see? She has always loved him—yes, *that*, for the story, 'pretty,' and he, saving, protecting, exempting his life (always, really, with and *for* the fear), has never known it. He likes her, talks to her, confides in her, sees her often—*la côtoie*, as to her hidden passion, but never guesses. She meanwhile, all the time, sees his life as it is. It is to her that he tells his fear—yes, she is the '2d consciousness.' At first she *feels*, herself, for him, his feeling of his fear, and is tender, reassuring, protective. Then she reads, as I say, his real case, and is, though unexpressedly, *lucid*. The years go by and *she sees the thing not happen*. At last one day they are somehow, some day, face to face over it, and then she speaks. 'It *has*, the great thing you've always lived in dread of, had the foreboding of—it *has* happened to you.' He wonders—when, how, what? 'What is it?—why, it is that *nothing* has happened!' Then, later on, I think, to keep up the prettiness, it must be that HE sees, that he understands. She has loved him always—and *that* might have happened. But it's too late—she's dead. That, I think, at least, he comes to later on, after an interval, after her death. She is dying, or ill, when she says it. He *then* DOESN'T understand, doesn't see—or so far, only, as to agree with her, ruefully, that that very well *may* be it: that nothing has happened. He goes back; she is gone; she is dead. *What* she has said to him has in a way, by its truth, created the need for her, made him want her, *positively* want her, more. But she is gone, he has lost her, and *then* he sees all she has meant. She has loved him. (*It must come for the* READER *thus, at this moment.*) With his base safety and shrinkage he never knew. *That* was what might have happened, and what *has* happened is that it didn't.

[The Beast in the Jungle, *running to about seventeen thousand words, was of a length that James was finding less and less placeable. It did not see publication, therefore, prior to* The Better Sort *(1903). In his collected edition he arranged it as a companion piece to* The Altar of the Dead. *But* The Beast in the Jungle *is concerned not so much with the dead as with the passions that 'might have been,' about which he had made an entry half a dozen years before (pp. 182-4 above). He refers, in his preface, to this present entry as containing the subject 'but as a recorded conceit and an accomplished fact.' James' absorption, to the end of his career, with giving embodiment to such a formalized spiritual and psychological pattern is again a token of his enduring kinship with Hawthorne. But James had progressed beyond Hawthorne's method of presenting, as in* Ethan Brand, *an allegory of the Unpardonable Sin. The Beast in the Jungle* is one of the most striking examples of how James could intensify his effect through the repetition of a dominant symbol.*

John Marcher is possessed at first not so much with fear as with the sense 'of being kept for something rare and strange,' of being destined to have 'felt and vibrated . . . more than any one else.' But this sense passes gradually into a dread that he may miss having that exposure, and he longs for the hidden beast to spring. But only beside the grave of May Bartram does he feel the beast finally upon him, crushing through the egotism that had kept him for so many years from perceiving May Bartram's love. Then only does he realize with horror that his selfish blindness has brought upon him the destiny of having been 'the man to whom nothing on earth was to have happened.']

L.H., August 29th, 1901.

SAME DATE. Note more fully than I can now the small *conte* suggested by W.'s mention of Edmund T<weedy> and 'Margaret,' Aunt M.'s *garde-malade* and attendant whóm he inherited after the latter's death. She has been with him—or lately *had*—ever since then—and as his eyes were, with his 87th, 88th, and so, year, supposed to be failing, it became a part of her duty to read to him—a part of regular evening routine. *La voilà*, then, settled down to this, feeling it, however, an effort and a charge, until *her* eyes gave out—with the odd and unexpected result that *he* then began to read to *her*. I seem to see the point of tiny *conte* in that situation. I *s*ee it told by a friend—the author is the observer. E.T. *likes* to read aloud—on finding that he *can* (with one of those flickers of life in old age that make his previously-incapable sight no longer an obstacle) and they thus sit together with

Margaret having to listen and her *corvée* now changed to *that*. It is worse than the other—she tells me—she complains. If *she* could only read now—that would be the less evil. Could I *arrange* it? Could I put it back as it was before? Well, I try, I approach him on it, but he won't *hear* of it—he is so proud of his *ability*, his powers, which are indeed, at his age, uncanny and unnatural. So I have to leave her to her fate. 'He will read to you till he dies.' 'Ah, but when will he die?' 'Well, you must wait. Now—(here he comes) go and sit down.' And he opens the book and I leave her trying to listen.

October 19th, 1901, Lamb House.

Something in reference to man who, like W.D.H. (say), has never known *at all* any woman BUT his wife—and at 'time of 'life' somehow sees it, is face to face with it: little situation *on* it. *Ça rentre*, however, rather, into the idea (is a small side of it) of *The Ambassadors*. But *never*, NEVER—in any degree to call a relation at all: *and on American lines.* x x x x x

Something like the man who subscribes to an agency for 'clippings'— a Romeike, or whatever, *quelconque*, to send him everything 'that appears about him,' and finds that nothing ever appears, that he never receives anything. x x x x x

And connection between that and notion suggested by little case of woman writing to me (to fill in some paper) on behalf of *Outlook*. The case of the newspaper girl or man who *needs* your reply, your taking *some* notice—suggesting once the little antithesis for tale: the would-be newspaperite whom, by a *guignon*, of his, of hers, people never answer (and sadness of that); and the other who finds that they never fail, that they leap, bound at him, press, surge, scream to be advertised; and ugliness of *that*. Awfully good little possibility seems to me to abide in it, as contrast and link between them—different shows of human egotism and the newspaper scramble: or even in the opposition, conjunction, *rencontre* of failure-girl and man first-named.

[*This 'awfully good little possibility' grew to an unwieldy thirty-six thousand word tale, The Papers, included in 1903 in The Better Sort, but not in the collected edition. The publicity seeker who gets no attention and the unsuccessful reporter are both balanced by contrasted characters. The girl journalist who fails has a suitor who is a notoriously successful newspaper man; a man who glows in journalistic limelight is set off against the one on whom no ray of public notice*

[313]

ever shines. The story emerges from the 'contrast and link' between the two journalists and their moral responses to the 'different shows of human egotism and the newspaper scramble.' Starting from the idea of a 'little antithesis,' James enlarged and squared the pattern, but then used the neat structure as no more than the formal foundation for a tale in which the interest centers on an analysis of a human relationship colored and determined by the monstrous inhumanity of the 'Papers.'

The remaining pages of Notebook VI contain entries of much later date than Notebook VII, which are printed later in their proper chronological place.]

NOTEBOOK VII

11 December 1904–30 March 1905 [1]

. . . expressively (articulatedly) to the kindly eyes: 'See, see, we are getting older, we are getting almost old—old enough; we are taking it on and entering into the beauty of time and the dignity of life—we are at last beginning. We don't look *now* like anything *else*, do we?' —etc., etc. And, then, oh golly!, the question of the Gate and the enclosure, and what that would easily give me if it didn't give me too much. It does—and so does that reference I should like to make to the effect of Sargent's portrait of H<enry> H<igginson>, rather dimly made out in that 1st 'gloaming' at the Union, and *se rattachant* so to the still-living vividness of the emotions of 23 years ago, when I was, the winter of Father's death, for a month or two in N.Y. and in Washington.

x   x   x   x   x

[*As James continues to dwell on his reminiscences, he conjures up not only the material that he used in* The American Scene, *but also some of the old Cambridge and Boston 'ghosts' whom he was to evoke, several years later, in his* Notes of a Son and Brother.]

December 11th, 1904. I came back from New York last night after (36 hours after) Harvey's Dinner and I snatch this intensely cold, but as intensely sunny, Sunday a.m. to try to catch on a little again to the interrupted foregoing. The lapse of each day, save the last <3?> days' rough and lurid vision of N.Y., gives me more and more the sense of what there is to be done, of the affluence of the Impression and the Reflection, of 'the fortune there *is* in it, upon my honour'—I being meanwhile only a little nervous about the amount of overtaking and catching up that I have now upon my hands. As I feared, the 'New England 11' gives me a marked *muchness* of material to deal with, but the only way is to let it *all* come—that serves me well; to drop

1. James marked this notebook 'H. James Jr. Journal, March 1905, "Journal III." It contains his renewed response to America after his long absence, and begins with what is obviously a continuation of an entry in some other manuscript volume that does not seem to have survived.

[315]

every thing into my pot and then pick out such pieces as I can place. These Cambridge, these Boston *concetti* are already receding things, but let me get back a little to where I broke off, too many days ago—to where I was reaching out to little connections for which I then made, on a loose leaf, for reference today, a brief memorandum—I was fumbling, I was groping through the little Cambridge haze that I was, by the same stroke, trying to make 'golden,' and I noted for my recall 'The Gates—questions of the Gates and of the fact of *enclosure* and of disclosure in general—the so importunate American question (of *Dis*-closure—call it so!) above all.' This, with some possible peep (but *how* and *where?*) of my vision of the old high Cambridge and Oxford *grilles* and their admirable office of making things look *interesting*—MAKE so—by their intervention, a *concetto* worth developing just *un brin*; as for instance how, *within* the College Yard, its elements and items gain presence by what has been done (little as it is, of enclosure —with a glance at the *old* misery!) and how I may put it that the less 'good' thing enclosed, approached, *defined*, often looks better than the less good thing *not* enclosed, not defined, not approached. With all of which, too, I was reaching out to Sargent *à propos* of the H.H. portrait—and the impression of the Union—which in its turn is a connection, the vision and sentiment (mine!) of the Union—with other things, and a sort of hook-on, possibly, for use, to that small bit about the *Stadium*, the foot-ball (Dartmouth) match,[1] and the way the big white arena *loomed* at me, in the twilight, ghostly and queer, from across the river, during the ½ hour, the wonderful, the unforgettable, that afternoon's end that I spent in the C<ambridge> C<emetery>. Do that (the picture) with the pink winter sunset and the ghosts, the other Lowells', Longfellow's and Wm. Story's. I swim a little, in fancy, in imagination, in association, in the Sargent connection—for its other ramifications—but there are so many of these. There is the one with the Boit picture, and there is the one with Mrs. G<ardner>'s portrait, and there is above all the one with the Boston Pub<lic> Lib<rary>, making—this one perhaps—a bridge straight across to the *Boston* compartment of my little subject, into which I so, with a happy economy, plunge in the midmost manner—though I don't want to be there till I have got quite out of Cambridge. I mustn't come *back* to C., with all that there is waiting, and with all there is to do for these other matters: therefore tack Cambridge in as you can, *mon bon*; make of it something pretty that you won't have, by the time you cross that bridge, to touch again. Surely the different little *clous* (for C.) *doivent* —with my imperative economy—*tous y'être*. I seem to hang over the

---

1. James originally wrote 'game,' and crossed it out.

'massing larger' and what that means; I seem to hang over the *concetto* of the largeness, all the great largenesses of development before the University, and for which I should like some SPECIAL FIGURE, of a fine high application; something about the way such an (American) institution sits and looks across the high unobstructed table-land of its future in a manner all its own—with a kind of incalculability in the probable, the logically-unsolved extent of its resources—and an horizon so receding, so undetermined, that one sees not—scarce sees—the lowest or faintest blue line. THAT, something of that—which calls up within me, however, such a desire for the glimmer of a glance at the 'sinister,' the ominous 'Münsterberg' possibility—the sort of class of future phenomena repres<en>ted by the 'foreigner' coming in and taking possession; the union of the large purchasing power with the absence of prejudice—of certain prejudices; the easy submission to foreign imposition (of attitude, etc.) and the very sovereign little truth that no branch, no phase, no face, nor facet is perhaps more 'interesting' (than this) of the question that hangs so forever before one here, and *more and more the more one sees:* that of what the effect of the great Infusion (call it that) is going to be. *This* particular light on it—this Harvard professor-of-the-future light, this determined high Harvard absence-of-prejudice light. In addition to which I seem to myself to 'hang over' 2 other interwoven strands—my own little personal harking back to the small old superseded Law-School (in presence of the actual —the big new *modern*); and some sort of glance at one's old vision of Memorial Hall—with something to be gouged out of it—as a ramification of the image and suggestion of the Union. Then the Cambridge fantastication seems to have only too much to 'give'—God help me! It gives and gives; everything seems to give and give as I artfully press it. And what pressure of mine *isn't* artful?—by the divine diabolical law under which I labour!!—Well then, I am thus taking for granted that my bridge across to Boston is represented by the flying leap from the (H.H.) Sargent at the Union to the other Sargent, the Boston one and the Abbeys, etc.—and thereby to the MIDDLE of my Boston business.

x   x   x   x   x

Coronado Beach, Cal., Wednesday, March 29th, 1905.

I needn't take precious time with marking and re-marking here how the above effort to catch up with my 'impressions' of the early winter was condemned to speedy frustration and collapse. I struggled but it all got beyond me—any opportunity for the process of this little precious, this sacred little record and register—but the history is written in my troubled and anxious, my always so strangely more or less aching, doubting, yearning, yet also more or less triumphant, or at least uplifted, heart. *Basta!* I sit here, after long weeks, at any rate, in front of my arrears, with an inward accumulation of material of which I feel the wealth, and as to which I can only invoke my familiar demon of patience, who always comes, doesn't he?, when I call. He is here with me in front of this green Pacific—he sits close and I feel his soft breath, which cools and steadies and inspires, on my cheek. Everything sinks in: nothing is lost; everything abides and fertilizes and renews its golden promise, making me think with closed eyes of deep and grateful longing when, in the full summer days of L<amb> H<ouse>, my long dusty adventure over, I shall be able to <plunge> my hand, my arm, *in,* deep and far, and up to the shoulder—into the heavy bag of re-membrance—of suggestion—of imagination—of art—and fish out every little figure and felicity, every little fact and fancy that can be to my purpose. These things are all packed away, now, thicker than I can penetrate, deeper than I can fathom, and there let them rest for the present, in their sacred cool darkness, till I shall let in upon them the mild still light of dear old L<amb> H<ouse>—in which they will begin to gleam and glitter and take form like the gold and jewels of a mine. x x x x x

The question, however, is with, is of, what I want now, and how I need to hark back, and hook on, to those very 1st little emotions and agitations and stirred sensibilities of the first Cambridge hours and days and even weeks—though it's really a matter for any *acuteness,* for any quality, of *but* the hours, the very first, during which the charms of the brave handsome autumn (I coax it, stretching a point with soft names) lingered and hung about, and made something of a little medium for the sensibility to act in. That was a good moment, genuine so far as it went, and just enough, no doubt, under an artful economy, to conjure with. What it is a question of at present is the putting together with some blessed little nervous intensity of patience, of a third Part to the *New England: an Autumn Impression* now begun in the N.A. Review. I drop out Boston—to come in later (next), into *Three Cities*—the three being B., Philadelphia, and Washington. There is absolutely no room *here* to squeeze in a stinted, starved little Boston picture. Oh, the division is good, I see—the 'three' will do beautifully and so for winding up the little *New England,* will Cambridge and its accessories. I feel as if I could *spread* on C., and that is my danger, as it's my danger everywhere. For *my* poor little personal C., of the far-off unspeakable past years, hangs there behind, like a pale pathetic ghost, hangs there behind, fixing me with tender, pleading eyes, eyes of such exquisite pathetic appeal and holding up the silver mirror, just faintly dim, that is like a sphere peopled with the old ghosts. How can I speak of Cambridge at all, e.g., without speaking of dear J. R. L<owell> and even of the early *Atlantic*, by, oh, such a delicate, ironic implication?—to say nothing of the *old* Shady Hill and the old Quincy St. and those days that bring tears, and the figure for Shady Hill, the figure and presence, of J<ane> N<orton>, and of S<ara> N<orton>, and even of G<eorge> W<illiam> C<urtis>, and the reminiscences of that night of Dickens, and the *emotion*, abiding, that it left with me. How it *did* something for my thought of him and his work—and would have done more without the readings, the hard charmless readings (or *à peu près*) that remained with me. (This is, of course, an impossible side-issue, but one just catches there the tip of the tail of *such* an old emotion of the throbbing prime!) The point for me (for fatal, for impossible expansion) is that I knew there, *had* there, in the ghostly old C. that I sit and write of here by the strange Pacific on the other side of the continent, *l'initiation première* (the divine, the unique), there and in Ashburton Place (which I just came in time to have that October or November glimpse of before seeing its site swept bare a month ago). Ah, the 'epoch-making' weeks of the spring of 1865!—from the 1st days of April or so on to the summer (partly spent at Newport, etc., partly at North Conway)! Something—some fine, superfine, supersubtle mystic breath of that may come in perhaps in the *Three Cities*, in relation to any reference to the remembered Boston of the 'prime.' Ah, that pathetic, heroic little *personal* prime of my own, which stretched over into the following summer at Swampscott—'66—that of the Seven Weeks War, and of unforgettable gropings and findings and sufferings and strivings and play of sensibility and of inward passion there. The hours, the moments, the days, come back to me—on into the early autumn before the move to Cambridge and with the sense, still, after such a lifetime, of particular little thrills and throbs and daydreams there. I can't help, either, just touching with my pen-point (here, here, only here) the recollection of that (probably August) day when I went up to Boston from Swampscott and called in Charles St. for news of O. W. H<olmes>, then on his 1st flushed and charming visit to England, and saw his mother in the cool dim matted drawingroom of that house (passed, *never*, since, without the *sense*), and got the news, of all his London, his general English, success and felicity, and *vibrated* so with the wonder and romance and curiosity and dim weak tender (oh, tender!) envy of it, that my walk up the hill, afterwards, up Mount Vernon St. and probably to Athenaeum was all coloured and gilded, and humming with it, and the emotion, exquisite of its kind, so remained with me that I always think of that occasion, that hour, as a sovereign contribution to the germ of that inward romantic principle which was <to> determine, so much later on (ten years!), my own vision-haunted migration. I recall, I can FEEL now, the empty August st., the Mt. Vernon St. of the closed houses and absent 'families' and my slow, upward, sympathetic, excited stroll there, and my sense of the remainder of the day in town—before the old 'cars' for the return home—so innocently to make a small adventure—vision-haunted as I was already even then—linking on to which somehow, moreover, too, is the memory of lying on my bed at Swampscott, later than that, somewhat, and toward the summer's end, and reading, in ever so thrilled a state, George Eliot's *Felix Holt*, just out, and of which I was to write, and *did* write, a review in the *Nation*. (I had just come back from a bad little 'sick' visit to the Temples somewhere—I have forgotten the name of the place—in the White Mountains; and the Gourlays were staying with us at S., and I was miserably stricken by my poor broken, all but unbearable, and unsurvivable *back* of those [and still, under fatigue, even of these] years.) To read over the opening pages of *Felix Holt* makes even now the whole time softly and shyly live again. Oh, strange little intensities of history, of ineffaceability; oh, delicate little odd links in the long chain, kept unbroken for the fingers of one's tenderest touch! Sanctities, pieties, treasures, abysses! x x x x x

But these are wanton lapses and impossible excursions; irrelevant strayings of the pen, in defiance of every economy. My subject awaits me, all too charged and too bristling with the most artful economy possible. What I seem to feel is that the Cambridge *tendresse* stands in the path like a waiting lion—or, more congruously, like a cooing dove that I shrink from scaring away. I want a little of the *tendresse*, but it trembles away over the whole field—or would if it could. Yet to present these accidents is what it is to be a *master*: that and that only. Isn't the highest deepest note of the whole thing the never-to-be-lost memory of that evening hour at Mount Auburn—at the Cambridge Cemetery when I took my way alone—after much waiting for the favouring hour—to that unspeakable group of graves. It was late, in November; the trees all bare, the dusk to fall early, the air all still (at Cambridge, in general, *so* still), with the western sky more and more turning to that terrible, deadly, pure polar pink that shows behind American winter woods. But I can't go over this—I can only, oh, so gently, so tenderly, brush it and breathe upon it—breathe upon it and brush it. It was the moment; it was the hour; it was the blessed flood of emotion that broke out at the touch of one's sudden *vision* and carried me away. I seemed then to know why I had done this; I seemed then to know why I had *come*—and to feel how not to have come would have been miserably, horribly to miss it. It made everything right—it made everything priceless. The moon was there, early, white and young, and seemed reflected in the white face of the great empty Stadium, forming one of the boundaries of Soldiers' Field, that looked over at me, stared over at me, through the clear twilight, from across the Charles. Everything was there, everything *came;* the recognition, stillness, the strangeness, the pity and the sanctity and the terror, the breath-catching passion and the divine relief of tears. William's inspired transcript, on the exquisite little Florentine urn of Alice's ashes, William's divine gift to us, and to *her,* of the Dantean lines—

> *Dopo lungo exilio e martiro*
> *Viene a questa pace—*

took me so at the throat by its penetrating *rightness,* that it was as if one sank down on one's knees in a kind of anguish of gratitude before something for which one had waited with a long, deep *ache.* But why do I write of the all unutterable and the all abysmal? Why . does my pen not drop from my hand on approaching the infinite pity and tragedy of all the past? It does, poor helpless pen, with what it meets of the ineffable, what it meets of the cold Medusa-face of life, of all the life *lived,* on every side. *Basta, basta!* x x x x x

There remains what one may, what one *must,* not pass without looking at it. But the infinite pity of dear J.R.L.—that is a vision of mine, a vision all faithful and tender, that both challenges and defies expression in the same troubled tormenting way. I don't know why, but there rises from it, with a rush that is like a sob, a sudden vividness of the old *Whitby* days, Whitby walks and lounges and evenings, with George Du M<aurier>—bathed, bathed in a bitter-sweet of ghostliness too. *Basta, basta.* The word about Elmwood—that is all it can, at the very most, come back to; with the word about Longfellow's house, and about poor W. W. Story's early one—and the reminiscence of that evening—late afternoon—walk with William, while the earlier autumn still hung on, through all the umbrageous 'new' part of Cambridge; up to where Fresh Pond, where I used to walk on Sunday afternoon with Howells, once *was!* (Give a word if possible, to *that* mild memory—yet without going to smash on the rock of autobiography.) That return, with William, from the Country Club, hangs somehow in my mind, with the sense that one had, at the time, of the quality of this added grace to life—a note in the general concert of the larger *amenity* surrounding this generation. The type of thing, the pleasant type, the large old country ('colonial') house, with its view, its

verandahs, its grounds, its sports, its refreshments, its service, its civilization, and what these things give that wasn't there before, in the old
thinner New England air and more meagre New England scheme.
There is too much—I am piling up matter; but I seem to remember
certain reflections, certain images that came to me there in the sense
of the more chances, the larger liberality, again, surrounding the young,
the generation of today, than in *my* time—I seem to remember vaguely
feeling, on the spot, on the wide verandah, among the old trees (the
growth of all the fine umbrage, everywhere), that there would be some
small report, or effect, to be made of it. A mere vignette is enough,
but my thing can be *only* all small vignettes throughout. A small
vignette for every little item, any little item: keep the thing down
to that, and my paper is done. But the thing is to catch just the notes
that were IN that country club 'value.' Wasn't the 'sport' image of
the young people, the straight brown young men, with strong good
figures and homely faces, one of them? I mean as associated with that
of the strong, charmless (*work* that 'charmless' right), stalwart, slangy
girls, in whom one feels the intimation, the consequence, of the absence
of danger, from the men—as one feels throughout, in the N.E., in
each sex, the absence of a sense, the absence of the consciousness, of,
or of the existence of, danger from the other. Other echoes and trailing
lights, too, does one seem to gather in from the kindly after-sense of
that afternoon—where, on one of the large overhanging verandahs,
we talked, W. and I, with good Scotch Mr. Muirhead—isn't he?—
who is the author of the excellent American Baedeker. The sense of
the American *club*, which was to be so handsomely confirmed for
me, and which certainly has in it to contribute a page—here and
there, throughout a paragraph—or two: *that* I probably entertained,
in germ, on that occasion. And there must have come to me then
too, as we went back, my 1st good vision of the striking symptoms,
so new to me, of the admirable Boston 'Park system,' which was to
become more emphatic, more vivid, during the time I afterwards
spent with Mrs. Gardner (ah, to squeeze a little, a little of what I felt,
out of *that*, too!) at Brookline, at her really so quite *picturable* Green
Hill—which would yield a 'vignette,' I think, whereof I fully possess
all the elements. The way the large, the immense 'Park' roads of the
new System unrolled themselves in their high type during 2 or 3 of
the drives I took with Mrs. G.—and the way the 'value' of the road,
as an earnest and a promise and a portent, stood up and seemed to
'tell.' The *material* civilization—'don't doubt—with these things everything is possible.' But I abound too much, as usual; I waste my art;
I do my thing in too costly a way—I damn the expense too consistently,
too heroically, too ruinously. Still, I dabble a moment longer in the

mild soft afterglow of that little excursion with William, at the end of which we walked home (after alighting from the tram) through the still summerish twilight of the region (of Cambridge) that I used to know as the region *near* the region (about the 'Fayerweather St.,' etc.) where the dear Gurneys anciently lived. Whenever one is with William one receives such an immense accession of suggestion and impression that the memory of the episode remains bathed for one in the very liquidity of his extraordinary play of mind; and I seem to recollect, thus, how he gave life and light, as it were, to the truth, the interest, of the change wrought all about there, by the two facts of the immense rise in the type and scope and scale of the American house, as it more and more multiplies, and of the special amenity of the effect, for the 'streets,' of the large tree-culture. The over-arching clustered trees, the way dignity and style were helped by them, the embowered city—cities—of the future. I recall a little *those* vibrating chords. But, ah, all this suffices, surely suffices above all, if I make my point that to an inordinate degree, alas, all this pleasantry of picture and evocation has a truth only as applied to the summer and autumn alone. The way with the winter bareness all one's remarks are falsified and all the meanness and ugliness comes out. The transformation is complete, and even the 2 or 3 elements of winter beauty do little to save the picture, do almost everything to betray it. The snow, the sunshine, light up and pauperize all the wooden surfaces, all the mere paint and pasteboard paltriness. The one fine thing are the winter sunsets, the blood on the snow, the pink crystal of the west, the wild frankness, wild sadness (?)—so to speak—of the surrender.

x   x   x   x   x

I was tackling (when I broke off this at Cambridge so long ago) the question of whether I mightn't let my little current float me into the presence of J.S.S., for the space of ten lines, by the way of his splendid portrait of H.H.—floated into the presence of *that*, as one was, by the impulse to do something with one's 1st impression of the *Union*, and its great high Hall; do it, really, too, as a part of that one *first and only afternoon ramble* there with H., blessed boy,[1] to which the small poetry, the small sharper or intenser sensibility of my renewal of impression really reduces or refers itself. (It was when I came back with him—or rather to him—from Chocorua, the day before I went on to Cotuit and Howard S<turgis>.) He was alone there, in Irving St., and had come to meet me, all blessedly, in Boston, and it was that same afternoon, I judge, that we made a brief simplified little tour, before

1. William James' oldest son, Henry.

dusk—having tea afterwards with Mrs. Gibbens. So I reconstitute it, but what was above all with me at the time was the then feeling that *that,* the quality just simply of that little moment, would be very possibly about all the general Cambridge fact, in short, would have to give me. It was just the last of the 'Long,' as they would say at Oxford—the place was still empty, but everything was furbishing and preparing for Term. He took me to the great new Law School—and I lived back feebly in to my melancholy little years (oh, so heart breaking) at the old, so primitive and archaic; and I saw John Gray, afar off, reading in the great new Library, and I wondered, on the spot, if I mightn't be able to make something of that!

Thursday, March 30th, 1905 (Coronado Beach).

So much as the foregoing I scrabbled yesterday, and it has given me a sense of getting on—done for me, in its degree, what the 'process,' the intimate, the sacred, the divine, always does (ah, how it *grew,* in those 'wasted' years!): floated me back into relation with the idea, with the possibility, into relation again with my task and my life. But *voyons, voyons.* The other pieces of my little tapestry hang there before me—the figures and bits I must work in, to eke out the effect of Cam<bridge>. There was Dedham, where I went in a pouring rain, to dine with Sam Warren—went with Mrs. G., who took me there, from my Brookline visit to her, as she took me to that other strange place, on another day, Blue Hill or wherever, to see Wm. Hunt's daughters. And then there is my day, my 2 different days (but the first the best) with Bob at Concord; and there is my small and adequate scrap of a stop over.

NOTEBOOK VIII

22 August 1907—1 October 1909

[*James seems to have been thinking at this time of a continuation of his earlier sketches, which he had recently collected into a volume, English Hours (1905). Just before his visit to America he had promised to write, according to Edmund Gosse, '"a romantical-psychological-pictorial-social" book about London, and in November 1905, he returned to this project with vivacity. . . Westminster was to have been the core of the matter, which was to circle out concentrically to the City and the suburbs.' He did not complete this undertaking.*]

August 22d, Spring Gardens.

While I linger to look, in front of the great demolitions and temporary hoardings: the old houses, few, very few, that survive, the good old brick fronts, the spoiled windows; the 2 or 3 with good 18th century doors and door-tops behind the back of the hideous new Admiralty extension. One of these, this late summer afternoon, with such a pretty misty London light, is open into dusty chambers or offices: and a cat lies sleeping in the sun, vague dim pretty sunshine, while the large red glazed door-top—like this [1] but higher—makes little old-world effect as of a homelier time. What has just struck me, *à propos* of the long new Mall is the extraordinary typical charm today of the London August light. The far away blue haze on the *low* palace front (where the monument is not yet) almost as of some 'blue distance,' some hill-horizon, in the country. The *silvery*, watery, misty light—or say misty, watery, silvery—*that* order. And my *liking* this time the pleasant high *cossus* (English-opulent) backs of Carlton Terrace. The note of association here—the amusement to me, as I find—and now I catch *on* to it—of the feeling *for*, about, what is being (even so poorly) attempted for the greater greatness of poor dear old London; the kind of affectionate sense of property, the sentimental *stake* in it. Came back to this vista, to the Horseguards, to St. James's Park. Looking at the backs of Carlton Terrace—near the Russell Sturgis's old house—I find I don't

1. Here James made a very crude sketch of a fan-light window.

[325]

know what little 'handsomeness,' little London domestic or 'social' charm, in the way each second floor window, between the Corinthian pillars of its Colonnade, has its own solid little under-bracketed, stuccoed balcony. But the deplorable Boer monument, opposite, in the little garden under the new Admiralty, and the at present so *bête* and common curve of the—bulge of the—face of the Grand Hotel (round into Whitehall). *Passages* in London, however, make vistas, and just at this hour I catch a little specimen of it and of the way that they make a little charm and a little picture. There is an opening at the end of the terrace through into Trafalgar Square at the end of (the shortness of) which just a bit of the Nat<ional> Gall<ery>, the ugly cupola itself, sits up and *speaks* to one. Speaks to one, that is, if one have the old London sense, the feeling and the fondness. How *all* one's appreciations here need that: nothing so fine, beautiful or artistic, as to work for much without it. The way the 'mean' little Roman warrior's statue of Jacobus Secundus—iron, lead?—that used to stand behind the Banqueting Hall in Whitehall, has been placed just before the part of the Admiralty Extension that looks on the small garden like some unwelcome household ornament put away at last—though originally expensive, most expensive—in a bad back room. The whole thing, here, the Horseguards back, and the house—old grey-black house, off to the right—identifying—with its HIGH second story and rococo pediment—never so 'precious' for old-times.

August 23d. Good and 'pretty' this noon the *mouth* of Walbrook, beside the Mansion House, with the narrow slightly *grouillant* dusky vista formed by the same with the second-hand book shop let into the base of St. Stephen's (*plaqué* over with a dirty little stucco front) and the rather bad spire above—very bad, rough masonry and *mean* pinnacle. Interior (all alone here this cool summer noon) very much better than poor smothered outside (smothered in passages and by the high rear of the Mansion House) gives a hint of—very fine *quadrillé*-panelled with old grey plaster rosettes and garlands—Dome—quite far and high, and today, with the florid old oak pulpit and canopy, the high old sallow sacred picture opposite, the 18th century memorial slabs, the place is quite the *retreat*, with the vague city hum outside, as they all get it, of the ghostly sense, the disembodied presences of the old London. There is an old grey print of the interior of the uniform—horizontally uniform—upper windows (not *clerestory* which are higher) before the hideous modern glass; dedicated to C.W., Esq. (Wren's son), as a view of one 'of the noble proofs of his father's superior genius.'[1]

1. Here a page is cut out in the manuscript.

Out of the space beyond the Mansion House, where the (dishonoured) ch. of St. Swithin's (??) stands, opens St. Swithin's[1] x x x x x St. Swithin's, no, is in Cannon St. with London Stone let into it, and the Lane is parallel to Walbrook and runs from the E. side of the Mansion H., as Walbrook from the W., down to Cannon St. Station. Very pretty *enfoncement* of court and front of Salters' Hall in St. Swithin's Lane, on right—which I must visit early in autumn.

x   x   x   x   x

The Tower so *pretty* today from the River, with one's back turned (on the steamboat) to the terrible Tower Bridge. (Yet right and *fine* symbol of our time), the whole low clustered mass so interesting, with its *ruddy* tinges of colour, a sort of suffused human complexion given by the long centuries. The *terrace* open to the public now—so long closed after an 'outrage,' and with many people, the whole thing was (just now, I write this on the boat) pleasant, I mean almost incongruously charming. But the *Pool* of London, all around me now as I write —the little tugs and tenders drawing the flat-bottomed barges—the little steamboats with their noses up as if their shrill whistle came through them, and the churn of the greasy brown flood kicked up by their <tread?, travel?>. This whole steamboat thing to be done again—much better than when I did it last. The vast black fuliginous south bank impossible to deal with—but fortunately I am limited by Southwark. Only I don't quite *see* my Southwark—as yet. *Ça viendra.* I am stopping on the boat this amusing afternoon—just to *do* the River to Greenwich now that *j'y suis* (Aug. 23d—saw Bill off to Quebec this a.m.). My only day—at this season—for months to come. Moreover, fortunately, I haven't to deal with it.

x   x   x   x   x

The barges, drawn up—I mean *especially* those drawn up—on the *Verge*, and the hollow flat-boats; such pretty things to *draw*. I have been as far as Greenwich—the grey—silver grey—hospital looking quite superb and archaic and *interesting*, but have caught a boat back, and now, 3:30, am on the return—so as to face toward London, which is the right way. The *blunt* barges—blunt, say: 'blunt' is good. The North shore awfully picturesque—a great *fouillis* of black and brown and russet odds and ends between Limehouse pier—in fact just above it. x x x x x

1. Presumably James' 'dishonoured' refers to the fact that the church of St. Swithin, built by Wren, had been modernized.

Have tried (4 p.m.) to get into St. Magnus the Martyr, close under London Bridge, and just south of the *Fire* column—but it's closed. The face of the grey stone columnar building at N.W. side of London Bridge—Fishmongers' Hall wharf—rather fine—but the Thames St. squalor here of the worst (base of Fish St. Hill).

August 24th. Have turned this a.m. into St. Clement Danes, the 2d church facing W. at end of Strand and opposite Arundel St. The interior, where I sit writing this, very elegant and charming with its light galleries vaulted—so [1]—on Corinthian capitals of the pillars; its (caved?) 'barrel-roofed' ceiling and elaborate *stucchi*, fruited garlands and cherubs' heads. Also its very long high deep set windows springing continuously from just above pavement to roof and passing behind gallery. But the thing all very much over done up, with stars (gilt) and [2] etc., now. x x x x x

I have come out of it into the big newish public green or garden beside the W. side of the Law-Courts—where you see the rich architecture and whence the tower and spire of St. Clement's in profile are pleasing. But newness—large dull legal newness builds in this little expanse, spaciously, all round. There are highish steps at the end, to which I've climbed, and it's all very enlightened and commodious (reverse order) and the grey stone of the Law-Courts is in a good stage of that dusky-silvering which is the best that London buildings can look for in the so operative, so tormenting (no, find the right kindly, affectionate word) air—which so deals with things (as a [fussy] family tone [no, not fussy]) deals with its members. The steps terminate in big stone and iron screen or *grille* opening into other grave clear Law precincts, into *Serle St.*, with its dear old square windowed, square paned 18th century backs (of old chambers) all dingy red brick—more delectable than the new red (Butterfieldian) priggish (self-conscious— *why* self-conscious?) architecture of New Court all perpendicular round-about, but this a.m. rather charming with vivid green and geraniums at the centre. I have walked on to Lincoln's Inn Fields and am writing this in the large central garden or square, where, this moist summer, the lawns, the turf, are extraordinary and where some of the trees are more magnificent (are they the ash?) than I knew. But Lincoln's Inn Fields and the Soane Museum are a bit by themselves—they will give me something, the right little page, when I want it. x x x x x

I missed a little way back a little *joli motif* on the south side of St. Clement Danes, the note of the New London in the circular, the

1. Here James made an outline of a vault.
2. An indecipherable word is omitted here.

shallow-curved street where the big statued insurance building (or whatever) is replacing the little old sordidries that were yet the old world where that pleasant bookshop (Buxton Forman's), publisher, some time vanished, used to be. The suggestions of the—in the—change to a London bristling with statued fronts. x x x x x

New Square, Lincoln's Inn, still delightful; *do* New Square. x x x x x

Funny little smothered red brick St. Mary Abchurch—with its crooked yard, one of the myriad 'short cuts' of the City, just out of Cannon St. E. of St. Swithin's. Look it up. (St. M.A. and St. Lawrence Pountney.) I never (before this time) discovered St. Augustine and St. Faith just under the back of St. Paul's, and the queer interview of narrow streets, lanes, Watling St., Old Change, Friday St., Bread St. x x x x x

St. Margaret Pattens is the church in Eastcheap, the way from London Bridge to the Tower—the featureless old brown church standing back on the left, with the fire escape in front of it, etc. x x x x x

Here I come suddenly, this same charming day (Aug. 24th) on delightfully placed old St. Dunstan's in the East (the mate of which, St. D. in West, Fleet St., I tried to get into, under the image of Queen Elizabeth, an hour ago). I never chanced upon this one before —just out of Eastcheap, on the way to the Tower, and beyond (south) the little St. Margaret Pattens. High 'fine' Gothic tower and spire, and built as it is on the steep hill down to the river the little old disused and voided churchyard is raised on deep southward substructions under the south wall of the church and employed as a small sitting-place for the specimens of the grimy public—*such* infinitely miserable specimens—who are dozing and gnawing bones (2 tramps under the south wall together doing *that*) in it now. The noise of drays from riverward, the clang of wheels, etc., harsh in the enclosed, built-in space; but the tall (3 or 4) thin trees (a lime and a locust?) make a green shade—and the clock in the tower, or at least the bell, gives out an immense deep note (2 o'ck.). Come back of course—get in. All these city churches have their *hours* on notices at doors. Make record of these.

October 8th, 1907. The site of Garroway's's Coffee House in Change Alley (rebuilt 1874). The place (C.A.) with its old opening from the traffic (of Lombard St.) looks as if it were going to be 'something' but is only a mere modernized desolation which even its crookedness

[329]

doesn't save—all big office windows and white-tiled walls for the dif-
fusion of light.

October 8th, 1907. St. Edmund, King and Martyr, and St. Nicholas
Acon, little grey old squat-towered church in Lombard St., opposite
Clement's Lane and just further than Change Alley. x x x x x

Often passed St. Michael's, Cornhill, without taking it in—I mean the
'importance' of its big square grey Gothic tower. *See* it and make small
scrap, if possible, of the effect of tower—good way it rises over interposing lower objects as seen from George Yard (out of Lombard St.)
beyond it—poor 'gone' G.Y., leading into Michael's Lane. The little
quad or court in the flank of the court, out of Lane, an almost 'gone'
thing too. The 2 renewed or scraped marble memorial slabs in side
wall of church do—verily—nothing. The little intricacies of tortuous
business—lanes and courts and nooks are characteristic—Simpson's
tavern and chop-rooms—are a note; but the big grey Cornhill Tower as
seen from corner by Bumpus's small, almost hidden, book shop, is the
only strong bit. 'Bengal Court (modern)—late White Lion court?'
Value of *names* even when all the rest is gone. How one likes *both*.
Allhallows Church in Lombard St. open 10-4. Close to Gracechurch
St. x x x x x

Look at St. Mary at Hill, out of Love Lane (Eastcheap)—poor little
dingy temple—and the idea of the poor little dingy place *being* Love
Lane at all! Go round to *Back*—opposite St. Margaret Pattens. The
funny long passage—internal corridor all indoors, bearing name G.
Mincing Lane—and going to M.L. from Eastcheap. *The feeling of
old London,* through, and in spite of, everything, in the City at night
—try and make some good morsel—some passage about it—at night
and in the dusk of this October day (6 o'ck.).

[*The following entries are from Notebook VI, inserted here in their
chronological order.*]

Lamb House, December 26th, 1908.

Mrs. F.F. (of Budd's Withersham, where Aleck [1] and I have just
been spending Xmas) mentioned to me little local fact that strikes me
as good small 'short-story' *donnée* of the orthodox type. (It was told
her of some small working or shop-keeping person there.) The man

1. William James' youngest son.

had engaged himself to a young woman, but afterwards had thought better of it and had backed out, to her great indignation and resentment, so that she threatened him *bel et bien* with an action for breach of promise of marriage—and so menacingly, and with such a prospect or presumption of success that he, scared, afraid of the scandal and injury, etc., agreed to 'compromise' and pay her two hundred Pounds of damages—her own valuation, etc. This he did, but with the effect for years afterward of staggering under the load of the obligations he had contracted to raise the money. His whole life blighted by it, impoverished, etc.—and the years going by. In the Withersham case—as she heard—he had married somebody else, etc.; after which, his wife dying, he had come round somehow to *her*, his early fiancée again— or she to *him*—and they had patched it up somehow and married. What I seem to see in it is *her* life and behaviour—her subsequent action. She has got her £200—she has been thrifty and canny; she has found work (off perhaps as a domestic servant in London); she has kept her money and added to it—she has led her life. She waited and watched in short—watched the hero of her early episode—from afar— or I seem to see her rather designedly and consciously doing it—almost on a calculation of what may happen. She *sees* him suffer—sees him burdened and collapsing—sees him pay for what he has done to her; and she measures and follows this, as if determined to let it go a certain time. In the little story, as I see it take its turn, they finally meet again—and they then marry. She has kept the money—she has it for him, gives it back to him augmented—she has been keeping it for him till the day when only this will save him. I seem to see her come to him—it isn't that he goes to *her*; never! And at first he won't look at her. They must have met before—he seen her prosperous, etc. Then he has hated her, etc. The thing given him by her in the end as all her own plan, design, etc. She has taken the money because she has known he would want money badly—later on; and she has kept it although other men have made up to her for it. She tells him she has refused to marry—so that the money shouldn't be got at by her husband. He has known of a case—a fellow she has known before she knew him and *whom she has refused or chucked, jilted, in order to become engaged* to him—and whom she supposes that now she *will* marry (now that she has the money); he sees her refuse this man just *because* she has, and wishes to keep, the money—and he's mystified and hasn't understood—thinks the money has made her 'proud'— and mean. But she has just thus remained single for him. At last, when he (the 'hero') learns that she has the money, *then* he accepts her charity, then he marries her.

[331]

[The Bench of Desolation, *the last short* nouvelle *that James produced, ran in* Putnam's Magazine *(October 1909—January 1910). It was too late to put it in his collected edition, as was also the case with the other stories he printed in* The Finer Grain *(1910). He followed his sketched plot very closely to produce another variation on the theme of suffering. After Herbert Dodd's wife and children have died and his little bookshop in a south-coast watering place has long since failed, Kate Cookham comes back to find him sitting, as he so often does, on his lonely bench at the far end of the promenade along the beach. As she tells him the strange story of how she has saved his money for him through all these years, she declares: 'You've suffered and you've worked—which, God knows, is what I've done! Of course you've suffered . . . you inevitably had to! We have to . . . to do or to be or to get anything.'*]

Same date. Noting this has brought back to me the little *donnée, à la Mary Wilkins,* etc., which I took mental note of here 10 years ago —the situation mentioned to me in relation to W.D. and his drinking-habits, etc., by (I think) Mrs. E.S. That surely is do-able—and I see it from the 'point of view of the woman,' don't I?—effectively enough. She traces, *views,* notes, follows, records, *reflects* (by observations and anxiety) the effect upon her rejected suitor, of the marriage she *has* made—his beginning to be seen to drink, then his getting worse, etc. She sees it herself at her wedding feast—on her wedding day. It makes her glad she *didn't* choose him—yet she yearns over him too till he gets worse. Then she declines responsibility—or assures herself she does. And I seem to see it 'told' through some—through 'certain'— passages between herself and a 'confidant'; not her husband, not the man she has accepted (that *complicates*), but her trustee, adviser, elderly bachelor friend or whatever, *qui lui rapporte* and talks over with him the facts involved. He has hoped she'll 'take' W.D. Then when she doesn't he fears something; and it's only through him she has news of the rejected one (I think). In fact this *has* to be for brevity. It goes on in a series of 'conversations'—or whatever. I see *this, par exemple,* in an 'easy' 5000. Surely I do. It's the very *type,* at least—it has *that* for it. And its predecessor noted here—that *ils ont pour eux* if nothing else. They are rather too much alike to be done as a pair. But I see the one before this in '5 of 5'—five little sections of 5 pages each: 25 in all, and 5000 words, through each section being of 1000 words—200 to a page. The present, the 'W.D.' one, seems to cut itself, say perhaps, rather in 3 or 4 parts. *Voyons alors.*

Same date. I find on loose page an allusion to what I call G.L.G.'s (and 'Colonel' H.'s) story. Ah *that!*

Names. Parkyn—Dummett—Sugg—Gaymer (or Gamer)—Properly.

Lamb House, February 10th, 1909.

A sense with me, divine and beautiful, of hooking on again to the 'sacred years' of the old D.V. Gdns. time, the years of the whole theatric dream and the 'working out' sessions, all ineffable and uneffaceable, that went with that, and that still live again, somehow (indeed I *know* how!) in their ashes:—that sense comes to me, I say, over the *concetto* of fingering a little what I call the C.F. and Katrina B. subject—that <of> the Prsa. de M. and de G. connection and of the 'humiliations' of Mrs. B. without her *amanti*—in the midst of the *amanti* of the others—that's what C.F. very intelligently said to me one day, put vividly before me.

[*The text now reverts to Notebook VIII.*]

September 21st, 1909. Just back from Overstrand—beautiful September day. Turned in to St. Bride's Fleet St.—great ample handsome empty 'Palladian' church, mercilessly modernized, brightened, decorated, painted and gilded—but so still in the roaring City—with the *rumeur* outside all softened and faint—so respectable, so bourgeois—such a denial of any cognizance of passions, remorses, compassions, appeals—anything but mildest contritions and most decorous prostrations. But big and square and clear and reverend—in all its simplicity and with no altar to speak—neither book nor bell nor cross nor candle. It is one of Wren's churches and the little baptismal font was saved from the Fire. Immense and massive tower to great height, with superpositions of stages in spire atop—*diminuendo*—like a tower of cards.

Same day. St. Martin Ludgate—on L. Hill at left, just before or below St. Paul's—small dim dark wainscoted church sideways to street and evidently of poor squeezed site—more of the sound of the city—but with 2 or 3 youngish very middle class men in prolonged and absorbed prayer, as at St. Bride's—and here one young girl, in great prostration. Much more favorable than St. B.'s. Poor charmless architectural effort —or accommodation.

Same afternoon again. Wandered up into St. Paul's—which was very full of trippers—but fine and dim and worthy—something to be done with it; and then off Ludgate hill (westward) past the Old Bailey (the new substitute for old Newgate) to St. Bartholomew's hospital. Into the wide grey court where patients were laid out on beds to take the air and talked with such a nice young fellow with charming face (26) laid up with hip disease.

In the Crypt of St. Paul's, October 1st, 1909, a.m.

— The homely lowly slab-tomb of C. Wren, 'the builder of this Cath. Church of St. Paul' (*ob.* 1723); also the pretty little florid rococo slab (mural) indicating the resting place of his wife. All about here the pavement-slabs of the painters—Turner, Millais, Leighton, Opie, Fuseli, our Pennsylvanian B. West, P.R.A.; [1] Reynolds, Fuseli, Landseer, and others; and in the wall a rather handsome mural monument to Frk. Holl (*ob.* 1888). Also very charming one to Randolph Caldecott of a child holding a medallion: touching memorials, both of them, in the place, to *young* infelicities. Make something of the spacious, vast *cheerful* effect of this crypt—*admirable* Valhalla in its way—with the great temple above it and the London sounds of only the ghostliest faintness. —The War Correspondents, a mural brass, collective; and then W. H. Russell and Archibald Forbes, identical mural monuments. There is also a 'dog' mural monument to Landseer—all right for the dog— mourning by a coffin (relief). The *tombs* of Wellington and of Nelson are great guarded sarcophagi and funereal urns isolated (guarded) in the dim centre of the great Crypt and looming through the deeper shade impressively enough. Say how the vastness of the Crypt gives the measure of the *area* of the Cathedral more than the Cath. itself. And note the memorial slabs to W. Besant, Charles Reade, Barham, George Smith, George Cruikshank, and the fine Rodin bronze bust to W. E. Henley. The mural things *memorial* (as of Holl, Caldecott, etc.); the pavement slabs only sepulchral.

The Library most interesting and charming in high aloofness in the upper vastness of the church—such space in these vast upper areas; and almost *elegant*—very with G. Gibbons's carvings—with the London uproar rising more audibly, and yet fitful and *estompé*, than as it comes, or *doesn't* come, to the Crypt. Come up if only to see the great copy of Luther's Bible, and to read in the Book of Donations for the rebuilding after the Fire, Charles II's autograph in the pale amber coloured ink: 'I will give one thousand pounds a yeare' and James's: 'I will give two hundred pounds a year to begin from midsummer.'

1. President of the Royal Academy.

Same day. Paul's Alley boring so narrowly into Paternoster Row, and so across into Ivy Lane so queerly named.

The insincere recesses and niches, of Wren's, in the high outer and so beautiful sides of cathedral (*so* in the grand manner as the traveller of old used to see them from top of bus).

2 p.m. In the old churchyard of St. Giles to look at the bastion of the old City Wall—'restored' alas, after fire in 1897, but massive and quaint. The large churchyard, with separated (business) passage through it, in itself interesting: with strong and sturdy aspect of tower from it; with so fresh green of turf and plants that have replaced all the burial-stones, after this wet summer. No city churchyard has held its own better, more amply; with hideous workhouses and offices pressing hard, it seems still to bid them stand off—keep their distance civilly, and respect a little the precious history of things.

NOTEBOOK IX

21 April 1911—10 May 1911

April 21st, 1911.

Just to seize the tip of the tail of the idea that I noted a longish time <ago>,[1] given me by Alice, a reminiscence of something, I think, that had happened at Weymouth, Mass., in her childhood; the incident of the woman waked up at night by some sound, below stairs, that shows there is some one in the house, on which she wakes up her husband. They listen, they consider—they become convinced that a burglar, a thief, a malefactor of some sort has made his way in and is operating with great precautions, which have yet not prevented their hearing him. It is obvious the husband must go down and see—but the wife perceives, at first with surprise and then with resentment, that he is not at all inclined to. She appeals to him, to his self-respect, to his common courage, but he remains unmoved and unshamed—whereupon she feels that she really now, in the light of this deplorable exhibition, knows him for the first time. It's a shock and a disgust to her, and in the irritation it produces, and by way of putting him to the blush, she determines to go down herself. She does so—though he protests (so not to the point, however, of preventing her by mustering pluck himself); she goes down, she faces the intruder—whom she finds to be a young man of the town whom she knows, whom she *has* known. I seem to see, yes, that they are old acquaintances or friends, that something has passed between them several years before: when she was a girl of twenty, say; she being now 30 and (but) these 2 or 3 years married. He, the man, has had a sort of 'lower-orders' flirtation with her—they've kept company for a little, or whatever—she having given him up or broken with him because of his bad habits, his being wild or idle, his not inspiring her with due confidence. Then she has lost sight of him—he has left the place. Behold then now she sees him again, after the interval, in this extraordinary situation —that of his standing there in her kitchen at 2 o'clk in the morning. I am assuming thus at any rate that they have had this relation—

1. Page 303 above.

but *il faudra voir;* just as I seem to see that the scene must—had best
—be a London suburb. Well, she confronts him—whether recognizing
him or not (*as* an old—a young—acquaintance); and in either case their
interview is a curious, an odd one. It takes a remarkable, an anomalous
turn. Decidedly, they *must* have met before; the economy of the tale
as a short thing demands it. The great fact is that he is unexpectedly
mild and accommodating and reasonable—he doesn't threaten or bully
or browbeat her, and she, on her side, doesn't (after a bit) threaten
him with exposure. He attempts to explain and justify—to make out
that he only stole in, through the temptation of seeing a window un-
latched or whatever, to get some food. (His pretext, apology or whatever, to be worked out; as also the question of *his* surprise and the
question of whether he knew the house to be hers, her husband's, or
only *happened* to have, by an extraordinary coincidence, picked out
theirs as the subject of his attempt.) Probably he must have *observed*
they were there and so chosen: this is what she accuses him of—of
resentfully playing on her and on the man she has married this belated
vengeance, to make her pay for her old contempt of him. Something
of that sort. He a poor *raté,* of course—essentially a vagabond, but
with redeeming traits; and of course I can only pretend here to the
barest skeleton. She feeds him and gets rid of him—it's of course of
the essence that the scene mustn't be too prolonged—as that makes
her husband's not coming down quite too unnatural. If she stays
below—while he sharply listens above—beyond a certain point, he
will of course come down to see what she's doing—unless indeed one
can put it that her non-return and apparent non-departure of the
burglar constitutes an additional ground for fear by seeming to indicate that she may somehow have been nefariously dealt with. At any
rate the passage between the two takes place, and the great point of it
is that she is *interested.* The young man somehow or other produces that
effect; so that though she does give him something to eat and lets
him off safely—I mean gets rid of him for a very bad character—she
keeps hold of him to the extent of not absolutely refusing to see
him again in some wholly different way—and of even getting from
him some indication of where and how he can again be got at. His
plea is that her old treatment of him had ruined him, that she has
been the prime cause of his perversion. She can still help him, he
pretends, by being 'kind' to him, and he leaves her with a measure
of assurance that she will be. She goes up again to her husband, flushed,
as it were, with the success of the boldness she has shown, and pro-
portionately the more disillusioned and disdainful at the sort of figure
that, through it, her lord and master has made. (He is a 'city-clerk'
or such like—and they are in the position of keeping a servant who

has been that night absent on a necessity of some sort or a holiday.) When he asks his wife what has happened below—who was there and what she—or he—did, she only looks at him from the depths of her disgust—at first without answering, and as if amazed and additionally nauseated at his asking. Then she has an inspiration. 'I won't tell you.' And on his pressure, his urgency: 'Nothing would induce me to.' He has to take it then, and they go to bed; but on the morrow he returns to the question—he wants so abjectly to know. As she sees this it gives her her cue—she sees that she can punish him for his poltroonery by balking his curiosity. 'You shall *never* know— you shall never, never, never get it out of me.' As she sees the curiosity work in him she determines he never shall, and she will attend to it that he shall not in any way find out. To this end she sees her young man again—she judges that she must *tell* him how she is dealing with her husband on the question of what happened between them that night—how he is never to know: so that he, the young man, shall keep *his* mouth absolutely closed about it. I seem to see that I must somehow or other make the irruption comparatively innocuous and innocent—as having some colour of need. He may have thought them absent and come in to help himself to something—only *what?*—that he was very much in want of. They have been absent and just got back—he not knowing of their return (that evening). The idea of the small thing comes out then *there*—in the relation created between the wife and the young man, created *for* her with him, by his thus getting her to help him to conceal his act from the *possibility* of her husband's knowing—and by his knowing how she was dealing with her husband, and why she was so doing it. Happy thought—the young man isn't a burglar—he's a young man who has seen the burglar come in—or come out—and has come in himself, at some peril, to give the alarm. He's a young man she knows—he thinks they are away. The great thing is that the husband knows the other person, 'the man,' knows what a coward he has been. She tells him she has told the man. Therefore what man is it? His intense curiosity to know. It intensely and horridly works in him. The growth of his suspicion of the 'relation'; not a relation formed, to his imagination, for 'illicit' purposes, but made up of their knowing together, she and the man, the abject little facts about him. If he can only know, if he can only learn, who her participant in this is—while the fact that he doesn't, that the other man gives no sign, and the sense therefrom proceeding of the 'hold' she accordingly has upon the unknown only irritates and haunts him the more. Well, so far so good—if 'good' at all; but the question is, what does it, the situation, lead to, and where is one's little issue, climax or denouement? It must arrive somewhere, or it's

[338]

without form and void. I ask myself, but nothing very much seems to come—and with my small prospect of ever using any such small scrap of a *donnée*, after all the humiliation and pain and inconvenience I've been through over this question of my small pieces—the end of the matter scarce seems worth gouging out now. However, I hate to touch things only to leave them, and the appeal of the little old consecrated idea of the application of the particular firm and gentle pressure that has seen me, in the past, through so many dark quandaries, difficult moments, hours of more or less anguish ('artistic' at least), that appeal throbs within me, or before me, again, and pleads and penetrates. I seem to see it glimmer to me that one's climax here is in some effect of the husband's finding out, identifying the man. He finds out *and*— well, what comes of it and how does he do it? I seem to want it to be somehow to his advantage and not to that of his wife—or at least I seem to want it to be to the advantage of the 'man,' the wife's fellow-conspirator or concealer. *Mettons* that he is bored by the fuss the woman makes over their secret at last—and *mettons* that at this stage the husband 'spots' him as *the* man. The way the husband spots him to be worked out; it would be arrangeable. The husband then lets him know that he has so spotted him, but *asks him not to let the wife know he has* done so. The man consents, promises, and the husband believes him, and that, in a way, makes a case—given the *how and the why* the husband recognizes and sees. The man is affected by the husband, pityingly, humorously or however—and I don't see perhaps—or do I see?—why the story shouldn't, as the best economy possibly, and the best vividness, which *is* the best economy, be *told* by the man himself—*of* himself, *of* the wife and the husband. Doesn't the latter somehow show the man that if it's only *he* of whom the wife is so keeping the identity from him—if it's so only *he*—why he doesn't care a bit. Say then that he proposes *this* to the man—that they two now make a compact, as it were, to keep the wife in the dark—in the dark about her husband having spotted the man and brought his identity home to him; about what has passed between them on that head—so that she may still think, still believe, his own, the husband's, obscurity and worriment complete and continuous and continual. Say the 'man' feels, on grounds of his own—these to be presented—the force or the oddity, the 'quaintness,' of this appeal, and that he is somehow touched and tempted (though isn't it all rather thin?) and that, in a word, he agrees to what the husband asks of him, and sees that the husband sees (as *we* see) that he will keep his promise. He does so, and the husband's sense of it is somehow the latter's revenge—on the wife. He has befooled her, taken her in, *l'a mise dedans*. For she all the while *thinks*, believes, and the man now deceives her—and that is the husband's *revanche*.

Now that I have so threshed it out—*à propos*—I can't say it strikes <me> as much of a matter—but such is the only way to lay these hovering little ghosts of motives. Attempt to *state* them—and then one sees. This *test* of the statement is moreover in any case such an exquisite thing that it's always worth making, if only for the way it brings back the spell of the old sacred days. The more I seem to fix the little stuff, such as it is, the more I seem to make out that the only way is to make the 'man' narrate it, make it *his* adventure. The wife, coming down, TELLS him what has happened above stairs—she gives her husband away to him;—and she may thus have seen him (*he* can make that right) for the 1st time. That, from the 1st, sticks in his crop a little and makes him wonder—even while he consents to do what she asks. He doesn't like it—for she, after all, *needn't* have told him—she might have pretexted, or whatever. Thus it lays a kind of basis, from the 1st, for the evolution of his feeling, and the turn of the climax— though, ah me, perhaps, what grand names! x x x x x

April 25th, 1911, 95 Irving St.

And then there is the little fantasy of the young woman (as she came into my head the other month) who remains so devoted to her apparently chronically invalid Mother, so attached to her bedside and so piously and exhaustedly glued there, to her waste of youth and strength and cheer, that certain persons, the doctor, the friend or two, the other relation or two, are unanimous as to the necessity that something be done about it—that is, that the daughter be got away, that she be saved while yet there is time. Say she is 35—or, perhaps (for the mother's being young enough), 32 or 33, and has been fast at her post for 10, 12, 14 years. She has always refused to move, under whatever pressure; she has been almost sublimely *entêtée* about it; but, visibly, she *is* worn and spent, she is withering on the stem—that is, more or less fading and fainting and perishing, at her post. Thus it is that the others intervene—and again I see that the little story must be told *more mea* by a witness, by an agent and spectator, by one of the interveners, interferers, man or woman, but most probably by a man— one of those who have been partly responsible. He relates it as an odd, almost as a droll, case. Well, what happens, by my *concetto*, is that the young woman consents under this extreme benevolent and sympathetic pressure, to *take* the holiday, to go away, to go abroad, for a time—say, as the case is put to her, for 6 months. (Of course the locus must be American—New Englandish.) She resigns herself, makes the effort, goes. It is the person who takes her place *auprès de la mère souffrante* who tells the tale—THAT clearly shines out; THAT is the obviously designated economy. So it goes; only *this* identity for the narrator surely, after all, makes that person a woman. 'I' (narrating) then take my place by the mother, and my poor cousin or whatever, my heroine in short, starts for Europe in consonance with arrangements made for her. What happens in 3 words (for I mustn't draggle *this* out here) is that in the first place Betty or whoever (to give her a stopgap name) doesn't come home in 6 months but prolongs her absence to 12 or 15; and that in the second place, when she does come, she shows herself absolutely detached and indifferent. She has been cured of her devotion—the holiday has acted but too well; the world has entered into her, and to see more of it, and thereby shed and shuffle off her burden, is the one thought that now possesses her. She has, in a word, a wholly changed consciousness, and the change is what I chronicle. That is the *subject* of the small stuff—that I see what we have done and that we have produced our effect only too well. 'The state—*of absolute indifference,* ONLY THAT AT 1ST—we have brought about in her by her experiences *là-bas*—so that what in the world can they, can these have been?' That is but the 1st half of the matter, however; for obviously there must be a development and a supplement, complement, to make a drama and a climax—to complete the case. What then shall this be? It has already come to me: the irony of the thing resides in the effect on the mother of this change of Betty's state. It would of course be in the last degree stupid and ugly and uninteresting that it should be simply a *bad* effect—the effect of the mother's sinking or suffering under neglect or cruelty. I see it as quite *another* effect— I assist at it as such; and therein seems to <be> a very pretty and curious and amusing situation. The mother realises that the daughter doesn't want to come back to her and *is* at 1st wounded, wronged, staggered; but then rallies from that under the effect of circumstances. Won't it be, *inter alia,* that Betty has made a little *héritage,* a sufficient one to give her her freedom if she is disposed to use it? She uses it then—and what the mother rallies under the effects of is the positive fascinations of the new character and new activity that Betty has taken on. Betty's 'heartlessness,' the *degree* of her detachment, itself fascinates her—makes her 'sit up.' She sits up 1st for surprise—then for a sort of resentful and even vindictive curiosity and interest. She becomes in her way as changed, as re-animated (and thereby as capable and convalescent) as Betty herself. My idea, my narrative vision, is that as Betty turns from her she ravenously turns after her. As Betty flees from her she rises from her long sofa and eagerly pursues. The fascinations, the resentment, the bringing B. to justice (partly—and partly the curiosity, the participating) give her that strength. Betty dashes off to Europe again, and before I know it, the mother, shaking *me* clear, has dashed after. I see, I hear of, the elder, following the younger woman like the tail of a kite or a comet. This must go more or less on—it must in fact all go on for 2 or 3 years (I getting echoes, gleams, rumours, reports, glimpses of it) in Europe. Then I see Betty return, breathless, having outstripped her mother. Then I see the mother arrive, breathless also, to overtake, to rejoin, Betty. Then I see Betty start afresh for Europe (dash away absolutely in secret) and, the next thing, see the mother take a following steamer—stream away after her: which makes my climax, the last *recorded* note of the drama and the point where I leave them. The thing necessitates, of course, the *recency* of the record; the narrator's having somehow brought it up to yesterday. That is all there is of it.

May 10th, 1911, 95 Irving St.

Can I catch hold—if it be in the least worth the effort?—of a very small fantasy that came to me the other month in New York?—but which, as I look at <it> a minute or so, seems to say to me that it has almost nothing to give. I mean the little idea about the good little picture in the bad sale, the small true and authentic old thing that the 'hero' of the sale recognizes in a sham collection, a *ramassis* of false attributions that are on show previous to being put up at auction. The idea came to me on my going in to one of the extraordinary places—for the pompous flourishing look in which humbugging masterpieces are offered to view—and recognizing that it was an array of wretched counterfeits and imitations. But the idea seems already to have slipped away—practically. I imagined that in such a show, in such company, after going (very quickly and easily) from one thing to another, I (the person narrating the anecdote) suddenly recognize a little thing which *is* a genuine old master, a primitive, perhaps—or something else, and seeing how lost in the heap, and compromised by its associations it is—pity it for the company it keeps x x x x x But I break down—letting the thing for the moment go.

THE 'K.B.' CASE and 'MRS. MAX'

['K.B.'—as Leon Edel has suggested—may very well refer to Katherine Bronson,[1] whom James had known in Venice. The ensuing discussion, left among James' manuscripts, bears out what he wrote to H. G. Wells in 1902: 'A plan for myself, as copious and developed as possible. I always do draw up . . . a preliminary private outpouring. But this . . . voluminous effusion is, ever, so extremely familiar, confidential and intimate—in the form of an interminable garrulous letter addressed to my own fond fancy—that, though I always, for easy reference, have it carefully typed, it isn't a thing I would willingly expose to any eye but my own.' The notes that Percy Lubbock printed with his editions of The Ivory Tower and The Sense of the Past are fuller examples of James' fertile colloquy with himself.

James seems not to have carried 'The "K.B." Case' beyond the first pages for an opening chapter, though, as we noted in our Introduction, he was to use some of the same names for his characters in The Ivory Tower.]

Note for the 'K.B.' Case

Splendid for the K.B. case that the 'sympathetic American' whom I've been thinking of should come to play the part I want for him in the foreign, in the cosmopolite *milieu*, through this process: that he is brought to see that if he doesn't some other man, *an* other man, will —a particular other dangerous (foreign?—or domestic, *badly* domestic) personage will, and that so it is he decides and, as it were, lends himself, to wear the appearance—which is all *she* wants, as an antidote to her humiliations, and yet save her from the absolute peril of accepting the service from the other fellow, who would, to a certainty, take some base advantage of it. I see him as 'put up' to this—I mean see the situation interpreted and lighted and made clear for him by an indispensable personage of the interpretative appreciative yet functional sort, woman or man, but woman probably, friend of my Heroine's, whom the Action must gather in. Yet, ah, *so* functional too must this

1. See also p. 333 above.

[343]

figure be—in the sense, I mean, of what will depend on it; which is the *only* sense of the functional.

x   x   x   x   x

I just jot down here that I seem to see as *characters* off-hand something like:

> My Heroine
> Her Mother-in-law
> The important Friend—1st in N.Y., then in Florence—(The American Type in Florence).
> The young (unmarried) American girl (in love with Other Man) who beats them so easily both.
> The Foreign Woman (Great Person).
> The Hero (American).
> The Other Man (interested Party) do. (1st 'danger').
> The Foreign Man. 'Danger' (2d).
> The American Husband (Type of the Type).
> The Young Man (English or other attached to the 'Important friend').

> The Hero is the *Cousin* of the Deceased Husband and Young Agent, etc., of the Mother-in-law's Property.

The Mother-in-law, in Book 1, gets her *early* impression of Important Friend—they have Heroine's situation a bit 'out'—and I immediately see, here, how young unmarried New York woman is indispensable, functionally, here—to prepare her effect, etc. The Interested (Other) Man already wants to marry her. She cares nothing for him, but already dreams of Hero, who, she believes, cares nothing for *her*. The Important friend urges her coming abroad (thinks she's not dangerous and *may* be convenient). The Mother-in-law suspects, fears, alone. Isn't 1st scene between Girl (of 25) and Other Man?

Mrs. Max

Anne Drabney ⎱ 1	Horton Crimper ⎱ 4	
(Nan Drabney) ⎰	(Haughty Crimper) ⎰	
Augusta Bradham ⎱ 2	Basil Hunn 5	
(Gussy Bradham) ⎰	Davy Bradham ⎱ 6	
Cissy Foy ⎱ 3	1 Bradham ⎰	
(Cecelia Foy) ⎰	Mrs. Drabney 7	

1. James has crossed out 'Conny (Constant).'

Graham Riser (Gray Riser)		Wenty Hinch	
Fielder		Cantopher	
Finder		Augerer	
Hincher	*Betterman*	Grey Bradham	
Clencham	Harold Rising	Kate Augerer	
Grabham		Cornard Cossingham	
Wrencher	Alan Wrencher	'Cornard Rosemary' [1]	
Grey Riser		Perrot	
Grey Fielder		Romper, Finder, Shimple	
Bright Riser		Moyra Ruddle	
Shimple—Kate Shimple		Bruit, Ode	
Moyra Brandish		Brasher, Oddsley	
Brinting Kate Crimple		Grabham	
Grey Bradham		Mention	
Alan Wrencher		Toyt	
Kate Crimple		Bulpit	
Mr. Betterman		Peregrine (King) (P. Roy)	
Wentworth Hinch			

December 17th, 1909. The receipt of a letter from F. A. Duneka about
a serial Fiction for Harpers comes in at an odd psychological moment
and with an odd psychological coincidence today—when I have been
literally in the very act of sitting down to a statement of the little idea
that I have for these few years past carried in my brooding brain as
the 'K.B.' (Venice) idea—struck out some longish little time ago now
in a talk about K.B. with C.F., who had had for years a great deal of
acute observation of her, and who struck out something, as a little
significant truth of her case, the formulation of an aspect of her situation, which immediately began to shine for me, in an appealing ironic
light, as a little subject, a particular and interesting case indeed, out
of which something might be made. And last winter, when I couldn't
do it, it came up for me again—with *more* of its little vivid intensity,
with developments and a whole picture, relations and elements and
aspects falling into their place and conspiring together; so that at
present it seems quite to cry out to me, with touching clearness and
confidence and trust, to take pity on it and disengage it from its comparative confused limbo; thresh and worry it out a little, see what is
really in it, set it down, in fine, in the old devout sacred way, for appreciation and constructibility, as I haven't hitherto had time or freedom
of mind to do. To this small fond prayer and twitching of my sleeve
on its part I have been, as I say, on the very edge of responding, when

1. This name was added in another hand than James'.

Duneka's letter comes in and seems, I confess, in spite of whatever other hostile preoccupations, rather movingly to force my hand. But I can only consider for the Harpers, at present, the question of a *short novel*—80 to 100 thousand words—and various throbbing possibilities crowd upon me in respect to my working out a plan for the use of this material, and the use of it in the only way in which it seems now pretty clear that I shall henceforth be able, with any vital, or any artistic, economy, to envisage my material at all—that is in the 'dramatic' way. *That* more and more imposes itself, and madness seems to me simply to lie in the direction of the unspeakable running of the '2 hares' at once—by which one means of course alternately. More than ever then, at any rate, does it seem to me worth my while to cipher out the subject of this thing for the possible 'serialised' employment, after the manner of my late so absorbing and endearing plunge into the whole process of the *Outcry* (to say nothing of *tutti quanti*, in the old, the ineffable, the exquisite, the pathetic and tragic 'sacred' days); from the moment, that is, that no *prima facie* presumption of the 'dramatic' value or plasticity of the *donnée* in question doesn't look me at all directly in the face. It doesn't here, thank God; and it doesn't for this reason—that I've seen my stuff—from the moment I began to get at all embracingly nearer to it—as peculiarly (*that's* the point) an Action, and that, for me, now, surely when an Action plants itself before me, it ceases to be a question of whether it '*can*' be Dramatic (in the splendid and whole sense—and in that only—in which I use the word) and becomes a question simply of what other form and *allure* it could conceivably take on. The process of the *Outcry* has been of enormous benefit and interest to me in all this connection—it has cast so large and rich and vivid a light upon my path: the august light, I mean, of the whole matter of method. I don't in the least see thus—beforehand!— how or why my 'K.B.' Case, as I may call it for convenience, should *se soustraire* from the application of that method and not be positively responsive to that treatment. Its having commended itself to me as peculiarly an action from the moment I began really to look at it is an enormous argument in favour of this possibility—and in fact, truly, would seem to settle the question. Of course I myself see *all* my stuff—I mean see it in each case—as an action; but there are degrees and proportions and *kinds* of plasticity—and everything isn't theatrically (using the term scientifically and, ah, so non-vulgarly!) workable to what I call the peculiar and special and ideal tune. At the same time one doesn't know—ideally—till one has got into real close quarters with one's proposition by absolutely ciphering it out, by absolutely putting to the proof and to the test what it will give.

What then do I see my K.B. case, under the pressure and the screw, as susceptible of giving? *Any* way I want to see; but *if* the way that has begun to glimmer and flush before me does appear to justify itself, what infinite *concomitant* advantages and blessings and inspirations will then be involved in it! Porphyro grows faint really as he thinks of them.

Just stated, first of all, in its most crude and lumpish, its most *sommaire* form, then, my question is that of a still youngish and still 'living' American woman who is suddenly thrown upon the world, and upon her first real freedom, by the death of a husband with whom she has had a bad time and as to whom she has yet been, by her nature and her conscience, devoted and irreproachable. She has nursed him through ten years of ill-health brought on by his bad habits —his vices; she has given up her young life, very much, all in New York, so that he should be tended and kept going to his very poor tune at best. She is not, it should be said, a woman considered either very pretty or very clever—but she has a personality (or for some few), a charm of her own. She has some oddity of appearance—something that doesn't attract the *plupart*. But she longs for experience and freedom and initiation—in her own way; she has no children; she has some money—just enough; and she somehow takes for granted, after what has happened, some new freedom and some new chance. The question is what she shall '*do*' (I think she must be 35 *or* 36)—and she's the sort of person (childless—2 children lost) as to whom it's assumed that she *may*—though not too easily—marry again. She has a little money of her own, but the rest depends on her mother-in-law, a figure of importance, *much* importance, in the scheme; the 'rest' being that lady's own fortune, which the deceased son and husband has only had an allowance—a very good allowance—from, during his lifetime, that has all depended on his Mother's discretion. *She* is a person who may possibly still live a longish time.

x   x   x   x   x

January 4th, 1910. I take this up again after an interruption—I in fact throw myself upon it this a.m. under the *secousse* of its being brought home to me even more than I expected that my urgent material reasons for getting settled at productive work again are of the very most imperative. *Je m'entends*—I have had a discomfiture (through a stupid misapprehension of my own, indeed); and I must now take up projected tasks—this long time *entrevus* and brooded over—with the firmest possible hand. I needn't expatiate on this—on the sharp consciousness of this hour of the dimly-dawning New Year, I mean; I simply invoke and appeal to all the powers and forces and divinities to whom I've

[347]

ever been loyal and who haven't failed me yet—after all: never, never yet! Infinitely interesting—and yet somehow with a beautiful sharp poignancy in it that makes it strange and rather exquisitely formidable, as with an unspeakable deep agitation, the whole artistic question that comes up for me in the train of this idea of a new short serial for the Harpers, of the *donnée* for a situation that I began here the other day to fumble out. I mean I come back, I come back yet again and again, to my only seeing it in the dramatic way—as I can only see everything and anything now; the way that filled my mind and floated and uplifted me when a fortnight ago I gave my few indications to Duneka. Momentary sidewinds—things of no real authority—break in every now and then to put their inferior little questions to me; but I come back, I come back, as I say, I all throbbingly and yearningly and passionately, oh, *mon bon,* come back to this way that is clearly the only one in which I can do anything now, and that will open out to me more and more and that has overwhelming reasons pleading all beautifully in its breast. What really happens is that the closer I get to the problem of the application of it in any particular case, the more I get *into* that application, so the more doubts and torments fall away from me, the more I know where I am, the more everything spreads and shines and draws me on and I'm justified of my logic and my passion.

x   x   x   x   x

What I seem to see then is the drawingroom of Mrs. Bradham's New York house on a Sunday afternoon in April or May—three or <four> weeks after her husband's death, and on the first occasion of her ever 'receiving,' in her bereavement and her mourning, even those immediately near her. I make out a number of them there now, and I see by their means my situation constitute and foreshadow itself. I see in other words my Exposition made perfect—see the thing as almost the Prologue, after the manner in which the first Book is the Prologue in *The Other House*. Oh, blest *Other House*, which gives me thus at every step a precedent, a support, a divine little light to walk by. *Causons, causons, mon bon*—oh celestial, soothing, sanctifying process, with all the high sane forces of the sacred time fighting, through it, on my side! Let me fumble it gently and patiently out— with fever and fidget laid to rest—as in all the old enchanted months! It only looms, it only shines and shimmers, *too* beautiful and too interesting; it only hangs there too rich and too full and with too much to give and to pay; it only presents itself too admirably and too vividly, too straight and square and vivid, as a little organic and effective Action. In consequence of my impulse always to make the 1st step of my situation place itself only and exactly where that situation may be conceived as really beginning to show, I seem to have a sight of my 'young unmarried American woman' and my 'Husband of Important Woman—American Husband—type,' as laying together the first squared stones of my basis; this I mean if I can make them functional—and whether I can make them functional I shall be able to worry out only by patiently and wisely fumbling on. It commends itself to my perception at once that Martha Bradham (Bertha Bradham?) must have an appendage or a belonging of some sort—one absolutely foresees the need of that—and the most *like<ly>* sort is embodied for me in this glimmering of the attached and appended Girl, *un peu de ses parents*, whom it's a question of her taking to Europe with her, and whom I see in the forefront on this important, this decisive, Sunday afternoon. It's the What is Nan to do?—it's the How is Nan to live?—it's the Discussion of the Future of Nan, that gives its stamp to the occasion and that I see thus ushered in. I see it, I *have* it so, that I even ask myself—! But *pazienza*, and step by step. The two houses, Mrs. Drabney's and her Daughter's-in-Law, communicate—by a passage along the covered verandah or balcony behind. The two women are at Mrs. Drabney's, looking over old things, young things, of the dead husband's: we have these facts, as we have others, given us by Cissy Foy as she gives them to Davy Bradham, who calls early in the afternoon—rather early—hoping to find his wife, whom he is to pick up there, by arrangement, to call elsewhere, a call of importance and decency (on some one of his people, his aunt) with her. She has not come, but Cissy, bored and unoccupied, waiting, hoping for eventualities of her own, passes the time, the moments, with him—much to our amusement and his; much to our edification and information; much to the illustration of the character and situation of each. Well I lay *dès maintenant* the basis of the question of *de quoi il s'agit*, dramatically and *actionally*, in this first Act. I have already to some extent stated it in speaking of the issue as the question of what Nan Drabney will now 'do'—which comes round a good deal—and part of the function of the act is to show *how* it comes round—to that of what her late husband's traditionally predominant and strenuous mother (with her whole theory of Nan's character, history, situation, liabilities, etc.) takes her stand on in respect to their relation, their common bereavement, their proper observance of it—and her own possible intentions. *She* has (the) money; she is rich; the fortune (hers) being partly her own and partly that left her by her late husband, Maxwell Drabney's Father; left her outright, wholly to dispose of—with an allowance made their son, in whom he had no faith, and whose bad habits, eventuating in the long illness through which Nan has nursed him—ten years of it, ten deadly years, mainly spent in the country—gave him all-sufficient grounds. Nan has some means of her own—enough, in strictness, modestly to live on; with presumptions of a continuation by her mother-in-law of the allowance made to Maxwell. This, and Mrs. Drabney's further and eventual dispositions, testamentary and other, as well as her general attitude and general employment of her own life —and even possible bestowal of her own *hand* (?)—depend much (this is one of the functions of all these preliminary parts to demonstrate) on how Nan—now for the first time free and at all at ease to display herself, attest and reveal herself, 'pans out.' It comes over me that I may find an indispensable use and value for (in) making Mrs. Drabney's own possible remarriage a contributive issue: which demands, however, a bit of looking at. What makes this worth weighing is my glimmering vision of the final grab of her hand and fortune by Horton Crimper—on finding that Nan has dished herself and doesn't get the latter—has every appearance of having it withheld from her in consequence of the events in Florence. But it seems to me that what is determinant—largely—in this connection is Mrs. Max's age; and my action involves her not being less than 35. Say she has been older than her husband by 3 years—that is possible and easy—he will have died at 33. Say they had been married eleven years, and her long sacrifice to him, her incarceration and sequestration with him, have gone on for about 9—upwards of 10. Say accordingly that he—well, say that Mrs. Drabney is 56 at the beginning, or even 55; and she needn't be more. Ah no, stay—if he has died at 32, she, his mother, to have married quite early and had him at 21 or 22, needn't be *more* than 56. There *is* the resource of my making him her *stepson*—whereby he may have died older, and Nan's *épreuve* been longer and harsher— a bigger sacrifice; whereby I can add a valuable year or two—making her 37—to her age. This is worth thinking of, and the only thing against it is the diminution of pious *motive* on that basis—though I think I see a sufficiency of that element as presentable. Mrs. Drabney has had no child—Nan has had two and lost them. Her husband *left* her his son to do her best for—and she has been important about the charge; making him thus her own. Say he was ten when she married his Father; she may have had him all for 15 years, he marrying at 25 and dying at 40. If I don't make Max's long illness the result of vice— but I really think I see this, with its advantages. I can at any rate try it and see how it works out. I *posit* Mrs. Drabney's own marriageability and her suspicion, her circumspection, her jealousy, her exaggerated claim of mourning, on the article of Maxwell's widow. If I make him in fact 'innocent'—only infinitely tiresome and selfish and suffering— I put truth into Mrs. Drabney's motive and into her retroactive sentiments of the order I intend. Cissy Foy puts it that she thinks him, poor Max, *now* so much more wonderful and herself so much more devoted, than was really the case;—just as she also passes the sponge over the extent to which she worked poor Nan during the whole dozen years, and the extent to which poor Nan consented to be workable. Well, so I leave this element; except that I seem to see, the more I think, that Maxwell must have been *good*—only impossible. Isn't Mrs. Drabney's idea that they shall mourn him together in a very crapy and conventional way—and that her step-daughter-in-law shall in particular give herself for an indefinite future time to these rites and this attitude? She makes assumptions of this sort; she is full of them— and *what pervades them all is the sense of Nan's dependence on her for the* LARGER *footing of life.* Nan has her own 7 or 8 thousand (dols.) a year, yes; but the allowance from Mrs. Drabney may be stinted or ample, handsomer or more meagre, or definitely *nil*, according to the manner in which Mrs. Max, at this crisis of her career, presents herself. One of Mrs. Drabney's assumptions is that, united as they are by their bereavement and their mourning, whatever Nan does she does it *with* her. She will go abroad with her—yes, in their common crape; but she'll be startled by any pretension on Nan's part to go alone—as it were; to enjoy herself and see the world. This has come up for Nan—this sense of her own yearning and reaching out, and yet sense of her own oppression; and the Function of this Exposition, as it were, the individual Action of this First, is to clear up the whole air of this question—to present the question, give it its development and deal with it. What is here my particular climax? What is my *dénouement d'acte*? Why, as I see it, that Nan decides, selects, takes to her own feet and invokes her adventure. She decides, that is, to break with Mrs. Drabney, and the latter's companionship and surveillance, to the extent of starting off without her—taking Cissy Foy with her as a companion instead. Everything must contribute to my making this an all efficient objective, as it were, a climax of the right emphasis and promise. My act then, its function and interest and entertainment, consists of the course and process I follow to arrive logically and thrillingly at that determination of the elements. I show by and through what and by and through whom the climax in question is brought about. The persons involved are Mrs. Drabney herself and, for women, Mrs. Bradham and Cissy Foy; and for men Basil Hunn, Horton Crimper, and Davy Bradham. I see the process pretty vividly; it glimmers before me, but it will glimmer more and more; and let me at any rate, *en attendant*, just dash down here provisionally 2 or 3 elements of the matter of which I thus just catch the tip of the tail. Nan is 'in love' with Basil Hunn—for whom she herself has no attraction of that sort whatever. Free now—ah, she'd marry him in a minute; that would be *her* solution of her future. He is her late husband's relative—cousin, a young New York lawyer (*à la* Harry—or older, more developed and more New York); and has had, from considerably back, charge of her own little fortune. She has not spent that, and he has taken care of it for her while she has lived with her sick husband and nursed him, on the income made them by Mrs. Drabney's allowance. Basil Hunn, kind to her, sorry for her, even liking her and feeling interested in her up to a certain point, but not conscious of any real person<al> charm (that appeals to himself) in her, has so fostered her little interests and resources that they have increased and multiplied. He has come to see her this Sunday afternoon for that purpose—she having sent for him. Her recent bereavement (6 or 8 weeks previous—or I think even less) has kept her, Mrs. Drabney's attitude aiding, a bit inaccessible and barricaded hitherto; and this day is a new day, a date or an epoch, marking her re-communications with the outer world. Seizing things, irrespective of their order here as yet and just as they come to me, I seem to see the *clou* of the act (or one of two *clous*) the *scène à faire*, as it were, in this appeal that she makes to him, as a friend as well as a Trustee, to know just where she is, how she may regard her outlook, what feel herself able to do. She doesn't *know* herself, she looks out upon her future with curiosities and anxieties, uncertainties—she feels that he somehow can tell her things, give her informations, warnings, advice, that will help. She *sounds* him, I say, as it were—but only to feel that, kind as he is, there is nothing intimately personal for her to look to from him, and she turns away with a certain pang of disappointment and humiliation. She is really romantic—deeply and foolishly romantic—though she half knows that it doesn't in the least fit her type, and that, given her type, the show of it will make her, *must* make her, more or less ridiculous. She wonders if she is ridiculous to *him*. But she can't find out—he doesn't let her know or show her anything of that kind; he is only awfully obliging and clear and kind and inspeakable <*sic*>—and she (deep within) is in love with him and desirous of him more than ever. It is thus, however, that he really answers the general question that she puts to him, and that is the question of what she had better 'do.' He answers it in the sense, that is, that she is perfectly free to go away—'for all *him!*' She would be willing to stay—she would ask nothing better than to stay—on the least word or hint received from him to the effect that he would like it. She puts to him the question of whether it is important she should be near him (near him is so what she would give her eyes to be) so as to communicate better about her interests; and he smiling, reassuring her, as a little amused at her simplicity, assures her that everything will go on quite as well and easily if she is on the other side of the Atlantic. He even says to her that she'll marry again—says it, without any bad or false note in it, in the key of the seriousness and clearness and kindness and wisdom she has appeared to demand of him. She'll marry again, still young, provided, attractive, interesting as she is: the only thing he hopes is that she won't marry a foreigner. Save for that it will be natural, inevitable, happy. He quite understands what a long ordeal, what a devil of a life she has had—and his idea is all for her having a change, a relief, a new start, etc. This it is that 'settles' her—his very kindness, the very imagination he is so good as to expend on her behalf and as to what will be good for her, has so little of any quality it would so deeply touch her by having. She completely controls herself, observing all the forms of serenity—but the scene is crucial. Don't I therefore all the more want to make something hang in the balance here for her, and with this—the absolute concrete form and dramatic value of the question which it's the function of the Act to present and then push to its solution? To ask this is of course to say immensely, Yes—and what I accordingly want is the most concrete form of my question possible, is the greatest dramatic value the connection will give. Well, pressing gently and firmly in the old ineffable way, I seem to get something like this, which I just note in its main items, the links and *liaisons* of it, and all roughly, first; to catch it.

(1) Nan's quasi-acceptance of her 'fate,' her common mourning, with Mrs. D.—combined with her (romantic) yearning to throw off the oppression of it.

(2) The fact that she would accept anything, any quantity of Mrs. D. now—in order to remain 'near' Basil Hunn, as it were; give up going abroad altogether, or go only with *her* if (through his looking after Mrs. Drabney's affairs too) this might keep her more in touch with him by the chance (Mrs. Drabney's affairs being so much bigger than hers) of its perhaps occasionally bringing him out to her. That they absolutely need have no personal meetings and communions over her own, he has struck her as perfectly emphatic and definite and 'hopeless' about. This is a kind of a blow—and she feels herself then and there, and utterly, give up all hope; and not only this but (since he affects her as absolutely shipping her off) knows, in her bitterness, dissimulated as it is, what moves those women who, slighted, jilted, *dépitées* by the man they have really cared for, respond, by a ricochet, to the advances, to the next one who approaches them. Don't I see her as (tentatively—indirectly and 'delicately,' *vu* her fresh mourning) approached at this juncture or moment by Horton Crimper, who is interested in her 'expectations' and believes in them and wants, as it were, to put down

his name, stick in his pin and reserve his place. He approaches her to give her to understand that when they *can* talk of it—well, there is something that he only wants to say. At the same time he feels that her 'expectations' are much bound up in her keeping well with Mrs. Drabney—and what he is really taking upon himself is to guard that interest. His idea is that they shall go abroad together and that he shall go with them—and that practically is what he proposes to Nan. Under the effect and the impression of her scene with Hunn she rather assents to it—she is responsive partly as she would be under the sting of the *spretae injuria formae* in the other quarter. But he asks from her some definite word—so that he may, as he says, act; something that may serve as a sort of pledge. She says she'll think— she'll let him know—as it might, or may be, before he goes, and he says he'll come back to her—come back, that is, from having tea off in another room into which the scene opens: tea served by Cissy Foy, and at which Davy Bradham, also perhaps his wife and two or three other persons who have 'come round' with Mrs. Drabney (to say nothing of Mrs. D. herself—??? disapprovingly studious of the more or less shocking Cissy—for Cissy is 28) are present. (That tea a great convenience and resource; that tea, and the approach through the other house, and the coming to it thence of those wanting it and yet to whom as by reason of her mourning, Mrs. Drabney doesn't give it—which help the movement of my Act.) *Je dois bien noter* that Horton Crimper has known Max Drabney from early days, and has seen something—a little—of his wife, even under their sequestration during the few previous years, and that he intimates—he shows—that he understands her feeling Mrs. Drabney, and her tie with Mrs. Drabney, rather a burden. He enters into that; he's clever and plausible and agreeable and diplomatic; he's everything but sincere and straight— and everything but in the least *really* cared for by Nan. But he takes for granted the fact, and the importance, of her union with Mrs. Drabney—if only, a little avowedly even, for the benefit of the way the former lives. What he assumes is that she will continue her allowance to Nan—a large allowance; making it the same as she made it to Maxwell; and this even if she (Nan) marries him—an old good friend of her stepson's. What he is really concerned to do is to see that she doesn't marry a foreigner. And he has, as it were, a rendezvous for this—for her last, her reflective word on the 'abroad' plan—before leaving her. What their scene is terminated by belongs to an order of considerations that I haven't yet, in this mere scrambling scrabble, even begun to fumble out. What I at any rate get hold of here is that Mrs. Bradham is now projected upon her, to make her—again *interestedly*, in a great measure—a very different sort of appeal—and one which so

[354]

makes all the difference. It's a sort of 'irony of her fate' that these people—almost every one alike (Basil Hunn and the girl, Cissy Foy, being the main *exceptions*)—see her, and in one way and another try to practise on her, to 'work' her, as a Value; which is what she so awfully little sees herself as being, *really*—though she tries a little, flutteredly, romantically, to take it from them that she *is*—and it's part of her little drama, in its pathos and its 'poignancy'—also a good bit in its comedy and its irony—that she discovers by the demonstration of life, by the demonstration of her adventure, that she isn't. This is what she comes to—what Basil Hunn, at the end, sees her, compassionately, kindly, humanly, sees her come to: this sense, under the discipline of events, that she *isn't* a Value, a hard, fine firm *worldly* Value, at all—by the real measure of such calculations and imaginations as Flora Bradham's—and also, in its degree, Horton Crimper's. *Mrs. Bradham's* motived and interested demonstration to her in Act I reposes on the fallacy (the *vulgar* fallacy on Flora's part) that she is going to be. Well, *here* it is that I seem to want the effect of Basil Hunn—his effect as to determining her accessibility to such an influence, an eloquence, a logic, as Flora Bradham's—give it the additional chance with her of her seeing, of her directly gathering, of her intimately feeling, that there's nothing for her to hope from *him*. Roughly speaking, and so far as this first mixed glimmer goes, I seem to want to put them—her and him—*twice* in presence; once before her scene with Flora B., and once after. It is her scene with him—and I think her first—that *settles* for <her> that she'll lend herself to Flora's representations; make up her mind to see them as attractively determinant. She is to wait to tell her—which involves a second scene (for Flora B.) with her; this second one, after her first with Basil (or shall I call him *Conrad*—Conrad Hunn? does it go?) being the one in which she lets him know how she has closed, in a manner, with the Bradhams, and in which, confirmatory, congratulatory, he strikes her as fairly shipping her off. I seem thus to have a second scene with Flora appointed for her, in which she lets the latter know that she has decided—that she will go. I thus seem to get, for the Act, I note, three *pairs* of scenes, at least; three occasions on which the second scene, later on, in the same place, and in respect to matters, to a question, to an aspect of the situation *entamé* in the first, the second is preappointed; after which at its right moment it takes place. So it is for Nan with Horton Crimper; so it is with her for Flora Bradham; so it is with her for Conrad Hunn. And this leaves out the possibility of something of the same sort for her with Cissy Foy—her Confidante really, all through—besides leaving out the element of Cissy's sentiment for and relation with Horton Crimper—to say nothing of Cissy's expositional scene with Davy Bradham. Above all it doesn't as yet take account of the question of Mrs. Drabney's appearances and aspects—of the way in which my case involves the due and vivid presentation of her; the way in which I seem to see for her, as a pair of clean wheels in the action, a scene with Conrad and a scene with Nan. I seem to want her to be present at some exhibition of Mrs. Bradham's tone and life—to be seen, in a manner, seeing and realising what may lurk in all that picture. But above all it's with Conrad on one side and Nan herself on the other that I see her mainly concerned. She has her sense of the *romantic* in Nan—her sense of the frivolous, of latent laxities and dangers. *Si elle le laisse entrevoir,* or *le laisse deviner,* to Hunn, he is however amused—with even a little sceptical compassionate hope for the poor woman (Nan herself) that she *may* be so qualified. And then there is (what I make out I must lay the ground for) the element of Mrs. Drabney's relation with Horton Crimper—whom (Mrs. D.) my denouement involves his marrying in 4th Act—or being made to successfully cause himself to be accepted by! Perhaps —it comes to me as I go—this qualification of Nan by Mrs. Drabney—this exhibition of her view and attitude—must in a measure come off between the latter and *Crimper* as part of *their* relation—his and Mrs. D.'s—and as expressible by her to him from the moment that they treat together of Nan at all. And that they do so treat together seems invoked, doesn't it, on the face of the matter, in my situation—he taking the favourable view, he *having,* up to Nan's disconcerting (to *him*) contrary determination, taken it, of the two women's remaining and acting together, going to Europe together, with Nan's consequent retention of advantages: that is of pecuniary ones. This is essentially what he has put before Mrs. Max in his scene of approach, scene of intimation to her, scene, as it were, of *sounding* her (as to his own chances, profit and advantage) early in the Act. Don't I—as it just now strikes me?—want to make this passage between these 2 occur after her, Nan's, 1st scene with Hunn, so that with her soreness, her vague hidden *blessure,* as it were, she may be shown as trying to lend herself to Horton's insidious appeal; after the manner of a wounded woman who, even while she hides her wound, turns almost to any kindness. She does just turn faintly to *his*—enough to show the difference as made by Mrs. Bradham's appeal later on—when she has just a little the air of *going back on* what she has first said to him: going back in the *second* scene I imagine between them. Thus do I get Hunn's 1st scene with her placed by my scheme, so far as it seems to shape, rather *early* in the act—and with that, too, in its degree prepared for. I have my provision of Cissy Foy and Davy Bradham there (rich in expositional power) all this time, I must remember—I have *them* there at any rate; and there glimmers upon me as sequent to them the question of the possibility of Mrs. Drabney before any appearance by Nan herself. I postulate this as prepared for—*mayn't* I just, this way, *mon bon?*—1st by Cissy and Davy Bradham together (ah, I see them a little as preparing for *Everything!*) and then Cissy and Horton Crimble (Davy having *gone*, to come back if I want him).

Thus perhaps I get:

i. Cissy Foy, Davy Bradham.
ii. Cissy, Davy, Horton Crimble.
iii. Cissy, Horton Crimble.
iv. Cissy, Horton, Mrs. Drabney.
v. Horton, Mrs. Drabney.

Thus just these first little wavings of the oh so tremulously passionate little old wand (now!) make for me, I feel, a sort of promise of richness and beauty and variety; a sort of portent of the happy presence of the elements. The good days of last August and even my broken September and my better October come back to me with their gage of divine possibilities, and I welcome these to my arms, I press them with unutterable tenderness. I seem to emerge from these recent bad days—the fruit of blind accident (Jan. 1910)—and the prospect clears and flushes, and my poor blest old Genius pats me so admirably and lovingly on the back that I turn, I screw round, and bend my lips to passionately, in my gratitude, kiss its hand. It somehow comes to me that if I have Mrs. Drabney on early, as it were, the relations of place inevitably so determine themselves—shifting a little from what seemed 1st to flush; determine themselves to her being in her daughter-in-law's house—*having* been there till her entrance, with Nan, upstairs; instead of Nan's being, and having been, upstairs with *her* in the older Drabney house. This seems to me to provide better for her, Mrs. D.'s, exit and return, etc.: she goes *back* to her own—and comes *from* it again as I want her—with the immense resource of Cissy Foy's administration of tea in the other rooms—*dans le fond*, etc., aiding and coming in to my aid for almost everything. (I *see* an immense hostility, let me here just parenthetically—bracketedly—throw off, between Cissy and Mrs. Drab—[Cissy *calls* them Mrs. Max and Mrs. Drab]; and it's a sharp little element of the matter that if, or when, the determination of Nan's choice and preference takes place—her virtual rupture with Mrs. Drab on the 'Europe' ground—the alternative presented by her to her mother-in-law is that of *Cissy's* companionship, countenance and comfort; her starting forth, as it were, under Cissy's guidance. Cissy has been a great deal in Europe—Cissy *knows*; above all she *thinks* she knows. Mrs. Drab immensely *se méfie d'elle*. She is archi-modern; she is the Europeanized American girl. She is

Julia Tucker—of the *neiges d'antan*. Oh, how *pretty* it seems to me all this can be!) But I, just before I knock off to go out (Jan. 14th, 1910), clutch the tip of the tail of *this*, that I have—*may* have—here my vii as between Mrs. Drab and Conrad Hunn. This makes:

vi. Mrs. Drab, Horton, Hunn.

vii. Mrs. Drab, Hunn.

Shan't I—all speculatively!—have provided for Crimper's exit (and return) by an understanding on his part with Cissy that he will join her there at tea? Or even join her *chez* Mrs. Drab (work this out as a convenience).

viii. Mrs. Drab, Hunn, Nan. Mrs. Drab goes off on *arrangement* with Hunn—previous to Nan's entrance—that she shall see him again. She goes to her own house and own people—and when he has had his scene with Nan *he* goes to Cissy Foy. That is, he has his scene with Nan—and she asks him to wait—to go to tea with Cissy. Yes—that's right. Crimper comes in, comes back to Nan—yes, that's it—*after—on*—her scene with Hunn; and then it is that Hunn's exit is determined. He does what both the women have asked of him—he goes to wait. Crimper then has his scene with Nan—unless I can avoid these 2's and 2's—*all* 2's and 2's—run *something* of this together. Let me see at any rate (as I've already seen it) what it makes. It makes viii, as I say, Mrs. Drab, Hunn, Nan. And then:—

ix. Nan, Hunn, with:—

x. Nan, Hunn, Crimper (Hunn's Exit) and:—

xi. Nan, Crimper.

She arranges for his return. He goes out. *He rejoins Mrs. Drab.* But he doesn't do this till Flora Bradham arrives; and I think I see the Part, the ½ Book, end—that is, the Act reach its mid-moment—with the arrival of Flora Bradham prepared for—*immensely* prepared for—by Cissy and Davy. This determines Horton's exit and leaves Nan and Flora face to face. So the Part terminates, making Scene xii and having xiii started.

[*At this point James began a draft for the first chapter of 'Mrs. Max.'*]

I

Cissy Foy was to see afterwards how the whole history, the succession of interesting, if often bewildering, matters to be eventually unfolded to her sense, had exactly taken its start with Davy Bradham's turning up in Madison Avenue that Sunday afternoon of the eventful Spring and finding her more or less in charge of the situation. Mrs. Drab, as she was apt a trifle cynically to call her Cousin Nan's immediate neighbour and ostensible mother-in-law—Mrs. Drabney more properly speaking—had appointed the earlier hours of the day for an 'overhauling' (as Cissy's irreverence again viewed the circumstance) of material memories, intimate properties, sacred relics; the process above stairs and in the adjacent house (from which, on two floors, an aperture had been made, for convenience, within recent years) had apparently dragged itself out, so that Nan wasn't yet back to preside at luncheon for her guest and this young woman had but vaguely nibbled in solitude. The two others, the bereaved wife and the afflicted and deprived stepmother—as Mrs. Drab merely was, after all—were still occupied together in the melancholy rite; in spite of which, let me add, Cissy had begun to flatter herself, with Mr. Bradham's arrival, that the occasion wouldn't hang heavy on her hands. She had her particular view of it—a little project of her own that would be put to the proof—and was sharply interested in this distinctly bold experiment. Though she had been but a fortnight in the house—having joined her distressed relative there a month after Maxwell Drabney's death and when his own people, great ralliers at dreary junctures and at such almost only, had had time to disperse—she had begun to believe that she saw her way, and that her happy thought, one of the happiest she had ever had, was going, as she would have said, to be put through. This conviction quickened and enriched for her the charming gathered light of the end of April, reflected at a hundred points, to an effect of high elegance and cheer, by poor long-suffering dismally dead Max's relinquished 'things'; which he had enjoyed so little in life, but which it was Cissy Foy's private intention that as many of his survivors as possible, and his sacrificed wife most of all, who had profited by them quite as little, and without his so good and so tragic reasons for it, should now proceed to testify to the value of —hideous after all as some of the objects were. Yes, she thought most of them dreadful—as how couldn't things be toward the acquisition of which Mrs. Drab had had a voice?—but their type of ugliness didn't invalidate them as resources, and to the appraisement of resources in general Cissy's own difficult history had been such as to direct her very straight.

Even New York itself, at any rate, was pretty enough for almost anything on such a day and in that quarter; a positively crude atmospheric optimism broke in with the shining afternoon—to the degree even of causing Mr. Bradham to figure fairly as a promise of help. He had never in his life, she felt sure, presented himself under that aspect to anyone, but she had her present reasons for quite clutching at him, and as he appeared she tossed down her lemon-covered French volume (not of fiction, but of criticism: she paid the awful shade of Mrs. Drab, which always loomed there, the tribute of this discrimination) without even sticking in a folder. It was impossible to give less the impression of a weight to apply than this sleek image of social accommodation; but her impulse was none the less to press him on the spot into her service. He immediately explained that he had been expecting to find his wife with Mrs. Max—they were to pay a call together, and his instructions had been definite: he was to pick her up there not later than four, she coming on from some place where she would have lunched. The quarter past four had sounded, but bringing with it of course no Flora; something abject in his surrender to the possible further implications of which fact was noted by Cissy as a fresh example of his inveterate humility as a husband. Whatever her husband should be, poor man, he wasn't to be humble after the conspicuous Bradham fashion, and nothing could prove better that Flora wasn't 'really clever' than that she should so little mind having reduced him to such a state in the eyes of those nations of the earth whose society they frequented. No society worth speaking of could be anything but disagreeably affected by the humble husband—when it didn't feel him, that is, either as preparing his revenge or as doing penance for his crimes. She didn't believe in Davy's crimes, though crimes in general so interested her that she was easily disposed to 'posit' them; the only question left therefore was whether he would ever be capable of revenge. If he would help her to what *she* wanted she would be willing to help him to that. But did he suffer? She doubted it—though there might some day be fun in finding out that he exquisitely did. He took refuge at any rate meanwhile in the appearance of thinking Flora very very nearly as fine as she clearly thought herself.

THE SENSE OF THE PAST

[*James gave up work on* The Sense of the Past *in 1900 (see p. 302 above) after he had written two and a half sections and had carried the story to the middle of the hero's talk with the Ambassador, who was drawn, as appears here, from James Russell Lowell. But the 'fine little silver thread of association' kept the idea dangling in his mind, and in the winter of 1914 he took it up again, 'having found,' says Mr. Lubbock, 'that in the conditions he could not then go on with* The Ivory Tower *and hoping that he might be able to work upon a story of remote and phantasmal life.' He sent to Rye for the original manuscript and while waiting for it wrote this 'preliminary' sketch for the novel. Later, after he had revised what he had written in 1900, he drew up a fuller statement of his plan, which was published in 1917, as an appendix to the unfinished book. In the novel he stuck to his first idea of showing 'the modern young man in a bygone world,' made the '1820 young man' an American, and gave up the brevity he had once hoped for. In 1900 he had felt that for the sake of 'simplification' the story must be told in the first person, but he abandoned this when he realized that too much compression would prevent the full expression of his theme. He needed space to bring out adequately the central point—the revelation of his 'hero,' translated in time, who is a source of 'terror' to the other characters as well as the victim of it himself, a man at once haunting and haunted.*]

First Statement: (Preliminary)

The idea of trying if something won't still be done with it has come back to me within a few days, under pressure of our present disconcerting conditions, and yet the desire, combined with that pressure, and forming indeed part of it, to try and get back to some form of work adjustable in a manner to one's present state of consciousness. I put the old beginning away, under frustration at the time, with a sense that there was something in it, a good deal in fact, of its kind, and it now rises a bit confusedly, and even dimly before me, as matter for possible experiment. I remember both the interest with which it inspired me and the sense of an intimate difficulty connected with it, which it would be yet splendid, however, to overcome, and how I just groped my way into it, a certain number of steps over the threshold, as it were, after a somewhat loose and speculative, perhaps also somewhat sceptical, fashion. When I get my old MS. beginning back I must try to recapture some sort of little grasp of my specific idea. It was complicated—I remember that I felt that, which however more inspired than discouraged: the beauty of it was just that it was complicated, if it shouldn't prove too much so to become splendidly clear, that is to give out all its value of intention. With the somewhat treacherous, or at least considerate, failure of further backing from Rottingdean, I remember suddenly coming to a stop—the thing was too difficult to try on a mere chance, and it appeared to be only in the name of a mere chance, after all, that I had been set in motion. So I put my beginning piously away—though as I seem to find now with a fine, fine little silver thread of association serving to let it dangle in the chamber of the mind. To jump straight to where I seem to recollect having got to and stopped, I see my young man, the hero of the thing, the young American primarily conceived and presented, coming to tell his story to the American Minister (of the period of Ministers, though I had dear J.R.L. in mind as his suppositious listener and critic); *there* it was, about in the middle of that interview, as I remember, that the pen dropped, so to speak, from my hand—partly because of my hearing, stupidly and vulgarly, as I thought, from the Doubleday man, and partly, no doubt, by reason of the rather sharp incidence there of a projected hard knot or two that would have to be as sharply faced and untied. I saw, so far as I remember, the young man's call at the Legation, his extraordinary closeting with J.R.L., as the end and climax of what was to figure as my Introduction or Prologue; which presented itself as of not inconsiderable length, and the jump from which to the far off time, from the present period to the 'Past,' involved in the title, was going to have to be somehow bridged. I don't think I quite saw the bridge; I was groping my way to it with difficulty—and there it was at any rate, as I say, that I gave up insisting. The recovery and reperusal of my MS., and above all the re-writing of it, if in face of the test of renewed acquaintance this seems worth while, will doubtless bring back some of my intentions to me—to which I have during all these years lost the clue. I ask myself for instance what the purpose, the conscious ground or necessity, of the visit to J.R.L., the particular reason for it in a word, may have very exactly been. I recollect thinking it at the time a happy dodge, a very good way of providing for, or, so to speak, against, what was immediately next to come; yet only dimly, dimly now, while I thus vaguely recur to it, does the workable connection seem to come. The scene occurs after what has taken place a night or two before in the empty house in the old London Square: the phenomenon on which the whole thing hinges: namely, the sight by my hero of the young man of the portrait, the full length portrait he has so fondly and intently studied—the sight of him one night that he goes back and lets himself in quietly, and passes upstairs, the sight of him in the room, the other room, with a door and a vista open between them, standing there as in life and looking at him and then moving toward him. I seem to remember that I ended my chapter, or dropped my curtain, with that effect—beyond which nothing directly or, so to speak, crudely related could go; and resorted for the sequel to what my young man comes to the Minister to relate, as his prodigious and unprecedented case. It's all difficult to recover; too far from me and not without the aid of what I at the time wrote to be brought really nearer. Still I like just to play with it and sniff or hover about it a little, just to see what may, under a fond pleading invitation, come back a little of itself. My idea of course—and that's what seems to me really so fine—that of the exchange of identity between my young American of today and his relative of upwards of a hundred years ago, or whatever, on the ground of the latter's reviving for the former under the prodigy of the actual man's so intense and so invoked and so fostered historic faculty, clumsily so to dub it, or in other words his sense of the past, the thing he has always wanted to have still more than historic records can give it, the thing forming the title, as the early part of the Introduction gives it, of the remarkable Essay or Study that he has published, a distinguished and striking little effort, and which we have learnt about to begin with. Yes, it glimmers back to me that at sight of the picture in the London house—all his comings back to see which, to come in for which, have also from the first been dealt with—he has had the extraordinary emotion of recognizing himself, his very self in the person of an ancestor, as if nothing but his clothes had been altered, to the dress of the time, and it is himself who looks out recognizingly *at* himself, just as the so interestingly painted image looks out recognizingly at *him*. My fantastic idea deals then with the phenomenon of the conscious and understood fusion, or exchange, that takes place between them; in connection with which I seize again the tip of the tail of the notion which seemed, which *must* have seemed to me a superior find, and which makes the basis, the mechanism or the logic, so to speak, of the prodigy. My actual young man, my young yearning and budding historian, who in the first chapter of all has been rejected by the young woman in New York (was she a young widow?—I forget!) because her heart is set all on a man of action and adventure, some sort of a type like that, and not on a sedentary student or whatever, my young man, I briefly note again, has been galled and humiliated by this attitude in her and I kind of make out that he has parted with her on a sort of understanding that she may be open to conquest, or to another appeal, if he succeeds in having about as great an adventure, and coming through with it, as any man ever had—or rather a much greater. I see he can't have known of course at all at that moment what this was going to be; the chapter with the young woman serves at any rate in my MS. as the introduction to the Introduction. Well, the sublime idea thrown up by the passage in the London house comes back to me as *this:* that there, face to face with my tremendously engaged and interested hero is this *alter ego* of a past generation of his 'race,' the inward passion of whose also yearning mind and imagination was the sense of the future—he having so nursed and cherished that, wanted so to project himself into it, that it makes him the very counterpart of his eventual descendant. It may be that they are not ascendant and descendant, but only collaterals, so to speak—that's a detail of no importance now. The strain of blood may be none the less effective in producing the relation—a minor question, as I say. What is involved in my prodigy, and makes the real drama, story or situation of it, is that one or the other of the young men in consequence of what so supernaturally passes between them, steps back or steps forward, into the life of the other exactly as that life is at that moment constituted, at that moment going on and being enacted, representing each the other for the persons, the society about him, concerned but with the double consciousness the representation of which makes the thrill and the curiosity of the affair, the consciousness of being the other and yet himself also, of being himself and yet the other also. What appealed to me as of an intensely effective note of the supernatural and sinister kind was this secret within his breast, that is within the hero's breast (for the two, in the 'situation,' are reduced to one) of his abnormal nature and of the effect on others that a dim, vague, attached and yet rather dreadful and distressful sense of it produces on *them*. I might be a little handicapped if I chose to think so by the fact of my having made use of a scrap of that fantasy in *The Jolly Corner*—distinctly do I remember saying to myself in writing that thing that I was filching in a small way this present put-away one and might conceivably afterwards regret it. But I don't mean to regret it if I prove not to want to, or to consider my idea at all compromised by the *J.C.*: the whole thing is so different and so much more ample, and precautions in short can be taken. Let the above rough indication of the core of the thing serve for the moment: the point is that it brings me at once of course to the action, its very self, of my drama: that is, takes up my hero in the alien, the borrowed, the 'past,' as I at first took it for granted, situation, and shows what he makes of it. The situation has of course to be intensely concrete, intensely exhibitional, compact and rounded, the exact right case. *But* here I am nose to nose with *the* difficulty, the crucial, the one I felt awaiting me, and that I seemed to hold off from, in imagination, as if for very dread. The production of the 'old world' atmosphere, the constitution of the precise milieu and tone I wanted, that seemed so difficult in anything of a short compass, and the book in question oughtn't at the very biggest stretch to exceed a hundred thousand words. Eighty thousand would be better—but that's again a detail. Now I remember beating about for the possible apprehension of an alternative—not the showing of the modern young man in the other world, to put it bravely, but the showing of the ancient young man in the actual; this because it would seem easier to do. The other on the other hand was what I first took for granted —and contains much more, probably, the true fruits of one's idea. In fact it stands out, from the moment one gets at all nearer and nearer, as the only form or aspect that *can* give what I want; and I have a sort of feeling already even, on taking up the old faded fancy again, that the intrinsic difficulties *must* probably yield to soft persistent and penetrating pressure, if this be but rightly applied. I think my passage from what I figure as the meeting of the two young men, each the *alter ego* of the other, as I conceive it, to the report of that matter by the living one, so to discriminate, to the extremely bewildered and confounded, yet extremely interested Minister, a really admirable *coup*, for my getting on, and not to be feared, the more it hovers before me, as putting too formidably the question of a transition in itself. If I can but do it as I seem to see it, it will need no transition but the 'jump,' as I figure the matter; its own effective climax, *if* perfectly effective, furnishing all the preparation, all the bridge over, that I shall require. What does he come to see the Minister *for?* I ask above: why, he comes to see him as a man on the eve of a great adventure, from which he perhaps may and perhaps mayn't return, takes certain precautions in advance, gives as it were, in some responsible or possibly in the event helpful quarter, some account of what he may intend or incur; so that in a word there may be some record or clue. In short I have this perfectly present; and I see as immediately sequent and making a new Book, as I suppose I should call it, our vision of him as transported a hundred years back and engaged in the 'then,' the then living and playing complexity of the particular case, the case of his *alter ego* of 1820, say. Turning it over I don't see why 1820 shouldn't respond to my need without the complication of my going further back. I want the moment of time to be far enough off for the complete old-world sense, and yet not so far as to be worrying from the point of view of aspects, appearances, details of tone, of life in general; accordingly if I see my 'present' hour, as really recent, as of 1910, say, I get upwards of a century of 'difference,' which is in all conscience enough—with the comparative nearness so simplifying certain apprehended difficulties.

Well then, what *is* the personal and then existing situation or predicament into which my young man emerges as from below, after the fashion of a swimmer who has dived or sunk or been dragged down for the minute and who comes up to the surface, recovering breath with difficulty at first and then gets by a few strokes more onto the fact of terra firma, where he feels his feet and can stand erect and look about and know where he is? Without my absent MS. I feel I lack a helpful hint or two as to this—though I must remember also how little, up to where my sketchiness had got, I had in the least consistently worked that question out. Roughly, roughly I now recover it, it seemed to come, though very unponderedly, to something like *this:* in connection with which my approach to which, however, I must at once mention, what I think I haven't hereabove, that my notion must have been quite that the 1820 young man, the real one, had anticipated more or less exactly the act or the fact of the 1910; that is, had done just what the latter is doing; which at once, I have to keep straight before me, has to make him a young American too. There immediately crops up a vision of 'difficulty'—which I am not however going for a moment to allow to worry me. They are easily settled from the moment I have so rigidly to respect my limits of space, and thereby my absolute, which I may call also admirable, need to generalise and foreshorten, to take all helpful leaps and jumps. The 'romantic' of course has essentially to be allowed for, but what on earth is the whole thing but the pure essence of the romantic and to be bravely faced and exploited as such? *Romantically* therefore I face the music, as I say, and get over any obstacle by simply working that note or grasping, so to speak, squeezing as hard as I can, that nettle. If asked what sort of young American it could be who in 1820 would come over to make the acquaintance of English relations, come over, that is, so comparatively soon after the wars and animosities between the two countries, I either make up my mind that 1820 isn't, or wasn't, too soon, or that my young man was, like so many, many thousands of his countrymen and above all townsmen, for he comes indispensably from New York, of Tory or Loyalist brood, and therefore never really effectively dissevered. The trouble, in a manner, with this would be that the Loyalists were all ruined, banished or scattered, and that his therefore coming from the States in anything like

[366]

that character at that period, 'swears' somewhat with the public and historic facts. However, the question is *la moindre des choses*; the merest flicker of ingenuity can settle it. In 1820, after all, more than thirty-five years had elapsed since the end of the Revolution, and even if the 'family,' the people in question, had been gravely incommoded and dispersed Loyalists, they may within the term of years have come back to the country and recovered themselves, various possibilities aiding; or otherwise a different footing is conceivable and arrangeable. What the footing was is a part, that is a touch or two, of what my modern young man communicated to the American Minister. I put it in there as I may, I put it in enough—as part of what he has entered into possession of at the nocturnal meeting in the London house—the London house in which, with the aid probably of a villa out of town, near town by our measure now, but quite rurally out of it then, the action of my affair takes place. Let me at any rate get at once to the point that I want most of all to express to myself, to make my little statement of as the very central beauty of the thing—this not to postpone it for the moment to anything else, everything else being so placeable and arrangeable, as I hope I don't too fatuously think, in relation to it. What his miraculous excursion into the past, his escapade into the world of that Sense of it that he has so yearned for, what it does to him most of all, he speedily becomes aware with sick dismay, is to make him feel far more off and lost, far more scared, as it were, and terrified, far more *horribly*, that is, painfully and nostalgically misplaced and disconnected, than had ever entered into the play of his imagination about the matter. His whole preconception has been that it would, that it should, be an excursion and nothing more, from which as by the pressure of a spring or a stop, the use of some effective password or charm, he might get out and away again, get back to his own proper consciousness, his own time and place and relation to things. What is terrible, he perceives after a bit, is that he feels immersed and shut in, lost and damned, as it were, beyond all rescue; and that in proportion as this is the case his relation to the other actors in the drama into the centre of which he, as I have said, crops or pops up, becomes of the last difficulty and dreadfulness, of something that I like to figure him thinking of as the most appalling danger. Just *with* which it is that I put my finger on what originally struck me as the very centre of my subject, and the element in it that I spoke hereabove of my having a bit discounted in the stuff of the *Jolly Corner*. The most intimate idea of *that* is that my hero's adventure there takes the form so to speak of his turning the tables, as I think I called it, on a 'ghost' or whatever, a visiting or haunting apparition otherwise qualified to appal *him*; and thereby winning a sort of victory by the appearance, and the evidence, that this personage or presence was more overwhelmingly affected by him than he by *it*. That is what the analogy amounts to—but let me dismiss any sense of inconvenience from it once for all. I have free use of everything I originally caught at in that connection on behalf of my present youth. He feels, after he has a bit taken things in, the particular things about him, he feels *cut off*, as I say, and lost: he is only too much immersed and associated and identified, and that—he couldn't 'realise' it till he should know how it felt—fills him with an anguish that it seems to him he can neither betray nor suppress. If he betrays it and thereby, so to speak, who and what he really is, he is in danger of passing for a madman, or some unspeakable kind of supernatural traitor, to others, and if he accepts the situation, that is, accepts the terror of his consciousness, he becomes the same sort of thing to himself. But what I seem to myself to have wanted most of all is to represent the drama of the whole outward effect (merely outward up to a certain point) of his 'success'; its effect in making him, for all his precautions, his successful ones, seem different and strange, at first attractively strange, to the others and then this in a degree and to a tune that becomes sinister to them, as who should say, even while he wants, for dear life, also, as who should say, to keep it from doing so; intensely wanting as he does to keep things consonant to his safety, his recovery, so to speak, his escape, that is, his return to his own age. His homesickness, as it were, becomes, as I say, appalling, and to fall short of escape identical for him, as it seems, with damnation. In short I see all there is and may be made to be in this; or shall, that is, when I have disposed of a question still hanging about it, but which indeed the only way probably to dispose of is by bringing to the concrete, absolutely, the relation with him, or the inter-relations, of the 'others,' the persons, the three or four, the four or five at most, for I can't afford space for many, in whom my 'rounded' action is embodied. Well then, roughly and roughly enough, what I seemed to see was his intermixture with two sisters, his relatives, though distant, as it were—meaning when I say 'his' those of the real young man of 1820; for whom, to put it platitudinously, they so completely, and yet so more and more worriedly, take him. What I saw without working it out was that he must somehow from the first have found himself in question as the suitor, as the pretended and predestined, of one of the sisters, but not of the one he finds himself caring for most. I haven't got at all at the machinery of this —that must come, and will, being but a matter of ingenuity, but what my *donnée* seemed to be giving me when I left it so many years ago was that they both fall in love with him, that the one designed for him is the wrong one by his measure, that she expresses her state of feeling, that the other, the 'sacrificed' one, doesn't and hasn't and can't, and is thereby but the more sacrificed—she however being contracted by her family to another young man, whom she doesn't like, whom she likes still less from the moment she has seen *ours* and who forms one of my 4 or 5 figures. I see a mother, a hard, pretty awful, and awful to the tune of 1820, mother—the father being dead; and I see, provisionally, such two or three other subsidiary figures. Above all I see—

THE AMBASSADORS

[James wrote to Wells in the fall of 1902: 'Those wondrous . . . preliminary statements (of my fictions that are to be) don't really exist in any form in which they can be imparted. I think I know to whom you allude as having seen their semblance—and indeed their very substance; but in two exceptional (as it were) cases. In these cases what was seen was the statement drawn up on the basis of the serialization of the work—drawn up in one case with extreme detail and at extreme length (in 20,000 words!) Pinker [1] saw that: it referred to a long novel, afterwards (this more than a year) written and finished, but not yet, to my great inconvenience, published; but it went more than two years ago to America, to the Harpers, and there remained and has probably been destroyed. Were it here I would with pleasure transmit it to you; for, though I say it who should not, it was, the statement, full and vivid, I think, as a statement could be, of a subject as worked out.'

This 'project' for The Ambassadors was not destroyed, although James says in this same letter that he himself did away with the comparable but shorter outline for The Wings of the Dove, since that novel having failed of serialization, he had 'no occasion to preserve' its synopsis. The following 'scenario' is therefore unique among James' manuscripts, and lets us have, for the work that he regarded as his best, four successive visions of it: his first record of its 'germ' (p. 225 above), this detailed synopsis, the novel itself, and the preface that he composed six or seven years after the book's completion.

The detailed comparison among these successive stages of The Ambassadors must be left to the reader, but it may be noted that the 'scenario' contains James' amplest account of how a 'dropped seed' germinated, as well as a revelatory indication of how much the physical setting for Howells' remark in 'the old-fashioned' part of Paris contributed to the stimulus to James' imagination. The synopsis itself is the most substantial example of the thoroughness with which he worked out his donnée. He made concrete for himself all the relevant elements in his characters' backgrounds—why he chose such a city as Worcester for the prototype of his Woollett, where the Newsomes' money came from, and so on. In some instances, as in the details of

1. James' literary agent.

Maria Gostrey's occupation as a special kind of guide to Europe, he put more into his outline than into his finished book. The fact that he had established so solidly all the documentation for the Pococks, the new 'ambassadors' who replace Strether, enabled him, when he came to that phase, to work with a much lighter hand than the outline suggests.

The most conspicuous omission of a theme dwelt on both in James' initial notebook entry and in the synopsis is Strether's failure to have understood with enough sympathy his own long since dead son. Strether's regret for this failure was to have been one of the contributory causes for his eagerness to do justice now to Chad's situation, as it unfolds unexpectedly before him. But in the novel the deaths of Strether's wife and son are barely mentioned, and the son is described merely as a 'little dull' schoolboy whom Strether had neglected in his grief for his wife. These losses are signs of Strether's general failure to have 'lived' hitherto, but James seems to have decided that any development of Strether's sense of what he had neglected and lost would have carried his story too far afield. Nevertheless, the strength with which James had imagined Strether's regret, though unexpressed in the novel, added to the intensity with which he did express there Strether's belated Indian summer of awakening. In a comparable, though more indirect, manner, James' feeling for 'the old houses' of Paris entered into his portrayal of Madame de Vionnet's house and the quality of life which emanated from it.

As he created the structure of his novel, James altered his proposed order and treatment of several episodes. Strether encounters first Maria Gostrey, not Waymarsh, and it is to her that he first mentions Chad's situation—both changes designed to utilize Maria's function as a ficelle. In the portion after the arrival of the Pococks, the final third of the novel, James showed a masterly foreshortening by such significant changes as making Sarah Pocock deliver her ultimatum and break with Strether before and not after his glimpse of Chad and Madame de Vionnet together on the river, and by arranging in a different sequence the final conversations between Strether and Madame de Vionnet and between Strether and Chad.

In the act of composing his serial, James also utilized his stipulated option of twelve rather than ten parts, and went about thirty-five thousand words above his outside limit of a hundred and twenty thousand. At many points, quite beyond the possibility of any synopsis to suggest, he solved his technical problems in a way that made a virtue out of the necessity of the serial form. His whole first part or book at Chester is a unit that strikes the theme of 'Europe,' and his successive climaxes are handled deftly within the limitations of a month's installment.

Particularly skillful is Chad's first entrance, at the back of Strether's and Maria's box at the Comédie. The climax of one chapter consists of Strether's intense awareness of his presence, and then, at the play's conclusion, comes the end of the installment, and the anticipatory break of a month before Strether's first talk with him. To such an extent could James make the acceptance of even the unlikely conventions of serialization a challenge to his 'architectural' balance of form.

That being the case, H. M. Alden's memo for Harper's on James' 'project' is a masterpiece of miscomprehension: "The scenario is interesting, but it does not promise a popular novel. The tissues of it are too subtly fine for general appreciation. It is subjective, fold within fold of a complex mental web, in which the reader is lost if his much-wearied attention falters. A good proportion of the characters are American, but the scene is chiefly in Paris. The story (in its mere plot) centres about an American youth in Paris who has been captivated by a charming French woman (separated from her husband) and the critical situations are developed in connection with the efforts of his friends and relatives to rescue him. The moral in the end is that he is better off in this captivity than in the conditions to which his friends would restore him. I do not advise acceptance. We ought to do better.'

One could hardly ask for a more distilled expression of the problems encountered by an artist in dealing with the editor of a 'popular' magazine. All the stock prejudices against James' international material are there, and no indication that Strether, whose central consciousness marks James' final perfection of his method, even figures in the novel. Nevertheless, The Ambassadors, after long delay, was ultimately serialized in the North American Review (January–December 1903).

James' heading for his manuscript read 'Project of Novel by Henry James.']

It occurs to me that it may conduce to interest to begin with a mention of the comparatively small matter that gave me, in this case, the germ of my subject—as it is very often comparatively small matters that do this; and as, at any rate, the little incident in question formed, for my convenience, my starting-point, on my first sketching the whole idea for myself.

A friend (of perceptions almost as profound as my own!) had spoken to me, then—and really not measuring how much it would strike me or I should see in it—something that had come under his observation a short time before, in Paris. He had found himself, one Sunday afternoon, with various other people, in the charming old garden attached to the house of a friend (also a friend of mine) in a particularly old-fashioned and pleasantly quiet part of the town; a garden that, with two or three others of the same sort near it, I myself knew, so that I could easily focus the setting. The old houses of the Faubourg St.-Germain close round their gardens and shut them in, so that you don't see them from the street—only overlook them from all sorts of picturesque excrescences in the rear. I had a marked recollection of one of these wondrous concealed corners in especial, which was contiguous to the one mentioned by my friend: I used to know, many years ago, an ancient lady, long since dead, who lived in the house to which it belonged and whom, also on Sunday afternoons, I used to go to see. On one side of that one was another, visible from my old lady's windows, which was attached to a great convent of which I have forgotten the name, and which I think was one of the places of training for young missionary priests, whom we used to look down on as they strolled, always with a book in hand, in the straight alleys. It endeared to me, I recall, the house in question—the one where I used to call—that Madame Récamier had finally lived and died in an apartment of the *rez-de-chaussée;* that my ancient friend had known her and waited on her last days; and that the latter gave me a strange and touching image of her as she lay there dying, blind, and bereft of Chateaubriand, who was already dead. But I mention these slightly irrelevant things only to show that I *saw* the scene of my young friend's anecdote.

This anecdote then—to come to it—was simply in something said to him, on the spot and on the occasion, by a person who had joined the little party in his company and who was still another acquaintance of my own: an American, distinguished and mature, who had been in Europe before, but comparatively little and very 'quietly,' and to whom, at all events, the note of everything that actually surrounded them in the charming place was practically as new, as up-to-that-time-unrevealed (as one may say) as it was picturesque and agreeable. This rather fatigued and alien compatriot, whose wholly, exclusively professional career had been a long, hard strain, and who could only be—given the place, people, tone, talk, circumstances—extremely 'out of it' all, struck my reporter as at first watching the situation in rather a brooding, depressed and uneasy way; which my reporter, moreover, quite followed, allowed for and understood. He understood and followed still better when our preoccupied friend happened at last, under some determining impression, some accumulation of suggestions, to lay his hand on his shoulder and make him the small speech from the echo of which my subject took its flight. But think of the place itself again first—the charming June afternoon in Paris, the tea under the trees, the 'intimate' nook, consecrated to 'artistic and literary' talk,

[373]

types, freedoms of (for the *désorienté* elderly American) an unprecedented sort; think above all of the so-possible presence of a charming
woman or two, of peculiarly 'European' tradition, such as it had never
yet been given him to encounter. Well, this is what the whole thing,
as with a slow rush the sense of it came over him, made him say:—
'Oh, *you're* young, you're blessedly young—be glad of it; be glad of it
and *live*. Live all you can: it's a mistake not to. It doesn't so much
matter what you do—but live. This place and these impressions, as well
as many of those, for so many days, of So-and-So's and So-and-So's
life, that I've been receiving and that have had their abundant message,
make it all come over me. I see it now. I haven't done so enough
before—and now I'm old; I'm, at any rate, too old for what I see. Oh,
I *do* see, at least—I see a lot. It's too late. It has gone past me. I've lost
it. It couldn't, no doubt, have been different for me—for one's life takes
a form and holds one: one lives as one can. But the point is that
you have time. That's the great thing. You're, as I say, damn you, so
luckily, so happily, so hatefully young. Don't be stupid. Of course I
don't dream you *are*, or I shouldn't be saying these awful things to
you. Don't, at any rate, make *my* mistake. Live!'

I amplify and improve a little, but that was the essence and the
tone. They immediately put before me, with the communicative force,
the real magic of the *right* things (those things the novelist worth his
salt knows and responds to when he sees them), an interesting situation, a vivid and workable theme. To *prove* it workable, indeed, I had
to work it out; which is what I have done and what I now give the
results of. But I thought it might amuse you to take in also the dropped
seed from which they were to spring.

I

My subject may be most simply described, then, as the picture of
a certain momentous and interesting period, of some six months or
so, in the history of a man no longer in the prime of life, yet still able
to live with sufficient intensity to be a source of what may be called
excitement to himself, not less than to the reader of his record.
Lambert Strether (to give him, for our purpose here, a name, even if
it be not final) has behind him so much past that I perforce accept
him, and undertake to create on his behalf all the romantic sympathy
necessary, just as his fifty-fifth year has struck. He is an American, of
the present hour and of sufficiently typical New England origin, who
has, at the point of his career that he has reached, the consciousness
of a good deal of prolonged effort and tension, the memory of a good

many earnest and anxious experiments—professional, practical, intellectual, moral, personal—to look back upon, without, for himself, any
very proportionate sense of acknowledged or achieved success. However,
he is, in the rather provincial, the somewhat contracted world in which
he lives, a highly esteemed figure and influence. Educated, with excellent gifts, intelligent, having passed, for the most part, as exceptionally
'clever,' he has had a life by no means wasted, but not happily concentrated; and rather makes on himself the impression of having
come in for many of the drawbacks, even perhaps for the little of the
discredit, of an incoherent existence, without, unfortunately, any of the
accompanying entertainment or 'fun.' He feels tired, in other words,
without having a great deal to show for it; disenchanted without having
known any great enchantments, enchanters, or, above all, enchantresses;
and even before the action in which he is engaged launches him, is
vaguely haunted by the feeling of what he has missed, though this
is a quantity, and a quality, that he would be rather at a loss to name.
His traditions, associations, sympathies, have all been the liberal and
instructed sort, on a due basis of culture and curiosity; he has not
been too much mixed up with vulgar things; he has always been occupied, and preoccupied, in one way and another, but has always, in all
relations and connections, been ridden by his 'New England conscience.'
He has known no extremes of fortune; has never been very poor, yet
still less had any but the most limited enjoyment of money; has had
always rather urgently to 'do something,' yet has never been without
the thing—in a decently remunerative way—to do.

So much for him in a very general way, for everything that further
concerns us about his conditions and antecedents is given, immediately,
by the unfolding of the action itself—the action of which my story
essentially consists and which of itself involves and achieves all presentation and explanation. This action takes him up at the moment of his
arrival, one evening of early spring, in England—arrival in connection
with a matter, and as the first note of a situation, with everything
that has prepared and led up to which we become *dramatically*, so to
speak, acquainted. My first Part or two are expository, presentative
(on these lines of present picture and movement); and are primar<il>y
concerned with his encounter and relation with two persons his por-
trayed intercourse with whom throws up to the surface what it concerns us to learn. One of these persons is an old friend, also an American,
a college-mate, much lost sight of, through separations and interruptions, in recent years, but between whom and Strether the tradition
of an old-time alliance, an approach to an intimacy, still exists. The
men are of the same age, and with similarities of history and situation,

and Waymark,[1] the friend, has been abroad, already, some two or three months—fatigued, overworked, threatened with nervous prostration and taking, somewhat against the grain, a fidgety, discomfortable rest. In communication with Strether, and hearing beforehand of *his* destined arrival, Waymark has thus fidgeted back from the Continent to be in England to meet him, with intentions of rather forlornly clinging and cleaving somewhat marked from the first. They come together, by my notion, at the picturesque old town of Chester, where they spend a Sunday—a Sunday pre-arranged by Strether's having wired from Queenstown: 'No—not Liverpool; wait for me at Chester—like awfully to be with you there a day or two.' The latter has been in Europe once or twice, briefly, with a sense of insufficiency, in earlier years, and has a recollection, very pleasant and charming, of a summer evening spent at Chester—a sweet, melancholy summer afternoon caught there the last thing, then, before re-embarking from Liverpool. It has come back to him as an impression he should like to renew.

Well, they have it there, the two men together; and a due quantity of preparation, explication, implication, comes up between them. They walk through the old 'Rows' and on the old town-walls together; they talk, talk, talk, as they have scarce had a chance of doing for years; they have fallen happily on an early foretaste of a beautiful season; Strether at least surrenders himself freely, quite gaily—for *him* —to a charming renewal of acquaintance with the English spring at its best, as well as with various other impressions. He has not known till now what a sense of holiday he was to have, and is only a little pulled up, or pulled down, by something backward and out of tune in his companion, whose way of taking things he finds to resemble his own rather less than he has been taking for granted. He somehow feels from the first that he is, after long years, after a great deal of grind and not much free play of anything, on the verge of an experience that (in spite of troublous things—prospectively, possibly so— latent and lurking within it) will be rather a fraud if it fails of enabling him also to forget, a little, and merely lounge, break awhile with the actual. I strike here the note that it's 'borne in' upon Strether that his differences with his old friend have come out a good deal in separation, and that if they are to be more or less together for the duration of his stay in Europe, they may yet find themselves not quite perfectly in step. This, in fine, is but part of a slight and comparatively subordinate feature of my business; a minor current, I may call it; the

1. Waymark becomes Waymarsh in the novel. The only other change in a character's name here is from Glenn Burbage to John Little Bilham, who, generally referred to by his last two names, takes on thus something of the diminutive quality James wanted for his 'young artist-man.'

exhibition of the two men as affected in wholly different ways by an experience considerably identical. It's 'too late,' in a manner, for each alike; but one, my hero, has, with imagination, perception, humour, melancholy, the interesting and interested sense of this—sense of what he has lost, or only caught the last whisk of the tip of the tail of; while the other, unamenable, unadjustable, to a new and disarranging adventure (Waymark's never having, previous to this, been out of his lifelong setting at all), fails to react, fails of elasticity, of 'amusement,' throws himself back on suspicion, depreciation, resentment really; the sense of exteriority, the cultivation of dissent, the surrender to unbridgeable difference. Waymark's office in the subject is, in other words, that of a contrast and foil to Strether—of an aid to the illustration and exhibition of many things; but it is also, at junctures, and precisely at the present, the initial, that of an active aid to what, in these opening passages, with the future course of our affair all before them, comes out, under the impressions, in the old town, on the old walls and from the new talks, between the two men.

But another agent, operative on this expository ground, as well as throughout the remainder, promptly comes into play in the person of a lady met by them on the rampart—strolling and looking, as they stroll and look; only unaccompanied, detached, with no one to talk of it to, and coming back to Strether as soon as he sees her, as a person already noticed by him, though with no great intensity, at the hotel at Liverpool, where she was occupied with a companion, another lady, whom she seemed to have come to 'see off' by the outgoing American steamer. She evidently, as they pass, knows Strether's face again; but she takes in at the same moment that of the gentleman he is with, and this—after she has gone on a few steps—determines her, with her uncertainty vanishing, to pull up, while Strether remarks to Waymark that he, Waymark, is evidently known to her. The two men, with this turn round, and a recognition—of Waymark—is what has in fact, on the lady's part, occurred. Waymark doesn't at first recognize her, but she recalls herself, and he places her; so that she presently has joined them and, in the course of a short time, become, as it were, for the moment, their travelling-companion. Waymark's contact with her proves, however, not to have been previously at all close; they have met on occasion, but superficially, and the connection is sufficiently explained. Waymark is an overworked lawyer in an American business community also, like Strether's, not of the first magnitude, but flourishing and important, and his situation in which has been such as to engender for him many responsibilities and much tension. He is a 'prominent man,' there, in his own way; and it is as a prominent man that Miss Gostrey has known him during some family visit or otherwise-de-

[377]

termined frequentation. This young woman—young as a slightly battered unmarried woman of five-and-thirty can be—is a study, as it were, of a highly contemporary and quasi-cosmopolite feminine type, and has her high utility in my little drama. The more immediate phase of that utility is that, the three being now together for several days, first at Chester, then in London (before Strether goes on to Paris, which is his specially-constituted objective), she is drawn into a relation with her new acquaintance—that is, with Strether, that makes, in its order, for our illumination. It is the accident of her knowing Waymark that has brought about their combination; but Waymark speedily drops out of it, and the congruity, the amusing affinity, that establishes itself for her, is altogether with Strether. They hit it off, in their degree—especially in Strether's limited one—from the first; they strike up a comradeship which proves full of profit for future lucidity. An American spinster left by the accidents of life free to wander, and having wandered and re-wandered from an early time, Miss Gostrey, clever, independent, humourous, shrewd, a little battered, a little hard, both highly unshockable and highly incorruptible, and many other things besides, is above all full of initiations and familiarities, full of Europe, full of ways and means, full of everything and everywhere. Active and energetic, interested in the human predicament and full of divination of it and a semi-cynical helpfulness *about* it, she has no one directly dependent on her, and so finds a happy exercise of her temperament in cultivating a protective attitude when she sees a chance for one. She is inordinately modern, the fruit of actual, international conditions, of the growing polyglot Babel. She calls herself the universal American agent. She calls herself the general amateur-courier. She comes over with girls. She goes back with girls. She meets girls at Liverpool, at Genoa, at Bremen—she has even been known to meet boys. She sees people through. She shops with them in Paris. She shops with them in London, where she has a tailor of her 'very own.' She knows all the trains. She meets a want. In short she has a very especial and, in her way, wonderful person. She takes an extraordinary fancy to Strether from the first; and the fancy that she takes to him is a secondary thread in the web, a little palpable gold thread that plays through all the pattern. She tries, after she has little by little got hold of his situation and entered into it, to help him, to 'do' for him in all sorts of ways, and he much appreciates it, responds to it, and likes her for it, so that with all she positively (mere lone, lean, migratory spinster as she is, but living in her world of reverberations) *shows* him and puts him up to, she is really, for him, quite one of the phenomena of his episode; he remaining for herself, as I say, still more, the job, of all she has ever undertaken, to which she has most zest to offer. He is better than any of the girls, better even than any of the boys, she has yet 'met'; better than the most bloated and benighted of the California billionairesses she has ever seen through the great round of the Paris purchases. What comes of this relation is for later on; at this point it is but the preliminary of the preliminary; definitely functional, as I·say, in the way of eliciting for us luminously the conditions in which Strether is involved.

This cluster of circumstances has two faces, the more immediate, the less private of which has already bared itself, from the first as between himself and Waymark. He has had to give the latter some explanation of why and how he is directed so straight upon Paris; so that we have, betimes, that thread in our hand. He has come out on a friendly mission—to render, that is, a service, doubtless rather delicate and difficult, to a friend at home, a friend who couldn't come. He has come out to take a look at 'Chad' (Chadwick) Newsome, Mrs. Newsome's son, her only one, these several years in Europe and recalcitrant to every appeal to return: Waymark will not be wholly ignorant of who Mrs. Newsome is. Who she is comes up, at any rate, lucidly, for ourselves; and with it, in brief, the full evocation of Strether's background and setting. These things put before us, by their implications, an American city of the second order—not such a place either as New York, as Boston or as Chicago, but a New England 'important local centre' like Providence, R.I., like Worcester, Mass., or like Hartford, Conn.; an old and enlightened Eastern community, in short, which is yet not the seat of one of the bigger colleges (which for special reasons I don't want). The place of course to be designated with sufficient intensity. Mrs. Newsome is the widow, there domiciled and dominant, of one of the local rich men, a man known to Strether in his time—and not all too agreeably or handsomely; the late Mr. Newsome, hard, sharp and the reverse of overscrupulous, not having left a name (for those who know—and Strether is abundantly one of them) of a savour ideally sweet. Mrs. Newsome herself, however, is a very different affair and a really remarkable woman: high, strenuous, nervous, 'intense' (oh, a type!)—full of ideals and activities, many of them really, in respect to her husband's career, of a decidedly fine expiatory or compensatory nature. She is many other things besides; invalidical, exalted, depressed, at once shrill and muffled, at once extremely abounding and extremely narrow, and of an especial austerity (in spite of herself almost, as it were, and of some of her imaginations), an especial refined hardness and dryness of grain and strain. She is old enough to have had by her early marriage, a marriage when she was barely twenty, two children, a son now of about twenty-eight, the one who remains in Europe, and predominantly in

Paris, where she can't, for reasons, get at him; and a daughter of thirty, Mrs. Pocock, who lives in the same place as her mother and near her, in close communion with her, being married, to a man somewhat older than herself, actually a partner in the considerable family business, a business, the manufacture of some small, convenient, homely, in fact distinctly vulgar article of domestic use (to be duly specified), to which the late Newsome gave in his time such an impulse that his family derive a large income from it and will continue to do so if their interests are sharply guarded and the working of the thing thoroughly kept up. This charge he, before his death, has laid, by testamentary and other injunction, very strenuously, on his son—who, practically, however, has not shown himself, as yet, as at all adequately responding to it. There are special conditions as to the son's share in the concern, contingencies as to forfeiture of the same in case of non-compliance, and other similar circumstances helping to constitute, with what he may gain and what he may lose, a special situation for the young man. The young man has none the less, however, as it happens, his considerable measure of financial independence through the possession of means inherited from his maternal grandfather; another sharp old local worthy as to whom Strether has also not been without his lights. Mrs. Newsome has thus likewise means of *her* own, coming to her from the same shrewd source and forming a property distinct from her anxious, responsible share in her husband's concern. It is this fact of having been benefited by his grandfather that has placed young Newsome on the footing of being able to act in considerable defiance of everyone and everything.

This practical defiance has been, for his mother, the greatest source of anxiety, for some time, in a life of which strenuous anxiety and responsibility, restless, nervous, and at the same time imperious, conscientiousness, has been the leading note. She has had her ideas and her fears, her suspicions and worries, and indeed, more than all these, her certitudes and convictions. She doesn't approve of Chad's long absence—purposeless, idle, selfish and worse than frivolous. She has all the more ground for regarding it as positively immoral as she is definitely aware of some of the facts of his career and has a horror of the company he keeps. There is a dreadful woman in particular —a woman with whom she knows him to have been living, and as to whom she is divided between the dread that he will marry her—which will be awful—and the dread that he will go on living with her without marrying her—which will be more awful still. She regards him as under a spell, a blight, a dark and baffling influence. He writes, he is kind, he is in ways of his own even reassuring; but she can really get nothing out of him, and she feels that he is not only elusive, but already all but veritably *lost*. She has her theory of the *why*—it's all the dreadful woman. The dreadful woman looms large to her, is a perpetual monstrous haunting image in her thoughts, grotesquely enlarged and fantastically coloured. Details, particular circumstances have come to her—they form, about the whole connection, a mass of portentous lurid fable, in which the poor lady's own real ignorance of life and of the world infinitely embroiders and revolves. The person in Paris is above all a *low* person, a mere mercenary and ravening adventuress of the basest stamp. She would have gone out herself long since were it not that the same highly nervous conditions that prompt and urge also dissuade, deter, detain. She is a particularly intense and energetic invalid, moreover, but still an invalid, never sure of herself in advance, and with recollections of Europe gathered from an early infelicitous round or two with her late husband, memories not of an order to leave traditions of ease. In short, for two or three years past she has, from year to year and from month to month, failed to achieve the move; in connection with which there has been another deterrent still. This deterrent has been the part more and more played in her life by Lambert Strether (full name Lewis Lambert Strether), and to which we catch on wholly through the lights given us by Strether himself. What we have is his depicted, betrayed, communicated consciousness and picture of it. We see Mrs. Newsome, in fine, altogether in this reflected manner, as she figures in our hero's relation to her and in his virtual projection, for us, *of* her. I may as well say at once, that, lively element as she is in the action, we deal with her presence and personality only as an affirmed influence, only in their deputed, represented form; and nothing, of course, can be more artistically interesting than such a little problem as to make her always out of it, yet always *of* it, always absent, yet always felt. But the realities, the circumstances—as they are evoked by Strether first for Waymark—are not the less distinctly before us. Waymark doesn't learn all—it's Miss Gostrey who presently makes all *out*; but Waymark elicits a good deal. Mrs. Newsome has begun by being immensely indebted to Strether, but Strether has also ended by contracting a sense of no small obligation to herself. He has helped her originally with her charities, her reforms, her good works—twenty manifestations of that restless conscience which I have called in a measure unwittingly expiatory; he has been advisory, sympathetic, suggestive, been an influence, for her, making in fact altogether for sanity and success. He has controlled and moderated her, been, in short, in these connections, exactly the clever, competent man needed by a peculiarly high-strung woman. Cleverness, competence, soundness, the thing to do and the thing not to, the way and the way not—these have been, by a happy constitution in our interesting friend, matters easy and natural to him; so that he has played, without great inconvenience to himself, and with an interest too in her subjects and ideals, straight into the current of his earnest neighbour's activity.

What we further learn about him helps to explain it. He himself has, in the New England way, married young, married, at an age not much greater than Mrs. Newsome's (who at present, I've omitted to note, is in her fifty-first year), emphatically for love, married happily for all save the fact of the death of his wife, in a second confinement, at the end of some five years. Left with a little boy of less than that age, Strether has then known such a period of helpless and discomfortable paternity as has deepened the bitterness of his bereavement; a period at once unrelieved and unspoiled by a second marriage, but brought to a term by the death—through an accident (while swimming)—of his boy at the age of about sixteen, an age sufficient to have unfortunately marked the fact that they (the boy and he) had not wholly hit it off together. There have been special facts about the boy, his nature, temperament, tendencies, that Strether has subsequently accused himself, with bitter compunction, of not having understood and allowed for, not handled with sufficient tenderness and tact. Deep and silent penance has he privately performed ever since; and the loss of his son, and the particular conditions and particular consequent feelings, are things that have constituted one of the sharpest elements of his life. It's all a history as to which Mrs. Newsome has repeatedly accused him of being morbid—as if, it is true, in a measure to make up as she can for all the occasions on which he has called *her* the same. He has thought her a little so—or in fact a good deal so—about her son, though holding a good deal himself the impression that Chad, whom he has known a bit as a boy, and in earlier youth, is not a little, really, alas, of an egotist and even a brute. He has *his* theory about Chad, which differs from the mother's, and is, as he considers, the theory of a man of the world as distinguished from such a person as Mrs. Newsome of Hartford, Conn. His own boy, at all events, *wasn't* a brute; he has ached, at times, with the sense that he himself was, in the doomed relation, the brute —unconscious of tender and sensitive things in the lad, stupidly, harshly blundering about them.

And there have been other things in his career—but things of labour and effort mainly, things in which he has tried to steep his disappointments, disillusionments, depressions. It had been his idea of himself, above all, that he has been fundamentally indifferent and detached, fatally unable really to care for anything. What more proof of it has he needed, to his own mind, than that he has tried half-a-dozen things and successively, rather, as he calls it to himself, sneakingly given them up? He tutored at college, after graduating, for a while, and gave that up. He studied law, and was admitted, and provincially, drearily practised for a time, but made little of that, had hankerings for 'study,' for serious literature, for serious journalism, and threw himself, with characteristic intensity, into experiments in that direction. They failed, in a manner, yet left him still with his yearnings, so that even after accepting and exercising, with a good deal of continuity, a salaried, an authoritative post in connection with the control of a large 'Home,' or some such other beneficent or economic institution founded, patronised, promoted by Mrs. Newsome these aspirations have again, a few years previous to our opening, in the form of an expensive Review, devoted to serious questions and inquiries, economic, social, sanitary, humanitary, Strether carries with some financial ruefulness and Mrs. Newsome subsidises with much public pride.[1] She gave him his chance, at a given moment, and he accepted it from her. Between them they keep the thing going. It has been an alliance, a united superior effort. What they both feel about it is that the thing is of course too good, too enlightened to succeed, but not, uncontestably, to *do* good. It's a great beneficent endeavour, equally honourable to both. It has, moreover, a few hundred subscribers, and all the colleges, all the cultivated groups scattered about the country, take it in and esteem it. It goes to Europe—where they believe it to have attracted attention in high quarters. Strether's name, as the editor, is on the cover, where it has been one of the few frank pleasures of his somewhat straightened life to have liked to see it. He is known by that pale, costly cover—it has become his principal identity. A man of moods and of a very variable imagination, he has sometimes thought this identity small, poor, miserable; while at others thinking it as good as most of the others around him. It's on the cover, at any rate, that Mrs. Newsome has liked to see him—this has been a greater joy to her than she has ever even betrayed; and the common interest, the most especial of many, has done much to bind them together. The feelings connected for her with this intimacy form precisely the subject of my reference just above to her practically deterred condition in respect to breaking in and going off. She has been under a spell from poor fine melancholy, missing, striving Strether. To be plain (though we are not plain at first), she's in love with him. She's fifty, and he's fifty-five; but he's the secret romance—secret, that is, up to

1. This sentence is printed as it appears in the original typescript made from James' dictation. Either he lost track of the development of his sentence, and omitted a word or words necessary to the sense, or his typist reproduced incorrectly what he said.

a given point; then sufficiently public—that she has never otherwise had. To say that she plays a similar part very exactly for himself would be to say too much; but he likes, admires and esteems her; she is much the most remarkable woman, in her way the most distinguished, the highest, keenest spirit, within his social range; and in their sufficiently 'awake' community she passes for very remarkable indeed. She is *the* personage, almost the great lady, certainly the 'prominent woman' of that community. Indeed her name is in the local papers much more than he, secretly, can like. However, *she* likes it, and the upshot of everything (for I am expatiating here, for you, far too much) is that, certain things having, at home, happened in certain ways, certain symptoms in regard to Chad, in Paris, having multiplied—in regard to Chad and in regard to other matters besides— the situation has taken the form of Strether's having offered Mrs. Newsome the service, as a loyal and grateful friend, of coming out to Paris to see what, in the premises, he can do. There has been a plan of *her* coming, but many personal and other things, complications, of sorts, indisposition, nervousness, moral and other apprehensions, have interposed and again checked her; a particular consideration which presently comes out for us has in fact above all interfered. There had been a question, if she *had* come, of Strether's coming with her; then there had been a question of her coming, as it were, with *him.* But the particular consideration I speak of has interposed especially as to *that*; and in the event Strether, tired, overstrained, chronically deficient in holidays and in 'a little change,' has taken his course by himself. It fits in, in short, with a kind of crisis in his personal history, which it may, in a manner, contribute to ease off, to produce an interruption, a suspension, a possible practical evaporation of. He comes on a kind of moral and sentimental mission, but committed to nothing more than to get hold of Chad tactfully, kindly, to try to fish him out of his deep waters. He is to act only within his full discretion, and he is to report on the situation and enlighten Mrs. Newsome's darkness. In particular, at any rate, they have both fully felt, and in almost equal good faith, that it will have been, on the possible bad issue, but a small honour to them if the boy be lost without some earnest, some practical, personal effort to save him. The case has been virtually as simple for them as that. Perdition on one side, salvation on the other.

But I am suffering this sketch already to reach such proportions that I must bear more lightly, must more sternly foreshorten. There is a situation between the three persons thus introduced—Strether, Waymark and Miss Gostrey—which floats us through the episode at Chester and carries us with them up to London, where my Prologue,

as it were, culminates. Before it is over I have marked the development of the curious and interesting relation between Strether and Miss
Gostrey—a development of which the rapidity is amusing in a high
degree to themselves, proceeding as it has done by the liveliest bounds,
by a kind of mutual half-tender, half-ironic recognition, and which
makes them spectators, commentators, critics together, of those al-
ready-marked signs and symptoms in their companion's state which
are to result in that demonstration of his case (his case 'in Europe')
as a case sharply opposed, representing the opposite pole of possibility,
to Strether's own, which I have somewhere above glanced at. Things
have, in London, on the eve of the separation of the two men from
Miss Gostrey (they going on to Paris together, and she destined to
turn up there after a brief interval) that she extracts from Strether (it's
the proof of her success with him) the communication of a very
private fact of which he has said nothing, even in their mutual expansion, to Waymark.[1] She is by this time, of course, completely *au
courant* of what his 'mission' in Paris amounts to; and after a fashion
that would be rather pushing, or have struck him as such, if it hadn't
struck him as rather pleasant, she has put to him many questions:
all of which have vividly illustrated for him her general human awareness and competence. If they haven't, by the same token, fully illustrated for him the kind of turn her interest in himself may be
apprehended as capable of taking, that is because he doesn't in general
jump rapidly to such conclusions. He only finds in talking with her
the special note of a kind of entertainment—almost a vague excitement—that really, yes, quite literally, he doesn't remember ever having
known. Full, at all events, of quickened shrewdness and sympathy,
full of perceptions and divinations that have given her the courage
of her curiosity, she ultimately elicits from him that his relation with
Mrs. Newsome has practically become, on the eve of his departure
from Worcester (or wherever) Mass., an 'engagement.' She has in
fact—she, Miss Gostrey, I mean—pointed the pistol at him; having
already elicited so much that it amounts to an implication of the
supreme fact. 'If you do it—if you come out all right—she'll marry
you?' And then, before they have gone many steps further, leaping
from peak to peak, she brings out the rest. 'It's *she* who proposed it
to you. *You* didn't—you wouldn't have thought of it. But since she
has—well, you're flattered. Oh, you needn't deny—and you needn't
confess either. It doesn't matter how, if you only do it; for she'll be
awfully good to you. She'll take a lot of things off you—personal
worries of your own, I mean; which is exactly what ought to be.'

1. Compare footnote on page 383 above.

[385]

He is really touched at the way Miss Gostrey has entered into his life—at the feeling <s>he has about certain things in it. He does deny —deny the offer as directly made by Mrs. Newsome, but his new friend makes what she likes of that. She has the whole thing—she reconstructs and fairly illumines it. She puts it all there to him—almost as if speaking of others. She even urges with exaggeration, almost with extravagance, his not disappointing a person who has made such an effort for him. Of course she's in love with him, Mrs. Newsome; but for many women that wouldn't have availed—the proceeding would have been too unusual. She herself, she, Miss Gostrey, would really like to know the person capable of it: she must be quite too wonderful. She will be, at all events, clearly, this heroic lady, his providence. Rich, clever, powerful, she will look after him in all sorts of charming ways, and guarantee and protect his future. Therefore he mustn't let her back out. He must *do* the thing he came out for. He must carry the young man home in triumph and be led to the altar as his reward. She gives the whole thing a humourous turn but we get from it all we need. Strether disclaims, deprecates, but really shows himself as so bewildered—that is, so affected both with dazzlement and doubt— over this particular element of his situation, that his condition constitutes of itself a kind of testimony. Yet, superficially, he refuses to recognize in Miss Gostrey's picture anything but a free joke; and to make his disclaimer appear the more sincere, he abounds in her sense and jokes *with* her. 'She won't then, you feel, if I *don't*?'

'Won't, you mean, stick to her offer if you don't capture the child? Surely not, no song no supper. So you *must* capture him. Oh, I see what you're thinking—that Paris is an awful place, and that it may be awfully difficult. But it will be all the more fun.'

'Fun?' poor Strether rather ruefully echoes.

'It's just the sort of job,' she replies, 'that's really, I assure you, in my line and that I should be quite ready to hand in an estimate for. Upon my word, I'd take the order.'

'I wish to goodness then you would!' her companion laughs. 'It would save me a lot of trouble!'

'Well, I'll save you,' she responds, 'all the trouble I can.' And the little scene, with its climax, marks the culmination, as I have indicated, of my Preliminary.

II

In Paris, after his arrival, he has at first such a rush, such an increase of the sense of rest, refreshment, change, long-deferred amusement and ease, without something immediately to do and some responsibility to meet, that he for the moment abandons himself to a certain regret, which he at the same time rebukes as pusillanimous, at his not having come with a wholly free hand, at his really being committed to a responsibility and having very presently a duty to take up and an effort to make. It has all come over him since his disembarkment at Liverpool that he responds to his holiday more even than he had expected, and that he is now responding—after the first few days —to a still quicker tune. He immediately informs himself about Chad, to whom he is of course not wholly without a clue, and learns with a certain relief that the young man is out of town. He sees, immediately, however, meets by an accident, a young man, a young artist-man, a young American art-student, who is his friend and who has a certain amount of perhaps rather visibly reserved news to give about him; a youth who, moreover, immediately rather interests Strether on his own account. This youth—Burbage by name and who is, by the way, three or four years older than Chad—constitutes the first note struck for Strether in a direction destined much to open out to him; being, the young man, a very Parisianised—in respect to the art-world—product, the product, in fact, altogether of an air of which Strether has never yet, directly, tasted a mouthful. Glenn likes him—in fact I'm afraid I shall represent everyone, rather monotonously, as liking Strether (which is a bad note for his intensity of identity, though we must risk it); is communicative, talkative, sociable, immensely 'modern,' and he takes him—takes the two men, Waymark and our hero, about together while they wait for what next happens. They are affected in different ways, as we know, the two men; but it is Strether who so predominantly concerns us that I drop here the notation (drop it, I mean, out of my synopsis) of what refers to Waymark, as it puts on my hands too many things for your patience, and even, perhaps, with all respect, for your intelligence. Burbage is, in short, one of the several agents in Strether's fermentation (besides being a marked type in himself)—and these are an essential part of our drama. Our hero sees Paris a little, accordingly, before Chad turns up, before Miss Gostrey again turns up, before anything particular happens save that he, in a general way, takes the somewhat uneasy measure—a little more face to face—of his deputed duty. He makes out things from Burbage, whom he yet is scrupulous not to seem to invite or to expect to bear witness; but it only adds to his vague sense as of something that looms; they bewilder, these impressions, and only seem, as he soon finds, originally to mislead— they carry him on further than his feet feel sure. The result is a sense that Chad must be 'in' pretty deep—in below all possible immediate sounding. Strether is a little shy with his new young artist-man friend—literally a trifle indisposed to betray ignorances and mistakes too marked; so he half the time feels that he absolutely doesn't under-

[387]

stand him. It's a good little moment, however—a sort of lull at cafés, at restaurants, at theatres, even at the Folies-Bergère, at the wondrous Louvre and at old bookstalls by the Seine, before the too-probable struggle.

After a little, however, Chad comes on the scene; with which Strether is immediately more or less in the presence of his business and his problem. He has grown, by reason of indications gathered, inductions made, during the few days, a little nervous about them beforehand; seems to make out that the image of the actual Chad doesn't fit with the image preconceived by themselves at home, or with that remembered in regard to the boy's earlier time. He has felt that there will probably be differences—marked ones, as is indeed only natural; but the differences when he *sees* the young man and has spent half an hour with him, are such as to give him the sense of really not having known what in the least to expect. What Chad seems to be has the effect, as it were, of so imposing itself, that any previous mistake about it, any mere sense of miscalculation, fades away as irrelevant. There he is, *with* more differences than Strether can at first at all catalogue, and really presenting himself as a positive prodigy in the sphere of transformation. Strether at first so feels that he's 'transformed,' that it must take time to find out *what* he's transformed to. He has vaguely expected, at any rate, to find him coarsened—that would have been mainly the word he would use; brutalised, perverted, poisoned—all in some rather obvious and distressing way; he has braced himself for being distressed about him—and on somehow, surprisingly, becoming conscious that he's *not* distressed, doesn't quite know what to do *with* the 'bracing.' It's as if a good deal of rather fine and serious preparation for the event had been wasted; though indeed he plucks up courage and tries to say to himself that if the corruption, as it were, is so extremely insidious, so therefore the salvation must be supersubtle to match it. For of one thing he *has* satisfied himself—that there has been a horrible woman, *the* horrible woman, that Chad has been quite helpless in her clutches, and, for all he knows, may be as much so as ever. All the same there are inscrutabilities, mysteries, things shading off into the vague. The young man is 'easy' for him and with him to a degree which in itself is a surprise; his manners at least have extraordinarily improved; and altogether the question of tackling him has to adjust itself, feels grounds for finding itself a more complex one. Literally, for a little, Strether rather lets it drop, on the theory of just playing a waiting game till he is so possessed of more of the facts as not to be in danger of making a grave mistake. He has told the young man at first, frankly, amicably, handsomely, that he has come out to represent to him his mother's earnest wish that he shall come home, and to put the whole issue seriously before him; but Chad has been charming about *this* even, goodnaturedly indifferent, cheerfully postponing and adjourning discussion, granting that it's quite worth talking about, but really talking about anything, everything else. Chad is, of course, like everyone else in the whole business a special figure —difficult to do, but to be unmistakeably done; and I don't pretend here to construct him for you. For that you must wait for the book. I repeat that for Strether, at first, the note of the *changed* creature is so strong in the youth that, by itself, it overlies everything else. He feels himself, in the presence of it, to be in the presence of one of the most striking and curious phenomena—in the human and personal order—that he has ever met or had to reckon with.

Meanwhile, at all events, Miss Gostrey reappears—coming back to Paris, where she has quite given Strether rendezvous, looking him up, with frank comradeship, as soon as she arrives, and so presenting herself in short as to become again, inevitably, the receptacle of some of his overflow. She is placed, by this connection, in the presence of Chad, and Strether promptly enough derives a sensible relief, a kind of convenience, from her share of his hopes and fears, contemplations, hesitations, speculations. They continue, the two, more or less, to have some of these things out together, and it's an especial convenience to him that, in Chad's presence, as I say, she catches on still more to *that* particular situation. Some of Strether's views of it amuse her, some of hers amuse him; they hold sundry theories diametrically opposed about it, and Miss Gostrey, certainly, is soon ready to assert that she has sounded it to the bottom. With characteristic acuteness, she has immediately found the true word. It affects Strether himself as the true one—and rather disconcertingly even, before they either of them really know more. 'Save him, my dear man? Why, what are you talking about? There's nothing more about him *to* save. He *is* saved.'

'Ah, but I'm not a bit less convinced than ever,' Strether returns, 'that some woman, playing a great part in his life, and more or less feeding on him, hasn't still hold on him.'

'Exactly then; it *would* be some woman; it's only they who do that sort of thing.' Miss Gostrey, as she goes on, is immensely struck with it. 'It's *she* who has saved him.'

This discomposes Strether's theory of a rescue, precisely, *from* such a person; and the thing is at any rate the first note, is a view of the matter with which he has more and more to count. Miss Gostrey has, by a miracle, not happened to know Chad, to have met him before; a fact that by itself speaks a good deal for his having lived out of the eye of the light. But she now sees him for herself and feels sure that she understands him; and a combination of the three briefly takes place. Chad has meanwhile, after an hesitation, a measurable delay, spoken to Strether of some good friends of his own, awfully charming people, a mother and a young daughter—the mother almost herself *as* young—whom he wants him to know. They are the people he himself likes best in Paris and, as it were, sees most of; and the motive of his recent absence has precisely been a period spent near them in the south of France. He has quitted them, to come up to Paris on purpose to see Strether; but they are soon also to arrive, and he will then speedily arrange a meeting for his visitor, who will be as sure to like them as they will be to like *him*. Strether sees, in fact, several things in this programme—some of which he submits to his friendly Egeria: among them, in any case, is the circumstance, distinguishable to him, that Chad has waited to report (after seeing him, after renewing a blurred young impression of him)—waited to communicate with the ladies in the south, giving his judgement on him and not speaking without their assent. This Strether mentions to Miss Gostrey, who thinks it highly probable and who immediately leaps, in consequence, at the perception of two facts. One of these is that Chad finds Strether awfully 'possible,' much more possible than he had dreamed; and that if he does mean to show him to his friends Strether may take that quite as a tribute. Strether looks at it—or tries to—accordingly, at her direction, in this light, and somehow feels that, at any rate, it may be—this 'possibility' of his—but a mixture the more. For through a hundred channels the 'mixture' in poor Strether's consciousness has already begun to threaten to become tolerably thick. Sensations, impressions, a whole inert or dormant world of feeling or side of life, find themselves awake and sitting up around him; and so, in short, he goes on. But the second of these conclusions, embraced at a glance —on her interpretations of the symptoms—by Miss Gostrey, is that the lady of whom Chad has spoken has put her hand on him for her daughter, is arranging, as fast as possible, a marriage for the girl with the rich, the flattered, the manageable young American.

'Then it's she,' says Strether rather struck, 'who has saved him.'

But his friend doesn't seem so sure. 'Who? The mother?'

Strether wonders, but without quite seeing *that*. 'Well—the girl. The beautiful pure maiden.' And he wonders again. 'Suppose *that's* what one has come upon. Won't it be possibly a little awkward?'

'Oh,' says Miss Gostrey, 'don't be too sure, in advance, of the shade of your awkwardness. There are many kinds; of every colour and every price. But perhaps!'

Chad meanwhile introduces Strether to other friends; Miss Gostrey, on her side, produces a type or two out of her own store; and the business of our hero's enjoying himself—to a degree almost scandalous indeed to Waymark who doesn't enjoy himself at all, but really not in the least, goes on apace. And yet the enjoyment is singularly imperfect, for our friend is haunted with an inward *malaise*; the whole question of his regular report to Mrs. Newsome being, on the evidence before him, more and more difficult to meet. He is fairly ashamed—for it comes to that—of the case of coarseness Mrs. Newsome and he together had made out so luridly, over there, the palpable grossness that they had, as it were, fairly mapped out as the young man's necessary state, the presumable depravity they had (as now seems to him) positively hugged the conception of as the colour of his connection. Poor Strether almost feels as if these things had been the fault of his own mind; the discomfort arises from his having, as he turns things over, to say to himself that they do him little honour. But he tries at least to tell his friend at home, to whom he profusely writes, as much as he can; secretly a little disappointed that he has nothing for her as yet quite bad enough. Sometimes he brushes away the vision of her fine, cold strenuous face and general high-pitched essence. He feels, he scarce knows why, a little false to her; feels even a little afraid of himself. The little spectacle that Chad has meanwhile amiably and thoughtfully evoked for him is largely that of some of the young man's own 'artistic' ramifications. He knows painters, sculptors, studios; knows a celebrity or two; puts Strether in relation—superficial, momentary, but very interesting to Strether— with them: brings about in particular an occasion of contact with a prime celebrity, of a very special note: all of which results in a Sunday-afternoon visit of the type of the one alluded to in my few preliminary pages. There is in other words a particular occasion on which everything—by which I mean a lot of accumulated perception and emotion —seems to culminate for Strether. I 'do' the occasion and the picture, evoke the place and influences, multiply so far as may be, the different sources of impression for our poor fermenting friend—the persons, figures, strangenesses, newnesses there present; give, above all, the wonderful intensity, oddity, amenity of the general intellectual, colloquial air. It's a real date for Strether. Chad's two friends, Mme de Vionnet and her daughter, are, happily, at last there; and there it is, very much in the same beautiful old garden that my original anecdote gives me, that our hero's introduction to them takes place. But this is an occasion on which, through relations already existing for her, Miss Gostrey is also on the ground; whereupon, lo and behold, once in presence, it turns out that Mme de Vionnet is a person she has already known, an acquaintance of a previous time—a time both previous to Mme de Vionnet's marriage and subsequent to it—whom she has lost sight of. The identity of this lady—through Strether's not having got her name right in speaking of her, or having forgotten it or not pronounced it—has not, antecedently to this encounter, come up between them sharply enough for Miss Gostrey to have been guided: so that when she does meet, in Strether's company, Chad's vaunted ladies, she finds it a surprise to be able to fit them in to facts actually known to her. These facts she produces afterwards for Strether, and they are indeed all to Mme de Vionnet's credit—in spite of the circumstance that she is living apart from her husband. By the time, at any rate, they are known in this measure to Strether, the impression, as it were, has been made upon him by the charming woman herself: inasmuch as it now becomes of the essence of the business, becomes vividly and importantly so, that Mme de Vionnet *is* charming, and that he fully recognizes her as such. She is young (that is, she is thirty-eight), bright, graceful, kind, sympathetic, interesting—and doesn't alarm him by being dazzlingly clever (which is the cleverest thing *in* her!). Without having anything that he immediately feels to be positive beauty, she has a face, and a general air and aspect, that singularly speak to him. He likes no less, also, the way she receives him, lends herself to the reference made to him by Chad for her, and to the reference made to *her* by Chad for Strether himself. She lends herself to everything, in short, with the friendliest ease, and strikes our hero from the first —which is the most particular note of all—as a kind of person he has absolutely never seen, nor ever, with any distinctness, dreamed of.

And yet it's not in the least that he has fallen in love with her, or is at all likely to do so. Her charm is independent of that for him, and gratifies some more distinctively disinterested aesthetic, intellectual, social, even, so to speak, historic sense in him, which has never yet been *à pareille fête*, never found itself so called to the front. She shows him her daughter, a girl of seventeen, who strikes him as almost as much of a revelation; a little tender flower of shy and exquisite good-breeding; different again, in her way and degree, from pretty little girls of seventeen as hitherto known to him. Above all she speaks to him of Chad after a fashion that intensifies his consciousness, his suspicion, as it were, of differences. Chad's being in confirmed relation with her at all, her being interested in Chad and at all socially bound up with him: these things have for Strether—and with all due deference, with all allowance made, for the young man's improved and transformed state—an element of mystification, of slight perplexity, even from the first hour: such an odd sort of personal, or social promotion or transposition do they seem to represent for the boy as known to him in other lights. However, this whole occasion puts so many new meanings into things, does its little part toward shifting so many landmarks and confounding so many small assumptions, that perhaps one case of ambiguity doesn't count much more than another. His judgments, conclusions, discriminations are more or less in solution—in the pot, on the fire, stewing and simmering again, waiting to come up in what will be doubtless new combinations. This whole occasion, I repeat, is a picture and an admonition for him; and among the things it does, it throws him again with the young artist-man, Chad's friend, whom he likes, who is acuter, more 'intellectual' and aesthetic, than Chad, and with whom he has some amusing and suggestive moments. With his enlarged and intensified vision of a life containing —though indeed, by what he makes out, also more or less lacking— ingredients and influences closed to him and, at his actual age, forfeited and foregone, the 'too late' comes immensely home to him, yet only to stir in him the impulse to do the whole thing at least an imaginative justice. He can't, at such a time of day, begin to live—for he feels, besides, with all the rush of the reaction against his past, that he *hasn't* lived: yet there stirs in him a dumb passion of desire, of rebellion, of God knows what, in respect to his still snatching a little super-sensual hour, a kind of vicarious joy, in that *freedom of another* which he has found himself, by an extraordinary turn of the wheel, committed to weigh in the balance: a connection not, however, on the spot, so much taking in Chad's case as that of young Burbage before-mentioned, whose own sense of his opportunities strikes him as perhaps not quite adequate. It's to young Burbage, at any rate, that he indulges in some such little outburst as the one retailed in my preliminary pages—the conditions and effect of which my story more or less reproduces. I leave nothing untouched in fine, that may make of this Sunday afternoon in the old Paris garden, in a circle profuse in intimations, the kind of moral 'dishing' for Strether that I have already glanced at.

When they separate he feels that a relation, a link, of a sort, that will have both more to give him and to ask of him, has formed itself for him with Mme de Vionnet. She asks him to come and see her; she wants to see him again; she is gracious, encouraging, benevolent: and yet all for what? Mysteries, mysteries: he stands in a world of mystery. He doesn't at all know her really—he feels that; but queerer yet is it that he feels he doesn't at all really, at this time of day, know even himself. Has she addressed herself to some conception of him purely delusive and erroneous?—or to some element in him of which he has himself been unconscious, but which she has, with prodigious penetration, made out, in half an hour, as a possibility? Well, he will see.

He walks away, through the grave and impressive old streets of the Faubourg Saint-Germain, with Miss Gostrey, and as soon as they have got, after a spell of silence at first, to a certain distance, he puts her, stopping short, the abrupt question, full of tacit references: '*Isn't it for her daughter . . . ?*'

'That she's nursing your young friend?' They have stopped on a quiet corner of the Rue de l'Université; the day and the hour are tranquil there, and the straight, narrow vista of the austere, aristocratic street stretches before them. For a moment they look at each other, and Strether's companion just visibly hesitates. 'Yes,' she then brings out with decision; and after their eyes have again met they resume their walk; in the course of which—for he sees her home—she is very interesting about Mme de Vionnet, whom she also particularly rejoices to have encountered again. Their acquaintance goes back to old days of school at Geneva, where this charming woman was a *pensionnaire* slightly older, but not much, than herself; a rather isolated young thing, the daughter of a French father and an English mother who, left a widow, had married again—married some second foreigner. The girl was then clever, already charming, polyglot, speaking French and English, and even German, equally well, doing everything, in fact, well that she touched. Afterwards, however, it appeared that she had not had a happy hand at marrying. Miss Gostrey, after a considerable interval, had again met her; by which time her mother, otherwise engaged and entangled, impatient, preoccupied, precipitate, had made for her a summary match, assisted by her possession of a certain sufficient *dot*, with a Frenchman of supposedly the best condition, who yet, in spite of it, had not at all turned out well. Miss Gostrey has lights on the Comte de Vionnet, with whom his young wife was still living at the moment of this second period of observation. But things had even then been ominous, and the tolerably prompt separation, of which she had also heard, was not a thing to surprise her. She believes the husband still to be living and the pair to be on irreconcileable terms; but she also knows how little there can be a question for them of divorce, each of them belonging to the kind of *monde* that, in France, doesn't practise it. Of the kind of *monde* they do belong to she gives Strether all due, all manageable or communicable, notion, putting the presumptions before him vividly and interestingly enough. She particularises, makes him understand it—all of which, however, are processes rather concerning the author than the reader. Strether's acquaintance with Mme de Vionnet, and the conditions of the lady's identity and existence, are, in fine, ushered in—as to which it is sufficient that Miss Gostrey is helpful. Strether, at all events, on the occasion I speak of, sees her home, but doesn't go in, having at the moment another engagement. So, before her door, reverting, taking things up again, they have another word. 'Yes, you *do* see,' he asks, 'don't you? that charming little girl as having done it?' But she is not, for the instant, all there. 'Done what?'

'Why, saved Chad.'

'Oh yes—as we said. One sees it. The charming little girl has done it. It's *she* who has saved Chad.' And on this they separate.

Strether forms a theory which more or less fits the case—the theory that Chad is more or less in love with Mlle de Vionnet, that her mother has much fostered it, that the young man is a good deal—and not unnaturally—under that charming person's influence, and that he wants to make an end of past complications and mistakes. He wants to marry, thinks it the best thing for himself, and sees in this young girl so highly civilised and so perfectly brought up, so amiable, so pretty, so attractive, an opportunity with much in its favour. But he is afraid, a little; hangs off, is waiting to have quite made up his mind and thereby be strong: all on account of his mother. He has his instinct, his conviction, that his mother will be inimically affected toward such a marriage, as mixing him up exactly with elements—the elements of absence, preparation, 'Europe'—against which she has so much been pleading; and he doesn't want to have the inevitable battle with her before his mind is wholly made up. Strether puts him indeed the question, and he meets it with a negative: denies that he is either in love with the young lady or intending to marry her. But meanwhile Strether has had to report to his mother—finding it more and more difficult to do so with lucidity; and meanwhile, further, he has been to see Mme de Vionnet. From this latter moment his own attitude, mission, simplicity and cogency of position on the whole question in which his presence in Paris has originated—from this latter moment these things undergo inevitable modification. A whole process begins to take form in him which is of the core of the subject, and the steps and shades in the representation of which I cannot pretend here to adumbrate. Chad's case becomes for him a concrete case in a kind of big general question that his actual experience keeps more and more putting to him; so that he finds himself each day more in the presence of a responsibility much less simple than the one he had braced himself to incur. And Mme de Vionnet becomes the most determinant cause of this revolution, this interesting process—becomes so simply by being, and by showing herself, exactly what she is. Though there are always, and more than enough, round about Strether, mysteries, ambiguities and things equivocal, yet one or two convictions and impressions thicken for him, stiffen, harden—and one of these is the estimate of the value of such a relation, for any young man, as such a woman as Mme de Vionnet represents. The value of this relation grows clear and high, to his eyes; and almost grotesque becomes the kind of revision he has to make of the bundle of notions with which he started from home. They all cluster about a woman, and there *is* a woman, most unmistakeably and strikingly. But it's a different thing from what he has mapped out to come to plead, to come to pull, against *her*. The person of most personal charm, indisputably, that poor Strether has ever met, arrays herself on one side, and the group of interests and associations on behalf of which he has proposed to carry Chad off arrays itself on the other. The bustling business at home, the mercantile mandate, the counter, the ledger, the bank, the 'advertising interest,' embody mainly the special phase of civilization to which he must recall his charge—and a totally other cluster of forces weave the adverse tangle. Singularly, admirably Mme de Vionnet comes after a little to stand, with Strether, for most of the things that make the *charm* of civilization as he now revises and imaginatively reconstructs, morally reconsiders, so to speak, civilization.

This is a summary sketch of what takes place in my hero's spirit in consequence of this new contact—and I needn't insist on the necessity weighing on the author to paint the contact in a manner to justify it. The whole thing must more or less stand or fall by the way in which both Strether and Mme de Vionnet are done. The latter, of course, is a magnificent little subject, and the artist must be left alone with her. There is much in her—alas, for the artist's ease, *too* much. But the thing none the less works out. One of its workings is that, even to Strether's consciousness, she *knows* what she wishes and tries for. She isn't spoiled for him by his analysis of the situation. What is spoiled for him, on the other hand, is his freedom of communication with Mrs. Newsome, which he has sought to make possible by making it really candid, by throwing his whole vision of the matter upon her intelligence and her sympathy. He tells her what he sees. He tells her what he does. He tells her what he thinks. He tells her what he feels. The more, at this point, everything grows, the more he tries, by letter, to keep her in touch with it. Of course he reflects that, after all, what he is doing isn't the very definite thing he came out to do—which was to bring Chad home. Instead of there being representable for her in his life a detachment, a removal, from the female element, there can only strike her as being a greater and stranger abundance of it, and in forms difficult to give her, really, a just notion of. As things go, none the less, Strether has by this time been in a manner frank with Chad as well—only, by the time that hour is able to strike, the young man is shrewd enough himself to make out that, for consistency on his friend's part, the assault is made, the charge sounded, too late. Chad has had a kind of happy instinct in making things play on to the juncture at which poor Strether has become sceptical—at which, accordingly, consequently, he can only do his business at a sore disadvantage. The young man declines to meet any of the propositions with which his visitor is charged—and yet has the covert triumph of seeing that visitor not throw up the game. Strether doesn't break off and go home—Strether stays on and fairly consecrates the situation by his anxious presence. This is what Chad sees, and what Mme de Vionnet sees, and what Strether himself sees, and sees that they see, and sees above all that the lady at home sees. He isn't straight, as it may be called, and he knows it; isn't at all straight after he finds himself not only consenting, but liking, to discuss the question with Mme de Vionnet herself—or even with Miss Gostrey. It isn't a question he came out to discuss at all. He came out to do what he could, but everything is altered for him by the fact that nothing, damn it, is as simple as his scheme. Chad was to have been simple, for instance; but even Chad isn't. Least of all is he now himself. What would have been straight would have been so almost equally, as it were, in either case. If it would have been simple to be able to 'write back': 'It's all right; he consents to come; I come with him, I bring him, only just taking a little turn off with him—perhaps to Norway and Sweden; in which case we sail about the middle of next month': so likewise it would have been comparatively plain-going to have to say: 'He absolutely won't come at all—and you'll have to come out yourself; so that, so far as I'm concerned, it's a failure, and I shall just look about me a bit on my own hook and take ship to rejoin you three or four weeks hence'—so likewise, I repeat, *that* would have been, though disappointing, yet manageable, natural and final. But somehow, on what *does* take place everything is different. Nothing is manageable, nothing final—nothing, above all, for poor Strether, natural. I repeat that he has almost a sense of the uncanny. I repeat, as a good little note of his fallacious forecast, that he has really thought, as a 'resource,' as a clever stroke, of the way it might have eased difficulties off just to *coax* Chad aside for some small sanitary and, as it were, disinfecting jaunt through some one of those regions vaguely figuring to Strether as the more marked homes and haunts of earnestness. If there are smiles for this *naïveté* later, the first smiles are yet all his very own. There is a passage of irony for him, in the connection, with Miss Gostrey. Well, he finds himself sinking, as I say, up to his middle in the Difference—difference from what he expected, difference in Chad, difference in everything; and the Difference, I also again say, is what I give.

'No: Chad won't come'—he has, accordingly, presently to communicate that. But what he has *not* to communicate with it is that he will therefore reappear without him. He won't reappear without him —that is practically what he has very soon to let Mrs. Newsome see; and as he can't reappear *with* him the complication is one that takes, so far as she is concerned, a good deal of explaining. Candid and explicit as he meanwhile tries to be, there are things he *can't* explain. It has been part of his characteristic understanding with the lady at home, and part of her own with him, that if Chad is really, as may be so well on the cards, painfully unamenable, he himself is not—out of any excessive conscience in respect to service or duty owing, to remain too long mixed up, too long in a state of contact that was originally at best rather to be deprecated. That last is a distinct note, one of a great many even, in the relation of Strether and Mrs. Newsome—the feeling she has so much had *for* him, the anxious, scrupulous feeling; which is not wholly unlike, moreover, the state of mind he has really, beforehand, rather been in about himself. They have between them—they had it, at least, to begin with almost equally—a sense that he can't morally, or even personally, cheapen himself too much in the business, can't too long hang about it, rub against it, give himself away for it. *She*, in fact, is very high and fine in all this view of it; is very high and fine indeed altogether—to the point even of being ready rather to let Chad go than to regard with any complacency the prostitution, so to speak, of poor Strether. Reflections and reverberations of all this play over the scene. Chad has meanwhile continued to deny, however, to our friend that he has his eye on Mlle de Vionnet, that her mother has, to any such end, hers on him, and that the question of his marrying the girl has come up between them. They are simply all three the best of friends, and they have made for him a kind of charming second home. Isn't that enough? He puts the case to Strether with every appearance of frankness— pleads quite explicitly for the kind of privilege it is to be *as* he is with *ces dames*, who weren't at all likely to have taken up with one of his type, and who have been, simply, incredibly nice and charming to him. He speaks of the matter as really quite a recognized anomaly— but that doesn't diminish the value he sets on it. His effect on Strether is, curiously, that of moving him without really quite convincing him; the latter assents, in a word, without quite believing. He throws himself moreover again, as it were, on Miss Gostrey; and she again tells him to let her shrewdness answer for it that the question of the marriage is really—though disavowed for whatever reasons of prudence and diplomacy, whatever precautions required by the possible interference of the obnoxious Monsieur de Vionnet—the tie. Strether takes this from her, fitting it fairly into impressions of his own; though there is one thing that does stick in his crop: the question, namely, of why Chad won't at least go home for long enough to see his mother her-self and have things out with her at Worcester. Chad promises of course to do this—admits the propriety of it; yet evidently has no intention of doing it at all soon. His perpetual postponement has therefore a motive—is the result of some obscure coercion; and Strether of course connects Mme de Vionnet with it. Yet at the same time he doesn't see her own reasons, or why she should have so peculiarly much to fear. In fine he goes on from day to day and from week to week; only, when he has done so a certain time, he finds himself landed in the *volte-face* in which the process I have described as taking place in him is practically to culminate. Various special things, a business-chance of importance in particular, depend for Chad upon an immediate change of life, a general radical rupture; and yet one fine day, in the presence of news from home that has brought every-thing immensely to a head, Strether's emphatic word to him is sud-denly: 'No then—don't. I seem to see my "mission" differently. Stay as you are.'

'And will you then,' says the young man, wonderfully pleased and impressed, 'see me through?'

Strether-has to think another moment; then he takes his jump. 'I'll see you through.'

But immediately afterwards, to make up for this grave inconsequence, he cables to his friend at home that his recommendation to her is, if she at all conveniently can, to come straight out. He more than half then, for a day or two, expects her; but two or three things may happen, and he holds himself in suspense—as also in readiness. She will either cable that she starts, or she will cable to him, more or less emphatically, and rather more than less, to come straight back to *her*. He has thought it over, and if she does so, believes that he will do it: though now really seeing how little he wants to. However, at the expectant word from her he *will*—yes, positively, he will. He gets no answer for three or four days, during which he is awfully restless, and yet with it all has a queer sense of freedom hitherto unknown to him. He *will* go— yes, again, if she calls; but even if he does go things will be somehow, and rather strangely, different: and his sense of freedom is partly just in *that*. Then at the end of the waiting a reply comes. But it proves to be neither a summons to Strether nor an announcement of Mrs. Newsome's embarkation. It is different—something he hadn't thought of. It announces the immediate departure of the Pococks—which is a surprise. But Strether sees a good deal in it—sees more the more he thinks.

Mrs. Pocock, as has been mentioned, is the daughter of Mrs. Newsome, Chad's elder sister, married to a partner in the family business, whose own young sister, a girl of about the same age as Mlle de Vionnet, accompanies them. They promptly arrive—a young couple of extremely marked attributes—as little Mamie Pocock is, in her way, the same: a lively (in their way) young American pair, who have been to Europe once before—immediately after their marriage; and consider (so far at least as Mrs. Pocock is concerned) that they know it very well. I can't 'do' this trio for you here—and they will take all proper doing in the book, where they will be adequately attended to; I limit myself to designating their office, which is in a manner that of rather tacitly, coldly and austerely superseding and suspending Strether in *his* function; that at all events of representing Mrs. Newsome on the spot and putting in their plea on behalf of the business, on behalf of the family, on behalf of propriety, on behalf of his country, on behalf of all the claims that Strether appears to have handled so ineffectually. As Mrs. Newsome remains personally out of the action, so now she is represented in it by these fresh emissaries. But Mrs. Pocock herself is the one who principally, or exclusively, counts in this respect; Mrs. Pocock is a sharp type and (D.V.) a vivid picture; Mrs. Pocock makes for interest and entertainment. She brings, as it were, her mother's ultimatum—which is that if Chad doesn't come home immediately he needn't, so far as his material advantage is concerned, ever come home at all; Mrs. Newsome being in possession of options and having command of alternatives upon which she is actually free to close. Strether is confronted thus with the whole crisis and, most sharply of all, with what it means for himself. This latter element is more or less implied—or even, doubtless, I shall make it explicit; the remarkable young woman, who has nothing in common with her brother, being fully *au courant* of the state of affairs between her mother and their friend, and empowered to speak and act, conscientiously, lucidly, indignantly, if necessary, *for* that lady. Mrs. Pocock arrives, in other words, with a great deal of accumulated resentment, disapproval, virtue, surprise. Her husband, in truth, is on quite another foot; her husband is an example, in characteristically vulgar form, and with all due humourous effect, of the same 'fatal' effect of European opportunities on characters giving way too freely, which Strether more subtly embodies. Pocock, a traitor in the camp, a humorous, surreptitious backer of his brother-in-law and their friend does, in short, all he can to amuse us. He has his personal function, in a word—for which he must be trusted. All the complexities of the

drama deepen here; things grow closer and more tense. Poor Waymark, thrown off from Strether, whose strange laxities and perversities
he deplores, whose general sensibility and surrender, as he can't help
thinking them, he regards as the reverse of edifying, rebounds to Mrs.
Pocock, who strikes up with him an alliance that they both regard
as rather a fine, free intimacy—almost a 'European' affair. They stand
together, they confer together, they exult and lament together, go
about together generally, hold the same opinions and invoke the same
conclusions, cheer and comfort and sustain each other. The whole
comedy, or tragedy, the drama, whatever we call it, of Strether's and
Chad's encounter of the new complications and relations springing
from the Pococks' presence, from the necessity, for instance, bravely
to confront them with Mme de Vionnet and her daughter, and to
confront Mme de Vionnet and her daughter with *them*—this is a
thing, I need scarcely say, I am not trying thus, *currente calamo*, to
formulate. Mme de Vionnet, in it all, is magnificent; Mme de Vionnet
is wonderful; but these things are no more than what she is throughout.
I repeat that, little as I project her here—for the smallest development
of that attempt would take me too far—I must be trusted with her.
Mrs. Newsome and Mrs. Pocock have hatched it between them
that *one* aid to the recovery of Chad may be possibly just this putting
in his path of the little Pocock girl. Strange and ignorant complacencies, fathomless fallacies, have attended this idea. She is thus produced in Paris for the young man's benefit, and is thus seen to figure
face to face with and in opposition to the little Vionnet girl—who is as
wonderful, in her way, about this introduced representative of a different type of manners, as her mother. Contrasts and oppositions
naturally here play straight up. The Vionnets and the Pococks, Chad
and his sister, Pocock and his brother-in-law, Chad and Pocock's
sister, Strether and Pocock, Pocock and Strether, Strether and everyone and everything, but Strether and Mrs. Pocock in especial, with
everything brought to a head by *her*—there is no lack of stuff; above
all as, on the very eve of the last-named lady's arrival, a sharp thing
has happened for Strether.

It has suddenly then come out—suddenly to *his* mind—that Mlle
de Vionnet is engaged to be married, only not a bit to Chad. To
a very different person, a Frenchman of 'position'—a match markedly
congruous and suitable, a candidate presented by her father, unexpectedly insistent, and in whom the proper conditions meet. Strether's
theory has therefore sharply broken down—the theory, moreover, which
Miss Gostrey has so backed up. The last thing that has happened before the apparition of the Pococks has been precisely a scene with
that lady on the question of this so unexpected issue. It takes place,

as happens, also on the eve of a departure of her own for a temporary absence. Strether, rather annoyed and disconcerted, charges her with the grossness of her mistake. But the way she meets the charge surprises him the more. She is astonishing. 'It was no mistake. I didn't believe it.'

'Didn't really believe what you said, what you made *me* believe—and therefore consciously misled me?'

She faces it—has to brace herself to confess. 'Yes, my poor dear man—monster as you must think me. I saw that what was going on for Chad wasn't at all, whatever it might be, *that*. And yet I thought it best to make *you* think otherwise.'

'To make a fool of me?'

'Oh, you know—for your good.'

'But I don't know at all. What "good" are you talking about? Why did you do such a thing?' He is troubled—having quite, in the teeth of some difficulties, cherished the theory in question, which has given him another leg to stand on.

Challenged thus, then, she has one of her odd hesitations, evasions, embarrassments. 'Well, I'll tell you when I come back.'

But he insists. 'What the deuce then *is* going on?'

It is, however, for the moment, all he can get from her. 'I'll tell you when I come back.'

She has gone, but meanwhile the fact of Chad's definite *non*-engagement, and with it the breakdown of the most presentable of the grounds for promoting, for condoning, his recalcitrance has had to be produced, has had inevitably to come straight up, for Mrs. Pocock. It facilitates, of course, her position, puts an arm in her hand. What motive that can conceivably remain *is* then presentable? She is moreover more fully armed now—or by so much the less obstructed—in respect to her putting forward her little sister-in-law. But we see what comes of that. *She* sees, and has to make her mother see—constantly, as she is, communicating and cabling (nothing having ever been known like the cabling that goes on—alarming even to Chad, immensely amusing to Pocock, fraught with strange possibilities for Strether and prodigious to Mme de Vionnet). Precipitated thus is the kind of *crux* in his position that Mrs. Pocock's manner of acting for her mother has already prepared. More than she has yet done, as it were, she has it out with Strether why they have come. She puts it in its light, and she gives him the warning that she herself believes to be admirably disinterested and magnanimous, purely conscientious and solicitous. I should premise that her brother has put it to her, on her having to recognize the humiliating futility of her attempt to catch him with any such bait as Miss Pocock, that, in respect to his consenting to do what appears to them all so imperative at home, he will stand or fall then by what Strether now says, will let the latter absolutely answer for him, determine his line, determine, quite, as it practically is, his fate. This is a special and superior stroke of Chad's —this inspiration of throwing himself, at the psychological moment, thus completely on our friend. But the inspiration has come, he has taken the measure of the dependence that, for backing him up, he can really place on Strether; and now, acting *on* that dependence, he passes to his sister his word of honour. The scene between them moreover has had other elements—elements rather confounding to some of Mrs. Pocock's complacencies: he really lets fly at her, that is, for the folly of her supposing him amenable to her ridiculous view of the little Pocock. He is fairly angry with her—in respect to what she has thus taken *him* for; and, though he has, to do him justice, tried not to be rude, he has raised for her a sufficiently startling and bewildering curtain, revealed to her, in a manner that she feels to be quite lurid and that makes her shudder off across the sea, the intimate difference now existing in their standards of value. She is *proud* of the little Pocock. *Why* the inspiration just mentioned—the inspiration of standing or falling by Strether's final word—has thus operated in Chad, we also interestingly know. The reason is partly the result of definite passages between them—at one of which I have already glanced; passages from which Chad had eagerly snatched Strether's general sense that, really, the young man has succeeded in growing, by whatever obscure, whatever nefarious process, comparatively too civilized for *him*, Strether, to find it in his responsible conscience to urge as a substitute for that process a mere relapse to the precious place— beautiful business-place, with a big chance for any, for every, new assertion of the paternal smartness, though it may be—which has, at much inconvenience to the family interest, been kept, or rather been all but lost, for him at home. That vision of Strether's attitude is part of the ground, I say, on which Chad's stand to Mrs. Pocock is made; but he has also been confirmed and illuminated by the so considerable acuter judgement and observation of Mme de Vionnet, who has not lost, not wasted her time with Strether, and has answered to Chad for the degree to which they can count on him. She has worked, in fine, and the necessary effect has been produced. What takes place accordingly is, as I have indicated, Mrs. Pocock's supreme appeal to their good friend, in which she gives her point, all her deputed meaning, its full value.

We know what this full value is, what Strether 'stands to lose' by any perversity or, as Mrs. Newsome's daughter really takes upon herself to brand it, disloyalty. 'If he doesn't look out, doesn't take care, etc., etc.'—why, he need scarcely, she supposes, dot the i's for him in respect to the natural consequences. If he doesn't, in a word, look out and take care, he forfeits everything comfortable and pleasant that his prospect of marriage with Mrs. Newsome has caused to cluster so richly about his future: the confidence, the esteem, the affection of a noble woman, the good opinion, frankly, for that matter, of a noble community; and at any rate the promise of ease and security, a refined, and even a luxurious, home for the rest of his days. Mrs. Pocock goes so far as to be even a trifle vulgar—in her emphasis and impressiveness—on this article of the luxury, on that of poor Strether's exposed time of life, and, in fine, on that of his having perhaps never yet, by any marked success made, in the course of his variegated career, of anything, created the presumption that he will be able to retire on honours, still less on more substantial accumulations, due to his own abilities. She goes further still—glances for him at her own and her brother's different, but natural, view of the marked favour shown him, conspicuous benefits showered on him, by their mother; and makes the point that he surely owes her—*her*, Mrs. Pocock—something for that indulgence of his interests to which she has lent herself even at the expense of her sense of her own. She also makes the point that, if he were only himself really awake to the former, he would perhaps make out that the game played by Chad is, after all, in essence, but a game calculated to produce such an embroilment, and thereby such a consequent rupture (rupture between their mother and the object of her infatuation) as he himself may pecuniarily profit by. She draws Strether's attention, in other words, both to the way she has—in deference to him—kept her hands off Mrs. Newsome's strange, slightly ridiculous (as many people would, and do, think it) project, at such an age, of a second marriage; and to the perfectly discernible circumstance that if Chad had been acting precisely from a masked hostility to such a consummation, such an admission of an outsider to the privilege of 'pickings,' he couldn't have acted—well, a bit differently. She leaves him, finally, to pronounce as to which of them strikes him as having—to a truly discriminating view—the more fortunate effect upon his personal opportunity. He is accordingly so left then, Strether, and he takes these arguments in, looks them completely in the face, and is, by the turn of that screw, moved so much the nearer to the *crux* of his case. There is even at this point one definitely simple thing for him to do; which is to place himself immediately on Mrs. Pocock's side, signify to her that he can do nothing more in Paris, and that he believes *she* can do nothing, and so, accelerating, determining, her renouncement and her retreat, confess to their common failure and return with her to America. The failure will not, over there, positively have helped him, helped the Review, helped his other employments and emoluments, with Mrs. Newsome; but, at least, with earnest effort earnestly shown, with proper patience properly recorded, with final impatience, not to say moral disgust, in-evitably triumphant and determinant, his prospects need not be found to be irrecoverably dished. Chad will be thrown overboard, practically, by such a course; but Strether will at any rate himself have testified to a zeal in Mrs. Newsome's service sufficient to enable him to count on her appointing, as his reward, the too-long delayed day of their nuptials. These things, as I say, he can only turn well over—which we assist (as we assist at everything) at the process of his doing. The upshot is, none the less, only the intenser impossibility, to his spirit, of the step just defined. He *can't* go home with Mrs. Pocock, he *won't* go home with Mrs. Pocock; above all it's impossible to him to throw Chad over. He has given him his word that he will see him through—though, at the same time, Chad has given Mrs. Pocock *his* word that he will surrender, once his summons is distinctly pro-nounced, to Strether's decision. Strether has, in this tighter squeeze of his crisis, to take again a little time, to put every question to him-self once again, and clear up, so far as he can, his ambiguities. There are one or two that won't clear up: the fact that the supposition of Chad's designs on Mlle de Vionnet has been dispelled leaves, for instance, a vague residuum of the discomfortable, the equivocal, that he doesn't quite know what to do with. What does anything, what does everything, in the intimacy of a youth after all comparatively crude and a woman after all much older and admirably fine and subtle, mean if it doesn't mean—well, what it might at the worst? There is one thing indeed that it *may* signify, and to this explanation Strether sufficiently clings. It *is*, in the light of it, the mother, not the daughter, that Chad has all the while been in love with, and it's in respect to the mother that he is hanging on and on. He has the inextinguishable hope of some turn of the situation that may render their marriage possible. She may consent to a divorce, or M. de Vionnet may, by a kind and just Providence, suddenly and happily be snuffed out. Such are conceivably, to Chad's mind, by Strether's interpretation, the pos-sibilities; and others, that match them, may prevail in that of Mme de Vionnet herself: though *her* 'hanging on' is, at the best, a phe-nomenon requiring at once more analysis and more elucidation. What requires very little of either, however, and what thereby has most to contribute to our friend's growing stiffness of back, is that—con-found the whole thing—he has by this time *seen* too much, felt too much, to retrace his steps to his old standpoint. The distance that separates him from it is, measured by mere dates, of the slightest, but it is virtually ground that he has got for ever behind him. He is conscious of his evolution; he likes it—wouldn't for the world not have had it; albeit that he fully sees how fatal, in a manner, it has been for him. But if he's dished, he *is*, and all that is left for him is to say what he can as mere interesting, inconvenient experience. He is out of pocket by it, clearly, materially; but he has a handful of gold-pieces for imagination and memory. Mrs. Pocock has signified to him that she awaits his supreme reply, awaits his final beneficent inter-position with Chad; and, for congruity, he conforms by appearing to take three days for the benefit of the doubt. His intention is to culti-vate, during this period, such detachment as he may; to get off some-where by himself; to see, for a little, nothing of Chad, of Mme de Vionnet, or of Mrs. Newsome's representative—and then come back with his reply. He's rather bored with them all, *en fin de compte*, as the people about him say; he is even a little overdone with other people's adventures, and wouldn't mind a trifling one on his own account, which should yield him a little less worry. Miss Gostrey, after the absence on the eve of which he took leave of her, has, to his knowledge, returned; but he doesn't want particularly to see even *her*. Still less does he wish to see Waymark, who, for that matter, has ended, as a result of the spectacle of his behaviour, by cultivating an estrangement from him that makes Strether half melancholy (so almost insanely odd, or madly morbid, it is) and half merry.

What does in fact befall during this little interval is that he tumbles for two or three days, in spite of himself, into the arms of poor soli-tarily-prowling Pocock, whom the preoccupations of the latter's wife, her earnest exchange of impressions and convictions with Waymark in especial, have left at the mercy of a good deal of more or less <con-soled?> [1] leisure. Strether is kind to him, easy with him, amused at him, and, above all, abundantly conscious of *his* reactions and 'game.' Pocock doesn't at all really want Chad brought back—doesn't believe in him as an active element in the business, and doesn't require him as an additional participant in what has been roughly denominated the general and particular 'pickings.' But this is one side, and Pocock has his mixture. He is amused at his mother-in-law's baffled state—a state rare for her and which he has never known the joy, so much as he would have liked it, of directly promoting. All his instinct is to pro-mote it now by acting on his rather coarse divination of the nature of Strether's independence, and above all on his still livelier perception of the character of Chad's own. For Strether, at all events, he performs the present function, while they go about together and Strether shows

1. The typescript reads 'concoled.'

him bits of Paris, things in it that he mightn't otherwise see—though not always the very things he wants; performs the function of representing as vulgarly as possible the whole particular mass of interests at home on behalf of which the long arm has reached itself out for Chad. Strether, as I have noted, has known the late Newsome and been well aware of what he didn't like about him and what he hasn't, since then, liked to think of and to remember in him and of him; but Pocock, in their walks and talks—Pocock will do nothing but talk of matters at home—happens to bring to his acquaintance two or three facts, illustrative of the deceased's character and practises, of which he has been unwitting and that excite in him a still more marked approach to disgust. They complete his vision, his memory, his theory of the late Newsome. It's the voice of the late Newsome that, as it were, from beyond the tomb, makes the demand of Chad, reaches out the arm to draw him back to the supervision of the 'advertising department.' It's as if there were two elements in the youth (as to whom I should take this occasion, hitherto neglected, to parenthesise that my situation requires in him, more perhaps than I have adequately noted, a certain element of the plastic and the wavering, a rigour of attitude not wholly unqualified, so that the drop of the balance for him may, after all, just be a matter of a push, administered with due force, from another hand). One of these elements is discernibly of the none-too-edifying paternal strain, while it is the other, singularly different, that his recent, his actual, situation happens, however deleteriously from some points of view, the point of view in especial of the home-circle, to have fostered on lines not, at any rate, prevailingly vulgar. Pocock, the contact of Pocock, the mind, the manners, the conversation, allusions, ideals, general atmosphere of Pocock, rub into Strether afresh the discomfortable truth that it is in the name of the paternal heritage that he has been launched upon his own errand. At the risk of seeming here to repeat what I may have already repeated, I note further Strether's consciousness, so unwittingly stimulated by Pocock, that the general heritage of the late Newsome is what has above all enabled his widow to render *him* her signal services as well as to diffuse her conspicuous general benefits; so that if he does marry a rich woman, it will be a woman rich in just these connections that have now begun somehow to change their look, to grow ugly and smell badly, for him. These things are all aggravations, attenuations, features and forms of his 'responsibility.' The thing presents itself to him anew in the hardness and clearness of its essential simplicity, and, hammering away for you thus for lucidity's sake, I once more re-formulate his intenser impression of it. Chad is to 'take up' something, and if he doesn't take it up, there is something, something important, a chance, a share, a haul, that he thereby loses. If he does take it up he takes it under Strether's influence; and this favourable exercise of Strether's influence confirms and consecrates the latter's own personal chance and tie at Worcester. I reiterate these things here on Strether's behalf, in order to intensify the fact that, as he acts now, he does so on full reflection. What this reflection, roughly stated, amounts to then is: 'No, I'll be hanged if I purchase the certainty of being coddled for the rest of my days by going straight against the way in which all these impressions and suggestions of the last three months have made me feel, and like to feel, and want to feel. Whatever is the matter with Chad, it strikes me as having done more for him as a man and a gentleman than would have been done, or than will yet be done, by his having remained in, or being again introduced and compressed into, the box that we have flattered ourselves can be once more made to contain him. It has really made him quite over. As between Mme de Vionnet and the advertising-department, then, I decide for Mme de Vionnet, and if my expression, my action *is* to tip down the scale, why, let it tip, and I'll take the consequences. They will really, whatever they may be, immensely interest, and in their way, doubtless, even amuse me. They will represent something—meagre and belated and indirect and absurd as it may be—that I shall have done for my poor old infatuated and imaginative self. I didn't know I had it in me, and it's worth all the journey and all the worry to have found out. It will have cost me—I feel sure, it's in my bones, I forecast the whole thing—everything that my engagement to that wonderful woman at home, so full of high qualities too, represents and promises; but I'm not going to let such a circumstance prevent me. I'll keep my promise to Chad; I'll say to him: "Do as the interest of your situation *here* most prescribes—and say frankly and freely that it's the sense in which I've positively advised you." I stand by that—and *vogue la galère!*'

He breaks away from Pocock, not being able to 'stand,' in the state of his nerves, much more of him; breaks away on the third or fourth day of this little episode, and it's in the course of a day—a day 'off'—that he does succeed in getting by himself, that another incident, full of further significance, of a very complicating kind, presents itself. The situation is now, I recall, that the question of Chad's engagement to Mlle de Vionnet is quite disposed of by the latter's otherwise-appointed nuptials; and that Mme de Vionnet knows—with Chad solicited, restless, precarious in her hands—that Strether has really, in effect, the casting vote for him, and for *her* so far as her fate is (so oddly, so mystifyingly) bound up with the young man's. Strether has made up his mind, and he is to see Mrs. Pocock, in accordance with it, so to speak, on the morrow; he is to give her that answer to her ultimatum on behalf of her mother, as it were, that she has signified to him that she awaits. Strether has it then, as I say, all ready, and in this condition he has taken the train to one of the suburbs of Paris quite at random, scarce knowing, and not much caring, where he is. The effect of his complete decision is a queer sense of freedom and almost of amusement. It's a lovely day of early summer; the aspect of things is such as to charm and beguile him—the air full of pictures and felicities and hints for future memory. Suddenly, with these predispositions, in a suburban village by the river, a place where people come out from Paris to boat, to dine, to dance, to make love, to do anything they like, he comes upon Mme de Vionnet and Chad together—Mme de Vionnet and Chad presented somehow in a light that, in spite of all preparation and previous perplexity, of all embarrassing questions and satisfactory and unsatisfactory answers, considerably startles and pulls him up. The case shows them, somehow, as they have not yet been shown; it represents them as positively and indubitably intimate with the last intimacy; it is, in a word, full, for Strether, of informing and convincing things. He meets it then and there as he can—which is the way they also, conscious, inconvenienced, but carrying the whole thing bravely off, deal, on their side, with the encounter. Each side acquits itself with such discretion and ease as it can command; and the passage between them is in fine full of interest. Of course I am not attempting in any degree whatever to represent or render it here, or to do more than thus glance at it and pass. They separate, on pretexts, and Strether goes back to Paris alone. But he goes back with a deeper and stranger sense, a sense that his responsibility is verily deep and sharp. It staggers him a little, and he has to brace himself afresh; he doesn't back down from his decision, but he rather wishes the incident hadn't occurred. At the same time he feels rather ashamed—ashamed, I mean, of his regret; for the essence of his attitude to himself on the whole business has been that what he *is* moved to he wants not to shirk. Here is a beautiful chance then not to shirk. He looks what he has seen in the face; he passes a discomfortable night on it; that is one way not to shirk. There are other ways too, and he vigorously cultivates them, for the next twenty-four hours, all. He shakes himself, snubs and scolds himself, brings himself sternly and rigidly into line. Why should he pusillanimously wish he mightn't so sharply have *known*, since all the value of his total episode, and all the enjoyment of it, has precisely been that 'knowing' was the effect of it? He is, all the same, rather inconsequently disposed not to go to Mrs. Pocock that very day with his answer; and while, exactly, he is hesitating as to the positively final immediacy and urgency of this step, another incident, not, superficially, at least, more simplifying than the previous, somewhat surprisingly overtakes him. He receives a visit from Mme de Vionnet, and Mme de Vionnet's visit is a wonderful affair, but which, again, I can, beyond naming it, really give you here no more than I have given you anything else. It gives her away to him—which is the last thing he had expected anything to do; and gives her away as the consequence of her fears. It's her fears, her weakness now, her surprising spilling of her cards, that definitely tell him, face to face, what he had previously neither really made out for himself, nor really dismissed: the strange fact—of an order both so obscure and so recorded—of the passion of this accomplished woman of almost forty for their so imperfectly accomplished young friend of a dozen years less. Strether is in the presence of more things than he has yet had to count with, things by no means, doubtless, explicitly in his book; but with which, pitying the remarkable woman all the more that her present proceeding reduces her, for the hour, in some respects, to a tolerably common category, he does his best to get, as it were, into relation. He sees and understands, and such is the force in him of his alien and awkward tradition, that he has, almost like a gasping spectator at a thrilling play, to *see* himself see and understand. Mme de Vionnet is, precisely like some woman less clever and less rare, in a 'funk' about the possible loss of Chad. He has become a cherished necessity to her. Her passion simplifies and abases her; ranges her in a category; presents her as a case; does, in short, more things than I can now enumerate. Infinite tact and delicacy of *presentation* of course lavished on all this. But the upshot of it, after all, is but to confirm Strether's vision of the influence and the benefit the situation has represented for Chad. If he has found him transformed, that effect ceases to be wonderful in the presence, so vividly, of the forces making for it. Mme de Vionnet's visit is at any rate a frightened appeal. She comes to entreat him to *keep* Chad for her. They have both got scared the day before, but she in particular, and the more, all night, her fears and her imagination have dwelt on it, as to the way their friend may be practically affected by the impression they were conscious of making on him. She beseeches him not to be practically affected. She tells him, shows him, proves to him, how good she is for Chad. He is rueful as to assenting to that, but he is helpless as to denying it, and, not to multiply my words here, he at all events dismisses her with the reassurance that his view is his view, that he doesn't mean to take back any word he has given, that his mind was in fact, the day before, all made up to confirm it; and that, in fine, no 'impression' of anything or anybody now will have made any difference. Besides, for that matter, what has she supposed he had supposed? He has, really and truly, in his 'secret heart,' not known what he has supposed—and hence his sharp emotion, the upset to his nerves, on the previous day. But he doesn't tell Mme de Vionnet that.

She leaves him, and he does nothing that day—Chad, meanwhile, 'lying low' very markedly; but on the morrow he goes and reports himself to Mrs. Pocock. If his responsibility has been complicated and thickened it proves, none the less, not, after all, too much for him. He tells her —and the announcement is practically made to Mrs. Newsome—that he has thought over everything he has owed it to her to think over since their last interview, but that his attitude remains just what he was then obliged to let her fear it to be. He 'sides,' so to speak, with Chad; he holds that Chad, by meeting his mother's views, will give up more than he gains, and he has frankly expressed himself to him in that sense. He recognizes the effect his words, of which he has counted the cost, will probably have; but he has not been able to act in any other way. I pass briefly, for you, over this juncture, and over the effect of it on the Pocock party, who, with Waymark, shocked and scandalised—approximately or vulgarly speaking—in their train, are quickly determined by it to departure and disappearance. They withdraw from the scene, they return straightway home, with all the proper circumstances and concomitants. Strether has immediately afterwards gone to Chad and told him what he has done; his sentiment about him being that he can't quite, all the same, wash his hands of him. On the other hand, what can he do more for him than he has already done? He lingers in Paris a little—he has wanted to see the situation 'through.' But with the direction events have taken from him, it sufficiently comes over him that they *are* through. His imagination of them drops, and if he rather glosses over for the pair the quantity they have cost him, the last tribute strikes him, at last, as the very most he can manage. He does gloss it over—with Chad at least; he carries out, to his utmost, the spirit of his promise to 'make it all right.' That is a pious misrepresentation, in the interest of Chad's stability, absolutely precious, now, to Strether's imagination: but it is a part of the amusement and the harmless *panache* of his proceeding. He measures exactly, himself, the situation. He knows he won't make it all right. He knows he can't make it all right. He knows that, for Mrs. Newsome, it's all hideously wrong and must remain so. But he only (that is as with Chad) knows this; and he misrepresents, as I say, the question with what he believes to be a certain success—making the matter, at all events, and without much difficulty, none of Chad's business. It's the last thing moreover, naturally, that he conceives Chad as being touched by, or conceives, with any intensity, Mme de Vionnet.

[411]

After these things have happened, however, and especially after the departure of the Pococks, he has a kind of moral and intellectual drop or arrest—of the whole range of feeling that has kept him up hitherto—which makes him feel that his work is done, that his so strange, half-bitter, half-sweet experience is at an end, that what has happened, through him, has really happened *for* him, for his own spirit, for his own queer sense of things, more than for anyone or anything else, and that now he has no reason for stopping any longer. Now he *will* go back, and he gathers himself up, and he's ready. He has waited till the moment he wished—he couldn't have gone before; the whole affair had become as a thing of his own that he had to watch and accompany, as it were, out of a deep inward necessity, sympathy, curiosity, perversity, if need were, to its conclusion; but he recognizes the conclusion, so far as *he* is concerned with it, when he sees it—recognizes that his hour has sounded. The sound is like the bell of the steamer calling him, from its place at the dock, aboard again, and by the same act ringing down the curtain on the play. He goes back to all the big Difference, over there, that he foresees—the big Difference of his having spoiled himself for any future favour from Mrs. Newsome, and spoiled the poor fatuous Review, as an implication and a consequence, for any future subsidy. These things, and many more things, are before him—evoked, projected, made vivid, made certain. But before he goes, on the eve of his departure, two other things happen which mark, to the extent of their interest and importance, that the curtain has *not* yet quite dropped, the play is not *yet* quite over. The first of these is an interview that he has with Mme de Vionnet, who either comes to see him again or addresses him an earnest request, which he complies with, to come to *her* (I've not yet determined which) after that last scene with Chad to which I have just referred. Of what has passed between them on this occasion she has, of course, immediately received from Chad all tidings, and, affected by it in more than one interesting manner, and moved, in particular, to the deepest gratitude, she has placed herself, in what she feels to be for the last time, in relation with him. On what Chad has told her, repeated to her, of his making everything 'all right,' as regards himself, his personal situation and responsibility, at home, she has her own impressions, suspicions, divinations, and, though she can do nothing *for* poor Strether, as it were, though she sees in him and in his behaviour more things than she can even be explicit about with him, she obeys an irresistible instinct in desiring once more to see him and, however poorly, to thank him. He has not, frankly, from a feeling quite absolute, though difficult to justify or—in this place, for instance—explain, wanted any further vision of Chad or contact with him, and he seeks none, and practically makes any, for the young man himself, impossible, after the just-above-mentioned passage. He has done with *him*, or at any rate feels that Chad has done, and that Chad (immensely, though perhaps after all a trifle ruefully, just a shade regretfully and anxiously, obliged) is ready, on his side, to let him pass away. But as to Mme de Vionnet, it's another affair, and to just a last sight of everything in her that he has found wonderful and abysmal, strange and charming, beautiful and rather dreadful, he thus finally adjusts and treats himself. The meeting, the scene, then, takes place, and is the happy and harmonious *pendant* (from the point of view, I mean, of interest and effect) of the previous one, the one referred to a moment ago, the scene of 'appeal' after Strether's encounter with the pair in the country and her consequent apprehension and commotion. But don't imagine I pretend to give it to you here. I merely mark it with this little cross as probably the most beautiful and interesting morsel in the book, and I would say most handsomely 'done'—say so did I admit that there can be any *difference* of morsels in any self-respecting work-of-art, where the morsel *not* handsomely done simply incurs one's own pity long before the critic—if there *were* a critic!—has cut the eye-teeth of any knowledge of *how* competently to kick it. You must leave me accordingly with this passage and with my treatment of it. It is really the climax—for all it can be made to give and to do, for the force with which it may illustrate and illuminate the subject —toward which the action marches straight from the first. So there it is.

The second of the two situations of which the one just noted is the first deals scarcely less handsomely with Strether's relation with poor Maria Gostrey, and with hers with him—taking it up again effectively, I should say, if it were correct to speak of it as having really at all dropped. But it hasn't really at all dropped; it has only seemed, here, to fall into the background through my not wanting to risk too much to confuse and complicate my statement by insistence, at every point, on its quite continuous function. I have not named Miss Gostrey in sketching the stages of the business after the arrival of the Pococks, but it is, from step to step, with the aid of her confirmed relation to Strether that I show what I need to show. It's a relation the fortunate friction of which projects light, the light of interpretation and illustration, upon all that passes before them, upon all causes and effects. After his question is settled, after the Pococks have gone and Waymark, as a sequel to a final brush with Strether and a presumably-not-at-all final sign from Mrs. Pocock, has gone with them; after Strether has seen Chad for the wind-up I have noted and then, as it were, washed his hands of him; after he has seen Mme de Vionnet on corresponding lines, there are two things he is left face to face with. One of these is what I have already so much more than sufficiently evoked, his end, the end of his play, of his stay, and his domestic penalty and consequences—all another business, all for him, on the spot, only taken for granted and accepted; the other is the presence, the personality, the general form and pressure of Maria Gostrey. *She* is his residuum—that of the three or four months' experience and drama after everything else has come and gone. He is there with her in Paris now alone, as it were; and I see a particular moment of the place and season: the midsummer emptiness reached, the flight of everyone, the rather stale hot, empty city—but with the sense of freedom and of a now strangely full initiation interfusing it all, which the pair seem, as it were, to have quite to themselves. Miss Gostrey, poor dear, but vivid and all herself to the last, is informed with the principle of standing by her friend, so to speak, to the end, and the meaning and moral of what she has done for him, the play of the circumstance that, all the while, she has just purely and simply fallen in love with him— these things gild with their declining rays this last of his complications. Here again I have something that I can't fully trot out for you; here again I can only put in the picture with a single touch of the brush. It will be brushed in another fashion in its order and proper light. Fate gives poor Strether, before she has done with him, just this other chance; and we see him see it and look it in the face and hold out his hand to it with half a kindness and half a renouncement; we see him all touched and intelligent about it, but we don't do anything so vulgar as make him 'take up,' save for a friendship that he quite sincerely hopes may last, with poor convenient, amusing, unforgettable, impossible Gostrey. Very pretty, very charming and pleasant and droll and sad all this concluding but I don't want to represent every woman in the book, beginning with Mrs. Newsome, as having, of herself, 'made up' to my hero; for vivid and concrete and interesting as I desire to make him, the mark of the real never ceases to show in him, and with the real only the real—of verisimilitude, of consistency— consorts. But it's none the less a fact that Mrs. Newsome, Miss Gostrey, and poor magnificent Mme de Vionnet herself (though this last is a secret of secrets) have been, in the degree involved, agreeably and favourably affected by him. Mrs. Newsome has—as we fairly figure to ourselves—'proposed.' Mme de Vionnet has been, only, exquisite over what *might* have been! Miss Gostrey, at all events, doesn't repeat Mrs. Newsome by proposing, but Strether has as clear a vision of his opportunity as if she did—and he has even his moment of hesitation. This moment of hesitation is what we get—what I give. He shows her that he has it—that is, that he sees he can marry her on the morrow if he will—at all events on the morrow of his return to America, or (since she in that case will follow) on the morrow of *that*; is, as I say, everything that is pleasant and appreciative about it—everything but what he would be if he assented or accepted. He *can't* accept or assent. He won't. He doesn't. It's too late. It mightn't have been, sooner—but it is, yes, distinctly, now. He has come so far through his total little experience that he has come out on the other side—on the other side, even, of a union with Miss Gostrey. He must go back as he came— or rather, really, so quite other that, in comparison, marrying Miss Gostrey would be almost of the old order. Yes, he goes back other— and to other things. We see him on the eve of departure, with whatever awaits him *là-bas*, and their lingering, ripe separation is the last note.

P.S.—I should mention that I see the foregoing in a tolerable certitude of Ten Parts, each of 10,000 words, making thus a total of 100,000. But I should very much like my option of stretching to 120,000 if necessary—that is, adding an Eleventh and Twelfth Parts. Each Part I rather definitely see in Two Chapters, and each very full, as it were, and charged—like a rounded medallion, in a series of a dozen, hung, with its effect of high relief, on a wall. Such are my general lines. Of course there's a lot to say about the matter that I haven't said—but I have doubtless said a great deal more than it may seem to you at first easy to find your way about in. The way is really, however, very straight. Only the difficulty with one's having made so very full a Statement as the present is that one seems to have gone far toward saying *all*: which I needn't add that I haven't in the least pretended to do. Reading these pages over, for instance, I find I haven't at all placed in a light what I make of the nature of Strether's feeling—his affianced, indebted, and other, consciousness—about Mrs. Newsome. But I need scarcely add, after this, that everything will in fact be in its place and of its kind.

Henry James

September 1st 1900.

APPENDIX

OF TEXTUAL EMENDATIONS

As explained in the 'Note on the Text,' some editorial emendations, not covered by the general principles stated there, have not been indicated in the printed text, but are listed here. In each case a reference to the page and line of the printed text has been given, followed by the emended version and then by the original manuscript reading.

10:24, some time—some time time
15:16, *a—an*
16:35, him—her
25:6, Atlantic—*Atlantic*
31:38, *quarto piano*—4° Po
35:24-5, In spite of it—In spite of it in spite of it
35:34, vision—visions
39:33, to—of
40:33, for—to for
47:11-12, disappointment—disappointed
71:38, Misses Claremont—Miss Claremont's
83:19, her tell him—him tell her
88:5, me—be
90:40, how—how I
92:30, Comédie Française—Comédie Frsce
97:21, or as that—or of that
104:40, few words—few words few words
107:43, his—this
111:18, any rate—anything
114:28, he—she
117:15, on—on on
119:5, making—make
137:18, a woman—and woman
147:16-17, was that of the—was that of that the
151:24, man—manner
155:3, 1894—1869

158:30, He meets—The meets
180:12, *première—1ᵉʳᵉ*
188:23, to call it)—to call it, the)
192:4, *Primo—1°; Secondo—2°*
197:22, from—by
201:37, of—of of
205:19, has—has has
208:21, 1st—1°
220:28, it—in
227:20-21, supposing him—supposing him to
227:35, is dead—is a dead
233:40, sit—sat
235:16, 6—4
241:16-17, the condition—the the condition
241:22, is (in—is with (in
243:32, relative to—of relative to
243:37, to see—to to see
249:26, do it—to do it
249:27, her his word—her on his word
251:27, 1896—1895
253:41, Fleda's—Mona's
255:40, Fleda—Mona
259:10, the theatre—the the theatre
266:16, 13—12
267:20 *L'honnête—La'honnête*
269:40, what is it—what it is it
270:19, care—care care
283:29, this—this a

[417]

290:24, Sometime—Sometimes
290:33, what—what what
291:25, the very—the the very
302:24, having—have
303:38, waked—walked
309:9, out—it
310:33, Mrs. W.—Mrs. Mrs. W.
312:28, 1901—1801
315:22, gives—give
316:14, its—or its
318:22, on, to—on, to to
320:15, by—as
321:28, George Du—George d.
323:18, truth—true
326:15, little—little little
326:17, before the—before the the
326:27, (plaqué—to (plaqué
326:35, with—with with
328:21, is in—in is in

329:34, 1907—1903
330:11, an—and
330:14, are—is
336:13, he—she
337:19, sort—sport
337:31, give him—him give him
337:38, him—her
338:24-5, by his—by her
339:14, be—me
342:30, pity—pities
345:19, F. A. Duneka—Duneka (F. A.)
350:6, as her—of her
351:36, is—are
358:19, can avoid—can to avoid
363:29, have—has
389:38, is a—in a
392:35, with her—with him
398:25, Mlle—Mme.

INDEX

Costa, Isaäc da, 62
Coulson, H. J. W., 25
Crackanthorpe, Mrs., 150
Crawfurd, Oswald, 241, 244
Cruikshank, George, 334
Curtis, Daniel S., 81, 85
Curtis, George W., 319

Daly, Augustin, 127
Daudet, Alphonse, 26, 48, 62
  L'Évangeliste, 47, 48, 67
  L'Immortel, 167
  Numa Roumestan, xv, 62
  Trente Ans de Paris, 87
Davis, Fay, 268
De Morgan, Miss, 181
Deacon, E., 116, 308
Dennery, Adolphe, 100
Dickens, Charles, 319
Du Maurier, George, 13, 97, 98, 101,
  102, 105, 321
  Peter Ibbetson, 98
  Trilby, 98
Dumas, Alexandre, 38
  Le Demi-Monde, 128
Duneka, F. A., 345, 346, 348

Earle, Mrs., 106
Edel, Leon, vii, 343
  Henry James, Les Années Dramat-
  iques, 100
Edgar, Pelham, 65
Eliot, George, 288
  Felix Holt, 320
Elliot, Maud Howe, 290
Estournelles, M. d', 113

Favart, Marie, 38
Fawkes, Guy, 132
Feuillet, Octave, 135
Fielding, Henry:
  Joseph Andrews, 104, 105
  Tom Jones, 103
Filon, Augustin, 191
Firdousi, 31
Flaubert, Gustave, xvii, 26, 150
Forbes, Archibald, 334
Forbes-Robertson, Sir Johnston, 186
Forman, Buxton, 329
France, Anatole, 102
Freeman, Mary Wilkins, *see* Wilkins,
  Mary
Frith, William, 102
Funck-Brentano, Frantz, *L'Affaire du*
  Collier, 309
Fuseli, John H., 334

Gamba, Countess, 72
Gardner, Jack, 39
Gardner, Mrs. John L., 60, 207, 316,
  322
Gaskell, Charles Milnes, 28, 29
Gautier, Théophile, *Les Vieux Por-*
  traits, 26
Gibbens, Mrs., 324
Gibbons, Grinling, 334
Gilder, Jeanette L., 98
Gilder, Joseph B., 98
Gilder, Richard W., 52
Gladstone, William, 34, 194
Godkin, Edwin L., 129
Goncourt, Edmond, 26
Gosse, Edmund, 57, 133, 269, 325
Gourlays, the, 320
Grant, Ulysses S., 59
Granville-Barker, Harley, 100
Gray, John C., 324
Greenough, Gordon, 289, 293
Greenough, Horatio, 289, 293
Gregory, Lady, 145, 146, 147
Griffin, Sir Lepel, 65
  The Great Republic, 66
Grignan, 'demoiselle de,' 19, 52
Grosvenor, Lord and Lady, 54
Grove, Archibald, 93, 95
Gryzanowski, E., 45
Gualdo, Luigi, 213, 265, 302, 306
Guiccoli, the, 72
Gurneys, the, 323

Hamlet, 11
Hare, Sir John, 39
Harland, Henry, 143, 149, 236
Harper, Henry, 167, 176, 187
Harvey, George, 315
Hawthorne, Julian, 83
Hawthorne, Nathaniel, xiv, 10, 14, 29,
  67, 151, 312
  Ethan Brand, 312
Henley, W. E., 334
Herter, Albert, 285
Higginson, Henry L., 315, 316, 317,
  323
Hill, F. H., 28
Holl, Frank, 334
Holland, Lady, 96
Holmes, Oliver Wendell (the younger),
  24, 319
Holmes, Mrs. Oliver Wendell (the
  younger), 24
Holmes, Mrs. Oliver Wendell (the
  elder), 319
Howard, George, 28
Howe, Julia Ward, 290, 291

[421]

THE EDITORS

The late F. O. Matthiessen was Professor of History and Literature at Harvard University and member of the board of the *New England Quarterly*. He is the author of many books, among them, *Sarah Orne Jewett; Translation: An Elizabethan Art; The Achievement of T. S. Eliot; Henry James: The Major Phase; The James Family; Theodore Dreiser;* and *The American Novels of Henry James.* In addition to the present volume, he edited *The Oxford Book of American Verse,* and *Stories of Writers and Artists,* by Henry James.

Kenneth B. Murdock is the author of *Increase Mather* and *Literature and Theology in Colonial New England.* Presently at Harvard as Higginson Professor of English Literature, he maintains a long-standing association with the University, one which began with his undergraduate studies, and includes service as Chairman of the Harvard Committees on General Education and on Educational Policy, as well as his recent appointment as Director of the *Villa i Tatti,* Harvard's new center for humanistic studies on the estate of the late Bernard Berenson near Florence, Italy.

GALAXY BOOKS

GALAXY BOOKS